STUDENT SOLUTIONS MANUAL

PIN NG
Northern Arizona University

D0085716

BASIC BUSINESS STATISTICS: CONCEPTS AND APPLICATIONS

THIRTEENTH EDITION

Mark L. Berenson
Montclair State University

David M. Levine
Baruch College, City University of New York

Kathryn A. Szabat
La Salle University

PEARSON

Boston   Columbus   Indianapolis   New York   San Francisco   Upper Saddle River
Amsterdam   Cape Town   Dubai   London   Madrid   Milan   Munich   Paris   Montreal   Toronto
Delhi   Mexico City   São Paulo   Sydney   Hong Kong   Seoul   Singapore   Taipei   Tokyo

The author and publisher of this book have used their best efforts in preparing this book. These efforts include the development, research, and testing of the theories and programs to determine their effectiveness. The author and publisher make no warranty of any kind, expressed or implied, with regard to these programs or the documentation contained in this book. The author and publisher shall not be liable in any event for incidental or consequential damages in connection with, or arising out of, the furnishing, performance, or use of these programs.

Reproduced by Pearson from electronic files supplied by the author.

Copyright © 2015, 2012, 2009, 2006 Pearson Education, Inc.
Publishing as Pearson, 75 Arlington Street, Boston, MA 02116.

All rights reserved. No part of this publication may be reproduced, stored in a retrieval system, or transmitted, in any form or by any means, electronic, mechanical, photocopying, recording, or otherwise, without the prior written permission of the publisher. Printed in the United States of America.

ISBN-13: 978-0-321-92670-8
ISBN-10: 0-321-92670-6

1 2 3 4 5 6 EBM 18 17 16 15 14

www.pearsonhighered.com

Table of Contents

Preface

The ***Student Solutions Manual*** consists of three major sections. The ***Objective*** section summarizes what is expected of a student after reading a chapter. The ***Overview and Key Concepts*** section provides an overview of the major topics covered in a chapter and lists the important key concepts. The overview and listing of the key concepts are meant not to replace but to supplement the textbook and to reinforce understanding. The ***Solutions to End of Section and Chapter Review Even Problems*** section provides extra detail in the problem solutions.

IMPORTANT THINGS TO LEARN FIRST

OBJECTIVES
- That the volume of data that exists in the world makes learning about statistics critically important
- That statistics is a way of thinking that can help you make better decisions
- How the DCOVA framework for applying statistics can help you solve business problems
- What business analytics is and how these techniques represent an opportunity for you
- How to make best use of this book
- How to prepare for using Microsoft Excel or Minitab with this book

OVERVIEW AND KEY CONCEPTS
What is Statistics?
Statistics is a way of thinking that can help you make better decisions based on data that have been collected. It helps transform data into useful information for decision makers.

Why Statistics in the Business World?
- To summarize and visualize business data
- To draw conclusions from the data
- To make reliable forecasts about business activities
- To improve business processes

How to Use Statistics in the Business World (DCOVA)?
The **D**efine **C**ollect **O**rganize **V**isualize **A**nalyze framework helps minimize possible errors of thinking and analysis.
- **D**efine the data that you want to study in order to solve a problem or meet an objective
- **C**ollect the data from appropriate sources
- **O**rganize the data collected by developing tables
- **V**isualize the data collected by developing charts
- **A**nalyze the data collected to reach conclusions and present those results

Key Definitions
- **Data:** The set of individual values associated with a variable.
- **Variable:** A characteristic of an item or individual.
- **Statistics:** The methods that help transform data into useful information for decision makers.

Business Analytics
Business analytics combine "traditional" statistical methods with methods and techniques from management science and information systems to form an interdisciplinary tool that supports fact-based management decision making. It enables a manager to
- Use statistical methods to analyze and explore data to uncover unforeseen relationships.
- Use management science methods to develop models that impact an organization's strategy, planning, and operations.
- Use information systems methods to collect and process data sets of all sizes, including very large data sets that would otherwise be hard to examine efficiently.

Copyright ©2015 Pearson Education, Inc.

CHAPTER 1

OBJECTIVES

- To understand the types of variables used in statistics
- To know the different measurement scales
- To know how to collect data
- To know the different ways to collect a sample
- To understand the types of survey errors

OVERVIEW AND KEY CONCEPTS

Key Definitions

- **Population (universe):** The whole collection of things under consideration, e.g., all the students enrolled at a university.
- **Sample:** A portion of the population selected for analysis, e.g., all the freshmen at a university.
- **Parameter:** A summary measure computed to describe a characteristic of the population, e.g., the population average weight of all the students enrolled at a university.
- **Statistic:** A summary measure computed to describe a characteristic of the sample, e.g., the average weight of a sample of freshmen at a university.
- **Recoded variable:** A new variable defined and created to supplement or replace the original variable in your analysis.

Relationship between Population and Sample

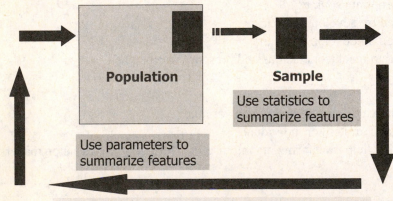

Population

Sample

Use statistics to summarize features

Use parameters to summarize features

Inference on the population from the sample

Copyright ©2015 Pearson Education, Inc.

The Different Types of Variables

- **Categorical (qualitative) variable**: A nonnumeric variable, e.g., male or female.
- **Numerical (quantitative) variable:** A numeric variable, e.g., weight, exam score.
- **Discrete variable:** A variable with only certain values, there are usually gaps between values, e.g., the number of cars a company owns.
- **Continuous variable:** A variable that can have any value within a specified range, e.g., atmospheric temperature.

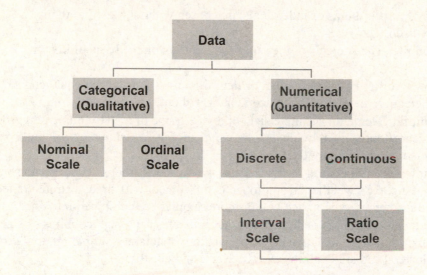

Levels of Measurement and Types of Measurement Scales

- **Nominal scale**: Categorical data that are classified into distinct categories in which no ranking is implied, e.g. male or female.
- **Ordinal scale:** Categorical data that are classified into distinct categories in which ranking is implied, e.g. student grades of A, B, C, D and F.
- **Interval scale:** Numerical data that are measured using an ordered scale in which the difference between measurements is meaningful but does not involve a true zero point, e.g. standardized exam score.
- **Ratio scale:** Numerical data that are measured using an ordered scale in which the difference between measurements is meaningful and involves a true zero point, e.g. height, weight.

The Different Types of Data Sources

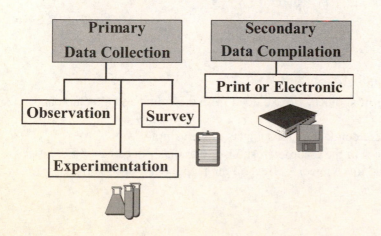

Copyright ©2015 Pearson Education, Inc.

Reasons for Drawing a Sample

- Less time consuming than a census
- Less costly to administer than a census
- Less cumbersome and more practical to administer than a census of the targeted population

The Different Methods of Sample Selection

- **A nonprobability sample:** Items or individuals are chosen without regard to their probability of occurrence.
- **A probability sample:** The subjects of the sample are chosen on the basis of known probabilities.
- **A simple random sample:** Every individual or item from the frame has an equal chance of being selected. Selection may be with replacement or without replacement.
- **A systematic sample:** Decide on a sample size, n; divide frame of N individuals into groups of k (rounded to nearest integer) individuals, $k = N/n$; randomly select one individual from the first group; select every k^{th} individual thereafter.
- **A stratified sample:** The population is divided into two or more groups according to some common characteristic, e.g., whether an employee is full-time or part-time; a simple random sample is selected from each group; then two or more samples are combined into one.
- **A cluster sample:** The population is divided into several "clusters", e.g., counties or election districts, in which each is representative of the population; then take a simple random sample of one or more clusters, and study all items in each selected cluster.

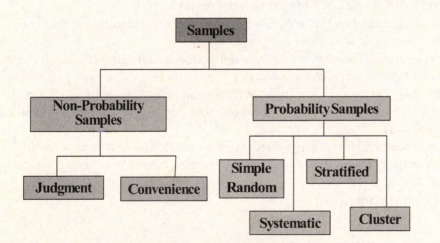

Evaluating Survey Worthiness

- What is the purpose of the survey?
- Is the survey based on a probability sample?
- **Coverage error:** Certain groups of subjects are excluded from the frame and have no chance of being selected in the sample.
- **Nonresponse error:** Failure to collect data on all subjects in the sample.
- **Measurement error:** Inaccuracies in the recorded responses that occur because of a weakness in question wording, an interviewer's effect on the respondent, or the effort made by the respondent.

Copyright ©2015 Pearson Education, Inc.

- **Sampling error:** The chance differences from sample to sample based on the probability of particular individuals or items being selected in the particular samples. Sampling error always exists in a survey.

Ethical Issues About Surveys

- Coverage error can result in selection bias if particular groups or individuals are purposely excluded from the frame so that the survey results are more favorable to the survey's sponsor.
- Nonresponse error can lead to nonresponse bias if the sponsor knowingly designs the survey so that particular groups or individuals are less likely than others to respond.
- Sampling error can result in a sponsored viewpoint that might otherwise be inappropriate when the results are purposely presented without reference to sample size and margin of error.
- Measurement error can become an ethical issue if: (1) a survey sponsor chooses leading questions that guide the respondent in a particular direction; (2) an interviewer, through mannerisms and tone, purposely makes a respondent obligated to please the interviewer or otherwise guides the respondent in a particular direction; or (3) a respondent willfully provides false information.

Copyright ©2015 Pearson Education, Inc.

SOLUTIONS TO END OF SECTION AND CHAPTER REVIEW EVEN PROBLEMS

1.2   Three sizes of U.S. businesses are classified into distinct categories—small, medium, and large—in which order is implied.

1.4   (a)   The number of cellphones is a numerical variable that is discrete because the outcome is a count. It is ratio scaled because it has a true zero point.

        (b)   Monthly data usage is a numerical variable that is continuous because any value within a range of values can occur. It is ratio scaled because it has a true zero point.

        (c)   Number of text messages exchanged per month is a numerical variable that is discrete because the outcome is a count. It is ratio scaled because it has a true zero point.

        (d)   Voice usage per month is a numerical variable that is continuous because any value within a range of values can occur. It is ratio scaled because it has a true zero point.

        (e)   Whether a cellphone is used for email is a categorical variable because the answer can be only yes or no. This also makes it a nominal-scaled variable.

1.6   (a)   Categorical, nominal scale.
        (b)   Numerical, continuous, ratio scale.
        (c)   Categorical, nominal scale.
        (d)   Numerical, discrete, ratio scale.
        (e)   Categorical, nominal scale.

1.8   (a)   numerical, continuous, ratio scale *
        (b)   numerical, discrete, ratio scale
        (c)   numerical, continuous, ratio scale *
        (d)   categorical, nominal
           *Some researchers consider money as a discrete numerical variable because it can be "counted."

1.10   The underlying variable, ability of the students, may be continuous, but the measuring device, the test, does not have enough precision to distinguish between the two students.

1.12   The answer depends on the chosen data set.

1.14   The answer depends on the specific story.

1.16   The information presented there is based mainly on a mixture of data distributed by an organization and data collected by ongoing business activities.

Copyright ©2015 Pearson Education, Inc.

1.18   Sample without replacement: Read from left to right in 3-digit sequences and continue
        unfinished sequences from end of row to beginning of next row.
        Row 05: 338 505 855 551 438 855 077 186 579 488 767 833 170
        Rows 05-06: 897
        Row 06: 340 033 648 847 204 334 639 193 639 411 095 924
        Rows 06-07: 707
        Row 07: 054 329 776 100 871 007 255 980 646 886 823 920 461
        Row 08: 893 829 380 900 796 959 453 410 181 277 660 908 887
        Rows 08-09: 237
        Row 09: 818 721 426 714 050 785 223 801 670 353 362 449
        Rows 09-10: 406
        Note: All sequences above 902 and duplicates are discarded.

1.20   A simple random sample would be less practical for personal interviews because of travel
        costs (unless interviewees are paid to attend a central interviewing location).

1.22   Here all members of the population are equally likely to be selected and the sample selection
        mechanism is based on chance. But not every sample of size 2 has the same chance
        of being selected. For example the sample "B and C" is impossible.

1.24   (a)   Row 16: 2323 6737 5131 8888 1718 0654 6832 4647 6510 4877
               Row 17: 4579 4269 2615 1308 2455 7830 5550 5852 5514 7182
               Row 18: 0989 3205 0514 2256 8514 4642 7567 8896 2977 8822
               Row 19: 5438 2745 9891 4991 4523 6847 9276 8646 1628 3554
               Row 20: 9475 0899 2337 0892 0048 8033 6945 9826 9403 6858
               Row 21: 7029 7341 3553 1403 3340 4205 0823 4144 1048 2949
               Row 22: 8515 7479 5432 9792 6575 5760 0408 8112 2507 3742
               Row 23: 1110 0023 4012 8607 4697 9664 4894 3928 7072 5815
               Row 24: 3687 1507 7530 5925 7143 1738 1688 5625 8533 5041
               Row 25: 2391 3483 5763 3081 6090 5169 0546
               Note: All sequences above 5000 are discarded. There were no repeating sequences.
        (b)   089 189 289 389 489 589 689 789 889 989
               1089 1189 1289 1389 1489 1589 1689 1789 1889 1989
               2089 2189 2289 2389 2489 2589 2689 2789 2889 2989
               3089 3189 3289 3389 3489 3589 3689 3789 3889 3989
               4089 4189 4289 4389 4489 4589 4689 4789 4889 4989
        (c)   With the single exception of invoice #0989, the invoices selected in the simple
               random sample are not the same as those selected in the systematic sample. It would
               be highly unlikely that a random process would select the same units as a systematic
               process.

1.26   Before accepting the results of a survey of college students, you might want to know, for
        example:
        Who funded the survey? Why was it conducted? What was the population from which the
        sample was selected? What sampling design was used? What mode of response was used: a
        personal interview, a telephone interview, or a mail survey? Were interviewers trained? Were
        survey questions field-tested? What questions were asked? Were they clear, accurate,
        unbiased, valid? What operational definition of "vast majority" was used? What was the
        response rate? What was the sample size?

Copyright ©2015 Pearson Education, Inc.

1.28   The results are based on an online survey. If the frame is supposed to be smart phone and tablet users, how is the population defined? This is a self-selecting sample of people who responded online, so there is an undefined nonresponse error. Sampling error cannot be determined since this is not a random sample.

1.30   Before accepting the results of the survey, you might want to know, for example: Who funded the study? Why was it conducted? What was the population from which the sample was selected? What sampling design was used? What mode of response was used: a personal interview, a telephone interview, or a mail survey? Were interviewers trained? Were survey questions field-tested? What other questions were asked? Were the questions clear, accurate, unbiased, and valid? What was the response rate? What was the margin of error? What was the sample size? What frame was used?

1.32   A statistic is a summary measure describing a sample whereas a parameter is a summary measure describing an entire population.

1.34   Discrete random variables produce numerical responses that arise from a counting process. Continuous random variables produce numerical responses that arise from a measuring process.

1.36   Both interval scaled and ratio scaled variables are numerical variables in which the difference between measurements is meaningful but an interval scaled variable does not involve a true zero such as standardized exam scores while a ratio scaled variable involves a true zero such as height.

1.38   Microsoft Excel or Minitab could be used to perform various statistical computations that were possible only with a slide-rule or hand-held calculator in the old days.

1.40   The answers to this question depend on which article and its corresponding data set is being selected.

1.42   The answers to this question depend on which data set is being selected.

1.44   (a)   The population of interest was the collection of all the 10,000 benefitted employees at the University of Utah when the study was conducted.
        (b)   The sample consisted of the 3,095 benefitted employees participated in the study.
        (c)   gender: categorical; age: numerical; education level: numerical; marital status: categorical; household income: numerical; employment category: categorical

Copyright ©2015 Pearson Education, Inc.

CHAPTER 2

OBJECTIVES

- To construct tables and charts for categorical variables
- To construct tables and charts for numerical variables
- To learn the principles of properly presenting graphs
- To organize and analyze many variables

OVERVIEW AND KEY CONCEPTS

Organizing A Single Categorical Variable

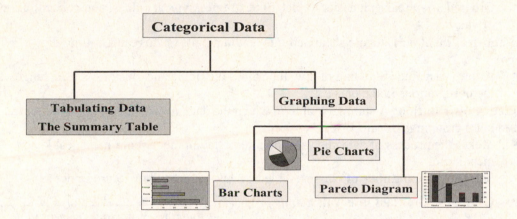

- **Summary table:** Similar to frequency distribution table for numerical data except there is no natural order of the classes
- **Bar chart:** Each category is depicted by a bar, the length of which represents the frequency or percentage of observations falling into a category
- **Pie chart:** The circle of 360^0 is divided into slices according to the percentage in each category
- **Pareto chart (diagram)**: A special type of vertical bar chart in which the categorized responses are plotted in the descending rank order of their frequencies and combined with a cumulative polygon on the same scale
  - Useful when the number of classification increases. Enables the separation of the "vital few" from the "trivial many"

Organizing Two or More Categorical Variables
- Contingency table (cross-classification table): Two-way table of cross-classification
- Side-by-side bar chart: Bar charts arranged side-by-side according to the different categories of the two categorical variables; useful when looking for patterns or relationship

Organizing A Single Numerical Variable

Copyright ©2015 Pearson Education, Inc.

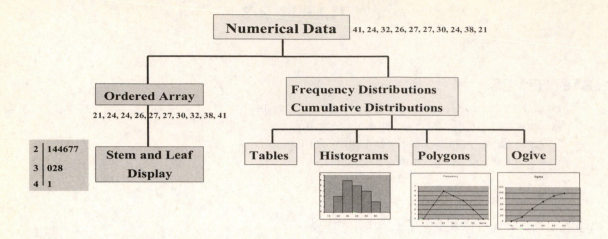

- **Ordered array:** Ordered sequence of raw data.
  - Ordered array makes it easier to pick out extremes, typical values, and concentrations of values.
- **Stem-and-leaf display:** Data are separated into leading digits (stems) and trailing digits (leaves).
  - Allows easy understanding of how the values distribute and cluster over the range of the observations in the data set.
- **Frequency distribution:** A summary table in which the data are arranged into numerically ordered class groupings or categories.
  - Makes the process of data analysis and interpretation much more manageable and meaningful
  - **Selecting the number of classes**: At least 5 but no more than 15 groupings
  - **Obtaining the class intervals:** $\text{width of interval} = \dfrac{\text{range}}{\text{number of desired class groupings}}$.
  - **Establishing the boundaries of the classes**: Non-overlapping classes must include the entire range of observations
  - **Class midpoint:** The point halfway between the boundaries of each class and is representative of the data within that class
- **Relative frequency distribution**: Formed by dividing the frequencies in each class of the frequency distribution by the total number of observations
  - Essential whenever one set of data is being compared with other sets of data if the number of observations in each set differs
- **Percentage distribution:** Formed by multiplying the relative frequencies by 100%
- **Cumulative distribution:** Formed from the frequency distribution, relative frequency distribution or percentage distribution by accumulating the frequencies, relative frequencies or percentages
  - It shows the number of observations below given values (lower class boundaries)
- **Histogram:** Vertical bar chart in which the rectangular bars are constructed at the boundaries of each class
- **Percentage polygon:** Formed by having the midpoint of each class represent the data in that class and then connecting the sequence of midpoints at their respective class percentages
  - Useful when comparing two or more sets of data
- **Cumulative polygon (Ogive):** Formed by plotting cumulative percentages against the lower boundaries of the classes and connecting the cumulative percentages

Copyright ©2015 Pearson Education, Inc.

- ▪ It is useful when comparing two or more sets of data

Graphing Two Numerical Variables
- **Scatter diagram (scatter plot):** Two-dimensional graph depicting how two numerical variables relate to each other
- **Time-series plot:** Two-dimensional graph that illustrates how a series of numerical data changes over time

Organizing Multidimensional Data
- Multidimensional contingency table: Tallies the responses of three or more categorical variables

Principles of Graphical Excellence
- Use a constant scale.
- A graph should not contain chartjunk, unnecessary adornments that convey no useful information.
- Any two-dimensional graph should contain a scale for each axis.
- The scale on the vertical axis should begin at zero.
- All axes should be properly labeled.
- The graph should contain a title.
- The simplest possible graph should be used for a given set of data.

Common Errors in Presenting Data
- Using "chart junk"
- No relative basis in comparing data between groups
- Compressing the vertical axis
- No zero point on the vertical axis

Copyright ©2015 Pearson Education, Inc.

SOLUTIONS TO END OF SECTION
AND CHAPTER REVIEW EVEN PROBLEMS

2.2   (a)   Table frequencies for all student responses

Student Major Categories

Gender	A	C	M	Totals
Male	14	9	2	25
Female	6	6	3	15
Totals	20	15	5	40

(b)   Table percentages based on overall student responses

Student Major Categories

Gender	A	C	M	Totals
Male	35.0%	22.5%	5.0%	62.5%
Female	15.0%	15.0%	7.5%	37.5%
Totals	50.0%	37.5%	12.5%	100.0%

Table based on row percentages

Student Major Categories

Gender	A	C	M	Totals
Male	56.0%	36.0%	8.0%	100.0%
Female	40.0%	40.0%	20.0%	100.0%
Totals	50.0%	37.5%	12.5%	100.0%

Table based on column percentages

Student Major Categories

Gender	A	C	M	Totals
Male	70.0%	60.0%	40.0%	62.5%
Female	30.0%	40.0%	60.0%	37.5%
Totals	100.0%	100.0%	100.0%	100.0%

2.4   (a)   The percentage of complaints for each automaker:

Automaker	Frequency	Percentage	Cumulative Pct.
General Motors	551	18.91%	18.91%
Other	516	17.71%	36.62%
Nissan Motors Corporation	467	16.03%	52.64%
Ford Motor Company	440	15.10%	67.74%
Chrysler LLC	439	15.07%	82.81%
Toyota Motor Sales	332	11.39%	94.20%
American Honda	169	5.80%	100.00%

(b)   General Motors has the most complaints, followed by Other, Nissan Motors Corporation, Ford Motor Company, Chryler LLC, Toyota Motor Sales and American Honda.

Copyright ©2015 Pearson Education, Inc.

2.4   (c)   The percentage of complaints for each category:
cont.

Category	Frequency	Percentage	Cumulative Pct.
Powertrain	1148	42.82%	42.82%
Steering	397	14.81%	57.63%
Interior Electronics/Hardware	279	10.41%	68.03%
Fuel/Emission/Exhaust System	240	8.95%	76.99%
Airbags and Seatbelts	201	7.50%	84.48%
Body and Glass	182	6.79%	91.27%
Brakes	163	6.08%	97.35%
Tires and Wheels	71	2.65%	100.00%

(d)   Powertrain has the most complaints, followed by steering, interior electronics/hardware, fuel/emission/exhaust system, airbags and seatbelts, body and glass, brakes, and, finally, tires and wheels.

2.6   (a)

Region	Oil Consumption (millions of barrels a day)	Percentag
Iran	3.53	4.00%
Saudi Arabia	9.34	10.58%
Other OPEC countries	22.87	25.91%
Non-OPEC countries	52.52	59.51%
Total	88.26	100.00%

(b)   More than half the oil produced is from non-OPEC countries. More than 25% is produced by OPEC countries other than Iran and Saudi Arabia..

2.8   (a)   Table of total percentages

ENJOY SHOPPING FOR CLOTHING FOR YOURSELF	GENDER		
	Male	Female	Total
Yes	22%	25%	47%
No	28%	25%	53%
Total	50%	50%	100%

Table of row percentages

ENJOY SHOPPING FOR CLOTHING FOR YOURSELF	GENDER		
	Male	Female	Total
Yes	46%	54%	100%
No	53%	47%	100%
Total	50%	50%	100%

Copyright ©2015 Pearson Education, Inc.

2.8   (a)   Table of column percentages
cont.

ENJOY SHOPPING FOR CLOTHING FOR YOURSELF	GENDER		
	Male	Female	Total
Yes	44%	51%	47%
No	56%	49%	53%
Total	100%	100%	100%

      (b)   A higher percentage of females enjoy shopping for clothing for themselves.

2.10   Social recommendations had very little impact on correct recall. Those who arrived at the link from a recommendation had a correct recall of 73.07% as compared to those who arrived at the link from browsing who had a correct recall of 67.96%.

2.12   Ordered array: 73 78 78 78 85 88 91

2.14   (a)   0 but less than 5 million, 5 million but less than 10 million, 10 million but less than 15 million, 15 million but less than 20 million, 20 million but less than 25 million, 25 million but less than 30 million.
       (b)   5 million
       (c)   2.5 million, 7.5 million, 12.5 million, 17.5 million, 22.5 million, and 27.5 million.

2.16   (a)

Electricity Costs	Frequency	Percentage
$80 to $99	4	8%
$100 to $119	7	14
$120 to $139	9	18
$140 to $159	13	26
$160 to $179	9	18
$180 to $199	5	10
$200 to $219	3	6

       (b)

Electricity Costs	Frequency	Percentage	Cumulative %
$99	4	8%	8%
$119	7	14%	22%
$139	9	18%	40%
$159	13	26%	66%
$179	9	18%	84%
$199	5	10%	94%
$219	3	6%	100%

       (c)   The majority of utility charges are clustered between $120 and $180.

Copyright ©2015 Pearson Education, Inc.

2.18 (a), (b)

Bin Cell	Frequency	Percentage	Cumulative Pctage.
695 but less than 705	3	2.10%	2.10%
705 but less than 715	12	8.39%	10.49%
715 but less than 725	12	8.39%	18.88%
715 but less than 735	19	13.29%	32.17%
735 but less than 745	18	12.59%	44.76%
745 but less than 755	24	16.78%	61.54%
755 but less than 765	22	15.38%	76.92%
765 but less than 775	20	13.99%	90.91%
775 but less than 785	10	6.99%	97.90%
795 but less than 795	3	2.10%	100.00%

(c)   The average credit scores are concentrated around 750.

2.20 (a), (b)

Bin	Frequency	Percentage	Cumulative %
8.310 -- 8.329	3	6.12%	6.12%
8.330 -- 8.349	2	4.08%	10.20%
8.350 -- 8.369	1	2.04%	12.24%
8.370 -- 8.389	4	8.16%	20.41%
8.390 -- 8.409	4	8.16%	28.57%
8.410 -- 8.429	15	30.61%	59.18%
8.430 -- 8.449	7	14.29%	73.47%
8.450 -- 8.469	5	10.20%	83.67%
8.470 -- 8.489	5	10.20%	93.88%
8.490 -- 8.509	3	6.12%	100.00%

(c)   All the troughs will meet the company's requirements of between 8.31 and 8.61 inches wide.

2.22 (a), (b) Manufacturer A:

Bin Cell	Frequency	Percentage	Cumulative Pctage.
6,500 but less than 7,500	3	7.50%	7.50%
7,500 but less than 8,500	5	12.50%	20.00%
8,500 but less than 9,500	20	50.00%	70.00%
9,500 but less than 10,500	9	22.50%	92.50%
10,500 but less than 11,500	3	7.50%	100.00%

Manufacturer B:

Bin Cell	Frequency	Percentage	Cumulative Pctage.
7,500 but less than 8,500	2	5.00%	5.00%
9,500 but less than 9,500	8	20.00%	25.00%
9,500 but less than 10,500	16	40.00%	65.00%
10,500 but less than 11,500	9	22.50%	87.50%
11,500 but less than 12,500	5	12.50%	100.00%

Copyright ©2015 Pearson Education, Inc.

2.22   (c)   Manufacturer B produces bulbs with longer lives than Manufacturer A. The
cont.   cumulative percentage for Manufacturer B shows 65% of its bulbs lasted less than
                 10,500 hours, contrasted with 70% of Manufacturer A's bulbs, which lasted less than
                 9,500 hours. None of Manufacturer A's bulbs lasted more than 11,499 hours, but
                 12.5% of Manufacturer B's bulbs lasted between 11,500 and 12,499 hours. At the
                 same time, 7.5% of Manufacturer A's bulbs lasted less than 7,500 hours, whereas all
                 of Manufacturer B's bulbs lasted at least 7,500 hours

2.24   (a)

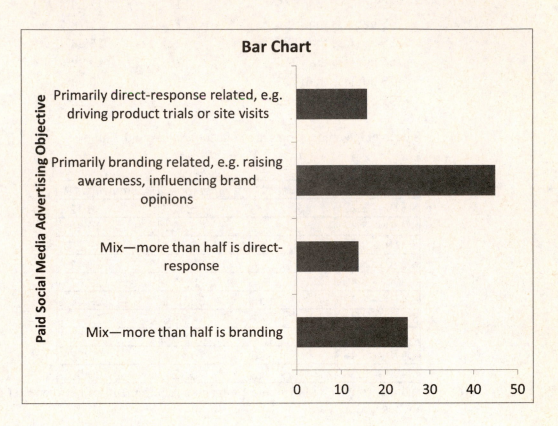

Copyright ©2015 Pearson Education, Inc.

2.24   (a)
cont.

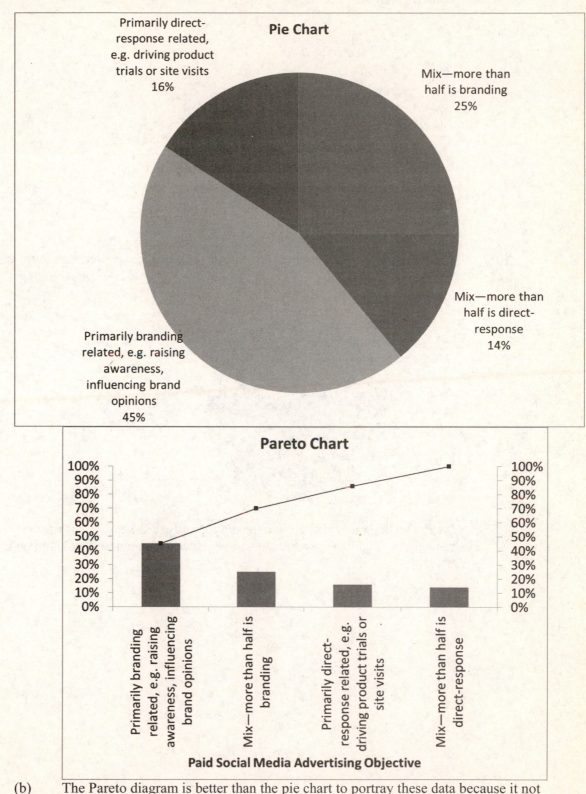

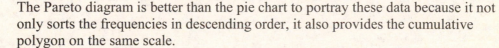

(b)   The Pareto diagram is better than the pie chart to portray these data because it not only sorts the frequencies in descending order, it also provides the cumulative polygon on the same scale.

Copyright ©2015 Pearson Education, Inc.

2.24   (c)   You can conclude that the "primarily branding related" objective accounts for the
cont.   largest percentage of 45%. When a mix of branding and direct response is added to
                primarily branding, this accounts for 84%.

2.26   (a)

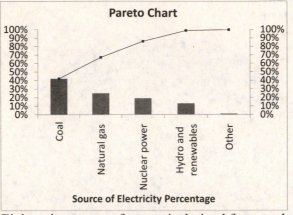

(b)   Eighty-six percent of power is derived from coal, nuclear power, or natural gas.

(c)

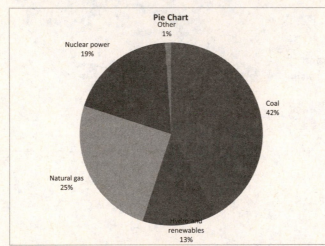

(d)   The Pareto diagram is better than the pie chart because it not only sorts the
        frequencies in descending order, it also provides the cumulative polygon on the same
        scale.

Copyright ©2015 Pearson Education, Inc.

2.28   (a)

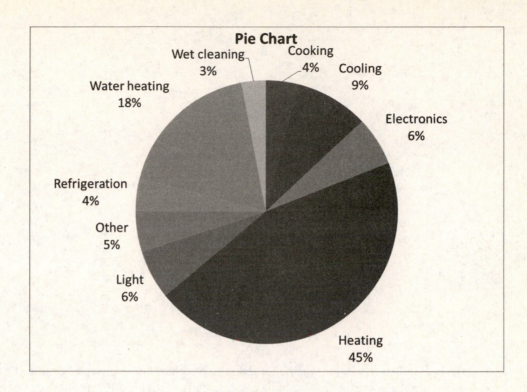

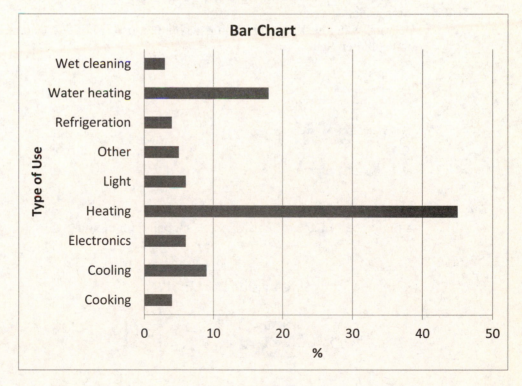

Copyright ©2015 Pearson Education, Inc.

2.28   (a)
cont.

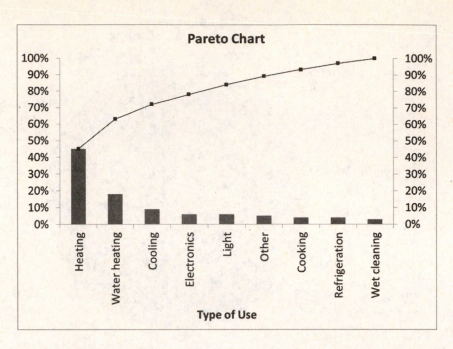

(b)   The Pareto diagram is better than the pie chart and bar chart because it not only sorts the frequencies in descending order; it also provides the cumulative polygon on the same scale.

(c)   Heating, water heating, and cooling accounted for 72% of the residential energy use in the United States.

2.30   (a)

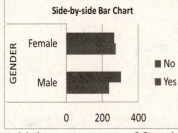

(b)   A higher percentage of females enjoy shopping for clothing.

2.32   (a)

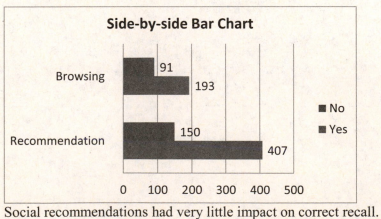

(b)   Social recommendations had very little impact on correct recall.

Copyright ©2015 Pearson Education, Inc.

2.34   Ordered array: 50   74   74   76   81   89   92

2.36   (a)

Statistics			Stem-and-Leaf Display	
			Stem unit 10	
Sample Size	30		14	6
Mean	207.6667		15	1 2 3
Median	197		16	0 6
Std. Deviation	48.81516		17	2 2 4 6
Minimum	146		18	4 4 5 7
Maximum	337		19	6 8
			20	
			21	3 7
			22	3 4 4 5 5
			23	0 3
			24	2
			25	7
			26	
			27	
			28	
			29	
			30	0
			31	
			32	4
			33	7

        (b)   The costs are concentrated between $172 and $225.

2.38   (a)

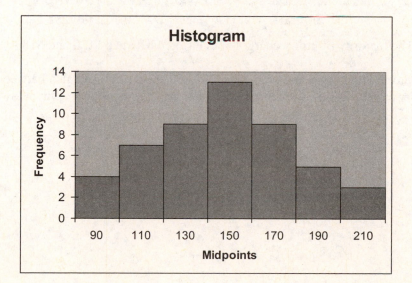

2.38   (a)
cont.

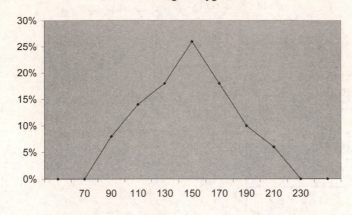

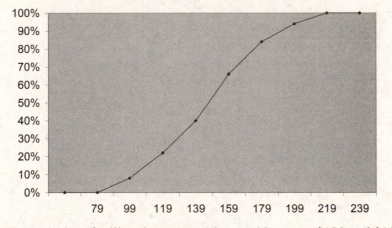

(b)

(c)   The majority of utility charges are clustered between $120 and $180.

2.40   Property taxes seem concentrated between $1,000 and $1,500 and also between $500 and $1,000 per capita. There were more states with property taxes per capita below $1,500 than above $1,500.

Copyright ©2015 Pearson Education, Inc.

2.42   (a)

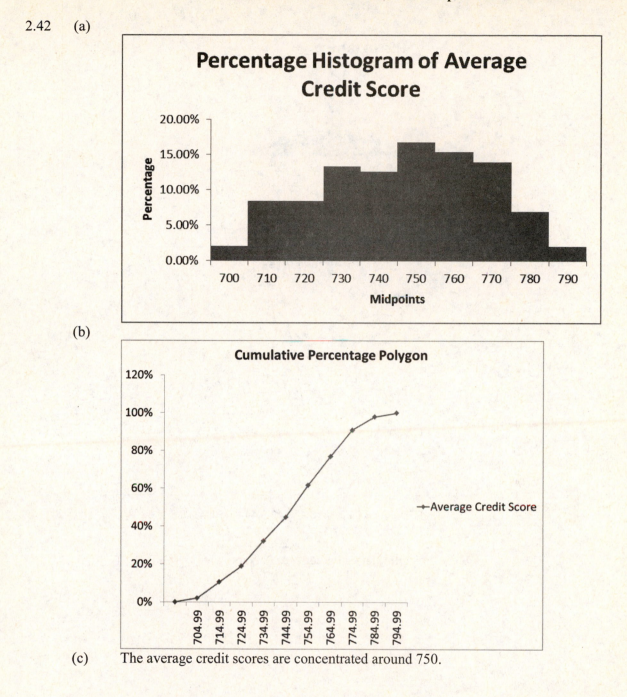

(c)   The average credit scores are concentrated around 750.

Copyright ©2015 Pearson Education, Inc.

2.44   (a)

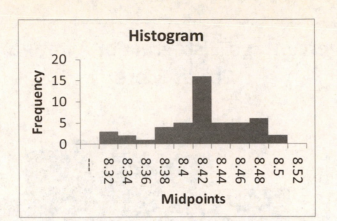

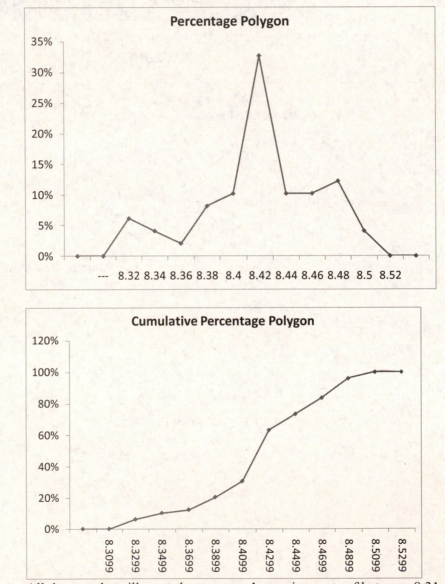

(b)

(c)   All the troughs will meet the company's requirements of between 8.31 and 8.61 inches wide.

Copyright ©2015 Pearson Education, Inc.

2.46   (a)

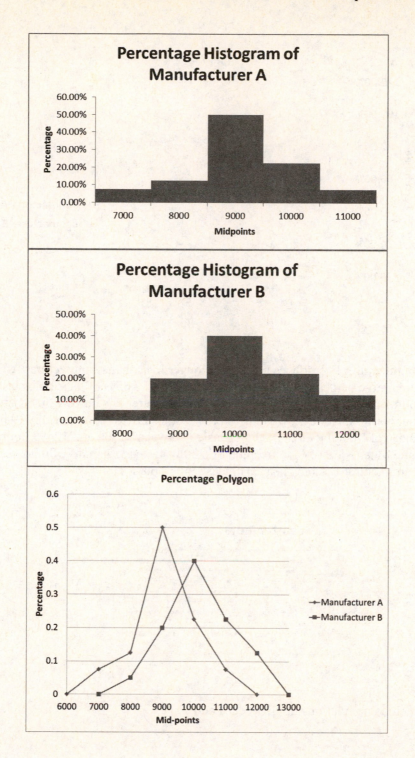

Copyright ©2015 Pearson Education, Inc.

2.46   (b)
cont.

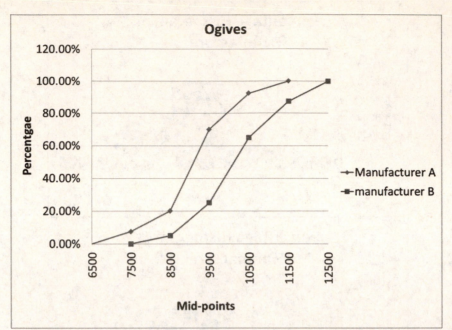

(c)   Manufacturer B produces bulbs with longer lives than Manufacturer A. The
cumulative percentage for Manufacturer B shows 65% of their bulbs lasted 10499
hours or less contrasted with 70% of Manufacturer A's bulbs which lasted 9499
hours or less. None of Manufacturer A's bulbs lasted more than 11499 hours, but
12.5% of Manufacturer B's bulbs lasted between 11500 and 12499 hours. At the
same time, 7.5% of Manufacturer A's bulbs lasted less than 7500 hours, while all of
Manufacturer B's bulbs lasted at least 7500 hours.

2.48   (a)

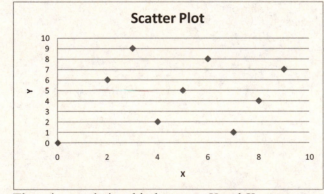

(b)   There is no relationship between X and Y.

Copyright ©2015 Pearson Education, Inc.

2.50   (a)

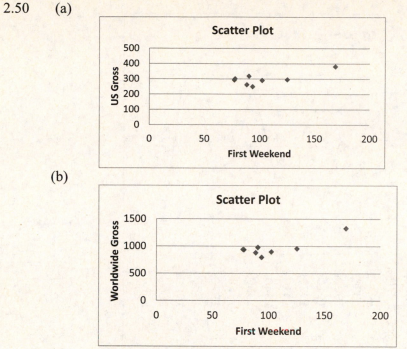

        (b)

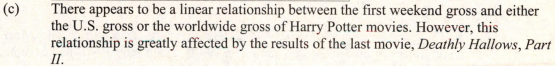

        (c)   There appears to be a linear relationship between the first weekend gross and either the U.S. gross or the worldwide gross of Harry Potter movies. However, this relationship is greatly affected by the results of the last movie, *Deathly Hallows*, *Part II*.

2.52   (a)   Yes, schools with higher revenues will also have higher coaches' total pay.
        (b)

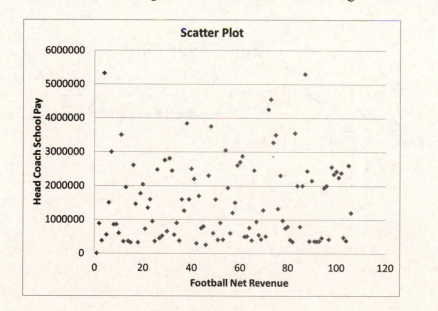

        (c)   The scatter plot contradicts your answer to (a).

Copyright ©2015 Pearson Education, Inc.

2.54   (a)   Excel output:

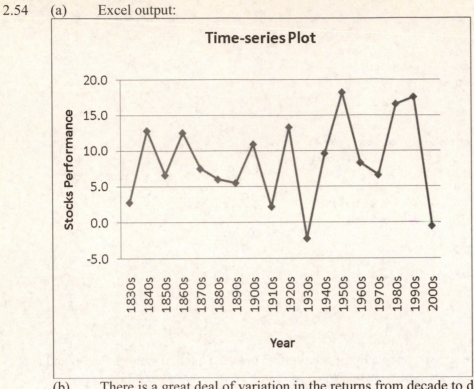

(b)   There is a great deal of variation in the returns from decade to decade. Most of the returns are between 5% and 15%. The 1950s, 1980s, and 1990s had exceptionally high returns, and only the 1930s and 2000s had negative returns.

2.56   (a)

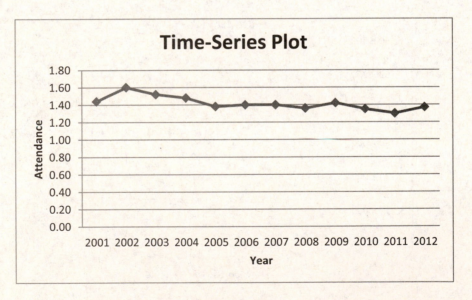

(b)   There was a slight decline in movie attendance between 2001 and 2012. During that time, movie attendance increased from 2001 to 2002 but then after 2004 began decreasing to levels below that in 2001.

Copyright ©2015 Pearson Education, Inc.

2.58   (a)   Pivotal table of tallies in terms of counts:

Count of 3YrReturn%	Star Rating					
Type	Five	Four	One	Three	Two	Grand Total
Growth	18	76	16	74	43	227
Large	9	31	5	37	21	103
Mid-Cap	7	28	4	20	13	72
Small	2	17	7	17	9	52
Value	5	22	7	36	19	89
Large	2	13	5	21	9	50
Mid-Cap	1	4		9	5	19
Small	2	5	2	6	5	20
Grand Total	23	98	23	110	62	316

Pivotal table of tallies in terms of % of grand total:

Count of 3YrReturn%	Star Rating					
Type	Five	Four	One	Three	Two	Grand Total
Growth	5.70%	24.05%	5.06%	23.42%	13.61%	71.84%
Large	2.85%	9.81%	1.58%	11.71%	6.65%	32.59%
Mid-Cap	2.22%	8.86%	1.27%	6.33%	4.11%	22.78%
Small	0.63%	5.38%	2.22%	5.38%	2.85%	16.46%
Value	1.58%	6.96%	2.22%	11.39%	6.01%	28.16%
Large	0.63%	4.11%	1.58%	6.65%	2.85%	15.82%
Mid-Cap	0.32%	1.27%	0.00%	2.85%	1.58%	6.01%
Small	0.63%	1.58%	0.63%	1.90%	1.58%	6.33%
Grand Total	7.28%	31.01%	7.28%	34.81%	19.62%	100.00%

(b)   Patterns of star rating conditioned on market cap:
For the growth funds as a group, most are rated as four-star, followed by three-star, two-star, five-star and one-star. The pattern of star rating is similar across the different market cap within the growth funds with most of the mid-cap funds receiving a four-star rating, followed by three-star, two-star, five-star and one-star, most of the small-cap funds receiving a four-star or three-star rating, followed by two-star, one-star and five-star while most of large cap funds receiving a three-star rating, followed by two-star, five-star and one-star.
For the value funds as a group, most are rated as three-star, followed by four-star, two-star, one-star and five-star. Within the value funds, the large-cap funds follow the same pattern as the value funds as a group. Most of the mid-cap funds are rated as three-star, followed by two-star, four-star, five-star and one-star while most of the small-cap funds are rated as three-star, followed by either two-star or four-star, and either one-star or five star.
Patterns of market cap conditioned on star rating:
Most of the growth funds are large-cap, followed by mid-cap and small-cap. The pattern is similar among the five-star, four-star, three-star and two-star growth funds but among the one-star growth funds, most are small-cap, followed by large-cap and mid-cap.

Copyright ©2015 Pearson Education, Inc.

2.58   (b)   The largest share of the value funds is large-cap, followed by small-cap and mid-cap.
cont.   The pattern is similar among the four-star and one-star value funds. Among the
               three-star value funds, most are large-cap, followed by mid-cap and then small-cap
               while most are large-cap, followed by equal portions of mid-cap and small-cap
               among the two-star value funds and most are either large-cap or small-cap followed
               by mid-cap among the five-star value funds.

2.60   (a)   Pivotal table of tallies in terms of counts:

Count of 3YrReturn%	Star Rating ▼					
Type ▼	Five	Four	One	Three	Two	Grand Total
⊟ Growth	18	76	16	74	43	227
Average	3	15	6	28	22	74
High		1	5	1	3	10
Low	15	60	5	45	18	143
⊟ Value	5	22	7	36	19	89
Average	1		3	7	6	17
High			2		1	3
Low	4	22	2	29	12	69
Grand Total	23	98	23	110	62	316

Pivotal table of tallies in terms of % of grand total:

Count of 3YrReturn%	Star Rating ▼					
Type ▼	Five	Four	One	Three	Two	Grand Total
⊟ Growth	5.70%	24.05%	5.06%	23.42%	13.61%	71.84%
Average	0.95%	4.75%	1.90%	8.86%	6.96%	23.42%
High	0.00%	0.32%	1.58%	0.32%	0.95%	3.16%
Low	4.75%	18.99%	1.58%	14.24%	5.70%	45.25%
⊟ Value	1.58%	6.96%	2.22%	11.39%	6.01%	28.16%
Average	0.32%	0.00%	0.95%	2.22%	1.90%	5.38%
High	0.00%	0.00%	0.63%	0.00%	0.32%	0.95%
Low	1.27%	6.96%	0.63%	9.18%	3.80%	21.84%
Grand Total	7.28%	31.01%	7.28%	34.81%	19.62%	100.00%

       (b)   Patterns of star rating conditioned on risk:
               For the growth funds as a group, most are rated as four-star, followed by three-star,
               two-star, five-star and one-star. The pattern of star rating is the same among the low-
               risk growth funds. The pattern is different among the high-risk and average-risk
               growth funds. Among the high-risk growth funds, most are rated as one-star,
               followed by two-star, equal portions of three-star and four-star with no five-star.
               Among the average-risk growth funds, most are rated as three-star, followed by two-
               star, four-star, one-star and five-star.
               For the value funds as a group, most are rated as three-star, followed by four-star,
               two-star, one-star and five-star. Among the average-risk value funds, most are three-
               star, followed by two-star, one-star, and five-star with no four-star. Among the high-
               risk value funds, most are one-star, followed by two-star with no three-star, four-star
               or five-star. Among the low-risk value funds, most are three-star, followed by four-
               star, two-star, five-star and one-star.
               Patterns of risk conditioned on star rating:

Copyright ©2015 Pearson Education, Inc.

2.60   (b)   Most of the growth funds are rated as low-risk, followed by average-risk and then
cont.   high-risk. The pattern is the same among the three-star, four-star and five-star
                   growth funds. Among the one-star growth funds, most are average-risk, followed by
                   equal portions of high-risk and low-risk. Among the two-star growth funds, most are
                   average-risk, followed by low-risk and high-risk.

                   Most of the value funds are rated as low-risk, followed by average-risk and then
                   high-risk. The pattern is the same among the two-star, three-star and five-star value
                   funds. Among the one-star value funds, most are average-risk, followed by equal
                   portions of high-risk and low-risk. Among the four-star value funds, all are low-risk
                   with no average-risk or high-risk.

2.66   (a)   There is a title.
        (b)   The simplest possible visualization is not used.
        (c)

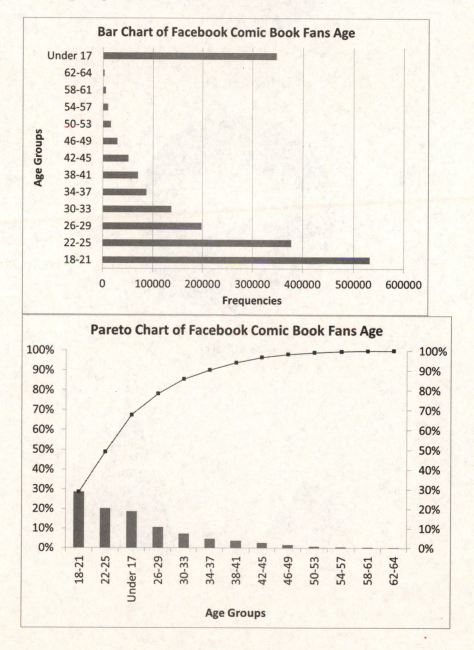

Copyright ©2015 Pearson Education, Inc.

2.70   (a)

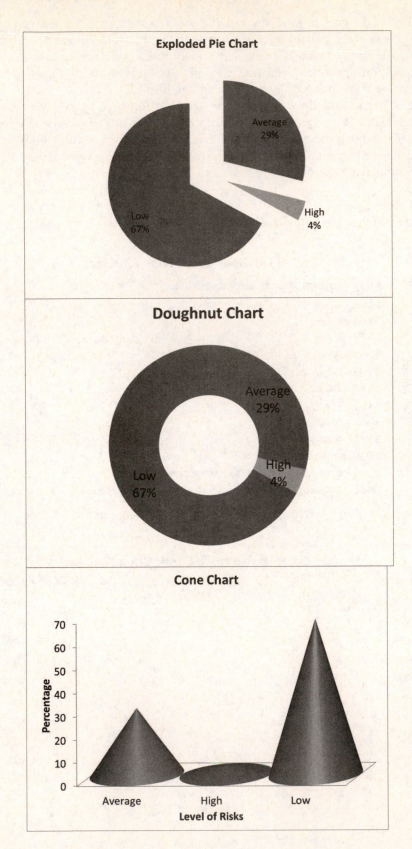

Copyright ©2015 Pearson Education, Inc.

2.70   (a)
cont.

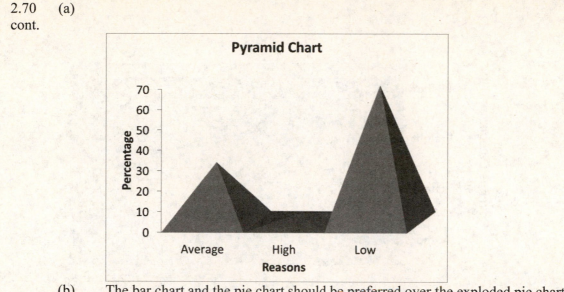

(b)   The bar chart and the pie chart should be preferred over the exploded pie chart, doughnut chart, the cone chart and the pyramid chart since the former set is simpler and easier to interpret.

2.72   A summary table allows one to determine the frequency or percentage of occurrences in each category.

2.74   The bar chart for categorical data is plotted with the categories on the vertical axis and the frequencies or percentages on the horizontal axis. In addition, there is a separation between categories. The histogram is plotted with the class grouping on the horizontal axis and the frequencies or percentages on the vertical axis. This allows one to more easily determine the distribution of the data. In addition, there are no gaps between classes in the histogram.

2.76   Because the categories are arranged according to frequency or importance, it allows the user to focus attention on the categories that have the greatest frequency or importance.

2.78   A contingency table contains information on two categorical variables whereas a multidimensional table can display information on more than two categorical variables.

Copyright ©2015 Pearson Education, Inc.

2.80   (a)

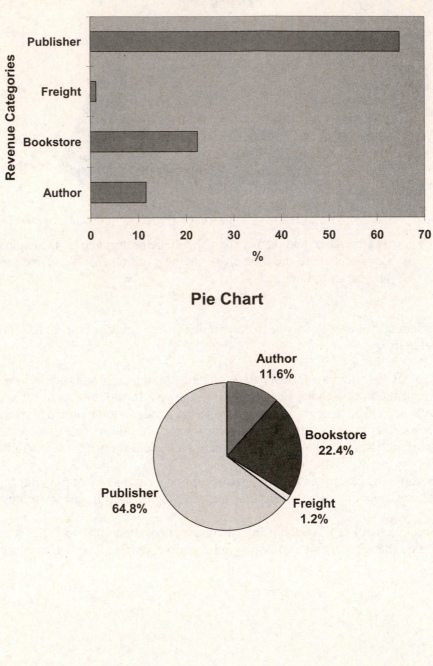

Bar Chart

Pie Chart

Copyright ©2015 Pearson Education, Inc.

2.80 (a)
cont.

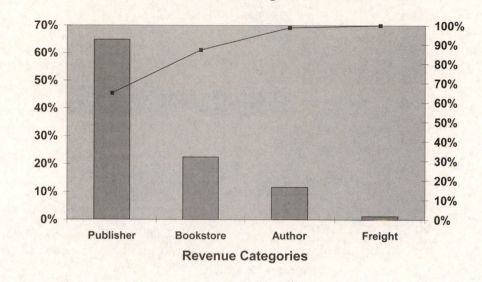

(b)

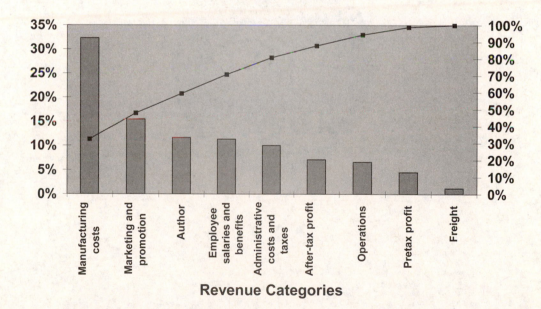

(c) The publisher gets the largest portion (64.8%) of the revenue. About half (32.3%) of the revenue received by the publisher covers manufacturing costs. The publisher's marketing and promotion account for the next largest share of the revenue, at 15.4%. Author, bookstore employee salaries and benefits, and publisher administrative costs and taxes each account for around 10% of the revenue, whereas the publisher after-tax profit, bookstore operations, bookstore pretax profit, and freight constitute the "trivial few" allocations of the revenue. Yes, the bookstore gets twice the revenue of the authors.

Copyright ©2015 Pearson Education, Inc.

2.82 (a)

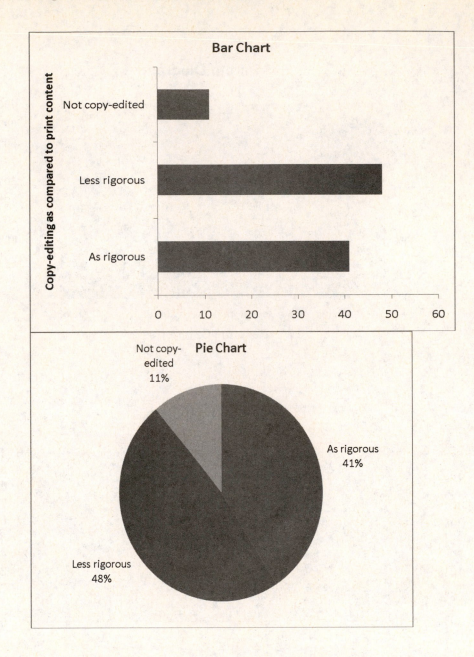

Copyright ©2015 Pearson Education, Inc.

2.82   (a)
cont.

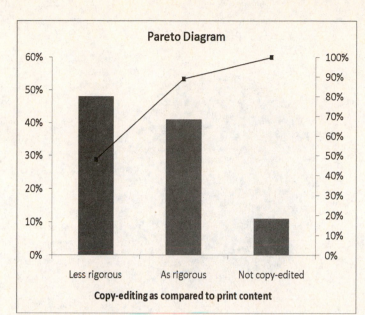

(b)   Since there are only three categories, all the three graphical methods are capable of portraying these data well. The Pareto diagram, however, is better than the pie chart and bar chart because it not only sorts the frequencies in descending order, it also provides the cumulative polygon on the same scale.

(c)

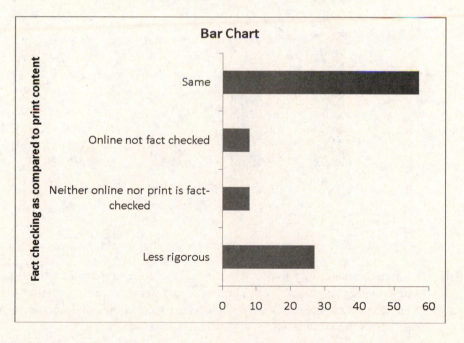

2.82 (c)
cont.

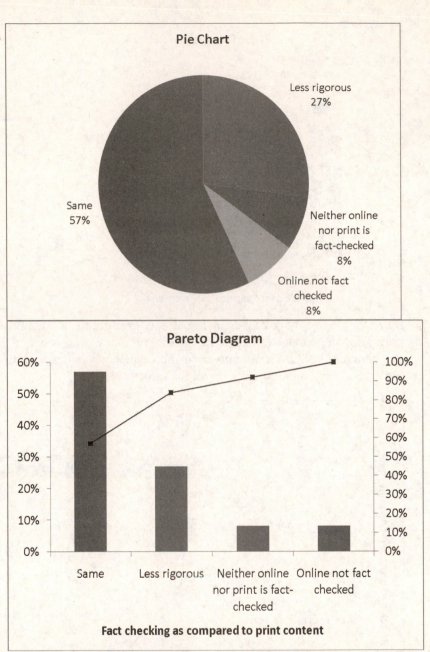

(d) Since there are only four categories, all the three graphical methods are capable of portraying these data well. The Pareto diagram, however, is better than the pie chart and bar chart because it not only sorts the frequencies in descending order, it also provides the cumulative polygon on the same scale.

(e) Based on the Pareto chart for copy-editing, about 50% of the contents in online consumer magazines receive less rigorous copy-editing. Based on the Pareto chart for fact-checking, more than 50% of the contents in online consumer magazines receive the same amount of fact-checking.

Copyright ©2015 Pearson Education, Inc.

2.84   (a)

Count of Dessert Ordered	Gender ⊷		
Desserts Ordered ⊷	Male	Female	Grand Total
Yes	34.25%	65.75%	100.00%
No	51.65%	48.35%	100.00%
Grand Total	47.62%	52.38%	100.00%

Count of Dessert Ordered	Gender ⊷		
Desserts Ordered ⊷	Male	Female	Grand Total
Yes	16.67%	29.09%	23.17%
No	83.33%	70.91%	76.83%
Grand Total	100.00%	100.00%	100.00%

Count of Dessert Ordered	Gender ⊷		
Desserts Ordered ⊷	Male	Female	Grand Total
Yes	7.94%	15.24%	23.17%
No	39.68%	37.14%	76.83%
Grand Total	47.62%	52.38%	100.00%

Count of Dessert Ordered	Beef Entrée ⊷		
Dessert Ordered ⊷	Yes	No	Grand Total
Yes	52.11%	47.89%	100.00%
No	25.20%	74.80%	100.00%
Grand Total	31.27%	68.73%	100.00%

Count of Dessert Ordered	Beef Entrée ⊷		
Dessert Ordered ⊷	Yes	No	Grand Total
Yes	37.56%	15.70%	22.54%
No	62.44%	84.30%	77.46%
Grand Total	100.00%	100.00%	100.00%

Count of Dessert Ordered	Beef Entrée ⊷		
Dessert Ordered ⊷	Yes	No	Grand Total
Yes	11.75%	10.79%	22.54%
No	19.52%	57.94%	77.46%
Grand Total	31.27%	68.73%	100.00%

(b)   If the owner is interested in finding out the percentage of joint occurrence of gender and ordering of dessert or the percentage of joint occurrence of ordering a beef entrée and a dessert among all patrons, the table of total percentages is most informative. If the owner is interested in the effect of gender on ordering of dessert or the effect of ordering a beef entrée on the ordering of dessert, the table of column percentages will be most informative. Since dessert will usually be ordered after the main entree and the owner has no direct control over the gender of patrons, the table of row percentages is not very useful here.

Copyright ©2015 Pearson Education, Inc.

2.84   (c)   16.67% of the men sampled ordered desserts compared to 29.09% of the women.
cont.   Women are almost twice as likely to order desserts as men. 37.56% of the patrons
              ordering a beef entree ordered dessert compared to less than 15.7% of patrons
              ordering all other entrees. Patrons ordering beef are better than 2.3 times as likely to
              order dessert as patrons ordering any other entree.

2.86   (a)

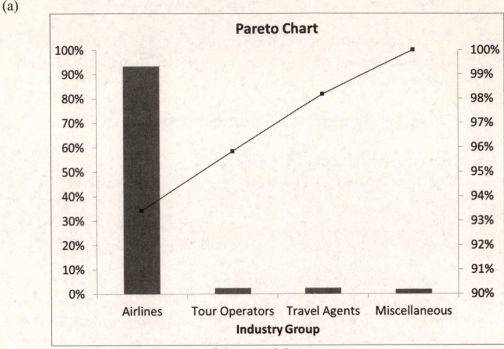

Airlines account for most of the complaints.

(b)

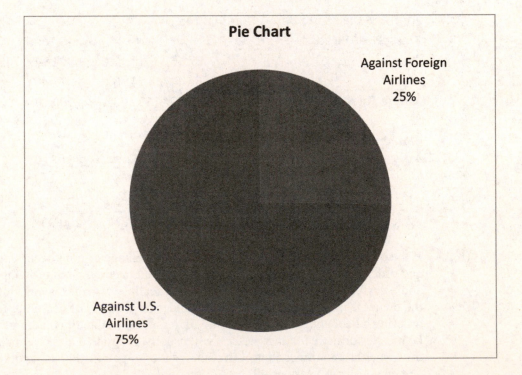

Copyright ©2015 Pearson Education, Inc.

2.86   (c)
cont.

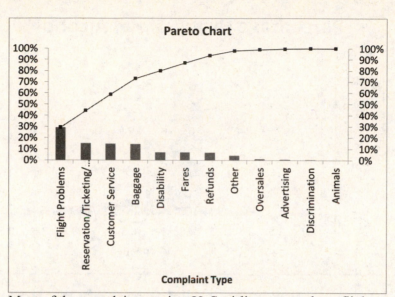

Most of the complaints against U. S. airlines were about flight problems, followed by reservations/ticketing/boarding, customer service, and baggage.

(d)   **Foreign airlines:**

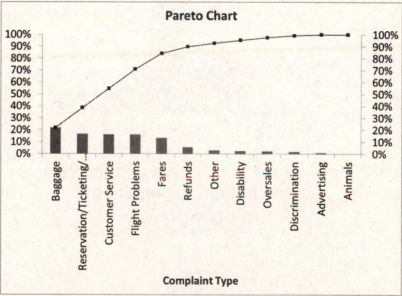

Most of the complaints against foreign airlines were about baggage, then reservations/ticketing/boarding, flight problems, and customer service.

Copyright ©2015 Pearson Education, Inc.

2.88   (a)

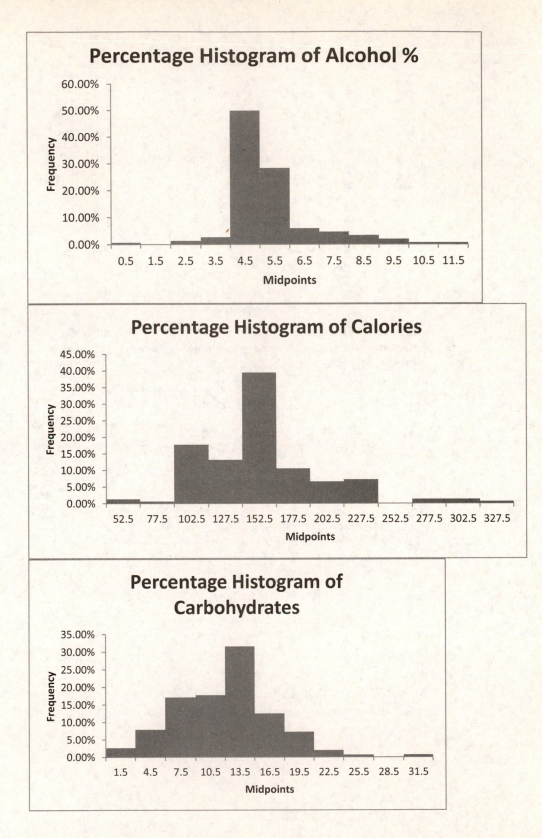

Copyright ©2015 Pearson Education, Inc.

2.88   (b)
cont.

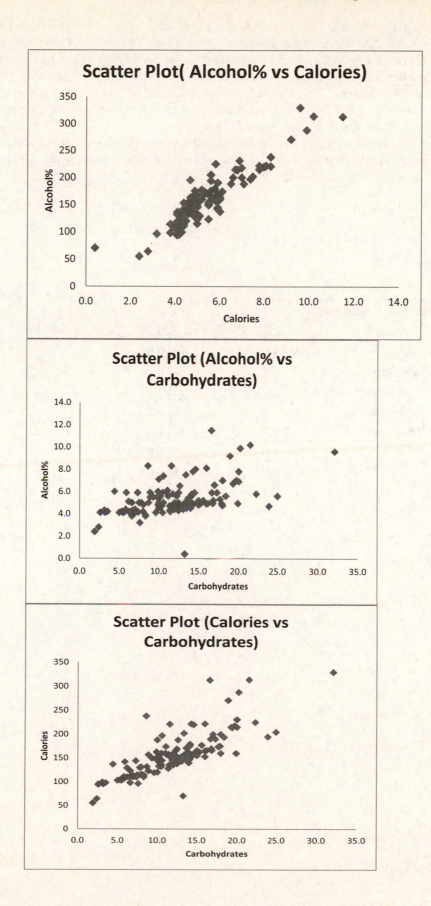

Copyright ©2015 Pearson Education, Inc.

2.88   (c)   The alcohol % is concentrated between 4 and 6, with more between 4 and 5. The
cont.   calories are concentrated between 140 and 160. The carbohydrates are concentrated
               between 12 and 15. There are outliers in the percentage of alcohol in both tails. The
               outlier in the lower tail is due to the non-alcoholic beer O'Doul's with only a 0.4%
               alcohol content. There are a few beers with alcohol content as high as around 11.5%.
               There are a few beers with calories content as high as around 327.5 and
               carbohydrates as high as around 31.5.
               There is a strong positive relationship between percentage alcohol and calories, and
               calories and carbohydrates and a moderately positive relationship between percentage
               alcohol and carbohydrates.

2.90   (a)   One-year CD:

Stem-and-Leaf Disp

Stem unit 0.1

Statistics		
Sample Size	23	
Mean	0.645652	
Median	0.8	
Std. Deviation	0.311051	
Minimum	0.1	
Maximum	1.05	

Stem	Leaf
1	05
2	05
3	005
4	0
5	
6	55
7	1
8	00089
9	00007
10	05

Copyright ©2015 Pearson Education, Inc.

2.90   (a)   5-year CD
cont.

		Stem-and-Leaf Displa
		Stem unit 0.1
Statistics		3 5
Sample Size	23	4 0
Mean	1.276087	5 0
Median	1.41	6
Std. Deviation	0.408998	7
Minimum	0.35	8
Maximum	1.85	9 5
		10 0 5
		11
		12 0 0 4 5
		13
		14 0 1 5
		15 0 1 2 2 4 5
		16 0 0
		17 6
		18 5

(b)

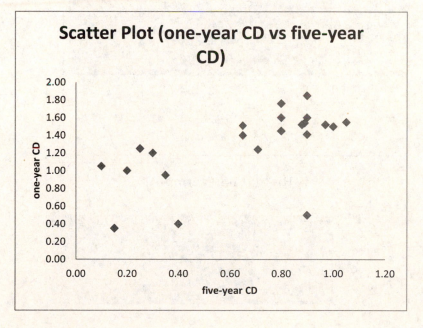

(c)   There appears to be a positive relationship between the yield of the one-year CD and
             the five-year CD.

Copyright ©2015 Pearson Education, Inc.

2.92   (a)

Frequencies (Boston)

Weight (Boston)	Frequency	Percentage
3015 but less than 3050	2	0.54%
3050 but less than 3085	44	11.96%
3085 but less than 3120	122	33.15%
3120 but less than 3155	131	35.60%
3155 but less than 3190	58	15.76%
3190 but less than 3225	7	1.90%
3225 but less than 3260	3	0.82%
3260 but less than 3295	1	0.27%

(b)

Frequencies (Vermont)

Weight (Vermont)	Frequency	Percentage
3550 but less than 3600	4	1.21%
3600 but less than 3650	31	9.39%
3650 but less than 3700	115	34.85%
3700 but less than 3750	131	39.70%
3750 but less than 3800	36	10.91%
3800 but less than 3850	12	3.64%
3850 but less than 3900	1	0.30%

(c)

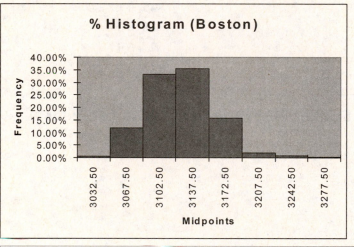

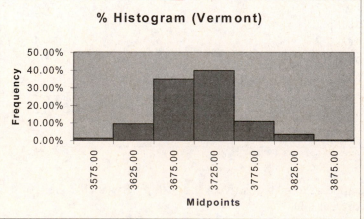

Copyright ©2015 Pearson Education, Inc.

2.92   (d)   0.54% of the "Boston" shingles pallets are underweight while 0.27% are overweight.
cont.   1.21% of the "Vermont" shingles pallets are underweight while 3.94% are
               overweight.

2.94   (a)

Calories	Frequency	Percentage	Percentage Less Than
50 up to 100	3	12%	12%
100 up to 150	3	12	24
150 up to 200	9	36	60
200 up to 250	6	24	84
250 up to 300	3	12	96
300 up to 350	0	0	96
350 up to 400	1	4	100

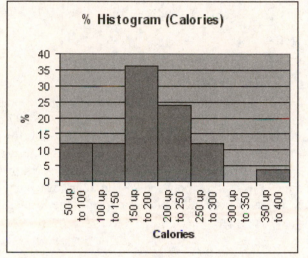

(b)

Cholesterol	Frequency	Percentage	Percentage Less Than
0 up to 50	2	8	8%
50 up to 100	17	68	76
100 up to 150	4	16	92
150 up to 200	1	4	96
200 up to 250	0	0	96
250 up to 300	0	0	96
300 up to 350	0	0	96
350 up to 400	0	0	96
400 up to 450	0	0	96
450 up to 500	1	4	100

Copyright ©2015 Pearson Education, Inc.

2.94   (b)
cont.

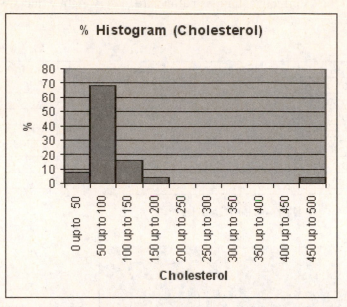

(c)   The sampled fresh red meats, poultry, and fish vary from 98 to 397 calories per serving, with the highest concentration between 150 to 200 calories. One protein source, spareribs, with 397 calories, is more than 100 calories above the next highest caloric food. The protein content of the sampled foods varies from 16 to 33 grams, with 68% of the data values falling between 24 and 32 grams. Spareribs and fried liver are both very different from other foods sampled—the former on calories and the latter on cholesterol content.

2.96   (a)

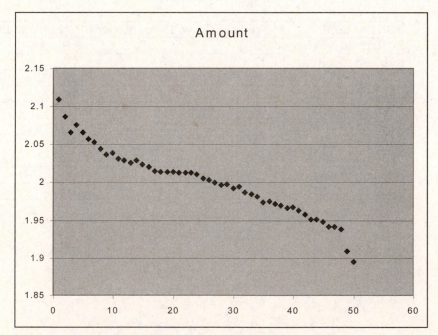

(b)   There is a downward trend in the amount filled.
(c)   The amount filled in the next bottle will most likely be below 1.894 liter.
(d)   The scatter plot of the amount of soft drink filled against time reveals the trend of the data, whereas a histogram only provides information on the distribution of the data.

Copyright ©2015 Pearson Education, Inc.

2.98   (a)

Variations	Percentage of Download
Original Call to Action Button	9.64%
New Call to Action Button	13.64%

(b)

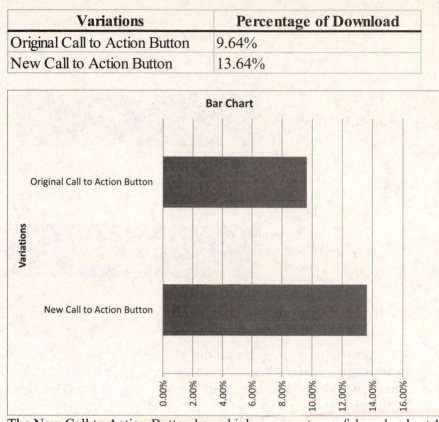

(c)   The New Call to Action Button has a higher percentage of downloads at 13.64% when compared to the Original Call to Action Button with a 9.64% of downloads.

(d)

Variations	Percentage of Downloads
Original web design	8.90%
New web design	9.41%

Copyright ©2015 Pearson Education, Inc.

2.98   (e)
cont.

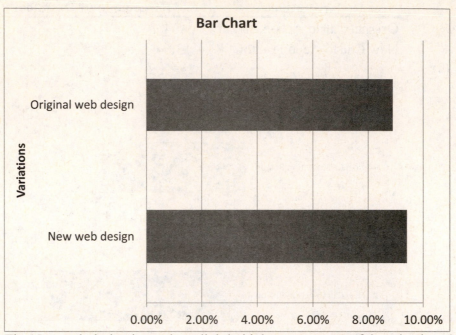

(f)   The New web design has only a slightly higher percentage of downloads at 9.41% when compared to the Original web design with an 8.90% of downloads.

(g)   The New web design is only slightly more successful than the Original web design while the New Call to Action Button is much more successful than the Original Call to Action Button with about 41% higher percentage of downloads.

(h)

Call to Action Button	Web Design	Percentage of Downloads
Old	Old	8.30%
New	Old	13.70%
Old	New	9.50%
New	New	17.00%

(i)   The combination of the New Call to Action Button and the New web design results in slightly more than twice as high a percentage of downloads than the combination of the Old Call to Action Button and Old web design.

(j)   The New web design is only slightly more successful than the Original web design while the New Call to Action Button is much more successful than the Original Call to Action Button with about 41% higher percentage of downloads. However, the combination of the New Call to Action Button and New web design results in more than twice as high a percentage of downloads than the combination of the Old Call to Action Button and Old web design.

Copyright ©2015 Pearson Education, Inc.

CHAPTER 3

OBJECTIVES

- To describe the properties of central tendency, variation, and shape in numerical data
- To construct and interpret a boxplot
- To compute descriptive summary measures for a population
- To compute the covariance and the coefficient of correlation

OVERVIEW AND KEY CONCEPTS

Measures of Central Tendency

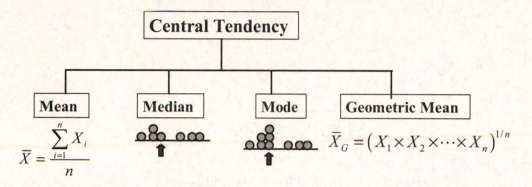

- **Arithmetic mean:** The sum of all the observations in a set of data divided by the total number of observations.

    - $$\bar{X} = \frac{\sum_{i=1}^{n} X_i}{n}$$

    - The arithmetic mean is the most common measure of central tendency.
    - It is very sensitive to extreme values, called outliers.
- **Median:** The value such that 50% of the observations are smaller and 50% of the observations are larger.

    - Median = $\frac{n+1}{2}$ ranked observation.

    - If n is odd, the median is the middle ranked observation.
    - If n is even, the median is the average of the two middle ranked observations.
    - The median is not affected by extreme values.
- **Mode:** The value that occurs most often in a set of data.
    - It is not affected by extreme values.
    - There may be several modes or there may be no mode in a set of data.
    - It can be used for either numerical or categorical data.
- **Geometric mean:** The nth root of the product of n values.
    - $\bar{X}_G = \left(X_1 \times X_2 \times \cdots \times X_n \right)^{1/n}$

    - It is useful in the measure of rate of change of a variable over time.

Copyright ©2015 Pearson Education, Inc.

- ▪ The geometric mean rate of return can be used to measure the status of an investment over time. $\bar{R}_G = \left[\left(1 + R_1 \right) \times \left(1 + R_2 \right) \times \cdots \times \left(1 + R_n \right) \right]^{1/n} - 1$
- **Quartiles:** The most widely used measures of noncentral location.
  - ▪ The ordered data is split into four equal portions.
  - ▪ The first quartile (Q_1) is the value for which 25% of the observations are smaller and 75% are larger.

    $Q_1 = \dfrac{n+1}{4}$ ordered observation.
  - ▪ The third quartile (Q_3) is the value for which 75% of the observations are smaller and 25% are larger.

    $Q_3 = \dfrac{3(n+1)}{4}$ ordered observation.
  - ▪ The median is the second quartile.

    $Q_2 = \dfrac{(n+1)}{2}$ ordered observation.

Measures of Variation

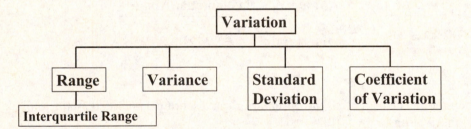

- **Range:** The largest value minus the smallest value.
  - ▪ The range ignores how the data are distributed.
  - ▪ It is very sensitive to extreme values.
- **Interquartile range (mid-spread):** The 3rd quartile minus the 1st quartile.
  - ▪ It is not affected by extreme values.
  - ▪ It measures the spread of the middle 50% of the observations.
- **Sample variance:** The sum of the squared differences around the arithmetic mean divided by the sample size minus 1.
  - ▪ $S^2 = \dfrac{\sum\limits_{i=1}^{n} \left(X_i - \bar{X} \right)^2}{n-1}$
  - ▪ Sample variance measures the average scatter around the mean.
- **Sample standard deviation:** The square root of the sample variance.
  - ▪ $S = \sqrt{\dfrac{\sum\limits_{i=1}^{n} \left(X_i - \bar{X} \right)^2}{n-1}}$
  - ▪ Sample standard deviation has the same units of measurement as the original data.

Copyright ©2015 Pearson Education, Inc.

- **Coefficient of Variation:** The standard deviation divided by the arithmetic mean, multiplied by 100%.

    - $$CV = \left(\frac{S}{\bar{X}}\right)100\%$$

        - It is a relative measure of variation.
        - It is used in comparing two or more sets of data measured in different units.

- **Z Scores:** The Z score of a data value is the difference between that value and the mean, divided by the standard deviation.

    - $$Z = \frac{X - \bar{X}}{S}$$

        - It measures how many standard deviations an observation is away from the sample mean in either direction.
        - As a general rule, a Z score that is less than -3.0 or greater than +3.0 indicates an outlier value.

Shape of a Distribution

- The shape describes how data are distributed.
- The shape of the distribution of data values can be described by two statistics: skewness and kurtosis.
- **Skewness** measures the extent to which the data values are not symmetrical around the mean.
- **Kurtosis** measures the extent to which values that are very different from the mean affect the shape of the distribution of a set of data.
    - Kurtosis affects the peakedness and the ends (tails) of the curve of the distribution.
    - A normal distribution has a kurtosis of zero.
    - Lepokurtic distribution: A sharper-rising center peak and fatter tails than a normal distribution has a positive kurtosis.
    - Platykurtic distribution: A slower-rising center peak and thinner tails than a normal distribution has a negative kurtosis.

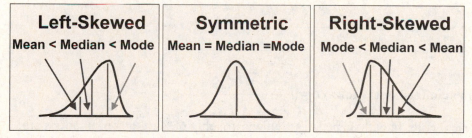

Exploratory Data Analysis

- A five-number summary consists of $X_{smallest}$, Q_1, Median, Q_3, $X_{largest}$.
- **Boxplot** provides a graphical representation of the data based on the five-number summary.

Copyright ©2015 Pearson Education, Inc.

Distribution Shape and Boxplot

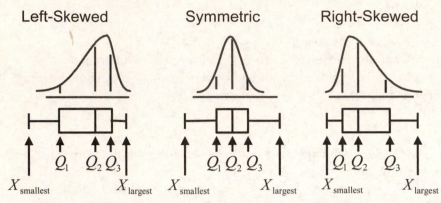

- In right-skewed distributions, the distance from the median to X_{largest} is greater than the distance from X_{smallest} to the median.
- In right-skewed distribution, the distance from Q_3 to X_{largest} is greater than the distance from X_{smallest} to Q_1.
- In left-skewed distributions, the distance from the median to X_{largest} is smaller than the distance from X_{smallest} to the median.
- In left-skewed distribution, the distance from Q_3 to X_{largest} is smaller than the distance from X_{smallest} to Q_1.

Obtaining Descriptive Summary Measures from a Population

- **Population mean:** $\mu = \dfrac{\sum_{i=1}^{N} X_i}{N}$

- **Population variance:** $\sigma^2 = \dfrac{\sum_{i=1}^{N} (X_i - \mu)^2}{N}$

- **Population standard deviation:** $\sigma = \sqrt{\dfrac{\sum_{i=1}^{N} (X_i - \mu)^2}{N}}$

- **The empirical rule:** In bell-shaped distributions, roughly 68% of the observations are contained within a distance of ± 1 standard deviation around the mean, approximately 95% of the observations are contained within a distance of ± 2 standard deviation around the mean and approximately 99.7% are contained within a distance of ± 3 standard deviation around the mean.

- **The Bienaymé-Chebyshev rule:** Regardless of how skewed a set of data is distributed, the percentage of observations that are contained within distances of k standard deviations around the mean must be at least $\left(1 - \dfrac{1}{k^2}\right)100\%$

  - At least 75% of the observations must be contained within distances of ± 2 standard deviation around the mean.
  - At least 88.89% of the observations must be contained within distances of ± 3 standard deviation around the mean.

Copyright ©2015 Pearson Education, Inc.

- ▪ At least 93.75% of the observations must be contained within distances of ± 4 standard deviation around the mean.

Covariance and Correlation Coefficient as a Measure of Strength between Two Numerical Variables

- • **Sample Covariance:** $\text{cov}(X,Y) = \dfrac{\sum\limits_{i=1}^{n}\left(X_i - \bar{X}\right)\left(Y_i - \bar{Y}\right)}{n-1}$

  - ▪ Measures the strength of a linear relationship between 2 numerical variables X and Y.
  - ▪ Is not unit free so cannot be used to determine the relative strength of the relationship.

- • **The coefficient of correlation:** $r = \dfrac{\sum\limits_{i=1}^{n}\left(X_i - \bar{X}\right)\left(Y_i - \bar{Y}\right)}{\sqrt{\sum\limits_{i=1}^{n}\left(X_i - \bar{X}\right)^2 \sum\limits_{i=1}^{n}\left(Y_i - \bar{Y}\right)^2}}$

  - ▪ Measures the strength of a linear relationship between 2 numerical variables X and Y.
  - ▪ Is unit free.
  - ▪ The values are between -1 and 1.
  - ▪ The closer r is to -1, the stronger the negative linear relationship.
  - ▪ The closer r is to $+1$, the stronger the positive linear relationship.
  - ▪ If r is close to 0, little or no linear relationship exists.
  - ▪ Correlation alone cannot prove that there is a causation effect—that is, that the change in the value of one variable caused the change in the other variable.
  - ▪ Causation implies correlation, but correlation alone does not imply causation.

Copyright ©2015 Pearson Education, Inc.

SOLUTIONS TO END OF SECTION
AND CHAPTER REVIEW EVEN PROBLEMS

3.2   (a)   Excel output:

X	
Mean	7
Median	7
Mode	7
Standard Deviation	3.286335
Sample Variance	10.8
Range	9
Minimum	3
Maximum	12
Sum	42
Count	6
First Quartile	4
Third Quartile	9
Interquartile Range	5
Coefficient of Variation	46.9476%

Mean = 7   Median = 7   Mode = 7

(b)   Range = 9   Variance = 10.8
Standard deviation = 3.286
Coefficient of variation = $(3.286/7) \cdot 100\% = 46.948\%$

(c)   Z scores: 0, -0.913, 0.609, 0, -1.217, 1.522
None of the Z scores is larger than 3.0 or smaller than -3.0. There is no outlier.

(d)   Since the mean equals the median, the distribution is symmetrical.

3.4   Excel output:

X	
Mean	2
Median	7
Mode	7
Standard Deviation	7.874007874
Sample Variance	62
Range	17
Minimum	-8
Maximum	9
Sum	10
Count	5
First Quartile	-6.5
Third Quartile	8
Interquartile Range	14.5
Coefficient of Variation	393.7004%

(a)   Mean = 2   Median = 7   Mode = 7

Copyright ©2015 Pearson Education, Inc.

3.4   (b)   Range = 17   Variance = 62
cont.   Standard deviation = 7.874   Coefficient of variation = (7.874/2)•100% = 393.7%
      (c)   Z scores: 0.635, -0.889, -1.270, 0.635, 0.889. No outliers.
      (d)   Since the mean is less than the median, the distribution is left-skewed.

3.6 $\bar{R}_G = \left[(1+0.2)(1-0.3)\right]^{1/2} - 1 = -8.348\%$

3.8   (a)

	Grade X	Grade Y
Mean	575	575.4
Median	575	575
Standard deviation	6.4	2.1

(b)   If quality is measured by central tendency, Grade X tires provide slightly better quality because X's mean and median are both equal to the expected value, 575 mm. If, however, quality is measured by consistency, Grade Y provides better quality because, even though Y's mean is only slightly larger than the mean for Grade X, Y's standard deviation is much smaller. The range in values for Grade Y is 5 mm compared to the range in values for Grade X, which is 16 mm.

(c)   Excel output:

Grade X		Grade Y	
Mean	575	Mean	577.4
Median	575	Median	575
Mode	#N/A	Mode	#N/A
Standard Deviation	6.403124	Standard Deviation	6.107373
Sample Variance	41	Sample Variance	37.3
Range	16	Range	15
Minimum	568	Minimum	573
Maximum	584	Maximum	588
Sum	2875	Sum	2887
Count	5	Count	5

	Grade X	Grade Y, Altered
Mean	575	577.4
Median	575	575
Standard deviation	6.4	6.1

When the fifth Y tire measures 588 mm rather than 578 mm, Y's mean inner diameter becomes 577.4 mm, which is larger than X's mean inner diameter, and Y's standard deviation increases from 2.1 mm to 6.1 mm. In this case, X's tires are providing better quality in terms of the mean inner diameter, with only slightly more variation among the tires than Y's.

Copyright ©2015 Pearson Education, Inc.

3.10   (a), (b)

Cost ($)	
Mean	7.093333
Median	6.8
Mode	6.5
Standard Deviation	1.406031
Sample Variance	1.976924
Range	4.71
Minimum	4.89
Maximum	9.6
Sum	106.4
Count	15
First Quartile	5.9
Third Quartile	8.3
CV	19.82%

(c)   The mean is only slightly larger than the median, so the data are only slightly right-skewed.

(d)   The mean amount spent is $7.09 and the median is $6.8. The average scatter of the amount spent around the mean is $1.41. The difference between the highest and the lowest amount spent is $4.71.

3.12   (a), (b)

MPG	
Mean	22.52941
Standard Error	0.446536
Median	22
Mode	22
Standard Deviation	1.841115
Sample Variance	3.389706
Kurtosis	0.340209
Skewness	0.525947
Range	7
Minimum	19
Maximum	26
Sum	383
Count	17
First Quartile	21.5
Third Quartile	23.5
CV	8.17%

Copyright ©2015 Pearson Education, Inc.

3.12   (a),(b)
cont.

MPG	Z Score	MPG	Z Score
22	-0.28755	19	-1.917
23	0.2556	22	-0.28755
21	-0.8307	22	-0.28755
22	-0.28755	26	1.885047
25	1.341898	23	0.2556
26	1.885047	24	0.798749
22	-0.28755	21	-0.8307
22	-0.28755	22	-0.28755
21	-0.8307		

(c)   The data appears to be symmetrical since the median is about the same as the mean.

(d)   The distribution of MPG of the sedans is slightly right-skewed while that of the SUVs is symmetrical. The mean MPG of sedans is 4.59 higher than that of SUVs. The average scatter of the MPG of sedans is almost 3 times that of SUVs. The range of sedans is slightly more than 2.5 times that of SUVs.

3.14   (a), (b)

Facebook Penetration	
Mean	36.27733
Standard Error	3.407431
Median	38.16
Mode	#N/A
Standard Deviation	13.19692
Sample Variance	174.1588
Kurtosis	0.745362
Skewness	-0.72185
Range	48.08
Minimum	5.37
Maximum	53.45
Sum	544.16
Count	15
First Quartile	30.12
Third Quartile	49.35
CV	36.38%

Copyright ©2015 Pearson Education, Inc.

3.14   (a), (b)
cont.

Country	Facebook Penetration	Z Score
United States	52.56	1.233823
Brazil	33.09	-0.24152
India	5.37	-2.34201
Indonesia	19.41	-1.27813
Mexico	32.52	-0.28471
Turkey	41.69	0.410146
United Kingdom	51.61	1.161836
Philippines	30.12	-0.46657
France	39.07	0.211615
Germany	30.62	-0.42869
Italy	38.16	0.14266
Argentina	49.35	0.990584
Canada	53.45	1.301263
Colombia	40.01	0.282844
Thailand	27.13	-0.69314

None of the Z scores are more than 3 standard deviations away from the mean so there is not any outlier.

(c)   The mean is only slightly smaller than the median, so the data are only slightly left-skewed.

(d)   The mean market penetration value is 36.2773 and the median is 38.16. The average scatter around the mean is 13.1969. The difference between the highest and the lowest value is 48.08.

3.16   (a), (b)

Cost(US$)	
Mean	155.75
Standard Error	4.565984
Median	158
Mode	158
Standard Deviation	12.91455
Sample Variance	166.7857
Kurtosis	-0.91399
Skewness	-0.51964
Range	36
Minimum	135
Maximum	171
Sum	1246
Count	8
First Quartile	141
Third Quartile	169
CV	8.29%

(c)   The mean price is $ 155.75 and the median is $ 158. The average scatter around the mean is $ 12.9146. The difference between the highest and the lowest value is $36.

Copyright ©2015 Pearson Education, Inc.

3.16   (d)   (a), (b)
cont.

Cost(US$)	
Mean	159.375
Standard Error	7.055741
Median	158
Mode	158
Standard Deviation	19.95665
Sample Variance	398.2679
Kurtosis	2.033271
Skewness	1.114906
Range	65
Minimum	135
Maximum	200
Sum	1275
Count	8
First Quartile	141
Third Quartile	169
CV	12.52%

(c)   The mean price is $159.375 and the median is $158. The average scatter
around the mean is $19.96. The difference between the highest and the
lowest value is $65.

The mean, standard deviation and range are sensitive to outliers. The higher
price at $200 raises the value of mean, standard deviation and range while
having no impact on the median.

3.18   Excel output:

Waiting Time	
Mean	7.114667
Median	6.68
Mode	#N/A
Standard Deviation	2.082189
Sample Variance	4.335512
Range	6.67
Minimum	3.82
Maximum	10.49
Sum	106.72
Count	15
First Quartile	5.64
Third Quartile	8.73
Interquartile Range	3.09
Coefficient of Variation	29.2662%

(a)   Mean = 7.114   Median = 6.68

Copyright ©2015 Pearson Education, Inc.

3.18   (b)   Variance = 4.336   Standard deviation = 2.082   Range = 6.67
cont.   Coefficient of variation = 29.27%

Waiting Time	Z Score
9.66	1.222431
5.90	-0.58336
8.02	0.434799
5.79	-0.63619
8.73	0.775786
3.82	-1.58231
8.01	0.429996
8.35	0.593286
10.49	1.62105
6.68	-0.20875
5.64	-0.70823
4.08	-1.45744
6.17	-0.45369
9.91	1.342497
5.47	-0.78987

   (b)   There is no outlier since none of the observations are greater than 3 standard deviations away from the mean.

   (c)   Because the mean is greater than the median, the distribution is right-skewed.

   (d)   The mean and median are both greater than 5 minutes. The distribution is right-skewed, meaning that there are some unusually high values. Further, 13 of the 15 bank customers sampled (or 86.7%) had waiting times greater than 5 minutes. So the customer is likely to experience a waiting time in excess of 5 minutes. The manager overstated the bank's service record in responding that the customer would "almost certainly" not wait longer than 5 minutes for service.

3.20   (a) $\bar{R}_G = \left[(1+0.024)(1+0.746)\right]^{1/2} - 1 = 33.71\%\%$

   (b)   If you purchased $1,000 of TASER stock at the start of 2011, its value at the end of 2012 was $1000(1+0.3371)^2 = \$ 1,787.904$.

   (c)   The result for Taser was better than the result for GE, which was worth $1188.41.

3.22   (a)

Year	Platinum	Gold	Silver
2012	8.7	0.1	7.1
2011	-21.1	10.2	-9.8
2010	21.5	29.8	83.7
2009	55.9	23.9	49.3
Geometric mean	12.90%	15.41%	27.58%

   (b)   Silver had the highest return, followed by gold and then platinum.

   (c)   Silver had a much higher return than the DJIA, the S&P 500, and the NASDAQ; gold's return was worse than the NASDAQ but better than the S&P 500 and DJIA; platinum's return was better than S&P 500 and DJIA but worse than NASDAQ.

Copyright ©2015 Pearson Education, Inc.

3.24   (a)

Average of 1YrReturn%	Star R					
Type	Five	Four	One	Three	Two	Grand Total
⊟ Growth	16.5544	15.2193	10.3575	13.9957	13.6058	14.2780
Large	18.0756	15.4971	12.3320	14.8743	17.1257	15.6771
Mid-Cap	15.5200	15.0400	10.0875	13.4140	8.7046	13.2160
Small	13.3300	15.0082	9.1014	12.7676	12.4722	12.9771
⊟ Value	17.2820	12.7295	13.4957	15.3603	15.4863	14.6982
Large	16.4150	11.7515	12.1120	14.5648	14.1633	13.5898
Mid-Cap	16.4400	16.1625		16.7267	17.4680	16.7879
Small	18.5700	12.5260	16.9550	16.0950	15.8860	15.4840
Grand Total	16.7126	14.6604	11.3126	14.4423	14.1821	14.3963

(b)

StdDev of 1YrReturn%	Star R					
Type	Five	Four	One	Three	Two	Grand Total
⊟ Growth	4.0813	3.6946	5.0187	3.8308	7.6709	5.0041
Large	4.3119	4.1374	4.6690	2.7064	7.4925	4.7615
Mid-Cap	3.3099	3.1017	8.7458	4.8023	7.6199	5.4705
Small	4.4265	3.9244	2.2479	4.3906	2.9127	4.0854
⊟ Value	6.9822	4.5679	4.3343	4.1815	3.6530	4.4651
Large	1.1384	3.6990	4.3732	4.5739	2.5803	4.0592
Mid-Cap	#DIV/0!	4.1910		3.1676	4.5127	3.4837
Small	13.7179	6.3546	1.6476	3.9994	4.1620	5.4861
Grand Total	4.6722	4.0202	4.9474	3.9820	6.7243	4.8551

(c)   The mean one-year return of small-cap value funds is higher than that of the small-cap growth funds across the different star ratings with the exception of those rated as four-star. On the other hand, the mean one-year return of large-cap value funds is lower than that of the growth funds across the different star ratings but the mid-cap value funds are higher across the different star ratings.

The standard deviation of the one-year return of growth funds is generally higher than that of the value funds across all the star ratings and market caps with the exception of the large-cap and three-star, mid-cap and five-star, mid-cap and four-star, mid-cap and one-star, small-cap and five-star, small-cap and four-star, and small-cap and two-star.

Copyright ©2015 Pearson Education, Inc.

3.26 (a)

Average of 1YrReturn%	Star Rating					
Type	Five	Four	One	Three	Two	Grand Total
⊟ **Growth**	**16.5544**	**15.2193**	**10.3575**	**13.9957**	**13.6058**	**14.2780**
Average	16.5333	16.2233	11.6467	13.0514	10.8005	13.0524
High		14.6100	9.3620	14.5900	33.7200	17.7170
Low	16.5587	14.9785	9.8060	14.5700	13.6822	14.6717
⊟ **Value**	**17.2820**	**12.7295**	**13.4957**	**15.3603**	**15.4863**	**14.6982**
Average	28.2700		13.9800	16.4786	17.5267	17.1012
High			12.0500		22.1400	15.4133
Low	14.5350	12.7295	14.2150	15.0903	13.9117	14.0751
Grand Total	**16.7126**	**14.6604**	**11.3126**	**14.4423**	**14.1821**	**14.3963**

(b)

StdDev of 1YrReturn%	Star Rating					
Type	Five	Four	One	Three	Two	Grand Total
⊟ **Growth**	**4.0813**	**3.6946**	**5.0187**	**3.8308**	**7.6709**	**5.0041**
Average	3.0735	4.9524	7.6948	4.9654	6.9272	6.0163
High		#DIV/0!	2.6945	#DIV/0!	0.2946	11.3821
Low	4.3448	3.3483	3.0114	2.8818	2.1220	3.3562
⊟ **Value**	**6.9822**	**4.5679**	**4.3343**	**4.1815**	**3.6530**	**4.4651**
Average	#DIV/0!		4.0506	2.9673	3.8277	4.4488
High			8.5843		#DIV/0!	8.4131
Low	3.8335	4.5679	0.5445	4.4251	2.4852	4.1475
Grand Total	**4.6722**	**4.0202**	**4.9474**	**3.9820**	**6.7243**	**4.8551**

(c) In general, the mean one-year return of the five-star rated growth funds is highest, followed by that of the four-star, three-star, two-star and one-star rated growth funds across the various risk levels. However, similar pattern does not hold through among the value funds.

There is no obvious pattern in the standard deviation of the one-year return.

3.28 (a) $Q_1 = 4$, $Q_3 = 9$, interquartile range = 5
(b) Five-number summary: 3 4 7 9 12
(c)

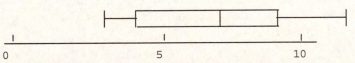

The distances between the median and the extremes are close, 4 and 5, but the differences in the tails are different (1 on the left and 3 on the right), so this distribution is slightly right-skewed.

(d) In 3.2 (d), because the mean and median are equal , the distribution is symmetric. The box part of the graph is symmetric, but the tails show right-skewness.

Copyright ©2015 Pearson Education, Inc.

3.30   (a) $Q_1 = -6.5$, $Q_3 = 8$, interquartile range = 14.5
        (b)   Five-number summary: -8 -6.5 7 8 9
        (c)

Box-and-whisker Plot

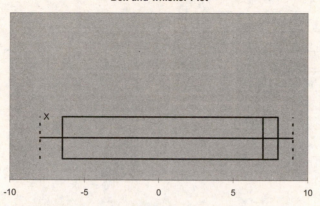

The distribution is left-skewed.
        (d)   This is consistent with the answer in 3.4 (d).

3.32   (a), (b)

Five-Number Summary	
Minimum	5.37
First Quartile	30.12
Median	38.16
Third Quartile	49.35
Maximum	53.45
Interquartile Range	19.23

        (c)

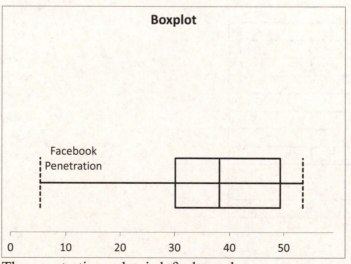

The penetration value is left-skewed.

Copyright ©2015 Pearson Education, Inc.

3.34   (a), (b)

Five-Number Summary	
Minimum	19
First Quartile	21.5
Median	22
Third Quartile	23.5
Maximum	26
Interquartile Range	2

(c)

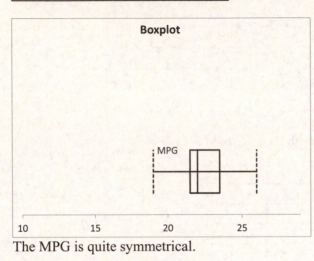

The MPG is quite symmetrical.

3.36   Excel output for Residential Area:

Waiting Time	
Mean	7.114667
Median	6.68
Mode	#N/A
Standard Deviation	2.082189
Sample Variance	4.335512
Range	6.67
Minimum	3.82
Maximum	10.49
Sum	106.72
Count	15
First Quartile	5.64
Third Quartile	8.73
Interquartile Range	3.09
Coefficient of Variation	29.2662%

Copyright ©2015 Pearson Education, Inc.

3.36
cont.

Excel output for Residential Area:

Box-and-whisker Plot	
Five-number Summary	
Minimum	3.82
First Quartile	5.64
Median	6.68
Third Quartile	8.73
Maximum	10.49

Excel output for Commercial District:

Waiting Time	
Mean	4.286667
Standard Error	0.422926
Median	4.5
Mode	#N/A
Standard Deviation	1.637985
Sample Variance	2.682995
Kurtosis	0.832925
Skewness	-0.83295
Range	6.08
Minimum	0.38
Maximum	6.46
Sum	64.3
Count	15
First Quartile	3.2
Third Quartile	5.55
Interquartile Range	2.35
Coefficient of Variation	38.2112%

Box-and-whisker Plot	
Five-number Summary	
Minimum	0.38
First Quartile	3.2
Median	4.5
Third Quartile	5.55
Maximum	6.46

(a)　　**Commercial district**: Five-number summary: 0.38 3.2 4.5 5.55 6.46
　　　　Residential area: Five-number summary: 3.82 5.64 6.68 8.73 10.49

Copyright ©2015 Pearson Education, Inc.

3.36   (b)   **Commercial district:**
cont.

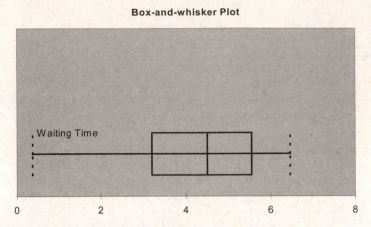

The distribution is skewed to the left.
Residential area:

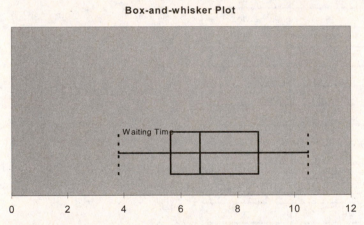

The distribution is skewed slightly to the right.

(c)   The central tendency of the waiting times for the bank branch located in the commercial district of a city is lower than that of the branch located in the residential area. There are a few longer than normal waiting times for the branch located in the residential area whereas there are a few exceptionally short waiting times for the branch located in the commercial area.

3.38   (a)   Population Mean = 6
        (b) $\sigma^2 = 2.8$ $\sigma = 1.67$

3.40   (a)   68%   (b)   95%   (c)   not calculable   75%   88.89%
        (d) $\mu - 4\sigma$ to $\mu + 4\sigma$ or -2.8 to 19.2

Copyright ©2015 Pearson Education, Inc.

3.42   Excel output:

Kilowatt Hours	
Mean	12999.22
Standard Error	546.9863
Median	13255
Mode	#N/A
Standard Deviation	3906.264
Sample Variance	15258895
Kurtosis	0.232784
Skewness	0.468115
Range	18171
Minimum	6396
Maximum	24567
Sum	662960
Count	51

(a)   mean = 12999.2158,   variance = 14959700.52,   std. dev. = 3867.7772

(b)   64.71%, 98.04% and 100% of these states have average per capita energy consumption within 1, 2 and 3 standard deviations of the mean, respectively.

(c)   This is consistent with the 68%, 95% and 99.7% according to the empirical rule.

(d)   Excel output:

Kilowatt Hours	
Mean	12857.74
Standard Error	539.0489
Median	12999
Mode	#N/A
Standard Deviation	3811.651
Sample Variance	14528684
Kurtosis	0.464522
Skewness	0.494714
Range	18171
Minimum	6396
Maximum	24567
Sum	642887
Count	50

(d)   (a)   mean = 12857.7402, variance = 14238110.67, std. dev. = 3773.3421

(b)   66%, 98% and 100% of these states have average per capita energy consumption within 1, 2 and 3 standard deviation of the mean, respectively.

(c)   This is consistent with the 68%, 95% and 99.7% according to the empirical rule.

Copyright ©2015 Pearson Education, Inc.

3.44   (a) $cov(X, Y) = 65.2909$

       (b) $S_X^2 = 21.7636$, $S_Y^2 = 195.8727$

$$r = \frac{cov(X, Y)}{\sqrt{S_X^2}\sqrt{S_Y^2}} = \frac{65.2909}{\sqrt{21.7636}\sqrt{195.8727}} = +1.0$$

       (c)   There is a perfect positive linear relationship between X and Y; all the points lie exactly on a straight line with a positive slope.

3.46   (a) $cov(X, Y) = 133.3333$

       (b) $S_X^2 = 2200$, $S_Y^2 = 11.4762$

$$r = \frac{cov(X, Y)}{S_X S_Y} = 0.8391$$

       (c)   The correlation coefficient is more valuable for expressing the relationship between calories and sugar because it does not depend on the units used to measure calories and sugar.

       (d)   There is a strong positive linear relationship between calories and sugar.

3.48   (a) $cov(X, Y) = 1.43478 \times 10^{13}$

       (b) $S_X^2 = 1.4339 \times 10^{12}$, $S_Y^2 = 2.3890 \times 10^{14}$

$$r = \frac{cov(X, Y)}{S_X S_Y} = 0.7752$$

       (c)   There is a positive linear relationship between the coaches' pay and revenue.

3.50   We should look for ways to describe the typical value, the variation, and the distribution of the data within a range.

3.52   The arithmetic mean is a simple average of all the values, but is subject to the effect of extreme values. The median is the middle ranked value, but varies more from sample to sample than the arithmetic mean, although it is less susceptible to extreme values. The mode is the most common value, but is extremely variable from sample to sample.

3.54   Variation is the amount of dispersion, or "spread," in the data.

3.56   The range is a simple measure, but only measures the difference between the extremes. The interquartile range measures the range of the center fifty percent of the data. The standard deviation measures variation around the mean while the variance measures the squared variation around the mean, and these are the only measures that take into account each observation. The coefficient of variation measures the variation around the mean relative to the mean. The range, standard deviation, variance and coefficient of variation are all sensitive to outliers while the interquartile range is not.

3.58   The Chebyshev rule applies to any type of distribution while the empirical rule applies only to data sets that are approximately bell-shaped. The empirical rule is more accurate than the Chebyshev rule in approximating the concentration of data around the mean.

3.60   The arithmetic mean is appropriate if you want to obtain a typical value and serves as a "balance point" in a set of data, similar to the fulcrum on a seesaw. The geometric mean is appropriate when you want to measure the rate of change of a variable over time.

Copyright ©2015 Pearson Education, Inc.

3.62   The covariance measures the strength of the linear relationship between two numerical variables while the coefficient of correlation measures the relative strength of the linear relationship. The value of the covariance depends very much on the units used to measure the two numerical variables while the value of the coefficient of correlation is totally free from the units used.

3.64   Excel output:

Time	
Mean	43.88889
Standard Error	4.865816
Median	45
Mode	17
Standard Deviation	25.28352
Sample Variance	639.2564
Range	76
Minimum	16
Maximum	92
First Quartile	18
Third Quartile	63
interquartile range	45
c.v	57.61%

(a)   mean = 43.89   median = 45   1st quartile = 18 3rd quartile = 63
(b)   range = 76   interquartile range = 45   variance = 639.2564
        standard deviation = 25.28   coefficient of variation = 57.61%
(c)

Box-and-whisker Plot

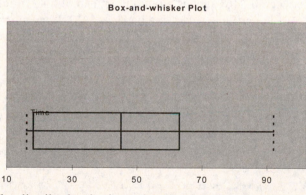

The distribution is skewed to the right because there are a few policies that require an exceptionally long period to be approved even though the mean is smaller than the median.

(d)   The mean approval process takes 43.89 days with 50% of the policies being approved in less than 45 days. 50% of the applications are approved between 18 and 63 days. About 67% of the applications are approved between 18.6 to 69.2 days.

Copyright ©2015 Pearson Education, Inc.

3.66   Excel output:

Width	
Mean	8.420898
Standard Error	0.006588
Median	8.42
Mode	8.42
Standard Deviation	0.046115
Sample Variance	0.002127
Kurtosis	0.035814
Skewness	-0.48568
Range	0.186
Minimum	8.312
Maximum	8.498
Sum	412.624
Count	49
First Quartile	8.404
Third Quartile	8.459
Interquartile Range	0.055
CV	0.55%

(a)   mean = 8.421, median = 8.42, range = 0.186 and standard deviation = 0.0461. On average, the width is 8.421 inches. The width of the middle ranked observation is 8.42. The difference between the largest and smallest width is 0.186 and majority of the widths fall between 0.0461 inches around the mean of 8.421 inches.

(b)   Minimum = 8.312, 1st quartile = 8.404, median = 8.42, 3rd quartile = 8.459 and maximum = 8.498

Box-and-whisker Plot

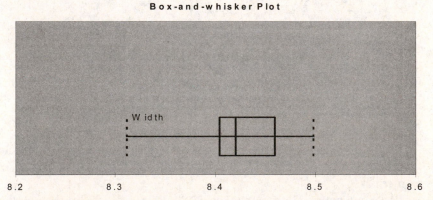

(c)   Even though the median is equal to the mean, the distribution is not symmetrical but skewed to the left.

(d)   All the troughs fall within the limit of 8.31 and 8.61 inches.

Copyright ©2015 Pearson Education, Inc.

3.68   (a), (b)

	Bundle Score	Typical Cost ($)
Mean	54.775	24.175
Standard Error	4.367344951	2.866224064
Median	62	20
Mode	75	8
Standard Deviation	27.62151475	18.12759265
Sample Variance	762.9480769	328.6096154
Kurtosis	-0.845357193	2.766393511
Skewness	-0.48041728	1.541239625
Range	98	83
Minimum	2	5
Maximum	100	88
Sum	2191	967
Count	40	40
First Quartile	34	9
Third Quartile	75	31
Interquartile Range	41	22
CV	50.43%	74.98%

(c)

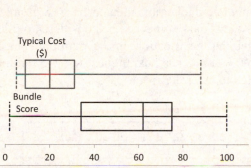

The typical cost is right-skewed, while the bundle score is left-skewed.

(d) $$r = \frac{\text{cov}(X, Y)}{S_X S_Y} = 0.3465$$

(e)   The mean typical cost is $24.18, with an average spread around the mean equaling $18.13. The spread between the lowest and highest costs is $83. The middle 50% of the typical cost fall over a range of $22 from $9 to $31, while half of the typical cost is below $20. The mean bundle score is 54.775, with an average spread around the mean equaling 27.6215. The spread between the lowest and highest scores is 98. The middle 50% of the scores fall over a range of 41 from 34 to 75, while half of the scores are below 62. The typical cost is right-skewed, while the bundle score is left-skewed. There is a weak positive linear relationship between typical cost and bundle score.

3.70   (a)   Excel output:
        Five-number Summary

	Boston	Vermont
Minimum	0.04	0.02
First Quartile	0.17	0.13
Median	0.23	0.2
Third Quartile	0.32	0.28
Maximum	0.98	0.83

Copyright ©2015 Pearson Education, Inc.

3.70   (b)
cont.

Box-and-whisker Plot

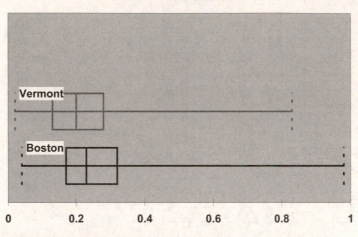

Both distributions are right skewed.

(c)   Both sets of shingles did quite well in achieving a granule loss of 0.8 gram or less. The Boston shingles had only two data points greater than 0.8 gram. The next highest to these was 0.6 gram. These two data points can be considered outliers. Only 1.176% of the shingles failed the specification. In the Vermont shingles, only one data point was greater than 0.8 gram. The next highest was 0.58 gram. Thus, only 0.714% of the shingles failed to meet the specification.

3.72   (a), (b), (c)

	Calories	Protein	Cholesterol
Calories	1		
Protein	0.464411	1	
Cholesterol	0.177665	0.141673	1

(d)   There is a rather weak positive linear relationship between calories and protein with a correlation coefficient of 0.46. The positive linear relationship between calories and cholesterol is quite weak at .178.

Copyright ©2015 Pearson Education, Inc.

3.74   (a), (b)

Property Taxes Per Capita ($)	
Mean	1332.235
Standard Error	80.91249
Median	1230
Mode	#N/A
Standard Deviation	577.8308
Sample Variance	333888.4
Kurtosis	0.539467
Skewness	0.918321
Range	2479
Minimum	506
Maximum	2985
Sum	67944
Count	51
First Quartile	867
Third Quartile	1633
Interquartile Range	766
6 * std.dev	3466.985
1.33 * std.dev	768.515

(c)

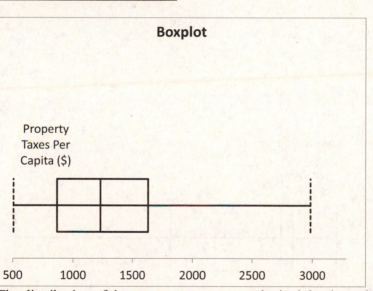

(d)   The distribution of the property taxes per capita is right-skewed with an average value of $1,332.24, a median of $1,230 and an average spread around the mean of $577.83. There is an outlier in the right tail at $2985 while the standard deviation is about 43.37% of the average. Twenty-five percent of the states have property taxes that fall below $864 while twenty-five percent have property taxes higher than $1,633.

Copyright ©2015 Pearson Education, Inc.

3.76   (a), (b)

	Abandonment rate in % (7:00AM-3:00PM)
Mean	13.86363636
Standard Error	1.625414306
Median	10
Mode	9
Standard Deviation	7.623868875
Sample Variance	58.12337662
Kurtosis	0.723568739
Skewness	1.180708144
Range	29
Minimum	5
Maximum	34
Sum	305
Count	22
First Quartile	9
Third Quartile	20
Interquartile Range	11
CV	54.99%

(c)

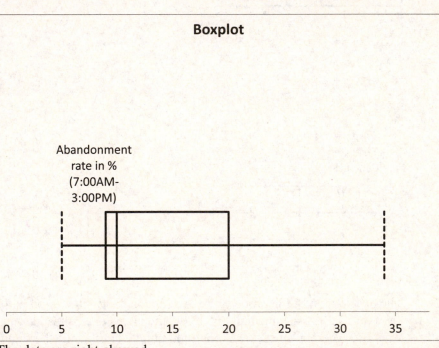

The data are right-skewed.

(d) $r = 0.7575$

(e)   The average abandonment rate is 13.86%. Half of the abandonment rates are less than 10%. One-quarter of the abandonment rates are less than 9% while another one-quarter are more than 20%. The overall spread of the abandonment rates is 29%. The middle 50% of the abandonment rates are spread over 11%. The average spread of abandonment rates around the mean is 7.62%. The abandonment rates are right-skewed.

Copyright ©2015 Pearson Education, Inc.

3.78   (a), (b)

Average Credit Score	
Mean	746.2238
Standard Error	1.821396
Median	749
Mode	760
Standard Deviation	21.78073
Sample Variance	474.4003
Kurtosis	-0.83035
Skewness	-0.22982
Range	89
Minimum	700
Maximum	789
Sum	106710
Count	143
First Quartile	730
Third Quartile	763
Interquartile Range	33
CV	2.92%

(c)

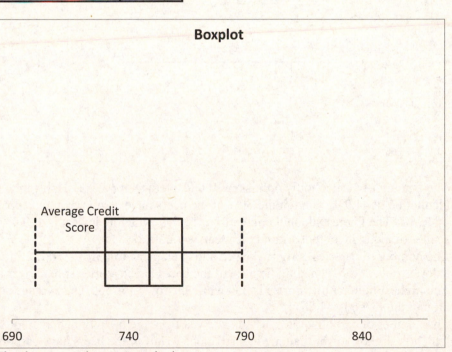

The data are quite symmetrical.

(d)   The average of the average credit scores is 746.2238. Half of the average credit scores are less than 749. One-quarter of the average credit scores are less than 730 while another one-quarter is more than 763. The overall spread of average credit scores is 89. The middle 50% of the average credit scores spread over 33. The average spread of average credit scores around the mean is 21.7807.

Copyright ©2015 Pearson Education, Inc.

3.80   Excel output:

	Alcohol %	Calories	Carbohydrates
Mean	5.235592105	154.3092105	11.96394737
Standard Error	0.115998617	3.616003621	0.399234292
Median	4.9	150	12.055
Mode	4.2	110	12
Standard Deviation	1.430126995	44.58108671	4.922090919
Sample Variance	2.045263223	1987.473292	24.22697902
Kurtosis	4.370842968	2.960631343	1.238172847
Skewness	1.434987665	1.211924335	0.478507837
Range	11.1	275	30.2
Minimum	0.4	55	1.9
Maximum	11.5	330	32.1
Sum	795.81	23455	1818.52
Count	152	152	152
First Quartile	4.4	129	8.3
Third Quartile	5.6	166	14.5
Interquartile Range	1.2	37	6.2
CV	27.32%	28.89%	41.14%

Boxplot

Carbohydrates

Calories

Alcohol %

0   50   100   150   200   250   300   350

The amount of % alcohol is right skewed and average at 5.24%. Half of the beers have % alcohol below 4.9%. The middle 50% of the beers have alcohol content spread over a range of 1.2%. The highest alcohol content is at 11.5% while the lowest is at 0.4%. The average scatter of alcohol content around the mean is 1.4301%.

The number of calories is right-skewed and average at 154.3092. Half of the beers have calories below 150. The middle 50% of the beers have calories spread over a range of 37. The highest number of calories is 330 while the lowest is 55. The average scatter of calories around the mean is 44.5811.

The number of carbohydrates is right-skewed from the boxplot and average at 11.9639, which is slightly lower than median at 12.055. Half of the beers have carbohydrates below 12.055. The middle 50% of the beers have carbohydrates spread over a range of 6.2. The highest number of carbohydrates is 32.1 while the lowest is 1.9. The average scatter of carbohydrates around the mean is 4.9221.

Copyright ©2015 Pearson Education, Inc.

CHAPTER 4

OBJECTIVES

- To understand basic probability concepts
- To learn about conditional probability
- To use Bayes' theorem to revise probabilities
- To learn various counting rules

OVERVIEW AND KEY CONCEPTS

Some Basic Probability Concepts

- **A priori probability:** The probability is based on prior knowledge of the process involved.
- **Empirical probability:** The probability is based on observed data.
- **Subjective probability:** Chance of occurrence assigned to an event by particular individual.
- **Sample space:** Collection of all possible outcomes, e.g., the set of all six faces of a die.
- **Simple event:** Outcome from a sample space with one characteristic, e.g., a red card from a deck of cards.
- **Joint event:** Involves two or more characteristics simultaneously, e.g., an Ace that is also a Red Card from a deck of cards.
- **Impossible event:** Event that will never happen, e.g., a club and diamond on a single card.
- **Complement event:** The complement of event A, denoted as A', includes all events that are not part of event A, e.g., If event A is the queen of diamonds, then the complement of event A is all the cards in a deck that are not the queen of diamonds.
- **Mutually exclusive events:** Two events are mutually exclusive if they cannot occur together. E.g., If event A is the queen of diamonds and event B is the queen of clubs, then both event A and event B cannot occur together on one card. An event and its complement are always mutually exclusive.
- **Collectively exhaustive events:** A set of events is collectively exhaustive if one of the events must occur. The set of collectively exhaustive events covers the whole sample space. E.g., Event A: all the aces, event B: all the black cards, event C: all the diamonds, event D: all the hearts. Then events A, B, C, and D are collectively exhaustive and so are events B, C, and D. An event and its complement are always collectively exhaustive.
- **Rules of probability:** (1) Its value is between 0 and 1; (2) the sum of probabilities of all collectively exhaustive and mutually exclusive events is 1.
- **The addition rule:** $P(A \text{ or } B) = P(A) + P(B) - P(A \text{ and } B)$
  - For two mutually exclusive events: $P(A \text{ and } B) = 0$
- **The multiplication rule:** $P(A \text{ and } B) = P(A \mid B) P(B) = P(B \mid A) P(A)$
- **Conditional probability:** $P(A \mid B) = \dfrac{P(A \text{ and } B)}{P(B)}$; $P(B \mid A) = \dfrac{P(A \text{ and } B)}{P(A)}$
- **Statistically independent events:** Two events are statistically independent if $P(A \mid B) = P(A)$, $P(B \mid A) = P(B)$ or $P(A \text{ and } B) = P(A) P(B)$. That is, any information about a given event does not affect the probability of the other event.

Copyright ©2015 Pearson Education, Inc.

- **Bayes' theorem:** $P(B_i \mid A) = \dfrac{P(A \mid B_i)P(B_i)}{P(A \mid B_1)P(B_1) + \cdots + P(A \mid B_k)P(B_k)} = \dfrac{P(B_i \text{ and } A)}{P(A)}$

  - **E.g.** We know that 50% of borrowers repaid their loans. Out of those who repaid, 40% had a college degree. Ten percent of those who defaulted had a college degree. What is the probability that a randomly selected borrower who has a college degree will repay the loan?

    Solution: Let R represent those who repaid and C represent those who have a college degree. $P(R) = 0.50$, $P(C \mid R) = 0.4$, $P(C \mid R') = 0.10$.

    $$P(R \mid C) = \frac{P(C \mid R)P(R)}{P(C \mid R)P(R) + P(C \mid R')P(R')} = \frac{(.4)(.5)}{(.4)(.5) + (.1)(.5)} = \frac{.2}{.25} = .8$$

  - Bayes' theorem is used if $P(A \mid B)$ is needed when $P(B \mid A)$ is given or vice-versa.

Viewing and Computing Marginal (Simple) Probability and Joint Probability Using a

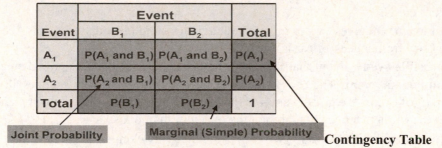

Contingency Table

Viewing and Computing Compound Probability Using a Contingency Table

$$P(A_1 \text{ or } B_1) = P(A_1) + P(B_1) - P(A_1 \text{ and } B_1)$$

Event	Event		
	B_1	B_2	Total
A_1	$P(A_1 \text{ and } B_1)$	$P(A_1 \text{ and } B_2)$	$P(A_1)$
A_2	$P(A_2 \text{ and } B_1)$	$P(A_2 \text{ and } B_2)$	$P(A_2)$
Total	$P(B_1)$	$P(B_2)$	1

For Mutually Exclusive Events: $P(A \text{ or } B) = P(A) + P(B)$

Copyright ©2015 Pearson Education, Inc.

Viewing and Computing Conditional Probability Using a Contingency Table

First setup the contingency table.

Type	Color		Total
	Red	Black	
Ace	2	2	4
Non-Ace	24	24	48
Total	26	26	52

Revised Sample Space

To find $P(\text{Ace|Red})$, we only need to focus on the revised sample space of $P(\text{Red}) = 26/52$.

Out of this, 2/52 belongs to Ace and Red.

Hence, $P(\text{Ace|Red})$ is the ratio of 2/52 to 26/52 or 2/26.

Likewise, $P(\text{Red | Ace}) = \dfrac{P(\text{Ace and Red})}{P(\text{Ace})} = \dfrac{2/52}{4/52} = \dfrac{2}{4}$

Applying Bayes' theorem Using a Contingency Table

- **E.g.** We know that 50% of borrowers repaid their loans. Out of those who repaid, 40% had a college degree. Ten percent of those who defaulted had a college degree. What is the probability that a randomly selected borrower who has a college degree will repay the loan?
  Solution: Let R represents those who repaid and C represents those who have a college degree. We know that $P(R) = 0.50$, $P(C \mid R) = 0.4$, $P(C \mid R') = 0.10$.

	Repay	$\overline{\text{Repay}}$	Total
College	.2	.05	.25
$\overline{\text{College}}$	.3	.45	.75
Total	.5	.5	1.0

First we fill in the marginal probabilities of $P(R) = 0.5$ and $P(R') = 0.5$ in the

contingency table. Then we make use of the conditional probability $P(C \mid R) = 0.4$. It says that if R has already occurred, the probability of C is 0.4. Since R has already occurred, we are restricted to the revised sample space of $P(R) = 0.5$. Forty percent or 0.4 of this

$P(R) = 0.5$ belongs to $P(C \text{ and } R)$. Hence, the $0.4(0.5) = 0.2$ for $P(C \text{ and } R)$ in the

contingency table. Likewise, given that R' has already occurred, the probability of C is 0.10. Hence, $P(C \text{ and } R')$ is 10% of $P(R') = 0.5$, which is 0.05. Utilizing the fact that the joint probabilities add up vertically and horizontally to their respective marginal probabilities, the contingency table is completed.

We want the probability of R given C. Now we are restricted to the revised sample space of $P(C) = 0.25$ since we know that C has already occurred. Out of this 0.25, 0.2 belongs to

$P(C \text{ and } R)$. Hence, $P(R \mid C) = \dfrac{0.2}{0.25} = 0.8$

Copyright ©2015 Pearson Education, Inc.

Counting Rules

- If any one of the k different mutually exclusive and collectively exhaustive events can occur on each of n trials, the number of possible outcomes is equal to k^n

- If there are k_1 events on the first trial, k_2 events on the second trials, …, and k_n events on the nth trial, then the number of possible outcomes is $(k_1)(k_2)\cdots(k_n)$

- The number of ways that all n objects can be arranged in order is $n! = n(n-1)\cdots(1)$
    - $n!$ is called *n factorial*
    - $0! = 1$

- **Permutation**: The number of ways of arranging X objects selected from n objects in order is
$$\frac{n!}{(n-X)!}$$

- **Combination**: The number of ways of selecting X objects out of n objects, irrespective or order, is $\binom{n}{X} = \dfrac{n!}{X!(n-X)!}$

Copyright ©2015 Pearson Education, Inc.

SOLUTIONS TO END OF SECTION
AND CHAPTER REVIEW EVEN PROBLEMS

4.2   (a)   Simple events include selecting a red ball.   (b)   Selecting a white ball
       (c)   The sample space is the collection of "a red ball being selected" and "a white ball
              being selected".

4.4   (a) $60/100 = 3/5 = 0.6$ (b) $10/100 = 1/10 = 0.1$
       (c) $35/100 = 7/20 = 0.35$ (d) $\dfrac{60}{100} + \dfrac{65}{100} - \dfrac{35}{100} = \dfrac{90}{100} = \dfrac{9}{10} = 0.9$

4.6   (a)   Mutually exclusive, not collectively exhaustive.
       (b)   Not mutually exclusive, not collectively exhaustive.
       (c)   Mutually exclusive, not collectively exhaustive.
       (d)   Mutually exclusive, collectively exhaustive

4.8   (a)   "Felt tense or stressed out at work"
       (b)   "Female felt tense or stressed out at work"
       (c)   "Did not feel tense or stressed out at work"
       (d)   "Male felt tense or stressed out a work" is a joint event because it consists of two
              characteristics.

4.10   (a)   A marketer who plans to increase use of LinkedIn.
       (b)   A B2B marketer who plans to increase use of LinkedIn.
       (c)   A marketer who does not plan to increase use of LinkedIn.
       (d)   A marketer who plans to increase use of LinkedIn and is a B2C marketer is a joint
              event because it consists of two characteristics, plans to increase use of LinkedIn and
              is a B2C marketer.

4.12   (a) P(indicates analyzing data as critical to his or her job) $= 8007/14074 = 0.5689$.
       (b) P(is a manager) $= 6264/14074 = 0.4451$
       (c) P(indicates analyzing data as critical to his or her job or is a manager)
              $= 8007/14074 + 6264/14074 - 3633/14074 = 0.7559$
       (d)   The probability of saying that analyzing data is critical or is a manager includes the
              probability of saying that analyzing data is critical plus the probability of being a
              manager minus the joint probability of saying that analyzing data is critical and is a
              manager.

4.14

Enjoy Shopping	Male	Female	Total
Yes	238	276	514
No	304	267	571
Total	542	543	1085

       (a) P(enjoys clothes shopping) $= 514/1085 = 0.4737$
       (b) P(female *and* enjoys clothes shopping) $= 276/1085 = 0.2544$
       (c) P(female *or* enjoys clothes shopping) $= (543+514-276)/1085 = 0.7198$

Copyright ©2015 Pearson Education, Inc.

(d) P(male *or* female) = 1085/1085 = 1.00

4.16   (a) $P(A \mid B) = 10/30 = 1/3 = 0.33$

(b) $P(A \mid B') = 20/60 = 1/3 = 0.33$

(c) $P(A' \mid B') = 40/60 = 2/3 = 0.67$

(d)   Since $P(A \mid B) = P(A) = 1/3$, events A and B are statistically independent.

4.18 $P(A \mid B) = \dfrac{P(A \text{ and } B)}{P(B)} = \dfrac{0.4}{0.8} = \dfrac{1}{2} = 0.5$

4.20   Since $P(A \text{ and } B) = .20$ and $P(A)\,P(B) = 0.12$, events A and B are not statistically independent.

4.22   (a) P(Increased use of LinkedIn | B2B marketer) = 1,478/1,945 = 0.7599

(b) P(Increased use of LinkedIn | B2C marketer) = 1,027/1,868 = 0.5498

(c) P(Increased use of LinkedIn) = 2,505/3,813 = 0.6570, which is not equal to P(Increased use of Linked | B2B marketer) = 0.7599. Therefore, increased use of LinkedIn and business focus are not independent.

4.24   (a) P(analyzing data is critical | is staff) = 4374/7810 = 0.5601

(b) P(analyzing data is not critical | is staff) = 3436/7810 = 0.4399

(c) P(analyzing data is critical | is a manager) = 3633/6264 = 0.5800

(d) P(analyzing data is not critical | is a manager) = 2631/6264 = 0.4200

4.26   (a) P(needs warranty repair | manufacturer based in U.S.) = 0.025/0.6 = 0.0417

(b) P(needs warranty repair | manufacturer not based in U.S.) = 0.015/0.4 = 0.0375

(c)   Since P(needs warranty repair | manufacturer based in U.S.) = 0.0417 and P(needs warranty repair) = 0.04, the two events are not statistically independent.

4.28   (a) $P(\text{both queens}) = \dfrac{4}{52} \cdot \dfrac{3}{51} = \dfrac{12}{2{,}652} = \dfrac{1}{221} = 0.0045$

(b) $P(\text{10 followed by 5 or 6}) = \dfrac{4}{52} \cdot \dfrac{8}{51} = \dfrac{32}{2{,}652} = \dfrac{8}{663} = 0.012$

(c) $P(\text{both queens}) = \dfrac{4}{52} \cdot \dfrac{4}{52} = \dfrac{16}{2{,}704} = \dfrac{1}{169} = 0.0059$

(d) $P(\text{blackjack}) = \dfrac{16}{52} \cdot \dfrac{4}{51} + \dfrac{4}{52} \cdot \dfrac{16}{51} = \dfrac{128}{2{,}652} = \dfrac{32}{663} = 0.0483$

4.30

$$P(B \mid A) = \frac{P(A \mid B) \cdot P(B)}{P(A \mid B) \cdot P(B) + P(A \mid B') \cdot P(B')}$$

$$= \frac{0.8 \cdot 0.05}{0.8 \cdot 0.05 + 0.4 \cdot 0.95} = \frac{0.04}{0.42} = 0.095$$

Copyright ©2015 Pearson Education, Inc.

4.32   (a) D = has disease T = tests positive

$$P(D\,|\,T) = \frac{P(T\,|\,D)\cdot P(D)}{P(T\,|\,D)\cdot P(D) + P(T\,|\,D')\cdot P(D')}$$

$$= \frac{0.9\cdot 0.03}{0.9\cdot 0.03 + 0.01\cdot 0.97} = \frac{0.027}{0.0367} = 0.736$$

(b)

$$P(D'\,|\,T') = \frac{P(T'\,|\,D')\cdot P(D')}{P(T'\,|\,D')\cdot P(D') + P(T'\,|\,D)\cdot P(D)}$$

$$= \frac{0.99\cdot 0.97}{0.99\cdot 0.97 + 0.10\cdot 0.03} = \frac{0.9603}{0.9633} = 0.997$$

4.34   (a) B = Base Construction Co. enters a bid
O = Olive Construction Co. wins the contract

$$P(B'\,|\,O) = \frac{P(O\,|\,B')\cdot P(B')}{P(O\,|\,B')\cdot P(B') + P(O\,|\,B)\cdot P(B)}$$

$$= \frac{0.5\cdot 0.3}{0.5\cdot 0.3 + 0.25\cdot 0.7} = \frac{0.15}{0.325} = 0.4615$$

(b) $P(O) = 0.175 + 0.15 = 0.325$

4.36   (a)   P(huge success | favorable review) = 0.099/0.459 = 0.2157
P(moderate success | favorable review) = 0.14/0.459 = 0.3050
P(break even | favorable review) = 0.16/0.459 = 0.3486
P(loser | favorable review) = 0.06/0.459 = 0.1307
(b)   P(favorable review) = 0.99(0.1) + 0.7(0.2) + 0.4(0.4) + 0.2(0.3) = 0.459

4.38 $3^{10} = 59049$

4.40   (a) $2^7 = 128$ (b) $6^7 = 279936$
(c)   There are two mutually exclusive and collectively exhaustive outcomes in (a) and six in (b).

4.42 $(8)(4)(3)(3) = 288$

4.44 $5! = (5)(4)(3)(2)(1) = 120$. Not all these orders are equally likely because the players are different in each team.

4.46 $n! = 6! = 720$

4.48 $_{10}C_4 = \dfrac{10!}{4!(6!)} = 210$

4.50 $\dfrac{n!}{X!(n-X)!} = \dfrac{100!}{2!(98!)} = \dfrac{(100)(99)}{2} = 4950$

Copyright ©2015 Pearson Education, Inc.

4.52   With a priori probability, the probability of success is based on prior knowledge of the process involved. With empirical probability, outcomes are based on observed data. Subjective probability refers to the chance of occurrence assigned to an event by a particular individual.

4.54   The general addition rule is used by adding the probability of A and the probability of B and then subtracting the joint probability of A and B.

4.56   If events A and B are statistically independent, the conditional probability of event A given B is equal to the probability of A.

4.58   Bayes' theorem uses conditional probabilities to revise the probability of an event in the light of new information.

4.60   (a)

SHARE HEALTH	AGE		
INFORMATION	18–24	45–64	Total
Yes	400	225	625
No	100	275	375
Total	500	500	1,000

    (b)   Simple event: "Shares health information through social media."
Joint event: "Shares health information through social media and is between 18 and 24 years old."

    (c)   P(Shares health information through social media) = 625/1,000 = 0.625

    (d)   P(Shares health information through social media and is in the 45-to-64-year-old group) = 225/1000 = 0.225

    (e)   P(is in the 46-to-64-year-old group) = 500/1000 = 0.5.
P(Shares health information through social media and is in the 45-to-64-year-old group) is not equal to P(Shares health information through social media) * P(is in the 46-to-64-year-old group); therefore, the events "age group" and "likely to share health information through social media" are not independent.

4.62   (a) P(cautious) = 84/200 = 0.42
    (b) P(optimistic or cautious) = (42+84)/200 = 126/200 = 0.63
    (c) P(male or hunkered-down) = (100+74-33)/200 = 141/200 = 0.705
    (d) P(male and hunkered-down) = 33/200 = 0.165
    (e) P(optimistic | female) = 16/100 = 0.16

4.64   (a) P(Big Data as critical to executing a customer-centric program) = 202/447 = 0.4519
    (b) P(Big Data as critical to executing a customer-centric program | Marketing) = 95/237 = 0.4008
    (c) P(Big Data as critical to executing a customer-centric program | IT) = 107/210 = 0.5095
    (d) P(functional silos block aggregation of customer data throughout the organization) = 217/447 = 0.4855
    (e) P(functional silos block aggregation of customer data throughout the organization | Marketing) = 122/237 = 0.5148
    (f) P(functional silos block aggregation of customer data throughout the organization | IT) = 95/210 = 0.4524

Copyright ©2015 Pearson Education, Inc.

4.64
cont.

(g) Identifying "Big Data as critical to executing a customer-centric program" and "executive group" are statistically dependent. Identifying "functional silos block aggregation of customer data throughout the organization" and "executive group" are statistically dependent also. Senior IT executives are more likely to identify Big Data as critical to executing a customer-centric program as compared to senior marketing executives. Senior marketing executives are more likely to identify that functional silos block aggregation of customer data throughout the organization as compared to senior IT executives.

Copyright ©2015 Pearson Education, Inc.

CHAPTER 5

OBJECTIVES

- To learn the properties of a probability distribution
- To compute the expected value and variance of a probability distribution
- To calculate the covariance and understand its use in finance
- To compute probabilities from the binomial, Poisson, and hypergeometric distributions
- To use the binomial, Poisson, and hypergeometric distributions to solve business problems

OVERVIEW AND KEY CONCEPTS

Some Basic Concepts of Discrete Probability Distribution

- **Random variable:** Outcomes of an experiment expressed numerically, e.g., Toss a die twice and count the number of times the number four appears (0, 1 or 2 times).
- **Discrete random variable:** A random variable that can have only certain distinct values. It is usually obtained by counting. E.g., Toss a coin five times and count the number of tails (0, 1, 2, 3, 4 or 5 tails).
- **Discrete probability distribution:** A mutually exclusive listing of all possible numerical outcomes for a discrete random variable such that a particular probability of occurrence is associated with each outcome.

Concepts of Expectation for a Discrete Random Variable

- **Expected value of a discrete random variable:** A weighted average over all possible outcomes.
  - The weights being the probabilities associated with each of the outcomes.
  - $$\mu = E(X) = \sum_{i=1}^{N} x_i P(X = x_i)$$

- **Variance of a discrete random variable:** The weighted average of the squared differences between each possible outcome and its mean
  - The weights being the probabilities of each of the respective outcomes.
  - $$\sigma^2 = \sum_{i=1}^{N} \left[x_i - E(X) \right]^2 P(X = x_i)$$

- **Standard deviation of a discrete random variable:** The square root of the variance.
  - $$\sigma = \sqrt{\sum_{i=1}^{N} \left[x_i - E(X) \right]^2 P(X = x_i)}$$

Covariance and Its Applications

- **Covariance:** $\sigma_{XY} = \sum_{i=1}^{N} \left[x_i - E(X) \right]\left[y_i - E(Y) \right] P(x_i y_i)$

  - A positive covariance indicates a positive relationship between the two discrete random variables.
  - A negative covariance indicates a negative relationship between the two discrete random variables.

Copyright ©2015 Pearson Education, Inc.

- ▪ The unit of the covariance depends on the units of the two discrete random variables, hence, its magnitude cannot be used to measure the strength of the relationship but only the direction of the relationship.
- **The expected value of the sum of two discrete random variables:** The expected value of the sum equals to the sum of the expected values.
  - ▪ $E(X+Y)=\mu_{X+Y}=E(X)+E(Y)=\mu_X+\mu_Y$
- **The variance of the sum of two discrete random variables:** The variance of the sum equals the sum of the variances plus twice the covariance.
  - ▪ $Var(X+Y)=\sigma_{X+Y}^2=\sigma_X^2+\sigma_Y^2+2\sigma_{XY}$
- **The standard deviation of the sum of two discrete random variables:**

$$\sigma_{X+Y}=\sqrt{\sigma_{X+Y}^2}$$

- **Portfolio expected return:** The portfolio expected returns for a two-asset investment is equal to the weight (w) assigned to asset X multiplied by the expected return of asset X plus the weight ($1-w$) assigned to asset Y multiplied by the expected return of asset Y.
  - ▪ $E(P)=\mu_P=wE(X)+(1-w)E(Y)$
- **Portfolio risk:** The standard deviation of the portfolio.
  - ▪ $\sigma_P=\sqrt{w^2\sigma_X^2+(1-w)^2\sigma_Y^2+2w(1-w)\sigma_{XY}}$
  - ▪ The smaller the value of σ_P, the less risky is an investment portfolio.

The Binomial Distribution

- **Properties of the binomial distribution:**
  - ▪ The sample has n observations.
  - ▪ Each observation is classified into one of the two mutually exclusive and collectively exhaustive categories, usually called *the event of interest* and *not the event of interest*.
  - ▪ The probability of getting an *event of interest* is π while the probability of getting *not an event of interest* is $(1-\pi)$.
  - ▪ The outcome (i.e., *the event of interest* or *not the event of interest*) of any observation is independent of the outcome of any other observation. This can be achieved by selecting each observation randomly either from an *infinite population without replacement* or from a *finite population with replacement*.
- **The binomial probability distribution function:**
  - ▪ $P(X=x)=\dfrac{n!}{x!(n-x)!}\pi^x(1-\pi)^{n-x}$

  where

  $P(X=x)$: probability of $X=x$ events of interest given n and π

  x: number of events of interest in the sample $(x=0,1,\cdots,n)$

  π: the probability of an event of interest

  $(1-\pi)$: the probability of not having an event of interest

  n: sample size
- **The mean and variance of a binomial distribution:**
  - ▪ $\mu=E(X)=n\pi$

Copyright ©2015 Pearson Education, Inc.

- $\sigma^2 = n\pi\left(1-\pi\right)$
- $\sigma = \sqrt{n\pi\left(1-\pi\right)}$

- **Applications:** Useful in evaluating the probability of X events of interest in a sample of size n drawn with replacement from a finite population or without replacement from an infinite population when the result of each draw is either an "event of interest" or "not event of interest".

The Poisson Distribution

- **Properties of the Poisson distribution:**
    1. The area of opportunity, in which the number of times a particular event occurs is of interest, is defined by time, length, surface area, etc.
    2. The probability that an event occurs in a given area of opportunity is the same for all of the areas of opportunity.
    3. The number of events that occur in one area of opportunity is independent of the number of events that occur in other areas of opportunity.
    4. The probability that two or more events will occur in an area of opportunity approaches zero as the area of opportunity becomes smaller.
- **The Poisson probability distribution function:**

    - $P\left(X = x \mid \lambda\right) = \dfrac{e^{-\lambda}\lambda^x}{x!}$

    where

    $P\left(X = x \mid \lambda\right)$: probability that $X = x$ events in an area of opportunity given λ

    X: number of events $\left(x == 0,1,2,\cdots,\infty\right)$

    λ: expected (average) number of events

    e: 2.71828 (base of natural logs)

- **The mean and variance of a Poisson Distribution**
    - $\mu = E\left(X\right) = \lambda$
    - $\sigma^2 = \lambda$
    - $\sigma = \sqrt{\lambda}$
- **Applications:** Useful in modeling the number of successes in a given continuous interval of time, length, surface area, etc.

The Hypergeometric Distribution

- **Properties of the hypergeometric distribution:**
    - There are "n" trials in a sample taken randomly from a finite population of size N.
    - The sample is drawn without replacement.
    - The "n" trials are dependent.
- **The hypergeometric probability distribution function:**

Copyright ©2015 Pearson Education, Inc.

- $$P\left(X = x \mid n, N, A\right) = \frac{\binom{A}{x}\binom{N-A}{n-x}}{\binom{N}{n}}$$

where

$P\left(X = x \mid n, N, A\right)$: the probability that x events of interest, given n, N, and A

n: sample size

N: population size

A: number of events of interest in the population

x: number of events of interest in the sample

$$\binom{A}{x} = {}_AC_x$$

$x \le A$

$x \le n$

- **The mean and variance of a hypergeometric distribution:**
  - $$\mu = E\left(X\right) = \frac{nA}{N}$$

  - $$\sigma = \sqrt{\frac{nA\left(N-A\right)}{N^2}}\sqrt{\frac{N-n}{N-1}}$$

- **Applications:** Useful in evaluating the probability of x events of interest in a sample containing n observations drawn without replacement from a finite population of N observations with A of those observations the event of interest.

Online Topic: Using the Poisson Distribution to Approximate the Binomial Distribution

- Use the Poisson distribution to approximate the binomial distribution when n is large and π is very small.

- $$P\left(X = x\right) \cong \frac{e^{-n\pi}\left(n\pi\right)^x}{x!}$$

where

$P\left(X = x\right)$ = probability of $X = x$ events of interest given the parameters n and π

n = sample size

π = probability of an event of interest

e = mathematical constant approximated by 2.71828

x = number of events of interest in the sample $\left(x = 0, 1, 2, \cdots, n\right)$

Copyright ©2015 Pearson Education, Inc.

SOLUTIONS TO END OF SECTION AND CHAPTER REVIEW EVEN PROBLEMS

5.2   PHStat output:

Probabilities & Outcomes:	P	X
	0.1	0
	0.2	1
	0.45	2
	0.15	3
	0.05	4
	0.05	5
Statistics		
E(X)	2	
E(Y)	0	
Variance(X)	1.4	
Standard Deviation(X)	1.183216	
Variance(Y)	0	
Standard Deviation(Y)	0	
Covariance(XY)	0	
Variance(X+Y)	1.4	
Standard Deviation(X+Y)	1.183216	

(a)-(b)

X	$P(x)$	$X*P(X)$	$(X-\mu_X)^2$	$(X-\mu_X)^2*P(X)$
0	0.10	0.00	4	0.40
1	0.20	0.20	1	0.20
2	0.45	0.90	0	0.00
3	0.15	0.45	1	0.15
4	0.05	0.20	4	0.20
5	0.05	0.25	9	0.45
	(a) Mean =	2.00	Variance =	1.40
			(b) Stdev =	1.18321596

5.4   (a)

X	$P(X)$
$-1	21/36
$+1	15/36

(b)

X	$P(X)$
$-1	21/36
$+1	15/36

(c)

X	$P(X)$
$-1	30/36
$+4	6/36

(d) $-0.167 for each method of play

Copyright ©2015 Pearson Education, Inc.

5.6   PHStat output:

Probabilities & Outcomes:	P	X
	0.125	0
	0.240385	1
	0.307692	2
	0.163462	3
	0.086538	4
	0.057692	5
	0.009615	6
	0.009615	7
Statistics		
E(X)	2.105769	
Variance(X)	2.152274	
Standard Deviation(X)	1.467063	

(a) $\mu = E(X) = 2.1058$

(b) $\sigma = 1.4671$

5.8   PHStat output:

Probabilities & Outcomes:	P	X	Y
	0.2	-100	50
	0.4	50	30
	0.3	200	20
	0.1	300	20
Weight Assigned to X	0.5		
Statistics			
E(X)	90		
E(Y)	30		
Variance(X)	15900		
Standard Deviation(X)	126.0952		
Variance(Y)	120		
Standard Deviation(Y)	10.95445		
Covariance(XY)	-1300		
Variance(X+Y)	13420		
Standard Deviation(X+Y)	115.8447		
Portfolio Management			
Weight Assigned to X	0.5		
Weight Assigned to Y	0.5		
Portfolio Expected Return	60		
Portfolio Risk	57.92236		

(a) $E(X) = (0.2)(\$-100) + (0.4)(\$50) + (0.3)(\$200) + (0.1)(\$300) = \$90$
        $E(Y) = (0.2)(\$50) + (0.4)(\$30) + (0.3)(\$20) + (0.1)(\$20) = \$30$

Copyright ©2015 Pearson Education, Inc.

5.8   (b)
cont.

$$\sigma_X = \sqrt{(0.2)(-100-90)^2 + (0.4)(50-90)^2 + (0.3)(200-90)^2 + (0.1)(300-90)^2}$$
$$= \sqrt{15900} = 126.10$$

$$\sigma_Y = \sqrt{(0.2)(50-30)^2 + (0.4)(30-30)^2 + (0.3)(20-30)^2 + (0.1)(20-30)^2}$$
$$= \sqrt{120} = 10.95$$

(c) $\sigma_{XY} = (0.2)(-100-90)(50-30) + (0.4)(50-90)(30-30)$
$$+ (0.3)(200-90)(20-30) + (0.1)(300-90)(20-30) = -1300$$

(d) $E(X+Y) = E(X) + E(Y) = \$90 + \$30 = \$120$

5.10   (a) $E(\text{total time}) = E(\text{time waiting}) + E(\text{time served}) = 4 + 5.5 = 9.5$ minutes

(b) $\sigma(\text{total time}) = \sqrt{1.2^2 + 1.5^2} = 1.9209$ minutes

5.12   PHStat output for (a)-(c):

Covariance Analysis			
Probabilities & Outcomes:	**P**	**X**	**Y**
	0.1	-100	50
	0.3	0	150
	0.3	80	-20
	0.3	150	-100
Statistics			
E(X)	59		
E(Y)	14		
Variance(X)	6189		
Standard Deviation(X)	78.6702		
Variance(Y)	9924		
Standard Deviation(Y)	99.61928		
Covariance(XY)	-6306		
Variance(X+Y)	3501		
Standard Deviation(X+Y)	59.16925		

(a) $E(X) = \sum_{i=1}^{N} x_i P(x_i) = 59$

$$E(Y) = \sum_{i=1}^{N} y_i P(y_i) = 14$$

(b)

$$\sigma_X = \sqrt{\sum_{i=1}^{N} \left[x_i - E(X) \right]^2 P(x_i)} = 78.6702$$

$$\sigma_Y = \sqrt{\sum_{i=1}^{N} \left[y_i - E(Y) \right]^2 P(y_i)} = 99.62$$

Copyright ©2015 Pearson Education, Inc.

5.12   (c) $\sigma_{XY} = \sum\limits_{i=1}^{N} \left[x_i - E(X) \right] \left[y_i - E(Y) \right] P(x_i, y_i) = -6306$

cont. (d)   Stock X gives the investor a lower standard deviation while yielding a higher
                expected return so the investor should select stock X.

5.14   PHStat output:

Probabilities & Outcomes:	P	X	Y
	0.1	-50	-100
	0.3	20	50
	0.4	100	130
	0.2	150	200
Statistics			
E(X)	71		
E(Y)	97		
Variance(X)	3829		
Standard Deviation(X)	61.87891		
Variance(Y)	7101		
Standard Deviation(Y)	84.26743		
Covariance(XY)	5113		
Variance(X+Y)	21156		
Standard Deviation(X+Y)	145.451		

(a) $E(X) = \$71$ $E(Y) = \$97$

(b) $\sigma_X = 61.88$ $\sigma_Y = 84.27$

(c) $\sigma_{XY} = 5113$

(d)   Stock Y gives the investor a higher expected return than stock X, but also has a
         higher standard deviation. Risk-averse investors would invest in stock X, whereas
         risk takers would invest in stock Y.

Copyright ©2015 Pearson Education, Inc.

5.16   (a)   PHStat output:

Covariance Analysis			
Probabilities & Outcomes:	**P**	**X**	**Y**
	0.01	-200	-999
	0.09	-70	-300
	0.15	30	-100
	0.35	80	100
	0.3	100	150
	0.1	120	350
Weight Assigned to X	0.5		
Statistics			
E(X)	66.2		
E(Y)	63.01		
Variance(X)	3273.56		
Standard Deviation(X)	57.21503		
Variance(Y)	38109.75		
Standard Deviation(Y)	195.2172		
Covariance(XY)	10766.74		
Variance(X+Y)	62916.79		
Standard Deviation(X+Y)	250.8322		
Portfolio Management			
Weight Assigned to X	0.5		
Weight Assigned to Y	0.5		
Portfolio Expected Return	64.605		
Portfolio Risk	125.4161		

Let X = corporate bond fund, Y = common stock fund.

(a) $E(X) = \$66.2$ $E(Y) = \$63.01.$

(b) $\sigma_X = \$57.2150$ $\sigma_Y = \$195.2172$

(c) $\sigma_{XY} = 10766.738$

(d) $CV(X) = 86.43\%$ $CV(Y) = 309.82\%$

The corporate bond fund gives the investor a slightly higher expected return than the common stock fund, and has a standard deviation about 1/3 of that of the common stock fund. An investor who does not like risk but desires a high expected return should invest in the corporate bond fund.

(e)   According to the probability of 0.01, it is highly unlikely that you will lose $999 of every $1,000 invested.

Copyright ©2015 Pearson Education, Inc.

5.18   (a)   0.5997
       (b)   0.0016
       (c)   0.0439
       (d)   0.4018

PHstat output for part (d):

Binomial Probabilities					
Data					
Sample size	6				
Probability of an event of interest	0.83				
Statistics					
Mean	4.98				
Variance	0.8466				
Standard deviation	0.920109				
Binomial Probabilities Table					
	X	P(X)	P(<=X)	P(<X)	P(>X)	P(>=X)
	0	2.41E-05	2.41E-05	0	0.999976	1
	1	0.000707	0.000731	2.41E-05	0.999269	0.999976
	2	0.008631	0.009362	0.000731	0.990638	0.999269
	3	0.056184	0.065546	0.009362	0.934454	0.990638
	4	0.205732	0.271277	0.065546	0.728723	0.934454
	5	0.401782	0.67306	0.271277	0.32694	0.728723
	6	0.32694	1	0.67306	0	0.32694

5.20   PHStat output for (a):

Data	
Sample size	4
Probability of an event of interest	0.1
Statistics	
Mean	0.4
Variance	0.36
Standard deviation	0.6

PHStat output for (b):

Data	
Sample size	4
Probability of an event of interest	0.4
Statistics	
Mean	1.6
Variance	0.96
Standard deviation	0.979796

Copyright ©2015 Pearson Education, Inc.

5.20
cont.   PHStat output for (c):

Data	
Sample size	5
Probability of an event of interest	0.8
Statistics	
Mean	4
Variance	0.8
Standard deviation	0.894427

PHStat output for (d):

Data	
Sample size	3
Probability of an event of interest	0.5
Statistics	
Mean	1.5
Variance	0.75
Standard deviation	0.866025

	Mean	Standard Deviation
(a)	0.40	0.60
(b)	1.60	0.980
(c)	4.00	0.894
(d)	1.50	0.866

5.22   Partial PHStat output:

Binomial Probabilities

Data	
Sample size	6
Probability of an event of interest	0.27

Statistics	
Mean	1.62
Variance	1.1826
Standard deviation	1.087474

Binomial Probabilities Table

X	P(X)	P(<=X)	P(<X)	P(>X)	P(>=X)
0	0.151334	0.151334	0	0.848666	1
1	0.335838	0.487172	0.151334	0.512828	0.848666
2	0.310535	0.797707	0.487172	0.202293	0.512828
3	0.15314	0.950847	0.797707	0.049153	0.202293
4	0.042481	0.993328	0.950847	0.006672	0.049153
5	0.006285	0.999613	0.993328	0.000387	0.006672
6	0.000387	1	0.999613	0	0.000387

Let X = number of tablets owned.

Copyright ©2015 Pearson Education, Inc.

5.22   (a) $P(X = 4) = 0.0425$

cont. (b) $P(X = 6) = 0.0004$

     (c) $P(X \geq 4) = 0.0492$

     (d) $E(X) = 1.62$ $\sigma_X = 1.0875$

     (e)   Each under-25-year-old either owns a tablet or does not own a tablet and that each person surveyed is independent of every other person.

5.24   Partial PHStat output:

Data	
Sample size	10
Probability of an event of interest	0.05

Statistics	
Mean	0.5
Variance	0.475
Standard deviation	0.689202

Binomial Probabilities Table

X	P(X)	P(<=X)	P(<X)	P(>X)	P(>=X)
0	0.598737	0.598737	0	0.401263	1
1	0.315125	0.913862	0.598737	0.086138	0.401263
2	0.074635	0.988496	0.913862	0.011504	0.086138
3	0.010475	0.998972	0.988496	0.001028	0.011504
4	0.000965	0.999936	0.998972	6.37E-05	0.001028
5	6.09E-05	0.999997	0.999936	2.75E-06	6.37E-05
6	2.67E-06	1	0.999997	8.2E-08	2.75E-06
7	8.04E-08	1	1	1.61E-09	8.2E-08
8	1.59E-09	1	1	1.87E-11	1.61E-09
9	1.86E-11	1	1	9.77E-14	1.87E-11
10	9.77E-14	1	1	0	9.77E-14

     (a) $P(X = 0) = 0.5987$

     (b) $P(X = 1) = 0.3151$

     (c) $P(X \leq 2) = 0.9885$

     (d) $P(X \geq 3) = 0.0115$

Copyright ©2015 Pearson Education, Inc.

5.26   PHStat output:

Binomial Probabilities

Data	
Sample size	3
Probability of an event of interest	0.83

Statistics	
Mean	2.49
Variance	0.4233
Standard deviation	0.650615

Binomial Probabilities Table

X	P(X)	P(<=X)	P(<X)	P(>X)	P(>=X)
0	0.004913	0.004913	0	0.995087	1
1	0.071961	0.076874	0.004913	0.923126	0.995087
2	0.351339	0.428213	0.076874	0.571787	0.923126
3	0.571787	1	0.428213	0	0.571787

Given $\pi = 0.83$ and $n = 3$,
(a) $P(X = 3) = 0.5718$
(b) $P(X = 0) = 0.0049$
(c) $P(X \geq 2) = 0.9231$
(d) $E(X) = n\pi = 2.49$

$$\sigma_X = \sqrt{n\pi(1-\pi)} = 0.6506$$

You can expect 2.49 orders to be filled with an average spread around the mean of 0.6506 orders.

5.28   (a)   Partial PHStat output:

Poisson Probabilities

Data	
Average/Expected number of successes:	2.5

Poisson Probabilities Table

X	P(X)	P(<=X)	P(<X)	P(>X)	P(>=X)
2	0.256516	0.543813	0.287297	0.456187	0.712703

Using the equation, if $\lambda = 2.5$, $P(X = 2) = \dfrac{e^{-2.5} \cdot (2.5)^2}{2!} = 0.2565$

Copyright ©2015 Pearson Education, Inc.

5.28 cont.

(b) Partial PHStat output:

Poisson Probabilities					
Data					
Average/Expected number of successes:			8		
Poisson Probabilities Table					
X	P(X)	P(<=X)	P(<X)	P(>X)	P(>=X)
8	0.139587	0.592547	0.452961	0.407453	0.547039

If $\lambda = 8.0$, $P(X = 8) = 0.1396$

(c) Partial PHStat output:

Poisson Probabilities					
Data					
Average/Expected number of successes:			0.5		
Poisson Probabilities Table					
X	P(X)	P(<=X)	P(<X)	P(>X)	P(>=X)
0	0.606531	0.606531	0.000000	0.393469	1.000000
1	0.303265	0.909796	0.606531	0.090204	0.393469

If $\lambda = 0.5$, $P(X = 1) = 0.3033$

(d) Partial PHStat output:

Poisson Probabilities					
Data					
Average/Expected number of successes:			3.7		
Poisson Probabilities Table					
X	P(X)	P(<=X)	P(<X)	P(>X)	P(>=X)
0	0.024724	0.024724	0.000000	0.975276	1.000000

If $\lambda = 3.7$, $P(X = 0) = 0.0247$

Copyright ©2015 Pearson Education, Inc.

5.30   PHStat output for (a) – (d)

Poisson Probabilities Table						
	X	P(X)	P(<=X)	P(<X)	P(>X)	P(>=X)
	0	0.006738	0.006738	0.000000	0.993262	1.000000
	1	0.033690	0.040428	0.006738	0.959572	0.993262
	2	0.084224	0.124652	0.040428	0.875348	0.959572
	3	0.140374	0.265026	0.124652	0.734974	0.875348
	4	0.175467	0.440493	0.265026	0.559507	0.734974
	5	0.175467	0.615961	0.440493	0.384039	0.559507
	6	0.146223	0.762183	0.615961	0.237817	0.384039
	7	0.104445	0.866628	0.762183	0.133372	0.237817
	8	0.065278	0.931906	0.866628	0.068094	0.133372
	9	0.036266	0.968172	0.931906	0.031828	0.068094
	10	0.018133	0.986305	0.968172	0.013695	0.031828
	11	0.008242	0.994547	0.986305	0.005453	0.013695
	12	0.003434	0.997981	0.994547	0.002019	0.005453
	13	0.001321	0.999302	0.997981	0.000698	0.002019
	14	0.000472	0.999774	0.999302	0.000226	0.000698
	15	0.000157	0.999931	0.999774	0.000069	0.000226
	16	0.000049	0.999980	0.999931	0.000020	0.000069
	17	0.000014	0.999995	0.999980	0.000005	0.000020
	18	0.000004	0.999999	0.999995	0.000001	0.000005
	19	0.000001	1.000000	0.999999	0.000000	0.000001
	20	0.000000	1.000000	1.000000	0.000000	0.000000

Given $\lambda = 5.0$,

(a) $P(X = 1) = 0.0337$
(b) $P(X < 1) = 0.0067$
(c) $P(X > 1) = 0.9596$
(d) $P(X \leq 1) = 0.0404$

Copyright ©2015 Pearson Education, Inc.

5.32   (a) – (c) Portion of PHStat output

	Data					
Average/Expected number of successes:			6			
Poisson Probabilities Table						
	X	P(X)	P(<=X)	P(<X)	P(>X)	P(>=X)
	0	0.002479	0.002479	0.000000	0.997521	1.000000
	1	0.014873	0.017351	0.002479	0.982649	0.997521
	2	0.044618	0.061969	0.017351	0.938031	0.982649
	3	0.089235	0.151204	0.061969	0.848796	0.938031
	4	0.133853	0.285057	0.151204	0.714943	0.848796
	5	**(b)** 0.160623	0.445680	**(a)** 0.285057	0.554320	**(c)** 0.714943
	6	0.160623	0.606303	0.445680	0.393697	0.554320
	7	0.137677	0.743980	0.606303	0.256020	0.393697
	8	0.103258	0.847237	0.743980	0.152763	0.256020
	9	0.068838	0.916076	0.847237	0.083924	0.152763
	10	0.041303	0.957379	0.916076	0.042621	0.083924
	11	0.022529	0.979908	0.957379	0.020092	0.042621
	12	0.011264	0.991173	0.979908	0.008827	0.020092
	13	0.005199	0.996372	0.991173	0.003628	0.008827
	14	0.002228	0.998600	0.996372	0.001400	0.003628
	15	0.000891	0.999491	0.998600	0.000509	0.001400
	16	0.000334	0.999825	0.999491	0.000175	0.000509
	17	0.000118	0.999943	0.999825	0.000057	0.000175

(a) $P(X < 5) = P(X = 0) + P(X = 1) + P(X = 2) + P(X = 3) + P(X = 4)$

$$= \frac{e^{-6}(6)^0}{0!} + \frac{e^{-6}(6)^1}{1!} + \frac{e^{-6}(6)^2}{2!} + \frac{e^{-6}(6)^3}{3!} + \frac{e^{-6}(6)^4}{4!}$$

$$= 0.002479 + 0.014873 + 0.044618 + 0.089235 + 0.133853 = 0.2851$$

(b) $P(X = 5) = \dfrac{e^{-6}(6)^5}{5!} = 0.1606$

(c) $P(X \geq 5) = 1 - P(X < 5) = 1 - 0.2851 = 0.7149$

(d) $P(X = 4 \text{ or } X = 5) = P(X = 4) + P(X = 5) = \dfrac{e^{-6}(6)^4}{4!} + \dfrac{e^{-6}(6)^5}{5!} = 0.2945$

5.34   Partial PHStat outputu:

Poisson Probabilities						
		Data				
Mean/Expected number of events of interest:			2.05			
Poisson Probabilities Table						
	X	P(X)	P(<=X)	P(<X)	P(>X)	P(>=X)
	0	0.128735	0.128735	0.000000	0.871265	1.000000
	1	0.263907	0.392641	0.128735	0.607359	0.871265
	2	0.270504	0.663146	0.392641	0.336854	0.607359
	3	0.184845	0.847990	0.663146	0.152010	0.336854

Copyright ©2015 Pearson Education, Inc.

5.34 $\lambda = 2.05$
cont.   (a) $P(X = 0) = 0.1287$ (b) $P(X \geq 1) = 0.8713$
        (c) $P(X \geq 2) = 0.6074$

5.36   Partial PHStat output:

Poisson Probabilities						
		Data				
Mean/Expected number of events of interest:			2.15			
Poisson Probabilities Table						
	X	P(X)	P(<=X)	P(<X)	P(>X)	P(>=X)
	0	0.116484	0.116484	0.000000	0.883516	1.000000
	1	0.250441	0.366925	0.116484	0.633075	0.883516
	2	0.269224	0.636149	0.366925	0.363851	0.633075

$\lambda = 2.15$
(a) $P(X = 0) = 0.1165$
(b) $P(X = 1) = 0.2504$
(c) $P(X > 1) = 0.6331$
(d) $P(X < 2) = 0.3669$

5.38   Partial PHStat output:

Poisson Probabilities						
		Data				
Mean/Expected number of events of interest:			1.12			
Poisson Probabilities Table						
	X	P(X)	P(<=X)	P(<X)	P(>X)	P(>=X)
	0	0.326280	0.326280	0.000000	0.673720	1.000000
	1	0.365433	0.691713	0.326280	0.308287	0.673720
	2	0.204643	0.896356	0.691713	0.103644	0.308287

(a) $P(X = 0) = 0.3263$
(b) $P(X \leq 2) = 0.8964$
(c)   Because Ford had a higher mean rate of problems per car in 2010 than Toyota, the probability of a randomly selected Ford having zero problems and the probability of no more than two problems are both lower than for Toyota.

Copyright ©2015 Pearson Education, Inc.

5.40   PHStat output:

Poisson Probabilities					
	Data				
Mean/Expected number of events of interest:			1.04		
Poisson Probabilities Table					
	X	P(X)	P(<=X)	P(<X)	P(>X)	P(>=X)
	0	0.353455	0.353455	0.000000	0.646545	1.000000
	1	0.367593	0.721048	0.353455	0.278952	0.646545
	2	0.191148	0.912196	0.721048	0.087804	0.278952

(a) $P(X = 0) = 0.3535$

(b) $P(X \le 2) = 0.9122$

(c)   Because Toyota had a lower mean rate of problems per car in 2009 compared to 2010, the probability of a randomly selected Toyota having zero problems and the probability of no more than 2 problems are both higher in 2009 than their values in 2010.

5.42   (a)   PHStat output:

Hypergeometric Probabilities		
Data		
Sample size	4	
No. of successes in population	5	
Population size	10	
Hypergeometric Probabilities Table		
	X	P(X)
	3	0.238095

$$P(X = 3) = \frac{\binom{5}{3}\binom{10-5}{4-3}}{\binom{10}{4}} = \frac{\dfrac{5 \cdot 4 \cdot 3!}{3! \cdot 2 \cdot 1} \cdot \dfrac{5 \cdot 4!}{4! \cdot 1!}}{\dfrac{10 \cdot 9 \cdot 8 \cdot 7 \cdot 6!}{6! \cdot 4 \cdot 3 \cdot 2 \cdot 1}} = \frac{5}{3 \cdot 7} = 0.2381$$

(b)   PHStat output:

Hypergeometric Probabilities		
Data		
Sample size	4	
No. of successes in population	3	
Population size	6	
Hypergeometric Probabilities Table		
	X	P(X)
	1	0.2
	2	0.6
	3	0.2

Copyright ©2015 Pearson Education, Inc.

5.42 (b)
cont.

$$P(X = 1) = \frac{\binom{3}{1} \cdot \binom{6-3}{4-1}}{\binom{6}{4}} = \frac{\frac{3 \cdot 2!}{2! \cdot 1} \cdot \frac{3!}{3! \cdot 0!}}{\frac{6 \cdot 5 \cdot 4!}{4! \cdot 2 \cdot 1}} = \frac{1}{5} = 0.2$$

(c) Partial PHStat output:

Hypergeometric Probabilities		
Data		
Sample size	5	
No. of successes in population	3	
Population size	12	
Hypergeometric Probabilities Table		
	X	P(X)
	0	0.159091

$$P(X = 0) = \frac{\binom{3}{0} \cdot \binom{12-3}{5-0}}{\binom{12}{5}} = \frac{\frac{3!}{3! \cdot 0!} \cdot \frac{9 \cdot 8 \cdot 7 \cdot 6 \cdot 5!}{5! \cdot 4 \cdot 3 \cdot 2 \cdot 1}}{\frac{12 \cdot 11 \cdot 10 \cdot 9 \cdot 8 \cdot 7!}{7! \cdot 5 \cdot 4 \cdot 3 \cdot 2 \cdot 1}} = \frac{7}{44} = 0.1591$$

(d) Partial PHStat output:

Hypergeometric Probabilities		
Data		
Sample size	3	
No. of successes in population	3	
Population size	10	
Hypergeometric Probabilities Table		
	X	P(X)
	3	0.008333

$$P(X = 3) = \frac{\binom{3}{3} \cdot \binom{10-3}{3-3}}{\binom{10}{3}} = \frac{\frac{3!}{3! \cdot 0!} \cdot \frac{7!}{7! \cdot 0!}}{\frac{10 \cdot 9 \cdot 8 \cdot 7!}{7! \cdot 3 \cdot 2 \cdot 1}} = \frac{1}{120} = 0.0083$$

Copyright ©2015 Pearson Education, Inc.

5.44   (a)   Partial PHStat outuput:

Hypergeometric Probabilities		
Data		
Sample size	6	
No. of successes in population	25	
Population size	100	
Hypergeometric Probabilities Table		
	X	P(X)
	0	0.168918
	1	0.361968
	2	0.305888
	3	0.130286
	4	0.029448
	5	0.003343
	6	0.000149

If $n = 6$, $E = 25$, and $N = 100$,

$$P(X \geq 2) = 1 - [P(X = 0) + P(X = 1)] = 1 - [\frac{\binom{25}{0}\binom{100-25}{6-0}}{\binom{100}{6}} + \frac{\binom{25}{1}\binom{100-25}{6-1}}{\binom{100}{6}}]$$

$$= 1 - [0.1689 + 0.3620] = 0.4691$$

(b)   Partial PHStat output:

Hypergeometric Probabilities		
Data		
Sample size	6	
No. of successes in population	30	
Population size	100	
Hypergeometric Probabilities Table		
	X	P(X)
	0	0.109992
	1	0.304593
	2	0.33459
	3	0.186438
	4	0.05552
	5	0.008368
	6	0.000498

If $n = 6$, $E = 30$, and $N = 100$,

$$P(X \geq 2) = 1 - [P(X = 0) + P(X = 1)] = 1 - [\frac{\binom{30}{0}\binom{100-30}{6-0}}{\binom{100}{6}} + \frac{\binom{30}{1}\binom{100-30}{6-1}}{\binom{100}{6}}]$$

$$= 1 - [0.1100 + 0.3046] = 0.5854$$

Copyright ©2015 Pearson Education, Inc.

5.44   (c)   Partial PHStat output:
cont.

Hypergeometric Probabilities		
Data		
Sample size	6	
No. of successes in population	5	
Population size	100	
Hypergeometric Probabilities Table		
	X	P(X)
	0	0.729085
	1	0.243028
	2	0.026706
	3	0.001161
	4	1.87E-05
	5	7.97E-08

If $n = 6$, $E = 5$, and $N = 100$,

$$P(X \geq 2) = 1 - [P(X=0) + P(X=1)] = 1 - [\frac{\binom{5}{0}\binom{100-5}{6-0}}{\binom{100}{6}} + \frac{\binom{5}{1}\binom{100-5}{6-1}}{\binom{100}{6}}]$$

$$= 1 - [0.7291 + 0.2430] = 0.0279$$

(d)   Partial PHStat output:

Hypergeometric Probabilities		
Data		
Sample size	6	
No. of successes in population	10	
Population size	100	
Hypergeometric Probabilities Table		
	X	P(X)
	0	0.522305
	1	0.368686
	2	0.096458
	3	0.011826
	4	0.000706
	5	1.9E-05
	6	1.76E-07

If $n = 6$, $E = 10$, and $N = 100$,

$$P(X \geq 2) = 1 - [P(X=0) + P(X=1)] = 1 - [\frac{\binom{10}{0}\binom{100-10}{6-0}}{\binom{100}{6}} + \frac{\binom{10}{1}\binom{100-10}{6-1}}{\binom{100}{6}}]$$

$$= 1 - [0.5223 + 0.3687] = 0.1090$$

Copyright ©2015 Pearson Education, Inc.

5.44   (e)   The probability that the entire group will be audited is very sensitive to the true
cont.   number of improper returns in the population. If the true number is very low ($E =$
               5), the probability is very low (0.0279). When the true number is increased by a
               factor of six ($E = 30$), the probability the group will be audited increases by a
               factor of almost 21 (0.5854).

5.46   PHStat output:

Data		
Sample size	**4**	
No. of successes in population	**4**	
Population size	**30**	
Hypergeometric Probabilities Table		
	X	**P(X)**
	0	**0.545521**
	1	**0.379493**
	2	**0.071155**
	3	**0.003795**
	4	**3.65E-05**

(a) $P(X = 4) = 3.6490 \times 10^{-5}$ (b) $P(X = 0) = 0.5455$
(c) $P(X \geq 1) = 0.4545$
(d) $E = 6$
       (a) $P(X = 4) = 0.0005$ (b) $P(X = 0) = 0.3877$
       (c) $P(X \geq 1) = 0.6123$

5.48   Partial PHStat output:

Hypergeometric Probabilities		
Data		
Sample size	**4**	
No. of events of interest in population	**6**	
Population size	**12**	
Hypergeometric Probabilities Table		
	X	**P(X)**
	0	**0.030303**
	1	**0.242424**
	2	**0.454545**
	3	**0.242424**
	4	**0.030303**

(a) $P(X = 1) = 0.2424$ (b) $P(X \geq 1) = 1 - P(X = 0) = 0.9697$
(c) $P(X = 3) = 0.2424$
(d)   Because the number of events of interest in the population is a smaller fraction of
       the population size in (c), the probability in (c) is smaller than that in Example
       5.7

Copyright ©2015 Pearson Education, Inc.

5.50   The four properties of a situation that must be present in order to use the binomial distribution are (i) the sample consists of a fixed number of observations, n, (ii) each observation can be classified into one of two mutually exclusive and collectively exhaustive categories, usually called "an event of interest" and "not an event of interest", (iii) the probability of an observation being classified as "an event of interest", π, is constant from observation to observation and (iv) the outcome (i.e., "an event of interest" or "not an event of interest") of any observation is independent of the outcome of any other observation.

5.52   The hypergeometric distribution should be used when the probability of an event of interest of a sample containing n observations is not constant from trial to trial due to sampling without replacement from a finite population.

5.54   Partial PHstat output:

Binomial Probabilities

Data	
Sample size	5
Probability of an event of interest	0.65

Statistics	
Mean	3.25
Variance	1.1375
Standard deviation	1.066536

Binomial Probabilities Table

X	P(X)	P(<=X)	P(<X)	P(>X)	P(>=X)
0	0.005252	0.005252	0	0.994748	1
1	0.04877	0.054023	0.005252	0.945978	0.994748
2	0.181147	0.235169	0.054022	0.764831	0.945978
3	0.336416	0.571585	0.235169	0.428415	0.764831
4	0.312386	0.883971	0.571585	0.116029	0.428415
5	0.116029	1	0.883971	0	0.116029

(a)   0.65   (b)   0.65

$\pi = 0.65$, $n = 5$

(c) $P(X = 4) = 0.3124$ (d) $P(X = 0) = 0.0053$

(e)   Stock prices tend to rise in the years when the economy is expanding and fall in the years of recession or contraction. Hence, the probability that the price will rise in one year is not independent from year to year.

Copyright ©2015 Pearson Education, Inc.

5.56   (a)   Partial PHStat output:

Data	
Sample size	13
Probability of an event of interest	0.5
Statistics	
Mean	6.5
Variance	3.25
Standard deviation	1.802776

Binomial Probabilities Table

X	P(X)	P(<=X)	P(<X)	P(>X)	P(>=X)
10	0.034912	0.98877	0.953857	0.01123	0.046143

If $\pi = 0.50$ and $n = 13$, $P(X \geq 10) = 0.0461$

(b)   Partial PHStat output:

Data	
Sample size	13
Probability of an event of interest	0.75

Statistics	
Mean	9.75
Variance	2.4375
Standard deviation	1.561249

Binomial Probabilities Table

X	P(X)	P(<=X)	P(<X)	P(>X)	P(>=X)
10	0.251651	0.667398	0.415747	0.332602	0.584253

If $\pi = 0.75$ and $n = 13$, $P(X \geq 10) = 0.5843$

5.58   Portion of the PHStat output:

Data	
Sample size	10
Probability of an event of interest	0.4

Statistics	
Mean	4
Variance	2.4
Standard deviation	1.549193

Binomial Probabilities Table

X	P(X)	P(<=X)	P(<X)	P(>X)	P(>=X)
0	0.006047	0.006047	0	0.993953	1
5	0.200658	0.833761	0.633103	0.166239	0.366897

(a) $P(X = 0) = 0.0060$
(b) $P(X = 5) = 0.2007$

Copyright ©2015 Pearson Education, Inc.

5.58   (c) $P(X > 5) = 0.1662$
cont.   (d) $\mu = 4$, $\sigma = 1.5492$

        (e)   Since the percentage of bills containing an error is lower in this problem, the
               probability is higher in (a) and (b) of this problem and lower in (c).

5.60   Partial PHStat output:

Data	
Sample size	20
Probability of an event of interest	0.41
Statistics	
Mean	8.2
Variance	4.838
Standard deviation	2.199545

Binomial Probabilities Table

X	P(X)	P(<=X)	P(<X)	P(>X)	P(>=X)
5	0.065636	0.107933	0.042296	0.892067	0.957704
10	0.126753	0.851976	0.725223	0.148024	0.274777

        (a) $\mu = n\pi = 8.2$ (b) $\sigma = \sqrt{n\pi(1-\pi)} = 2.1995$
        (c) $P(X = 10) = 0.1268$ (d) $P(X \le 5) = 0.1079$
        (e) $P(X \ge 5) = 0.9577$

5.62   (a) $\pi = 0.5$, $P(X \ge 35) = 6.91 \times 10^{-7}$
        Partial PHStat output:

Data	
Sample size	40
Probability of an event of interest	0.5
Statistics	
Mean	20
Variance	10
Standard deviation	3.162278

Binomial Probabilities Table

X	P(X)	P(<=X)	P(<X)	P(>X)	P(>=X)
35	5.98E-07	1	0.999999	9.29E-08	6.91E-07

Copyright ©2015 Pearson Education, Inc.

5.62   (b) $\pi = 0.7$, $P(X \geq 35) = 0.0086$
cont.   Partial PHStat output:

Data	
Sample size	40
Probability of an event of interest	0.7
Statistics	
Mean	28
Variance	8.4
Standard deviation	2.898275

Binomial Probabilities Table

X	P(X)	P(<=X)	P(<X)	P(>X)	P(>=X)
35	0.006057	0.997439	0.991382	0.002561	0.008618

(c) $\pi = 0.9$, $P(X \geq 35) = 0.7937$
Partial PHStat output:

Data	
Sample size	40
Probability of an event of interest	0.9
Statistics	
Mean	36
Variance	3.6
Standard deviation	1.897367

Binomial Probabilities Table

X	P(X)	P(<=X)	P(<X)	P(>X)	P(>=X)
35	0.16471	0.370982	0.206273	0.629018	0.793727

(d)   Based on the results in (a)-(c), the probability that the Standard & Poor's 500
         index will increase if there is an early gain in the first five trading days of the
         year is very likely to be close to 0.90 because that yields a probability of 79.37%
         that at least 35 of the 40 years the Standard & Poor's 500 index will increase the
         entire year.

Copyright ©2015 Pearson Education, Inc.

5.64   (a)   The assumptions needed are (i) the probability of questionable insurance claims in a given interval in a day is constant, (ii) the probability of questionable insurance claims in this interval approaches zero as the interval gets smaller, (iii) the probability of questionable insurance claims is independent from interval to interval.

Partial PHStat output:

Poisson Probabilities

Data				
Mean/Expected number of events of interest:				10

Poisson Probabilities Table

X	P(X)	P(<=X)	P(<X)	P(>X)	P(>=X)
5	0.037833	0.067086	0.029253	0.932914	0.970747
10	0.125110	0.583040	0.457930	0.416960	0.542070
11	0.113736	0.696776	0.583040	0.303224	0.416960

$\lambda = 10.0$

(b) $P(X = 5) = 0.0378$

(c) $P(X \leq 10) = 0.5830$

(d) $P(X \geq 11) = 0.4170$

Copyright ©2015 Pearson Education, Inc.

CHAPTER 6

OBJECTIVES

- To compute probabilities from the normal distribution
- To use the normal distribution to solve business problems
- To use the normal probability plot to determine whether a set of data is approximately normally distributed
- To compute probabilities from the uniform distribution
- To compute probabilities from the exponential distribution

OVERVIEW AND KEY CONCEPTS

Some Basic Concepts of Continuous Probability Density Function

- **Continuous random variable:** A variable that can take on an infinite number of values within a specific range, e.g. Weight, height, daily changes in closing prices of stocks, and time between arrivals of planes landing on a runway.
- **Continuous probability density function:** A mathematical expression that represents the continuous phenomenon of a continuous random variable, and can be used to calculate the probability that the random variable occurs within certain ranges or intervals.
- The probability that a continuous random variable is equal to a *particular value* is 0. This distinguishes continuous phenomena, which are measured, from discrete phenomena, which are counted. For example, the probability that a task can be completed in between 20 and 30 seconds can be measured. With a more precise measuring instrument, we can compute the probability that the task can be completed between a very small interval such as 19.99 to 20.01. However, the probability that the task can be completed in *exactly* 21 seconds is 0.
- Obtaining probabilities or computing expected values and standard deviations for continuous random variables involves mathematical expressions that require knowledge of integral calculus. In this book, these are achieved via special probability tables or computer statistical software like Minitab or PHStat.

The Normal Distribution

- **Properties of the normal distribution:**
  - Bell-shaped (and thus symmetrical) in its appearance.
  - Its measures of central tendency (mean, median, and mode) are all identical.
  - Its "middle spread" (interquartile range) is equal to 1.33 standard deviations.
  - Its associated random variable has an infinite range $(-\infty < X < +\infty)$.

Copyright ©2015 Pearson Education, Inc.

- **The normal probability density function:**

  - $$f(X) = \frac{1}{\sqrt{2\pi\sigma^2}} e^{-\frac{1}{2\sigma^2}(X-\mu)^2} \quad \text{where}$$

    $f(X)$: density of random variable X

    $\pi = 3.14159; \quad e = 2.71828$

    μ: population mean

    σ: population standard deviation

    X: value of random variable $(-\infty < X < \infty)$

  - A particular combination of μ and σ will yield a particular normal probability distribution.

- **Standardization or normalization of a normal continuous random variable:** By standardizing (normalizing) a normal random variable, we need only one table to tabulate the probabilities of the whole family of normal distributions.

- **The transformation (standardization) formula:** $Z = \dfrac{X - \mu}{\sigma}$

  - The standardized normal distribution is one whose random variable Z always has a mean 0 and a standard deviation 1.

- **Finding range probability of a normal random variable:**
  1. Standardize the value of X into Z.
  2. Look up the cumulative probabilities from the cumulative standardized normal distribution table.

     E.g., For $\mu = 5$ and $\sigma = 10$, $P(2.9 < X < 7.1) = ?$

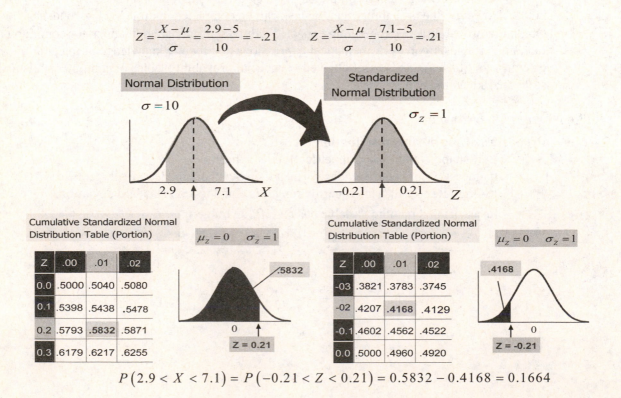

$$Z = \frac{X - \mu}{\sigma} = \frac{2.9 - 5}{10} = -.21 \qquad Z = \frac{X - \mu}{\sigma} = \frac{7.1 - 5}{10} = .21$$

$$P(2.9 < X < 7.1) = P(-0.21 < Z < 0.21) = 0.5832 - 0.4168 = 0.1664$$

Copyright ©2015 Pearson Education, Inc.

E.g., For $\mu = 5$ and $\sigma = 10$, $P(X \geq 8) = ?$

$$Z = \frac{X - \mu}{\sigma} = \frac{8 - 5}{10} = .30$$

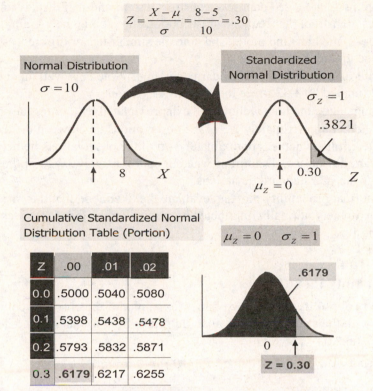

$$P(X \geq 8) = P(Z \geq 0.30) = 1 - 0.6179 = 0.3821$$

- **Recovering X values for known probabilities:**
    1. Look up the Z value from the cumulative standardized normal distribution table.
    2. Recover the value of X using the formula $X = \mu + Z\sigma$

E.g., For $\mu = 5$ and $\sigma = 10$, $P(X \leq A) = 0.6179$, what is the value of A?

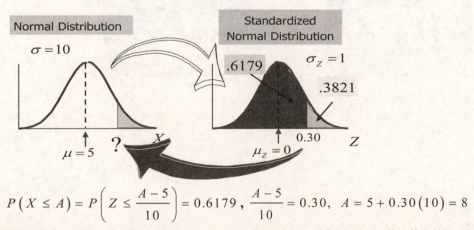

$$P(X \leq A) = P\left(Z \leq \frac{A - 5}{10}\right) = 0.6179, \quad \frac{A - 5}{10} = 0.30, \quad A = 5 + 0.30(10) = 8$$

- **Applications:** Many continuous random phenomena are either normally distributed or can be approximated by a normal distribution. Hence, it is important to know how to assess whether a distribution is normally distributed.

Copyright ©2015 Pearson Education, Inc.

Evaluating the Normality Assumption

- For small and moderate-sized data sets, construct a stem-and-leaf display and boxplot. For large data sets, construct the frequency distribution and plot the histogram or polygon.
- Obtain the mean, median, and mode, and note the similarities or differences among these measures of central tendency.
- Obtain the interquartile range and standard deviation. Note how well the interquartile range can be approximated by 1.33 times the standard deviation.
- Obtain the range and note how well it can be approximated by 6 times the standard deviation.
- Determine whether approximately 2/3 of the observations lie between the mean ± 1 standard deviation. Determine whether approximately 4/5 of the observations lie between the mean ± 1.28 standard deviations. Determine whether approximately 19/20 of the observations lie between the mean ± 2 standard deviations.
- Construct a normal probability plot and evaluate the likelihood that the variable of interest is at least approximately normally distributed by inspecting the plot for evidence of linearity (i.e., a straight line).

The Normal Probability Plot

- **The normal probability plot:** A two-dimensional plot of the observed data values on the vertical axis with their corresponding quantile values from a standardized normal distribution on the horizontal axis.

Left-Skewed
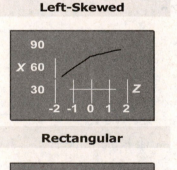

Right-Skewed
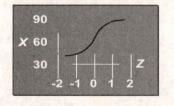

Rectangular
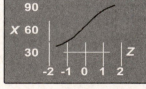

U-Shaped
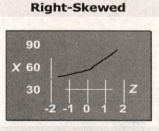

Copyright ©2015 Pearson Education, Inc.

The Uniform Distribution

- **Properties of the uniform distribution:**
  - The probability of occurrence of a value is equally likely to occur anywhere in the range between the smallest value a and the largest value b.
  - Also called the **rectangular distribution.**
  - $\mu = \dfrac{a+b}{2}$
  - $\sigma^2 = \dfrac{(b-a)^2}{12}$
  - $\sigma = \sqrt{\dfrac{(b-a)^2}{12}}$

- **The uniform probability density function:**
  - $f(X) = \dfrac{1}{b-a}$ if $a \leq X \leq b$ and 0 elsewhere, where

    a is the minimum value of X and b is the maximum value of X

- **Applications:** Selection of random numbers.

The Exponential Distribution

- **The exponential distribution:**

  $P(\text{arrival time} \leq X) = 1 - e^{-\lambda X}$

  where

  X : any value of continuous random variable

  λ : the population average number of arrivals per unit of time

  $1/\lambda$: average time between arrivals

  $e = 2.71828$

- **Applications:** The exponential distribution is useful in waiting line (or queuing) theory to model the length of time between arrivals in processes such as customers at fast-food restaurants, and patients entering a hospital emergency room.

Online Topic: The Normal Approximation to the Binomial Distribution

- Whenever $n\pi > 5$ and $n(1-\pi) > 5$, the normal distribution can be used to approximate the binomial distribution.
- For the discrete random variable X that has a binomial distribution, let A and B be integers. The various scenarios of computing the binomial probability using a normal approximation with a correction for continuity adjustment are presented below:
  - $P(A \leq X) = P((A - 0.5) \leq X) = P\left(\dfrac{(A - 0.5) - n\pi}{\sqrt{n\pi(1-\pi)}} \leq Z \right)$

Copyright ©2015 Pearson Education, Inc.

- $P(A < X) = P((A+1) \le X) = P((A+0.5) \le X) = P\left(\dfrac{(A+0.5) - n\pi}{\sqrt{n\pi(1-\pi)}} \le Z\right)$

- $P(X \le B) = P(X \le (B+0.5)) = P\left(Z \le \dfrac{(B+0.5) - n\pi}{\sqrt{n\pi(1-\pi)}}\right)$

- $P(X < B) = P(X \le (B-1)) = P(X \le (B-0.5)) = P\left(Z \le \dfrac{(B-0.5) - n\pi}{\sqrt{n\pi(1-\pi)}}\right)$

- $P(A \le X \le B) = P((A-0.5) \le X \le (B+0.5)) = P\left(\dfrac{(A-0.5) - n\pi}{\sqrt{n\pi(1-\pi)}} \le Z \le \dfrac{(B+0.5) - n\pi}{\sqrt{n\pi(1-\pi)}}\right)$

- $P(A < X < B) = P((A+1) \le X \le (B-1)) = P((A+0.5) \le X \le (B-0.5))$

  $= P\left(\dfrac{(A+0.5) - n\pi}{\sqrt{n\pi(1-\pi)}} \le Z \le \dfrac{(B-0.5) - n\pi}{\sqrt{n\pi(1-\pi)}}\right)$

- $P(A < X \le B) = P((A+1) \le X \le B) = P((A+0.5) \le X \le (B+0.5))$

  $= P\left(\dfrac{(A+0.5) - n\pi}{\sqrt{n\pi(1-\pi)}} \le Z \le \dfrac{(B+0.5) - n\pi}{\sqrt{n\pi(1-\pi)}}\right)$

- $P(A \le X < B) = P(A \le X \le (B-1)) = P((A-0.5) \le X \le (B-0.5))$

  $= P\left(\dfrac{(A-0.5) - n\pi}{\sqrt{n\pi(1-\pi)}} \le Z \le \dfrac{(B-0.5) - n\pi}{\sqrt{n\pi(1-\pi)}}\right)$

- $P(X = A) = P((A-0.5) \le X \le (A+0.5)) = P\left(\dfrac{(A-0.5) - n\pi}{\sqrt{n\pi(1-\pi)}} \le Z \le \dfrac{(A+0.5) - n\pi}{\sqrt{n\pi(1-\pi)}}\right)$

Copyright ©2015 Pearson Education, Inc.

SOLUTIONS TO END OF SECTION
AND CHAPTER REVIEW EVEN PROBLEMS

6.2   PHStat output:

Normal Probabilities				
Common Data				
Mean	0			
Standard Deviation	1			
			Probability for a Range	
Probability for X <=			From X Value	1.57
X Value	-1.57		To X Value	1.84
Z Value	-1.57		Z Value for 1.57	1.57
P(X<=-1.57)	0.0582076		Z Value for 1.84	1.84
			P(X<=1.57)	0.9418
Probability for X >			P(X<=1.84)	0.9671
X Value	1.84		P(1.57<=X<=1.84)	0.0253
Z Value	1.84			
P(X>1.84)	0.0329		**Find X and Z Given Cum. Pctage.**	
			Cumulative Percentage	84.13%
Probability for X<-1.57 or X >1.84			Z Value	0.999815
P(X<-1.57 or X >1.84)	0.0911		X Value	0.999815

(a) $P(-1.57 < Z < 1.84) = 0.9671 - 0.0582 = 0.9089$
(b) $P(Z < -1.57) + P(Z > 1.84) = 0.0582 + 0.0329 = 0.0911$
(c)   If $P(Z > A) = 0.025$, $P(Z < A) = 0.975$. $A = +1.96$.
(d)   If $P(-A < Z < A) = 0.6826$, $P(Z < A) = 0.8413$. So 68.26% of the area is captured between $-A = -1.00$ and $A = +1.00$.

6.4   PHStat output:

Normal Probabilities				
Common Data				
Mean	0			
Standard Deviation	1			
			Probability for a Range	
Probability for X <=			From X Value	-1.96
X Value	-0.21		To X Value	-0.21
Z Value	-0.21		Z Value for -1.96	-1.96
P(X<=-0.21)	0.4168338		Z Value for -0.21	-0.21
			P(X<=-1.96)	0.0250
Probability for X >			P(X<=-0.21)	0.4168
X Value	1.08		P(-1.96<=X<=-0.21)	0.3918
Z Value	1.08			
P(X>1.08)	0.1401		**Find X and Z Given Cum. Pctage.**	
			Cumulative Percentage	84.13%
Probability for X<-0.21 or X >1.08			Z Value	0.999815
P(X<-0.21 or X >1.08)	0.5569		X Value	0.999815

Copyright ©2015 Pearson Education, Inc.

6.4   (a) $P(Z > 1.08) = 1 - 0.8599 = 0.1401$
cont.   (b) $P(Z < -0.21) = 0.4168$
        (c) $P(-1.96 < Z < -0.21) = 0.4168 - 0.0250 = 0.3918$
        (d) $P(Z > A) = 0.1587, P(Z < A) = 0.8413. \quad A = +1.00.$

6.6   (a)   Partial PHStat output:

Common Data					
Mean	50				
Standard Deviation	4				
			Probability for a Range		
Probability for X <=			From X Value		42
X Value	42		To X Value		43
Z Value	-2		Z Value for 42		-2
P(X<=42)	0.0227501		Z Value for 43		-1.75
			P(X<=42)		0.0228
Probability for X >			P(X<=43)		0.0401
X Value	43		P(42<=X<=43)		0.0173
Z Value	-1.75				
P(X>43)	0.9599		**Find X and Z Given Cum. Pctage.**		
			Cumulative Percentage		5.00%
Probability for X<42 or X >43			Z Value		-1.644854
P(X<42 or X >43)	0.9827		X Value		43.42059

$$P(X > 43) = P(Z > -1.75) = 1 - 0.0401 = 0.9599$$

        (b) $P(X < 42) = P(Z < -2.00) = 0.0228$
        (c) $P(X < A) = 0.05,$

$$Z = -1.645 = \frac{A - 50}{4} \qquad A = 50 - 1.645(4) = 43.42$$

        (d)   Partial PHStat output:

Find X and Z Given Cum. Pctage.	
Cumulative Percentage	**80.00%**
Z Value	**0.841621**
X Value	**53.36648**

$$P(X_{\text{lower}} < X < X_{\text{upper}}) = 0.60$$
$$P(Z < -0.84) = 0.20 \text{ and } P(Z < 0.84) = 0.80$$

$$Z = -0.84 = \frac{X_{\text{lower}} - 50}{4} \qquad Z = +0.84 = \frac{X_{\text{upper}} - 50}{4}$$

$$X_{\text{lower}} = 50 - 0.84(4) = 46.64 \text{ and } X_{\text{upper}} = 50 + 0.84(4) = 53.36$$

6.8   Partial PHStat output:

Common Data	
Mean	50
Standard Deviation	12

Probability for X <=	
X Value	30
Z Value	-1.666667
P(X<=30)	0.0477904

Probability for X >	
X Value	60
Z Value	0.8333333
P(X>60)	0.2023

Probability for X<30 or X >60	
P(X<30 or X >60)	0.2501

Probability for a Range	
From X Value	34
To X Value	50
Z Value for 34	-1.333333
Z Value for 50	0
P(X<=34)	0.0912
P(X<=50)	0.5000
P(34<=X<=50)	0.4088

Find X and Z Given Cum. Pctage.	
Cumulative Percentage	20.00%
Z Value	-0.841621
X Value	39.90055

(a) $P(34 < X < 50) = P(-1.33 < Z < 0) = 0.4088$

(b) $P(X < 30) + P(X > 60) = P(Z < -1.67) + P(Z > 0.83)$
        $= 0.0475 + (1.0 - 0.7967) = 0.2508$

(c) $P(X > A) = 0.80$ $P(Z < -0.84) \cong 0.20$ $Z = -0.84 = \dfrac{A - 50}{12}$

        $A = 50 - 0.84(12) = 39.92$ thousand miles or 39,920 miles

(d)   Partial PHStat output:

Common Data	
Mean	50
Standard Deviation	10

Probability for X <=	
X Value	30
Z Value	-2
P(X<=30)	0.0227501

Probability for X >	
X Value	60
Z Value	1
P(X>60)	0.1587

Probability for X<30 or X >60	
P(X<30 or X >60)	0.1814

Probability for a Range	
From X Value	34
To X Value	50
Z Value for 34	-1.6
Z Value for 50	0
P(X<=34)	0.0548
P(X<=50)	0.5000
P(34<=X<=50)	0.4452

Find X and Z Given Cum. Pctage.	
Cumulative Percentage	20.00%
Z Value	-0.841621
X Value	41.58379

The smaller standard deviation makes the Z-values larger.

(a) $P(34 < X < 50) = P(-1.60 < Z < 0) = 0.4452$

(b) $P(X < 30) + P(X > 60) = P(Z < -2.00) + P(Z > 1.00)$
        $= 0.0228 + (1.0 - 0.8413) = 0.1815$

(c) $A = 50 - 0.84(10) = 41.6$ thousand miles or 41,600 miles

6.10   PHStat output:

Common Data	
Mean	73
Standard Deviation	8

Probability for X <=	
X Value	91
Z Value	2.25
P(X<=91)	0.9877755

Probability for X >	
X Value	81
Z Value	1
P(X>81)	0.1587

Probability for X<91 or X >81	
P(X<91 or X >81)	1.1464

Probability for a Range	
From X Value	65
To X Value	89
Z Value for 65	-1
Z Value for 89	2
P(X<=65)	0.1587
P(X<=89)	0.9772
P(65<=X<=89)	0.8186

Find X and Z Given Cum. Pctage.	
Cumulative Percentage	95.00%
Z Value	1.644854
X Value	86.15883

(a) $P(X < 91) = P(Z < 2.25) = 0.9878$

(b) $P(65 < X < 89) = P(-1.00 < Z < 2.00) = 0.9772 - 0.1587 = 0.8185$

(c) $P(X > A) = 0.05$ $P(Z < 1.645) = 0.9500$

$$Z = 1.645 = \frac{A - 73}{8}   \quad A = 73 + 1.645(8) = 86.16\%$$

(d)   Option 1: $P(X > A) = 0.10$ $P(Z < 1.28) \cong 0.9000$

$$Z = \frac{81 - 73}{8} = 1.00$$

Since your score of 81% on this exam represents a Z-score of 1.00, which is below the minimum Z-score of 1.28, you will not earn an "A" grade on the exam under this grading option.

Option 2: $Z = \frac{68 - 62}{3} = 2.00$

Since your score of 68% on this exam represents a Z-score of 2.00, which is well above the minimum Z-score of 1.28, you will earn an "A" grade on the exam under this grading option. You should prefer Option 2.

6.12   (a) $P(X > 60) = P(Z > 1.1429) = 0.1265$

Probability for X >	
X Value	60
Z Value	1.1428571
P(X>60)	0.1265

(b) $P(15 < X < 30) = P(-2.0714 < Z < -1) = 0.1395$

Probability for a Range	
From X Value	15
To X Value	30
Z Value for 15	-2.0714
Z Value for 30	-1
P(X<=15)	0.0192
P(X<=30)	0.1587
P(15<=X<=30)	0.1395

(c) $P(X < 15) = P(Z < -2.0714) = 0.0192$

Probability for X <=	
X Value	15
Z Value	-2.0714
P(X<=15)	0.0192

(d) $P(X < A) = 0.99$ $Z = 2.3263$ $A = 76.5689$

Find X and Z Given Cum. Pctage.	
Cumulative Percentage	99.00%
Z Value	2.3263
X Value	76.5689

6.14   With 39 values, the smallest of the standard normal quantile values covers an area under the normal curve of 0.025. The corresponding Z value is -1.96. The middle (20th) value has a cumulative area of 0.50 and a corresponding Z value of 0.0. The largest of the standard normal quantile values covers an area under the normal curve of 0.975, and its corresponding Z value is +1.96.

Copyright ©2015 Pearson Education, Inc.

6.16   (a)   Excel output:

MPG	
Mean	22.52941
Standard Error	0.446536
Median	22
Mode	22
Standard Deviation	1.841115
Sample Variance	3.389706
Kurtosis	0.340209
Skewness	0.525947
Range	7
Minimum	19
Maximum	26
Sum	383
Count	17
First Quartile	21.5
Third Quartile	23.5
Interquartile Range	2
CV	8.17%
6*std.dev	11.04669
1.33*std.dev	2.448683

The mean is about the same as the median. The range is smaller than 6 times the standard deviation and the interquartile range is smaller than 1.33 times the standard deviation.

(b)

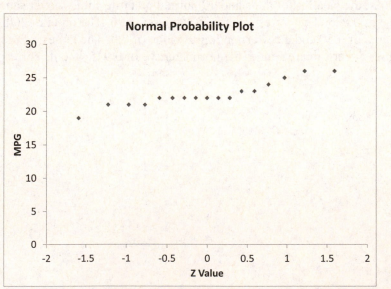

The normal probability plot indicates departure from normal distribution. The kurtosis is 0.3402, indicating a distribution that is slightly more peaked than a normal distribution, with more values in the tails. The skewness of 0.5259 indicates a slightly right-skewed distribution.

Copyright ©2015 Pearson Education, Inc.

6.18   Excel output:

Property Taxes Per Capita ($)	
Mean	1332.235
Standard Error	80.91249
Median	1230
Mode	#N/A
Standard Deviation	577.8308
Sample Variance	333888.4
Kurtosis	0.539467
Skewness	0.918321
Range	2479
Minimum	506
Maximum	2985
Sum	67944
Count	51
First Quartile	867
Third Quartile	1633
Interquartile Range	766
6 * std.dev	3466.985
1.33 * std.dev	768.515

(a)   Because the mean is slightly larger than the median, the interquartile range is slightly less than 1.33 times the standard deviation, and the range is much smaller than 6 times the standard deviation, the data appear to deviate from the normal distribution.

(b)

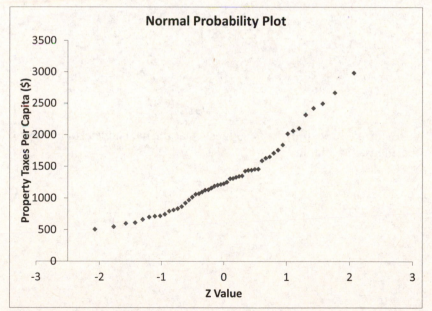

The normal probability plot suggests that the data appear to be right-skewed. The kurtosis is 0.5395 indicating a distribution that is slightly more peaked than a normal distribution, with more values in the tails. A skewness of 0.9183 indicates a right-skewed distribution.

Copyright ©2015 Pearson Education, Inc.

6.20   Excel output:

Error	
Mean	-0.00023
Median	0
Mode	0
Standard Deviation	0.001696
Sample Variance	2.88E-06
Range	0.008
Minimum	-0.003
Maximum	0.005
First Quartile	-0.0015
Third Quartile	0.001
1.33 Std Dev	0.002255
Interquartile Range	0.0025
6 Std Dev	0.010175

(a)   Because the interquartile range is close to 1.33S and the range is also close to 6S, the data appear to be approximately normally distributed.

(b)

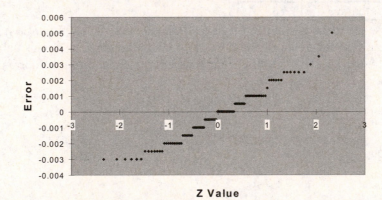

The normal probability plot suggests that the data appear to be approximately normally distributed.

Copyright ©2015 Pearson Education, Inc.

6.22   (a)   Five-number summary: 82   127   148.5   168   213   mean = 147.06
             range = 131   interquartile range = 41   standard deviation = 31.69
             The mean is very close to the median. The five-number summary suggests that the
             distribution is quite symmetrical around the median. The interquartile range is very
             close to 1.33 times the standard deviation. The range is about $50 below 6 times the
             standard deviation. In general, the distribution of the data appears to closely
             resemble a normal distribution.
             Note: The quartiles are obtained using PHStat without any interpolation.

      (b)

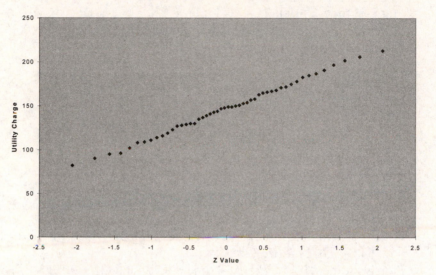

             The normal probability plot confirms that the data appear to be approximately
             normally distributed.

6.24   (a) $P(0 < X < 20) = (20 - 0)/120 = 0.1667$
      (b) $P(10 < X < 30) = (30 - 10)/120 = 0.1667$
      (c) $P(35 < X < 120) = (120 - 35)/120 = 0.7083$

      (d) $\mu = \dfrac{0 + 120}{2} = 60$ $\sigma = \sqrt{\dfrac{(120 - 0)^2}{12}} = 34.6410$

6.26   (a) $P(X < 19) = (19 - 18)/(24 - 18) = 0.1667$
      (b) $P(X < 23) = (23 - 18)/(24 - 18) = 0.8333$
      (c) $P(20 < X < 22) = (22 - 20)/(24 - 18) = 0.3333$

      (d) $\mu = \dfrac{(18 + 24)}{2} = 21$ $\sigma = \sqrt{\dfrac{(24 - 18)^2}{12}} = 1.7321$

Copyright ©2015 Pearson Education, Inc.

6.28   (a)   PHStat output:
         Exponential
         Probabilities

Data	
Mean	10
X Value	0.1

Results	
P(<=X)	0.6321

$P(\text{arrival time} < 0.1) = 1 - e^{-\lambda x} = 1 - e^{-(10)(0.1)} = 0.6321$

(b) $P(\text{arrival time} > 0.1) = 1 - P(\text{arrival time} \leq 0.1) = 1 - 0.6321 = 0.3679$

(c)   PHStat output:

         Exponential
         Probabilities

Data	
Mean	10
X Value	0.2

Results	
P(<=X)	0.8647

$P(0.1 < \text{arrival time} < 0.2) = P(\text{arrival time} < 0.2) - P(\text{arrival time} < 0.1)$
$= 0.8647 - 0.6321 = 0.2326$

(d) $P(\text{arrival time} < 0.1) + P(\text{arrival time} > 0.2) = 0.6321 + 0.1353 = 0.7674$

6.30   (a)   PHStat output:

Data	
Mean	5
X Value	0.3

Results	
P(<=X)	0.7769

$P(\text{arrival time} < 0.3) = 1 - e^{-(5)(0.3)} = 0.7769$

(b) $P(\text{arrival time} > 0.3) = 1 - P(\text{arrival time} < 0.3) = 0.2231$

(c)   PHStat output:

Data	
Mean	5
X Value	0.5

Results	
P(<=X)	0.9179

$P(0.3 < \text{arrival time} < 0.5) = P(\text{arrival time} < 0.5) - P(\text{arrival time} < 0.3)$
$= 0.9179 - 0.7769 = 0.1410$

(d) $P(\text{arrival time} < 0.3 \text{ or} > 0.5) = 1 - P(0.3 < \text{arrival time} < 0.5) = 0.8590$

Copyright ©2015 Pearson Education, Inc.

6.32   (a)   PHStat output:

**Exponential
Probabilities**

Data	
Mean	2
X Value	1

Results	
P(<=X)	0.8647

P(arrival time $\leq$ 1) = 0.8647

(b)   PHStat output:

**Exponential
Probabilities**

Data	
Mean	2
X Value	5

Results	
P(<=X)	0.999955

P(arrival time $\leq$ 5) = 0.99996

(c)   PHStat output:

**Exponential
Probabilities**

Data	
Mean	1
X Value	1

Results	
P(<=X)	0.6321

**Exponential
Probabilities**

Data	
Mean	1
X Value	5

Results	
P(<=X)	0.993262

If $\lambda = 1$, P(arrival time $\leq$ 1) = 0.6321,
P(arrival time $\leq$ 5) = 0.9933

Copyright ©2015 Pearson Education, Inc.

6.34   (a)   PHStat output:

Exponential Probabilit	
Data	
Mean	0.2
X Value	3
Results	
P(<=X)	0.4512

P(next call arrives in < 3) = 0.4512

(b)   PHStat output:

Exponential Probabilit	
Data	
Mean	0.2
X Value	6
Results	
P(<=X)	0.6988

P(next call arrives in > 6) = 1 - 0.6988 = 0.3012

(c)   PHStat output:

Exponential Probabilit	
Data	
Mean	0.2
X Value	1
Results	
P(<=X)	0.1813

P(next call arrives in < 1) = 0.1813

Copyright ©2015 Pearson Education, Inc.

6.36   (a)   PHStat output:

Exponential
Probabilities

Data	
Mean	8
X Value	0.25

Results	
P(<=X)	0.8647

P(arrival time ≤ 0.25) = 0.8647

(b)   PHStat output:

Exponential
Probabilities

Data	
Mean	8
X Value	0.05

Results	
P(<=X)	0.3297

P(arrival time ≤ 0.05) = 0.3297

(c)   PHStat output:

Exponential
Probabilities

Data	
Mean	15
X Value	0.25

Results	
P(<=X)	0.9765

Exponential
Probabilities

Data	
Mean	15
X Value	0.05

Results	
P(<=X)	0.5276

If $\lambda = 15$, P(arrival time ≤ 0.25) = 0.9765,
P(arrival time ≤ 0.05) = 0.5276

6.38   Using the tables of the normal distribution with knowledge of μ and σ along with the transformation formula, we can find any probability under the normal curve.

Copyright ©2015 Pearson Education, Inc.

6.40   Find the Z value corresponding to the given percentile and then use the equation
$X = \mu + z\sigma$.

6.42   Both the normal distribution and the uniform distribution are symmetric but the uniform distribution has a bounded range while the normal distribution ranges from negative infinity to positive infinity. The exponential distribution is right-skewed and ranges from zero to infinity.

6.44   The exponential distribution is used to determine the probability that the next arrival will occur within a given length of time.

6.46   (a)   Partial PHStat output:

Probability for a Range	
From X Value	1.9
To X Value	2
Z Value for 1.9	-2
Z Value for 2	0
P(X<=1.9)	0.0228
P(X<=2)	0.5000
P(1.9<=X<=2)	0.4772

$P(1.90 < X < 2.00) = P(-2.00 < Z < 0) = 0.4772$

(b)   Partial PHStat output:

Probability for a Range	
From X Value	1.9
To X Value	2.1
Z Value for 1.9	-2
Z Value for 2.1	2
P(X<=1.9)	0.0228
P(X<=2.1)	0.9772
P(1.9<=X<=2.1)	0.9545

$P(1.90 < X < 2.10) = P(-2.00 < Z < 2.00) = 0.9772 - 0.0228 = 0.9544$

(c)   Partial PHStat output:

Probability for X<1.9 or X >2.1	
P(X<1.9 or X >2.1)	0.0455

$P(X < 1.90) + P(X > 2.10) = 1 - P(1.90 < X < 2.10) = 0.0456$

(d)   Partial PHStat output:

Find X and Z Given Cum. Pctage.	
Cumulative Percentage	1.00%
Z Value	-2.326348
X Value	1.883683

$P(X > A) = P(Z > -2.33) = 0.99$ $A = 2.00 - 2.33(0.05) = 1.8835$

Copyright ©2015 Pearson Education, Inc.

6.46   (e)   Partial PHStat output:
cont.

Find X and Z Given Cum. Pctage.	
Cumulative Percentage	99.50%
Z Value	2.575829
X Value	2.128791

$P(A < X < B) = P(-2.58 < Z < 2.58) = 0.99$

$A = 2.00 - 2.58(0.05) = 1.8710$ \qquad $B = 2.00 + 2.58(0.05) = 2.1290$

6.48   (a)   Partial PHStat output:

Probability for X <=	
X Value	1000
Z Value	-1.0780
P(X<=1000)	0.1405

$P(X < 1000) = P(Z < -1.0780) = 0.1405$

(b)

Probability for a Range	
From X Value	2500
To X Value	3000
Z Value for 2500	1.9220
Z Value for 3000	2.922
P(X<=2500)	0.9727
P(X<=3000)	0.9983
P(2500<=X<=3000)	0.0256

$P(2500 < X < 3000) = P(1.9220 < Z < 2.922) = 0.0256$

(c)

Find X and Z Given Cum. Pctage.	
Cumulative Percentage	90.00%
Z Value	1.2816
X Value	2179.7758

$P(X < A) = P(Z < 1.2816) = 0.90$ \qquad $A = 1539 + 500(1.2816) = \$2,179.7758$

(d)

Find X and Z Given Cum. Pctage.	
Cumulative Percentage	90.00%
Z Value	1.2816
X Value	2179.7758

$P(A < X < B) = P(-1.2816 < Z < 1.2816) = 0.80$

$A = 1539 - 1.28(500) = \$898.2242$

$B = 1539 + 1.28(500) = \$2,179.7758$

Copyright ©2015 Pearson Education, Inc.

6.50 (a) Waiting time will more closely resemble an exponential distribution.
(b) Seating time will more closely resemble a normal distribution.
(c)

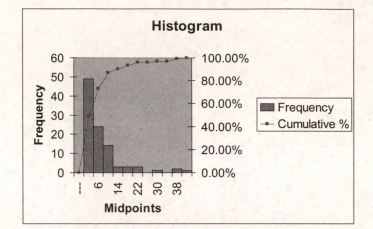

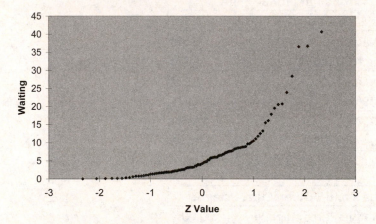

Both the histogram and normal probability plot suggest that waiting time more closely resembles an exponential distribution.

(d)

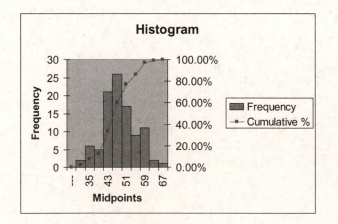

Copyright ©2015 Pearson Education, Inc.

6.50
cont.

Normal Probability Plot

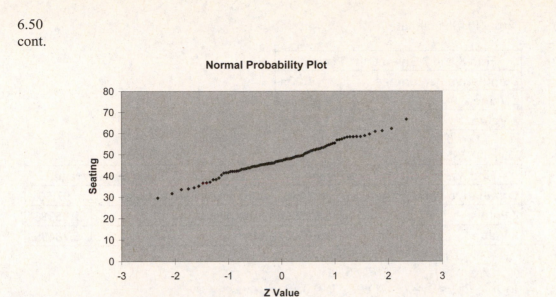

Both the histogram and normal probability plot suggest that seating time more closely resembles a normal distribution.

6.52   (a)   Partial PHStat output:

Probability for X <=	
X Value	2
Z Value	-1.720769
P(X<=2)	0.0426464

$P(X < 2) = P(Z < -1.7208) = 0.0426$

(b)   Partial PHStat output:

Probability for a Range	
From X Value	1.5
To X Value	2.5
Z Value for 1.5	-2.105385
Z Value for 2.5	-1.336154
P(X<=1.5)	0.0176
P(X<=2.5)	0.0907
P(1.5<=X<=2.5)	0.0731

$P(1.5 < X < 2.5) = P(-2.1054 < Z < -1.3362) = 0.0731$

(c)   Partial PHStat output:

Probability for X >	
X Value	1.8
Z Value	-1.874615
P(X>1.8)	0.9696

$P(X > 1.8) = P(Z > -1.8746) = 0.9696$

Copyright ©2015 Pearson Education, Inc.

6.52   (d)   Partial PHStat output:
cont.

Find X and Z Given Cum. Pctage.	
Cumulative Percentage	1.00%
Z Value	-2.326348
X Value	1.212748

$P(A < X) = 0.01$ $Z = -2.3263$ $A = 1.2127$

(e)   Partial PHStat output:

Find X and Z Given Cum. Pctage.		Find X and Z Given Cum. Pctage.	
Cumulative Percentage	2.50%	Cumulative Percentage	97.50%
Z Value	-1.959964	Z Value	1.959964
X Value	1.689047	X Value	6.784953

$P(A < X < B) = 0.95$ $Z = -1.9600$ $A = 1.6890$
$Z = 1.96$ $B = 6.7850$

(f)   (a) $P(X < 2) = (2 - 1)/(9 - 1) = 0.125$
       (b) $P(1.5 < X < 2.5) = (2.5 - 1.5)/(9 - 1) = 0.125$
       (c) $P(X > 1.8) = (9 - 1.8)/(9 - 1) = 0.9$

Copyright ©2015 Pearson Education, Inc.

CHAPTER 7

OBJECTIVES
- To learn about the concept of the sampling distribution
- To compute probabilities related to the sample mean and the sample proportion
- To understand the importance of the Central Limit Theorem

OVERVIEW AND KEY CONCEPTS

Some Basic Concepts on Sampling Distribution
- **Why do we study sampling distribution?**
  - Sample statistics are used to estimate population parameters, but different samples yield different estimates. The solution is to develop a theoretical basis based on a sampling distribution.
- **What is a sampling distribution?**
  - A sampling distribution is a theoretical probability distribution of a sample statistic. A sample statistic (e.g., sample mean, sample proportion) is a random variable because a different sample will yield a different value for the statistic, and, hence, a different estimate for the parameter of interest. The sampling distribution is the probability distribution of the sample statistic as a result of taking all possible samples of the same size from the population.

Sampling Distribution of the Sample Mean
- **Population mean of the sample mean**
  - $\mu_{\bar{X}} = \mu$
  - This is the unbiased property of the sample mean.
- **Standard error (population standard deviation) of the sample mean**
  - $\sigma_{\bar{X}} = \dfrac{\sigma}{\sqrt{n}}$
  - Standard error of the sample mean is smaller than the standard deviation of the population.
  - The larger the sample size, the smaller the standard error.
- **The central limit theorem:** As the sample size (i.e., the number of the observations in a sample) gets *large enough*, the sampling distribution of the mean can be approximated by the normal distribution regardless of the distribution of the individual values in the population.
- **The distribution of the sample mean**
  - If the population is normally distributed, the sampling distribution of the mean is normally distributed regardless of the sample size.
  - If the population distribution is fairly symmetrical, the sampling distribution of the mean is approximately normal if sample size is at least 15.
  - For most population distributions, regardless of the shape, the sampling distribution of the mean is approximately normally distributed if the sample size is at least 30.

Copyright ©2015 Pearson Education, Inc.

- **Online Topic: Finite population correction**
    - Use the finite population correction factor to modify the standard error if sample size n is large relative to the population size N, i.e. $n/N > 0.05$.

    - Standard error with finite population correction factor: $\sigma_{\bar{X}} = \dfrac{\sigma}{\sqrt{n}} \sqrt{\dfrac{N-n}{N-1}}$

Finding Range Probability of the Sample Mean

1. Standardize the value of the sample mean using $Z = \dfrac{\bar{X} - \mu_{\bar{X}}}{\sigma_{\bar{X}}} = \dfrac{\bar{X} - \mu}{\dfrac{\sigma}{\sqrt{n}}}$.

2. Look up the cumulative probabilities from the cumulative standardized normal distribution table.

    E.g., for $\mu = 8$, $\sigma = 2$, $n = 25$ and X normally distributed. $P\left(7.8 < \bar{X} < 8.2\right) = ?$

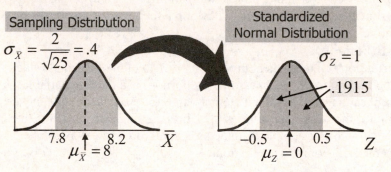

$$P\left(7.8 < \bar{X} < 8.2\right) = P\left(\frac{7.8 - 8}{2/\sqrt{25}} < \frac{\bar{X} - \mu_{\bar{X}}}{\sigma_{\bar{X}}} < \frac{8.2 - 8}{2/\sqrt{25}}\right) = P\left(-.5 < Z < .5\right) = .3830$$

Sampling Distribution of the Sample Proportion

- **Sample proportion:** $p = \dfrac{X}{n} = \dfrac{\text{number of items having the characteristic of interest}}{\text{sample size}}$

- **Population mean of the sample proportion**
    - $\mu_p = \pi$ where π is the population proportion.

- **Standard error of the sample proportion**
    - $\sigma_p = \sqrt{\dfrac{\pi(1-\pi)}{n}}$

- **The distribution of the sample proportion**
    - When $n\pi$ and $n(1-\pi)$ are each at least 5, the sampling distribution of the sample proportion can be approximated by the normal distribution with mean μ_p and standard deviation σ_p.

Copyright ©2015 Pearson Education, Inc.

- **Online Topic: Finite population correction**
    - Use the finite population correction factor to modify the standard error if sample size n is large relative to the population size N, i.e. $n/N > 0.05$.

    - Standard error with finite population correction factor: $\sigma_p = \sqrt{\dfrac{\pi(1-\pi)}{n}} \sqrt{\dfrac{N-n}{N-1}}$

Finding Range Probability of the Sample Proportion

1. Standardize the value of the sample proportion using $Z = \dfrac{p - \mu_p}{\sigma_p} = \dfrac{p - \pi}{\sqrt{\dfrac{\pi(1-\pi)}{n}}}$.

2. Look up the cumulative probabilities from the cumulative standardized normal distribution table.

E.g., for $n = 200$, $\pi = 0.4$. $P(p < 0.43) = ?$

$$P(p < .43) = P\left(\frac{p - \mu_p}{\sigma_p} < \frac{.43 - .4}{\sqrt{\dfrac{.4(1-.4)}{200}}} \right) = P(Z < .87) = .8078$$

Copyright ©2015 Pearson Education, Inc.

SOLUTIONS TO END OF SECTION
AND CHAPTER REVIEW EVEN PROBLEMS

7.2   PHStat output:

Common Data	
Mean	50
Standard Deviation	0.5

Probability for X <=	
X Value	47
Z Value	-6
P(X<=47)	9.866E-10

Probability for X >	
X Value	51.5
Z Value	3
P(X>51.5)	0.0013

Probability for X<47 or X >51.5	
P(X<47 or X >51.5)	0.0013

Probability for X >	
X Value	51.1
Z Value	2.2
P(X>51.1)	0.0139

Probability for a Range	
From X Value	47
To X Value	49.5
Z Value for 47	-6
Z Value for 49.5	-1
P(X<=47)	0.0000
P(X<=49.5)	0.1587
P(47<=X<=49.5)	0.1587

Find X and Z Given Cum. Pctage.	
Cumulative Percentage	65.00%
Z Value	0.38532
X Value	50.19266

(a) $P(\overline{X} < 47) = P(Z < -6.00) =$ virtually zero

(b) $P(47 < \overline{X} < 49.5) = P(-6.00 < Z < -1.00) = 0.1587 - 0.00 = 0.1587$

(c) $P(\overline{X} > 51.1) = P(Z > 2.20) = 1.0 - 0.9861 = 0.0139$

(d) $P(\overline{X} > A) = P(Z > 0.39) = 0.35$ $\overline{X} = 50 + 0.39(0.5) = 50.195$

Copyright ©2015 Pearson Education, Inc.

7.4   (a)   Sampling Distribution of the Mean for $n = 2$ (without replacement)

Sample Number	Outcomes	Sample Means $\overline{X}_i$
1	1, 3	$\overline{X}_1 = 2$
2	1, 6	$\overline{X}_2 = 3.5$
3	1, 7	$\overline{X}_3 = 4$
4	1, 9	$\overline{X}_4 = 5$
5	1, 10	$\overline{X}_5 = 5.5$
6	3, 6	$\overline{X}_6 = 4.5$
7	3, 7	$\overline{X}_7 = 5$
8	3, 9	$\overline{X}_8 = 6$
9	3, 10	$\overline{X}_9 = 6.5$
10	6, 7	$\overline{X}_{10} = 6.5$
11	6, 9	$\overline{X}_{11} = 7.5$
12	6, 10	$\overline{X}_{12} = 8$
13	7, 9	$\overline{X}_{13} = 8$
14	7, 10	$\overline{X}_{14} = 8.5$
15	9, 10	$\overline{X}_{15} = 9.5$

(a)   Mean of All Possible Sample Means: Mean of All Population Elements:

$$\mu_{\overline{X}} = \frac{90}{15} = 6 \qquad\qquad \mu = \frac{1+3+6+7+9+10}{6} = 6$$

Both means are equal to 6. This property is called unbiasedness.

Copyright ©2015 Pearson Education, Inc.

7.4   (b)   Sampling Distribution of the Mean for $n = 3$ (without replacement)
cont.

Sample Number	Outcomes	Sample Means $\overline{X}_i$
1	1, 3, 6	$\overline{X}_1 = 3\ 1/3$
2	1, 3, 7	$\overline{X}_2 = 3\ 2/3$
3	1, 3, 9	$\overline{X}_3 = 4\ 1/3$
4	1, 3, 10	$\overline{X}_4 = 4\ 2/3$
5	1, 6, 7	$\overline{X}_5 = 4\ 2/3$
6	1, 6, 9	$\overline{X}_6 = 5\ 1/3$
7	1, 6, 10	$\overline{X}_7 = 5\ 2/3$
8	3, 6, 7	$\overline{X}_8 = 5\ 1/3$
9	3, 6, 9	$\overline{X}_9 = 6$
10	3, 6, 10	$\overline{X}_{10} = 6\ 1/3$
11	6, 7, 9	$\overline{X}_{11} = 7\ 1/3$
12	6, 7, 10	$\overline{X}_{12} = 7\ 2/3$
13	6, 9, 10	$\overline{X}_{13} = 8\ 1/3$
14	7, 9, 10	$\overline{X}_{14} = 8\ 2/3$
15	1, 7, 9	$\overline{X}_{15} = 5\ 2/3$
16	1, 7, 10	$\overline{X}_{16} = 6$
17	1, 9, 10	$\overline{X}_{17} = 6\ 2/3$
18	3, 7, 9	$\overline{X}_{18} = 6\ 1/3$
19	3, 7, 10	$\overline{X}_{19} = 6\ 2/3$
20	3, 9, 10	$\overline{X}_{20} = 7\ 1/3$

$$\mu_{\overline{X}} = \frac{120}{20} = 6 \qquad \text{This is equal to } \mu, \text{ the population mean.}$$

(c)   The distribution for $n = 3$ has less variability. The larger sample size has resulted in sample means being closer to μ.

(d)   (a)   Sampling Distribution of the Mean for $n = 2$ (with replacement)

Copyright ©2015 Pearson Education, Inc.

7.4
cont.

Sample Number	Outcomes	Sample Means $\overline{X}_i$
1	1, 1	$\overline{X}_1 = 1$
2	1, 3	$\overline{X}_2 = 2$
3	1, 6	$\overline{X}_3 = 3.5$
4	1, 7	$\overline{X}_4 = 4$
5	1, 9	$\overline{X}_5 = 5$
6	1, 10	$\overline{X}_6 = 5.5$
7	3, 1	$\overline{X}_7 = 2$
8	3, 3	$\overline{X}_8 = 3$
9	3, 6	$\overline{X}_9 = 4.5$
10	3, 7	$\overline{X}_{10} = 5$
11	3, 9	$\overline{X}_{11} = 6$
12	3, 10	$\overline{X}_{12} = 6.5$
13	6, 1	$\overline{X}_{13} = 3.5$
14	6, 3	$\overline{X}_{14} = 4.5$
15	6, 6	$\overline{X}_{15} = 6$
16	6, 7	$\overline{X}_{16} = 6.5$
17	6, 9	$\overline{X}_{17} = 7.5$
18	6, 10	$\overline{X}_{18} = 8$
19	7, 1	$\overline{X}_{19} = 4$
20	7, 3	$\overline{X}_{20} = 5$
21	7, 6	$\overline{X}_{21} = 6.5$
22	7, 7	$\overline{X}_{22} = 7$
23	7, 9	$\overline{X}_{23} = 8$
24	7, 10	$\overline{X}_{24} = 8.5$
25	9, 1	$\overline{X}_{25} = 5$
26	9, 3	$\overline{X}_{26} = 6$
27	9, 6	$\overline{X}_{27} = 7.5$
28	9, 7	$\overline{X}_{28} = 8$
29	9, 9	$\overline{X}_{29} = 9$
30	9, 10	$\overline{X}_{30} = 9.5$
31	10, 1	$\overline{X}_{31} = 5.5$
32	10, 3	$\overline{X}_{32} = 6.5$
33	10, 6	$\overline{X}_{33} = 8$
34	10, 7	$\overline{X}_{34} = 8.5$
35	10, 9	$\overline{X}_{35} = 9.5$
36	10, 10	$\overline{X}_{36} = 10$

Copyright ©2015 Pearson Education, Inc.

7.4   (d)   (a)   Mean of All Possible   Mean of All
cont.   Sample Means: Population Elements:

$$\mu_{\bar X} = \frac{216}{36} = 6 \qquad\qquad \mu = \frac{1+3+6+7+7+12}{6} = 6$$

Both means are equal to 6. This property is called unbiasedness.

(b)   Repeat the same process for the sampling distribution of the mean for $n = 3$ (with replacement). There will be $6^3 = 216$ different samples.

$$\mu_{\bar X} = 6 \qquad\qquad \text{This is equal to } \mu, \text{ the population mean.}$$

(c)   The distribution for $n = 3$ has less variability. The larger sample size has resulted in more sample means being close to μ.

7.6   (a)   When $n = 4$, the shape of the sampling distribution of $\bar X$ should closely resemble the shape of the distribution of the population from which the sample is selected. Because the mean is larger than the median, the distribution of the sales price of new houses is skewed to the right, and so is the sampling distribution of $\bar X$ although it will be less skewed than the population.

(b)   If you select samples of $n = 100$, the shape of the sampling distribution of the sample mean will be very close to a normal distribution with a mean of \$291,200 and a standard deviation of $\sigma_{\bar X} = \dfrac{\sigma}{\sqrt{n}} = \$9,000$.

(c) $\sigma_{\bar X} = \dfrac{\sigma}{\sqrt{n}} = \dfrac{90000}{\sqrt{100}} = 9000$

PHStat output:

Probability for X <=	
X Value	315000
Z Value	2.6444444
P(X<=315000)	0.9959087

$P(\bar X < 315,000) = P(Z < 2.6444) = 0.9959$

(d)   PHStat output:

Probability for a Range	
From X Value	295000
To X Value	310000
Z Value for 295000	0.422222
Z Value for 310000	2.088889
P(X<=295000)	0.6636
P(X<=310000)	0.9816
P(295000<=X<=310000)	0.3181

$P(295,000 < \bar X < 310,000) = P(0.4222 < Z < 2.0889) = 0.3181$

Copyright ©2015 Pearson Education, Inc.

7.8   PHStat output:

Probability for X >	
X Value	26
Z Value	-1.0000
P(X>26)	0.8413

Find X and Z Given Cum. Pctage.	
Cumulative Percentage	85.00%
Z Value	1.0364
X Value	28.0364

(a) $P(\bar{X} > 26) = P(Z > -1.0) = 0.8413$

(b) $P(\bar{X} < A) = P(Z < 1.0364) = 0.85$ $\bar{X} = 27 + 1.0364\,(1) = 28.0364$

(c)   To be able to use the standard normal distribution as an approximation for the area under the curve, we must assume that the population is symmetrically distributed such that the central limit theorem will likely hold for samples of $n = 16$.

(d)   PHStat output:

Find X and Z Given Cum. Pctage.	
Cumulative Percentage	85.00%
Z Value	1.0364
X Value	27.51822

$P(\bar{X} < A) = P(Z < 1.0364) = 0.85$ $\bar{X} = 27 + 1.0364\,(0.5) = 27.5182$

7.10   (a) $p = 20/50 = 0.40$ (b) $\sigma_p = \sqrt{\dfrac{(0.45)(0.55)}{50}} = 0.0704$

7.12   (a) $\mu_p = \pi = 0.501$, $\sigma_p = \sqrt{\dfrac{\pi(1-\pi)}{n}} = \sqrt{\dfrac{0.501(1-0.501)}{100}} = 0.05$

Partial PHstat output:

Probability for X >	
X Value	0.55
Z Value	0.98
P(X>0.55)	0.1635

$P(p > 0.55) = P(Z > 0.98) = 1 - 0.8365 = 0.1635$

(b) $\mu_p = \pi = 0.60$, $\sigma_p = \sqrt{\dfrac{\pi(1-\pi)}{n}} = \sqrt{\dfrac{0.6(1-0.6)}{100}} = 0.04899$

Partial PHstat output:

Probability for X >	
X Value	0.55
Z Value	-1.020621
P(X>0.55)	0.8463

$P(p > 0.55) = P(Z > -1.021) = 1 - 0.1539 = 0.8461$

(c) $\mu_p = \pi = 0.49$, $\sigma_p = \sqrt{\dfrac{\pi(1-\pi)}{n}} = \sqrt{\dfrac{0.49(1-0.49)}{100}} = 0.05$

Partial PHstat output:

Probability for X >	
X Value	0.55
Z Value	1.2002401
P(X>0.55)	0.1150

$P(p > 0.55) = P(Z > 1.20) = 1 - 0.8849 = 0.1151$

(d)   Increasing the sample size by a factor of 4 decreases the standard error by a factor of 2.

Copyright ©2015 Pearson Education, Inc.

7.12   (d)   (a)   Partial PHstat output:
cont.

Probability for X >	
X Value	0.55
Z Value	1.9600039
P(X>0.55)	0.0250

$$P(p > 0.55) = P\ (Z > 1.96) = 1 - 0.9750 = 0.0250$$

(b)   Partial PHstat output:

Probability for X >	
X Value	0.55
Z Value	-2.041241
P(X>0.55)	0.9794

$$P(p > 0.55) = P\ (Z > -2.04) = 1 - 0.0207 = 0.9793$$

(c)   Partial PHstat output:

Probability for X >	
X Value	0.55
Z Value	2.4004801
P(X>0.55)	0.0082

$$P(p > 0.55) = P\ (Z > 2.40) = 1 - 0.9918 = 0.0082$$

If the sample size is increased to 400, the probably in (a), (b) and (c) is smaller, larger, and smaller, respectively because the standard error of the sampling distribution of the sample proportion becomes smaller and, hence, the sampling distribution is more concentrated around the true population proportion.

7.14   (a) $\mu_p = \pi = 0.80,\ \sigma_p = \sqrt{\dfrac{\pi(1-\pi)}{n}} = \sqrt{\dfrac{0.80(1-0.80)}{100}} = 0.04$

Partial PHStat output:

Probability for X <=	
X Value	0.85
Z Value	1.2500
P(X<=0.85)	0.8944

$$P(p < 0.85) = P\ (Z < 1.2500) = 0.8944$$

(b)   Partial PHStat output:

Probability for a Range	
From X Value	0.75
To X Value	0.85
Z Value for 0.75	-1.2500
Z Value for 0.85	1.2500
P(X<=0.75)	0.1056
P(X<=0.85)	0.8944
P(0.75<=X<=0.85)	0.7887

$$P(0.75 < p < 0.85) = P\ (-1.2500 < Z < 1.2500) = 0.7887$$

Copyright ©2015 Pearson Education, Inc.

7.14 cont.   (c)   Partial PHStat output:

Probability for X >	
X Value	0.82
Z Value	0.5000
P(X>0.82)	0.3085

$P(p > 0.82) = P(Z > 0.5000) = 0.3085$

(d) $\mu_p = \pi = 0.80,\ \sigma_p = \sqrt{\dfrac{\pi(1-\pi)}{n}} = \sqrt{\dfrac{0.80(1-0.80)}{400}} = 0.02$

(a)   Partial PHStat output:

Probability for X <=	
X Value	0.85
Z Value	2.5000
P(X<=0.85)	0.9938

$P(p < 0.85) = P(Z < 2.5000) = 0.9938$

(b)   Partial PHStat output:

Probability for a Range	
From X Value	0.75
To X Value	0.85
Z Value for 0.75	-2.5000
Z Value for 0.85	2.5000
P(X<=0.75)	0.0062
P(X<=0.85)	0.9938
P(0.75<=X<=0.85)	0.9876

$P(0.75 < p < 0.85) = P(-2.5000 < Z < 2.5000) = 0.9876$

(c)   Partial PHStat output:

Probability for X >	
X Value	0.82
Z Value	1.0000
P(X>0.82)	0.1587

$P(p > 0.82) = P(Z > 1.0000) = 0.1587$

Copyright ©2015 Pearson Education, Inc.

7.16   (a)   PHStat output:

Probability for a Range	
From X Value	0.12
To X Value	0.18
Z Value for 0.12	-1.1882
Z Value for 0.18	1.1882
P(X<=0.12)	0.1174
P(X<=0.18)	0.8826
P(0.12<=X<=0.18)	0.7652

Since $n = 200$, which is quite large, we use the sample proportion to approximate the population proportion and, hence, $\pi = 0.15$. Also the sampling distribution of the sample proportion will be close to a normal distribution according to the central limit theorem.

$$\mu_p = \pi = 0.15, \ \sigma_p = \sqrt{\frac{\pi(1-\pi)}{n}} = \sqrt{\frac{0.15(1-0.15)}{200}} = 0.0252$$

$P(0.12 < p < 0.18) = P(-1.1882 < Z < 1.1882) = 0.7652$

(b)

Find X and Z Given Cum. Pctage.	
Cumulative Percentage	5.00%
Z Value	-1.6449
X Value	0.1085

Find X and Z Given Cum. Pctage.	
Cumulative Percentage	95.00%
Z Value	1.6449
X Value	0.1915

$P(A < p < B) = P(-1.6449 < Z < 1.6449) = 0.90$
$A = 0.1085$
$B = 0.1915$

(c)   PHStat output:

Find X and Z Given Cum. Pctage.	
Cumulative Percentage	2.50%
Z Value	-1.9600
X Value	0.1005

Find X and Z Given Cum. Pctage.	
Cumulative Percentage	97.50%
Z Value	1.9600
X Value	0.1995

$P(A < p < B) = P(-1.96 < Z < 1.96) = 0.95$
$A = 0.1005$
$B = 0.1995$

7.18   (a) $\mu_p = \pi = 0.39, \ \sigma_p = \sqrt{\frac{\pi(1-\pi)}{n}} = \sqrt{\frac{0.39(1-0.39)}{100}} = 0.0488$

Partial PHStat output:

Probability for X <=	
X Value	0.3
Z Value	-1.8452
P(X<=0.3)	0.0325

$P(p < 0.3) = P(Z < -1.8452) = 0.0325$

Copyright ©2015 Pearson Education, Inc.

7.18 (b) $\mu_p = \pi = 0.39, \; \sigma_p = \sqrt{\dfrac{\pi(1-\pi)}{n}} = \sqrt{\dfrac{0.39(1-0.39)}{400}} = 0.0244$

cont.

Probability for X <=	
X Value	0.3
Z Value	-3.6904
P(X<=0.3)	0.0001

$P(p < 0.3) = P\,(Z < -3.6904) = 0.0001$

(c)   Increasing the sample size by a factor of 4 decreases the standard error by a factor of $\sqrt{4}$. The sampling distribution of the proportion becomes more concentrated around the true proportion of 0.39 and, hence, the probability in (b) becomes smaller than that in (a).

7.20   The variation of the sample means becomes smaller as larger sample sizes are taken. This is due to the fact that an extreme observation will have a smaller effect on the mean in a larger sample than in a small sample. Thus, the sample means will tend to be closer to the population mean as the sample size increases.

7.22   The population distribution is the distribution of a particular variable of interest, while the sampling distribution represents the distribution of a statistic.

7.24 $\mu_{\bar{X}} = 0.753 \qquad \sigma_{\bar{X}} = \dfrac{\sigma}{\sqrt{n}} = \dfrac{0.004}{5} = 0.0008$

PHStat output:

Common Data	
Mean	0.753
Standard Deviation	0.0008

Probability for X <=	
X Value	0.74
Z Value	-16.25
P(X<=0.74)	1.117E-59

Probability for X >	
X Value	0.76
Z Value	8.75
P(X>0.76)	0.0000

Probability for X<0.74 or X >0.76	
P(X<0.74 or X >0.76)	0.0000

Probability for a Range	
From X Value	0.75
To X Value	0.753
Z Value for 0.75	-3.75
Z Value for 0.753	0
P(X<=0.75)	0.0001
P(X<=0.753)	0.5000
P(0.75<=X<=0.753)	0.4999

Find X and Z Given Cum. Pctage.	
Cumulative Percentage	7.00%
Z Value	-1.475791
X Value	0.751819

Copyright ©2015 Pearson Education, Inc.

7.24
cont.

Probability for a Range	
From X Value	0.74
To X Value	0.75
Z Value for 0.74	-16.25
Z Value for 0.75	-3.75
P(X<=0.74)	0.0000
P(X<=0.75)	0.0001
P(0.74<=X<=0.75)	0.00009

(a) $P(0.75 < \bar{X} < 0.753) = P(-3.75 < Z < 0) = 0.5 - 0.00009 = 0.4999$

(b) $P(0.74 < \bar{X} < 0.75) = P(-16.25 < Z < -3.75) = 0.00009$

(c) $P(\bar{X} > 0.76) = P(Z > 8.75) =$ virtually zero

(d) $P(\bar{X} < 0.74) = P(Z < -16.25) =$ virtually zero

(e) $P(\bar{X} < A) = P(Z < -1.48) = 0.07$ $X = 0.753 - 1.48(0.0008) = 0.7518$

7.26 $\mu_{\bar{X}} = 4.7$ $\sigma_{\bar{X}} = \dfrac{\sigma_X}{\sqrt{n}} = \dfrac{0.40}{5} = 0.08$

PHstat output:

Common Data	
Mean	4.7
Standard Deviation	0.08

Probability for X >	
X Value	4.6
Z Value	-1.25
P(X>4.6)	0.8944

Find X and Z Given Cum. Pctage.	
Cumulative Percentage	23.00%
Z Value	-0.738847
X Value	4.640892

Find X and Z Given Cum. Pctage.	
Cumulative Percentage	15.00%
Z Value	-1.036433
X Value	4.6170853

Find X and Z Given Cum. Pctage.	
Cumulative Percentage	85.00%
Z Value	1.036433
X Value	4.782915

(a) $P(4.60 < \bar{X}) = P(-1.25 < Z) = 1 - 0.1056 = 0.8944$

(b) $P(A < \bar{X} < B) = P(-1.04 < Z < 1.04) = 0.70$
        $A = 4.70 - 1.04(0.08) = 4.6168$ ounces $X = 4.70 + 1.04(0.08) = 4.7832$ ounces

(c) $P(\bar{X} > A) = P(Z > -0.74) = 0.77$ $A = 4.70 - 0.74(0.08) = 4.6408$

7.28 $\mu_{\bar{X}} = \mu = 17.87, \ \sigma_{\bar{X}} = \dfrac{\sigma}{\sqrt{n}} = \dfrac{20}{\sqrt{16}} = 5$

(a)   PHStat output:

Probability for X <=	
X Value	0
Z Value	-3.5740
P(X<=0)	0.00017578

$P(\bar{X} < 0) = P(Z < -3.5740) = 0.0002$

Copyright ©2015 Pearson Education, Inc.

7.28   (b)   PHStat output:
cont.

Probability for a Range	
From X Value	-10
To X Value	10
Z Value for -10	-5.5740
Z Value for 10	-1.5740
P(X<=-10)	0.0000
P(X<=10)	0.0577
P(-10<=X<=10)	0.0577

$P(-10 < \overline{X} < 10) = P(0 < Z < 0.0577) = 0.0577$

(c)   PHStat output:

Probability for X >	
X Value	10
Z Value	-1.5740
P(X>10)	0.9423

$P(\overline{X} > 10) = P(Z > -1.5740) = 0.9423$

Copyright ©2015 Pearson Education, Inc.

CHAPTER 8

OBJECTIVES

- To construct and interpret confidence interval estimates for the mean and the proportion
- To determine the sample size necessary to develop a confidence interval estimate for the mean or proportion

OVERVIEW AND KEY CONCEPTS

Why We Need Confidence Interval Estimates in Addition to Point Estimates

- Confidence interval estimates take into consideration variation in sample statistics from sample to sample.
- They provide information about closeness to unknown population parameters.
- The interval estimates are always stated in level of confidence, which is lower than 100%.

Confidence Interval Estimate for the Mean when the Population Variance is Known

- **Assumptions:**
  - Population variance σ^2 is known.
  - Population is normally distributed or the sample size is large.
- **Point estimate for the population mean μ : $\bar{X}$**
- **Confidence interval estimate:**
  - $\bar{X} \pm Z_{\alpha/2} \dfrac{\sigma}{\sqrt{n}}$ where $Z_{\alpha/2}$ is the value corresponding to a cumulative area of

    $\left(1 - \dfrac{\alpha}{2}\right)$ from a standardized normal distribution, i.e., the right-tail probability of

    $\alpha/2$.
- **Elements of confidence interval estimate**
  - **Level of confidence:** Measures the level of confidence in which the interval will contain the unknown population parameter.
  - **Precision (range):** Represents the closeness to the unknown parameter.
  - **Cost:** The cost required to obtain a sample of size n.
- **Factors affecting interval width (precision)**
  - **Data variation measured by σ^2 :** The larger is the σ^2, the wider is the interval estimate.
  - **Sample size n:** The larger is the sample size, the narrower is the interval estimate.
  - **The level of confidence $100(1 - \alpha)\%$:** The higher is the level of confidence, the wider is the interval estimate.

Copyright ©2015 Pearson Education, Inc.

- **Interpretation of a** $100(1-\alpha)\%$ **confidence interval estimate:** If all possible samples of size n are taken and their sample means are computed, $100(1-\alpha)\%$ of the intervals contain the true population mean somewhere within the interval around their sample means and only $100(\alpha)\%$ of them do not.

Confidence Interval Estimate for the Mean when the Population Variance is Unknown

- **Assumptions:**
    - Population variance σ^2 is unknown.
    - Population is normally distributed or the sample size is large.
- **Confidence interval estimate:**
    - $\bar{X} \pm t_{\alpha/2}\dfrac{S}{\sqrt{n}}$ where $t_{\alpha/2,n-1}$ is the value corresponding to a cumulative area of

      $\left(1-\dfrac{\alpha}{2}\right)$ from a Student's t distribution with n-1 degrees of freedom, i.e., the right-tail probability of $\alpha/2$.
- **Online Topic: Confidence interval estimate for finite population:**
    - $\bar{X} \pm t_{\alpha/2}\dfrac{S}{\sqrt{n}}\sqrt{\dfrac{(N-n)}{(N-1)}}$ where N is the population size

Confidence Interval Estimate for the Proportion

- **Assumptions:**
    - Two categorical outcomes
    - Population follows Binomial distribution
    - Normal approximation can be used if $np \geq 5$ and $n(1-p) \geq 5$.
- **Point estimate for the population proportion of characteristic of interest** π : $p = \dfrac{X}{n}$
- **Confidence interval estimate:**
    - $p \pm Z_{\alpha/2}\sqrt{\dfrac{p(1-p)}{n}}$
- **Online Topic: Confidence interval estimate for finite population:**
    - $p \pm Z_{\alpha/2}\sqrt{\dfrac{p(1-p)}{n}}\sqrt{\dfrac{(N-n)}{(N-1)}}$ where N is the population size

Online Topic: Confidence Interval Estimate for the Total Amount (Application of Confidence Interval Estimate in Auditing)

- **Point estimate for population total:** $N\bar{X}$
- **Confidence interval estimate:**
    - $N\bar{X} \pm N(t_{\alpha/2})\dfrac{S}{\sqrt{n}}\sqrt{\dfrac{(N-n)}{(N-1)}}$

Copyright ©2015 Pearson Education, Inc.

Online Topic: Confidence Interval Estimate for the Total Difference (Application of Confidence Interval Estimate in Auditing)

- **Point estimate for total difference:** $N\bar{D}$ where $\bar{D} = \dfrac{\sum_{i=1}^{n} D_i}{n}$ is the sample average difference.
- **Confidence interval estimate:**

  - $$N\bar{D} \pm N\left(t_{\alpha/2,n-1}\right)\frac{S_D}{\sqrt{n}}\sqrt{\frac{(N-n)}{(N-1)}} \text{ where } S_D = \sqrt{\frac{\sum_{i=1}^{n}\left(D_i - \bar{D}\right)^2}{n-1}}.$$

Online Topic: One-sided Confidence Interval Estimate for the Proportion (Application of Confidence Interval Estimate in Auditing)

- **Confidence interval estimate:**

  - $$Upper\ Bound = p + Z_\alpha \sqrt{\frac{p(1-p)}{n}}\sqrt{\frac{N-n}{N-1}}$$ where Z_α is the value corresponding to a cumulative area of $(1-\alpha)$ from a standardized normal distribution, i.e., the right-tail probability of α.

Determining Sample Size

- **The sample size needed when estimating the population mean:**

  - $n_0 = \dfrac{Z_{\alpha/2}^2 \sigma^2}{e^2}$ where e is the acceptable sampling error and σ^2 is estimated from past data, by an educated guess or by the data obtained from a pilot study.

- **The sample size needed when estimating the population proportion:**

  - $n_0 = \dfrac{Z_{\alpha/2}^2 \pi(1-\pi)}{e^2}$ where e is the acceptable sampling error and π is estimated from past information, by an educated guess or use 0.5.

- **Online Topic: Sample size determination using the finite population correction factor:**

  - $n = \dfrac{n_0 N}{n_0 + (N-1)}$ where N is the population size

Online Topic: Bootstrapping

- Use the bootstrapping method to construct bootstrap confidence interval when the assumption of normality of the population is invalid.
- To construct the bootstrap confidence interval for the population mean:
  1. Select a random sample of size n without replacement from a population of size N.
  2. Resample the initial sample by selecting n values with replacement from the n values in the initial sample.
  3. Compute $\bar{X}$ from this resample.
  4. Repeat steps 2 and 3 m different times.

Copyright ©2015 Pearson Education, Inc.

5. Construct the resampling distribution of $\bar{X}$.
6. Construct an ordered array of the entire set of resampled means.
7. Find the value that cuts off the smallest $\alpha / 2 \times 100\%$ and the value that cuts off the largest $\alpha / 2 \times 100\%$. These values provide the lower and upper limits of the bootstrap confidence interval estimate of the population mean.

Copyright ©2015 Pearson Education, Inc.

SOLUTIONS TO END OF SECTION
AND CHAPTER REVIEW EVEN PROBLEMS

8.2 $\bar{X} \pm Z \dfrac{\sigma}{\sqrt{n}} = 125 \pm 2.58 \dfrac{24}{\sqrt{36}}$ $114.68 \le \mu \le 135.32$

8.4   Yes, it is true since 5% of intervals will not include the population mean.

8.6   (a)   You would compute the mean first because you need the mean to compute the standard deviation. If you had a sample, you would compute the sample mean. If you had the population mean, you would compute the population standard deviation.

 (b)   If you have a sample, you are computing the sample standard deviation not the population standard deviation needed in Equation 8.1. If you have a population, and have computed the population mean and population standard deviation, you don't need a confidence interval estimate of the population mean since you already have computed it.

8.8   Equation (8.1) assumes that you know the population standard deviation. Because you are selecting a sample of 100 from the population, you are computing a sample standard deviation, not the population standard deviation.

8.10   (a)

Confidence Interval Estimate for the Mean	
Data	
Population Standard Deviation	**1000**
Sample Mean	**7500**
Sample Size	**64**
Confidence Level	**95%**
Intermediate Calculations	
Standard Error of the Mean	125
Z Value	-1.9600
Interval Half Width	244.9955
Confidence Interval	
Interval Lower Limit	**7255.00**
Interval Upper Limit	**7745.00**

$\bar{X} \pm Z \cdot \dfrac{\sigma}{\sqrt{n}} = 7500 \pm 1.96 \cdot \dfrac{1000}{\sqrt{64}}$ $7255.00 \le \mu \le 7745.00$

 (b)   No. The manufacturer cannot support a claim that the bulbs last an average 8,000 hours with a 95% level of confidence because 8,000 does not fall inside the 95% confidence interval.

Copyright ©2015 Pearson Education, Inc.

8.10 (c)   No. Since σ is known and $n = 64$, from the Central Limit Theorem, we may assume
cont.   that the sampling distribution of $\bar{X}$ is approximately normal.

(d)   The confidence interval is narrower based on a process standard deviation of 800
       hours rather than the original assumption of 1000 hours.

(a) $\bar{X} \pm Z \cdot \dfrac{\sigma}{\sqrt{n}} = 7500 \pm 1.96 \cdot \dfrac{800}{\sqrt{64}}$ $7304.00 \le \mu \le 7696.00$

(b)   No. The manufacturer cannot support a claim that the bulbs last an average
       8,000 hours with a 95% level of confidence because 8,000 still does not fall
       inside the 95% confidence interval.

8.12 (a) $df = 9$, $\alpha = 0.05$, $t_{\alpha/2} = 2.2622$

(b) $df = 9$, $\alpha = 0.01$, $t_{\alpha/2} = 3.2498$

(c) $df = 31$, $\alpha = 0.05$, $t_{\alpha/2} = 2.0395$

(d) $df = 64$, $\alpha = 0.05$, $t_{\alpha/2} = 1.9977$

(e) $df = 15$, $\alpha = 0.1$, $t_{\alpha/2} = 1.7531$

8.14   Original data: $5.8571 \pm 2.4469 \cdot \dfrac{6.4660}{\sqrt{7}}$ $-0.1229 \le \mu \le 11.8371$

Altered data: $4.00 \pm 2.4469 \cdot \dfrac{2.1602}{\sqrt{7}}$ $2.0022 \le \mu \le 5.9978$

The presence of an outlier in the original data increases the value of the sample mean and
greatly inflates the sample standard deviation.

8.16 (a) $\bar{X} \pm t \cdot \dfrac{S}{\sqrt{n}} = 75 \pm 2.0049 \cdot \dfrac{9}{\sqrt{55}}$ $72.57 \le \mu \le 77.43$

Confidence Interval Estimate for the Mean	
Data	
Sample Standard Deviation	9
Sample Mean	75
Sample Size	55
Confidence Level	95%
Intermediate Calculations	
Standard Error of the Mean	1.213559752
Degrees of Freedom	54
t Value	2.0049
Interval Half Width	2.4330
Confidence Interval	
Interval Lower Limit	72.57
Interval Upper Limit	77.43

Copyright ©2015 Pearson Education, Inc.

8.16   (b)   You can be 95% confident that the population mean one-time gift donation is
cont.   somewhere between $72.57 and $77.43.

8.18   PHStat output:

Confidence Interval Estimate for the Mean

Data	
Sample Standard Deviation	1.406031226
Sample Mean	7.09
Sample Size	15
Confidence Level	95%

Intermediate Calculations	
Standard Error of the Mean	0.363035702
Degrees of Freedom	14
t Value	2.1448
Interval Half Width	0.7786

Confidence Interval	
Interval Lower Limit	6.31
Interval Upper Limit	7.87

(a) $\bar{X} \pm t \dfrac{S}{\sqrt{n}} = 7.09 \pm 2.1448 \dfrac{1.4060}{\sqrt{15}}$ $6.31 \le \mu \le 7.87$

(b)   You can be 95% confident that the population mean amount spent for lunch ($) at a
      fast-food restaurant is somewhere between $6.31 and $7.87.

8.20   PHStat output:

Confidence Interval Estimate for the Mean

Data	
Sample Standard Deviation	1.841115391
Sample Mean	22.52941176
Sample Size	17
Confidence Level	95%

Intermediate Calculations	
Standard Error of the Mean	0.446536072
Degrees of Freedom	16
t Value	2.1199
Interval Half Width	0.9466

Confidence Interval	
Interval Lower Limit	21.58
Interval Upper Limit	23.48

Copyright ©2015 Pearson Education, Inc.

8.20   (a) $\bar{X} \pm t\dfrac{S}{\sqrt{n}} = 22.5294 \pm 2.1199\left(\dfrac{1.8411}{\sqrt{17}}\right)$ $21.58 \leq \mu \leq 23.48$

cont.   (b)   You can be 95% confident that the population mean MPG of 2013 small SUVs is somewhere between 21.58 and 23.48.

      (c)   Because the upper limit of the 95% confidence interval for population mean miles per gallon of 2013 small SUVs is lower than the lower limit of the 95% confidence interval for population mean miles per gallon of 2013 family sedans, you are able to conclude that the population mean miles per gallon of 2013 small SUVs is lower than that of 2013 family sedans.

8.22   (a) $\bar{X} \pm t \cdot \dfrac{S}{\sqrt{n}} = 43.04 \pm 2.0096 \cdot \dfrac{41.9261}{\sqrt{50}}$ $31.12 \leq \mu \leq 54.96$

      (b)   The population distribution needs to be normally distribution.

      (c)

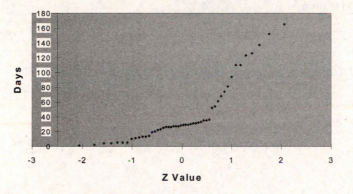

      (c)

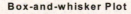

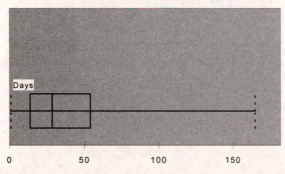

Both the normal probability plot and the boxplot suggest that the distribution is skewed to the right.

      (d)   Even though the population distribution is not normally distributed, with a sample of 50, the t distribution can still be used due to the Central Limit Theorem.

Copyright ©2015 Pearson Education, Inc.

8.24   (a)   PHStat output:

Confidence Interval Estimate for the Mean	
Data	
Sample Standard Deviation	13.19692305
Sample Mean	36.27733333
Sample Size	15
Confidence Level	95%
Intermediate Calculations	
Standard Error of the Mean	3.407430881
Degrees of Freedom	14
t Value	2.1448
Interval Half Width	7.3082
Confidence Interval	
Interval Lower Limit	28.97
Interval Upper Limit	43.59

$$\bar{X} \pm t\frac{S}{\sqrt{n}} = 36.2773 \pm 2.1448\left(\frac{13.1969}{\sqrt{15}}\right) \qquad 28.97 \leq \mu \leq 43.59$$

(b)   The population distribution needs to be normally distributed.

(c)

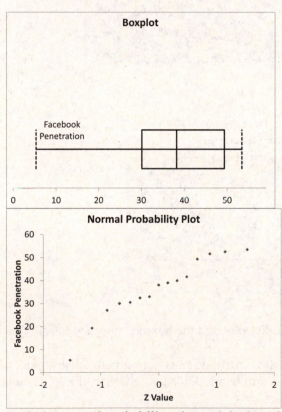

Both the normal probability plot and the boxplot show that the distribution is left-skewed, so with the small sample size, the validity of the confidence interval is in question.

Copyright ©2015 Pearson Education, Inc.

8.26 $p = \dfrac{X}{n} = \dfrac{50}{200} = 0.25$ $p \pm Z \cdot \sqrt{\dfrac{p(1-p)}{n}} = 0.25 \pm 1.96\sqrt{\dfrac{0.25(0.75)}{200}}$

$$0.19 \le \pi \le 0.31$$

8.28   (a)

	A	B
1	Purchase Additional Telephone Line	
2		
3	Sample Size	500
4	Number of Successes	135
5	Confidence Level	99%
6	Sample Proportion	0.27
7	Z Value	-2.57583451
8	Standard Error of the Proportion	0.019854471
9	Interval Half Width	0.05114183
10	Interval Lower Limit	0.21885817
11	Interval Upper Limit	0.32114183

$p = \dfrac{X}{n} = \dfrac{135}{500} = 0.27$ $p \pm Z \cdot \sqrt{\dfrac{p(1-p)}{n}} = 0.27 \pm 2.5758\sqrt{\dfrac{0.27(1-0.27)}{500}}$

$$0.22 \le \pi \le 0.32$$

(b)   The manager in charge of promotional programs concerning residential customers can infer that the proportion of households that would purchase a new cellphone if it were made available at a substantially reduced installation cost is between 0.22 and 0.32 with a 99% level of confidence.

8.30   (a)   PHStat output:

Confidence Interval Estimate for the Proportion	
Data	
Sample Size	500
Number of Successes	265
Confidence Level	95%
Intermediate Calculations	
Sample Proportion	0.53
Z Value	-1.9600
Standard Error of the Proportion	0.0223
Interval Half Width	0.0437
Confidence Interval	
Interval Lower Limit	0.4863
Interval Upper Limit	0.5737

$p = \dfrac{X}{n} = \dfrac{265}{500} = 0.53$ $p \pm Z \cdot \sqrt{\dfrac{p(1-p)}{n}} = 0.53 \pm 1.96\sqrt{\dfrac{0.53(1-0.53)}{500}}$

$$0.4863 \le \pi \le 0.5737$$

8.30   (b)   Since the 95% confidence interval contains 0.50, you cannot claim that more than
cont.   half of all social media sports fans would likely purchase a brand mentioned by an
               athlete on a social media site.

       (c)   (a) $p = \dfrac{X}{n} = \dfrac{2650}{5000} = 0.53$ $p \pm Z \cdot \sqrt{\dfrac{p(1-p)}{n}} = 0.53 \pm 1.96\sqrt{\dfrac{0.53(1-0.53)}{5000}}$

$$0.5162 \le \pi \le 0.5438$$

       (b)   Since the lower limit of the 95% confidence interval is greater than 0.50, you
              can claim that more than half of all social media sports fans would likely
              purchase a brand mentioned by an athlete on a social media site..

       (d)   The larger the sample size, the narrow is the confidence interval holding everything
              else constant.

8.32   (a)   PHStat output:

Confidence Interval Estimate for the Proportion	
Data	
Sample Size	1954
Number of Successes	743
Confidence Level	95%
Intermediate Calculations	
Sample Proportion	0.38024565
Z Value	-1.9600
Standard Error of the Proportion	0.0110
Interval Half Width	0.0215
Confidence Interval	
Interval Lower Limit	0.3587
Interval Upper Limit	0.4018

$$p = \frac{X}{n} = \frac{743}{1954} = 0.3802$$

$$p \pm Z \cdot \sqrt{\frac{p(1-p)}{n}} = 0.3802 \pm 1.96\sqrt{\frac{0.3802(1-0.3802)}{1954}}$$

$$0.3587 \le \pi \le 0.4018$$

Copyright ©2015 Pearson Education, Inc.

8.32   (b)   PHStat output:
cont.

Confidence Interval Estimate for the Proportion

Data	
Sample Size	1954
Number of Successes	430
Confidence Level	95%

Intermediate Calculations	
Sample Proportion	0.220061412
Z Value	-1.9600
Standard Error of the Proportion	0.0094
Interval Half Width	0.0184

Confidence Interval	
Interval Lower Limit	0.2017
Interval Upper Limit	0.2384

$$p = \frac{X}{n} = \frac{430}{1954} = 0.2201$$

$$p \pm Z \cdot \sqrt{\frac{p(1-p)}{n}} = 0.2201 \pm 1.96\sqrt{\frac{0.2201(1-0.2201)}{1954}}$$

$$0.2017 \le \pi \le 0.2384$$

(c)   Since the two confidence intervals do not overlap, you can conclude that with 95% confidence that the population proportion of adult cellphone owners who use their phone to keep themselves occupied during commercials or breaks in something they were watching on television is higher than the population proportion of adult cellphone owners who use their phone to check whether something they heard on television was true.

8.34 $n = \dfrac{Z^2\sigma^2}{e^2} = \dfrac{1.96^2 \cdot 15^2}{5^2} = 34.57$ Use $n = 35$

8.36 $n = \dfrac{Z^2\pi(1-\pi)}{e^2} = \dfrac{2.58^2(0.5)(0.5)}{(0.04)^2} = 1,040.06$ Use $n = 1,041$

8.38   (a) $n = \dfrac{Z^2\sigma^2}{e^2} = \dfrac{1.96^2 \cdot 400^2}{50^2} = 245.86$ Use $n = 246$

(b) $n = \dfrac{Z^2\sigma^2}{e^2} = \dfrac{1.96^2 \cdot 400^2}{25^2} = 983.41$ Use $n = 984$

Copyright ©2015 Pearson Education, Inc.

8.40 $n = \dfrac{Z^2 \sigma^2}{e^2} = \dfrac{1.96^2 \cdot (1000)^2}{(200)^2} = 96.04$ Use $n = 97$

8.42   (a) $n = \dfrac{Z^2 \sigma^2}{e^2} = \dfrac{2.5758^2 \cdot 10^2}{3^2} = 73.7211$ Use $n = 74$

    (b) $n = \dfrac{Z^2 \sigma^2}{e^2} = \dfrac{1.96^2 \cdot 10^2}{3^2} = 42.6829$ Use $n = 43$

8.44   (a) $n = \dfrac{Z^2 \sigma^2}{e^2} = \dfrac{1.96^2 \cdot 2^2}{0.25^2} = 245.85$ Use $n = 246$

    (b) $n = \dfrac{Z^2 \sigma^2}{e^2} = \dfrac{1.96^2 \cdot 2.5^2}{0.25^2} = 384.15$ Use $n = 385$

    (c) $n = \dfrac{Z^2 \sigma^2}{e^2} = \dfrac{1.96^2 \cdot 3.0^2}{0.25^2} = 553.17$ Use $n = 554$

    (d)   When there is more variability in the population, a larger sample is needed to accurately estimate the mean.

8.46   (a) $p = 0.18$ $p \pm Z\sqrt{\dfrac{p(1-p)}{n}} = 0.18 \pm 1.96\sqrt{\dfrac{0.18(1-0.18)}{300}}$

                                    $0.1365 \le \pi \le 0.2235$

    (b) $p = 0.13$ $p \pm Z\sqrt{\dfrac{p(1-p)}{n}} = 0.13 \pm 1.96\sqrt{\dfrac{0.13(1-0.13)}{300}}$

                                      $0.0919 \le \pi \le 0.1681$

    (c) $p = 0.09$ $p \pm Z\sqrt{\dfrac{p(1-p)}{n}} = 0.09 \pm 1.96\sqrt{\dfrac{0.09(1-0.09)}{300}}$

                                      $0.0576 \le \pi \le 0.1224$

    (d)   (a) $n = \dfrac{Z^2 \pi(1-\pi)}{e^2} = \dfrac{1.96^2(0.18)(1-0.18)}{0.02^2} = 1{,}417.4983$ Use $n = 1{,}418$

         (b) $n = \dfrac{Z^2 \pi(1-\pi)}{e^2} = \dfrac{1.96^2(0.13)(1-0.13)}{0.02^2} = 1{,}086.1725$ Use $n = 1{,}087$

         (c) $n = \dfrac{Z^2 \pi(1-\pi)}{e^2} = \dfrac{1.96^2(0.09)(1-0.09)}{0.02^2} = 786.5387$ Use $n = 787$

8.48   (a)   If you conducted a follow-up study to estimate the population proportion of individuals who say that banking on their mobile device is convenient, you would use p = 0.77 in the sample size formula because it is based on past information on the proportion.

    (b) $n = \dfrac{Z^2 \pi(1-\pi)}{e^2} = \dfrac{1.96^2(0.77)(1-0.77)}{0.03^2} = 755.9137$ Use $n = 756$

Copyright ©2015 Pearson Education, Inc.

8.50   The only way to have 100% confidence is to obtain the parameter of interest, rather than a sample statistic. From another perspective, the range of the normal and t distribution is infinite, so a Z or t value that contains 100% of the area cannot be obtained.

8.52   If the confidence level is increased, a greater area under the normal or t distribution needs to be included. This leads to an increased value of Z or t, and thus a wider interval.

8.54   (a)   Cellphone:

$$p \pm Z\sqrt{\frac{p(1-p)}{n}} = 0.8802 \pm 1.96\sqrt{\frac{0.8802(1-0.8802)}{2253}}$$

$$0.8667 \le \pi \le 0.8936$$

Desktop computer:

$$p \pm Z\sqrt{\frac{p(1-p)}{n}} = 0.5801 \pm 1.96\sqrt{\frac{0.5801(1-0.5801)}{2253}}$$

$$0.5597 \le \pi \le 0.6005$$

Laptop computer:

$$p \pm Z\sqrt{\frac{p(1-p)}{n}} = 0.6099 \pm 1.96\sqrt{\frac{0.6099(1-0.6099)}{2253}}$$

$$0.5897 \le \pi \le 0.6300$$

Ebook reader:

$$p \pm Z\sqrt{\frac{p(1-p)}{n}} = 0.1802 \pm 1.96\sqrt{\frac{0.1802(1-0.1802)}{2253}}$$

$$0.1643 \le \pi \le 0.1961$$

Tablet computer:

$$p \pm Z\sqrt{\frac{p(1-p)}{n}} = 0.1802 \pm 1.96\sqrt{\frac{0.1802(1-0.1802)}{2253}}$$

$$0.1643 \le \pi \le 0.1961$$

(b)   Most adults have a cellphone. Over half of sdults have a desktop computer and over half have a laptop. Less than 20% have an ebook reader and less than 20% have a tablet computer.

Copyright ©2015 Pearson Education, Inc.

8.56   (a)   PHStat output:

Confidence Interval Estimate for the Mean	
Data	
Sample Standard Deviation	3.5
Sample Mean	41
Sample Size	40
Confidence Level	95%
Intermediate Calculations	
Standard Error of the Mean	0.553398591
Degrees of Freedom	39
t Value	2.0227
Interval Half Width	1.1194
Confidence Interval	
Interval Lower Limit	**39.88**
Interval Upper Limit	**42.12**

$$39.88 \le \mu \le 42.12$$

(b)   PHStat output:

Confidence Interval Estimate for the Proportion	
Data	
Sample Size	40
Number of Successes	30
Confidence Level	95%
Intermediate Calculations	
Sample Proportion	0.75
Z Value	-1.9600
Standard Error of the Proportion	0.0685
Interval Half Width	0.1342
Confidence Interval	
Interval Lower Limit	**0.6158**
Interval Upper Limit	**0.8842**

$$0.6158 \le \pi \le 0.8842$$

(c) $n = \dfrac{Z^2 \cdot \sigma^2}{e^2} = \dfrac{1.96^2 \cdot 5^2}{2^2} = 24.01$ Use $n = 25$

(d) $n = \dfrac{Z^2 \cdot \pi \cdot (1 - \pi)}{e^2} = \dfrac{1.96^2 \cdot (0.5) \cdot (0.5)}{(0.06)^2} = 266.7680$ Use $n = 267$

(e)   If a single sample were to be selected for both purposes, the larger of the two sample sizes ($n = 267$) should be used.

Copyright ©2015 Pearson Education, Inc.

8.58   (a)   PHStat output:

Confidence Interval Estimate for the Mean

Data	
Sample Standard Deviation	7.3
Sample Mean	6.2
Sample Size	25
Confidence Level	95%

Intermediate Calculations	
Standard Error of the Mean	1.46
Degrees of Freedom	24
t Value	2.0639
Interval Half Width	3.0133

Confidence Interval	
Interval Lower Limit	3.19
Interval Upper Limit	9.21

$3.19 \le \mu \le 9.21$

(b)   PHStat output:

Confidence Interval Estimate for the Proportion

Data	
Sample Size	25
Number of Successes	13
Confidence Level	95%

Intermediate Calculations	
Sample Proportion	0.52
Z Value	-1.9600
Standard Error of the Proportion	0.0999
Interval Half Width	0.1958

Confidence Interval	
Interval Lower Limit	0.3242
Interval Upper Limit	0.7158

$0.3241 \le \pi \le 0.7158$

(c) $n = \dfrac{Z^2 \cdot \sigma^2}{e^2} = \dfrac{1.96^2 \cdot 8^2}{1.5^2} = 109.2682$ Use $n = 110$

(d) $n = \dfrac{Z^2 \cdot \pi \cdot (1 - \pi)}{e^2} = \dfrac{1.645^2 \cdot (0.5) \cdot (0.5)}{(0.075)^2} = 120.268$ Use $n = 121$

(e)   If a single sample were to be selected for both purposes, the larger of the two sample sizes ($n = 121$) should be used.

Copyright ©2015 Pearson Education, Inc.

8.60 (a) $p \pm Z \cdot \sqrt{\dfrac{p(1-p)}{n}} = 0.31 \pm 1.645 \cdot \sqrt{\dfrac{0.31(0.69)}{200}}$ $0.2562 \leq \pi \leq 0.3638$

(b) $\bar{X} \pm t \cdot \dfrac{S}{\sqrt{n}} = 3.5 \pm 1.9720 \cdot \dfrac{2}{\sqrt{200}}$ $3.22 \leq \mu \leq 3.78$

(c) $\bar{X} \pm t \cdot \dfrac{S}{\sqrt{n}} = 18000 \pm 1.9720 \cdot \dfrac{3000}{\sqrt{200}}$ $\$17,581.68 \leq \mu \leq \$18,418.32$

8.62 (a) $\bar{X} \pm t \cdot \dfrac{S}{\sqrt{n}} = \$38.54 \pm 2.0010 \cdot \dfrac{\$7.26}{\sqrt{60}}$ $\$36.66 \leq \mu \leq \$40.42$

(b) $p \pm Z \cdot \sqrt{\dfrac{p(1-p)}{n}} = 0.30 \pm 1.645 \cdot \sqrt{\dfrac{0.30(0.70)}{60}}$ $0.2027 \leq \pi \leq 0.3973$

(c) $n = \dfrac{Z^2 \cdot \sigma^2}{e^2} = \dfrac{1.96^2 \cdot 8^2}{1.5^2} = 109.27$ Use $n = 110$

(d) $n = \dfrac{Z^2 \cdot \pi \cdot (1-\pi)}{e^2} = \dfrac{1.645^2 \cdot (0.5) \cdot (0.5)}{(0.04)^2} = 422.82$ Use $n = 423$

(e) If a single sample were to be selected for both purposes, the larger of the two sample sizes ($n = 423$) should be used.

8.64 (a)

Confidence Interval Estimate for the Proportion

Data	
Sample Size	90
Number of Successes	51
Confidence Level	95%

Intermediate Calculations	
Sample Proportion	0.566666667
Z Value	-1.9600
Standard Error of the Proportion	0.0522
Interval Half Width	0.1024

Confidence Interval	
Interval Lower Limit	0.4643
Interval Upper Limit	0.6690

$p \pm Z \cdot \sqrt{\dfrac{p(1-p)}{n}} = 0.5667 \pm 1.96 \cdot \sqrt{\dfrac{0.5667(1-0.5667)}{90}}$

$0.4643 \leq \pi \leq 0.6690$

Copyright ©2015 Pearson Education, Inc.

8.64   (b)
cont.

Confidence Interval Estimate for the Mean

Data	
Sample Standard Deviation	1103.6491
Sample Mean	563.38
Sample Size	51
Confidence Level	95%

Intermediate Calculations	
Standard Error of the Mean	154.5417855
Degrees of Freedom	50
t Value	2.0086
Interval Half Width	310.4063

Confidence Interval	
Interval Lower Limit	252.97
Interval Upper Limit	873.79

$$\bar{X} \pm t \cdot \frac{S}{\sqrt{n}} = 563.38 \pm 2.0086\left(\frac{1103.6491}{\sqrt{51}}\right)$$ $\$252.97 \le \mu \le \$873.79$

8.66   (a) $\bar{X} \pm t \cdot \frac{S}{\sqrt{n}} = 8.4209 \pm 2.0106 \cdot \frac{0.0461}{\sqrt{49}}$ $8.41 \le \mu \le 8.43$

(b)   With 95% confidence, the population mean width of troughs is somewhere between 8.41 and 8.43 inches. Hence, the company's requirement of troughs being between 8.31 and 8.61 is being met with a 95% level of confidence.

(c)   The assumption is valid as the width of the troughs is approximately normally distributed.

8.68   (a) $\bar{X} \pm t \cdot \frac{S}{\sqrt{n}} = 0.2641 \pm 1.9741 \cdot \frac{0.1424}{\sqrt{170}}$ $0.2425 \le \mu \le 0.2856$

(b) $\bar{X} \pm t \cdot \frac{S}{\sqrt{n}} = 0.218 \pm 1.9772 \cdot \frac{0.1227}{\sqrt{140}}$ $0.1975 \le \mu \le 0.2385$

Copyright ©2015 Pearson Education, Inc.

8.68   (c)
cont.

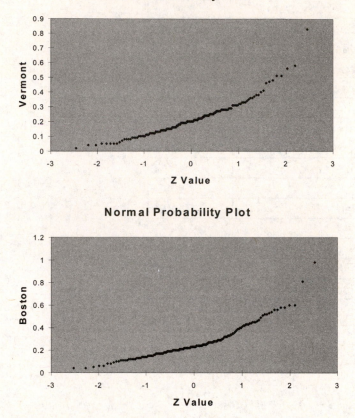

The amount of granule loss for both brands are skewed to the right but the sample sizes are large enough so the violation of the normality assumption is not critical.

(d)   Because the two confidence intervals do not overlap, you can conclude that the mean granule loss of Boston shingles is higher than that of Vermont shingles

Copyright ©2015 Pearson Education, Inc.

CHAPTER 9

OBJECTIVES
- To learn the basic principles of hypothesis testing
- To learn to use hypothesis testing to test a mean or proportion
- To know the assumptions of each hypothesis-testing procedure, how to evaluate them, and the consequences if they are seriously violated
- To be aware of the pitfalls and ethical issues involved in hypothesis testing
- To learn to avoid the pitfalls involved in hypothesis testing

OVERVIEW AND KEY CONCEPTS
Some Basic Concepts in Hypothesis Testing
- **Null hypothesis** (H_0): The hypothesis that is always tested.
  - The null hypothesis always refers to a specified value of the population parameter, not a sample statistic.
  - The statement of the null hypothesis always contains an equal sign regarding the specified value of the population parameter.
- **Alternative hypothesis:** The opposite of the null hypothesis and represents the conclusion supported if the null hypothesis is rejected.
  - The statement of the alternative hypothesis never contains an equal sign regarding the specified value of the population parameter.
- **Critical value:** A value or values that separate the rejection region or regions from the remaining values.
- **Type I error:** A Type I error occurs if the null hypothesis is rejected when in fact it is true and should not be rejected.
- **Type II error:** A Type II error occurs if the null hypothesis is not rejected when in fact it is false and should be rejected.
- **Level of significance** (α): The probability of committing a Type I error.
- **The β risk (the consumer's risk level):** The probability of committing a Type II error.
- **Factors that affect the β risk:** Holding everything else constant,
  - β increases when the difference between the hypothesized parameter and its true value decreases.
  - β increases when α decreases.
  - β increases when σ increases.
  - β increases when the sample size n decreases.
- **The confidence coefficient** $(1-\alpha)$: The probability that the null hypothesis is not rejected when in fact it is true and should not be rejected.
- **The confidence level:** $100(1-\alpha)\%$
- **The power of a test** $(1-\beta)$: The probability of rejecting the null hypothesis when in fact it is false and should be rejected.

Copyright ©2015 Pearson Education, Inc.

- **Risk in decision making:** There is a delicate balance between the probability of committing a Type I error and the probability of a Type II error.

H_0: Innocent

E.g. Jury Trial			Hypothesis Test		
	The Truth			**State of Nature**	
Verdict	Innocent	Not Innocent	**Decision**	H_0 True	H_0 False
Innocent	**Correct**	**Error**	Do Not Reject H_0	$1 - \alpha$	$\beta =$ P(Type II Error)
Not Innocent	**Error**	**Correct**	Reject H_0	$\alpha =$ P(Type I Error)	**Power = (1 - β)**

H_1: Not Innocent

- Reducing the probability of a Type I error will inevitably increase the probability of committing a Type II error holding everything else constant.
- One should choose a smaller Type I error when the cost of rejecting the maintained hypothesis is high.
- One should choose a larger Type I error when there is an interest in changing the status quo.
- ***p*-value (the observed level of significance):** The probability of obtaining a test statistic equal to or more extreme than the result obtained from the sample data, given the null hypothesis is true.
  - It is also the smallest level of significance at which the null hypothesis can be rejected.
  - Roughly speaking, it measures the amount of evidence against the null hypothesis. The smaller the *p*-value, the stronger is the evidence against the null hypothesis.
  - The statistical decision rule is to reject the null hypothesis if the *p*-value is less than the level of significance (α), and do not reject otherwise.

The Critical Value Approach to Hypothesis Testing

1. State the null hypothesis, H_0 and the alternative hypothesis, H_1.
2. Choose the level of significance, α and the sample size, *n*. The level of significance is specified according to the relative importance of the risks of committing Type I and Type II errors in the problem.
3. Determine the appropriate test statistic and sampling distribution.
4. Determine the critical values that divide the rejection and nonrejection regions.
5. Collect the data and compute the value of the test statistic.
6. Make the statistical decision and state the managerial conclusion. Compare the computed test statistic to the critical values. Reject H_0 when the computed test statistic falls in a rejection region; do not reject H_0 otherwise. The managerial conclusion is written in the context of the real-world problem.

Copyright ©2015 Pearson Education, Inc.

The *p*-Value Approach to Hypothesis Testing
1. State the null hypothesis, H_0 and the alternative hypothesis, H_1.
2. Choose the level of significance, α and the sample size, *n*. The level of significance is specified according to the relative importance of the risks of committing Type I and Type II errors in the problem.
3. Determine the appropriate test statistic and sampling distribution.
4. Collect the data, compute the value of the test statistic and obtain the *p*-value based on the computed test statistic.
5. Make the statistical decision and state the managerial conclusion. If the *p*-value is greater than or equal to α, you do not reject the null hypothesis H_0. If the *p*-value is less than α, you reject the null hypothesis. Remember the phrase, if the *p*-value is low, the H_0 must go. The managerial conclusion is written in the context of the real-world problem.

A Connection Between Confidence Interval Estimation and Hypothesis Testing
*   When performing a two-tail hypothesis test at an $100\alpha\%$ level of significance, you can reject the null hypothesis if the hypothesized value of the parameter does not fall within the $100(1-\alpha)\%$ confidence interval and do not reject otherwise.

Z Test for the Population Mean (μ) when σ is Known
*   **Assumptions:**
    *   Population is normally distributed or large sample size.
    * σ is known.
*   **Test statistic:**
    * $Z = \dfrac{\overline{X} - \mu_{\overline{X}}}{\sigma_{\overline{X}}} = \dfrac{\overline{X} - \mu}{\sigma/\sqrt{n}}$
    *   The alternative hypothesis can be one-tail with a right-tail rejection region, one-tail with a left-tail rejection region or two-tail with both right-tail and left-tail rejection regions.

t Test for the Population Mean (μ) when σ Is Unknown
*   **Assumptions:**
    *   Population is normally distributed or large sample size.
    * σ is unknown.
*   **Test statistic:**
    * $t = \dfrac{\overline{X} - \mu}{S/\sqrt{n}}$ with $(n-1)$ degrees of freedom.
    *   The alternative hypothesis can be one-tail with a right-tail rejection region, one-tail with a left-tail rejection region or two-tail with both right-tail and left-tail rejection regions.

Z Test for the Population Proportion (π)
*   **Assumptions:**
    *   Population involves 2 categorical values.
    *   Both *np* and *n*(1-*p*) are at least 5.

Copyright ©2015 Pearson Education, Inc.

- **Test statistic:**

  - $$Z = \frac{p - \mu_p}{\sigma_p} = \frac{p - \pi}{\sqrt{\dfrac{\pi(1-\pi)}{n}}}$$

    - The alternative hypothesis can be one-tail with a right-tail rejection region, one-tail with a left-tail rejection region or two-tail with both right-tail and left-tail rejection regions.

Potential Hypothesis-Testing Pitfalls
- To avoid potential hypothesis-testing pitfalls, you should:
  1. Consult with a person with substantial statistical training early in the process.
  2. Build in adequate controls from the beginning to avoid biases.
  3. Plan ahead by asking the following questions:
     i.   What is the goal of the survey, study, or experiment? How can you translate into a null hypothesis and an alternative hypothesis?
     ii. Is the hypothesis test a two-tail test or one-tail test?
     iii. Can you select a random sample from the underlying population of interest?
     iv. What kinds of measurements will you collect from the sample? Are the sampled outcomes numerical or categorical?
     v.   At what significance level, or risk of committing a Type I error, should you conduct the hypothesis test?
     vi. Is the intended sample size large enough to achieve the desired power of the test for the level of significance chosen?
     vii. What statistical test procedure should you use and why?
     viii. What conclusions and interpretations can you make from the results of the hypothesis test?

Ethical Issues
- Ethical considerations arise when the hypothesis-testing process is manipulated.
  - **Data collection method should be randomized:** The data must be the outcome of a random sample from a population or from an experiment in which a randomization process was used. Potential respondents should not be permitted to self-select for a study nor should they be purposely selected.
  - **Informed Consent from Human Respondents Being "Treated":** Any individual who is to be subjected to some "treatment" in an experiment should be made aware of the research endeavor and any potential behavioral or physical side effects. The subject should also provide informed consent with respect to participation.
  - **Type of Test—Two-Tail or One-Tail:** If prior information is available that leads you to test the null hypothesis against a specifically directed alternative, then a one-tail test is more powerful than a two-tail test. On the other hand, if you are interested only in differences from the null hypothesis, not in the direction of the difference, the two-tail test is the appropriate procedure to use.
  - **Choice of Level of Significance:** The level of significance should be selected before data collection occurs. It is also good practice to always report the *p*-value, not just the conclusions of the hypothesis test.
  - **Data Snooping:** It is unethical to perform a hypothesis test on a set of data, look at the results, and then decide on the level of significance or decide between a one-tail or two-tail test.

Copyright ©2015 Pearson Education, Inc.

- **Cleansing and Discarding of Data:** If a measurement is incomplete or grossly in error because of some equipment problem or unusual behavioral occurrence unrelated to the study, you can discard the value. In a well-designed experiment or study, you should decide, in advance, on all rules regarding the possible discarding of data.
- **Reporting of Findings:** In conducting research, you should document both good and bad results. It is inappropriate to report the results of hypothesis tests that show statistical significance but not those for which there is insufficient evidence in the findings.
- **Statistical Significance versus Practical Significance:** You need to make the distinction between the existence of a statistically significant result and its practical significance in the context within a field of application. Sometimes, due to a very large sample size, you will get a result that is statistically significant, but has little practical significance.

Copyright ©2015 Pearson Education, Inc.

SOLUTIONS TO END OF SECTION
AND CHAPTER REVIEW EVEN PROBLEMS

9.2   Decision rule: Reject H_0 if $Z_{STAT} < -1.96$ or $Z_{STAT} > +1.96$.
       Decision: Since $Z_{STAT} = +2.21$ is greater than the upper critical value of $+1.96$, reject H_0.

9.4   Decision rule: Reject H_0 if $Z_{STAT} < -2.58$ or $Z_{STAT} > +2.58$.

9.6 p-value $= 2(1 - .9772) = 0.0456$

9.8 p-value $= 0.1676$

9.10   Under the French judicial system, unlike ours in the United States, the null hypothesis
       assumes the defendant is guilty, the alternative hypothesis assumes the defendant is innocent.
       A Type I error would be not convicting a guilty person and a Type II error would be
       convicting an innocent person.

9.12 H_0: $\mu = 20$ minutes. 20 minutes is adequate travel time between classes.
       H_1: $\mu \neq 20$ minutes. 20 minutes is not adequate travel time between classes.

9.14   (a)   PHStat output:

Z Test of Hypothesis for the Mean	
Data	
Null Hypothesis $\mu=$	7500
Level of Significance	0.05
Population Standard Deviation	1000
Sample Size	64
Sample Mean	7250
Intermediate Calculations	
Standard Error of the Mean	125.0000
Z Test Statistic	**-2.0000**
Two-Tail Test	
Lower Critical Value	-1.9600
Upper Critical Value	1.9600
p-Value	0.0455
Reject the null hypothesis	

Copyright ©2015 Pearson Education, Inc.

9.14   (a) H_0: $\mu = 7500$. The mean life of a large shipment of light bulbs is equal to 7500 hours.
cont. H_1: $\mu \neq 7500$. The mean life of a large shipment of light bulbs differs from 7500 hours.

Decision rule: Reject H_0 if $|Z_{STAT}| > 1.96$

Test statistic: $Z_{STAT} = \dfrac{\bar{X} - \mu}{\sigma / \sqrt{n}} = $ -2.0000

Decision: Since $|Z_{STAT}| > 1.96$, reject H_0. There is enough evidence to conclude that the mean life of a large shipment of light bulbs differs from 7500 hours.

(b) p-value = 0.0455. If the population mean life of a large shipment of light bulbs is indeed equal to 7500 hours, the probability of obtaining a test statistic that is more than 2.0 standard error units away from 0 is 0.0455.

(c)   PHStat output:

Confidence Interval Estimate for the Mean	
Data	
Population Standard Deviation	1000
Sample Mean	7250
Sample Size	64
Confidence Level	95%
Intermediate Calculations	
Standard Error of the Mean	125.0000
Z Value	-1.9600
Interval Half Width	244.9955
Confidence Interval	
Interval Lower Limit	7005.00
Interval Upper Limit	7495.00

(c) $\bar{X} \pm Z_{a/2} \dfrac{\sigma}{\sqrt{n}} = 7250 \pm 1.96 \dfrac{1000}{\sqrt{64}}$ $7005.00 \leq \mu \leq 7495.00$

(d)   You are 95% confident that the population mean life of a large shipment of light bulbs is somewhere between 7005.00 and 7495.00 hours.
Since the 95% confidence interval does not contain the hypothesized value of 7500, you will reject H_0. The conclusions are the same.

Copyright ©2015 Pearson Education, Inc.

9.16   (a)   PHStat output:

Data	
Null Hypothesis $\mu =$	**1**
Level of Significance	**0.01**
Population Standard Deviation	**0.02**
Sample Size	**50**
Sample Mean	**0.995**
Intermediate Calculations	
Standard Error of the Mean	0.002828427
Z Test Statistic	**-1.767766953**
Two-Tail Test	
Lower Critical Value	**-2.575829304**
Upper Critical Value	**2.575829304**
p-**Value**	**0.077099872**
Do not reject the null hypothesis	

H_0: $\mu = 1$. The mean amount of water is 1 gallon.

H_1: $\mu \neq 1$. The mean amount of water differs from 1 gallon.

Decision rule: Reject H_0 if $|Z_{STAT}| > 2.5758$

(a)   Test statistic: $Z_{STAT} = \dfrac{\overline{X} - \mu}{\sigma / \sqrt{n}} = \dfrac{.995 - 1}{.02/\sqrt{50}} = -1.7678$

Decision: Since $|Z_{STAT}| < 2.5758$, do not reject H_0. There is not enough evidence to conclude that the mean amount of water contained in 1-gallon bottles purchased from a nationally known water bottling company is different from 1 gallon.

(b)   *p*-value = 0.0771. If the population mean amount of water contained in 1-gallon bottles purchased from a nationally known water bottling company is actually 1 gallon, the probability of obtaining a test statistic that is more than 1.7678 standard error units away from 0 is 0.0771.

(c)   PHStat output:

Data	
Population Standard Deviation	**0.02**
Sample Mean	**0.995**
Sample Size	**50**
Confidence Level	**99%**
Intermediate Calculations	
Standard Error of the Mean	0.002828427
Z Value	-2.5758293
Interval Half Width	0.007285545
Confidence Interval	
Interval Lower Limit	**0.987714455**
Interval Upper Limit	**1.002285545**

Copyright ©2015 Pearson Education, Inc.

9.16   (c) $\bar{X} \pm Z_{a/2} \dfrac{\sigma}{\sqrt{n}} = .995 \pm 2.5758 \dfrac{.02}{\sqrt{50}}$ $0.9877 \le \mu \le 1.0023$

cont.   You are 99% confident that population mean amount of water contained in 1-gallon bottles purchased from a nationally known water bottling company is somewhere between 0.9877 and 1.0023 gallons.

       (d)   Since the 99% confidence interval does contain the hypothesized value of 1, you will not reject H_0. The conclusions are the same.

9.18 $t_{STAT} = \dfrac{\bar{X} - \mu}{S / \sqrt{n}} = \dfrac{56 - 50}{12 / \sqrt{16}} = 2.00$

9.20   For a two-tailed test with a 0.05 level of confidence, the critical values are ± 2.1315.

9.22   No, you should not use the t test to test the null hypothesis that $\mu = 60$ on a population that is left-skewed because the sample size ($n = 16$) is less than 30. The t test assumes that, if the underlying population is not normally distributed, the sample size is sufficiently large to enable the test to be valid. If sample sizes are small ($n < 30$), the t test should not be used because the sampling distribution does not meet the requirements of the Central Limit Theorem.

9.24   PHStat output:

t Test for Hypothesis of the Mean	
Data	
Null Hypothesis $\mu =$	3.7
Level of Significance	0.05
Sample Size	64
Sample Mean	3.57
Sample Standard Deviation	0.8
Intermediate Calculations	
Standard Error of the Mean	0.1
Degrees of Freedom	63
t Test Statistic	-1.3
Two-Tail Test	
Lower Critical Value	-1.9983405
Upper Critical Value	1.9983405
p-Value	0.1983372
Do not reject the null hypothesis	

       (a) $H_0 : \mu = 3.7$ $H_1 : \mu \ne 3.7$

       Decision rule: Reject H_0 if $|t_{STAT}| > 1.9983$ *d.f.* = 63

       Test statistic: $t_{STAT} = \dfrac{\bar{X} - \mu}{S / \sqrt{n}} = \dfrac{3.57 - 3.7}{0.8 / \sqrt{64}} = -1.3$

       Decision: Since $|t_{STAT}| < 1.9983$, do not reject H_0. There is not enough evidence to conclude that the population mean waiting time is different from 3.7 minutes at the 0.05 level of significance.

Copyright ©2015 Pearson Education, Inc.

9.24   (b)   The sample size of 64 is large enough to apply the Central Limit Theorem and,
cont.   hence, you do not need to be concerned about the shape of the population
                 distribution when conducting the t-test in (a). In general, the t test is
                 appropriate for this sample size except for the case where the population is
                 extremely skewed or bimodal.

9.26   PHStat output:

t Test for Hypothesis of the Mean	
Data	
Null Hypothesis $\mu=$	50
Level of Significance	0.05
Sample Size	100
Sample Mean	58
Sample Standard Deviation	55
Intermediate Calculations	
Standard Error of the Mean	5.5000
Degrees of Freedom	99
t Test Statistic	1.4545
Two-Tail Test	
Lower Critical Value	-1.9842
Upper Critical Value	1.9842
p-Value	0.1490
Do not reject the null hypothesis	

    (a) $H_0 : \mu = \$50$ $H_1 : \mu \neq \$50$

           Decision rule: Reject H_0 if p-value < 0.05

           Test statistic: $t_{STAT} = \dfrac{\overline{X} - \mu}{S / \sqrt{n}} = 1.4545$

           p-value $= 0.1490$

           Decision: Since the p-value of $0.1490 > 0.05$, do not reject H_0. There is not enough
           evidence to conclude that the population mean savings for all showroomers who
           purchased a consumer electronics item is different from $50.

    (b)   The p-value is 0.1490. If the population mean is indeed $50, the probability of
           obtaining a test statistic that is more than 1.4545 standard error units away from 0 in
           either direction is 0.1490.

9.28   PHStat output:

t Test for Hypothesis of the Mean	
Data	
Null Hypothesis μ=	6.5
Level of Significance	0.05
Sample Size	15
Sample Mean	7.09
Sample Standard Deviation	1.406031226
Intermediate Calculations	
Standard Error of the Mean	0.3630
Degrees of Freedom	14
t Test Statistic	1.6344
Two-Tail Test	
Lower Critical Value	-2.1448
Upper Critical Value	2.1448
p-Value	0.1245
Do not reject the null hypothesis	

(a) $H_0 : \mu = \$6.50 \quad H_1 : \mu \neq \$6.50$

Decision rule: Reject H_0 if $|t_{STAT}| > 2.1448$ or p-value < 0.05

Test statistic: $t_{STAT} = \dfrac{\bar{X} - \mu}{S / \sqrt{n}} = 1.6344$

Decision: Since $|t_{STAT}| < 2.1448$, do not reject H_0. There is not enough evidence to conclude that the mean amount spent for lunch is different from $6.50.

(b)   The p-value is 0.1245. If the population mean is indeed $6.50, the probability of obtaining a test statistic that is more than 1.6344 standard error units away from 0 in either direction is 0.4069.

(c)   That the distribution of the amount spent on lunch is normally distributed.

(d)   With a sample size of 15, it is difficult to evaluate the assumption of normality. However, the distribution may be fairly symmetric because the mean and the median are close in value. Also, the boxplot appears only slightly skewed so the normality assumption does not appear to be seriously violated.

Copyright ©2015 Pearson Education, Inc.

9.30 (a) $H_0 : \mu = 2$ $H_1 : \mu \neq 2$ $d.f. = 49$

          Decision rule: Reject H_0 if $|t_{STAT}| > 2.0096$

          Test statistic: $t_{STAT} = \dfrac{\overline{X} - \mu}{S / \sqrt{n}} = \dfrac{2.0007 - 2}{0.0446 / \sqrt{50}} = 0.1143$

          Decision: Since $|t_{STAT}| < 2.0096$, do not reject H_0. There is not enough evidence to conclude that the mean amount of soft drink filled is different from 2.0 liters.

     (b) p-value = 0.9095. If the population mean amount of soft drink filled is indeed 2.0 liters, the probability of observing a sample of 50 soft drinks that will result in a sample mean amount of fill more different from 2.0 liters is 0.9095.

     (c)

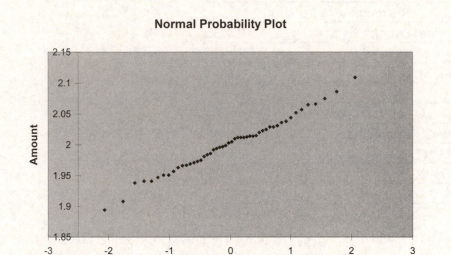

     (d)   The normal probability plot suggests that the data are rather normally distributed. Hence, the results in (a) are valid in terms of the normality assumption.

     (e)

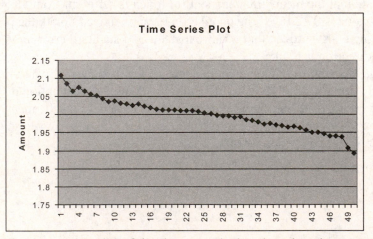

The time series plot of the data reveals that there is a downward trend in the amount of soft drink filled. This violates the assumption that data are drawn independently from a normal population distribution because the amount of fill in consecutive bottles appears to be closely related. As a result, the t test in (a) becomes invalid.

Copyright ©2015 Pearson Education, Inc.

9.32   (a) $H_0 : \mu = 8.46$ $H_1 : \mu \neq 8.46$

Decision rule: Reject H_0 if $|t_{STAT}| > 2.0106$ $d.f. = 48$

Test statistic: $t_{STAT} = \dfrac{\overline{X} - \mu}{S / \sqrt{n}} = \dfrac{8.4209 - 8.46}{0.0461 / \sqrt{49}} = -5.9355$

Decision: Since $|t_{STAT}| > 2.0106$, reject H_0. There is enough evidence to conclude that mean widths of the troughs is different from 8.46 inches.

(b)   The population distribution needs to be normal.

(c)

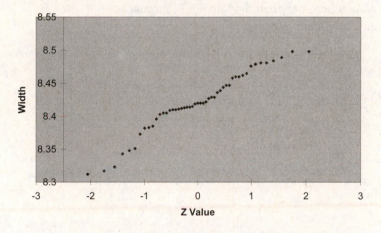

(c)

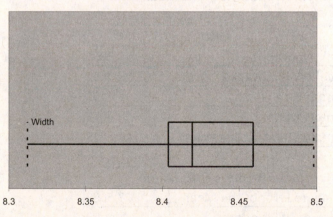

(d)   The normal probability plot and the boxplot indicate that the distribution is skewed to the left. Even though the population distribution is not normally distributed, the result obtained in (a) should still be valid due to the Central Limit Theorem as a result of the relatively large sample size of 49.

Copyright ©2015 Pearson Education, Inc.

9.34   (a) $H_0 : \mu = 5.5$ $H_1 : \mu \neq 5.5$

Decision rule: Reject H_0 if $|t_{STAT}| > 2.680$ $d.f. = 49$

Test statistic: $t_{STAT} = \dfrac{\overline{X} - \mu}{S / \sqrt{n}} = \dfrac{5.5014 - 5.5}{0.1058 / \sqrt{50}} = 0.0935$

Decision: Since $|t_{STAT}| < 2.680$, do not reject H_0. There is not enough evidence to conclude that the mean amount of tea per bag is different from 5.5 grams.

(b) $\overline{X} \pm t \cdot \dfrac{s}{\sqrt{n}} = 5.5014 \pm 2.6800 \cdot \dfrac{0.1058}{\sqrt{50}}$ $5.46 < \mu < 5.54$

With 99% confidence, you can conclude that the population mean amount of tea per bag is somewhere between 5.46 and 5.54 grams.

(c)   The conclusions are the same.

9.36 p-value $= 1 - 0.9772 = 0.0228$

9.38 p-value $= 0.0838$

9.40 p-value $= P(Z < 1.38) = 0.9162$

9.42 $t = 2.7638$

9.44 $t = -2.5280$

9.46   (a)   PHStat output:

t Test for Hypothesis of the Mean

Data	
Null Hypothesis μ=	3900
Level of Significance	0.05
Sample Size	100
Sample Mean	3975
Sample Standard Deviation	275

Intermediate Calculations	
Standard Error of the Mean	27.5000
Degrees of Freedom	99
t Test Statistic	2.7273

Upper-Tail Test	
Upper Critical Value	1.6604
p-Value	0.0038
Reject the null hypothesis	

Copyright ©2015 Pearson Education, Inc.

9.46   (a) $H_0 : \mu \le 36.5$ $H_1 : \mu > 36.5$
cont.
Decision rule: Reject H_0 if p-value < 0.05 $d.f. = 99$

Test statistic: $t_{STAT} = \dfrac{\bar{X} - \mu}{S / \sqrt{n}} = 2.7273$

p-value $= 0.0038$

Decision: Since the p-value of $0.0038 < 0.05$, reject H_0. There is enough evidence
to conclude that the population mean bus miles is more than 3,900 bus miles.

    (b)   The p-value is 0.0038. If the population mean is indeed no more than 3900 hours,
the probability of obtaining a test statistic that is more than 2.7273 is 0.0038.

9.48   PHStat output:

t Test for Hypothesis of the Mean	
Data	
Null Hypothesis μ=	25
Level of Significance	0.01
Sample Size	355
Sample Mean	23.05
Sample Standard Deviation	16.83
Intermediate Calculations	
Standard Error of the Mean	0.8932
Degrees of Freedom	354
t Test Statistic	-2.1831
Lower-Tail Test	
Lower Critical Value	-2.3369
p-Value	0.0148
Do not reject the null hypothesis	

    (a) H_0: $\mu \ge 25$ H_1: $\mu < 25$
Decision rule: If p-value < 0.01, reject H_0.

Test statistic: $t_{STAT} = \dfrac{\bar{X} - \mu}{S / \sqrt{n}} = = -2.1831$

p-value $= 0.0148$

Decision: Since p-value $= 0.0148 > 0.01$, do not reject H_0. There is not enough
evidence to conclude the population mean wait time is less than 25 minutes.

    (b)   The probability of obtaining a test statistic that is -2.1831 or lower when the null
hypothesis is true is essentially 0.0148.

Copyright ©2015 Pearson Education, Inc.

9.50   PHStat output:

t Test for Hypothesis of the Mean

Data		
Null Hypothesis $\mu =$		70
Level of Significance		0.01
Sample Size		55
Sample Mean		75
Sample Standard Deviation		9

Intermediate Calculations	
Standard Error of the Mean	1.2136
Degrees of Freedom	54
t Test Statistic	4.1201

Upper-Tail Test	
Upper Critical Value	2.3974
p-Value	0.0001
Reject the null hypothesis	

(a) H_0: $\mu \le \$70$

H_1: $\mu > \$70$

Decision rule: If the *p*-value < 0.01, reject H_0.

Test statistic: $t_{STAT} = \dfrac{\overline{X} - \mu}{S/\sqrt{n}} = 4.1201$

p-value = 0.0001

Decision: Since the *p*-value is less than 0.01, reject H_0. There is enough evidence to conclude that the mean one-time gift donation is greater than $70.

(b)   When the null hypothesis is true, the probability of obtaining a sample whose test statistic is 4.1201 or more is 0.0001.

9.52 $p = \dfrac{X}{n} = \dfrac{88}{400} = 0.22$

9.54 H_0: $\pi = 0.20$

H_1: $\pi \ne 0.20$

Decision rule: If $Z < -1.96$ or $Z > 1.96$, reject H_0.

Test statistic: $Z_{STAT} = \dfrac{p - \pi}{\sqrt{\dfrac{\pi(1-\pi)}{n}}} = \dfrac{0.22 - 0.20}{\sqrt{\dfrac{0.20(0.8)}{400}}} = 1.00$

Decision: Since $Z = 1.00$ is between the critical bounds of ± 1.96, do not reject H_0.

Copyright ©2015 Pearson Education, Inc.

9.56   (a)   PHStat output:

Z Test of Hypothesis for the Proportion	
Data	
Null Hypothesis $\pi =$	**0.2030**
Level of Significance	0.05
Number of Items of Interest	25
Sample Size	100
Intermediate Calculations	
Sample Proportion	0.25
Standard Error	0.0402
Z Test Statistic	**1.1685**
Upper-Tail Test	
Upper Critical Value	**1.6449**
***p*-Value**	**0.1213**
Do not reject the null hypothesis	

H_0: $\pi \leq 0.203$ H_1: $\pi > 0.203$
Decision rule: If *p*-value < 0.05, reject H_0.

Test statistic: $Z_{STAT} = \dfrac{p - \pi}{\sqrt{\dfrac{\pi(1-\pi)}{n}}} = 1.1685$ *p*-value = 0.1213

Decision: Since *p*-value > 0.05, do not reject H_0. There is not enough evidence that the market share for the Mozilla Firefox web browser at your university is greater than the worldwide market share of 20.3%.

(b)   PHStat output:

Z Test of Hypothesis for the Proportion	
Data	
Null Hypothesis $\pi =$	**0.2030**
Level of Significance	0.05
Number of Items of Interest	100
Sample Size	400
Intermediate Calculations	
Sample Proportion	0.25
Standard Error	0.0201
Z Test Statistic	**2.3370**
Upper-Tail Test	
Upper Critical Value	**1.6449**
***p*-Value**	**0.0097**
Reject the null hypothesis	

Copyright ©2015 Pearson Education, Inc.

9.56   (b) H_0: $\pi \leq 0.203$ H_1: $\pi > 0.203$
cont.   Decision rule: If p-value < 0.05, reject H_0.

Test statistic: $Z_{STAT} = \dfrac{p - \pi}{\sqrt{\dfrac{\pi(1-\pi)}{n}}} = 2.3370$ p-value $= 0.0097$.

Decision: Since p-value < 0.05, reject H_0. There is enough evidence that the market share for the Mozilla Firefox web browser at your university is greater than the worldwide market share of 20.3%.

(c)   A larger sample size reduces the standard error (variation) of the sample proportion and, hence, reduces the p-value and makes it easier to reject H_0 holding everything else constant.

(d)   You would be very unlikely to reject the null hypothesis with a sample of 20.

9.58   PHStat output:

Z Test of Hypothesis for the Proportion	
Data	
Null Hypothesis π =	0.3500
Level of Significance	0.05
Number of Items of Interest	328
Sample Size	801
Intermediate Calculations	
Sample Proportion	0.40948814
Standard Error	0.0169
Z Test Statistic	3.5298
Two-Tail Test	
Lower Critical Value	-1.9600
Upper Critical Value	1.9600
p-Value	0.0004
Reject the null hypothesis	

H_0: $\pi = 0.35$

H_1: $\pi \neq 0.35$

Decision rule: If $Z_{STAT} < -1.96$ or $Z_{STAT} > 1.96$ or if p-value < 0.05, reject H_0.

Test statistic: $Z_{STAT} = \dfrac{p - \pi}{\sqrt{\dfrac{\pi(1-\pi)}{n}}} = 3.5298$

Decision: Since $Z_{STAT} = 3.5298$ is greater than the upper critical bound of 1.96, reject H_0. You conclude that there is enough evidence the proportion of all LinkedIn members who plan to spend at least $1,000 on consumer electronics in the coming year is different from 35%.

Copyright ©2015 Pearson Education, Inc.

9.60   (a)

Z Test of Hypothesis for the Proportion	
Data	
Null Hypothesis π =	0.3100
Level of Significance	0.05
Number of Items of Interest	28
Sample Size	100
Intermediate Calculations	
Sample Proportion	0.28
Standard Error	0.0462
Z Test Statistic	**-0.6487**
Lower-Tail Test	
Lower Critical Value	-1.6449
p-Value	0.2583
Do not reject the null hypothesis	

H_0: $\pi \geq 0.31$

H_1: $\pi < 0.31$

(b)   Decision rule: If p-value < 0.05, reject H_0.

Test statistic: $Z_{STAT} = \dfrac{p - \pi}{\sqrt{\dfrac{\pi(1-\pi)}{n}}} = -0.6487,$ p-value = 0.2583

Decision: Since p-value = 0.2583 > 0.05, do not reject H_0. There is not enough evidence to show that the percentage is less than 31%.

9.62   A Type I error represents rejecting a true null hypothesis, while a Type II error represents not rejecting a false null hypothesis.

9.64   In a one-tailed test for a mean or proportion, the entire rejection region is contained in one tail of the distribution. In a two-tailed test, the rejection region is split into two equal parts, one in the lower tail of the distribution, and the other in the upper tail.

9.66   Assuming a two-tailed test is used, if the hypothesized value for the parameter does not fall into the confidence interval, then the null hypothesis can be rejected.

9.68   The following are the 5-step p-value approach to hypothesis testing: (1) State the null hypothesis, H_0, and the alternative hypothesis, H_1. (2) Choose the level of significance, α, and the sample size, n. (3) Determine the appropriate test statistic and the sampling distribution. (4) Collect the sample data, compute the value of the test statistic, and compute the p-value. (5) Make the statistical decision and state the managerial conclusion. If the p-value is greater than or equal to α, you do not reject the null hypothesis, H_0. If the p-value is less than α, you reject the null hypothesis.

Copyright ©2015 Pearson Education, Inc.

9.70   (a)   A Type I error occurs when a firm is predicted to be a bankrupt firm when it will not.

     (b)   A Type II error occurs when a firm is predicted to be a non-bankrupt firm when it will go bankrupt.

     (c)   The executives are trying to avoid a Type I error by adopting a very stringent decision criterion. Only firms that show significant evidence of being in financial stress will be predicted to go bankrupt within the next two years at the chosen level of the possibility of making a Type I error.

     (d)   If the revised model results in more moderate or large Z scores, the probability of committing a Type I error will increase. Many more of the firms will be predicted to go bankrupt than will go bankrupt. On the other hand, the revised model that results in more moderate or large Z scores will lower the probability of committing a Type II error because few firms will be predicted to go bankrupt than will actually go bankrupt.

9.72   (a)   PHStat output:

t Test for Hypothesis of the Mean	
Data	
Null Hypothesis $\mu=$	6.5
Level of Significance	0.05
Sample Size	60
Sample Mean	7.25
Sample Standard Deviation	1.75
Intermediate Calculations	
Standard Error of the Mean	0.2259
Degrees of Freedom	59
t Test Statistic	3.3197
Two-Tail Test	
Lower Critical Value	-2.0010
Upper Critical Value	2.0010
***p*-Value**	0.0015
Reject the null hypothesis	

H_0: $\mu = \$6.50$

H_1: $\mu \neq \$6.50$

Decision rule: *d.f.* = 59. If *p*-value < 0.05, reject H_0.

Test statistic: $t_{STAT} = \dfrac{\bar{X} - \mu}{S / \sqrt{n}} = = 3.3197$ *p*-value = 0.0015

Decision: Since *p*-value < 0.05, reject H_0. There is enough evidence to conclude that the mean amount spent differs from $6.50

     (b)   *p*-value = 0.0015.

Note: The-*p* value was found using Excel.

Copyright ©2015 Pearson Education, Inc.

9.72   (c)   PHStat output:
cont.

Z Test of Hypothesis for the Proportion	
Data	
Null Hypothesis π =	0.5
Level of Significance	0.05
Number of Items of Interest	31
Sample Size	60
Intermediate Calculations	
Sample Proportion	0.516666667
Standard Error	0.0645
Z Test Statistic	0.2582
Upper-Tail Test	
Upper Critical Value	1.6449
p-Value	0.3981
Do not reject the null hypothesis	

H_0: $\pi \leq 0.50$.
H_1: $\pi > 0.50$.
Decision rule: If p-value < 0.05, reject H_0.

Test statistic: $Z_{STAT} = \dfrac{p - \pi}{\sqrt{\dfrac{\pi\,(1 - \pi)}{n}}} = \ = 0.2582$ p-value $= 0.3981$

Decision: Since p-value > 0.05, do not reject H_0. There is not sufficient evidence to conclude that more than 50% of customers say they "definitely will" recommend the specialty coffee shop to family and friends.

Copyright ©2015 Pearson Education, Inc.

9.72   (d)   PHStat output:
cont.

t Test for Hypothesis of the Mean	
Data	
Null Hypothesis $\mu=$	**6.5**
Level of Significance	**0.05**
Sample Size	**60**
Sample Mean	**6.25**
Sample Standard Deviation	**1.75**
Intermediate Calculations	
Standard Error of the Mean	0.2259
Degrees of Freedom	59
t Test Statistic	**-1.1066**
Two-Tail Test	
Lower Critical Value	**-2.0010**
Upper Critical Value	**2.0010**
***p*-Value**	**0.2730**
Do not reject the null hypothesis	

H_0: $\mu = \$6.50$

H_1: $\mu \neq \$6.50$

Decision rule: *d.f.* = 59. If *p*-value < 0.05, reject H_0.

Test statistic: $t = \dfrac{\overline{X} - \mu}{S/\sqrt{n}} = \dfrac{6.25 - 6.5}{1.75/\sqrt{60}} = -1.1066$ *p*-value = 0.2730

Decision: Since the *p*-value > 0.05, do not reject H_0. There is not enough evidence to conclude that the mean amount spent differs from $6.50.

Copyright ©2015 Pearson Education, Inc.

9.72   (e)   PHStat output:
cont.

Z Test of Hypothesis for the Proportion	
Data	
Null Hypothesis π =	0.5
Level of Significance	0.05
Number of Items of Interest	39
Sample Size	60
Intermediate Calculations	
Sample Proportion	0.65
Standard Error	0.0645
Z Test Statistic	**2.3238**
Upper-Tail Test	
Upper Critical Value	1.6449
***p*-Value**	0.0101
Reject the null hypothesis	

H_0: $\pi \leq 0.50$.

H_1: $\pi > 0.50$.

Decision rule: If *p*-value < 0.05, reject H_0.

Test statistic: $Z_{STAT} = \dfrac{p - \pi}{\sqrt{\dfrac{\pi(1-\pi)}{n}}} = = 2.3238$ *p*-value = 0.0101

Decision: Since *p*-value < 0.05, reject H_0. There is sufficient evidence to conclude that more than 50% of customers say they "definitely will" recommend the specialty coffee shop to family and friends.

Copyright ©2015 Pearson Education, Inc.

9.74   (a) H_0: $\mu \geq 5$ minutes. The mean waiting time at a bank branch in a commercial district of the city is at least 5 minutes during the 12:00 p.m. to 1 p.m. peak lunch period.
H_1: $\mu < 5$ minutes. The mean waiting time at a bank branch in a commercial district of the city is less than 5 minutes during the 12:00 p.m. to 1 p.m. peak lunch period.
Decision rule: $d.f. = 14$. If $t_{STAT} < -1.7613$, reject H_0.

Test statistic: $t_{STAT} = \dfrac{\overline{X} - \mu}{S/\sqrt{n}} = \dfrac{4.286\overline{6} - 5.0}{1.637985/\sqrt{15}} = -1.6867$

Decision: Since $t_{STAT} = -1.6867$ is greater than the critical bound of -1.7613, do not reject H_0. There is not enough evidence to conclude that the mean waiting time at a bank branch in a commercial district of the city is less than 5 minutes during the 12:00 p.m. to 1 p.m. peak lunch period.

(b)   To perform the t-test on the population mean, you must assume that the observed sequence in which the data were collected is random and that the data are approximately normally distributed.

(c)   Normal probability plot:

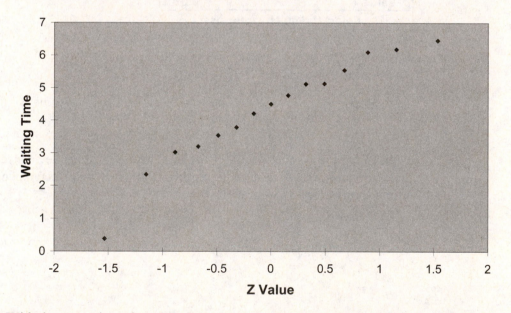

Normal Probability Plot

(d)   With the exception of one extreme point, the data are approximately normally distributed.

(e)   Based on the results of (a), the manager does not have enough evidence to make that statement.

Copyright ©2015 Pearson Education, Inc.

9.76 (a) $H_0 : \mu \geq 0.35$ $H_1 : \mu < 0.35$

Decision rule: Reject H_0 if $t_{STAT} < -1.690$ $d.f. = 35$

Test statistic: $t_{STAT} = \dfrac{\overline{X} - \mu}{S/\sqrt{n}} = \dfrac{0.3167 - 0.35}{0.1357/\sqrt{36}} = -1.4735$

Decision: Since $t_{STAT} > -1.690$, do not reject H_0. There is not enough evidence to conclude that the mean moisture content for Boston shingles is less than 0.35 pounds per 100 square feet.

(b) p-value = 0.0748. If the population mean moisture content is in fact no less than 0.35 pounds per 100 square feet, the probability of observing a sample of 36 shingles that will result in a sample mean moisture content of 0.3167 pounds per 100 square feet or less is .0748.

(c) $H_0 : \mu \geq 0.35$ $H_1 : \mu < 0.35$

Decision rule: Reject H_0 if $t_{STAT} < -1.6973$ $d.f. = 30$

Test statistic: $t_{STAT} = \dfrac{\overline{X} - \mu}{S/\sqrt{n}} = \dfrac{0.2735 - 0.35}{0.1373/\sqrt{31}} = -3.1003$

Decision: Since $t_{STAT} < -1.6973$, reject H_0. There is enough evidence to conclude that the mean moisture content for Vermont shingles is less than 0.35 pounds per 100 square feet.

(d) p-value = 0.0021. If the population mean moisture content is in fact no less than 0.35 pounds per 100 square feet, the probability of observing a sample of 31 shingles that will result in a sample mean moisture content of 0.2735 pounds per 100 square feet or less is .0021.

(e) In order for the t test to be valid, the data are assumed to be independently drawn from a population that is normally distributed. Since the sample sizes are 36 and 31, respectively, which are considered quite large, the t distribution will provide a good approximation to the sampling distribution of the mean as long as the population distribution is not very skewed.

Copyright ©2015 Pearson Education, Inc.

9.76   (f)
cont.

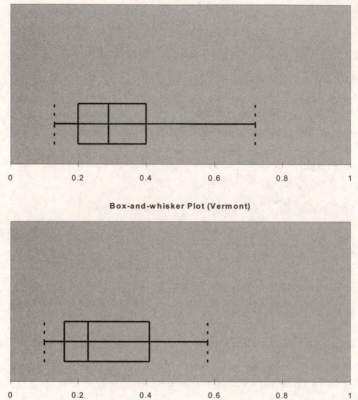

Both boxplots suggest that the data are skewed slightly to the right, more so for the Boston shingles. However, the very large sample sizes mean that the results of the t test are relatively insensitive to the departure from normality.

Copyright ©2015 Pearson Education, Inc.

9.78   (a) $H_0 : \mu = 0.3$ $H_1 : \mu \neq 0.3$

t Test for Hypothesis of the Mean

Data	
Null Hypothesis μ=	0.3
Level of Significance	0.05
Sample Size	170
Sample Mean	0.26
Sample Standard Deviation	0.142382504

Intermediate Calculations	
Standard Error of the Mean	0.0109
Degrees of Freedom	169
t Test Statistic	-3.2912

Two-Tail Test	
Lower Critical Value	-1.9741
Upper Critical Value	1.9741
p-Value	0.0012
Reject the null hypothesis	

Decision rule: Reject H_0 if $|t_{STAT}| > 1.9741$ $d.f. = 169$

Test statistic: $t_{STAT} = \dfrac{\bar{X} - \mu}{S / \sqrt{n}} = -3.2912,$ p-value = 0.0012

Decision: Since $t_{STAT} < -1.9741$, reject H_0. There is enough evidence to conclude that the mean granule loss for Boston shingles is different from 0.3 grams.

(b) p-value is virtually zero. If the population mean granule loss is in fact 0.3 grams, the probability of observing a sample of 170 shingles that will yield a test statistic more extreme than -3.2912 is 0.0012.

Copyright ©2015 Pearson Education, Inc.

9.78 (c) $H_0 : \mu = 0.5$ $H_1 : \mu \neq 0.5$
cont.

t Test for Hypothesis of the Mean	
Data	
Null Hypothesis μ=	0.3
Level of Significance	0.05
Sample Size	140
Sample Mean	0.22
Sample Standard Deviation	0.122698672
Intermediate Calculations	
Standard Error of the Mean	0.0104
Degrees of Freedom	139
t Test Statistic	-7.9075
Two-Tail Test	
Lower Critical Value	-1.9772
Upper Critical Value	1.9772
p-Value	0.0000
Reject the null hypothesis	

Decision rule: Reject H_0 if $|t_{STAT}| > 1.9772$ $d.f. = 139$

Test statistic: $t_{STAT} = \dfrac{\overline{X} - \mu}{S / \sqrt{n}} = -7.9075$

Decision: Since $t_{STAT} < -1.977$, reject H_0. There is enough evidence to conclude that the mean granule loss for Vermont shingles is different from 0.3 grams.

(d)   *p*-value is virtually zero. The probability of observing a sample of 140 shingles that will yield a test statistic more extreme than -1.977 is virtually zero if the population mean granule loss is in fact 0.3 grams.

(e)   In order for the *t* test to be valid, the data are assumed to be independently drawn from a population that is normally distributed. Both normal probability plots indicate that the data are slightly right-skewed. Since the sample sizes are 170 and 140, respectively, which are considered large enough, the *t* distribution will provide a good approximation to the sampling distribution of the mean even if the population is not normally distributed.

Copyright ©2015 Pearson Education, Inc.

CHAPTER 10

OBJECTIVES

- To compare the means of two independent populations
- To compare the means of two related populations
- To compare the proportions of two independent populations
- To compare the variances of two independent populations

OVERVIEW AND KEY CONCEPTS

Pooled-Variance t Test for Difference in Two Means $(\mu_1 - \mu_2)$

- **Assumptions:**
  - The two samples are randomly and independently drawn.
  - Both populations are normally distributed.
  - Population variances are unknown but assumed equal.
  - If the two populations are not normally distributed, large sample sizes are needed ($n_1 \geq 30$ and $n_2 \geq 30$).

- **Test statistic:**

  - $$t = \frac{(\overline{X}_1 - \overline{X}_2) - (\mu_1 - \mu_2)}{\sqrt{S_p^2\left(\dfrac{1}{n_1} + \dfrac{1}{n_2}\right)}} \text{ with } n_1 + n_2 - 2 \text{ degrees of freedom}$$

    where $S_p^2 = \dfrac{(n_1 - 1)S_1^2 + (n_2 - 1)S_2^2}{(n_1 - 1) + (n_2 - 1)}$

  - The alternative hypothesis can be one-tail with a right-tail rejection region, one-tail with a left-tail rejection region or two-tail with both right-tail and left-tail rejection regions.

- **Confidence interval estimate:** Use the $100(1 - \alpha)\%$ confidence interval for the difference in two means.

  - $$(\overline{X}_1 - \overline{X}_2) \pm t_{\alpha/2, n_1+n_2-2}\sqrt{S_p^2\left(\frac{1}{n_1} + \frac{1}{n_2}\right)}$$

Separate-Variance t Test for Difference in Two Means $(\mu_1 - \mu_2)$

- **Assumptions:**
  - The two samples are randomly and independently drawn.
  - Both populations are normally distributed.
  - Both population variances are unknown and assumed not equal.
  - If the two populations are not normally distributed, large sample sizes are needed.

Copyright ©2015 Pearson Education, Inc.

- **Test statistic:**
  - $t = \dfrac{(\bar{X}_1 - \bar{X}_2) - (\mu_1 - \mu_2)}{\sqrt{\dfrac{S_1^2}{n_1} + \dfrac{S_2^2}{n_2}}}$ with degrees of freedom ν taken to be the integer

    portion of $\nu = \dfrac{\left(\dfrac{S_1^2}{n_1} + \dfrac{S_2^2}{n_2}\right)^2}{\dfrac{\left(\dfrac{S_1^2}{n_1}\right)^2}{n_1 - 1} + \dfrac{\left(\dfrac{S_2^2}{n_2}\right)^2}{n_2 - 1}}$

  - The alternative hypothesis can be one-tail with a right-tail rejection region, one-tail with a left-tail rejection region or two-tail with both right-tail and left-tail rejection regions.

Paired t Test for the Mean Difference (μ_D) with Unknown Variance

- **Assumptions:**
  - Both populations are normally distributed.
  - Observations are matched or paired.
  - Variance is unknown.
  - The test is robust to the normal distribution assumption as long as the sample size is not too small and the population is not highly skewed.
- **Test statistic:**
  - $t = \dfrac{\bar{D} - \mu_D}{\dfrac{S_D}{\sqrt{n}}}$ with $n - 1$ degrees of freedom

    where $\bar{D} = \dfrac{\sum\limits_{i=1}^{n} D_i}{n}$ and $S_D = \sqrt{\dfrac{\sum\limits_{i=1}^{n} (D_i - \bar{D})^2}{n - 1}}$

  - The alternative hypothesis can be one-tail with a right-tail rejection region, one-tail with a left-tail rejection region or two-tail with both right-tail and left-tail rejection regions.
- **Confidence interval estimate:** Use the $100(1 - \alpha)\%$ confidence interval for the mean difference.
  - $\bar{D} \pm t_{\alpha/2, n-1} \dfrac{S_D}{\sqrt{n}}$

Z Test for Differences between Two Proportions $(\pi_1 - \pi_2)$

- **Assumptions:**
  - Samples are independently drawn.
  - Populations follow the binomial distribution.
  - Both sample sizes are large enough: $n_1 p_1 \geq 5$, $n_1(1 - p_1) \geq 5$, $n_2 p_2 \geq 5$,

    $n_2(1 - p_2) \geq 5$

Copyright ©2015 Pearson Education, Inc.

- **Test statistic:**

  - $Z = \dfrac{(p_1 - p_2) - (\pi_1 - \pi_2)}{\sqrt{\overline{p}(1 - \overline{p})\left(\dfrac{1}{n_1} + \dfrac{1}{n_2}\right)}}$ where $\overline{p} = \dfrac{X_1 + X_2}{n_1 + n_2}$ is the pooled estimate of the

    population proportion.
  - The alternative hypothesis can be one-tail with a right-tail rejection region, one-tail with a left-tail rejection region or two-tail with both right-tail and left-tail rejection regions.

- **Confidence interval estimate:** Use the $100(1 - \alpha)\%$ confidence interval for the difference in two proportions.

  - $(p_1 - p_2) \pm Z_{\alpha/2} \sqrt{\dfrac{p_1(1 - p_1)}{n_1} + \dfrac{p_2(1 - p_2)}{n_2}}$

F Test for the Ratio of Two Variances $\left(\dfrac{\sigma_1^2}{\sigma_2^2}\right)$

- **Assumptions:**
  - The two samples are randomly and independently drawn.
  - Both populations are normally distributed.
  - The test is not robust to violation of the normality assumption.
- **Test statistic:**

  - $F = \dfrac{S_1^2}{S_2^2}$ with $n_1 - 1$ numerator degrees of freedom and $n_2 - 1$ denominator degrees

    of freedom.
  - S_1^2 = variance of sample 1 (the larger sample variance)
  - S_2^2 = variance of sample 2 (the smaller sample variance)
  - n_1 = sample size selected from population 1
  - n_2 = sample size selected from population 2

Copyright ©2015 Pearson Education, Inc.

SOLUTIONS TO END OF SECTION
AND CHAPTER REVIEW EVEN PROBLEMS

10.2   **(a)** $S_p^{\,2} = \dfrac{(n_1 - 1) \cdot S_1^{\,2} + (n_2 - 1) \cdot S_2^{\,2}}{(n_1 - 1) + (n_2 - 1)} = \dfrac{(7) \cdot 4^2 + (14) \cdot 5^2}{7 + 14} = 22$

$t_{STAT} = \dfrac{\left(\overline{X}_1 - \overline{X}_2\right) - \left(\mu_1 - \mu_2\right)}{\sqrt{S_p^{\,2}\left(\dfrac{1}{n_1} + \dfrac{1}{n_2}\right)}} = \dfrac{(42 - 34) - 0}{\sqrt{22\left(\dfrac{1}{8} + \dfrac{1}{15}\right)}} = 3.8959$

     (b) $d.f. = (n_1 - 1) + (n_2 - 1) = 7 + 14 = 21$

     (c)   Decision rule: $d.f. = 21$. If $t_{STAT} > 2.5177$, reject H_0.

     (d)   Decision: Since $t = 3.8959$ is greater than the critical bound of 2.5177, reject H_0. There is enough evidence to conclude that the first population mean is larger than the second population mean.

10.4

$$\left(\overline{X}_1 - \overline{X}_2\right) \pm t\sqrt{S_p^{\,2}\left(\dfrac{1}{n_1} + \dfrac{1}{n_2}\right)} = (42 - 34) \pm 2.0796\sqrt{22\left(\dfrac{1}{8} + \dfrac{1}{15}\right)}$$

$$3.7296 \le \mu_1 - \mu_2 \le 12.2704$$

Copyright ©2015 Pearson Education, Inc.

10.6   PHStat output:

Data	
Hypothesized Difference	**0**
Level of Significance	**0.01**
Population 1 Sample	
Sample Size	**5**
Sample Mean	**42**
Sample Standard Deviation	**4**
Population 2 Sample	
Sample Size	**4**
Sample Mean	**34**
Sample Standard Deviation	**5**

Intermediate Calculations	
Population 1 Sample Degrees of Freedom	4
Population 2 Sample Degrees of Freedom	3
Total Degrees of Freedom	7
Pooled Variance	19.85714
Difference in Sample Means	8
t Test Statistic	**2.676242**

Upper-Tail Test	
Upper Critical Value	**2.997949**
p-Value	**0.015856**
Do not reject the null hypothesis	

H_0: $\mu_1 \leq \mu_2$ H_1: $\mu_1 > \mu_2$

Test statistic: $t_{STAT} = \dfrac{(\overline{X}_1 - \overline{X}_2) - (\mu_1 - \mu_2)}{\sqrt{S_p^2\left(\dfrac{1}{n_1} + \dfrac{1}{n_2}\right)}} = 2.6762$

Decision: Since $t_{STAT} = 2.6762$ is smaller than the upper critical bounds of 2.9979, do not reject H_0. There is not enough evidence of a difference in the means of the two populations.

Copyright ©2015 Pearson Education, Inc.

10.8   (a)   PHStat output:

Pooled-Variance *t* Test for the Difference Between Two Means				Confidence Interval Estimate	
(assumes equal population variances)				for the Difference Between Two Means	
Data					
Hypothesized Difference	0				
Level of Significance	0.05			**Data**	
Population 1 Sample				Confidence Level	95%
Sample Size	51				
Sample Mean	36			**Intermediate Calculations**	
Sample Standard Deviation	21.4			Degrees of Freedom	90
Population 2 Sample				*t* Value	1.9867
Sample Size	41			Interval Half Width	7.5384
Sample Mean	25				
Sample Standard Deviation	12.8			**Confidence Interval**	
				Interval Lower Limit	3.4616
Intermediate Calculations				Interval Upper Limit	18.5384
Population 1 Sample Degrees of Freedom	50				
Population 2 Sample Degrees of Freedom	40				
Total Degrees of Freedom	90				
Pooled Variance	327.2400				
Standard Error	3.7945				
Difference in Sample Means	11.0000				
t Test Statistic	2.8990				
Upper-Tail Test					
Upper Critical Value	1.6620				
p-Value	0.0024				
Reject the null hypothesis					

$H_0: \mu_1 \le \mu_2$ $H_1: \mu_1 > \mu_2$

where population 1 = children who watched the sports celebrity endorsed Walker
Crisps commercial
population 2 = children who watched the alternative food snack commercial
Decision rule: If *p*-value < 0.05, reject H_0.

Test statistic: $t_{STAT} = \dfrac{(\overline{X}_1 - \overline{X}_2) - (\mu_1 - \mu_2)}{\sqrt{S_p^2\left(\dfrac{1}{n_1} + \dfrac{1}{n_2}\right)}} = 2.8990$

p-value = 0.0024
Decision: Since the *p*-value is smaller than 0.05, reject H_0. There is enough evidence that
the mean amount of Walker Crisps crackers eaten was significantly higher for the
children who watched food ads.

10.8 **(b)** $\left(\bar{X}_1 - \bar{X}_2 \right) \pm t_{\alpha/2} \sqrt{S_p^2 \left(\dfrac{1}{n_1} + \dfrac{1}{n_2} \right)}$

cont.

$$3.4616 \leq \mu_1 - \mu_2 \leq 18.5384$$

10.10 **(a)** $H_0: \mu_1 = \mu_2$ where Populations: 1 = Southeast, 2 = Gulf Coast

$H_1: \mu_1 \neq \mu_2$

Pooled-Variance *t* Test for the Difference Between Two M	
(assumes equal population variances)	
Data	
Hypothesized Difference	0
Level of Significance	0.05
Population 1 Sample	
Sample Size	14
Sample Mean	40.07142857
Sample Standard Deviation	40.99055104
Population 2 Sample	
Sample Size	17
Sample Mean	27.94117647
Sample Standard Deviation	32.09063451
Intermediate Calculations	
Population 1 Sample Degrees of Freedom	13
Population 2 Sample Degrees of Freedom	16
Total Degrees of Freedom	29
Pooled Variance	1321.3748
Standard Error	13.1191
Difference in Sample Means	12.1303
t Test Statistic	0.9246
Two-Tail Test	
Lower Critical Value	-2.0452
Upper Critical Value	2.0452
p-Value	0.3628
Do not reject the null hypothesis	

Decision rule: If *p*-value < 0.05, reject H_0.

Test statistic:

$$t_{STAT} = \frac{\left(\bar{X}_1 - \bar{X}_2 \right) - \left(\mu_1 - \mu_2 \right)}{\sqrt{S_p^2 \left(\dfrac{1}{n_1} + \dfrac{1}{n_2} \right)}} = 0.9246 \qquad p\text{-value} = 0.3628$$

Decision: Since *p*-value > 0.05, do not reject H_0. There is not enough evidence of a difference between Southeast region accounting firms and Gulf Coast accounting firms with respect to the mean number of partners.

Copyright ©2015 Pearson Education, Inc.

10.10   (b)   The *p*-value = 0.3628. The probability of obtaining a sample that yields a *t* test
cont.   statistic farther away from 0 in either direction is 0.3628 if there is no difference
               between Southeast region accounting firms and Gulf Coast accounting firms with
               respect to the mean number of partners.

       (c)   In order to use the pooled-variance *t* test, you need to assume that the populations are
               normally distributed with equal variances.

10.12   (a) $H_0 : \mu_1 = \mu_2$ Mean waiting times of Bank 1 and Bank 2 are the same.

               $H_1 : \mu_1 \neq \mu_2$ Mean waiting times of Bank 1 and Bank 2 are different.

PHStat output:

t Test for Differences in Two Means	
Data	
Hypothesized Difference	0
Level of Significance	0.05
Population 1 Sample	
Sample Size	15
Sample Mean	4.286667
Sample Standard Deviation	1.637985
Population 2 Sample	
Sample Size	15
Sample Mean	7.114667
Sample Standard Deviation	2.082189
Intermediate Calculations	
Population 1 Sample Degrees of Freedom	14
Population 2 Sample Degrees of Freedom	14
Total Degrees of Freedom	28
Pooled Variance	3.509254
Difference in Sample Means	-2.828
t-Test Statistic	-4.13431
Two-Tailed Test	
Lower Critical Value	-2.04841
Upper Critical Value	2.048409
p-Value	0.000293
Reject the null hypothesis	

Since the *p*-value of 0.000293 is less than the 5% level of significance, reject the null
hypothesis. There is enough evidence to conclude that the mean waiting time is
different in the two banks.

       (b)   *p*-value = 0.000293. The probability of obtaining a sample that will yield a *t* test
               statistic more extreme than –4.13431 is 0.000293 if, in fact, the mean waiting times
               of Bank 1 and Bank 2 are the same.

       (c)   We need to assume that the two populations are normally distributed.

       (d) $$\left(\bar{X}_1 - \bar{X}_2 \right) + t \sqrt{S_p^2 \left(\frac{1}{n_1} + \frac{1}{n_2} \right)} = \left(4.2867 - 7.1147 \right) + 2.0484 \sqrt{3.5093 \left(\frac{1}{15} + \frac{1}{15} \right)}$$

               $$-4.2292 \leq \mu_1 - \mu_2 \leq -1.4268$$

               You are 95% confident that the difference in mean waiting time between Bank 1 and
               Bank 2 is between –4.2292 and –1.4268 minutes.

Copyright ©2015 Pearson Education, Inc.

10.14   (a) H_0: $\mu_1 = \mu_2$ H_1: $\mu_1 \neq \mu_2$

PHStat output:

Pooled-Variance *t* Test for the Difference Between Two Means				Confidence Interval Estimate	
(assumes equal population variances)				for the Difference Between Two Means	
Data					
Hypothesized Difference	0				
Level of Significance	0.05				
Population 1 Sample				**Data**	
Sample Size	15			Confidence Level	95%
Sample Mean	23.66667				
Sample Standard Deviation	28.29353			Intermediate Calculations	
Population 2 Sample				Degrees of Freedom	28
Sample Size	15			*t* Value	2.0484
Sample Mean	12.46667			Interval Half Width	15.5996
Sample Standard Deviation	8.331238				
				Confidence Interval	
Intermediate Calculations				Interval Lower Limit	-4.3996
Population 1 Sample Degrees of Freedom	14			Interval Upper Limit	26.7996
Population 2 Sample Degrees of Freedom	14				
Total Degrees of Freedom	28				
Pooled Variance	434.9667				
Standard Error	7.6155				
Difference in Sample Means	11.2000				
t Test Statistic	1.4707				
Two-Tail Test					
Lower Critical Value	-2.0484				
Upper Critical Value	2.0484				
p-Value	0.1525				
Do not reject the null hypothesis					

Decision: Since *p*-value = 0.1525 > 0.05, do not reject H_0. There is not enough evidence of a difference in the mean time required to start a business between developed countries and emerging countries.

(b)   *p*-value = 0.1525. The probability of obtaining two samples with a mean difference of 11.20 or more is 0.1525 if there is no difference in the mean time required to start a business between developed countries and emerging countries.

(c)   Since both sample sizes are smaller than 30, you need to assume that the population of time required to start a business of both developed countries and emerging countries is normally distributed.

(d)

$$\left(\bar{X}_1 - \bar{X}_2 \right) + t \sqrt{ S_p^2 \left(\frac{1}{n_1} + \frac{1}{n_2} \right) }$$

$$-4.3996 \leq \mu_1 - \mu_2 \leq 26.7996$$

You are 95% confident that the difference in the mean time required to start a business between developed countries and emerging countries is between -4.3996 and 26.7996.

Copyright ©2015 Pearson Education, Inc.

10.16 (a)   PHStat output:

(assumes equal population variances)

Data	
Hypothesized Difference	0
Level of Significance	0.05
Population 1 Sample	
Sample Size	30
Sample Mean	79
Sample Standard Deviatic	57.78079862
Population 2 Sample	
Sample Size	30
Sample Mean	157.1666667
Sample Standard Deviatic	205.7227936

Intermediate Calculations	
Population 1 Sample Deg|	29
Population 2 Sample Deg|	29
Total Degrees of Freedom	58
Pooled Variance	22830.24425
Standard Error	39.0130
Difference in Sample Me|	-78.16666667
t Test Statistic	-2.0036

Two-Tail Test	
Lower Critical Value	-2.0017
Upper Critical Value	2.0017
p-Value	0.0498
Reject the null hypothesis	

Confidence Interval Estimate	
for the Difference Between Two Means	
Data	
Confidence Level	95%
Intermediate Calculations	
Degrees of Freedom	58
t Value	2.0017
Interval Half Width	78.0931
Confidence Interval	
Interval Lower Limit	-156.2597
Interval Upper Limit	-0.0736

H_0: $\mu_1 = \mu_2$ H_1: $\mu_1 \neq \mu_2$

where Populations: 1 = female; 2 = male

Decision rule: If $|t_{STAT}| > 2.0017$ or p-value < 0.05, reject H_0.

Test statistic:

$$t_{STAT} = \frac{(\bar{X}_1 - \bar{X}_2) - (\mu_1 - \mu_2)}{\sqrt{S_p^2\left(\frac{1}{n_1} + \frac{1}{n_2}\right)}} = -2.0036 \qquad p\text{-value} = 0.0498$$

Decision: Since p-value < 0.05, reject H_0. There is enough evidence of a difference in the mean time spent on Facebook per day between males and females.

(b)   You must assume that each of the two independent populations is normally distributed.

10.18 $d.f. = n - 1 = 20 - 1 = 19$, where n = number of pairs of data

Copyright ©2015 Pearson Education, Inc.

10.20   Excel output:
        t-Test: Paired Two Sample for Means

	A	B
Mean	24	25.55555556
Variance	7	3.527777778
Observations	9	9
Pearson Correlation	0.85524255	
Hypothesized Mean Difference	0	
Df	8	
t Stat	-3.277152121	
P(T<=t) one-tail	0.00561775	
t Critical one-tail	1.859548033	
P(T<=t) two-tail	0.011235501	
t Critical two-tail	2.306004133	

(a)   Define the difference in summated rating as the rating on brand A minus the rating
     on brand B.

$$H_0 : \mu_D = 0 \quad \text{vs.} \quad H_1 : \mu_D \neq 0$$

Test statistic: $t_{STAT} = \dfrac{\overline{D} - \mu_D}{\dfrac{S_D}{\sqrt{n}}} = -3.2772$, p-value = 0.0112

Decision: Since the p-value = 0.0112 < 0.05, reject H_0. There is enough evidence
of a difference in the mean summated ratings between the two brands.

(b)   You must assume that the distribution of the differences between the two ratings is
     approximately normal.

(c) p-value is 0.0112. The probability of obtaining a mean difference in ratings that
     gives rise to a test statistic that deviates from 0 by 3.2772 or more in either direction
     is 0.0112 if there is no difference in the mean summated ratings between the two
     brands.

(d) $\overline{D} \pm t \dfrac{S_D}{\sqrt{n}} = -1.5556 \pm 2.3060 \dfrac{1.4240}{\sqrt{9}}$ $-2.6501 \leq \mu_D \leq -0.4610$

You are 95% confident that the mean difference in summated ratings between brand
A and brand B is somewhere between -2.6501 and -0.4610.

Copyright ©2015 Pearson Education, Inc.

10.22 (a)   Define the difference in price as the price of Super Target minus the price of Walmart.

PHStat output:

Paired *t* Test	
Data	
Hypothesized Mean Difference	**0**
Level of significance	**0.05**
Intermediate Calculations	
Sample Size	33
DBar	0.1494
Degrees of Freedom	32
S_D	0.4782
Standard Error	0.0832
t Test Statistic	**1.7948**
Upper-Tail Test	
Upper Critical Value	**1.6939**
p -Value	**0.0411**
Reject the null hypothesis	

$H_0: \mu_{\bar{D}} \leq 0$

$H_1: \mu_{\bar{D}} > 0$

Decision rule: If *p*-value < 0.05, reject H_0.

Test statistic: $t_{STAT} = \dfrac{\bar{D} - \mu_D}{\dfrac{S_D}{\sqrt{n}}} = 1.7948$ *p*-value = 0.0411

Decision: Since *p*-value < 0.05, reject H_0. There is enough evidence that the mean price of items is higher at Super Target than at Walmart.

(b)   You must assume that the distribution of the differences between the price of Super Target and price of Walmart is approximately normal.

(c)   *p*-value = 0.0411. The probability of obtaining a test statistic farther away from 0 is 0.0411 if the mean price of items is no higher at Super Target than at Walmart.

Copyright ©2015 Pearson Education, Inc.

10.24   (a)   Define the difference in bone marrow microvessel density as the density before the transplant minus the density after the transplant and assume that the difference in density is normally distributed.

$$H_0 : \mu_D \leq 0 \quad \text{vs.} \quad H_1 : \mu_D > 0$$

Excel output:
t-Test: Paired Two Sample for Means

	Before	After
Mean	312.1429	226
Variance	15513.14	4971
Observations	7	7
Pearson Correlation	0.295069	
Hypothesized Mean Difference	0	
df	6	
t Stat	1.842455	
P(T<=t) one-tail	0.057493	
t Critical one-tail	1.943181	
P(T<=t) two-tail	0.114986	
t Critical two-tail	2.446914	

Test statistic: $t_{STAT} = \dfrac{\overline{D} - \mu_D}{\dfrac{S_D}{\sqrt{n}}} = 1.8425$

Decision: Since $t_{STAT} = 1.8425$ is less than the critical value of 1.943, do not reject H_0. There is not enough evidence to conclude that the mean bone marrow microvessel density is higher before the stem cell transplant than after the stem cell transplant.

(b) p-value = 0.0575. The probability of obtaining a mean difference in density that gives rise to a t test statistic that deviates from 0 by 1.8425 or more is .0575 if the mean density is not higher before the stem cell transplant than after the stem cell transplant.

(c) $\overline{D} \pm t \dfrac{S_D}{\sqrt{n}} = 86.1429 \pm 2.4469 \dfrac{123.7005}{\sqrt{7}}$ $-28.26 \leq \mu_D \leq 200.55$

You are 95% confident that the mean difference in bone marrow microvessel density before and after the stem cell transplant is somewhere between -28.26 and 200.55.

(d)   You must assume that the distribution of differences between the mean density of before and after stem cell transplant is approximately normal.

Copyright ©2015 Pearson Education, Inc.

10.26 (a) H_0: $\mu_{\bar{D}} \geq 0$

H_1: $\mu_{\bar{D}} < 0$

Decision rule: $d.f. = 39$. If $t_{STAT} < -2.4258$, reject H_0.

Test statistic: $t_{STAT} = \dfrac{\bar{D} - \mu_D}{\dfrac{S_D}{\sqrt{n}}} = -9.372$

Decision: Since $t_{STAT} = -9.372$ is less than the critical bound of -2.4258, reject H_0. There is enough evidence to conclude that the mean strength is lower at two days than at seven days.

(b)   You must assume that the distribution of the differences between the mean strength of the concrete is approximately normal.

(c) p-value is virtually 0. The probability of obtaining a mean difference that gives rise to a test statistic that is -9.372 or less when the null hypothesis is true is virtually 0.

10.28 (a) $p_1 = \dfrac{X_1}{n_1} = \dfrac{45}{100} = 0.45$, $p_2 = \dfrac{X_2}{n_2} = \dfrac{25}{50} = 0.50$,

and $\bar{p} = \dfrac{X_1 + X_2}{n_1 + n_2} = \dfrac{45 + 25}{100 + 50} = 0.467$

H_0: $\pi_1 = \pi_2$ H_1: $\pi_1 \neq \pi_2$

Decision rule: If $Z < -2.58$ or $Z > 2.58$, reject H_0.

$Z_{STAT} = \dfrac{(p_1 - p_2) - (\pi_1 - \pi_2)}{\sqrt{\bar{p}(1 - \bar{p})\left(\dfrac{1}{n_1} + \dfrac{1}{n_2}\right)}} = \dfrac{(0.45 - 0.50) - 0}{\sqrt{0.467\,(1 - 0.467)\left(\dfrac{1}{100} + \dfrac{1}{50}\right)}} = -0.58$

Decision: Since $Z_{STAT} = -0.58$ is between the critical bound of ± 2.58, do not reject H_0. There is insufficient evidence to conclude that the population proportion differs for group 1 and group 2

(b)

$(p_1 - p_2) \pm Z\sqrt{\left(\dfrac{p_1(1 - p_1)}{n_1} + \dfrac{p_2(1 - p_2)}{n_2}\right)} = -0.05 \pm 2.5758\sqrt{\left(\dfrac{.45(.55)}{100} + \dfrac{.5(.5)}{50}\right)}$

$-0.2727 \leq \pi_1 - \pi_2 \leq 0.1727$

Copyright ©2015 Pearson Education, Inc.

10.30   (a) H_0: $\pi_1 \leq \pi_2$ H_1: $\pi_1 > \pi_2$
Population 1 = social media recommendation, 2 = only web browsing

(b)   PHStat output:

Z Test for Differences in Two Proportions	
Data	
Hypothesized Difference	0
Level of Significance	0.05
Group 1	
Number of Items of Interest	407
Sample Size	557
Group 2	
Number of Items of Interest	193
Sample Size	284
Intermediate Calculations	
Group 1 Proportion	0.73070018
Group 2 Proportion	0.679577465
Difference in Two Proportions	0.051122715
Average Proportion	0.713436385
Z Test Statistic	1.550652654
Upper-Tail Test	
Upper Critical Value	1.6449
p-Value	0.0605
Do not reject the null hypothesis	

(b)   Decision rule: If $Z_{STAT} > 1.6449$, reject H_0.
Test statistic:

$$Z_{STAT} = \frac{(p_1 - p_2) - (\pi_1 - \pi_2)}{\sqrt{\bar{p}(1 - \bar{p})\left(\dfrac{1}{n_1} + \dfrac{1}{n_2}\right)}} = 1.5507 \qquad\qquad p\text{-value} = 0.0605$$

Decision: Since *p*-value > 0.05, do not reject H_0. There is not sufficient evidence to conclude that brand recall is higher following a social media recommendation than with only web browsing.

(c)   No, the result in (b) does not make it appropriate to claim that brand recall is higher following a social media recommendation than by web browsing.

10.32   (a)   PHStat output:

Z Test for Differences in Two Proportions

Data	
Hypothesized Difference	0
Level of Significance	0.01
Group 1	
Number of Items of Interest	930
Sample Size	1000
Group 2	
Number of Items of Interest	230
Sample Size	1000
Intermediate Calculations	
Group 1 Proportion	0.93
Group 2 Proportion	0.23
Difference in Two Proportions	0.7
Average Proportion	0.58
Z Test Statistic	31.71351646
Two-Tail Test	
Lower Critical Value	-2.5758
Upper Critical Value	2.5758
p-Value	0.0000
Reject the null hypothesis	

Confidence Interval Estimate	
of the Difference Between Two Proportions	
Data	
Confidence Level	99%
Intermediate Calculations	
Z Value	-2.5758
Std. Error of the Diff. between two Proporti	0.0156
Interval Half Width	0.0401
Confidence Interval	
Interval Lower Limit	0.6599
Interval Upper Limit	0.7401

H_0: $\pi_1 = \pi_2$ H_1: $\pi_1 \neq \pi_2$

Population: 1 = Superbanked; 2 = Unbanked.

Decision rule: If $|Z_{STAT}| > 2.5758$ or p-value < 0.05, reject H_0.

Test statistic:

$$Z_{STAT} = \frac{(p_1 - p_2) - (\pi_1 - \pi_2)}{\sqrt{\overline{p}(1-\overline{p})\left(\frac{1}{n_1} + \frac{1}{n_2}\right)}} = 31.7135$$

Decision: Since p-value < 0.05, reject H_0. There is evidence of a difference in the proportion of Superbanked and Unbanked with respect to the proportion that use credit cards.

(b) p-value is virtually 0. The probability of obtaining a difference in proportions that gives rise to a test statistic below -31.7135 or above +31.7135 is 0.0000 if there is no difference in the proportion of Superbanked and Unbanked who use credit cards.

(c) $$(p_1 - p_2) \pm Z \sqrt{\left(\frac{p_1(1-p_1)}{n_1} + \frac{p_2(1-p_2)}{n_2}\right)} = 0.7 \pm 2.5758 \sqrt{\left(\frac{0.93(1-0.93)}{1000} + \frac{0.23(1-0.23)}{1000}\right)}$$

$$0.6599 \leq \pi_1 - \pi_2 \leq 0.7401$$

You are 99% confident that the difference in the proportion of Superbanked and Unbanked who use credit cards is between 0.6599 and 0.7401.

Copyright ©2015 Pearson Education, Inc.

10.34   (a) H_0: $\pi_1 = \pi_2$ H_1: $\pi_1 \neq \pi_2$

Z Test for Differences in Two Proportions	
Data	
Hypothesized Difference	0
Level of Significance	0.05
Group 1	
Number of Items of Interest	31
Sample Size	37
Group 2	
Number of Items of Interest	138
Sample Size	275
Intermediate Calculations	
Group 1 Proportion	0.837837838
Group 2 Proportion	0.501818182
Difference in Two Proportions	0.336019656
Average Proportion	0.5417
Z Test Statistic	**3.8512**
Two-Tail Test	
Lower Critical Value	-1.9600
Upper Critical Value	1.9600
***p*-Value**	0.0001
Reject the null hypothesis	

Decision rule: If *p*-value < 0.05, reject H_0.
Decision: Since *p*-value = 0.0001 < 0.05, reject H_0. There is sufficient evidence of a difference between gamification-user sales organizations and non-gamification-user sales organizations in the proportion that provide mobile access to CRM.

(b)   *p*-value is 0.0001. The probability of obtaining a difference in proportions that gives rise to a test statistic that deviates from 0 by 3.8512 or more in either direction is 0.0001 if there is not a difference between gamification-user sales organizations and non-gamification-user sales organizations in the proportion that provide mobile access to CRM.

10.36   (a) $\alpha = 0.10$, $n_1 = 16$, $n_2 = 21$, $F_{0.10/2} = 2.20$

(b) $\alpha = 0.05$, $n_1 = 16$, $n_2 = 21$, $F_{0.05/2} = 2.57$

(c) $\alpha = 0.01$, $n_1 = 16$, $n_2 = 21$, $F_{0.01/2} = 3.50$

10.38   (a)   You place the larger sample variance $S^2 = 25$ in the numerator of F_{STAT}.

(b) $F_{STAT} = \dfrac{S_1^{\,2}}{S_2^{\,2}} = \dfrac{25}{16} = 1.5625$

Copyright ©2015 Pearson Education, Inc.

10.40   The degrees of freedom for the numerator is 24 and for the denominator is 24.

10.42   Since $F_{STAT} = 1.2109$ is lower than $F_{0.05/2} = 2.27$, do not reject H_0. There is not enough evidence to conclude that the two population variances are different.

10.44   (a) H_0: $\sigma_1^2 = \sigma_2^2$ The population variances are the same.
        H_1: $\sigma_1^2 \neq \sigma_2^2$ The population variances are different.
        Decision rule: If $F_{STAT} > 3.18$ reject H_0.

        Test statistic: $F_{STAT} = \dfrac{S_1^2}{S_2^2} = \dfrac{47.3}{36.4} = 1.2995$

        Decision: Since $F_{STAT} = 1.2995$ is less than $F_{\alpha/2} = 3.18$, do not reject H_0. There is not enough evidence to conclude that the two population variances are different.

        (b) H_0: $\sigma_1^2 \leq \sigma_2^2$ The variance for population 1 is less than or equal to the variance for population 2.
        H_1: $\sigma_1^2 > \sigma_2^2$ The variance for population 1 is greater than the variance for population 2.
        Decision rule: If $F_{STAT} > 2.62$, reject H_0.

        Test statistic: $F_{STAT} = \dfrac{S_1^2}{S_2^2} = \dfrac{47.3}{36.4} = 1.2995$

        Decision: Since $F_{STAT} = 1.2995$ is less than the critical bound of $F_{\alpha} = 2.62$, do not reject H_0. There is not enough evidence to conclude that the variance for population 1 is greater than the variance for population 2.

10.46   (a) H_0: $\sigma_1^2 = \sigma_2^2$ The population variances are the same.
        H_1: $\sigma_1^2 \neq \sigma_2^2$ The population variances are different.

F Test for Differences in Two Variances	
Data	
Level of Significance	0.05
Larger-Variance Sample	
Sample Size	14
Sample Variance	1680.225275
Smaller-Variance Sample	
Sample Size	17
Sample Variance	1029.808824
Intermediate Calculations	
F Test Statistic	1.6316
Population 1 Sample Degrees of Freedom	13
Population 2 Sample Degrees of Freedom	16
Two-Tail Test	
Upper Critical Value	2.8506
p-Value	0.3509
Do not reject the null hypothesis	

Copyright ©2015 Pearson Education, Inc.

10.46 (a)   Decision rule: If p-value < 0.05, reject H_0.
cont.   Decision: Since p-value = 0.3509 > 0.05, do not reject H_0. There is not enough evidence of a difference in the variability in numbers of partners for Southeast region accounting firms and Gulf Coast accounting firms.

       (b) p-value = 0.3509. The probability of obtaining a sample that yields a test statistic more extreme than 1.6316 is 0.3509 if the null hypothesis that there is no difference in the two population variances is true.

       (c)   The test assumes that the two populations are both normally distributed.

       (d)   Based on (a) and (b), a pooled-variance t test should be used.

10.48 (a)   PHStat output:

F Test for Differences in Two Variances	
Data	
Level of Significance	0.05
Larger-Variance Sample	
Sample Size	7
Sample Variance	3366.7
Smaller-Variance Sample	
Sample Size	11
Sample Variance	881.82
Intermediate Calculations	
F Test Statistic	3.8179
Population 1 Sample Degrees of Freedo	6
Population 2 Sample Degrees of Freedo	10
Two-Tail Test	
Upper Critical Value	4.0721
p-Value	0.0609
Do not reject the null hypothesis	

H_0: $\sigma_1^2 = \sigma_2^2$ The population variances are the same.

H_1: $\sigma_1^2 \neq \sigma_2^2$ The population variances are different.

Decision rule: If $F_{STAT} > 4.0721$, reject H_0.

Test statistic: $F_{STAT} = \dfrac{S_1^2}{S_2^2} = 3.8179$

Decision: Since $F_{STAT} = 3.8179$ is less than the upper critical value of 4.0721, do not reject H_0. There is not enough evidence of a difference in the variability of the battery life between the two types of digital cameras.

       (b) p-value = 0.0609. The probability of obtaining a sample that yields a test statistic greater than 3.8179 is 0.0609 if the null hypothesis that there is no difference in the two population variances is true.

10.48   (c)   The test assumes that the two populations are both normally distributed.
cont.

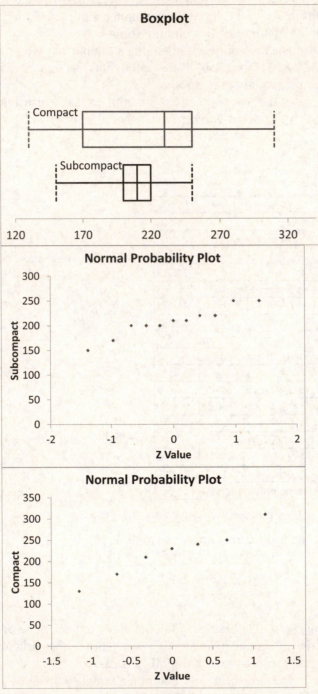

The boxplots appear fairly symmetrical and the skewness and kurtosis statistics are not dramatically different from 0. Thus, the distributions do not appear to be substantially different from a normal distribution.

(d)   Based on (a), a pooled-variance *t* test should be used.

Copyright ©2015 Pearson Education, Inc.

10.50   PHStat output:

F Test for Differences in Two Variances	
Data	
Level of Significance	0.05
Larger-Variance Sample	
Sample Size	10
Sample Variance	0.23556
Smaller-Variance Sample	
Sample Size	8
Sample Variance	0.203369643
Intermediate Calculations	
F Test Statistic	1.1583
Population 1 Sample Degrees of Freedom	9
Population 2 Sample Degrees of Freedom	7
Two-Tail Test	
Upper Critical Value	4.8232
p-Value	0.8658
Do not reject the null hypothesis	

H_0: $\sigma_1^2 = \sigma_2^2$ The population variances are the same.

H_1: $\sigma_1^2 \neq \sigma_2^2$ The population variances are different.

Decision rule: If *p*-value < 0.05, reject H_0.

Decision: Since *p*-value = 0.8658 > 0.05, do not reject H_0. There is not enough evidence of a difference in the variance of the yield of five-year CDs in the two cities.

10.52   The pooled variance *t*-test should be used when the populations are approximately normally distributed and the variances of the two populations are assumed equal.

10.54   With independent populations, the outcomes in one population do not depend on the outcomes in the second population. With two related populations, either repeated measurements are obtained on the same set of items or individuals, or items or individuals are paired or matched according to some characteristic.

10.56   They are two different ways of investigating the concern of whether there is significant difference between the means of two independent populations. If the hypothesized value of 0 for the difference in two population means is not in the confidence interval, then, assuming a two-tailed test is used, the null hypothesis of no difference in the two population means can be rejected.

Copyright ©2015 Pearson Education, Inc.

10.58   (a) H_0: $\sigma_1^2 = \sigma_2^2$ The population variances are the same.   1 = Green Belt
H_1: $\sigma_1^2 \neq \sigma_2^2$ The population variances are different.   2 = Black Belt
PHStat output:

F Test for Differences in Two Variances	
Data	
Level of Significance	0.05
Larger-Variance Sample	
Sample Size	26
Sample Variance	547513201
Smaller-Variance Sample	
Sample Size	121
Sample Variance	447999556
Intermediate Calculations	
F Test Statistic	1.2221
Population 1 Sample Degrees of Freedom	25
Population 2 Sample Degrees of Freedom	120
Two-Tail Test	
Upper Critical Value	1.7462
p-Value	0.4688
Do not reject the null hypothesis	

Decision rule: If p-value < 0.05, reject H_0.
Decision: Since p-value $= 0.4688 > 0.05$, do not reject H_0. There is not enough evidence of any difference in the variability of salaries between Black Belts and Green Belts.

(b)   Since there is not enough evidence of any difference in the variability of salaries between Black Belts and Green Belts, a pooled-variance t test should be used.

Copyright ©2015 Pearson Education, Inc.

10.58 (c) H_0: $\mu_1 \geq \mu_2$ H_1: $\mu_1 < \mu_2$ 1 = Green Belt, 2 = Black Belt

cont.

Pooled-Variance t Test for the Difference Between Two Mea	
(assumes equal population variances)	
Data	
Hypothesized Difference	0
Level of Significance	0.05
Population 1 Sample	
Sample Size	26
Sample Mean	74173
Sample Standard Deviation	23399
Population 2 Sample	
Sample Size	121
Sample Mean	93946
Sample Standard Deviation	21166
Intermediate Calculations	
Population 1 Sample Degrees of Freedom	25
Population 2 Sample Degrees of Freedom	120
Total Degrees of Freedom	145
Pooled Variance	465157081.0000
Standard Error	4662.0736
Difference in Sample Means	-19773.0000
t Test Statistic	-4.2412
Lower-Tail Test	
Lower Critical Value	-1.6554
p-Value	0.0000
Reject the null hypothesis	

Decision rule: If p-valu e< 0.05, reject H_0.

Decision: Since p-value = 0.0000 < 0.05, reject H_0. There is enough evidence that the mean salary of Green Belts is less than the mean salary of Black Belts.

Copyright ©2015 Pearson Education, Inc.

10.60   (a) H_0: $\sigma_1^2 = \sigma_2^2$ The population variances are the same.

H_1: $\sigma_1^2 \neq \sigma_2^2$ The population variances are different.

F Test for Differences in Two Variances	
Data	
Level of Significance	**0.01**
Larger-Variance Sample	
Sample Size	**100**
Sample Variance	**15625**
Smaller-Variance Sample	
Sample Size	**100**
Sample Variance	**10000**
Intermediate Calculations	
F Test Statistic	**1.5625**
Population 1 Sample Degrees of Freedo	99
Population 2 Sample Degrees of Freedo	99
Two-Tail Test	
Upper Critical Value	**1.6854**
p-Value	**0.0274**
Do not reject the null hypothesis	

Decision rule: If $F_{STAT} > 1.6854$, reject H_0.

Test statistic: $F_{STAT} = \dfrac{S_1^2}{S_2^2} = 1.5625$

Decision: Since $F_{STAT} = 1.5625$ is less than the upper critical bound of 1.6584, do not reject H_0. There is not enough evidence of a difference in the variances of the amount of time spent talking between women and men.

Copyright ©2015 Pearson Education, Inc.

10.60 (b)
cont.

It is more appropriate to use a pooled-variance t test.

Pooled-Variance t Test for the Difference Between	
(assumes equal population variances)	
Data	
Hypothesized Difference	0
Level of Significance	0.01
Population 1 Sample	
Sample Size	100
Sample Mean	818
Sample Standard Deviation	125
Population 2 Sample	
Sample Size	100
Sample Mean	716
Sample Standard Deviation	100
Intermediate Calculations	
Population 1 Sample Degrees of Freedom	99
Population 2 Sample Degrees of Freedom	99
Total Degrees of Freedom	198
Pooled Variance	12812.5
Standard Error	16.0078
Difference in Sample Means	102
t Test Statistic	6.3719
Two-Tail Test	
Lower Critical Value	-2.6009
Upper Critical Value	2.6009
p-Value	0.0000
Reject the null hypothesis	

$H_0: \mu_1 = \mu_2$ $H_1: \mu_1 \neq \mu_2$ Population 1 = women, Population 2 = men

Decision rule: If $|t_{STAT}| > 2.6009$, reject H_0.

Test statistic:

$$t_{STAT} = \frac{\left(\overline{X}_1 - \overline{X}_2\right) - \left(\mu_1 - \mu_2\right)}{\sqrt{S_p^2\left(\dfrac{1}{n_1} + \dfrac{1}{n_2}\right)}} = 6.3719$$

Decision: Since $t_{STAT} = 6.3719$ is larger than the upper critical bound of 2.6009, reject H_0. There is enough evidence of a difference in the mean amount of time spent talking between women and men.

Copyright ©2015 Pearson Education, Inc.

10.60   (c) H_0: $\sigma_1^2 = \sigma_2^2$ The population variances are the same.
cont. H_1: $\sigma_1^2 \neq \sigma_2^2$ The population variances are different.

F Test for Differences in Two Variances	
Data	
Level of Significance	0.01
Larger-Variance Sample	
Sample Size	100
Sample Variance	22500
Smaller-Variance Sample	
Sample Size	100
Sample Variance	15625
Intermediate Calculations	
F Test Statistic	**1.4400**
Population 1 Sample Degrees of Freedo	99
Population 2 Sample Degrees of Freedo	99
Two-Tail Test	
Upper Critical Value	1.6854
p-Value	0.0711
Do not reject the null hypothesis	

Decision rule: If $F_{STAT} > 1.6854$, reject H_0.

Test statistic: $F_{STAT} = \dfrac{S_1^2}{S_2^2} = 1.4400$

Decision: Since $F_{STAT} = 1.4400$ is lower than the upper critical bound 1.6854, do not reject H_0. There is not enough evidence of a difference in the variances of the number of text messages sent per month by women and men.

Copyright ©2015 Pearson Education, Inc.

10.60 (d)   It is more appropriate to use a pooled-variance t test.
cont. H_0: $\mu_1 = \mu_2$ H_1: $\mu_1 \neq \mu_2$ Population 1 = women, Population 2 = men

Pooled-Variance t Test for the Difference Between (assumes equal population variances)	
Data	
Hypothesized Difference	0
Level of Significance	0.01
Population 1 Sample	
Sample Size	100
Sample Mean	716
Sample Standard Deviation	150
Population 2 Sample	
Sample Size	100
Sample Mean	555
Sample Standard Deviation	125
Intermediate Calculations	
Population 1 Sample Degrees of Freedom	99
Population 2 Sample Degrees of Freedom	99
Total Degrees of Freedom	198
Pooled Variance	19062.5
Standard Error	19.5256
Difference in Sample Means	161
t Test Statistic	8.2456
Two-Tail Test	
Lower Critical Value	-2.6009
Upper Critical Value	2.6009
p-Value	0.0000
Reject the null hypothesis	

Decision rule: If $|t_{STAT}| > 2.6009$, reject H_0.
Test statistic:

$$t_{STAT} = \frac{(\bar{X}_1 - \bar{X}_2) - (\mu_1 - \mu_2)}{\sqrt{S_p^{\,2}\left(\dfrac{1}{n_1} + \dfrac{1}{n_2}\right)}} = 8.2456$$

Decision: Since $t_{STAT} = 8.2456$ is greater than the upper critical bound of 2.6009, reject H_0. There is enough evidence of a difference in the mean number of text messages sent per month by women and men.

Copyright ©2015 Pearson Education, Inc.

10.62   (a) H_0: $\mu \leq 10$ minutes. Introductory computer students required no more than a mean of 10 minutes to write and run a program in VB.NET.

H_1: $\mu > 10$ minutes. Introductory computer students required more than a mean of 10 minutes to write and run a program in VB.NET.

Decision rule: $d.f. = 8$. If $t_{STAT} > 1.8595$, reject H_0.

Test statistic: $t_{STAT} = \dfrac{\overline{X} - \mu}{S / \sqrt{n}} = \dfrac{12 - 10}{1.8028 / \sqrt{9}} = 3.3282$

Decision: Since $t_{STAT} = 3.3282$ is greater than the critical bound of 1.8595, reject H_0. There is enough evidence to conclude that the introductory computer students required more than a mean of 10 minutes to write and run a program in VB.NET.

(b) H_0: $\mu \leq 10$ minutes. Introductory computer students required no more than a mean of 10 minutes to write and run a program in VB.NET.

H_1: $\mu > 10$ minutes. Introductory computer students required more than a mean of 10 minutes to write and run a program in VB.NET.

Decision rule: $d.f. = 8$. If $t_{STAT} > 1.8595$, reject H_0.

Test statistic: $t_{STAT} = \dfrac{\overline{X} - \mu}{S / \sqrt{n}} = \dfrac{16 - 10}{13.2004 / \sqrt{9}} = 1.3636$

Decision: Since $t_{STAT} = 1.3636$ is less than the critical bound of 1.8595, do not reject H_0. There is not enough evidence to conclude that the introductory computer students required more than a mean of 10 minutes to write and run a program in VB.NET.

(c)   Although the mean time necessary to complete the assignment increased from 12 to 16 minutes as a result of the increase in one data value, the standard deviation went from 1.8 to 13.2, which in turn brought the t-value down because of the increased denominator.

(d) H_0: $\sigma_{IC}^{2} = \sigma_{CS}^{2}$ H_1: $\sigma_{IC}^{2} \neq \sigma_{CS}^{2}$

Decision rule: If $F_{STAT} > 3.8549$, reject H_0.

Test statistic: $F_{STAT} = \dfrac{S_{CS}^{2}}{S_{IC}^{2}} = \dfrac{2.0^{2}}{1.8028^{2}} = 1.2307$

Decision: Since $F_{STAT} = 1.2307$ is lower than the critical bound 3.8549, do not reject H_0. There is not enough evidence to conclude that the population variances are different for the Introduction to Computers students and computer majors. Hence, the pooled variance t test is a valid test to see whether computer majors can write a VB.NET program (on average) in less time than introductory students, assuming that the distributions of the time needed to write a VB.NET program for both the Introduction to Computers students and the computer majors are approximately normal.

Copyright ©2015 Pearson Education, Inc.

10.62 (d) H_0: $\mu_{IC} \leq \mu_{CS}$ The mean amount of time needed by Introduction to Computers
cont.   students is not greater than the mean amount of time needed by computer majors.
              H_1: $\mu_{IC} > \mu_{CS}$ The mean amount of time needed by Introduction to Computers
.   students is greater than the mean amount of time needed by computer majors.
              PHStat output:

Pooled-Variance *t* Test for the Difference Between Two Means	
(assumes equal population variances)	
Data	
Hypothesized Difference	0
Level of Significance	0.05
Population 1 Sample	
Sample Size	9
Sample Mean	12
Sample Standard Deviation	1.802776
Population 2 Sample	
Sample Size	11
Sample Mean	8.5
Sample Standard Deviation	2
Intermediate Calculations	
Population 1 Sample Degrees of Freedom	8
Population 2 Sample Degrees of Freedom	10
Total Degrees of Freedom	18
Pooled Variance	3.666667
Difference in Sample Means	3.5
***t* Test Statistic**	4.066633
Upper-Tail Test	
Upper Critical Value	1.734064
***p*-Value**	0.000362
Reject the null hypothesis	

Decision rule: $d.f. = 18$. If $t_{STAT} > 1.7341$, reject H_0.

Test statistic:

$$S_p^2 = \frac{(n_{IC}-1)\cdot S_{IC}^2 + (n_{CS}-1)\cdot S_{CS}^2}{(n_{IC}-1)+(n_{CS}-1)} = \frac{9\cdot 1.8028^2 + 11\cdot 2.0^2}{8+10} = 3.6667$$

$$t_{STAT} = \frac{\left(\overline{X}_{IC}-\overline{X}_{CS}\right)-\left(\mu_{IC}-\mu_{CS}\right)}{\sqrt{S_p^2\left(\dfrac{1}{n_{IC}}+\dfrac{1}{n_{CS}}\right)}} = \frac{12.0-8.5}{\sqrt{3.6667\left(\dfrac{1}{9}+\dfrac{1}{11}\right)}} = 4.0666$$

Decision: Since $t_{STAT} = 4.0666$ is greater than 1.7341, reject H_0. There is enough
evidence to support a conclusion that the mean time is higher for Introduction to
Computers students than for computer majors.

Copyright ©2015 Pearson Education, Inc.

10. 62   (e)   *p*-value = 0.0052. If the true population mean amount of time needed for
cont.   Introduction to Computer students to write a VB.NET program is indeed no more
                   than 10 minutes, the probability for observing a sample mean greater than the 12
                   minutes in the current sample is 0.0052, which means it will be a quite unlikely
                   event. Hence, at a 95% level of confidence, you can conclude that the population
                   mean amount of time needed for Introduction to Computer students to write a
                   VB.NET program is more than 10 minutes.

                   As illustrated in part (d) in which there is not enough evidence to conclude that the
                   population variances are different for the Introduction to Computers students and
                   computer majors, the pooled variance *t* test performed is a valid test to determine
                   whether computer majors can write a VB.NET program in less time than in
                   introductory students, assuming that the distributions of the time needed to write a
                   VB.NET program for both the Introduction to Computers students and the computer
                   majors are approximately normal.

10.64

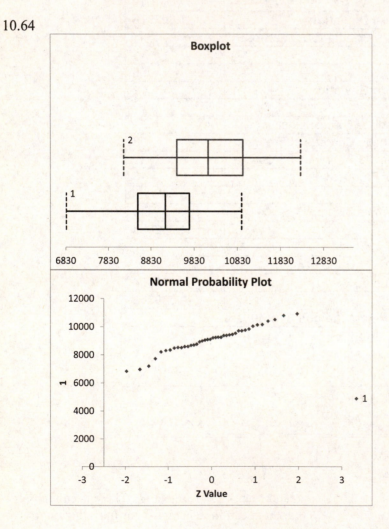

Copyright ©2015 Pearson Education, Inc.

10.64
cont.

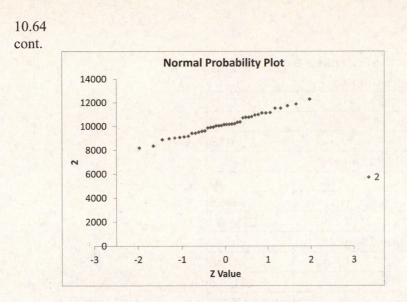

From the box plot and normal probability plots, both data seem to have come
from rather symmetrical distributions that are quite normally distributed.

The following F test for any evidence of difference between two population variances
suggests that there is insufficient evidence to conclude that the two population variances are
significantly different at 5% level of significance.

PHStat output:

F Test for Differences in Two Variances	
Data	
Level of Significance	0.05
Larger-Variance Sample	
Sample Size	40
Sample Variance	938987.4359
Smaller-Variance Sample	
Sample Size	40
Sample Variance	889346.4103
Intermediate Calculations	
F Test Statistic	1.0558
Population 1 Sample Degrees of Freedom	39
Population 2 Sample Degrees of Freedom	39
Two-Tail Test	
Upper Critical Value	1.8907
p-Value	0.8662
Do not reject the null hypothesis	

Since both data are drawn from independent populations, the most appropriate test for any
difference in the life of the bulbs between the two manufacturers is the pooled-variance t test.

Copyright ©2015 Pearson Education, Inc.

10.64   PHStat output:
cont.

Pooled-Variance *t* Test for the Difference Between Two M	
(assumes equal population variances)	
Data	
Hypothesized Difference	**0**
Level of Significance	**0.05**
Population 1 Sample	
Sample Size	**40**
Sample Mean	**9096.5**
Sample Standard Deviation	**943.0516477**
Population 2 Sample	
Sample Size	**40**
Sample Mean	**10183.5**
Sample Standard Deviation	**969.0136407**
Intermediate Calculations	
Population 1 Sample Degrees of Freedom	39
Population 2 Sample Degrees of Freedom	39
Total Degrees of Freedom	78
Pooled Variance	914166.9231
Standard Error	213.7951
Difference in Sample Means	-1087.0000
***t* Test Statistic**	**-5.0843**
Two-Tail Test	
Lower Critical Value	**-1.9908**
Upper Critical Value	**1.9908**
***p*-Value**	**0.0000**
Reject the null hypothesis	

Since the *p*-value < 0.05, at the 5% level of significance, there is sufficient evidence
to reject the null hypothesis of no difference in the mean life of the bulbs between the two
manufacturers. You can conclude that there is significant difference in the mean life of the
bulbs between the two manufacturers.

Copyright ©2015 Pearson Education, Inc.

10.66 H_0: $\pi_1 = \pi_2$ H_1: $\pi_1 \neq \pi_2$ where Populations: 1 = Males, 2 = Females
Decision rule: If p-value < 0.05, reject H_0.
Gender:
PHStat output:

Z Test for Differences in Two Proportions	
Data	
Hypothesized Difference	0
Level of Significance	0.05
Group 1	
Number of Items of Interest	50
Sample Size	300
Group 2	
Number of Items of Interest	96
Sample Size	330
Intermediate Calculations	
Group 1 Proportion	0.166666667
Group 2 Proportion	0.290909091
Difference in Two Proportions	-0.12424242
Average Proportion	0.2317
Z Test Statistic	**-3.6911**
Two-Tail Test	
Lower Critical Value	**-1.9600**
Upper Critical Value	**1.9600**
***p*-Value**	**0.0002**
Reject the null hypothesis	

Decision: Since the p-value is smaller than 0.05, reject H_0. There is enough evidence of a difference between males and females in the proportion who order dessert.

Copyright ©2015 Pearson Education, Inc.

10.66   **Beef Entrée:**
cont.   PHStat output:

Z Test for Differences in Two Proportions	
Data	
Hypothesized Difference	0
Level of Significance	0.05
Group 1	
Number of Items of Interest	74
Sample Size	197
Group 2	
Number of Items of Interest	68
Sample Size	433
Intermediate Calculations	
Group 1 Proportion	0.375634518
Group 2 Proportion	0.15704388
Difference in Two Proportions	0.218590638
Average Proportion	0.2254
Z Test Statistic	6.0873
Two-Tail Test	
Lower Critical Value	-1.9600
Upper Critical Value	1.9600
***p*-Value**	0.0000
Reject the null hypothesis	

Decision: Since the p-value = 0.0000 is smaller than 0.05, reject H_0. There is enough evidence of a difference in the proportion who order dessert based on whether a beef entrée has been ordered.

Copyright ©2015 Pearson Education, Inc.

10.68

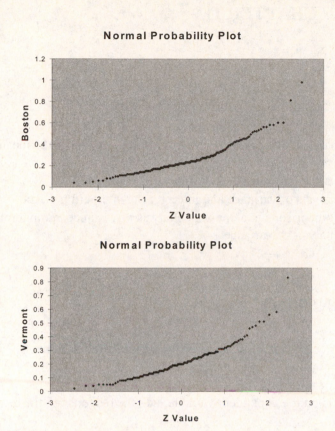

The normal probability plots suggest that the two populations are not normally distributed so an F test is inappropriate for testing the difference in two variances. The sample variances for Boston and Vermont shingles are 0.0203 and 0.015, respectively, which are not very different. It appears that a pooled-variance t test is appropriate for testing the difference in means.

$H_0 : \mu_B = \mu_V$ Mean granule loss of Boston and Vermont shingles are the same.

$H_1 : \mu_B \neq \mu_V$ Mean granule loss of Boston and Vermont shingles are different.

Excel output:
t-Test: Two-Sample Assuming Equal Variances

	Boston	Vermont
Mean	0.264059	0.218
Variance	0.020273	0.015055
Observations	170	140
Pooled Variance	0.017918	
Hypothesized Mean Difference	0	
Df	308	
t Stat	3.014921	
P(T<=t) one-tail	0.001392	
t Critical one-tail	1.649817	
P(T<=t) two-tail	0.002784	
t Critical two-tail	1.967696	

Since the p-value = 0.0028 is less than the 5% level of significance, reject H_0. There is sufficient evidence to conclude that there is a difference in the mean granule loss of Boston and Vermont shingles.

Copyright ©2015 Pearson Education, Inc.

CHAPTER 11

OBJECTIVES
- To introduce the basic concepts of experimental design
- To learn to use the one-way analysis of variance to test for differences among the means of several groups
- To learn when and how to use a randomized block design
- To learn to use the two-way analysis of variance and interpret the interaction effect
- To learn to perform multiple comparisons in a one-way analysis of variance, a randomized block design, and a two-way analysis of variance

OVERVIEW AND KEY CONCEPTS

General Experimental Setting
- Investigators have control over one or more independent variables called treatment variables or factors.
- Each treatment factor has two or more levels.
- Investigators observe the effects on the dependent variable, i.e., the response to the levels of the independent variable(s).
- **Experimental Design:** The plan used to test a hypothesis.

The Completely Randomized Design
- The experimental units (subjects) are assigned randomly to treatments.
- The subjects are assumed to be homogenous.
- There is only one factor or independent variable with two or more treatment levels.
- The completely randomized design will be analyzed by one-way ANOVA.

Some Important Identities in the Completely Randomized Design
- $SST = SSA + SSW$

- $SST = \sum_{j=1}^{c} \sum_{i=1}^{n_j} (X_{ij} - \bar{\bar{X}})^2$

- $SSA = \sum_{j=1}^{c} n_j (\bar{X}_j - \bar{\bar{X}})^2$

- $SSW = \sum_{j=1}^{c} \sum_{i=1}^{n_j} (X_{ij} - \bar{X}_j)^2$

- $MSA = \dfrac{SSA}{c-1}$

- $MSW = \dfrac{SSW}{n-c}$

Copyright ©2015 Pearson Education, Inc.

where n = the total number of observations in the sample

c = the number of groups

n_j = the number of observations in group j

X_{ij} = the ith observation in group j

$$\overline{\overline{X}} = \frac{\sum\limits_{j=1}^{c}\sum\limits_{i=1}^{n_j} X_{ij}}{n} : \text{the overall or grand mean}$$

$\overline{X}_j$ = the sample mean of group j

F Test for Differences in More than Two Means

- **Assumptions:**
  - Samples are randomly and independently drawn.
  - Populations are normally distributed. The F test is robust to violation of this assumption.
  - Populations have equal variances. The F test is less sensitive to violation of this assumption when samples are of equal size from each population.

- **The null and alternative hypotheses:**
  - $H_0 : \mu_1 = \mu_2 = \cdots = \mu_c$ There is no treatment effect
  - H_1 : Not all μ_j are the same. There is some treatment effect.

- **Test statistic:**
  - $F = \dfrac{MSA}{MSW}$ with $(c-1)$ numerator degrees of freedom and $(n-c)$ denominator degrees of freedom
  - The F test always has the rejection region in the right tail.

One-way ANOVA Summary Table

Source of Variation	Degrees of Freedom	Sum of Squares	Mean Squares (Variance)	F Statistic
Among (Factor)	$c - 1$	SSA	MSA = SSA/(c – 1)	MSA/MSW
Within (Error)	$n - c$	SSW	MSW = SSW/(n – c)	
Total	$n - 1$	SST = SSA + SSW		

Copyright ©2015 Pearson Education, Inc.

The Tukey-Kramer Procedure for the Completely Randomized Design

- A post hoc (a posteriori) procedure performed after rejection of the null hypothesis of equal means.
- Enables pair-wise comparison to see which pair of means is significantly different.
- **The Tukey-Kramer procedure:**

  1. Compute the absolute difference between any pair of sample means $\left| \bar{X}_j - \bar{X}_{j'} \right|$

  2. Compute the critical range for that pair of sample means using

     $$\text{Critical Range} = Q_\alpha \sqrt{\frac{MSW}{2}\left(\frac{1}{n_j} + \frac{1}{n_{j'}}\right)}$$ where Q_α is the upper-tail critical value from

     the Studentized range distribution with c numerator degrees of freedom and $(n - c)$

     denominator degrees of freedom, and n_j and n_j are the two sample sizes for the pair of

     samples.

  3. The population means of a specific pair are declared significantly different if $\left| \bar{X}_j - \bar{X}_{j'} \right|$

     is greater than the critical range.

Levene's Test for Homogeneity of Variance

- Used to test the assumption of equal group variances required in the F test for difference in more than two means.
- **The null and alternative hypotheses:**
  - $H_0 : \sigma_1^2 = \sigma_2^2 = \cdots = \sigma_c^2$ All group variances are the same.
  - H_1 : Not all σ_j^2 are the same. Not all group variances are the same.
- **The Levene's test procedure:**
  - For each observation in each group, obtain the absolute value of the difference between each observation and the median of the group.
  - Carry out a one-way analysis of variance on these absolute differences.

The Randomized Block Design

- Items are divided into blocks by matching individual items in different samples or taking repeated measurement of the same individuals to reduce within group variation (i.e. remove the effect of blocking before testing).
- Response of each treatment group is obtained.
- **Assumptions:**
  - Samples are randomly and independently drawn.
  - Populations are normally distributed. The F test is robust to violation of this assumption.
  - Populations have equal variances. The F test is less sensitive to violation of this assumption when samples are of equal size from each population.
  - There is no interaction between the levels of treatment and block.

Copyright ©2015 Pearson Education, Inc.

Some Important Identities in the Randomized Block Design

- $SST = SSA + SSBL + SSE$

- $SST = \sum_{j=1}^{c} \sum_{i=1}^{r} \left(X_{ij} - \bar{\bar{X}} \right)^2$

- $SSA = r \sum_{j=1}^{c} \left(\bar{X}_{\bullet j} - \bar{\bar{X}} \right)^2$

- $SSBL = c \sum_{i=1}^{r} \left(\bar{X}_{i\bullet} - \bar{\bar{X}} \right)^2$

- $SSE = \sum_{j=1}^{c} \sum_{i=1}^{r} \left(X_{ij} - \bar{X}_{i\bullet} - \bar{X}_{\bullet j} + \bar{\bar{X}} \right)^2$

- $MSA = \dfrac{SSA}{c-1}$

- $MSBL = \dfrac{SSBL}{r-1}$

- $MSE = \dfrac{SSE}{(r-1)(c-1)}$

where n = total number of observations ($n = rc$)

r = the number of blocks

c = the number of groups or levels

X_{ij} : the value of the ith block for the jth treatment

$$\bar{X}_{i\bullet} = \frac{\sum_{j=1}^{c} X_{ij}}{c} \text{ : the mean of all values in block } i$$

$$\bar{X}_{\bullet j} = \frac{\sum_{i=1}^{r} X_{ij}}{r} \text{ : the mean of all values for treatment level } j$$

$$\bar{\bar{X}} = \frac{\sum_{j=1}^{c} \sum_{i=1}^{r} X_{ij}}{rc} \text{ : the overall or grand mean}$$

The Randomized Block F Test for Differences in c Means

- **The null and alternative hypotheses:**
  - $H_0 : \mu_{\bullet 1} = \mu_{\bullet 2} = \cdots = \mu_{\bullet c}$ No treatment effect
  - H_1 : Not all $\mu_{\bullet j}$ are equal   There is some treatment effect

- **Test statistic:**
  - $F = \dfrac{MSA}{MSE}$ with $(c-1)$ numerator degrees of freedom and $(r-1)(c-1)$ denominator degrees of freedom.
  - The rejection region is always in the right tail.

Copyright ©2015 Pearson Education, Inc.

The Randomized Block F Test for Block Effect

- **The null and alternative hypotheses:**
  - $H_0 : \mu_{1\bullet} = \mu_{2\bullet} = \cdots = \mu_{r\bullet}$ There is no block effect
  - H_1 : Not all $\mu_{i\bullet}$ are equal   There is some block effect
- **Test statistic:**
  - $F = \dfrac{MSBL}{MSE}$ with $(r-1)$ numerator degrees of freedom and $(r-1)(c-1)$ denominator degrees of freedom.
  - The rejection region is always in the right tail.

ANOVA Table for the Randomized Block Design

Source of Variation	Degrees of Freedom	Sum of Squares	Mean Squares	F Statistic
Among Treatment	$c-1$	SSA	MSA = SSA/(c – 1)	MSA/ MSE
Among Block	$r-1$	SSBL	MSBL = SSBL/(r – 1)	MSBL/ MSE
Error	$(r-1) \bullet (c-1)$	SSE	MSE = SSE/[(r – 1)•(c– 1)]	
Total	$rc-1$	SST		

The Tukey-Kramer Procedure for the Randomized Block Design

- Similar to the Tukey-Kramer procedure for the completely randomized design except the critical range = $Q_\alpha \sqrt{\dfrac{MSE}{r}}$, in which Q_α has c degrees of freedom in the numerator and $(r-1)(c-1)$ degrees of freedom in the denominator.

The Two-Factor Factorial Design

- There is one dependent variable and two treatment factors.
- There can be interaction between the two treatment factors.
- **Assumptions:**
  - Populations are normally distributed.
  - Populations have equal variances.
  - Samples are drawn independently and randomly.

Some Important Identities in the Two-Factor Factorial Design

- $SST = SSA + SSB + SSAB + SSE$
- $SST = \displaystyle\sum_{i=1}^{r}\sum_{j=1}^{c}\sum_{k=1}^{n'}\left(X_{ijk} - \overline{\overline{X}}\right)^2$

Copyright ©2015 Pearson Education, Inc.

- $SSA = cn' \sum\limits_{i=1}^{r} \left(\bar{X}_{i \bullet \bullet} - \bar{\bar{X}} \right)^2$

- $SSB = rn' \sum\limits_{j=1}^{c} \left(\bar{X}_{\bullet j \bullet} - \bar{\bar{X}} \right)^2$

- $SSAB = n' \sum\limits_{i=1}^{r} \sum\limits_{j=1}^{c} \left(\bar{X}_{ij \bullet} - \bar{X}_{i \bullet \bullet} - \bar{X}_{\bullet j \bullet} + \bar{\bar{X}} \right)^2$

- $SSE = \sum\limits_{i=1}^{r} \sum\limits_{j=1}^{c} \sum\limits_{k=1}^{n'} \left(X_{ijk} - \bar{X}_{ij \bullet} \right)^2$

- $MSA = \dfrac{SSA}{r-1}$

- $MSB = \dfrac{SSB}{c-1}$

- $MSAB = \dfrac{SSAB}{(r-1)(c-1)}$

- $MSE = \dfrac{SSE}{rc(n'-1)}$

where n = total number of observations $(n = rcn')$

r = the number of level of factor A

c = the number of level of factor B

n' = the number of replication in each cell (combination of a particular level of factor A and a particular level of factor B)

X_{ijk} = the value of the kth observation for level i of factor A and level j of factor B

$$\bar{X}_{i \bullet \bullet} = \dfrac{\sum\limits_{j=1}^{c} \sum\limits_{k=1}^{n'} X_{ijk}}{cn'} \quad : \text{the mean of the } i^{\text{th}} \text{ level of factor } A$$

$$\bar{X}_{\bullet j \bullet} = \dfrac{\sum\limits_{i=1}^{r} \sum\limits_{k=1}^{n'} X_{ijk}}{rn'} \quad : \text{the mean of the } j^{\text{th}} \text{ level of factor } B$$

$$\bar{X}_{ij \bullet} = \sum\limits_{k=1}^{n'} \dfrac{X_{ijk}}{n'} : \text{mean of the cell } ij, \text{ the combination of the } i^{\text{th}} \text{ level of factor } A \text{ and } j^{\text{th}}$$

level of factor B

$$\bar{\bar{X}} = \dfrac{\sum\limits_{j=1}^{c} \sum\limits_{i=1}^{r} \sum\limits_{k=1}^{n'} X_{ijk}}{rcn'} : \text{the overall or grand mean}$$

Copyright ©2015 Pearson Education, Inc.

The Two-Factor Factorial Design F Test for Interaction

- **The null and alternative hypotheses:**
    - H_0 : The interaction of A and B is equal to zero
    - H_1 : The interaction of A and B is not equal to zero
- **Test statistic:**
    - $F = \dfrac{MSAB}{MSE}$ with $(r-1)(c-1)$ numerator degrees of freedom and $rc\left(n^{'}-1\right)$ denominator degrees of freedom.
    - The rejection region is always in the right tail.
    - In the two-factor factorial design, the test for interaction should be performed prior to the tests for factor A effect and factor B effect.
    - Only when there is no evidence of interaction will the test and interpretation of the main effect be meaningful.

The Two-Factor Factorial Design F Test for Factor A Effect

- **The null and alternative hypotheses:**
    - $H_0 : \mu_{1\bullet\bullet} = \mu_{2\bullet\bullet} = \cdots = \mu_{r\bullet\bullet}$ There is no factor A treatment effect
    - H_1 : Not all $\mu_{i\bullet\bullet}$ are equal   There is some factor A treatment effect
- **Test statistic:**
    - $F = \dfrac{MSA}{MSE}$ with $(r-1)$ numerator degrees of freedom and $rc\left(n^{'}-1\right)$ denominator degrees of freedom.
    - The rejection region is always in the right tail.
    - This main effect test should be performed only after the test for interaction has concluded that there is insufficient evidence of interaction between factor A and B.

The Two-Factor Factorial Design F Test for Factor B Effect

- **The null and alternative hypotheses:**
    - $H_0 : \mu_{\bullet 1\bullet} = \mu_{\bullet 2\bullet} = \cdots = \mu_{\bullet c\bullet}$ There is no factor B treatment effect
    - H_1 : Not all $\mu_{\bullet j\bullet}$ are equal   There is some factor B treatment effect
- **Test statistic:**
    - $F = \dfrac{MSB}{MSE}$ with $(c-1)$ numerator degrees of freedom and $rc\left(n^{'}-1\right)$ denominator degrees of freedom.
    - The rejection region is always in the right tail.
    - This main effect test should be performed only after the test for interaction has concluded that there is insufficient evidence of interaction between factor A and B.

Copyright ©2015 Pearson Education, Inc.

ANOVA Table for the Two-Factor Factorial Design

Source of Variation	Degrees of Freedom	Sum of Squares	Mean Squares	F Statistic
Factor A (Row)	$r - 1$	SSA	$MSA = SSA/(r - 1)$	MSA/MSE
Factor B (Column)	$c - 1$	SSB	$MSB = SSB/(c - 1)$	MSB/MSE
AB (Interaction)	$(r - 1)(c - 1)$	SSAB	$MSAB = SSAB/[(r - 1)(c - 1)]$	MSAB/MSE
Error	$r \cdot c \cdot (n' - 1)$	SSE	$MSE = SSE/[r \cdot c \cdot (n' - 1)]$	
Total	$r \cdot c \cdot n' - 1$	SST		

The Tukey-Kramer Procedure for the Two-Factor Factorial Design

- **For factor A:** Similar to the Tukey-Kramer procedure for the completely randomized design except the critical range $= Q_\alpha \sqrt{\dfrac{MSE}{rn'}}$, in which Q_α has $= r$ degrees of freedom in the numerator and $rc(n' - 1)$ degrees of freedom in the denominator.

- **For factor B:** Similar to the Tukey-Kramer procedure for the completely randomized design except the critical range $= Q_\alpha \sqrt{\dfrac{MSE}{rn'}}$, in which Q_α has $= c$ degrees of freedom in the numerator and $rc(n' - 1)$ degrees of freedom in the denominator.

- These multiple comparisons should be performed only after the test for interaction has concluded that there is insufficient evidence of interaction between factor A and B.

Online Topic: Fixed Effects Models, Random Effects Models, and Mixed Effects Models

- If the levels of a factor in the two-factor factorial design are specifically selected, the effect is called a fixed effect.
- If the levels of a factor in the two-factor factorial design are randomly selected from a population of levels, the effect is called a fixed effect.
- If each factor in the two-factor factorial design is a fixed effect, the model is called a fixed effects model.
- If each factor in the two-factor factorial design is a random effect, the model is called a fixed effects model.
- If the two-factor factorial design includes both fixed effects and random effects, it is called a mixed effects model.
- The F tests that are conducted for each of the factors differ in the fixed effects, random effects, and mixed effects models, and they are summarized below:

Copyright ©2015 Pearson Education, Inc.

Null Hypothesis	Fixed Effects (A and B fixed)	Random Effects (A and B random)	Mixed Effects (A fixed, B random)
No effect due to factor A	$F = \dfrac{MSA}{MSE}$	$F = \dfrac{MSA}{MSAB}$	$F = \dfrac{MSA}{MSAB}$
No effect due to factor B	$F = \dfrac{MSB}{MSE}$	$F = \dfrac{MSB}{MSAB}$	$F = \dfrac{MSB}{MSE}$
No interaction between factors A and B	$F = \dfrac{MSAB}{MSE}$	$F = \dfrac{MSAB}{MSE}$	$F = \dfrac{MSAB}{MSE}$

Copyright ©2015 Pearson Education, Inc.

SOLUTIONS TO END OF SECTION
AND CHAPTER REVIEW EVEN PROBLEMS

11.2　(a)　$SSW = SST - SSA = 210 - 60 = 150$

　　　(b)　$MSA = \dfrac{SSA}{c-1} = \dfrac{60}{5-1} = 15$

　　　(c)　$MSW = \dfrac{SSW}{n-c} = \dfrac{150}{35-5} = 5$

　　　(d)　$F_{STAT} = \dfrac{MSA}{MSW} = \dfrac{15}{5} = 3$

11.4　(a)　$df\ A = c - 1 = 3 - 1 = 2$

　　　(b)　$df\ W = n - c = 21 - 3 = 18$

　　　(c)　$df\ T = n - 1 = 21 - 1 = 20$

11.6　(a)　Decision rule: If $F_{STAT} > 2.95$, reject H_0.

　　　(b)　Since $F_{STAT} = 4$ is greater than the critical bound of 2.95, reject H_0.

　　　(c)　There are $c = 4$ degrees of freedom in the numerator and $n - c = 32 - 4 = 28$ degrees of freedom in the denominator. The table does not have 28 degrees of freedom in the denominator so use the next larger critical value, $Q_\alpha = 3.90$.

　　　(d)　To perform the Tukey-Kramer procedure, the critical range is

$$Q_\alpha \sqrt{\dfrac{MSW}{2}\left(\dfrac{1}{n_j} + \dfrac{1}{n_j}\right)} = 3.90\sqrt{\dfrac{20}{2}\left(\dfrac{1}{8} + \dfrac{1}{8}\right)} = 6.166.$$

11.8　(a)　$H_0: \mu_A = \mu_B = \mu_C = \mu_D$　　　H_1: At least one mean is different.

ANOVA						
Source of Variation	**SS**	**df**	**MS**	**F**	**P-value**	**F crit**
Between Groups	7854648.6000	3	2618216.2000	6.2265	0.0016	2.8663
Within Groups	15137801.8000	36	420494.4944			
Total	22992450.4000	39				
					Level of significance	0.05

Since p-value $= 0.0016 < 0.05$, you can reject H_0. There is sufficient evidence to conclude there is a difference in the mean cost of importing across the four global regions.

Copyright ©2015 Pearson Education, Inc.

11.8   (b)   PHStat output:
cont.

problem 11.8

Group	Sample Mean	Sample Size		Comparison	Absolute Difference	Std. Error of Difference	Critical Range	Results
1: East Asia & Pacific	632.9	10		Group 1 to Group 2	959.2	205.0596241	777.18	Means are different
2: Eastern Europe & Central Asia	1592.1	10		Group 1 to Group 3	1170.9	205.0596241	777.18	Means are different
3: Latin American & Carribbean	1803.8	10		Group 1 to Group 4	805.5	205.0596241	777.18	Means are different
4: Middle East & North Africa	1438.4	10		Group 2 to Group 3	211.7	205.0596241	777.18	Means are not different
				Group 2 to Group 4	153.7	205.0596241	777.18	Means are not different
Other Data				Group 3 to Group 4	365.4	205.0596241	777.18	Means are not different
Level of significance	0.05							
Numerator d.f.	4							
Denominator d.f.	36							
MSW	420494.5							
Q Statistic	3.79							

From the Tukey-Kramer procedure, there is a difference in mean cost of importing between East Asia & Pacific and Eastern Europe & Central Asia, between East Asia & Pacific and Latin American & Caribbean, and between East Asia & Pacific and Middle East & North Africa.

(c) H_0: $\sigma_A^2 = \sigma_B^2 = \sigma_C^2 = \sigma_D^2$ H_1: At least one variance is different.

ANOVA output for Levene's test for homogeneity of variance:

ANOVA

Source of Variation	SS	df	MS	F	P-value	F crit
Between Groups	1387853.3000	3	462617.7667	2.1757	0.1078	2.8663
Within Groups	7654784.8000	36	212632.9111			
Total	9042638.1000	39				
				Level of significance		0.05

Since the p-value = 0.1078 > 0.05, do not reject H_0. There is not sufficient evidence of a difference in the variation in cost of importing among the four global region.

(d)   From the results obtained in (a) and (b), you should consider East Asia & Pacific region because it has the lowest mean cost of importing.

11.10   (a) H_0: $\mu_A = \mu_B = \mu_C = \mu_D = \mu_E$ H_1: At least one mean is different.

PHStat output:
ANOVA

Source of Variation	SS	df	MS	F	P-value	F crit
Between Groups	377.8667	4	94.46667	12.56206	9.74E-06	2.758711
Within Groups	188	25	7.52			
Total	565.8667	29				

Since the p-value is essentially zero, reject H_0. There is evidence of a difference in the mean rating of the five advertisements.

Copyright ©2015 Pearson Education, Inc.

11.10   (b)
cont.

Tukey Kramer Multiple Comparisons				Absolute	Std. Error	Critical	
Group	Sample Mean	Sample Size	Comparison	Difference	of Difference	Range	Results
1	18	6	Group 1 to Group 2	0.333333	1.11952371	4.668	Means are not different
2	17.66667	6	Group 1 to Group 3	6.666667	1.11952371	4.668	Means are different
3	11.33333	6	Group 1 to Group 4	9	1.11952371	4.668	Means are different
4	9	6	Group 1 to Group 5	2.666667	1.11952371	4.668	Means are not different
5	15.33333	6	Group 2 to Group 3	6.333333	1.11952371	4.668	Means are different
			Group 2 to Group 4	8.666667	1.11952371	4.668	Means are different
Other Data			Group 2 to Group 5	2.333333	1.11952371	4.668	Means are not different
Level of significance	0.05		Group 3 to Group 4	2.333333	1.11952371	4.668	Means are not different
Numerator d.f.	5		Group 3 to Group 5	4	1.11952371	4.668	Means are not different
Denominator d.f.	25		Group 4 to Group 5	6.333333	1.11952371	4.668	Means are different
MSW	7.52						
Q Statistic	4.17						

There is a difference in the mean rating between advertisement A and C, between A and D, between B and C, between B and D and between D and E.

(c) H_0: $\sigma_A^2 = \sigma_B^2 = \sigma_C^2 = \sigma_D^2 = \sigma_E^2$ H_1: At least one variance is different.

ANOVA output for Levene's test for homogeneity of variance:
ANOVA

Source of Variation	SS	df	MS	F	P-value	F crit
Between Groups	14.13333	4	3.533333	1.927273	0.137107	2.758711
Within Groups	45.83333	25	1.833333			
Total	59.96667	29				

Since the p-value = 0.137 > 0.05, do not reject H_0. There is not enough evidence to conclude there is a difference in the variation in rating among the five advertisements.

(d)   There is no significant difference between advertisements A and B, and they have the
highest mean rating among the five and should be used. There is no significant difference between advertisements C and D, and they are among the lowest in mean rating and should be avoided.

11.12   (a)

Source	Degrees of Freedom	Sum of Squares	Mean Squares	F
Among groups	2	1.879	0.9395	8.7558
Within groups	297	31.865	0.1073	
Total	299	33.744		

(b) $H_0: \mu_1 = \mu_2 = \mu_3$ H_1: At least one mean is different.

Since $F_{Stat} = 8.7558 > 3.00$, reject H_0. There is evidence of a difference in the mean soft-skill score of the different groups.

(c)

Tukey-Kramer Multiple Comparisons

Group	Sample Mean	Sample Size		Comparison	Absolute Difference	Std. Error of Difference	Critical Range	Results
No coursework in lea	3.29	109		Group 1 to Group 2	0.072	0.032989588	0.1092	Means are not different
Certificate in leaders	3.362	90		Group 1 to Group 3	0.181	0.031908968	0.1056	Means are different
Degree in leadership	3.471	102		Group 2 to Group 3	0.109	0.033497634	0.1109	Means are not different

Other Data	
Level of significance	0.05
Numerator d.f.	3
Denominator d.f.	297
MSW	0.1073
Q Statistic	3.31

There is evidence of a difference in the mean soft-skill score between those who had no coursework in leadership and those who had a degree in leadership.

11.14   (a)   To test at the 0.05 level of significance whether there is any evidence of a difference in the mean distance traveled by the golf balls differing in design, you conduct an F test:

$H_0: \mu_1 = \mu_2 = \mu_3 = \mu_4$ H_1: At least one mean is different.

Decision rule: *df*: 3, 36. If $F_{STAT} > 2.866$, reject H_0.

PHStat output:

ANOVA

Source of Variation	SS	df	MS	F	P-value	F crit
Between Groups	2990.99	3	996.9966	53.02982	2.73E-13	2.866265
Within Groups	676.8244	36	18.80068			
Total	3667.814	39				

Since $F_{STAT} = 53.03$ is greater than the critical bound of 2.866, reject H_0. There is enough evidence to conclude that there is significant difference in the mean distance traveled by the golf balls differing in design.

Note: The critical bound of F is obtained using Excel. The critical bound of F using the Table in the text with 3 numerator and 30 denominator degrees of freedom is 2.92.

Copyright ©2015 Pearson Education, Inc.

11.14 (b)
cont.

To determine which of the means are significantly different from one another, you use the Tukey-Kramer procedure to establish the critical range:

$Q_\alpha = 3.79$

$$\text{critical range} = Q_\alpha \sqrt{\frac{MSW}{2}\left(\frac{1}{n_j}+\frac{1}{n_j}\right)} = 3.79\sqrt{\frac{18.8007}{2}\left(\frac{1}{10}+\frac{1}{10}\right)} = 5.1967$$

PHStat output:

Tukey Kramer Multiple Comparisons					
Group	Sample Mean	Sample Size	Comparison	Absolute Difference	Results
1	206.614	10	Group 1 to Group 2	11.902	Means are different
2	218.516	10	Group 1 to Group 3	19.974	Means are different
3	226.588	10	Group 1 to Group 4	22.008	Means are different
4	228.622	10	Group 2 to Group 3	8.072	Means are different
			Group 2 to Group 4	10.106	Means are different
MSW	18.800677		Group 3 to Group 4	2.034	Means are not different

At 5% level of significance, there is enough evidence to conclude that mean traveling distances between all pairs of designs are different with the only exception of the pair between design 3 and design 4.

(c) The assumptions needed in (a) are (i) the samples are randomly and independently drawn, (ii) populations are normally distributed, and (iii) populations have equal variances.

(d) To test at the 0.05 level of significance whether the variation within the groups is similar for all groups, you conduct a Levene's test for homogeneity of variance:

$H_0: \sigma_1^2 = \sigma_2^2 = \sigma_3^2 = \sigma_4^2$ H_1: At least one variance is different.

PHStat output:
ANOVA

Source of Variation	SS	df	MS	F	P-value	F crit
Between Groups	40.63675	3	13.54558	2.093228	0.118276	2.866265
Within Groups	232.9613	36	6.471147			
Total	273.598	39				

Since p-value = 0.1183 > 0.05, do not reject the null hypothesis. There is not enough evidence to conclude that there is any difference in the variation of the distance traveled by the golf balls differing in design.

(e) In order to produce golf balls with the farthest traveling distance, either design 3 or 4 can be used.

Copyright ©2015 Pearson Education, Inc.

11.16   (a) $SSE = SST - SSA - SSBL = 210 - 60 - 75 = 75$

(b) $= 15 \; MSA = \dfrac{SSA}{c-1} = \dfrac{60}{4} = 15$

$= 12.5 \; MSBL = \dfrac{SSBL}{r-1} = \dfrac{75}{6} = 12.5$

$= 3.125 \; MSE = \dfrac{SSE}{(r-1)(c-1)} = \dfrac{75}{6 \cdot 4} = 3.125$

(c) $F_{STAT} = \dfrac{MSA}{MSE} = \dfrac{15}{3.125} = 4.80$

(d) $F_{STAT} = \dfrac{MSBL}{MSE} = \dfrac{12.5}{3.125} = 4.00$

11.18   (a)   There are 5 degrees of freedom in the numerator and 24 degrees of freedom in the denominator.

(b) $Q_\alpha = 4.17$

(c)   critical range $= Q_\alpha \sqrt{\dfrac{MSE}{r}} = 4.17 \sqrt{\dfrac{3.125}{7}} = 2.786$

11.20   (a) $MSE = \dfrac{MSA}{F} = \dfrac{18}{6} = 3$

$SSE = (MSE)(df\,E) = (3)(12) = 36$

(b) $SSBL = (F)(MSE)(df\,BL) = (4)(3)(6) = 72$

(c) $SST = SSA + SSBL + SSE = 36 + 72 + 36 = 144$

(d)   Since $F_{STAT} = 6 < F_{0.01,2,12} = 6.9266$, do not reject the null hypothesis of no treatment effect. There is not enough evidence to conclude there is a treatment effect.
Since $F_{STAT} = 4.0 < F_{0.01,6,12} = 4.821$, do not reject the null hypothesis of no block effect. There is not enough evidence to conclude there is a block effect.

11.22   (a)   Decision rule: If $F_{STAT} > 3.07$, reject H_0.
Decision: Since $F_{STAT} = 5.185$ is greater than the critical bound 3.07, reject H_0. There is enough evidence to conclude that the treatment means are not all equal.

(b)   Decision rule: If $F_{STAT} > 2.49$, reject H_0.
Decision: Since $F_{STAT} = 5.000$ is greater than the critical bound 2.49, reject H_0. There is enough evidence to conclude that the block means are not all equal.

Copyright ©2015 Pearson Education, Inc.

11.24   (a) $H_0: \mu_{.1} = \mu_{.2} = \mu_{.3}$

where 1 = TV, 2 = Phone, 3 = Internet

H_1: Not all $\mu_{.j}$ are equal where j = 1, 2, 3

Excel Output:

ANOVA						
Source of Variation	SS	df	MS	F	P-value	F crit
Rows	1028.256	12	85.68803	29.16509	2.23E-11	2.18338
Columns	540.1538	2	270.0769	91.92436	5.62E-12	3.402826
Error	70.51282	24	2.938034			
Total	1638.923	38				

F_{STAT} = 91.9244. Since the p-value is virtually 0 < 0.05, reject H_0. There is evidence of a difference in the mean rating between TV, phone, and Internet.

(b)   Excel output for the Tukey procedure:

Tukey-Kramer Multiple Comparisons

Group	Sample Mean	Sample Size		Comparison	Absolute Difference	Std. Error of Difference	Critical Range	Results
1: TV	64.84615	13		Group 1 to Group 2	8.9230769	0.475397339	1.6782	Means are different
2: Phone	73.76923	13		Group 1 to Group 3	2.8461538	0.475397339	1.6782	Means are different
3: Internet	67.69231	13		Group 2 to Group 3	6.0769231	0.475397339	1.6782	Means are different

Other Data	
Level of significance	0.05
Numerator d.f.	3
Denominator d.f.	24
MSW	2.938034
Q Statistic	3.53

The mean rating for the three services are significantly different from each other with TV at the lowest, followed by Internet, and finally Phone.

11.26   (a) $H_0: \mu_{.1} = \mu_{.2} = \mu_{.3} = \mu_{.4}$

where 1 = Money Market, 2 = One Year CD, 3 = Two Year CD, 4 = Five Year CD

H_1: Not all $\mu_{.j}$ are equal where j = 1, 2, 3, 4

Excel output:

ANOVA						
Source of Variation	SS	df	MS	F	P-value	F crit
Rows	4.854975	15	0.323665	12.21774	3.07E-11	1.894875
Columns	7.931888	3	2.643963	99.8046	6.6E-20	2.811544
Error	1.192113	45	0.026491			
Total	13.97898	63				

F_{STAT} = 99.8046. Since the p-value is virtually 0, reject H_0. There is evidence of a difference in the mean rates for these investments.

Copyright ©2015 Pearson Education, Inc.

11.26   (b)
cont.
The assumptions needed are: (i) samples are randomly and independently drawn, (ii) populations are normally distributed, (iii) populations have equal variances and (iv) no interaction effect between treatments and blocks.

(c)   Excel output of the Tukey procedure:

Tukey-Kramer Multiple Comparisons

Group	Sample Mean	Sample Size		Comparison	Absolute Difference	Std. Error of Difference	Critical Range	Results
1: Money Market	0.31875	16		Group 1 to Group 2	0.196875	0.040690439	0.1542	Means are different
2: One Year CD	0.515625	16		Group 1 to Group 3	0.5275	0.040690439	0.1542	Means are different
3: Two Year CD	0.84625	16		Group 1 to Group 4	0.928125	0.040690439	0.1542	Means are different
4: Five Year CD	1.246875	16		Group 2 to Group 3	0.330625	0.040690439	0.1542	Means are different
				Group 2 to Group 4	0.73125	0.040690439	0.1542	Means are different
Other Data				Group 3 to Group 4	0.400625	0.040690439	0.1542	Means are different
Level of significance	0.05							
Numerator d.f.	4							
Denominator d.f.	45							
MSW	0.026491							
Q Statistic	3.79							

Using $Q_\alpha = 3.79$ for numerator d.f. = 4 and denominator d.f. = 40, the mean rates of these investments are all different with Money Market being the lowest, followed by One Year CD, Two Year CD and finally Five Year CD.

(d) H_0: $\mu_{1.} = \mu_{2.} = \cdots = \mu_{16.}$

H_1: Not all $\mu_{i.}$ are equal where $i = 1, 2, \cdots, 16$

$F_{STAT} = 12.2177$. Since the p-value is virtually 0, reject H_0. There is enough evidence of a significant block effect in this experiment. The blocking has been advantageous in reducing the experimental error.

11.28   (a) H_0: $\mu_1 = \mu_2 = \mu_3$ where 1 = 2 days, 2 = 7 days, 3 = 28 days

H_1: At least one mean differs.

Decision rule: If $F_{STAT} > 3.114$, reject H_0.

ANOVA

Source of Variation	SS	df	MS	F	P-value	F crit
Rows	21.17006	39	0.542822	5.752312	2.92E-11	1.553239
Columns	50.62835	2	25.31417	268.2556	1.09E-35	3.113797
Error	7.360538	78	0.094366			
Total	79.15894	119				

Test statistic: $F = 268.26$

Decision: Since $F_{STAT} = 268.26$ is greater than the critical bound 3.114, reject H_0. There is enough evidence to conclude that there is a difference in the mean compressive strength after 2, 7 and 28 days.

(b)   From Table E.10, $Q_\alpha = 3.4$.

$$\text{critical range} = Q_\alpha \sqrt{\frac{MSE}{r}} = 3.4\sqrt{\frac{0.0944}{40}} = 0.1651$$

$\left| \bar{X}_1 - \bar{X}_2 \right| = 0.5531^*$ $\left| \bar{X}_1 - \bar{X}_3 \right| = 1.5685^*$ $\left| \bar{X}_2 - \bar{X}_3 \right| = 1.0154^*$

Copyright ©2015 Pearson Education, Inc.

11.28   (b)   At the 0.05 level of significance, all of the comparisons are significant. This is
cont.   consistent with the results of the *F*-test indicating that there is significant difference
                 in the mean compressive strength after 2, 7 and 28 days.

(c)

$$RE = \frac{(r-1)MSBL + r(c-1)MSE}{(rc-1)MSE} = \frac{39 \cdot 0.5428 + 40 \cdot 2 \cdot 0.0943}{119 \cdot 0.0943} = 2.558$$

(d)

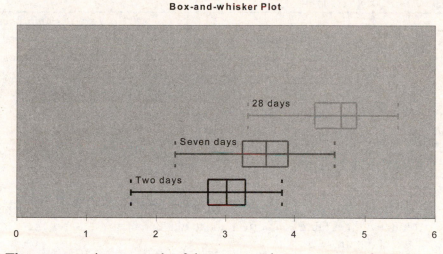

Box-and-whisker Plot

(e)   The compressive strength of the concrete increases over the 3 time periods.

11.30

Source	df	SS	MS	F
Factor *A*	2	120	(b) 120 ÷ 2 = 60	60 ÷ 10 = 6
Factor *B*	2	110	(b) 110 ÷ 2 = 55	55 ÷ 10 = 5.5
Interaction, *AB*	4	(a) 540–120–110–270=40	(c) 40 ÷ 4 = 10	10 ÷ 10 = 1
Error, *E*	27	270	(d)270 ÷ 27 = 10	
Total, *T*	35	540		

11.32 $F_{(2, 27)} = 3.35$ $F_{(4, 27)} = 2.73$
(a)   Decision: Since $F_{STAT} = 6.00$ is greater than the critical bound of 3.35, reject H_0.
        There is evidence of a difference among factor *A* means.
(b)   Decision: Since $F_{STAT} = 5.50$ is greater than the critical bound of 3.35, reject H_0.
        There is evidence of a difference among factor *B* means.
(c)   Decision: Since $F_{STAT} = 1.00$ is less than the critical bound of 2.73, do not reject H_0.
        There is insufficient evidence to conclude there is an interaction effect.

11.34

Source	df	SS	MS	F
Factor *A*	2	2 x 80 = 160	80	80 ÷ 5 = 16
Factor *B*	8 ÷ 2 = 4	220	220 ÷ 4 = 55	11
Interaction, *AB*	8	8 x 10 = 80	10	10 ÷ 5 = 2
Error, *E*	30	30 x 5 = 150	55 ÷ 11 = 5	
Total, *T*	44	160+220+80+150 = 610		

Copyright ©2015 Pearson Education, Inc.

11.36 Excel Two-way ANOVA output:

ANOVA						
Source of Variation	SS	df	MS	F	P-value	F crit
Sample	214.2635	1	214.2635	1.8496	0.1890	4.3512
Columns	1095.2557	1	1095.2557	9.4549	0.0060	4.3512
Interaction	394.2272	1	394.2272	3.4032	0.0799	4.3512
Within	2316.8107	20	115.8405			
Total	4020.5571	23				
					Level of significance	0.05

(a) H_0: There is no interaction between die temperature and die diameter.

H_1: There is an interaction between die temperature and die diameter.

Decision: Since $F_{STAT} = 3.4032 < 4.3512$, do not reject H_0. There is insufficient evidence to conclude that there is any interaction between die temperature and die diameter.

(b) H_0: $\mu_{145..} = \mu_{155..}$ H_1: $\mu_{145} \neq \mu_{155}$

Decision: Since $F_{STAT} = 1.8496 < 4.3512$, do not reject H_0. There is insufficient evidence to conclude that there is an effect due to die temperature.

(c) H_0: $\mu_{.3mm.} = \mu_{.4mm.}$ H_1: $\mu_{.3mm} \neq \mu_{.4mm}$

Decision: Since $F_{STAT} = 9.4549 > 4.3512$, reject H_0. There is sufficient evidence to conclude that there is an effect due to die diameter.

(d) Excel output:

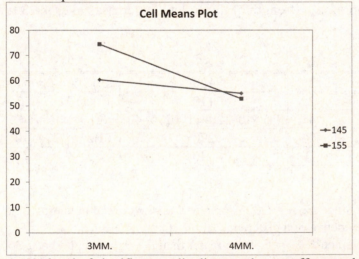

(e) At 5% level of significance, die diameter has an effect on the density while the die temperature does not have any impact on the density. There is no significant interaction between die diameter and die temperature.

Copyright ©2015 Pearson Education, Inc.

11.38   Excel Two-way ANOVA output:

Source of Variation	SS	df	MS	F	P-value	F crit
Sample	24274.85	1	24274.85	1986.507	7.07E-20	4.413863
Columns	356.0027	2	178.0014	14.56656	0.000173	3.554561
Interaction	506.3104	2	253.1552	20.7167	2.14E-05	3.554561
Within	219.9576	18	12.21986			
Total	25357.12	23				

(a) H_0: There is no interaction between brand and water temperature.

H_1: There is an interaction between brand and water temperature.

$$MSAB = \frac{SSAB}{(r-1)(c-1)} = \frac{506.3104}{(1)(2)} = 253.1552$$

$$F = \frac{MSAB}{MSE} = \frac{253.1552}{12.2199} = 20.7167$$

$F_{0.05,2,18} = 3.555$

Since $F_{STAT} = 20.7167 > 3.555$ or the p-value $= 2.14E-05 < 0.05$, reject H_0. There is evidence of an interaction between brand of pain-reliever and temperature of the water.

(b)   Since there is an interaction between brand and the temperature of the water, it is inappropriate to analyze the main effect due to brand.

(c)   Since there is an interaction between brand and the temperature of the water, it is inappropriate to analyze the main effect due to water temperature.

(d)   Excel output:

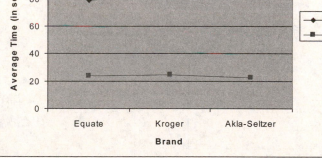

(e)   The difference in the mean time a tablet took to dissolve in cold and hot water depends on the brand with Alka-Seltzer having the largest difference and Equate with the smallest difference.

Copyright ©2015 Pearson Education, Inc.

11.40   (a) H_0: There is no interaction between the brake discs and the gauges.
H_1: There is an interaction between the brake discs and the gauges.
Decision rule: If p-value < 0.05, reject H_0.
Test statistic: $F_{STAT} = 0.1523$, p-value $= 0.9614$
Decision: Since p-value $= 0.9614 > 0.05$, do not reject H_0. There is not enough evidence to conclude that there is an interaction between the brake discs and the gauges.
Excel output:
ANOVA

Source of Variation	SS	df	MS	F	P-value	F crit
Sample	72207.55	4	18051.89	7.770119	3.06E-05	2.502656
Columns	340.3125	1	340.3125	0.146482	0.70308	3.977779
Interaction	1415	4	353.75	0.152265	0.96138	2.502656
Within	162627.1	70	2323.245			
Total	236590	79				

(b) H_0: $\mu_{1..} = \mu_{2..} = \mu_{3..} = \mu_{4..} = \mu_{5..}$ H_1: At least one mean differs.

Decision rule: If p-value < 0.05, reject H_0.
Test statistic: $F_{STAT} = 7.7701$, p-value is virtually 0.
Decision: Since p-value < 0.05, reject H_0. There is sufficient evidence to conclude that there is an effect due to brake discs.

(c) H_0: $\mu_{.1.} = \mu_{.2.}$ H_1: At least one mean differs.

Decision rule: If p-value < 0.05, reject H_0.
Test statistic: $F_{STAT} = 0.1465$, p-value $= 0.7031$.
Decision: Since p-value $= 0.7031 > 0.05$, do not reject H_0. There is inadequate evidence to conclude that there is an effect due to the gauges.

(d)

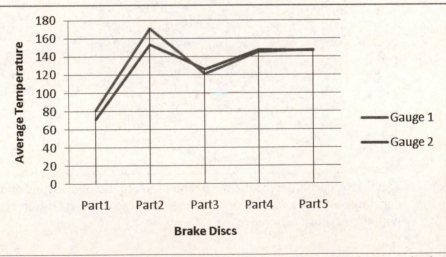

(e)   It is obvious from the plot that there is no obvious interaction between brake discs and gauges. There is no obvious difference in average temperature across the gauges either. It appears that Part 1 has the lowest, Part 3 the second lowest while Part 2 has the highest average temperature.

Copyright ©2015 Pearson Education, Inc.

11.42   The completely randomized design evaluates one factor of interest, in which sample observations are randomly and independently drawn. The randomized block design also evaluates one factor of interest, but sample observations are divided into blocks according to common characteristics to reduce within group variation.

11.44   The major assumptions of ANOVA are randomness and independence, normality, and homogeneity of variance.

11.46   When the ANOVA has indicated that at least one of the groups has a different population mean than the others, you should use multiple comparison procedures for evaluating pairwise combinations of the group means. In such cases, the Tukey-Kramer procedure should be used to compare all pairs of means.

11.48   The one-way ANOVA F test for a completely randomized design is used to test for the existence of treatment effect of the treatment variable on the mean level of the dependent variable, while the Levene test is used to test whether the amounts of variation of the dependent variable are the same across the different categories of the treatment variable.

11.50   Interaction measures the difference in the effect of one variable for the different levels of the second factor. If there is no interaction, any difference between levels of one factor will be the same at each level of the second factor.

11.52   (a)   PHStat output of Two-Way ANOVA:

ANOVA						
Source of Variation	*SS*	*df*	*MS*	*F*	*P-value*	*F crit*
Sample	6.9722	1	6.9722	0.8096	0.3750	4.1491
Columns	134.3488	3	44.7829	5.1999	0.0049	2.9011
Interaction	0.2868	3	0.0956	0.0111	0.9984	2.9011
Within	275.5920	32	8.6123			
Total	417.1998	39				
					Level of significance	0.05

H_0: There is no interaction
H_1: There is an interaction
Decision: Since $F_{STAT} = 0.0111 < 2.9011$, do not reject H_0. There is not enough evidence to conclude that there is an interaction between supplier and loom.

(b) H_0: $\mu_{jetta..} = \mu_{turk..}$ H_1: At least one mean differs.

Decision: Since $F_{STAT} = 0.8096 < 4.1491$, do not reject H_0. There is insufficient evidence to conclude that there is an effect due to loom.

(c) H_0: $\mu_{.1.} = \mu_{.2.} = \mu_{.3.} = \mu_{.4.}$ H_1: At least one mean differs.

Decision: Since $F_{STAT} = 5.1999 > 2.9011$, reject H_0. There is adequate evidence to conclude that there is an effect due to suppliers.

Copyright ©2015 Pearson Education, Inc.

11.52   (d)
cont.

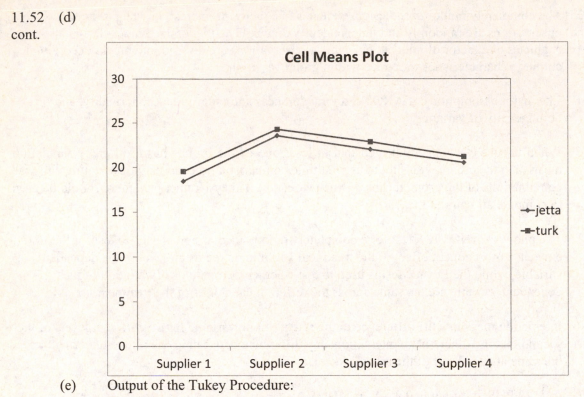

(e)   Output of the Tukey Procedure:
For different suppliers, $Q_\alpha = 3.84$ with numerator d.f. = 4 and denominator d.f. = 32.

Tukey-Kramer Multiple Comparisons

Group	Sample Mean	Sample Size		Comparison	Absolute Difference	Std. Error of Difference	Critical Range	Results
1: Supplier 1	18.97	10		Group 1 to Group 2	4.93	0.92802209	3.5636	**Means are different**
2: Supplier 2	23.9	10		Group 1 to Group 3	3.44	0.92802209	3.5636	**Means are not different**
3: Supplier 3	22.41	10		Group 1 to Group 4	1.86	0.92802209	3.5636	**Means are not different**
4: Supplier 4	20.83	10		Group 2 to Group 3	1.49	0.92802209	3.5636	**Means are not different**
				Group 2 to Group 4	3.07	0.92802209	3.5636	**Means are not different**
Other Data				Group 3 to Group 4	1.58	0.92802209	3.5636	**Means are not different**
Level of significance	0.05							
Numerator d.f.	4							
Denominator d.f.	32							
MSE	8.61225							
Q Statistic	3.84							

There is a difference in mean strength between supplier 1 and supplier 2 only.

Copyright ©2015 Pearson Education, Inc.

11.52   (f)   Excel Output for the one-factor ANOVA:
cont.

ANOVA						
Source of Variation	**SS**	**df**	**MS**	**F**	**P-value**	**F crit**
Between Groups	134.3488	3	44.7829	5.6998	0.0027	2.8663
Within Groups	282.8510	36	7.8570			
Total	417.1998	39				
					Level of significance	0.05

H_0: $\mu_1 = \mu_2 = \mu_3 = \mu_4$ H_1: At least one mean differs.

Decision: Since $F_{STAT} = 5.6998 > 2.8663$, reject H_0. There is adequate evidence to conclude that there is an effect due to suppliers.

Output of Tukey-Kramer Procedure:

Tukey-Kramer Multiple Comparisons								
Group	**Sample Mean**	**Sample Size**		**Comparison**	**Absolute Difference**	**Std. Error of Difference**	**Critical Range**	**Results**
1: Supplier 1	18.97	10		Group 1 to Group 2	4.93	0.88639564	3.3594	Means are different
2: Supplier 2	23.9	10		Group 1 to Group 3	3.44	0.88639564	3.3594	Means are different
3: Supplier 3	22.41	10		Group 1 to Group 4	1.86	0.88639564	3.3594	Means are not different
4: Supplier 4	20.83	10		Group 2 to Group 3	1.49	0.88639564	3.3594	Means are not different
				Group 2 to Group 4	3.07	0.88639564	3.3594	Means are not different
Other Data				Group 3 to Group 4	1.58	0.88639564	3.3594	Means are not different
Level of significance	0.05							
Numerator d.f.	4							
Denominator d.f.	36							
MSW	7.856972							
Q Statistic	3.79							

The result is consistent with that in (b) and (e) except the Turkey-Kramer Procedure in the one-way ANOVA concludes that not only there is a difference in mean strength between supplier 1 and supplier 2, but there is also a difference in mean strength between supplier 1 and suppler 3.

11.54   (a)   To test the homogeneity of variance, you perform a Levene's Test.

H_0: $\sigma_1^2 = \sigma_2^2 = \sigma_3^2$ H_1: Not all σ_j^2 are the same

Excel output:

ANOVA						
Source of Variation	*SS*	*df*	*MS*	*F*	*P-value*	*F crit*
Between Groups	0.07	2	0.035	0.07468	0.928383	3.682317
Within Groups	7.03	15	0.468667			
Total	7.1	17				

Since the p-value = 0.928 > 0.05, do not reject H_0. There is not enough evidence of a significant difference in the variances of the breaking strengths for the three air-jet pressures.

Copyright ©2015 Pearson Education, Inc.

11.54   (b) H_0: $\mu_1 = \mu_2 = \mu_3$ H_1: At least one of the means differs.
cont.   Decision rule: If $F_{STAT} > 3.68$, reject H_0.

One-way ANOVA: BreakStr versus Pressure

```
Source      DF      SS      MS      F       P
Pressure    2     8.074   4.037   4.09   0.038
Error       15   14.815   0.988
Total       17   22.889
```

```
S = 0.9938   R-Sq = 35.28%   R-Sq(adj) = 26.65%
```

Test statistic: $F_{STAT} = 4.09$

Decision: Since $F_{STAT} = 4.09$ is greater than the critical bound of 3.68, reject H_0.
There is enough evidence to conclude that the mean breaking strengths differ for the
three air-jet pressures.

   (c) $Q_\alpha = 3.67$

```
Tukey 95% Simultaneous Confidence Intervals
All Pairwise Comparisons among Levels of Pressure

Individual confidence level = 97.97%


Pressure = 30 subtracted from:

Pressure    Lower    Center    Upper    -----+---------+---------+---------
+-----
40         -2.7890   -1.3000   0.1890      (------------*------------)
50         -3.0057   -1.5167  -0.0277   (------------*------------)
                                         -----+---------+---------+---------
+-----
                                         -2.4      -1.2      0.0       1.2


Pressure = 40 subtracted from:

Pressure    Lower    Center    Upper    -----+---------+---------+---------+-
---
50         -1.7057   -0.2167   1.2723            (------------*------------)
                                         -----+---------+---------+---------+-
---
                                         -2.4      -1.2      0.0       1.2
```

$$\text{critical range} = Q_\alpha \sqrt{\frac{MSW}{2}\left(\frac{1}{n_j} + \frac{1}{n_{j'}}\right)} = 3.67 \sqrt{\frac{0.988}{2}\left(\frac{1}{6} + \frac{1}{6}\right)} = 1.489$$

The pair of means that differs at the 0.05 level is marked with * below.

$\left|\bar{X}_{30} - \bar{X}_{40}\right| = 1.30$ $\left|\bar{X}_{30} - \bar{X}_{50}\right| = 1.516*$ $\left|\bar{X}_{40} - \bar{X}_{50}\right| = 0.216$

Breaking strength scores under 30 psi are significantly higher than those under 50
psi.

   (d)   Other things being equal, use 30 psi.

Copyright ©2015 Pearson Education, Inc.

11.56   Two-way ANOVA output from Excel:
ANOVA

Source of Variation	SS	Df	MS	F	P-value	F crit
Sample	112.5603	1	112.5603	30.4434	3.07E-06	4.113165
Columns	46.01025	1	46.01025	12.4441	0.001165	4.113165
Interaction	0.70225	1	0.70225	0.1899	0.665575	4.113165
Within	133.105	36	3.697361			
Total	292.3778	39				

(a) H_0: There is no interaction between type of breakfast and desired time.
H_1: There is an interaction between type of breakfast and desired time.
Decision rule: If $F_{STAT} > 4.1132$, reject H_0.
Test statistic: $F_{STAT} = 0.1899$.
Decision: Since $F_{STAT} = 0.1899$ is less than the critical bound of 4.1132, do not reject H_0. There is insufficient evidence to conclude that there is any interaction between type of breakfast and desired time.

(b) H_0: $\mu_1 = \mu_2$ H_1: $\mu_1 \neq \mu_2$ Population 1 = Continental, 2 = American
Decision rule: If $F_{STAT} > 4.1132$, reject H_0.
Test statistic: $F_{STAT} = 30.4434$.
Decision: Since $F_{STAT} = 30.4434$ is greater than the critical bound of 4.1132, reject H_0. There is sufficient evidence to conclude that there is an effect that is due to type of breakfast.

(c) H_0: $\mu_1 = \mu_2$ H_1: $\mu_1 \neq \mu_2$ Population 1 = Early, 2 = Late
Decision rule: If $F_{STAT} > 4.1132$, reject H_0.
Test statistic: $F_{STAT} = 12.4441$.
Decision: Since $F_{STAT} = 12.4441$ is greater than the critical bound of 4.1132, reject H_0. There is sufficient evidence to conclude that there is an effect that is due to desired time

Copyright ©2015 Pearson Education, Inc.

11.56   (d)
cont.

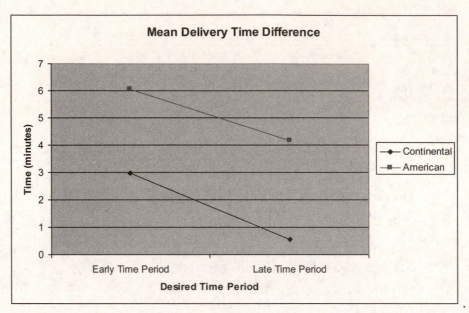

(e)   At the 5% level of significance, both the type of breakfast ordered and the desired time have an effect on delivery time difference. There is no interaction between the type of breakfast ordered and the desired time.

11.58 H_0: There is no interaction between the size of the pieces and the can fill height.
             H_1: There is an interaction between the size of the pieces and the can fill height.
             Decision rule: If p-value < 0.05, reject H_0.

ANOVA

Source of Variation	SS	df	MS	F	P-value	F crit
Sample	100.6658	1	100.6658	842.2242	7.2E-43	3.96676
Columns	25.94642	1	25.94642	217.0816	5.61E-24	3.96676
Interaction	0.02592	1	0.02592	0.216861	0.642774	3.96676
Within	9.08381	76	0.119524			
Total	135.722	79				

Test statistic: $F_{STAT} = 0.2169$
Decision: Since p-value is 0.6428, do not reject H_0. There is not sufficient evidence to conclude there is an interaction between the size of the pieces and the can fill height.

H_0: $\mu_1 = \mu_2$ H_1: $\mu_1 \neq \mu_2$ Populations: 1 = low fill, 2 = current

ANOVA

Source of Variation	SS	df	MS	F	P-value	F crit
Between Groups	25.94642	1	25.94642	18.43598	5.01E-05	3.963472
Within Groups	109.7756	78	1.407379			
Total	135.722	79				

Copyright ©2015 Pearson Education, Inc.

11.58
cont.

Decision rule: If p-value < 0.05, reject H_0.

Test statistic: $F_{STAT} = 18.4360$

Decision: Since p-value is virtually 0, reject H_0. There is evidence of an effect due to fill height. The low fill height has a lower difference in coded weight.

H_0: $\mu_1 = \mu_2$ H_1: $\mu_1 \neq \mu_2$.   Populations: 1 = fine piece size, 2 = current

ANOVA

Source of Variation	SS	df	MS	F	P-value	F crit
Between Groups	100.6658	1	100.6658	223.9817	1.23E-24	3.963472
Within Groups	35.05615	78	0.449438			
Total	135.722	79				

Decision rule: If p-value < 0.05, reject H_0.

Test statistic: $F_{STAT} = 223.9817$

Decision: Since p-value is virtually 0, reject H_0. There is evidence of an effect due to piece size. The fine piece size has a lower difference in coded weight.

11.60 **1-year Returns:**

Population 1 = Short-term, 2 = Long-term, 3 = World

The design of the experiment satisfies the randomness and independence requirement for a one-way F test.

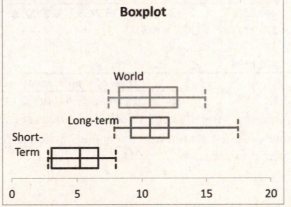

The boxplots reveal that the 1-year returns of short-term bond funds and long-term bond funds are somewhat right-skewed, hence, a violation of the normality assumption needed for the one-way F test to be valid.

To test the homogeneity of variance, you perform a Levene's Test

Copyright ©2015 Pearson Education, Inc.

11.60 $H_0: \sigma_1^2 = \sigma_2^2 = \sigma_3^2$ $\qquad\qquad$ $H_1:$ Not all σ_j^2 are the same
cont.

Output of the Levene test:

ANOVA

Source of Variation	SS	df	MS	F	P-value	F crit
Between Groups	3.3749	2	1.6875	0.6661	0.5220	3.3541
Within Groups	68.4042	27	2.5335			
Total	71.7791	29				
				Level of significance		0.05

Test statistic: $F_{STAT} = 0.6661$ $\qquad\qquad$ p-value $= 0.5220$

Decision: Since the p-value $= 0.5220 > 0.05$, do not reject H_0. There is insufficient evidence to show a difference in the variance of return among the 3 different types of bond funds at a 5% level of significance.

Since the data for the 1-year returns of short-term bond funds and long-term bond funds are right-skewed, a nonparametric test like the Kruskal-Wallis rank test described in Chapter 12 might be more appropriate.

A one-way F test yields the following results.

$H_0: \mu_1 = \mu_2 = \mu_3$ $\qquad$ $H_1:$ Not all μ_j are the same

Decision rule: If p-value > 0.05, reject H_0.

ANOVA

Source of Variation	SS	df	MS	F	P-value	F crit
Between Groups	244.4213	2	122.2106	18.7258	0.0000	3.3541
Within Groups	176.2111	27	6.5263			
Total	420.6324	29				
				Level of significance		0.05

Test statistic: $F_{STAT} = 18.7258$ $\qquad\qquad$ p-value $= 0.0000$

Decision: Since the p-value is virtually zero, reject H_0. There is sufficient evidence to show a difference in the mean 1-year returns among the 3 different types of bond funds at a 5% level of significance.

11.60   PHStat output for the Tukey-Kramer procedure:
cont.

Tukey-Kramer Multiple Comparisons

Group	Sample Mean	Sample Size		Comparison	Absolute Difference	Std. Error of Difference	Critical Range	Results
1: Short-Term	5.046	10		Group 1 to Group 2	6.319	0.807857477	2.8194	Means are different
2: Long-term	11.365	10		Group 1 to Group 3	5.751	0.807857477	2.8194	Means are different
3: World	10.797	10		Group 2 to Group 3	0.568	0.807857477	2.8194	Means are not different

Other Data	
Level of significance	0.05
Numerator d.f.	3
Denominator d.f.	27
MSW	6.526337
Q Statistic	3.49

At the 5% level of significance, there is sufficient evidence that the mean one-year returns of the long-term bond funds and world funds is significantly higher than that of the short-term bond funds.

3-year Returns:

Population 1 = Short-term, 2 = Long-term, 3 = World
The design of the experiment satisfies the randomness and independence requirement for a one-way F test.

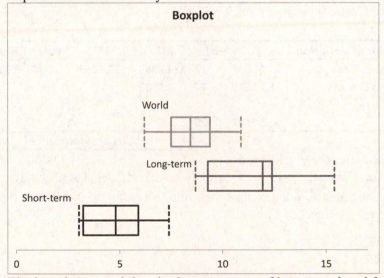

The boxplots reveal that the 3-year returns of long-term bond funds and short-term bond funds are right-skewed, hence, a violation of the normality assumption needed for the one-way F test to be valid.

Copyright ©2015 Pearson Education, Inc.

11.60
cont.

To test the homogeneity of variance, you perform a Levene's Test

$H_0: \sigma_1^2 = \sigma_2^2 = \sigma_3^2 = \sigma_4^2 = \sigma_5^2$ H_1: Not all σ_j^2 are the same

ANOVA						
Source of Variation	*SS*	*df*	*MS*	*F*	*P-value*	*F crit*
Between Groups	2.1407	2	1.0703	1.0557	0.3619	3.3541
Within Groups	27.3730	27	1.0138			
Total	29.5137	29				
					Level of significance	0.05

Test statistic: $F_{STAT} = 1.0557$ p-value $= 0.3619$

Decision: Since the p-value $= 0.3619 > 0.05$, do not reject H_0. There is insufficient evidence to show a difference in the variance of return among the 3 different types of bond funds at a 5% level of significance.   The equal variance assumption of one-way ANOVA F test is holding up.

Since the data for the 3-year returns of long-term bond funds and short-term bond funds are right-skewed, a nonparametric test like the Kruskal-Wallis rank test described in Chapter 12 might be more appropriate.

A one-way F test yields the following results.

$H_0: \mu_1 = \mu_2 = \mu_3$ H_1: Not all μ_j are the same

Decision rule: If p-value > 0.05, reject H_0.

ANOVA						
Source of Variation	*SS*	*df*	*MS*	*F*	*P-value*	*F crit*
Between Groups	229.3687	2	114.6843	37.1365	0.0000	3.3541
Within Groups	83.3810	27	3.0882			
Total	312.7497	29				
					Level of significance	0.05

Test statistic: $F_{STAT} = 37.1365$ p-value $= 0.0000$

Decision: Since the p-value is virtually zero, reject H_0. There is sufficient evidence to show a difference in the mean 3-year returns among the 3 different types of bond funds at a 5% level of significance.

Copyright ©2015 Pearson Education, Inc.

11.60   PHStat output for the Tukey-Kramer procedure:
cont.

Tukey-Kramer Multiple Comparisons									
Group	Sample Mean	Sample Size		Comparison	Absolute Difference	Std. Error of Difference	Critical Range	Results	
1: Short-term	4.82	10		Group 1 to Group 2	6.77	0.555714422	1.9394	Means are different	
2: Long-term	11.59	10		Group 1 to Group 3	3.56	0.555714422	1.9394	Means are different	
3: World	8.38	10		Group 2 to Group 3	3.21	0.555714422	1.9394	Means are different	

Other Data	
Level of significance	0.05
Numerator d.f.	3
Denominator d.f.	27
MSW	3.088185
Q Statistic	3.49

At the 5% level of significance, there is sufficient evidence that the mean three-year returns of the short-term bond funds is significantly lower than the world bond funds, which in turn is significantly lower than the long-term bond funds.

Copyright ©2015 Pearson Education, Inc.

CHAPTER 12

OBJECTIVES

- To learn when to use the chi-square test for contingency tables
- To learn to use the Marascuilo procedure for determining pairwise differences when evaluating more than two proportions
- To learn to use nonparametric tests

OVERVIEW AND KEY CONCEPTS

χ^2 Test for Differences in Two Proportions (Independent Samples)

- **Assumptions:**
    - Independent samples
    - Large sample sizes: All expected frequencies ≥ 5.
- **Test statistic:**

    - $$\chi^2 = \sum_{\text{All Cells}} \frac{\left(f_0 - f_e\right)^2}{f_e} \text{ with 1 degree of freedom}$$

        where

        f_o = observed frequency in a cell

        f_e = [(row total)(column total)]/n : expected frequency in a cell

    - The rejection region is always in the right tail.

χ^2 Test for Differences among More Than Two Proportions

- **Assumptions:**
    - Independent samples
    - Large sample sizes: All expected frequencies ≥ 1.
- **Test statistic:**

    - $$\chi^2 = \sum_{\text{All Cells}} \frac{\left(f_0 - f_e\right)^2}{f_e} \text{ with } \left(c - 1\right) \text{ degree of freedom}$$

        where

        f_o = observed frequency in a cell

        f_e = [(row total)(column total)]/n: expected frequency in a cell.

    - The rejection region is always in the right tail.

Marascuilo Procedure

- Enable one to make comparison between all pairs of groups.
- **The Marascuilo multiple comparison procedure:**

1. Compute the absolute differences $\left| p_j - p_j \right|$ among all pairs of groups.

Copyright ©2015 Pearson Education, Inc.

2.   The critical range for a pair where $j \neq j^{'}$ is $\sqrt{\chi_{\alpha}^{2}} \sqrt{\dfrac{p_{j}\left(1-p_{j}\right)}{n_{j}} + \dfrac{p_{j^{'}}\left(1-p_{j^{'}}\right)}{n_{j^{'}}}}$ where

χ_{α}^{2} is the upper-tail critical value from a χ^{2} distribution with $(c-1)$ degrees of freedom.

3.   A specific pair is considered significantly different if $\left|p_{j}-p_{j^{'}}\right| >$ critical range.

χ^{2} Test of Independence

- **Assumptions:**
  - One sample is drawn with two factors; each factor has two or more levels (categories) of responses.
  - Large sample sizes: All expected frequencies ≥ 1.
- **Test statistic:**
  - $\chi^{2} = \displaystyle\sum_{\text{All Cells}} \dfrac{\left(f_{0}-f_{e}\right)^{2}}{f_{e}}$ with $(r-1)(c-1)$ degrees of freedom

    where

    f_{o} = observed frequency in a cell

    f_{e} = [(row total)(column total)]/n: expected frequency in a cell

    r = the number of rows in the contingency table.

    c = the number of columns in the contingency table.

  - The rejection region is always in the right tail.
  - The χ^{2} test does not show the nature of any relationship nor causality.

Wilcoxon Rank Sum Test for Difference in Two Medians $\left(M_{1}-M_{2}\right)$

- **Assumptions:**
  - Both populations do not need to be normally distributed. It is a distribution free procedure.
  - The two samples are randomly and independently drawn.
  - The test is also appropriate when only ordinal data is available.
- **Test procedure:**
  1.   Assign ranks, $R_{1}, R_{2}, \cdots, R_{n_{1}+n_{2}}$, to each of the $n_{1}+n_{2}$ sample observations.

      - If sample sizes are not the same, let n_{1} refer to the smaller sample size.
      - Assign average rank for any ties.
  2.   Compute the sum of the ranks, T_{1} and T_{2}, for each of the two samples.
  3.   Test statistic: The sum of ranks of the smaller sample, T_{1}.
  4.   Obtain the critical value(s), T_{1L}, T_{1U} or both, from a table.
  5.   Compare the test statistic T_{1} to the critical value(s).
  6.   Make a statistical decision.
  7.   Draw a conclusion.

Copyright ©2015 Pearson Education, Inc.

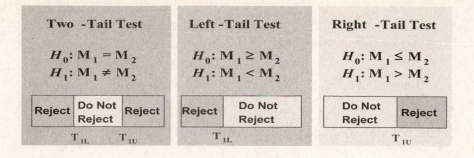

Wilcoxon Rank Sum Test for Difference in Two Medians $(M_1 - M_2)$, Large Sample

- **Test statistic:**
    - For large sample (at least one sample size > 10), the test statistic T_1 is approximately normally distributed with mean $\mu_{T_1} = \dfrac{n_1(n+1)}{2}$ and standard deviation

$$\sigma_{T_1} = \sqrt{\dfrac{n_1 n_2 (n+1)}{12}} \text{ where } n_1 \leq n_2 \text{ and } n = n_1 + n_2$$

    - $Z = \dfrac{T_1 - \mu_{T_1}}{\sigma_{T_1}}$ has a standard normal distribution.

The Kruskal-Wallis Rank Test: Nonparametric Analysis for the One-Way ANOVA

- It is used to analyze the completely randomized design.
- This is an extension of the Wilcoxon rank sum test for difference in two medians.
- It is a distribution free test procedure without any distribution assumption on the population.
- **The null and alternative hypotheses:**
    - $H_0 : M_1 = M_2 = \cdots = M_c$
    - H_1 : Not all M_j are the same.

- **Assumptions:**
    - Samples are randomly and independently drawn.
    - The dependent variable is a continuous variable.
    - Data may be ranked both within and among samples.
    - Each sample group size is greater than five.
    - The populations have the same variation and shape.
    - The test is robust to the same variation and shape assumption.
- **The Kruskal-Wallis rank test procedure:**
1. Obtain the ranks of the observations.
2. Add the ranks for each of the c groups.
3. Compute the H statistic: $H = \left[\dfrac{12}{n(n+1)} \sum\limits_{j=1}^{c} \dfrac{T_j^2}{n_j} \right] - 3(n+1)$ where $n = n_1 + n_2 + \cdots + n_c$.
4. The distribution of the H test statistic can be approximated by a χ^2 distribution with $(c-1)$ degrees of freedom if each sample group size is greater than 5
5. The rejection region is in the right tail.

Copyright ©2015 Pearson Education, Inc.

Online Topic: McNemar Test for the Difference between Two Proportions (Related Samples)

- **Assumptions:**
  - Related samples; repeated measurements on the same set of respondents
- **Test statistic:**

  - $$Z = \frac{B - C}{\sqrt{B + C}}$$

    where

    B: number of respondents that answer yes to condition 1 and no to condition 2

    C: number of respondents that answer no to condition 1 and yes to condition 2
  - The test statistic Z is approximately distributed as a standardized normal distribution.
  - The alternative hypothesis can be one-tail with a right-tail rejection region, one-tail with a left-tail rejection region or two-tail with both right-tail and left-tail rejection regions.

Online Topic: χ^2 Test for the Population Variance $\left(\sigma^2\right)$ or Standard Deviation (σ)

- **Assumption:**
  - Population is normally distributed.
- **Test statistic:**

  - $\chi^2 = \dfrac{(n-1)S^2}{\sigma^2}$ with $(n-1)$ degrees of freedom.

  - The alternative hypothesis can be one-tail with a right-tail rejection region, one-tail with a left-tail rejection region or two-tail with both right-tail and left-tail rejection regions.

Online Topic: Wilcoxon Signed Ranks Test for Median Difference $\left(M_D\right)$: A Nonparametric Test for Two Related Populations

- **Assumptions:**
  - The observed data either constitute a random sample of n independent items or individuals, each with two measurements, one taken before and the other taken after the presentation of some treatment or the observed data constitute a random sample of n independent pairs of items or individuals with values for each member of the match pair ($i = 1, 2, …, n$).
  - The underlying variable of interest is continuous.
  - The observed data are measured on an ordinal, interval or ratio level.
  - The distribution of the population of difference scores between repeated measurements or between matched items or individuals is approximately symmetric.
- **Test procedure:**
  1. For each item in a sample of n items, compute a difference score D_i between the two paired values.
  2. Neglect the "+" and "−" signs and compute a set of n absolute differences $|D_i|$.
  3. Omit from further analysis any absolute difference score of zero, thereby yielding a set of n' nonzero absolute difference scores, where $n' \le n$. After you remove values with absolute difference scores of zero, n' becomes the actual sample size.

Copyright ©2015 Pearson Education, Inc.

4.   Assign ranks R_i from 1 to n' to each of the $|D_i|$ such that the smallest absolute difference score gets rank 1 and the largest gets rank n'. If two or more $|D_i|$ are equal, assign each of them the mean of the ranks they would have been assigned individually had ties in the data not occurred.

5.   Reassign the symbol "+" or "−" to each of the n' ranks R_i, depending on whether D_i was originally positive or negative.

6.   Compute the Wilcoxon test statistic W as the sum of the positive ranks:

$$W = \sum_{i=1}^{n'} R_i^{(+)}.$$

7.   For small sample size, $n' \le 20$, obtain the critical value(s), W_L, W_U or both, from Table 12.19.

8.   Compare the test statistic W to the critical value(s).

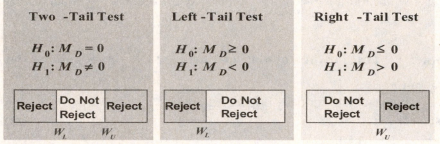

9.   Make a statistical decision.
10. Draw a conclusion.

Online Topic: Wilcoxon Signed Rank Test for Median Difference (M_D), Large Sample

- **Test statistic:**
  - For large sample $(n' > 20)$, the test statistic W is approximately normally distributed with mean $\mu_W = \dfrac{n'(n'+1)}{4}$ and standard deviation $\sigma_W = \sqrt{\dfrac{n'(n'+1)(2n'+1)}{24}}$

  - $Z_{STAT} = \dfrac{W - \mu_W}{\sigma_W}$ has a standard normal distribution.

Online Topic: Friedman Rank Test: Nonparametric Analysis for the Randomized Block Design

- It is used to analyze a randomized block design.
- It is a distribution free test procedure without any distribution assumption on the population.
- It can be used when the data collected are only in rank form within each block.
- **The null and alternative hypotheses:**
  - $H_0 : M_{.1} = M_{.2} = \cdots = M_{.c}$
  - H_1: Not all $M_{.j}$ are the same.
- **Assumptions:**
  - The r blocks are independent.
  - The underlying random variable of interest is continuous.

Copyright ©2015 Pearson Education, Inc.

  ▪ The observed data constitute at least an ordinal scale of measurement within **each of** the r blocks.
  ▪ There is no interaction between the r blocks and the c treatment levels.
  ▪ The c populations have the same variability.
  ▪ The c populations have the same shape.

- **The Friedman rank test procedure:**

1. In each of the r independent blocks, the c observations are replaced by their corresponding ranks such that rank 1 is given to the smallest observation in the block **and** rank c to the largest. If any values in a block are tied, they are assigned the average **of** the ranks that they would otherwise have been given.

2. **Test statistic:** $F_R = \dfrac{12}{rc(c+1)} \displaystyle\sum_{j=1}^{c} R_{\cdot j}^2 - 3r(c+1)$

   where $R_{\cdot j}^2$ is the square of the rank total for group j ($j = 1, 2, \ldots, c$)

   r is the number of independent blocks
   c is the number of groups or treatment levels

3. F_R can be approximated by the chi-square distribution with $(c-1)$ degrees of **freedom** when $r > 5$.

4. The rejection region is in the right tail.

Copyright ©2015 Pearson Education, Inc.

SOLUTIONS TO END OF SECTION
AND CHAPTER REVIEW EVEN PROBLEMS

12.2 (a)   For $df = 1$ and $\alpha = 0.05$, $\chi^2 = 3.841$.

     (b)   For $df = 1$ and $\alpha = 0.025$, $\chi^2 = 5.024$.

     (c)   For $df = 1$ and $\alpha = 0.01$, $\chi^2 = 6.635$.

12.4 (a)

Observed Freq	*Expected Freq*	Observed Freq	*Expected Freq*	Total Obs, Row 1
20	25	30	25	50
chi-sq contrib= 1.00		chi-sq contrib= 1.00		
Observed Freq	*Expected Freq*	Observed Freq	*Expected Freq*	Total Obs, Row 2
30	25	20	25	50
chi-sq contrib= 1.00		chi-sq contrib= 1.00		
Total Obs, Col 1		Total Obs, Col 2		GRAND TOTAL
50		50		100

     (b)   Decision rule: If $\chi^2 > 3.841$, reject H_0.

Test statistic: $\chi^2_{STAT} = \sum_{\text{All Cells}} \frac{(f_0 - f_e)^2}{f_e} = 1.00 + 1.00 + 1.00 + 1.00 = 4$

Decision: Since $\chi^2_{STAT} = \sum_{\text{All Cells}} \frac{(f_0 - f_e)^2}{f_e} = 4$ is greater than the critical value of 3.841,

it is significant at the 5% level of significance.

Copyright ©2015 Pearson Education, Inc.

12.6   PHStat output:

Chi-Square Test			

Observed Frequencies			
	Correctly Recall the Brand		
Arrival Method	Yes	No	Total
Recommendation	407	150	557
Browsing	193	91	284
Total	600	241	841

Expected Frequencies			
	Correctly Recall the Brand		
Arrival Method	Yes	No	Total
Recommendation	397.3840666	159.6159334	557
Browsing	202.6159334	81.38406659	284
Total	600	241	841

Data	
Level of Significance	0.05
Number of Rows	2
Number of Columns	2
Degrees of Freedom	1

Results	
Critical Value	3.841458821
Chi-Square Test Statistic	2.404523655
p-Value	0.120984946
Do not reject the null hypothesis	

(a) H_0: $\pi_1 = \pi_2$ H_1: $\pi_1 \neq \pi_2$

(b)   Decision rule: $df = 1$. If $\chi^2_{STAT} > 3.8415$ or p-value < 0.05, reject H_0.

Test statistic: $\chi^2_{STAT} = 2.4045$

Decision: Since $\chi^2_{STAT} = 2.4045$ is less than the upper critical bound of 3.8415, do not reject H_0. There is not enough evidence a difference in brand recall between viewers who arrived by following a social media recommendation and those who arrived by web browsing.

(c)   You should not compare the results in (a) to those of Problem 10.30 part (b) because Problem 10.30 was a one-tail test.

Copyright ©2015 Pearson Education, Inc.

12.8   (a) $H_0: \pi_1 = \pi_2$ $H_1: \pi_1 \ne \pi_2$

PHStat output with computation:

Chi-Square Test			
Observed Frequencies			
		Customers	
Use Credit Card	Superbanked	Unbanked	Total
Yes	930	230	1160
No	70	770	840
Total	1000	1000	2000

Expected Frequencies			
		Customers	
Use Credit Card	Superbanked	Unbanked	Total
Yes	580	580	1160
No	420	420	840
Total	1000	1000	2000

Data	
Level of Significance	0.01
Number of Rows	2
Number of Columns	2
Degrees of Freedom	1

Results	
Critical Value	6.634896601
Chi-Square Test Statistic	1005.747126
p-Value	1.0117E-220
Reject the null hypothesis	

Decision rule: $df = 1$. If $\chi^2_{STAT} > 6.6349$, reject H_0.

Test statistic: $\chi^2_{STAT} = \sum_{\text{All Cells}} \dfrac{(f_0 - f_e)^2}{f_e} = 1005.7471$

Decision: Since $\chi^2_{STAT} = 1005.7471$ is greater than the upper critical bound of 6.6349, reject H_0. There is enough evidence of a significant difference between the Superbanked and the Unbanked with respect to the proportion that use credit cards.

(b)   p-value is virtually 0. The probability of obtaining a difference in proportions that gives rise to a test statistic above 1,005.7471 is 0.0000 if there is no difference in the proportion of Superbanked and Unbanked who use credit cards..

(c)   The results of (a) and (b) are exactly the same as those of Problem 10.32. The χ^2_{STAT} in (a) and the Z_{STAT} in Problem 10.32 (a) satisfy the relationship that $\chi^2_{STAT} = 1005.7471 = (Z_{STAT})^2 = (31.7135)^2$ and the p-value in Problem 10.32 (b) is exactly the same as the p-value obtained in (b).

12.10   (a), (b) $H_0: \pi_1 = \pi_2$ $H_1: \pi_1 \neq \pi_2$

PHStat output with computation:

Chi-Square Test

	Observed Frequencies		
	gamification-user organizations		
provide mobile access to CRM	Yes	No	Total
Yes	31	138	169
No	6	137	143
Total	37	275	312

	Expected Frequencies		
	gamification-user organizations		
provide mobile access to CRM	Yes	No	Total
Yes	20.04166667	148.9583333	169
No	16.95833333	126.0416667	143
Total	37	275	312

Data	
Level of Significance	0.05
Number of Rows	2
Number of Columns	2
Degrees of Freedom	1

Results	
Critical Value	3.841458821
Chi-Square Test Statistic	14.83186062
p-Value	0.000117533
Reject the null hypothesis	

Decision rule: $df = 1$. If $\chi^2_{STAT} > 3.841$, reject H_0.

Test statistic: $\chi^2_{STAT} = \sum_{\text{All Cells}} \dfrac{(f_0 - f_e)^2}{f_e} = 14.8319$

Decision: Since $\chi^2_{STAT} = 14.8319 > 3.841$, reject H_0. There is enough evidence of a difference between gamification-user sales organizations and non-gamification-user sales organizations in the proportion that provide mobile access to CRM.

(c)   *p*-value = 0.0001. The probability of obtaining a test statistic of = 14.8319 or larger when the null hypothesis is true is 0.0001.

(d)   The results of (a) and (b) are exactly the same as those of Problem 10.34. The χ^2_{STAT} in (a) and the Z_{STAT} in Problem 10.34 (a) satisfy the relationship that $\chi^2_{STAT} = $ $14.8319 = (Z_{STAT})^2 = (3.8512)^2$ and the *p*-value in Problem 10.34 (b) is exactly the same as the *p*-value obtained in (b).

12.12   (a)   The expected frequencies in the first row are 20, 30, and 40.
The expected frequencies in the second row are 30, 45, and 60.

(b) $\chi^2_{STAT} = 12.500$. The critical value with 2 degrees of freedom and $\alpha = 0.05$ is 5.991.
The result is deemed significant.

12.14   PHStat output:

Chi-Square Test

		Observed Frequencies						
		Age Groups						
Buy Lunch		18 to 24	25 to 34	35 to 44	45 to 54	55 to 64	65+	Total
	Yes	150	154	144	116	114	110	788
	No	50	46	56	84	86	90	412
	Total	200	200	200	200	200	200	1200

		Expected Frequencies						
		Age Groups						
Buy Lunch		18 to 24	25 to 34	35 to 44	45 to 54	55 to 64	65+	Total
	Yes	131.3333	131.3333	131.3333	131.3333	131.3333	131.3333	788
	No	68.66667	68.66667	68.66667	68.66667	68.66667	68.66667	412
	Total	200	200	200	200	200	200	1200

Data	
Level of Significance	0.05
Number of Rows	2
Number of Columns	6
Degrees of Freedom	5

Results	
Critical Value	11.0705
Chi-Square Test Statistic	44.65034
p-Value	1.71E-08
Reject the null hypothesis	

(a) $H_0: \pi_1 = \pi_2 = \pi_3 = \pi_4 = \pi_5 = \pi_6$ $H_1:$ Not all π_j are equal.

Test statistic: $\chi^2_{STAT} = \sum_{\text{All Cells}} \frac{(f_0 - f_e)^2}{f_e} = 44.6503$

Decision: Since the calculated test statistic 44.6503 is greater than the critical value of 11.0705, you reject H_0 and conclude that there is evidence of a difference among the age groups in the preference for lunch.

(b)   p-value is virtually zero. The probability of obtaining a data set which gives rise to a test statistic of 44.6503 or more is virtually zero if there is no difference among the age groups in the preference for lunch.

Copyright ©2015 Pearson Education, Inc.

12.14   (c)   Excel output of the Marascuilo procedure:
cont.

Marascuilo Procedure			
Level of Significance	0.05		
Square Root of Critical Value	3.327235744		
Sample Proportions			
Group 1	0.75		
Group 2	0.77		
Group 3	0.72		
Group 4	0.58		
Group 5	0.57		
Group 6	0.55		
MARASCUILO TABLE			
Proportions	**Absolute Differences**	**Critical Range**	
| Group 1 - Group 2 |	0.02	0.142061667	Not significant
| Group 1 - Group 3 |	0.03	0.146757123	Not significant
| Group 1 - Group 4 |	0.17	0.15447478	Significant
| Group 1 - Group 5 |	0.18	0.154743292	Significant
| Group 1 - Group 6 |	0.2	0.155171945	Significant
| Group 2 - Group 3 |	0.05	0.144782552	Not significant
| Group 2 - Group 4 |	0.19	0.152600105	Significant
| Group 2 - Group 5 |	0.2	0.152871909	Significant
| Group 2 - Group 6 |	0.22	0.153305794	Significant
| Group 3 - Group 4 |	0.14	0.156980661	Not significant
| Group 3 - Group 5 |	0.15	0.157244894	Not significant
| Group 3 - Group 6 |	0.17	0.157666745	Significant
| Group 4 - Group 5 |	0.01	0.164471156	Not significant
| Group 4 - Group 6 |	0.03	0.164874519	Not significant
| Group 5 - Group 6 |	0.02	0.165126121	Not significant

The 18–24 and 25–34 groups are different from the 45–54, 55–64 and 65+ groups, and the 35–44 group is different from the 65+ group.

Copyright ©2015 Pearson Education, Inc.

12.16 (a) $H_0 : \pi_1 = \pi_2 = \pi_3$, H_1 : at least one proportion differs

where population $1 = 18\text{-}34$, $2 = 35\text{-}64$, $3 = 65+$

PHStat output:

Chi-Square Test

Observed Frequencies				
	Age			
Use of Mobile Phone	**18-34**	**35-64**	**65+**	**Total**
Yes	118	72	26	216
No	82	128	174	384
Total	200	200	200	600

Expected Frequencies				
	Age			
Use of Mobile Phone	18-34	35-64	65+	Total
Yes	72	72	72	216
No	128	128	128	384
Total	200	200	200	600

Data	
Level of Significance	0.05
Number of Rows	2
Number of Columns	3
Degrees of Freedom	2

Results	
Critical Value	5.991465
Chi-Square Test Statistic	91.84028
p-Value	1.14E-20
Reject the null hypothesis	

Decision rule: $df = (c - 1) = (3 - 1) = 2$. If $\chi^2_{STAT} > 5.9915$, reject H_0.

Test statistic: $\chi^2_{STAT} = \sum_{\text{All Cells}} \frac{(f_0 - f_e)^2}{f_e} = 91.8403$

Decision: Since $\chi^2_{STAT} = 91.8403$ is greater than the upper critical bound of 5.9915, reject H_0. There is enough evidence of a difference among the age groups with respect to use of mobile phone for accessing social networking.

(b) p-value $= 0.0000$. The probability of obtaining a sample that gives rise to a test statistic that is equal to or more than 91.8403 is 0.0000 if there is no difference among the age groups with respect to use of mobile phone for accessing social networking.

Copyright ©2015 Pearson Education, Inc.

12.16   (c)
cont.

Marascuilo Procedure				
Level of Significance	0.05			
Square Root of Critical Value	2.447746831			
Sample Proportions				
Group 1	0.59			
Group 2	0.36			
Group 3	0.13			
MARASCUILO TABLE				
Proportions	Absolute Differences	Critical Range		
| Group 1 - Group 2 |	0.23	0.118948911	Significant	
| Group 1 - Group 3 |	0.46	0.103125407	Significant	
| Group 2 - Group 3 |	0.23	0.101441315	Significant	

There is a significant difference between all the groups.

(d)   Marketers can use this information to target their marketing to the 18- to 34-year-old group since they are most likely to use their cellphones to access social media..

Copyright ©2015 Pearson Education, Inc.

12.18   PHStat output:

Chi-Square Test

Observed Frequencies				
		Owners		
Use Phones	Urban	Suburban	Rural	Total
Yes	171	516	251	938
No	145	477	306	928
Total	316	993	557	1866

Expected Frequencies				
		Owners		
Use Phones	Urban	Suburban	Rural	Total
Yes	158.8467	499.1608	279.9925	938
No	157.1533	493.8392	277.0075	928
Total	316	993	557	1866

Data	
Level of Significance	0.05
Number of Rows	2
Number of Columns	3
Degrees of Freedom	2

Results	
Critical Value	5.991465
Chi-Square Test Statistic	9.048512
p-Value	0.010843
Reject the null hypothesis	

(a) $H_0: \pi_1 = \pi_2 = \pi_3$ H_1 Not all π_j are equal.

Test statistic: $\chi^2_{STAT} = \sum_{\text{All Cells}} \frac{(f_0 - f_e)^2}{f_e} = 9.0485$

Decision: Since the calculated test statistic 9.0485 is greater than the critical value of 5.9915, you reject H_0 and conclude that there is evidence of a significant difference among the urban, suburban, and rural American cellphone owners with respect to the proportion who use their phone to engage in several activities while watching TV.

(b)   p-value = 0.0108. The probability of obtaining a data set which gives rise to a test statistic of 9.0485 or more is 0.0108 if there is no difference among the urban, suburban, and rural American cellphone owners with respect to the proportion who use their phone to engage in several activities while watching TV.

Copyright ©2015 Pearson Education, Inc.

12.18   (c)   PHStat output of the Marascuilo procedure:
cont.

Marascuilo Procedure			
Level of Significance	0.05		
Square Root of Critical Value	2.447746831		
Sample Proportions			
Group 1	0.541139241		
Group 2	0.519637462		
Group 3	0.450628366		
MARASCUILO TABLE			
Proportions	Absolute Differences	Critical Range	
| Group 1 - Group 2 |	0.021501778	0.078829511	Not significant
| Group 1 - Group 3 |	0.090510874	0.085854183	Significant
| Group 2 - Group 3 |	0.069009096	0.064568146	Significant

The rural group is different from both the urban and suburban groups.

12.20 $df = (r-1)(c-1) = (3-1)(4-1) = 6$

12.22 H_0: There is no relationship between type of dessert and type of entrée.
        H_1: There is a relationship between type of dessert and type of entrée.

Test statistic: $\chi^2_{STAT} = \sum_{All\ Cells} \frac{(f_0 - f_e)^2}{f_e} = 92.1028$

Decision: Since the calculated test statistic 92.1028 is larger than the critical value of 16.9190, you reject H_0 and conclude that there is enough evidence of a relationship between type of dessert and type of entrée.

Copyright ©2015 Pearson Education, Inc.

12.24 H_0: There is no relationship between frequency of posting on Facebook and age.

H_1: There is a relationship between frequency of posting on Facebook and age.

PHStat output:

Chi-Square Test

Observed Frequencies

	AGE GROUP					
FREQUENCY	**18-22**	**23-35**	**36-49**	**50 -65**	**65+**	**Total**
Several times a day	20	22	9	2	1	54
About once a day	28	37	14	4	1	84
3–5 days per week	32	46	31	7	2	118
1–2 days per week	32	69	35	17	7	160
Every few weeks	22	66	47	28	6	169
Less often	16	59	56	61	18	210
Never	6	15	42	66	23	152
Total	156	314	234	185	58	947

Expected Frequencies

	AGE GROUP					
FREQUENCY	18-22	23-35	36-49	50 -65	65+	Total
Several times a day	8.895459	17.90496	13.34319	10.5491	3.307286	54
About once a day	13.83738	27.85216	20.75607	16.40971	5.144667	84
3–5 days per week	19.43823	39.12566	29.15734	23.05174	7.227033	118
1–2 days per week	26.35692	53.05174	39.53537	31.2566	9.799366	160
Every few weeks	27.83949	56.0359	41.75924	33.01478	10.35058	169
Less often	34.59345	69.63041	51.89018	41.02429	12.86167	210
Never	25.03907	50.39916	37.55861	29.69377	9.309398	152
Total	156	314	234	185	58	947

Data	
Level of Significance	**0.01**
Number of Rows	7
Number of Columns	5
Degrees of Freedom	24

Results	
Critical Value	42.97982
Chi-Square Test Statistic	229.7554
p-Value	1.64E-35
Reject the null hypothesis	

Copyright ©2015 Pearson Education, Inc.

12.24   Decision rule: If $\chi^2_{STAT} > 42.9798$, reject H_0.

cont.   Test statistic: $\chi^2_{STAT} = \sum\limits_{\text{All Cells}} \dfrac{(f_0 - f_e)^2}{f_e} = 229.7554$

Decision: Since $\chi^2_{STAT} = 229.7554 > 42.9798$, reject H_0. There is enough evidence to conclude there is a relationship between frequency of posting on Facebook and age.

12.26 H_0: There is no relationship between consumer segment and geographic region.
H_1: There is a relationship between consumer segment and geographic region.

Chi-Square Test

Observed Frequencies

Consumer Segment	Midwest	Northeast	South	West	Total
Optimistic	67	23	60	63	213
Cautious	101	57	127	133	418
Hunkered down	83	46	115	125	369
Total	251	126	302	321	1000

Expected Frequencies

Consumer Segment	Midwest	Northeast	South	West	Total
Optimistic	53.463	26.838	64.326	68.373	213
Cautious	104.918	52.668	126.236	134.178	418
Hunkered down	92.619	46.494	111.438	118.449	369
Total	251	126	302	321	1000

Data	
Level of Significance	0.05
Number of Rows	3
Number of Columns	4
Degrees of Freedom	6

Results	
Critical Value	12.59159
Chi-Square Test Statistic	6.687621
p-Value	0.350704
Do not reject the null hypothesis	

Decision rule: $d.f. = 6$.   If $\chi^2_{STAT} > 12.5916$ or p-value < 0.05, reject H_0.

Test statistic: $\chi^2_{STAT} = 6.6876$

Decision: Since the $\chi^2_{STAT} = 6.6876$ is lower than the critical bound of 12.5916, do not reject H_0. There is not enough evidence of a significant relationship between consumer segment and geographic region.

Copyright ©2015 Pearson Education, Inc.

12.28   (a)   The lower critical value is 31.
   (b)   The lower critical value is 29.
   (c)   The lower critical value is 27.
   (d)   The lower critical value is 25.

12.30   The lower and upper critical values are 40 and 79, respectively.

12.32   (a)   The ranks for Sample 1 are 1, 2, 4, 5, and 10, respectively.
    The ranks for Sample 2 are 3, 6.5, 6.5, 8, 9, and 11, respectively.
   (b) $T_1 = 1 + 2 + 4 + 5 + 10 = 22$
   (c) $T_2 = 3 + 6.5 + 6.5 + 8 + 9 + 11 = 44$
   (d) $T_1 + T_2 = \dfrac{n(n+1)}{2} = \dfrac{11(12)}{2} = 66 \qquad T_1 + T_2 = 22 + 44 = 66$

12.34   Decision: Since $T_1 = 22$ is greater than the lower critical bound of 20, do not reject H_0.

12.36   (a)   The data are ordinal.
   (b)   The two-sample t-test is inappropriate because the data are ordinal, the sample size is small and the distribution of the ordinal data is not normally distributed.
   (c) $H_0: M_1 = M_2$ where Populations: 1 = California,   2 = Washington
    $H_1: M_1 \neq M_2$

PHStat output:

Data	
Level of Significance	0.05
Population 1 Sample	
Sample Size	8
Sum of Ranks	47
Population 2 Sample	
Sample Size	8
Sum of Ranks	89
Intermediate Calculations	
Total Sample Size n	16
T1 Test Statistic	47
T1 Mean	68
Standard Error of T1	9.521905
Z Test Statistic	-2.20544
Two-Tailed Test	
Lower Critical Value	-1.95996
Upper Critical Value	1.959964
p-value	0.027423
Reject the null hypothesis	

(c)

$$\mu_{T1} = \frac{n_1(n+1)}{2} = \frac{8(16+1)}{2} = 68$$

$$\sigma_{T_1} = \sqrt{\frac{n_1 n_2 (n+1)}{12}} = \sqrt{\frac{8(8)(16+1)}{12}} = 9.5219$$

$$Z_{STAT} = \frac{T_1 - \mu_{T_1}}{\sigma_{T_1}} = -2.2054$$

Decision: Since $Z_{STAT} = -2.2054$ is lower than the lower critical bounds of -1.96, reject H_0. There is enough evidence of a significant difference in the median rating of California Cabernets and Washington Cabernets.

Copyright ©2015 Pearson Education, Inc.

12.38   (a) $H_0: M_1 = M_2$ where Populations: 1 = Wing A,   2 = Wing B

               $H_1: M_1 \neq M_2$

                      PHStat output:

Data	
Level of Significance	0.05
Population 1 Sample	
Sample Size	20
Sum of Ranks	561
Population 2 Sample	
Sample Size	20
Sum of Ranks	259
Intermediate Calculations	
Total Sample Size n	40
$T1$ Test Statistic	561
$T1$ Mean	410
Standard Error of $T1$	36.96846
Z Test Statistic	4.084563
Two-Tailed Test	
Lower Critical Value	-1.95996
Upper Critical Value	1.959964
p-value	4.42E-05
Reject the null hypothesis	

$$\mu_{T_1} = \frac{n_1(n+1)}{2} = \frac{20(40+1)}{2} = 410$$

$$\sigma_{T_1} = \sqrt{\frac{n_1 n_2(n+1)}{12}} = \sqrt{\frac{20(20)(40+1)}{12}} = 36.9685$$

$$Z_{STAT} = \frac{T_1 - \mu_{T_1}}{\sigma_{T_1}} = 4.0846$$

Decision: Since $Z_{STAT} = 4.0846$ is greater than the upper critical bound of 1.96, reject H_0. There is enough evidence of a difference in the median delivery time in the two wings of the hotel.

    (b)   The results of (a) conclude that there is enough evidence of a difference in the median delivery time in the two wings of the hotel while the results of Problem 10.65 conclude that there is enough evidence of a difference in the mean delivery time in the two wings of the hotel.

Copyright ©2015 Pearson Education, Inc.

12.40 (a) H_0: $M_1 = M_2$ where Populations: 1 = Technology,   2 = Financial Institutions
          H_1: $M_1 \neq M_2$

Wilcoxon Rank Sum Test	
Data	
Level of Significance	**0.05**
Population 1 Sample	
Sample Size	16
Sum of Ranks	366
Population 2 Sample	
Sample Size	22
Sum of Ranks	375
Intermediate Calculations	
Total Sample Size n	38
$T1$ Test Statistic	366
$T1$ Mean	312
Standard Error of $T1$	33.823069
Z Test Statistic	**1.5965435**
Two-Tail Test	
Lower Critical Value	**-1.9600**
Upper Critical Value	**1.9600**
p-Value	**0.1104**
Do not reject the null hypothesis	

Decision rule: If $|Z_{STAT}| > 1.96$ or p-value < 0.05, reject H_0.
Test statistic:

$$Z_{STAT} = \frac{T_1 - \mu_{T_1}}{\sigma_{T_1}} = 1.5965$$

Decision: Since $|Z_{STAT}| = |1.5965| < 1.96$, do not reject H_0. There is not enough evidence of a difference in the median brand value between the two sectors.

(b)   You must assume approximately equal variability in the two populations.

(c)   Using the pooled-variance t-test allowed you to reject the null hypothesis and conclude in Problem 10.17 that there is evidence of a difference between the technology sector and the financial institutions sector with respect to mean brand value while using the separate-variance t-test did not allow you to reject the null hypothesis and conclude in that there is not enough evidence of a difference between the technology sector and the financial institutions sector with respect to mean brand value. In this test using the Wilcoxon rank sum test with large-sample Z-approximation also allowed you to reject the null hypothesis and conclude that there is enough evidence of a difference in the median brand value between the two sectors.

12.42   (a) $H_0: M_1 = M_2$ where population 1 = Subcompact, 2 = Compact
                 $H_1: M_1 \neq M_2$
                 PHStat output:

Wilcoxon Rank Sum Test	
Data	
Level of Significance	0.05
Population 1 Sample	
Sample Size	11
Sum of Ranks	96.5
Population 2 Sample	
Sample Size	7
Sum of Ranks	74.5
Intermediate Calculations	
Total Sample Size n	18
$T1$ Test Statistic	74.5
$T1$ Mean	66.5
Standard Error of $T1$	11.041588
Z Test Statistic	0.7245335
Two-Tail Test	
Lower Critical Value	-1.9600
Upper Critical Value	1.9600
p-Value	0.4687
Do not reject the null hypothesis	

$$Z_{STAT} = \frac{T_1 - \mu_{T_1}}{\sigma_{T_1}} = 0.7245$$

Decision: Since $Z_{STAT} = 0.7245$ is between the critical bounds of -1.96 and 1.96, do not reject H_0. There is not enough evidence of a difference in the median battery life between subcompact cameras and compact cameras.

(b)   You must assume approximately equal variability in the two populations.

(c)   Using the pooled-variance t-test, you do not reject the null hypothesis ($t = -0.6181$ > -2.1190; p-value = 0.5452 > 0.05) and conclude that there is not enough evidence of a difference in the mean battery life between the two types of digital cameras in Problem 10.11(a).

12.44   (a)   Decision rule: If $H > \chi_\alpha^2 = 15.086$, reject H_0.

(b)   Decision: Since $H_{calc} = 13.77$ is less than the critical bound of 15.086, do not reject H_0.

Copyright ©2015 Pearson Education, Inc.

12.46   PHStat output of Kruskal-Wallis rank test:

Data	
Level of Significance	0.05
Group 1	
Sum of Ranks	640
Sample Size	15
Group 2	
Sum of Ranks	291
Sample Size	15
Group 3	
Sum of Ranks	468
Sample Size	15
Group 4	
Sum of Ranks	431
Sample Size	15
Intermediate Calculations	
Sum of Squared Ranks/Sample Size	59937.73
Sum of Sample Sizes	60
Number of groups	4
H Test Statistic	13.51716
Test Result	
Critical Value	7.814728
p-Value	0.003642
Reject the null hypothesis	

(a) $H_0: M_{main} = M_{Sat1} = M_{Sat2} = M_{Sat3}$ H_1: At least one of the medians differs.
Since the p-value = 0.0036 is lower than 0.05, reject H_0. There is sufficient evidence
of a difference in the median waiting time in the four locations.

(b)   The results are consistent with those of Problem 11.9.

12.48   PHStat output of Kruskal-Wallis rank test:

Data	
Level of Significance	0.05
Intermediate Calculations	
Sum of Squared Ranks/Sample Size	8705.333
Sum of Sample Sizes	30
Number of Groups	5
Test Result	
H Test Statistic	19.32688
Critical Value	9.487729
p-Value	0.000678
Reject the null hypothesis	

(a) $H_0: M_A = M_B = M_C = M_D = M_E$ H_1: At least one of the medians differs.
Since the p-value = 0.0007 < 0.05, reject H_0. There is sufficient evidence of a
difference in the median rating of the five advertisements.

(b)   In (a), you conclude that there is evidence of a difference in the median rating of the
five advertisements, while in problem 11.10 (a), you conclude that there is evidence
of a difference in the mean rating of the five advertisements.

(c)   Since the combined scores are not true continuous variables, the nonparametric
Kruskal-Wallis rank test is more appropriate because it does not require the scores to
be normally distributed.

Copyright ©2015 Pearson Education, Inc.

12.50   PHStat output:

Kruskal-Wallis Rank Test for Differences in Medians

Data	
Level of Significance	0.05

Intermediate Calculations	
Sum of Squared Ranks/Sample Size	19821.55
Sum of Sample Sizes	40
Number of Groups	4

Test Result	
H Test Statistic	22.03573171
Critical Value	7.814727903
p-Value	6.41239E-05
Reject the null hypothesis	

Group	Sample Size	Sum of Ranks	Mean Ranks
1	10	57.5	5.75
2	10	255.5	25.55
3	10	277	27.7
4	10	230	23

(a) H_0: $M_1 = M_2 = M_3 = M_4$ H_1: At least one of the medians differs.
Since the p-value is virtually zero, reject H_0. There is sufficient evidence of a
difference in the median cost associated with importing a standardized cargo of
goods by sea transport.

(b)   In (a), you conclude that there is sufficient evidence of a difference in the median
cost associated with importing a standardized cargo of goods by sea transport while
in problem 11.8, you conclude that there is sufficient evidence of a difference in the
mean cost associated with importing a standardized cargo of goods by sea transport.

12.52   The Chi-square test can be used for c populations as long as all expected frequencies are at
least one.

12.54   The Wilcoxon rank sum test should be used when you are unable to assume that each of two
independent populations are normally distributed.

12.56   (a) H_0: There is no relationship between a student's gender and his/her pizzeria selection.
H_1: There is a relationship between a student's gender and his/her pizzeria selection.
Decision rule: $d.f. = 1$. If $\chi^2_{STAT} > 3.841$, reject H_0.   Test statistic: $\chi^2_{STAT} = 0.412$

Decision: Since the $\chi^2_{STAT} = 0.412$ is smaller than the critical bound of 3.841, do not
reject H_0. There is not enough evidence to conclude that there is a relationship
between a student's gender and his/her pizzeria selection.

(b)   Test statistic: $\chi^2_{STAT} = 2.624$

Decision: Since the $\chi^2_{STAT} = 2.624$ is less than the critical bound of 3.841, do not
reject H_0. There is not enough evidence to conclude that there is a relationship
between a student's gender and his/her pizzeria selection.

Copyright ©2015 Pearson Education, Inc.

12.56   (c) H_0: There is no relationship between price and pizzeria selection.
cont. H_1: There is a relationship between price and pizzeria selection.

Decision rule: $d.f. = 2$.   If $\chi^2_{STAT} > 5.991$, reject H_0.   Test statistic: $\chi^2_{STAT} = 4.956$

Decision: Since the $\chi^2_{STAT} = 4.956$ is smaller than the critical bound of 5.991, do not reject H_0. There is not enough evidence to conclude that there is a relationship between price and pizzeria selection.

(d) p-value = 0.0839. The probability of obtaining a sample that gives a test statistic equal to or greater than 4.956 is 0.0839 if the null hypothesis of no relationship between price and pizzeria selection is true.

12.58   (a) H_0: There is no relationship between the attitudes of employees toward the use of self-managed work teams and employee job classification.
H_1: There is a relationship between the attitudes of employees toward the use of self-managed work teams and employee job classification.

Decision rule: If $\chi^2_{STAT} > 12.592$, reject H_0.

Test statistic: $\chi^2_{STAT} = 11.895$

Decision: Since $\chi^2_{STAT} = 11.895$ is less than the critical bound 12.592, do not reject H_0. There is not enough evidence to conclude that there is a relationship between the attitudes of employees toward the use of self-managed work teams and employee job classification.

(b) H_0: There is no relationship between the attitudes of employees toward vacation time without pay and employee job classification.
H_1: There is a relationship between the attitudes of employees toward vacation time without pay and employee job classification.

Decision rule: If $\chi^2_{STAT} > 12.592$, reject H_0.

Test statistic: $\chi^2_{STAT} = 3.294$

Decision: Since $\chi^2_{STAT} = 3.294$ is less than the critical bound 12.592, do not reject H_0. There is not enough evidence to conclude that there is a relationship between the attitudes of employees toward vacation time without pay and employee job classification.

Copyright ©2015 Pearson Education, Inc.

CHAPTER 13

OBJECTIVES

- To learn to use regression analysis to predict the value of a dependent variable based on the value of an independent variable
- Understand the meaning of the regression coefficients b_0 and b_1
- To learn to evaluate the assumptions of regression analysis and what to do if the assumptions are violated
- To make inferences about the slope and correlation coefficient
- To estimate mean values and predict individual values

OVERVIEW AND KEY CONCEPTS

Purpose of Regression Analysis

- Regression analysis is used for predicting the values of a dependent (response) variable based on the value of at least one independent (explanatory) variable.

The Simple Linear Regression Model

- The relationship between the dependent variable (Y) and the explanatory variable (X) is described by a linear function.
- The change in the explanatory (independent) variable explains the change in the response (dependent) variable.
- The value of the explained variable depends on the explanatory variable.
- The population linear regression: $Y_i = \beta_0 + \beta_1 X_i + \varepsilon_i$ where β_0 is the intercept and β_1 is the slope of the population regression line $\mu_{Y|X} = \beta_0 + \beta_1 X_i$ and ε_i is called the error term.

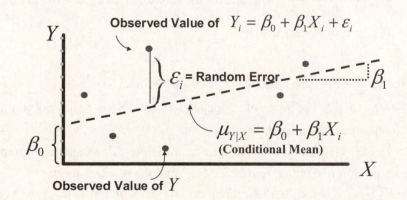

- The parameters β_0 and β_1 are unknown and need to be estimated.

Copyright ©2015 Pearson Education, Inc.

- The least squares estimates for β_0 and β_1 are b_0 and b_1, respectively, obtained by minimizing the sum of squared residuals, $\sum_{i=1}^{n}\left(Y_i - \left(b_0 + b_1 X_i\right)\right)^2 = \sum_{i=1}^{n} e_i^2$.

- The sample linear regression: $Y_i = b_0 + b_1 X_i + e_i$ where b_0 is the intercept and b_1 is the slope of the simple linear regression equation $\hat{Y} = b_0 + b_1 X_i$ and e_i is called the residual.

- The simple linear regression equation (sample regression line) $\hat{Y} = b_0 + b_1 X_i$ can be used to predict the value of the dependent variable for a given value of the independent variable X.

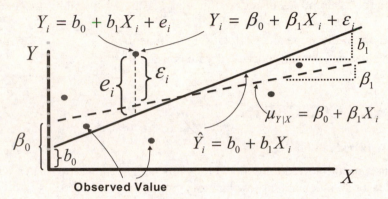

Interpretations of β_0, β_1, b_0 and b_1

- $\beta_0 = E\left(Y \mid X = 0\right) = \mu_{Y\mid X=0}$ is the average value of Y when the value of X is zero.

- $b_0 = \hat{E}\left(Y \mid X = 0\right) = \hat{Y}(X = 0)$ is the **estimated** average value of Y when the value of X is zero.

- $\beta_1 = \dfrac{\text{change in } E\left(Y \mid X\right)}{\text{change in } X} = \dfrac{\text{change in } \mu_{Y\mid X}}{\text{change in } X}$ measures the change in the average value of Y as a result of a one-unit change in X.

- $b_1 = \dfrac{\text{change in } \hat{E}\left(Y \mid X\right)}{\text{change in } X} = \dfrac{\text{change in } \hat{Y}}{\text{change in } X}$ measures the **estimated** change in the average value of Y as a result of a one-unit change in X.

Some Important Identities in the Simple Linear Regression Model

- $Y_i = \beta_0 + \beta_1 X_i + \varepsilon_i = \mu_{Y\mid X} + \varepsilon_i$. The value of the dependent variable is decomposed into the value on the population regression line and the error term.

- $Y_i = b_0 + b_1 X_i + e_i = \hat{Y}_i + e_i$. The value of the dependent variable is decomposed into the value on the sample regression line (fitted regression line) and the residual term.

- $\mu_{Y\mid X} = \beta_0 + \beta_1 X_i = E\left(Y \mid X\right)$ is the population regression line, which measures the average value of the dependent variable Y for a particular value of the independent variable X. Hence, it is also sometimes called the conditional mean regression line.

Copyright ©2015 Pearson Education, Inc.

- $\hat{Y}_i = b_0 + b_1 X_i$ is the sample regression line (simple linear regression equation), which measures the **estimated** average value of the dependent variable Y for a particular value of the independent variable X. It also provides prediction for the value of Y for a given value of X.

- $\varepsilon_i = Y_i - \mu_{Y|X} = Y_i - (\beta_0 + \beta_1 X_i)$ is the error.

- $e_i = Y_i - \hat{Y}_i = Y_i - (b_0 + b_1 X_i)$ is the residual.

- $SST = \sum_{i=1}^{n} (Y_i - \bar{Y})^2$ is the total sum of squares.

- $SSR = \sum_{i=1}^{n} (\hat{Y}_i - \bar{Y})^2$ is the regression (explained) sum of squares.

- $SSE = \sum_{i=1}^{n} (Y_i - \hat{Y}_i)^2 = \sum_{i=1}^{n} e_i^2$ is the error (residual) sum of squares.

- $MSR = \dfrac{SSR}{k} = \dfrac{SSR}{1}$ where k is the number of the independent variable, which is 1 in the simple linear regression model.

- $MSE = \dfrac{SSE}{n-k-1} = \dfrac{SSE}{n-2}$

- The coefficient of determination

  - $r^2 = \dfrac{SSR}{SST} = \dfrac{\text{Regression Sum of Squares}}{\text{Total Sum of Squares}}$

  - The coefficient of determination measures the proportion of variation in Y that is explained by the independent variable X in the regression model.

- Standard error of estimate

  - $S_{YX} = \sqrt{\dfrac{SSE}{n-2}} = \sqrt{\dfrac{\sum_{i=1}^{n}(Y - \hat{Y}_i)^2}{n-2}}$

  - The standard error of estimate is the standard deviation of the variation of observations around the sample regression line $\hat{Y}_i = b_0 + b_1 X_i$.

The ANOVA Table for the Simple Linear Regression Model as Presented in Excel

ANOVA					
	df	**SS**	**MS**	**F**	**Significance F**
Regression	k	SSR	$MSR=SSR/k$	MSR/MSE	p-value of the F Test
Residuals	$n-k-1$	SSE	$MSE=SSE/(n-k-1)$		
Total	$n-1$	SST			

Copyright ©2015 Pearson Education, Inc.

Assumptions Needed for the Simple Linear Regression Model

- Normality of error: The errors around the population regression line are normally distributed at each X value. This also implies that the dependent variable is normally distributed at each value of the independent variable.
- Homoscedasticity: The variance (amount of variation) of the errors around the population regression line is the same at each X value.
- Independence of errors: The errors around the population regression line are independent for each value of X.

Residual Analysis

- Residual analysis is used to evaluate whether the regression model that has been fitted to the data is an appropriate model.
- **Residual analysis for linearity:**

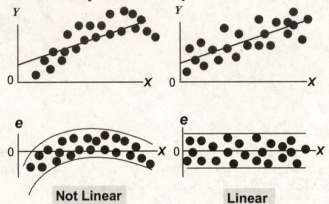

- **Residual analysis for homoscedasticity:**

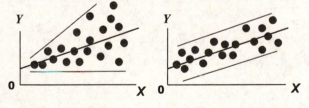

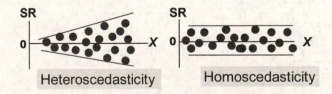

Copyright ©2015 Pearson Education, Inc.

- **Residual analysis for independence:**

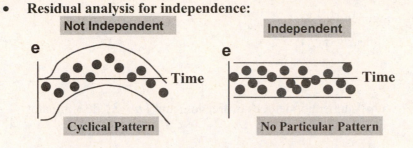

Residual Is Plotted Against Time to Detect Any Autocorrelation

- **Residual analysis for independence using Durbin-Watson statistic:**

    1. H_0: No autocorrelation (error terms are independent)

        H_1: There is autocorrelation (error terms are not independent)

    2. Compute the Durbin-Watson statistic $D = \dfrac{\sum_{i=2}^{n}(e_i - e_{i-1})^2}{\sum_{i=1}^{n}e_i^2}$

    3. Obtain the critical values d_L and d_U from a table.

    4. Compare the Durbin-Watson statistic with the critical values.

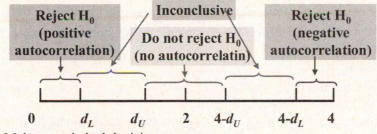

    5. Make a statistical decision.

    6. Draw a conclusion.

t Test for the Slope Parameter β_1

- $H_0 : \beta_1 = 0$ (Y does not depend on X)

    $H_1 : \beta_1 \neq 0$ (Y depends linearly on X)

- **Test statistic:**

    - $t = \dfrac{b_1 - \beta_1}{S_{b_1}}$ with $(n-2)$ degrees of freedom, where $S_{b_1} = \dfrac{S_{YX}}{\sqrt{\sum_{i=1}^{n}(X_i - \bar{X})^2}}$

    - The t test can also be a one-tail test for a one-tail alternative.

- **Confidence interval estimate:** Use the $100(1-\alpha)\%$ confidence interval for the slope parameter β_1.

    - $b_1 \pm t_{\alpha/2, n-2} S_{b_1}$

Copyright ©2015 Pearson Education, Inc.

F Test for the Slope Parameter β_1

- $H_0 : \beta_1 = 0$ (Y does not depend on X)

  $H_1 : \beta_1 \neq 0$ (Y depends linearly on X)

- **Test statistic:**

  - $F = \dfrac{\dfrac{SSR}{1}}{\dfrac{SSE}{(n-2)}}$ with 1 numerator degrees of freedom and $(n-2)$ denominator degrees of freedom.

  - The F test always has a right-tail rejection region and can only be used for the two-tail alternative.

The Relationship between the t Test and F Test for the Slope Parameter β_1

- For $H_0 : \beta_1 = 0$ vs $H_1 : \beta_1 \neq 0$, $t^2 = F$ and the p-value of the t test is identical to the p-value of the F test.

Correlation Analysis

- Correlation analysis is concerned with the strength of any linear relationship between 2 quantitative variables.
- There is no causal effect implied in a correlation analysis.
- The population correlation coefficient ρ is used to measure the strength of the linear relationship between the variables while the sample correlation coefficient r provides an estimate of the strength.
- **Features of ρ and r:**
  - They are unit free.
  - Their values range between –1 and 1.
  - The close is the value to –1, the stronger is the negative linear relationship.
  - The close is the value to +1, the stronger is the positive linear relationship.
  - The close is the value to 0, the weaker is any linear relationship.

t Test for a Linear Relationship

- **Hypotheses:**
  - $H_0 : \rho = 0$ (There is no linear relationship)
  - $H_1 : \rho \neq 0$ (There is some linear relationship)
- **Test statistic:**

  - $t = \dfrac{r - \rho}{\sqrt{\dfrac{1-r^2}{n-2}}}$ with $(n-2)$ degrees of freedom, where

    $r = \sqrt{r^2} = \dfrac{\sum\limits_{i=1}^{n} (X_i - \bar{X})(Y_i - \bar{Y})}{\sqrt{\sum\limits_{i=1}^{n} (X_i - \bar{X})^2 \sum\limits_{i=1}^{n} (Y_i - \bar{Y})^2}}$.

  - The t test can be a one-tail test for a one-tail alternative.

Copyright ©2015 Pearson Education, Inc.

Confidence Interval Estimate for the Mean of Y $\left(\mu_{Y|X}\right)$

- The point estimate for $\mu_{Y|X=X_i}$ is $\hat{Y}_i$

- The confidence interval estimate for $\mu_{Y|X}$ is $\hat{Y}_i \pm t_{\alpha/2,n-2} S_{YX} \sqrt{\dfrac{1}{n} + \dfrac{(X_i - \bar{X})^2}{\displaystyle\sum_{i=1}^{n}(X_i - \bar{X})^2}}$

Prediction Interval for an Individual Response Y

- The point prediction for an individual response Y_i at a particular X_i, denoted as $Y_{X=X_i}$ is

  $\hat{Y}_i = b_0 + b_1 X_i$

- The prediction interval for an individual response Y_i is

  $\hat{Y}_i \pm t_{\alpha/2,n-2} S_{YX} \sqrt{1 + \dfrac{1}{n} + \dfrac{(X_i - \bar{X})^2}{\displaystyle\sum_{i=1}^{n}(X_i - \bar{X})^2}}$

Common Pitfalls in Regression Analysis

- Lacking an awareness of the assumptions underlying least-squares regression
- Not knowing how to evaluate the assumptions
- Not knowing what the alternatives to least-squares regression are if a particular assumption is violated
- Using a regression model without knowledge of the subject matter
- Extrapolating outside the relevant range
- Concluding that a significant relationship identified in an observational study is due to a cause-and-effect relationship

Strategy for Avoiding the Pitfalls in Regression

- Always start with a scatter plot to observe the possible relationship between X and Y
- Check the assumptions of the regression after the regression model has been fit, before moving on to using the results of the model
- Plot the residuals versus the independent variable to determine whether the model fit to the data is appropriate and check visually for violations of the homoscedasticity assumption
- Use a histogram, stem-and-leaf display, boxplot, or normal probability plot of the residuals to graphically evaluate whether the normality assumption has been seriously violated
- If the evaluations indicate violations in the assumptions, use alternative methods to least-squares regression or alternative least-squares models (quadratic or multiple regression) depending on what the evaluation has indicated
- If the evaluations do not indicate violations in the assumptions, then the inferential aspects of the regression analysis can be undertaken, tests for the significance of the regression coefficients can be done, and confidence and prediction intervals can be developed

Copyright ©2015 Pearson Education, Inc.

- Avoid making predictions and forecasts outside the relevant range of the independent variable
- Always note that the relationships identified in observational studies may or may not be due to a cause-and-effect relationship, and remember that while causation implies correlation, correlation does not imply causation

Copyright ©2015 Pearson Education, Inc.

SOLUTIONS TO END OF SECTION
AND CHAPTER REVIEW EVEN PROBLEMS

13.2   (a)   yes,   (b) no,   (c) no,   (d) yes

13.4   (a)

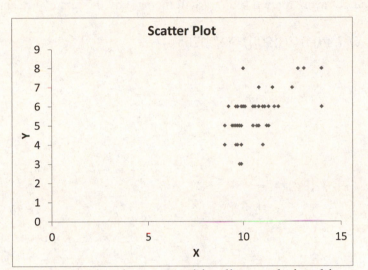

             The scatter plot shows a positive linear relationship.

    (b)   For each % increase in alcohol content, there is an expected increase in quality of an estimated 0.5624.

    (c) $\hat{Y} = -0.3529 + 0.5624X = -0.3529 + 0.5624(10) = 5.2715$

    (d)   There appears to be a positive linear relationship between quality and % alcohol content. For each % increase in alcohol content, there is an expected increase in quality of an estimated 0.5624.

13.6   (a)

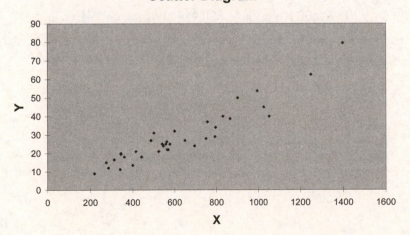

Copyright ©2015 Pearson Education, Inc.

13.6   (b)   Partial Excel output:
cont.

	Coefficients	Standard Error	t Stat	P-value
Intercept	-2.3697	2.0733	-1.1430	0.2610
Feet	0.0501	0.0030	16.5223	0.0000

(c)   The estimated mean amount of labor will increase by 0.05 hour for each additional cubic foot moved.

(d) $\hat{Y} = -2.3697 + 0.0501(500) = 22.6705$

13.8   (a)

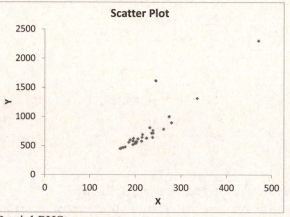

(b)   Partial PHStat output:

	Coefficients	Standard Error	t Stat	P-value
Intercept	-601.9291	122.1578	-4.9275	0.0000
Revenue	5.9316	0.5218	11.3668	0.0000

$b_0 = -601.9291$ $b_1 = 5.9316$

(c)   For each additional million dollars increase in revenue, the mean annual value will increase by an estimated 5.9316 million dollars. Literal interpretation of b_0 is not meaningful because an operating franchise cannot have zero revenue.

(d) $\hat{Y} = -601.9291 + 5.9316(250) = 880.9832$ million dollars

(e)   You would tell a group considering an investment in a major league baseball team that there appears to be a positive relationship between revenue and the value of a team.

Copyright ©2015 Pearson Education, Inc.

13.10   (a)

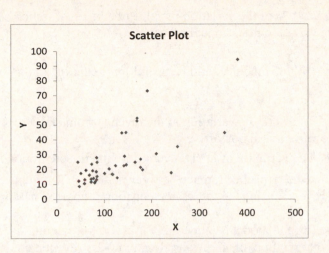

(b)

	Coefficients	Standard Error	t Stat	P-value
Intercept	4.8445	3.6648	1.3219	0.1935
Gross	0.1631	0.0249	6.5626	0.0000

$$\hat{Y} = b_0 + b_1 X = 4.8445 + 0.1631X$$

(c)   For each increase of one additional million dollars of box office gross, the estimated mean revenue of DVDs sold will increase by 0.1631 million dollars.

(d) $\hat{Y} = b_0 + b_1 X = 4.8445 + 0.1631(100) = 21.1588$ million dollars.

(e)   There appears to be a positive linear relationship between movie gross and DVD revenue. So movie gross can be a good predictor for DVD revenue.

13.12 $SST = 40$ and $r^2 = 0.90$. So, 90% of the variation in the dependent variable can be explained by the variation in the independent variable.

13.14 $r^2 = 0.75$. So, 75% of the variation in the dependent variable can be explained by the variation in the independent variable.

13.16   (a) $r^2 = \dfrac{SSR}{SST} = 0.3417$. So, 34.17% of the variation in wine quality can be explained by the variation in alcohol content.

(b) $S_{YX} = \sqrt{\dfrac{SSE}{n-2}} = \sqrt{\dfrac{\sum_{i=1}^{n}\left(Y_i - \hat{Y}_i\right)^2}{n-2}} = 0.9369$

(c)   Based on (a) and (b), the model should be moderately useful for predicting wine quality.

13.18   (a) $r^2 = 0.8892$. So, 88.92% of the variation in labor hours can be explained by the variation in cubic feet moved.

(b) $S_{YX} = 5.0314$

(c)   Based on (a) and (b), the model should be very useful for predicting labor hours.

Copyright ©2015 Pearson Education, Inc.

13.20   (a) $r^2 = 0.8219$. So, 82.19% of the variation in value of a baseball franchise can be explained by the variation in its annual revenue.

        (b) $S_{YX} = 165.3106$

        (c)   Based on (a) and (b), the model should be useful for predicting the value of a baseball franchise.

13.22   (a) $r^2 = 0.5123$. So, 51.23% of the variation in the revenue from DVD revenue can be explained by the variation in box office gross.

        (b) $S_{YX} = 12.2279$. The variation of DVD revenue around the prediction line is $12.2279 million. The typical difference between actual DVD revenue and the predicted DVD revenue using the regression equation is approximately $12.2279 million.

        (c)   Based on (a) and (b), the model is moderately useful for predicting DVD revenue.

        (d)   Other variables that might explain the variation in DVDs revenue could be the amount spent on advertising, the timing of the release of the DVDs and the type of movie.

13.24   A residual analysis of the data indicates a pattern, with sizable clusters of consecutive residuals that are either all positive or all negative. This pattern indicates a violation of the assumption of linearity. A curvilinear model should be investigated.

13.26

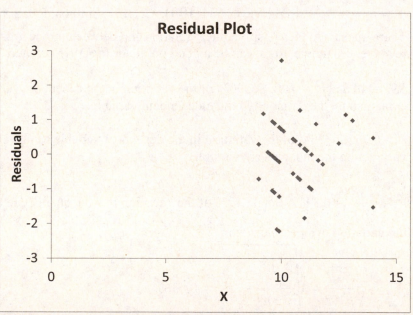

Based on the residual plot, there does not appear to be a pattern in the residual plot. The linearity and equal variance assumptions appear to be holding up.

Copyright ©2015 Pearson Education, Inc.

13.26
cont.

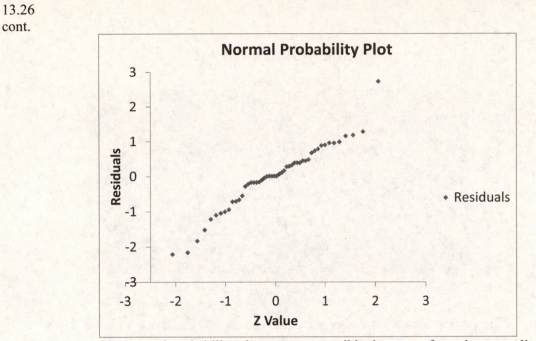

Normal Probability Plot

The normal probability plot suggests possible departure from the normality assumption.

13.28

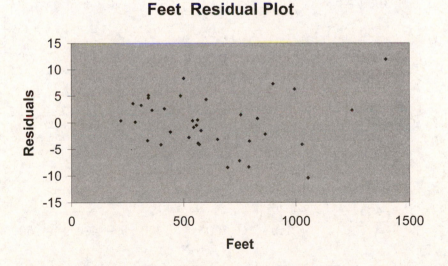

Feet Residual Plot

Based on the residual plot, there does not appear to be a curvilinear pattern in the residuals.

Copyright ©2015 Pearson Education, Inc.

310 Chapter 13: Simple Linear Regression

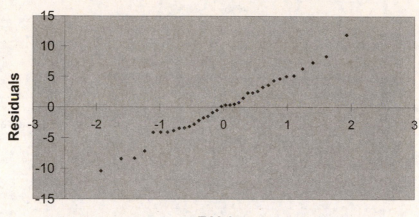

The assumptions of normality and equal variance do not appear to be seriously violated.

13.30

The linearity assumption might have been violated.

Copyright ©2015 Pearson Education, Inc.

13.30
cont.

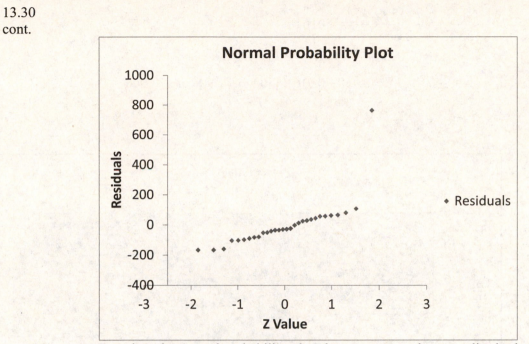

Based on the normal probability plot, there appears to be an outlier in the residuals so the normality assumption might have been violated.

13.32   (a)

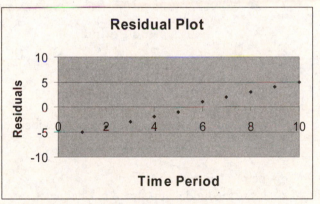

An increasing linear relationship exists.

(b)   There appears to be strong positive autocorrelation among the residuals.

13.34   (a)   No, it is not necessary to compute the Durbin-Watson statistic since the data have been collected for a single period for a set of bags.

(b)   If a single bag-sealing equipment was studied over a period of time and the amount of plate gap varied over time, computation of the Durbin-Watson statistic would be necessary.

Copyright ©2015 Pearson Education, Inc.

13.36   (a) $b_1 = \dfrac{SSXY}{SSX} = \dfrac{201399.05}{12495626} = 0.0161$

$b_0 = \bar{Y} - b_1\bar{X} = 71.2621 - 0.0161(4393) = 0.458$

(b) $\hat{Y} = 0.458 + 0.0161X = 0.458 + 0.0161(4500) = 72.908$ or \$72,908

(c)

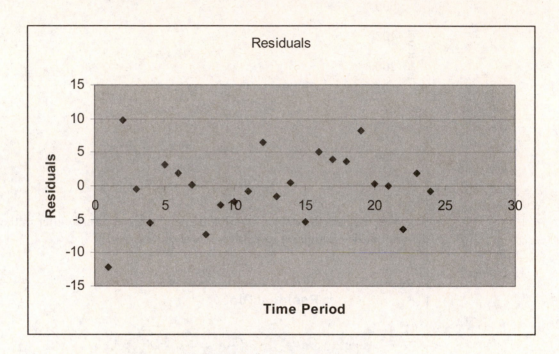

(d) $D = \dfrac{\sum\limits_{i=2}^{n}(e_i - e_{i-1})^2}{\sum\limits_{i=1}^{n}e_i^2} = \dfrac{1243.2244}{599.0683} = 2.08 > 1.45.$ There is no evidence of positive

autocorrelation among the residuals.

(e)   Based on a residual analysis, the model appears to be adequate.

(f)   It appears that the number of orders affects the monthly distribution costs.

Copyright ©2015 Pearson Education, Inc.

13.38   (a) $b_0 = -2.535$, $b_1 = 0.060728$

(b) $\hat{Y} = -2.535 + 0.060728X = -2.535 + 0.060728(83) = 2.5054$ or \$2505.40

(c)

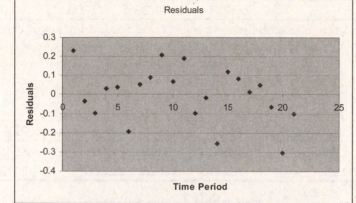

(d) $D = 1.64 > 1.42$. There is no evidence of positive autocorrelation among the residuals.

(e)   The plot of the residuals versus time period shows some clustering of positive and negative residuals for intervals in the domain, suggesting a nonlinear model might be better. Otherwise, the model appears to be adequate.

(f)   There appears to be a positive relationship between sales and atmospheric temperature.

13.40   (a) $H_0 : \beta_1 = 0 \qquad H_1 : \beta_1 \neq 0$

Test statistic: $t_{STAT} = (b_1 - 0)/s_{b_1} = 4.5/1.5 = 3.00$

(b)   With $n = 18$, df $= 18 - 2 = 16$, $t_{0.05/2} = \pm 2.1199$.

(c)   Reject H_0. There is evidence that the fitted linear regression model is useful.

(d) $b_1 - t_{0.05/2} s_{b_1} \leq \beta_1 \leq b_1 + t_{0.05/2} s_{b_1}$

$4.5 - 2.1199(1.5) \leq \beta_1 \leq 4.5 + 2.1199(1.5)$

$1.32 \leq \beta_1 \leq 7.68$

13.42   (a) $H_0 : \beta_1 = 0 \qquad H_1 : \beta_1 \neq 0$

	Coefficients	Standard Error	t Stat	P-value	Lower 95%	Upper 95%
Intercept	-0.3529	1.2000	-0.2941	0.7700	-2.7656	2.0599
alcohol	0.5624	0.1127	4.9913	0.0000	0.3359	0.7890

$t_{STAT} = \dfrac{b_1 - \beta_1}{S_{b_1}} = 4.9913$ with a p-value $= 0.0000 < 0.05$. Reject H_0. There is enough

evidence to conclude that the fitted linear regression model is useful.

(b) $b_1 \pm t_{\alpha/2} S_{b_1}$ $\qquad\qquad$ $0.3359 \leq \beta_1 \leq 0.7890$

13.44   (a) $t_{STAT} = 16.5223 > t_{0.05/2} = 2.0322$ for $\alpha = 0.05$. Reject H_0. There is evidence that the fitted linear regression model is useful.

(b) $b_1 \pm t_{\alpha/2} S_{b_1}$ $\qquad\qquad$ $0.0439 \leq \beta_1 \leq 0.0562$

Copyright ©2015 Pearson Education, Inc.

13.46   (a) $H_0 : \beta_1 = 0$ $H_1 : \beta_1 \neq 0$

	Coefficients	Standard Error	t Stat	P-value	Lower 95%	Upper 95%
Intercept	-601.9291	122.1578	-4.9275	0.0000	-852.1581	-351.7001
Revenue	5.9316	0.5218	11.3668	0.0000	4.8627	7.0006

Since the *p*-value is essentially zero, reject H_0 at 5% level of significance. There is evidence of a linear relationship between annual revenue sales and franchise value.

(b) $b_1 \pm t_{\alpha/2} S_{b_1}$ $4.8627 \leq \beta_1 \leq 7.0006$

13.48   (a) $H_0 : \beta_1 = 0$ $H_1 : \beta_1 \neq 0$

	Coefficients	Standard Error	t Stat	P-value	Lower 95%	Upper 95%
Intercept	4.8445	3.6648	1.3219	0.1935	-2.5567	12.2457
Gross	0.1631	0.0249	6.5626	0.0000	0.1129	0.2133

Since $t_{STAT} = \dfrac{b_1 - \beta_1}{S_{b_1}} = 6.5626$ with a *p*-value = 0.0000 < 0.05, reject H_0 at 5% level

of significance. There is enough evidence of a linear relationship between box office gross and DVD revenue.

(b) $b_1 \pm t_{\alpha/2} S_{b_1}$ $0.1129 \leq \beta_1 \leq 0.2133$

13.50   (a)   (% weekly change in MDU) = 0.0 + 3.0 (% weekly change in S & P Midcap 400)
        (b)   If the S & P Midcap 400 gains 10% in a year, the MDU is expected to gain an estimated 30% on average.
        (c)   If the S & P Midcap 400 loses 20% in a year, the MDU is expected to lose an estimated 60% on average.
        (d)   Risk takers will be attracted to leveraged funds, but risk averse investors will stay away.

13.52   (a)   **First weekend gross and the U. S. gross**
                $r = 0.7284$. There appears to be a strong positive linear relationship.
                First weekend gross and the worldwide gross
                $r = 0.8233$. There appears to be a strong positive linear relationship.
                U. S. gross, and worldwide gross
                $r = 0.9642$ There appears to be a very strong positive linear relationship.
        (b)   **First weekend gross and the U. S. gross**
                Since $t_{stat} = 2.6042 > 2.4469$ and *p*-value = 0.0404 < 0.05, reject H_0. At the 0.05 level of significance, there is evidence of a linear relationship between first weekend sales and U.S. gross.
                First weekend gross and the worldwide gross
                Since $t_{stat} = 3.5532 > 2.4469$ and *p*-value = 0.0120 < 0.05, reject H_0. At the 0.05 level of significance, there is evidence of a linear relationship between first weekend sales and worldwide gross.
                U. S. gross, and worldwide gross
                Since $t_{stat} = 8.9061 > 2.4469$ and *p*-value = 0.0001 < 0.05, reject H_0. At the 0.05 level of significance, there is evidence of a linear relationship between U.S. gross and worldwide gross.

Copyright ©2015 Pearson Education, Inc.

13.54   (a) $r = 0.7042$. There appears to be a strong positive linear relationship between GDP and social media usage.

(b) $t = 4.3227$, p-value $= 0.0004 < 0.05$. Reject H_0. At the 0.05 level of significance, there is a significant linear relationship between GDP and social media usage.

(c)   There is a significant linear relationship between GDP and social media usage and the positive linear relationship is considered as strong.

13.56   (a)   When $X = 4$, $\hat{Y} = 5 + 3X = 5 + 3(4) = 17$

$$h = \frac{1}{n} + \frac{(X_i - \overline{X})^2}{\displaystyle\sum_{i=1}^{n}(X_i - \overline{X})^2} = \frac{1}{20} + \frac{(4-2)^2}{20} = 0.25$$

95% confidence interval: $\hat{Y} \pm t_{0.05/2} s_{YX} \sqrt{h} = 17 \pm 2.1009 \cdot 1 \cdot \sqrt{0.25}$

$$15.95 \le \mu_{Y|X=4} \le 18.05$$

(b)   95% prediction interval: $\hat{Y} \pm t_{0.05/2} s_{YX} \sqrt{1+h} = 17 \pm 2.1009 \cdot 1 \cdot \sqrt{1.25}$

$$14.651 \le Y_{X=4} \le 19.349$$

(c)   The intervals in this problem are wider because the value of X is farther from $\overline{X}$.

13.58   (a) $4.9741 \le \mu_{Y|X=10} \le 5.568984094$

(b) $3.3645 \le Y_{X=10} \le 7.178609919$

(c)   Part (b) provides a prediction interval for the individual response given a specific value of the independent variable, and part (a) provides an interval estimate for the mean value, given a specific value of the independent variable. Because there is much more variation in predicting an individual value than in estimating a mean value, a prediction interval is wider than a confidence interval estimate.

13.60   (a) $20.7990 \le \mu_{Y|X=500} \le 24.5419$

(b) $12.2755 \le Y_{X=500} \le 33.0654$

(c)   Part (b) provides an interval prediction for the individual response given a specific value of the independent variable, and part (a) provides an interval estimate for the mean value given a specific value of the independent variable. Since there is much more variation in predicting an individual value than in estimating a mean value, a prediction interval is wider than a confidence interval estimate holding everything else fixed.

13.62   (a) $814.3841 \le \mu_{Y|X=250} \le 947.5823$

(b) $535.8727 \le Y_{X=250} \le 1226.0937$

(c)   Part (b) provides an interval prediction for the individual response given a specific value of the independent variable, and part (a) provides an interval estimate for the mean value given a specific value of the independent variable. Since there is much more variation in predicting an individual value than in estimating a mean value, a prediction interval is wider than a confidence interval estimate holding everything else fixed.

Copyright ©2015 Pearson Education, Inc.

13.64   The slope of the line, b_1, represents the estimated expected change in Y per unit change in X. It represents the estimated mean amount that Y changes (either positively or negatively) for a particular unit change in X. The Y intercept b_0 represents the estimated mean value of Y when X equals 0.

13.66   The unexplained variation or error sum of squares (SSE) will be equal to zero only when the regression line fits the data perfectly and the coefficient of determination equals 1.

13.68   Unless a residual analysis is undertaken, you will not know whether the model fit is appropriate for the data. In addition, residual analysis can be used to check whether the assumptions of regression have been seriously violated.

13.70   The normality of error assumption can be evaluated by obtaining a histogram, boxplot, and/or normal probability plot of the residuals. The homoscedasticity assumption can be evaluated by plotting the residuals on the vertical axis and the X variable on the horizontal axis. The independence of errors assumption can be evaluated by plotting the residuals on the vertical axis and the time order variable on the horizontal axis. This assumption can also be evaluated by computing the Durbin-Watson statistic.

13.72   The confidence interval for the mean response estimates the mean response for a given X value. The prediction interval estimates the value for a single item or individual.

13.74   (a) $b_0 = 24.84$, $b_1 = 0.14$

   (b)   24.84 is the portion of estimated mean delivery time that is not affected by the number of cases delivered. For each additional case, the estimated mean delivery time increases by 0.14 minutes.

   (c) $\hat{Y} = 24.84 + 0.14X = 24.84 + 0.14(150) = 45.84$

   (d)   No, 500 cases is outside the relevant range of the data used to fit the regression equation.

   (e) $r^2 = 0.972$. So, 97.2% of the variation in delivery time can be explained by the variation in the number of cases.

   (f)   Based on a visual inspection of the graphs of the distribution of residuals and the residuals versus the number of cases, there is no pattern. The model appears to be adequate.

   (g) $t = 24.88 > t_{0.05/2} = 2.1009$ with 18 degrees of freedom for $\alpha = 0.05$. Reject H_0. There is evidence that the fitted linear regression model is useful.

   (h) $44.88 \leq \mu_{Y|X=150} \leq 46.80$

   $41.56 \leq Y_{X=150} \leq 50.12$

Copyright ©2015 Pearson Education, Inc.

13.76   (a)
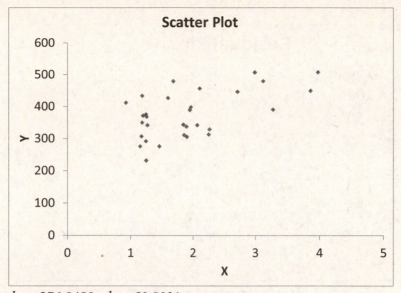

$b_0 = 276.8480$ $b_1 = 50.8031$

(b)   For each additional square foot increase in size, the estimated mean assessed value of a house increases by 50.8031 thousand dollars. The estimated mean assessed value of a house with a 0 size is 276.8480 thousand dollars. However, this interpretation is not meaningful in the current setting since the size cannot be 0 square foot for a house.

(c) $\hat{Y} = 276.8480 + 50.8031X = 276.8480 + 50.8031(2000) = 101,883.0335$
thousand dollars

(d) $r^2 = 0.3273$. So, 32.73% of the variation in assessed value can be explained by the variation in the size of the house.

Copyright ©2015 Pearson Education, Inc.

13.76 (e)
cont.

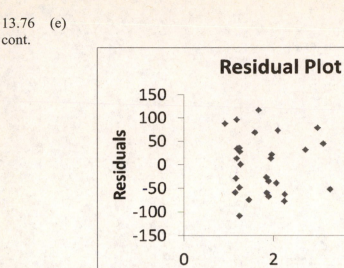

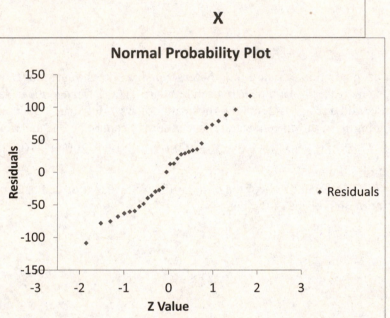

Both the residual plot and the normal probability plot do not reveal any potential violation of the linearity, equal variance and normality assumptions.

(f)

	Coefficients	Standard Error	t Stat	P-value	Lower 95%	Upper 95%
Intercept	276.8480	28.8074	9.6103	0.0000	217.8388	335.8572
Size(000 sq. ft.	50.8031	13.7628	3.6913	0.0009	22.6113	78.9949

Since $t_{STAT} = 3.6913$ with a p-value = $0.0009 < 0.05$, reject H_0. There is evidence of a linear relationship between assessed value and size.

(g) $22.6113 \leq \beta_1 \leq 78.9949$

(h) There appears to be a moderately positive relationship between assessed value and size.

Copyright ©2015 Pearson Education, Inc.

13.78   (a)

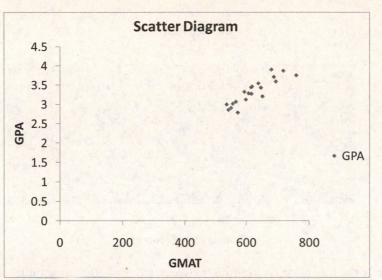

$b_0 = 0.30$, $b_1 = 0.00487$

(b)   0.30 is the portion of estimated mean GPI index (GPA) that is not affected by the GMAT score. The mean GPI index of a student with a zero GMAT score is estimated to be 0.30, which does not have practical meaning. For each additional point on the GMAT score, the estimated GPI increases by an average of 0.00487.

(c) $\hat{Y} = 0.30 + 0.00487\ X = 0.30 + 0.00487\ (600\ ) = 3.222$

(d) $r^2 = 0.7978$. 79.78% of the variation in the GPI can be explained by the variation in the GMAT score.

(e)   Based on a visual inspection of the graphs of the distribution of residuals and the residuals versus the GMAT score, there is no pattern. The model appears to be adequate.

(f) $t = 8.428 > t_{0.05/2} = 2.1009$ with 18 degrees of freedom for $\alpha = 0.05$. Reject H_0.
There is evidence that the fitted linear regression model is useful.

(g) $3.144 \leq \mu_{Y|X=600} \leq 3.301$

$2.886 \leq Y_{X=600} \leq 3.559$

(h) $0.00366\ \leq \beta_1 \leq 0.00608$

Copyright ©2015 Pearson Education, Inc.

13.80   (a)

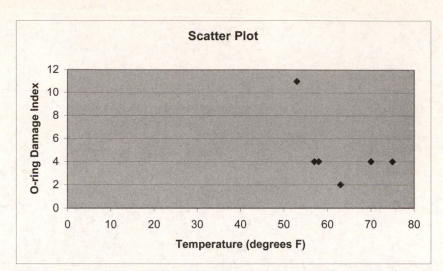

There is not any clear relationship between atmospheric temperature and O-ring damage from the scatter plot.

(b),(f)

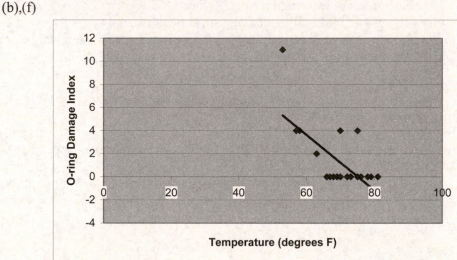

(c)   In (b), there are 16 observations with an O-ring damage index of 0 for a variety of temperatures. If one concentrates on these observations with no O-ring damage, there is obviously no relationship between O-ring damage index and temperature. If all observations are used, the observations with no O-ring damage will bias the estimated relationship. If the intention is to investigate the relationship between the degrees of O-ring damage and atmospheric temperature, it makes sense to focus only on the flights in which there was O-ring damage.

(d)   Prediction should not be made for an atmospheric temperature of 31 ^{0}F because it is outside the range of the temperature variable in the data. Such prediction will involve extrapolation, which assumes that any relationship between two variables will continue to hold outside the domain of the temperature variable.

(e) $\hat{Y} = 18.036 - 0.240X$

(g)   A nonlinear model is more appropriate for these data.

Copyright ©2015 Pearson Education, Inc.

13.80   (h)
cont.

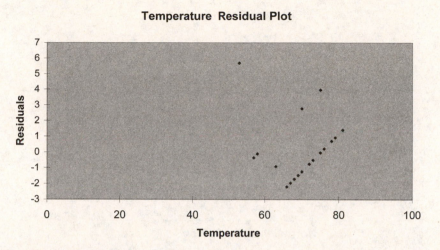

The string of negative residuals and positive residuals that lie on a straight line with a positive slope in the lower-right corner of the plot is a strong indication that a nonlinear model should be used if all 23 observations are to be used in the fit.

13.82   (a)

Regression Statistics	
Multiple R	0.9143
R Square	0.8360
Adjusted R Square	0.8301
Standard Error	78.2884
Observations	30

ANOVA

	df	SS	MS	F	Significance F
Regression	1	874546.7072	874546.7072	142.6881	0.0000
Residual	28	171614.2595	6129.0807		
Total	29	1046160.9667			

	Coefficients	Standard Error	t Stat	P-value	Lower 95%	Upper 95%
Intercept	-132.5114	55.5767	-2.3843	0.0241	-246.3551	-18.6676
Revenue ($mil)	5.2286	0.4377	11.9452	0.0000	4.3320	6.1252

$b_0 = -132.5114 \; b_1 = 5.2286$

(b)   For each additional million-dollars of revenue generated, the mean value of the franchise will increase by an estimated $5.2286 million. Literal interpretation of the intercept is not meaningful because an operating franchise cannot have zero revenue.

(c) $\hat{Y} = -132.5114 + 5.2286X = -132.5114 + 5.2286(150) = \$ 651.7731 \text{ millions}$

(d) $r^2 = 0.8360$. So, 83.60% of the variation in the value of an NBA franchise can be explained by the variation in its annual revenue.

Copyright ©2015 Pearson Education, Inc.

13.82   (e)
cont.

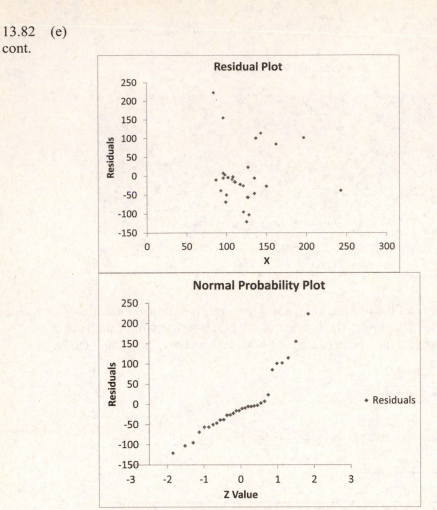

The normal probability plot suggests possible departure from the normality assumption.

(f) $t_{STAT} = 11.9452$ with a p-value that is approximately zero, reject H_0 at the 5% level of significance. There is evidence of a linear relationship between annual revenue and franchise value.

(g) 613.6103 millions $\leq \mu_{Y|X=150} \leq$ 689.9359 millions

(h) 486.9282 millions $\leq Y_{X=150} \leq$ 816.6180 millions

(i)   The strength of the relationship between revenue and value is stronger for NBA franchises than for European soccer teams and Major League Baseball teams.

Copyright ©2015 Pearson Education, Inc.

13.84   (a)

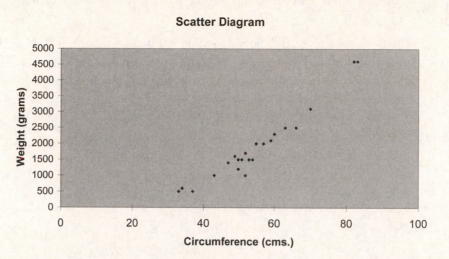

Scatter Diagram

$$\hat{Y} = -2629.222 + 82.4717X$$

(b)   For each increase of one centimeter in circumference, the estimated mean weight of a pumpkin will increase by 82.4717 grams.

(c) $\hat{Y} = -2629.222 + 82.4717(60) = 2319.080$ grams.

(d)   There appears to be a positive relationship between weight and circumference of a pumpkin. It is a good idea for the farmer to sell pumpkins by circumference instead of weight for circumference is a good predictor of weight, and it is much easier to measure the circumference of a pumpkin than its weight.

(e) $r^2 = 0.9373$.   93.73% of the variation in pumpkin weight can be explained by the variation in circumference.

(f)

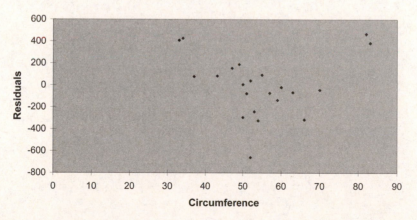

Circumference Residual Plot

There appears to be a nonlinear relationship between circumference and weight.

(g) p-value is virtually 0. Reject H_0. There is sufficient evidence to conclude that there is a linear relationship between the circumference and the weight of a pumpkin.

(h) $72.7875 < \beta_1 < 92.1559$

Copyright ©2015 Pearson Education, Inc.

13.86 (a)   The correlation between compensation and the investment return is 0.1719.

     (b) $H_0 : \rho = 0$ vs. $H_1 : \rho \neq 0$

          The t_{STAT} value is 2.2615 with a p-value $= 0.0250 < 0.05$, reject H_0. The correlation between compensation and the investment return is statistically significant.

     (c)   The small correlation between compensation and stock performance was surprising (or maybe it should not have been!).

Copyright ©2015 Pearson Education, Inc.

CHAPTER 14

OBJECTIVES

- To learn to develop a multiple regression model
- To learn to interpret the regression coefficients
- To learn to determine which independent variables to include in the regression model
- To learn to determine which independent variables are most important in predicting a dependent variable
- To learn to use categorical independent variables in a regression model
- To use logistic regression to predict a categorical dependent variable
- To learn to identify individual observations that may be unduly influencing the multiple regression model

OVERVIEW AND KEY CONCEPTS

The Multiple Regression Model

- The multiple regression model describes the relationship between one dependent variable and 2 or more independent variables in a linear function.

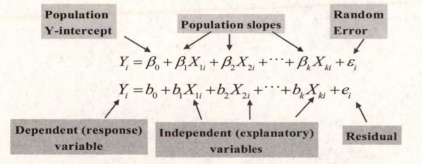

$$Y_i = \beta_0 + \beta_1 X_{1i} + \beta_2 X_{2i} + \cdots + \beta_k X_{ki} + \varepsilon_i$$

$$Y_i = b_0 + b_1 X_{1i} + b_2 X_{2i} + \cdots + b_k X_{ki} + e_i$$

The Simple Linear Regression and Multiple Regression Compared

- Coefficients in a simple regression pick up the impact of that variable plus the impacts of other variables that are correlated with it and the dependent variable.
- Coefficients in a multiple regression net out the impacts of other variables in the equation. Hence, they are called *net regression coefficients*.

Interpretation of the Estimated Coefficients

- **The *Y* intercept** (b_0) **:** The estimated average value of Y_i when all $X_i = 0$.

- **Slope** (b_i) **:** Estimated that the average value of Y changes by b_i for each one-unit increase in X_i holding constant the effect of all other independent variables.

Copyright ©2015 Pearson Education, Inc.

Predicting the Dependent Variable Y

- Use the estimated sample regression equation (multiple linear regression equation):

$$\hat{Y}_i = b_0 + b_1 X_{1i} + \cdots + b_k X_{ki}$$

The Venn Diagram and Explanatory Power of the Multiple Regression Model

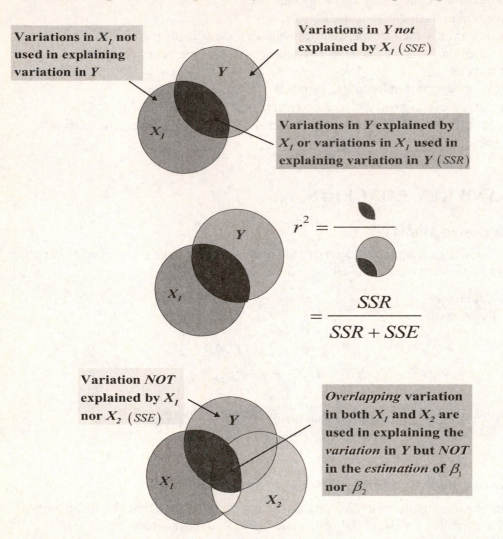

Coefficient of Multiple Determination

- Coefficient of multiple determination measures the proportion of total variation in Y explained by all X variables taken together.

- $r_{Y \bullet 12 \cdots k}^2 = \dfrac{SSR}{SST} = \dfrac{\text{Explained Variation}}{\text{Total Variation}}$

Copyright ©2015 Pearson Education, Inc.

- It never decreases when an additional X variable is added to the model, which is a disadvantage when comparing among models.

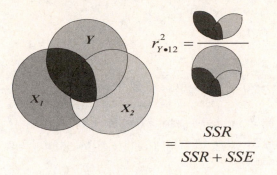

$$r^2_{Y \bullet 12} = \frac{}{}$$

$$= \frac{SSR}{SSR + SSE}$$

Adjusted Coefficient of Multiple Determination

- It measures the proportion of variation in Y explained by all X variables adjusted for the number of X variables used.
- $r^2_{adj} = 1 - \left[\left(1 - r^2_{Y \bullet 12 \cdots k} \right) \dfrac{n-1}{n-k-1} \right]$
- It penalizes excessive use of independent variables.
- It is smaller than $r^2_{Y \bullet 12 \cdots k}$.
- It is useful in comparing among models.
- It can have a negative value.
- Its value can decrease when an additional explanatory variable is added to the existing model.

Interpretation of Coefficient of Multiple Determination

- $r^2_{Y \bullet 12 \cdots k}$ measures the proportion of total variation in Y that can be explained by all X variables.
- r^2_{adj} measures the proportion of total variation in Y that can be explained by all X variables after adjusting for the number of independent variables and sample size.

F Test for the Significance of the Entire Multiple Regression Model

- **The hypotheses:**
    - $H_0 : \beta_1 = \beta_2 = \cdots = \beta_k = 0$ (There is no linear relationship)
    - $H_1 :$ At least one $\beta_i \neq 0$ (At least one independent variable affects Y)
- **Test statistic:**
    - $F = \dfrac{MSR}{MSE} = \dfrac{SSR\left(\text{all} \right) / k}{SSE\left(\text{all} \right) / \left(n - k - 1 \right)}$ with k numerator degrees of freedom and

      $\left(n - k - 1 \right)$ denominator degrees of freedom.
    - The rejection region is always in the right tail.

Copyright ©2015 Pearson Education, Inc.

t Test for the Significance of Individual Variables

- **The hypotheses:**
  - $H_0 : \beta_i = 0$ (X_i does not affect Y)
  - $H_1 : \beta_i \neq 0$ (X_i affects Y)
- **Test statistic:**
  - $t = \dfrac{b_j - \beta_j}{S_{b_j}}$ with $(n - k - 1)$ degrees of freedom.
    - The *t* test can also be a one-tail test for a one-tail alternative.
- Confidence interval estimate for β_j : Use the $100(1 - \alpha)\%$ confidence interval for β_j .
  - $b_j \pm t_{\alpha/2, n-k-1} S_{b_j}$

Contribution of a Single Independent Variable X_j

- The contribution of an independent variable X_j to the regression model is measured by

$$SSR\left(X_j \mid \text{all variables except } X_j\right)$$

$$= SSR\left(\text{all variables including } X_j\right) - SSR\left(\text{all variables except } X_j\right)$$

The Partial *F* Test for Determining the Contribution of an Independent Variable

- **The hypotheses:**
  - H_0 : Variable X_j does not significantly improve the model after all the other X have been included
  - H_1 : Variable X_j significantly improve the model once all the other X have been included
- **Test statistic:**
  - $F = \dfrac{SSR\left(X_j \mid \text{all variables except } X_j\right)}{MSE(\text{all})}$ with 1 and $(n - k - 1)$ degrees of freedom.
  - The rejection region is always in the right tail.
  - This partial *F* test statistic $F_{1, n-k-1}$ always equals to the squared of the *t* test statistic for the significance of X_j , i.e., $\left(t_{n-k-1}\right)^2 = F_{1, n-k-1}$.

Coefficient of Partial Determination

- It measures the proportion of variation in the dependent variable that is explained by X_j while controlling for (holding constant) the other independent variables.

Copyright ©2015 Pearson Education, Inc.

- $r^2_{Yj\bullet \text{ all variables except } X_j} = \dfrac{SSR\left(X_j \mid \text{all variables except } X_j\right)}{SST - SSR\left(\text{all variables including } X_j\right) + SSR\left(X_j \mid \text{all variables except } X_j\right)}$

Two independent variables model

$SSR(X_1 \mid X_2)$

$r^2_{Y1\bullet 2} =$

$\dfrac{SSR(X_1 \mid X_2)}{SST - SSR(X_1, X_2) + SSR(X_1 \mid X_2)}$

$=$

Dummy-Variable Model and Interactions

- Dummy variables are used to represent categorical explanatory variables with two or more levels.
- A dummy variable is always coded as 0 and 1.
- The number of dummy variables needed is equal to the number of levels minus 1.
- **Interpretation of the estimated slope coefficient of a dummy variable:** The slope coefficient of a dummy variable measures the estimated average incremental effect of the presence of the characteristic captured by the dummy variable holding constant the effect of all other independent variables.
- In the dummy-variable model, it is assumed that the slope of the dependent variable Y with an independent variable X is the same for each of the two levels of the dummy variable.
- To test whether the slope of the dependent variable Y with an independent variable X is the same for each of the two levels of the dummy variable, we can introduce the interaction term and test for the significance of this interaction term.

  E.g., Let X_1 and X_2 be two numerical independent variables, and X_3 be a dummy variable.

  To test whether the slopes of Y with X_1 and/or X_2 are the same for each of the two levels of X_3, the regression model is $Y_i = \beta_0 + \beta_1 X_{1i} + \beta_2 X_{2i} + \beta_3 X_{3i} + \beta_4 X_{1i} X_{3i} + \beta_5 X_{2i} X_{3i} + \varepsilon_i$

  - **The hypotheses:**

    $H_0 : \beta_4 = \beta_5 = 0$ (no interaction of X_1 with X_3 or X_2 with X_3)

    $H_1 : \beta_4$ and/or $\beta_5 \neq 0$ (X_1 and/or X_2 interacts with X_3)

  - **Partial F test statistic:** $F = \dfrac{\left(SSR(X_1, X_2, X_3, X_4, X_5) - SSR(X_1, X_2, X_3)\right)/2}{MSE(X_1, X_2, X_3, X_4, X_5)}$

    with 2 and $(n - 6)$ degrees of freedom.

- To test only whether the slope of Y with X_1 is the same for each of the two level of X_3, we can perform a t test on $H_0 : \beta_4 = 0$ vs. $H_1 : \beta_4 \neq 0$. Likewise, to test only whether the slope

Copyright ©2015 Pearson Education, Inc.

of Y with just X_2 along is the same for each of the two level of X_3, one can perform a t test on $H_0 : \beta_5 = 0$ vs. $H_1 : \beta_5 \neq 0$.

- If all the independent variables are numerical variables, the above analysis can be extended to test for whether the independent variables interact with each other.

  E.g., Let X_1, X_2 and X_3 be three numerical independent variables. To evaluate possible interaction between the independent variables, the regression model to use is

  $$Y_i = \beta_0 + \beta_1 X_{1i} + \beta_2 X_{2i} + \beta_3 X_{3i} + \beta_4 X_{1i} X_{2i} + \beta_5 X_{1i} X_{3i} + \beta_6 X_{2i} X_{3i} + \varepsilon_i$$

  - To test whether the three interaction terms significantly improve the regression model:
    - ❑ **The hypotheses**:

      $H_0 : \beta_4 = \beta_5 = \beta_6 = 0$ (There are no interaction among X_1, X_2 and X_3)

      $H_1 : \beta_4 \neq 0$ and/or $\beta_5 \neq 0$ and/or $\beta_6 \neq 0$ (X_1 interact with X_2, and/or X_1 interacts with X_3, and/or X_2 interacts with X_3)

    - ❑ **Partial F test statistic:**

      $$F = \frac{\left(SSR(X_1, X_2, X_3, X_4, X_5, X_6) - SSR(X_1, X_2, X_3) \right)/3}{MSE(X_1, X_2, X_3, X_4, X_5, X_6)} \text{ with 3 and}$$

      $(n - 7)$ degrees of freedom.

  - To test the contribution of each interaction separately to determine which interaction terms should be included in the model, we can perform separate t test.

Logistic Regression

- **Odds ratio:** $\text{Odds ratio} = \dfrac{\text{probability of an event of interest}}{1 - \text{probability of an event of interest}}$

- **Logistic regression model:** $\ln(\text{odds ratio}) = \beta_0 + \beta_1 X_{1i} + \beta_2 X_{2i} + \cdots + \beta_k X_{ki} + \varepsilon_i$

- **Logistic regression equation:** $\ln(\text{estimated odds ratio}) = b_0 + b_1 X_{1i} + b_2 X_{2i} + \cdots + b_k X_{ki}$

- **Estimated odds ratio:** $e^{\ln(\text{estimated odds ratio})}$

- **Estimated probability of an event of interest:** $\dfrac{\text{estimated odds ratio}}{1 + \text{estimated odds ratio}}$

- **Interpretation of the estimated slope coefficient** b_j **:** b_j measures the estimated change in the natural logarithm of the odds ratio as a result of a one unit change in X_j holding constant the effects of all the other independent variables.

Testing whether the Logistic Regression is a Good-Fitting Model

- **The hypotheses:**
  - H_0 : The model is a good-fitting model
  - H_1 : The model is not a good-fitting model
- **Test statistic:**
  - The *deviance statistic* has a χ^2 distribution with $(n - k - 1)$ degrees of freedom.

Copyright ©2015 Pearson Education, Inc.

▪ The rejection region is always in the right tail.

Testing whether an Independent Variable Makes a Significant Contribution to a Logistic Model

- **The hypotheses:**
    - ▪ $H_0 : \beta_j = 0$ (X_j does not make a significant contribution to the logistic model)
    - ▪ $H_1 : \beta_j \neq 0$ (X_j makes a significant contribution to the logistic model)
- **Test statistic:**
    - ▪ The **Wald statistic** is normally distributed.
    - ▪ This is a two-tail test with left and right-tail rejection regions.

Influence Analysis

- Three measures of the influence of individual values.
    - ▪ The hat matrix elements, h_i
    - ▪ The Studentized deleted residuals, t_i
    - ▪ Cook's distance statistic, D_i
    - ▪ Currently, no consensus exists as to which statistic is the best one to use.
    - ▪ Most statisticians will agree to remove an observation if all the three measures suggest that the observation is influential.
- The hat matrix elements, h_i
    - ▪ If $h_i > 2(k+1)/n$, where k is the number of independent variables in the model, then X_i is an influential observation and is a candidate for removal from the model.
- The Studentized deleted residuals:
    - ▪ $$t_i = e_i \sqrt{\frac{n-k-1}{SSE(1-h_i)-e_i^2}}$$

    where

    e_i = residual for the observation i

    k = number of independent variables

    SSE = error sum of squares of the regression model fitted

    h_i = hat matrix diagonal element for observation i
    - ▪ If $t_i > \left| t_{\alpha/2} \right|$, with $\alpha = 0.1$, then observation i is highly influential on the regression equation and is a candidate for removal.
- Cook's distance statistic:
    - ▪ $$D_i = \frac{e_i^2}{k(MSE)} \left[\frac{h_i}{(1-h_i)^2} \right]$$

Copyright ©2015 Pearson Education, Inc.

where

e_i = residual for the observation i

k = number of independent variables

MSE = mean square error of the regression model fitted

h_i = hat matrix diagonal element for observation i

- If $D_i > F_\alpha$ (the critical value of the F distribution having $k + 1$ degrees of freedom in the numerator and $n - k - 1$ degrees of freedom in the denominator at a 0.50 level of significance), the observation is candidate for removal.

Copyright ©2015 Pearson Education, Inc.

SOLUTIONS TO END OF SECTION
AND CHAPTER REVIEW EVEN PROBLEMS

14.2   (a)   Holding constant the effect of X_2, for each increase of one unit in X_1, the response variable Y is estimated to decrease an average of 2 units. Holding constant the effect of X_1, for each increase of one unit in X_2, the response variable Y is estimated to increase an average of 7 units.

       (b)   The Y-intercept 50 is the estimate of the mean value of Y if X_1 and X_2 are both 0.

14.4   (a) $\hat{Y} = -2.72825 + 0.047114 X_1 + 0.011947 X_2$

       (b)   For a given number of orders, each increase of $1,000 in sales is estimated to result in a mean increase in distribution cost of $47.114. For a given amount of sales, each increase of one order is estimated to result in a mean increase in distribution cost of $11.95.

       (c)   The interpretation of b_0 has no practical meaning here because it would have been the estimated mean distribution cost when there were no sales and no orders.

       (d) $\hat{Y}_i = -2.72825 + 0.047114(400) + 0.011947(4500) = 69.878$ or $69,878

       (e) $\$66,419.93 \le \mu_{Y|X} \le \$73,337.01$

       (f) $\$59,380.61 \le Y_X \le \$80,376.33$

       (g)   Since there is much more variation in predicting an individual value than in estimating a mean value, a prediction interval is wider than a confidence interval estimate holding everything else fixed.

       (h)   The model uses both the number of orders and the amount of sales to predict warehouse distribution cost. This may produce a better model than if only one of these independent variables is included.

14.6   (a) $\hat{Y} = 156.4 + 13.081 X_1 + 16.795 X_2$

       (b)   For a given amount of newspaper advertising, each increase of $1000 in radio advertising is estimated to result in a mean increase in sales of $13,081. For a given amount of radio advertising, each increase of $1000 in newspaper advertising is estimated to result in the mean increase in sales of $16,795.

       (c)   When there is no money spent on radio advertising and newspaper advertising, the estimated mean amount of sales is $156,430.44.

       (d)   According to the results of (b), newspaper advertising is more effective as each increase of $1000 in newspaper advertising will result in a higher mean increase in sales than the same amount of increase in radio advertising.

14.8   (a) $\hat{Y} = 532.2883 + 407.1346 X_1 - 2.8257 X_2$ where $X_1 = $ Land, $X_2 = $ Age

       (b)   For a given age, each increase by one acre in land area is estimated to result in a mean increase in fair market value of $407.1346 thousands. For a given acreage, each increase of one year in age is estimated to result in the mean decrease in fair market value of $2.8257 thousands.

       (c)   The interpretation of b_0 has no practical meaning here because it would have meant the estimated mean fair market value of a new house that has no land area.

       (d) $\hat{Y} = 532.2883 + 407.1346(.25) - 2.8257(55) = \$478.6577$ thousands.

Copyright ©2015 Pearson Education, Inc.

14.8 (e) $446.8367 \le \mu_{Y|X} \le 510.4788$

cont. (f) $307.2577 \le Y_X \le 650.0577$

14.10 (a) $MSR = SSR/k = 30/2 = 15$
$MSE = SSE/(n - k - 1) = 120/10 = 12$

(b) $F_{STAT} = MSR/MSE = 15/12 = 1.25$

(c) $F_{STAT} = 1.25 < F_{U(2,13-2-1)} = 4.103$. Do not reject H_0. There is not sufficient evidence of a significant linear relationship.

(d) $r^2 = \dfrac{SSR}{SST} = \dfrac{30}{150} = 0.2$

(e) $r_{adj}^2 = 1 - \left[\left(1 - r_{Y.12}^2\right) \dfrac{n-1}{n-k-1} \right] = 0.04$

14.12 (a) $F_{STAT} = 97.69 > F_{U(2,15-2-1)} = 3.89$. Reject H_0. There is evidence of a significant linear relationship with at least one of the independent variables.

(b) p-value = virtually zero. The probability of obtaining an F test statistic of 97.69 or larger is virtually zero if H_0 is true.

(c) $r_{Y.12}^2 = SSR/SST = 12.6102/13.38473 = 0.9421$. So, 94.21% of the variation in the long-term ability to absorb shock can be explained by variation in forefoot absorbing capability and variation in midsole impact.

(d) $r_{adj}^2 = 1 - \left[(1 - r_{Y.12}^2) \dfrac{n-1}{n-k-1} \right] = 1 - \left[(1 - 0.9421) \dfrac{15-1}{15-2-1} \right] = 0.93245$

14.14 (a) $MSR = SSR/k = 3368.087/2 = 1684.04$
$MSE = SSE/(n - k - 1) = 477.043/21 = 22.72$

$F_{STAT} = MSR/MSE = 1684/22.7 = 74.13$

$F_{STAT} = 74.13 > F_{U(2,24-2-1)} = 3.467$. Reject H_0. There is evidence of a significant linear relationship.

(b) p-value = virtually zero. The probability of obtaining an F test statistic of 74.13 or larger is virtually zero if H_0 is true.

(c) $r_{Y.12}^2 = SSR/SST = 3368.087/3845.13 = 0.8759$. So, 87.59% of the variation in distribution cost can be explained by variation in sales and variation in number of orders.

(d) $r_{adj}^2 = 1 - \left[(1 - r_{Y.12}^2) \dfrac{n-1}{n-k-1} \right] = 1 - \left[(1 - 0.8759) \dfrac{24-1}{24-2-1} \right] = 0.8641$

Copyright ©2015 Pearson Education, Inc.

14.16   (a) $MSR = SSR / k = 2,028,033 / 2 = 1,014,016$

$MSE = SSE / (n - k - 1) = 479,759.9 / 19 = 25,251$

$F_{STAT} = MSR / MSE = 1,014,016 / 25,251 = 40.16$

$F_{STAT} = 40.16 > F_{\alpha} = 3.522$. Reject H_0. There is evidence of a significant linear relationship.

(b) p-value < 0.001. The probability of obtaining an F test statistic of 40.16 or larger is less than 0.001 if H_0 is true.

(c) $r_{Y.12}^2 = SSR / SST = 2,028,033 / 2,507,793 = 0.8087$. So, 80.87% of the variation in sales can be explained by variation in radio advertising and variation in newspaper advertising.

(d) $r_{adj}^2 = 1 - \left[(1 - r_{Y.12}^2) \dfrac{n-1}{n-k-1} \right] = 1 - \left[(1 - 0.8087) \dfrac{22-1}{22-2-1} \right] = 0.7886$

14.18   (a)

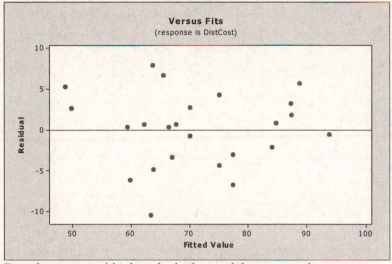

Based upon a residual analysis the model appears adequate.

(b)

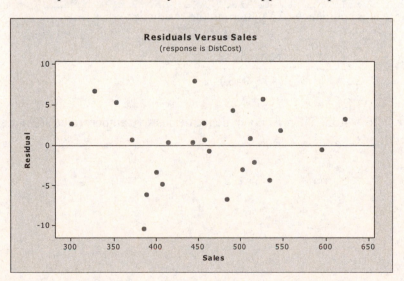

Copyright ©2015 Pearson Education, Inc.

14.18   (c)
cont.

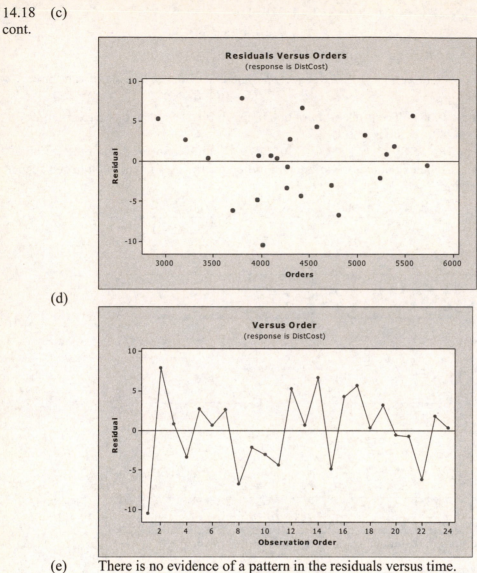

(d)

(e)   There is no evidence of a pattern in the residuals versus time.

(f) $$D = \dfrac{\displaystyle\sum_{i=2}^{n}\left(e_i - e_{i-1}\right)^2}{\displaystyle\sum_{i=1}^{n} e_i^2} = \dfrac{1077.0956}{477.0430} = 2.26$$

(g) $D = 2.26 > 1.55$. There is no evidence of positive autocorrelation in the residuals.

Copyright ©2015 Pearson Education, Inc.

14.20   (a)

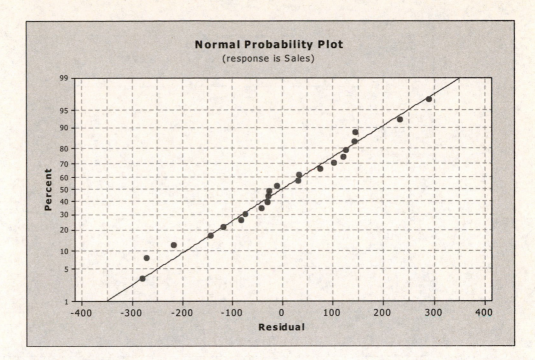

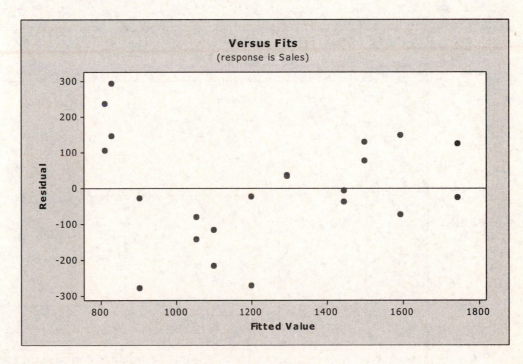

Copyright ©2015 Pearson Education, Inc.

14.20   (a)
cont.

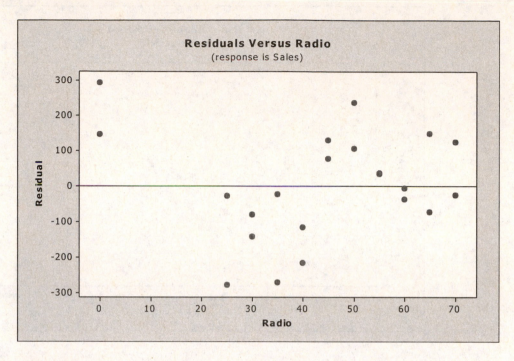

Minitab output:

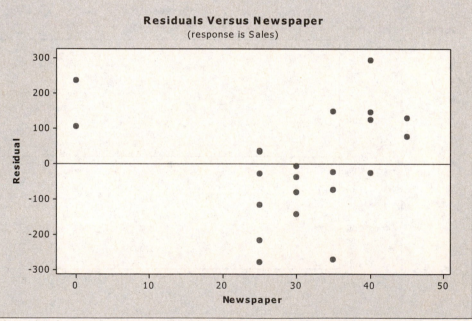

(b)   Since the data set is cross-sectional, it is inappropriate to compute the Durbin-Watson statistic.

(c)   There appears to be a quadratic relationship in the plot of the residuals against the fitted value and both radio and newspaper advertising. Thus, quadratic terms for each of these explanatory models should be considered for inclusion in the model. The normal probability plot suggests that the distribution of the residuals is very close to a normal distribution.

Copyright ©2015 Pearson Education, Inc.

14.22   (a)

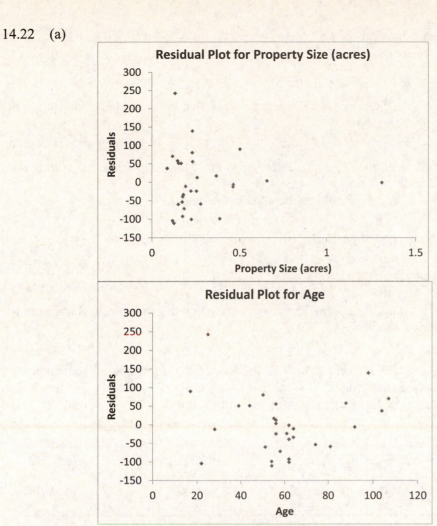

The residual analysis reveals no patterns.
   (b)   Since the data set is cross-sectional, the Durbin-Watson test is not appropriate.
   (c)   There are no apparent violations of the assumptions.

14.24   (a)   The slope of X_2 in terms of the t statistic is 3.75 which is larger than the slope of X_1 in terms of the t statistic which is 3.33.

   (b)   95% confidence interval on β_1 : $b_1 \pm t_{n-k-1} s_{b_1}$, $4 \pm 2.1098(1.2)$

$$1.46824 \leq \beta_1 \leq 6.53176$$

   (c)   For X_1: t_{STAT} $= b_1 / s_{b_1}$ $= 4/1.2 = 3.33 > t_{17}$ $= 2.1098$ with 17 degrees of freedom for $\alpha = 0.05$. Reject H_0. There is evidence that the variable X_1 contributes to a model already containing X_2.
   For X_2: t_{STAT} $= b_2 / s_{b_2}$ $= 3/0.8 = 3.75 > t_{17}$ $= 2.1098$ with 17 degrees of freedom for $\alpha = 0.05$. Reject H_0. There is evidence that the variable X_2 contributes to a model already containing X_1.
   Both variables X_1 and X_2 should be included in the model.

Copyright ©2015 Pearson Education, Inc.

14.26   (a)   95% confidence interval on β_1 : $b_1 \pm t_{n-k-1}s_{b_1}$, $0.0471 \pm 2.0796(0.0203)$

$$0.00488 \leq \beta_1 \leq 0.08932$$

(b)   For X_1: $t_{STAT} = b_1 / s_{b_1} = 0.0471 / 0.0203 = 2.32 > t_{21} = 2.0796$ with 21 degrees of freedom for $\alpha = 0.05$. Reject H_0. There is evidence that the variable X_1 contributes to a model already containing X_2.

For X_2: $t_{STAT} = b_2 / s_{b_2} = 0.01195 / 0.00225 = 5.31 > t_{21} = 2.0796$ with 21 degrees of freedom for $\alpha = 0.05$. Reject H_0. There is evidence that the variable X_2 contributes to a model already containing X_1.

Both variables X_1 and X_2 should be included in the model.

14.28   (a)   95% confidence interval on β_1 : $b_1 \pm t_{n-k-1}s_{b_1}$, $13.0807 \pm 2.093(1.7594)$

$$9.398 \leq \beta_1 \leq 16.763$$

(b)   For X_1: $t_{STAT} = b_1 / s_{b_1} = 13.0807 / 1.7594 = 7.43 > t_{19} = 2.093$ with 19 degrees of freedom for $\alpha = 0.05$. Reject H_0. There is evidence that the variable X_1 contributes to a model already containing X_2.

For X_2: $t_{STAT} = b_2 / s_{b_2} = 16.7953 / 2.9634 = 5.67 > t_{19} = 2.093$ with 19 degrees of freedom for $\alpha = 0.05$. Reject H_0. There is evidence that the variable X_2 contributes to a model already containing X_1.

Both variables X_1 and X_2 should be included in the model.

14.30   (a)

	Coefficients	Standard Error	t Stat	P-value	Lower 95%	Upper 95%
Intercept	532.2883	48.6661	10.9376	0.0000	432.4338	632.1428
Property Size (acres	407.1346	64.8028	6.2827	0.0000	274.1702	540.0990
Age	-2.8257	0.6813	-4.1475	0.0003	-4.2236	-1.4278

$274.1702 \leq \beta_1 \leq 540.0990$

(b)   For X_1: $t_{STAT} = b_1 / s_{b_1} = 6.2827$ and p-value = 0.0000. Since p-value < 0.05, reject H_0. There is evidence that the variable X_1 contributes to a model already containing X_2.

For X_2: $t_{STAT} = b_2 / s_{b_2} = -4.1475$ and p-value = 0.0003. Since p-value < 0.05, reject H_0. There is evidence that the variable X_2 contributes to a model already containing X_1.

Both variables X_1 and X_2 should be included in the model.

Copyright ©2015 Pearson Education, Inc.

14.32 (a) For X_1: $SSR\left(X_1\middle|X_2\right) = SSR\left(X_1\text{ and }X_2\right) - SSR\left(X_2\right) = 30 - 15 = 15$

$$F_{STAT} = \frac{SSR\left(X_1\middle|X_2\right)}{MSE} = \frac{15}{120\,/10} = 1.25 < F_{U(1,10)} = 4.965 \text{ with 1 and 10 degrees}$$

of freedom and $\alpha = 0.05$. Do not reject H_0. There is not sufficient evidence that the variable X_1 contributes to a model already containing X_2.

For X_2: $SSR\left(X_2\middle|X_1\right) = SSR\left(X_1\text{ and }X_2\right) - SSR\left(X_1\right) = 30 - 20 = 10$

$$F_{STAT} = \frac{SSR\left(X_2\middle|X_1\right)}{MSE} = \frac{10}{120\,/10} = 0.833 < F_{U(1,10)} = 4.965 \text{ with 1 and 10 degrees}$$

of freedom and $\alpha = 0.05$. Do not reject H_0. There is not sufficient evidence that the variable X_2 contributes to a model already containing X_1.

Neither independent variable X_1 nor X_2 makes a significant contribution to the model in the presence of the other variable. Also the overall regression equation involving both independent variables is not significant:

$$F_{STAT} = \frac{MSR}{MSE} = \frac{30\,/2}{120\,/10} = 1.25 < F_{U(2,10)} = 4.103$$

Neither variable should be included in the model and other variables should be investigated.

(b) $$r_{Y1.2}^2 = \frac{SSR\left(X_1\middle|X_2\right)}{SST - SSR\left(X_1\text{ and }X_2\right) + SSR\left(X_1\middle|X_2\right)} = \frac{15}{150 - 30 + 15}$$

= 0.1111. Holding constant the effect of variable X_2, 11.11% of the variation in Y can be explained by the variation in variable X_1.

$$r_{Y2.1}^2 = \frac{SSR\left(X_2\middle|X_1\right)}{SST - SSR\left(X_1\text{ and }X_2\right) + SSR\left(X_2\middle|X_1\right)} = \frac{10}{150 - 30 + 10}$$

= 0.0769. Holding constant the effect of variable X_1, 7.69% of the variation in Y can be explained by the variation in variable X_2.

14.34 (a) For X_1:

$$SSR\left(X_1\middle|X_2\right) = SSR\left(X_1\text{ and }X_2\right) - SSR\left(X_2\right) = 3368\,.087 - 3246\,.062 = 122\,.025$$

$$F_{STAT} = \frac{SSR\left(X_1\middle|X_2\right)}{MSE} = \frac{122\,.025}{477\,.043\,/21} = 5.37 > F_{U(1,21)} = 4.325 \text{ with 1 and 21}$$

degrees of freedom and $\alpha = 0.05$. Reject H_0. There is evidence that the variable X_1 contributes to a model already containing X_2.

For X_2:

$$SSR\left(X_2\middle|X_1\right) = SSR\left(X_1\text{ and }X_2\right) - SSR\left(X_1\right) = 3368\,.087 - 2726\,.822 = 641\,.265$$

$$F_{STAT} = \frac{SSR\left(X_2\middle|X_1\right)}{MSE} = \frac{641\,.265}{477\,.043\,/21} = 28.23 > F_{U(1,21)} = 4.325 \text{ with 1 and 21}$$

degrees of freedom and $\alpha = 0.05$. Reject H_0. There is evidence that the variable X_2 contributes to a model already containing X_1.

Since each independent variable, X_1 and X_2, makes a significant contribution to the model in the presence of the other variable, the most appropriate regression model for this data set should include both variables.

Copyright ©2015 Pearson Education, Inc.

14.34 (b)
cont.

$$r_{Y1.2}^2 = \frac{SSR(X_1 | X_2)}{SST - SSR(X_1 \ and \ X_2) + SSR(X_1 | X_2)}$$

$$= \frac{122.025}{3845.13 - 3368.087 + 122.025} = 0.2037.$$ Holding constant the effect of the number of orders, 20.37% of the variation in Y can be explained by the variation in sales.

$$r_{Y2.1}^2 = \frac{SSR(X_2 | X_1)}{SST - SSR(X_1 \ and \ X_2) + SSR(X_2 | X_1)}$$

$$= \frac{641.265}{3845.13 - 3368.087 + 641.265} = 0.5734.$$ Holding constant the effect of sales, 57.34% of the variation in Y can be explained by the variation in the number of orders.

14.36 (a) For X_1:

$$SSR(X_1 | X_2) = SSR(X_1 \ and \ X_2) - SSR(X_2) = 2,028,033 - 632,259.4 = 1,395,773.6$$

$$F_{STAT} = \frac{SSR(X_1 | X_2)}{MSE} = \frac{1,395,773.6}{479,759.9/19} = 55.28 > F_{U(1,21)} = 4.381 \text{ with 1 and 19}$$

degrees of freedom and $\alpha = 0.05$. Reject H_0. There is evidence that the variable X_1 contributes to a model already containing X_2.

For X_2:

$$SSR(X_2 | X_1) = SSR(X_1 \ and \ X_2) - SSR(X_1) = 2028033 - 1216940 = 811093$$

$$F_{STAT} = \frac{SSR(X_2 | X_1)}{MSE} = \frac{811,093}{479,759.9/19} = 32.12 > F_{U(1,19)} = 4.381 \text{ with 1 and 19}$$

degrees of freedom and $\alpha = 0.05$. Reject H_0. There is evidence that the variable X_2 contributes to a model already containing X_1.

Since each independent variable, X_1 and X_2, makes a significant contribution to the model in the presence of the other variable, the most appropriate regression model for this data set should include both variables.

(b)

$$r_{Y1.2}^2 = \frac{SSR(X_1 | X_2)}{SST - SSR(X_1 \ and \ X_2) + SSR(X_1 | X_2)}$$

$$= \frac{1,395,773.6}{2,507,793 - 2,028,033 + 1,395,773.6} = 0.7442.$$ Holding constant the effect of newspaper advertising, 74.42% of the variation in Y can be explained by the variation in radio advertising.

$$r_{Y2.1}^2 = \frac{SSR(X_2 | X_1)}{SST - SSR(X_1 \ and \ X_2) + SSR(X_2 | X_1)}$$

$$= \frac{811,093}{2,507,793 - 2,028,033 + 811,093} = 0.6283.$$ Holding constant the effect of radio advertising, 62.83% of the variation in Y can be explained by the variation in newspaper advertising.

Copyright ©2015 Pearson Education, Inc.

14.38 (a) Holding constant the effect of X_2, the estimated mean value of the dependent variable will increase by 4 units for each increase of one unit of X_1.

(b) Holding constant the effects of X_1, the presence of the condition represented by $X_2 = 1$ is estimated to increase the mean value of the dependent variable by 2 units.

(c) $t = 3.27 > t_{17} = 2.1098$. Reject H_0. The presence of X_2 makes a significant contribution to the model.

14.40 (a) $\hat{Y} = 243.7371 + 9.2189\ X_1 + 12.6967\ X_2$, where X_1 = number of rooms and X_2 = neighborhood (east = 0).

(b) Holding constant the effect of neighborhood, for each additional room, the selling price is estimated to increase by a mean of 9.2189 thousands of dollars, or \$9218.9. For a given number of rooms, a west neighborhood is estimated to increase mean selling price over an east neighborhood by 12.6967 thousands of dollars, or \$12,696.7.

(c) $\hat{Y} = 243.7371 + 9.2189\ (9) + 12.6967\ (0) = 326.70758$ or \$326,707.58

$\$309,560.04 \le Y_{X=X_i} \le \$343,855.11$ $\$321,471.44 \le \mu_{Y|X=X_i} \le \$331,943.71$

(d)

Normal Probability Plot

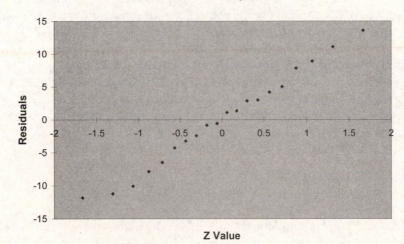

14.40   (d)
cont.

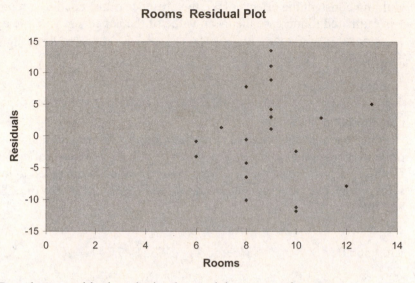

Rooms Residual Plot

Based on a residual analysis, the model appears adequate.

(e) $F_{STAT} = 55.39$, p-value is virtually 0. Since p-value < 0.05, reject H_0. There is evidence of a significant relationship between selling price and the two independent variables (rooms and neighborhood).

(f)   For X_1: $t_{STAT} = 8.9537$, p-value is virtually 0. Reject H_0. Number of rooms makes a significant contribution and should be included in the model.
For X_2: $t_{STAT} = 3.5913$, p-value $= 0.0023 < 0.05$. Reject H_0. Neighborhood makes a significant contribution and should be included in the model.
Based on these results, the regression model with the two independent variables should be used.

(g) $7.0466 \leq \beta_1 \leq 11.3913$,

(h) $5.2378 \leq \beta_2 \leq 20.1557$

(i) $r_{adj}^2 = 0.851$

(j) $r_{Y1.2}^2 = 0.825$. Holding constant the effect of neighborhood, 82.5% of the variation in selling price can be explained by variation in number of rooms. $r_{Y2.1}^2 = 0.431$.
Holding constant the effect of number of rooms, 43.1% of the variation in selling price can be explained by variation in neighborhood.

(k)   The slope of selling price with number of rooms is the same regardless of whether the house is located in an east or west neighborhood.

(l) $\hat{Y} = 253.95 + 8.032 X_1 - 5.90 X_2 + 2.089 X_1 X_2$.
For $X_1 X_2$: the p-value is 0.330. Do not reject H_0. There is no evidence that the interaction term makes a contribution to the model.

(m)   The two-variable model in (f) should be used.

(n)   The real estate association can conclude that the number of rooms and the neighborhood both significantly affect the selling price, but the number of rooms has a greater effect.

Copyright ©2015 Pearson Education, Inc.

14.42   (a) $\hat{Y} = 8.0100 + 0.0052X_1 - 2.1052X_2$, where $X_1 =$ depth (in feet) and $X_2 =$ type of drilling (wet = 0, dry = 1).

(b)   Holding constant the effect of type of drilling, for each foot increase in depth of the hole, the additional drilling time is estimated to increase by a mean of 0.0052 minute . For a given depth, a dry drilling is estimated to reduce mean additional drilling time over wet drilling by 2.1052 minutes.

(c)   Dry drilling: $\hat{Y} = 8.0101 + 0.0052\,(100) - 2.1052 = 6.4276$ minutes.

   $6.2096 \le \mu_{Y|X=X_i} \le 6.6457$, $4.9230 \le Y_{X=X_i} \le 7.9322$

(d)

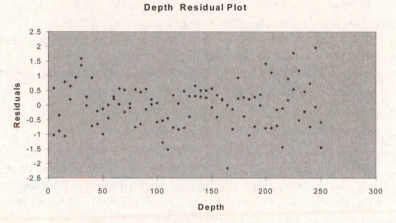

Based on a residual analysis, the model appears adequate.

(e) $F_{STAT} = 111.109$ with 2 and 97 degrees of freedom, $F_{2,97} = 3.09$ using Excel. p-value is virtually 0. Reject H_0 at 5% level of significance. There is evidence of a relationship between additional drilling time and the two dependent variables.

(f)   For X_1: $t_{STAT} = 5.0289 > t_{97} = 1.9847$. Reject H_0. Depth of the hole makes a significant contribution and should be included in the model.
   For X_2: : $t_{STAT} = -14.0331 < t_{97} = -1.9847$. Reject H_0. Type of drilling makes a significant contribution and should be included in the model.
   Based on these results, the regression model with the two independent variables should be used.

(g) $0.0032 \le \beta_1 \le 0.0073$

(h) $-2.4029 \le \beta_2 \le -1.8075$

(i) $r^2_{adj} = 0.6899$

(j) $r^2_{Y1.2} = 0.2068$. Holding constant the effect of type of drilling, 20.68% of the variation in additional drilling time can be explained by variation in depth of the hole.
   $r^2_{Y2.1} = 0.6700$. Holding constant the effect of the depth of the hole, 67% of the variation in additional drilling time can be explained by variation in type of drilling.

(k)   The slope of additional drilling time with depth of the hole is the same regardless of whether it is a dry drilling hole or a wet drilling hole.

(l) $\hat{Y} = 7.9120 + 0.0060X_1 - 1.9091X_2 - 0.0015X_1 X_2$.
   For X_1X_2: the p-value is 0.4624 > 0.05. Do not reject H_0. There is not evidence that the interaction term makes a contribution to the model.

(m)   The two-variable model in (a) should be used.

Copyright ©2015 Pearson Education, Inc.

14.42   (n)   Both variables affect the drilling time. Dry drilling holes should be used to reduce the
cont.   drilling time.

14.44   (a) $\hat{Y} = 31.5594 - 0.0296\,X_1 + 0.0041\,X_2 + 1.7159 \cdot 10^{-5} X_3$.

where X_1 = sales, X_2 = orders, $X_3 = X_1 X_2$
For X_1X_2: the p-value is $0.3249 > 0.05$. Do not reject H_0. There is not enough
evidence that the interaction term makes a contribution to the model.

(b)   Since there is not enough evidence of any interaction effect between sales and orders,
the model in problem 14.4 should be used.

14.46   (a) $\hat{Y} = -1293.3105 + 43.6600X_1 + 56.9335X_2 - 0.8430X_3$.

where X_1 = radio advertisement, X_2 = newspaper advertisement, $X_3 = X_1 X_2$
For X_1X_2: the p-value is $0.0018 < 0.05$. Reject H_0. There is enough evidence that the
interaction term makes a contribution to the model.

(b)   Since there is enough evidence of an interaction effect between radio and newspaper
advertisement, the model in this problem should be used.

14.48   (a) $\hat{Y} = 250.4237 + 0.0127X_1 - 1.4785X_2 + 0.004X_3$.

where X_1 = staff present, X_2 = remote hours, $X_3 = X_1 X_2$
For X_1X_2: the p-value is $0.2353 > 0.05$. Do not reject H_0. There is not enough
evidence that the interaction term makes a contribution to the model.

(b)   Since there is not enough evidence of an interaction effect between total staff present
and remote hours, the model in problem 14.7 should be used.

14.50   Holding constant the effect of other variables, the natural logarithm of the estimated odds
ratio for the dependent categorical response will increase by a mean of 2.2 for each unit
increase in the independent variable to which the coefficient corresponds.

14.52   Estimated Probability of Success = Estimated Odds Ratio / (1 + Estimated Odds Ratio)
$= 0.75/(1 + 0.75) = 0.4286$

14.54   (a)   ln(estimated odds ratio) $= -6.94 + 0.13947X_1 + 2.774X_2$
$= -6.94 + 0.13947(36) + 2.774(0) = -1.91908$
Estimated odds ratio $= e^{-1.91908} = 0.1467$
Estimated Probability of the Event of Interest
$=$ Estimated Odds Ratio / (1 + Estimated Odds Ratio) $= 0.1467/(1 + 0.1467) = 0.1280$

(b)   From the text discussion of the example, 70.16% of the individuals who charge
$36,000 per annum and possess additional cards can be expected to purchase the
premium card. Only 12.80% of the individuals who charge $36,000 per annum and
do not possess additional cards can be expected to purchase the premium card. For a
given amount of money charged per annum, the likelihood of purchasing a premium
card is substantially higher among individuals who already possess additional cards
than for those who do not possess additional cards.

Copyright ©2015 Pearson Education, Inc.

14.54   (c)   ln(estimated odds ratio) $= -6.94 + 0.13947X_1 + 2.774X_2$
cont. $= -6.94 + 0.13947(18) + 2.774(0) = -4.42954$
Estimated odds ratio $= e^{-4.42954} = 0.0119$
Estimated Probability of the Event of Interest
$=$ Estimated Odds Ratio / (1 + Estimated Odds Ratio) $= 0.0119/(1 + 0.0119) =$
0.01178

(d)   Among individuals who do not purchase additional cards, the likelihood of
purchasing a premium card diminishes dramatically with a substantial decrease in the
amount charged per annum.

14.56   (a)   PHStat output:

Binary Logistic Regression				
Predictor	Coefficients	SE Coef	Z	p-Value
Intercept	-47.4821	12.0173	-3.9512	0.0001
fixed acidity	1.310179398	0.4139	3.1656	0.0015
chlorides	90.57937563	22.643	4.0003	0.0001
pH	9.779258829	2.9743	3.288	0.0010
Deviance	54.45564087			

(b)   Holding constant the effects of chlorides and pH, for each increase of one unit of
fixed acidity, ln(odds) increases by an estimate of 1.3102. Holding constant the
effects of fixed acidity and pH, for each increase of one unit in chlorides, ln(odds)
increases by an estimate of 90.5794. Holding constant the effects of fixed acidity and
chlorides, for each increase of one unit in pH, ln(odds) increases by an estimate of
9.7793.

(c)   ln(estimated odds ratio) $= -47.4821 + 1.3102X_1 + 90.5794X_2 + 9.7793X_3 = -$
0.4603
Estimated odds ratio $= e^{-0.4603} = 0.6311$
Estimated Probability of the Event of Interest = Estimated Odds Ratio / (1 +
Estimated Odds Ratio) $= 0.6311/(1 + 0.6311) = 0.3869$

(d)   The deviance statistic is 54.4556, which has a p-value of 0.9998. Do not reject H_0.
The model is a good fitting model.

(e)   For fixed acidity: $Z_{STAT} = 3.1656$ with a p-value $= 0.0015$. Reject H_0. There is
sufficient evidence that fixed acidity makes a significant contribution to the model.
For chlorides: $Z_{STAT} = 4.0003$ with a p-value $= 0.0001$. Reject H_0. There is sufficient
evidence that the amount of chlorides makes a significant contribution to the model.
For pH: $Z_{STAT} = 3.2880$ with a p-value $= 0.0010$. Reject H_0. There is sufficient
evidence that pH makes a significant contribution to the model.

(f)   Based on the p-values corresponding to the Z-values for the variable coefficients in
the
logistic regression equation and corresponding to the deviance statistics, the model
that includes fixed acidity, chlorides and pH should be used to predict whether the
wine is red.

Copyright ©2015 Pearson Education, Inc.

14.58 (a) PHStat output:

Predictor	Coefficients	SE Coef	Z	p-Value
Intercept	-0.6048	0.4194	-1.4421	0.1493
claims/year	0.093769442	0.5029	0.1865	0.8521
new business (1=yes, 0=no):1	1.810770296	0.8134	2.2261	0.0260
Deviance	119.4353239		p-value	0.0457

(b) Holding constant the effects of whether the policy is new, for each increase of the number of claims submitted per year by the policy holder, ln(odds) increases by an estimate of 0.0938. Holding constant the number of claims submitted per year by the policy holder, ln(odds) is estimated to be 1.8108 higher when the policy is new as compared to when the policy is not new.

(c) ln(estimated odds ratio) $= -0.6048 + 0.0938(1) + 1.8108(1) = 1.2998$

Estimated odds ratio $= e^{1.2998} = 3.6684$
Estimated Probability of the Event of Interest = Estimated Odds Ratio / (1 + Estimated Odds Ratio) $= 0.7858$

(d) The deviance statistic is 119.4353 with a χ^2 distribution of 95 d.f. and p-value = $0.0457 < 0.05$. Reject H_0. The model is not a good fitting model.

(e) For claims/year: $Z_{STAT} = 0.1865$, p-value = $0.8521 > 0.05$. Do not eject H_0. There is not sufficient evidence that the number of claims submitted per year by the policy holder makes a significant contribution to the logistic model.
For new business: $Z_{STAT} = 2.2261$, p-value = $0.0260 < 0.05$. Reject H_0. There is sufficient evidence that whether the policy is new makes a significant contribution to the logistic model.

(f) PHStat output:

Predictor	Coefficients	SE Coef	Z	p-Value
Intercept	-1.0125	0.3888	-2.6042	0.0092
claims/year	0.992742206	0.3367	2.9481	0.0032
Deviance	125.0102452		p-value	0.0250

(g) PHStat output:

Predictor	Coefficients	SE Coef	Z	p-Value
Intercept	-0.5423	0.2515	-2.1563	0.0311
new business	1.928618927	0.5211	3.7008	0.0002
Deviance	119.4701921		p-value	0.0526

(h) The deviance statistic for (f) is 125.0102 with a χ^2 distribution of 96 d.f. and p-value = $0.0250 < 0.05$. Reject H_0. The model is not a good fitting model.

The deviance statistic for (g) is 119.4702 with a χ^2 distribution of 96 d.f. and p-value = $0.0526 > 0.05$. Do not reject H_0. The model is a good fitting model.
The model in (g) should be used to predict a fraudulent claim.

Copyright ©2015 Pearson Education, Inc.

14.60   Observations 14 ($h_i = 0.3568$) and 19 ($h_i = 0.2828$) are influential as they have
$h_i > 2(k+1)/n = 2(2+1)/24 = 0.25$.

Observations 1, 2, and 14 had an effect on the model: $\left|t_1^*\right| = 2.5783$, $\left|t_2^*\right| = 1.8465$, and
$\left|t_{14}^*\right| = 1.8429$. All of these values exceed $t_{\alpha/2} = 1.7247$.

The largest value for Cook's D_i is 0.5637, which is less than $F_\alpha = 0.8149$. Using the 3
criteria, there is insufficient evidence for removal of any observation from the model.

14.62   Observations 1 ($h_i = 0.2924$), 2 ($h_i = 0.2924$), 13 ($h_i = 0.3564$) and 14 ($h_i = 0.3564$) are
influential as they have $h_i > 2(k+1)/n = 2(2+1)/22 = 0.2727$.

Observations 2, 4, 7, and 13 had an effect on the model: $\left|t_2^*\right| = 2.44$, $\left|t_4^*\right| = 1.98$, $\left|t_7^*\right| = 1.87$,
and $\left|t_{13}^*\right| = 1.96$. All of these values exceed $t_{\alpha/2} = 1.7341$.

The largest value for Cook's D_i is 0.652 for Observation 2, which is less than $F_\alpha = 0.8177$.
Using the 3 criteria, there is insufficient evidence for removal of any observation from the
model.

14.64   Observations 12 ($h_i = 0.7027$) is influential as it has $h_i > 2(k+1)/n = 2(2+1)/30 = 0.2$.

Observations 6 and 10 have an effect on the model: $\left|t_6^*\right| = 1.9048$ and $\left|t_{10}^*\right| = 3.9433$. All of
these values exceed $t_{\alpha/2} = 1.7056$ with d.f. = 26.

None of the observations have a Cook's $D_i > F_\alpha = 0.8089$ with d.f. = 3 and 27.

Using the 3 criteria, there is insufficient evidence for removal of any observation from the
model.

14.66   In the case of the simple linear regression model, the slope b_1 represents the change in the
estimated mean of Y per unit change in X and does not take into account any other variables.
In the multiple linear regression model, the slope b_1 represents the change in the estimated
mean of Y per unit change in X_1, taking into account the effect of all the other independent
variables.

14.68   The coefficient of partial determination measures the proportion of variation in Y explained
by a particular X variable holding constant the effect of the other independent variables in the
model. The coefficient of multiple determination measures the proportion of variation in Y
explained by all the X variables included in the model.

14.70   You test whether the interaction of the dummy variable and each of the independent variables
in the model make a significant contribution to the regression model.

14.72   It is assumed that the slope of the dependent variable Y with an independent variable X is the
same for each of the two levels of the dummy variable.

14.74   The hat matrix diagonal element h_i reflects the possible influence of X_i on the regression
equation while the Studentized deleted residuals measures the difference of each Y_i from the
value predicted by a model that includes all observations except observation X_i.

Copyright ©2015 Pearson Education, Inc.

14.76   (a) $\hat{Y} = -3.9152 + 0.0319\ X_1 + 4.2228\ X_2$, where X_1 = amount of cubic feet moved and X_2 = number of pieces of large furniture.

(b)   Holding constant the number of pieces of large furniture, for each additional cubic foot moved, the mean labor hours are estimated to increase by 0.0319. Holding constant the amount of cubic feet moved, for each additional piece of large furniture, the mean labor hours are estimated to increase by 4.2228.

(c) $\hat{Y} = -3.9152 + 0.0319\ (500) + 4.2228\ (2) = 20.4926$

(d)

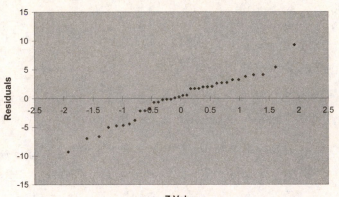

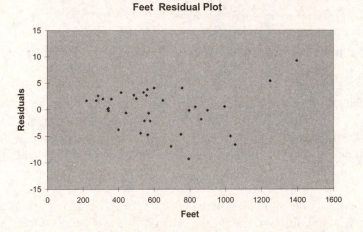

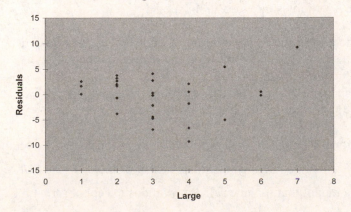

Copyright ©2015 Pearson Education, Inc.

14.76 (d)   Based on a residual analysis, the errors appear to be normally distributed. The equal
cont.   variance assumption might be violated because the variances appear to be larger
             around the center region of both independent variables. There might also be
             violation of the linearity assumption. A model with quadratic terms for both
             independent variables might be fitted.

(e) $F_{STAT} = 228.80$, p-value is virtually 0. Since p-value < 0.05, reject H_0. There is
      evidence of a significant relationship between labor hours and the two independent
      variables (the amount of cubic feet moved and the number of pieces of large
      furniture).

(f)   The p-value is virtually 0. The probability of obtaining a test statistic of 228.80 or
      greater is virtually 0 if there is no significant relationship between labor hours and the
      two independent variables (the amount of cubic feet moved and the number of pieces
      of large furniture).

(g) $r_{Y.12}^2 = 0.9327$. 93.27% of the variation in labor hours can be explained by variation
      in the amount of cubic feet moved and the number of pieces of large furniture.

(h) $r_{adj}^2 = 0.9287$

(i)   For X_1: $t_{STAT} = 6.9339$, p-value is virtually 0. Reject H_0. The amount of cubic feet
      moved makes a significant contribution and should be included in the model.
      For X_2: $t_{STAT} = 4.6192$, p-value is virtually 0. Reject H_0. The number of pieces of large
      furniture makes a significant contribution and should be included in the model.
      Based on these results, the regression model with the two independent variables
      should be used.

(j)   For X_1: $t_{STAT} = 6.9339$, p-value is virtually 0. The probability of obtaining a sample
      that will yield a test statistic farther away than 6.9339 is virtually 0 if the amount of
      cubic feet moved does not make a significant contribution holding the effect of the
      number of pieces of large furniture constant.
      For X_2: $t_{STAT} = 4.6192$, p-value is virtually 0. The probability of obtaining a sample
      that will yield a test statistic farther away than 4.6192 is virtually 0 if the number of
      pieces of large furniture does not make a significant contribution holding the effect of
      the amount of cubic feet moved constant.

(k) $0.0226 \leq \beta_1 \leq 0.0413$. We are 95% confident that the mean labor hours will
      increase by somewhere between 0.0226 and 0.0413 for each additional cubic foot
      moved holding constant the number of pieces of large furniture. In Problem 13.44,
      we are 95% confident that the mean labor hours will increase by somewhere between
      0.0439 and 0.0562 for each additional cubic foot moved regardless of the number of
      pieces of large furniture.

(l) $r_{Y1.2}^2 = 0.5930$. Holding constant the effect of the number of pieces of large furniture,
      59.3% of the variation in labor hours can be explained by variation in the amount of
      cubic feet moved.
      $r_{Y2.1}^2 = 0.3927$. Holding constant the effect of the amount of cubic feet moved,
      39.27% of the variation in labor hours can be explained by variation in the number of
      pieces of large furniture.

(m)   Both the number of cubic feet moved and the number of large pieces of furniture are
      useful in predicting the labor hours, but the cubic feet removed is more important.

Copyright ©2015 Pearson Education, Inc.

14.78 (a)

	Coefficients	Standard Error	t Stat	P-value
Intercept	257.9033	66.0000	3.9076	0.0006
Size(000 sq. ft.	53.3606	16.1075	3.3128	0.0026
Age	0.2521	0.7871	0.3203	0.7512

$\hat{Y} = 257.9033 + 53.3606 X_1 + 0.2521 X_2$

(b) Holding constant the age of the house, for each additional thousand square feet in size, the mean assessed value is estimated to increase by 53.3606 thousand dollars. Holding constant the size of a house, for each additional year in the age of the house, the mean assessed value is estimated to increase by 0.2521 thousand dollars.

(c) $\hat{Y} = 257.9033 + 53.3606(2) + 0.2521(55) = 378.4893$ thousand dollars

(d)

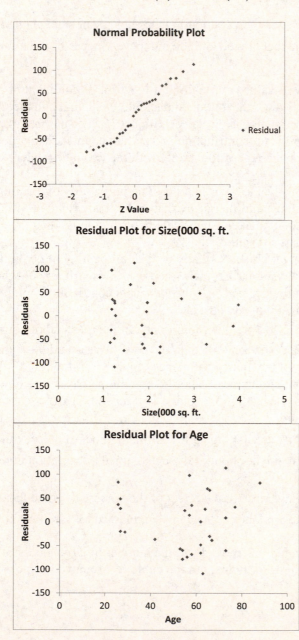

Copyright ©2015 Pearson Education, Inc.

14.78	(d)	Based on a residual analysis, the model appears adequate.
cont.	(e)	$F = 6.6459$, p-value $= 0.0045$. Since p-value < 0.05, reject H_0. There is evidence of a significant relationship between assessed value and the two independent variables (size and age).
	(f)	The p-value $= 0.0045$. The probability of obtaining a test statistic of 6.6459 or greater is 0.0045 if there is no significant relationship between assessed value and the two independent variables (size and age).
	(g)	$r_{Y.12}^2 = 0.3299$. 32.99% of the variation in selling price can be explained by variation in size and age.
	(h)	$r_{adj}^2 = 0.2803$
	(i)	For X_1: $t = 3.3128$, p-value $= 0.0026$. Reject H_0. The size of a house makes a significant contribution and should be included in the model. For X_2: $t = 0.3203$, p-value $= 0.7512 > 0.05$. Do not reject H_0. The age of a house does not make a significant contribution and should be included in the model. Based on these results, the regression model with the size of a house should be used.
	(j)	For X_1: $t = 3.3128$, p-value $= 0.0026$. The probability of obtaining a sample that will yield a test statistic farther away from 0 is 0.0026 if the size does not make a significant contribution holding age constant. For X_2: $t = 0.3203$, p-value $= 0.7512$. The probability of obtaining a sample that will yield a test statistic farther away from 0 is 0.3203 if the age does not make a significant contribution holding the effect of size constant.
	(k)	$20.3109 \le \beta_1 \le 86.4104$. We are 95% confident that the mean assessed value will increase by an amount somewhere between 20.3109 thousand dollars and 86.4104 thousand dollars for each additional thousand square feet increase in size holding constant the age. In Problem 13.76, we are 95% confident that the mean assessed value will increase by an amount somewhere between 22.6113 thousand dollars and 78.9949 thousand dollars for each additional thousand square feet increase size regardless of the age.
	(l)	$r_{Y1.2}^2 = 0.2890$. Holding constant the effect of the age, 28.90% of the variation in assessed value can be explained by variation in the size. $r_{Y2.1}^2 = 0.0038$. Holding constant the effect of the size, 0.38% of the variation in assessed value can be explained by variation in the age.
	(m)	Only the size of a house has a significant effect on the assessed value.
14.80	(a)	$\hat{Y} = 694.9557 + 8.6059 X_1 + 2.0690 X_2$, where X_1 = assessed value and X_2 = age.
	(b)	Holding constant the age, for each additional thousand dollars of assessed value, the taxes are estimated to increase by a mean of 8.6059 dollars. Holding constant the assessed value, for each additional year, the taxes are estimated to increase by a mean of 2.0690 dollars.
	(c)	$\hat{Y} = 694.9557 + 8.6059(400) + 2.0690(50) = 4240.75$ dollars

Copyright ©2015 Pearson Education, Inc.

14.80 (d)
cont.

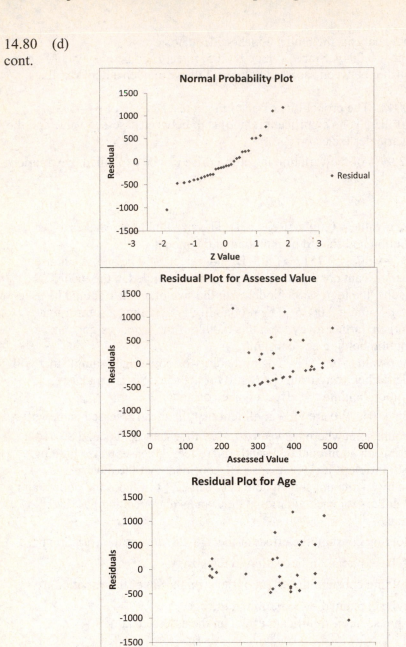

(d) Based on a residual analysis, the errors does not appear to be normally distributed. The equal variance assumption appears to be holding up.

(e) $F_{STAT} = 22.0699$, p-value = 0.0000. Since p-value < 0.05, reject H_0. There is evidence of a significant relationship between taxes and the two independent variables (size and age).

(f) The p-value = 0.0000. The probability of obtaining a test statistic of 22.0699 or greater is virtually 0 if there is no significant relationship between taxes and the two independent variables (assessed value and age).

(g) $r^2 = 0.6205$. 62.05% of the variation in taxes can be explained by variation in assessed value and age.

Copyright ©2015 Pearson Education, Inc.

14.80   (h) $r^2_{adj} = 0.5924$

cont.   (i)   For X_1: $t_{STAT} = 6.5271$, p-value $= 0.0000 < 0.05$. Reject H_0. The assessed value of a house makes a significant contribution and should be included in the model.

For X_2: $t_{STAT} = 0.3617$, p-value $= 0.7204 > 0.05$. Do not reject H_0. The age of a house does not make any significant contribution and should not be included in the model. Based on these results, the regression model with only the assessed value should be used.

(j)   For X_1: p-value $= 0.0000$. The probability of obtaining a sample that will yield a test statistic farther away from 0 is 0.0000 if the assessed value of a house does not make a significant contribution holding age constant.

For X_2: p-value $= 0.7204$. The probability of obtaining a sample that will yield a test statistic farther away from 0 is 0.7204 if the age of a house does not make a significant contribution holding the effect of the assessed value constant.

(k) $5.9005 \le \beta_1 \le 11.3112$. We are 95% confident that the mean taxes will increase by an amount somewhere between 5.9005 dollars and 11.3112 dollars for each additional thousand dollars increase in assessed value of a house holding constant the age. In Problem 13.77, you estimated that for each additional thousand dollars increase in the assessed value of a house, the mean taxes increases by 8.4915 dollars without taking into consideration the age of the house.

(l) $r^2_{Y1.2} = 0.6121$. Holding constant the effect of age, 61.21% of the variation in taxes can be explained by variation in assessed value.

$r^2_{Y2.1} = 0.0048$. Holding constant the effect of assessed value, 0.48% of the variation in taxes can be explained by variation in age.

(m)   Based on your answers to (a) through (l), the age of a house does have an effect on its taxes.

14.82   Excel output:

Regression Statistics	
Multiple R	0.8378
R Square	0.7019
Adjusted R Square	0.6798
Standard Error	6.7531
Observations	30

ANOVA

	df	SS	MS	F	Significance F
Regression	2	2898.6937	1449.3468	31.7812	0.0000
Residual	27	1231.3063	45.6039		
Total	29	4130.0000			

	Coefficients	Standard Error	t Stat	P-value	Lower 95%	Upper 95%
Intercept	163.8291	10.4638	15.6567	0.0000	142.3591	185.2991
E.R.A.	-20.0106	2.5249	-7.9253	0.0000	-25.1913	-14.8300
League	-4.8622	2.4951	-1.9487	0.0618	-9.9816	0.2573

Copyright ©2015 Pearson Education, Inc.

14.82 (a) $\hat{Y} = 163.8291 - 20.0106 X_1 - 4.8622 X_2$, where X_1 = ERA and X_2 = League
cont.   (American = 0).

(b)   Holding constant the effect of the league, for each additional ERA, the number of wins is estimated to decrease by a mean of 20.0106. For a given ERA, a team in the National League is estimated to have a mean of 4.8622 fewer wins than a team in the American League.

(c) $\hat{Y} = 163.8291 - 20.0106(4.5) - 4.8622(0) = 73.7813$ wins = 74 wins

(d)   PHStat output:

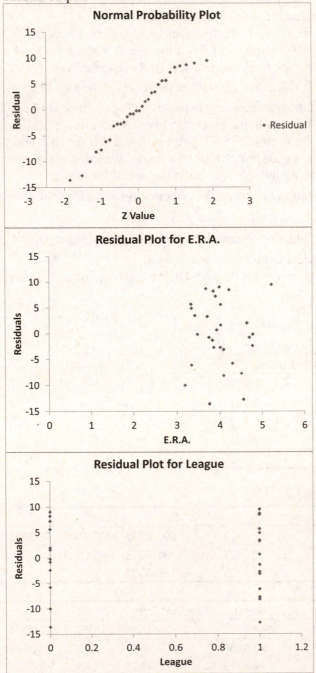

14.82 (d)   Based on a residual analysis, there is no pattern in the errors. There is no apparent
cont.   violation of other assumptions.

(e) F_{STAT} = 31.7812, p-value = 0.0005. Since p-value < 0.05, reject H_0. There is evidence of a significant relationship between wins and the two independent variables (ERA and league).

(f)   For X_1: t_{STAT} = -7.9253, p-value = 0.0000 < 0.05. Reject H_0. ERA makes a significant contribution and should be included in the model.
For X_2: t_{STAT} = -1.9487, p-value = 0.0618 > 0.05. Do not reject H_0. The league does not make a significant contribution and should not be included in the model.
Based on these results, the regression model with only the ERA as the independent variable should be used.

(g) $-25.1913 \le \beta_1 \le -14.8300$

(h) $-9.9816 \le \beta_2 \le 0.2573$

(i) r^2_{adj} = 0.6798. So 67.98% of the variation in wins can be explained by the variation in ERA and league after adjusting for number of independent variables and sample size.

(j) $r^2_{Y1.2}$ = 0.6994. Holding constant the effect of league, 69.94% of the variation in number of wins can be explained by the variation in ERA.
$r^2_{Y2.1}$ = 0.1233. Holding constant the effect of ERA, 12.33% of the variation in number of wins can be explained by the variation in league.

(k)   The slope of the number of wins with ERA is the same regardless of whether the team belongs to the American or the National League.

(l)   Excel output:

	Coefficients	Standard Error	t Stat	P-value
Intercept	155.0925	15.6995	9.8788	0.0000
E.R.A.	-17.8704	3.8200	-4.6781	0.0001
League	10.6201	20.7575	0.5116	0.6132
E.R.A. X League	-3.8496	5.1232	-0.7514	0.4592

For $X_1 X_2$: the p-value is 0.4592 > 0.05. Do not reject H_0. There is no evidence that the interaction term makes a contribution to the model.

(m)   The one-variable model in (f) should be used.

Copyright ©2015 Pearson Education, Inc.

14.84   Excel output:

Regression Statistics	
Multiple R	0.2540
R Square	0.0645
Adjusted R Square	0.0247
Standard Error	3.4367
Observations	50

ANOVA

	df	SS	MS	F	Significance F
Regression	2	38.2915	19.1458	1.6211	0.2085
Residual	47	555.0989	11.8106		
Total	49	593.3904			

	Coefficients	Standard Error	t Stat	P-value	Lower 95%	Upper 95%
Intercept	98.7920	15.7539	6.2709	0.0000	67.0992	130.4848
Pressure	-0.0075	0.0350	-0.2150	0.8307	-0.0779	0.0629
Temp	-0.3210	0.1806	-1.7773	0.0820	-0.6843	0.0423

The r^2 of the multiple regression is very low at 0.0645. Only 6.45 of the variation in thickness can be explained by the variation of pressure and temperature.

The F test statistic for the combined significant of pressure and temperature is 1.621 with a p-value of 0.2085. Hence, at a 5% level of significance, there is not enough evidence to conclude that both pressure and temperature affect thickness.

The p-value of the t test for the significance of pressure is 0.8307, which is larger than 5%. Hence, there is not sufficient evidence to conclude that pressure affects thickness holding constant the effect of temperature. The p-value of the t test for the significance of temperature is 0.0820, which is also larger than 5%. There is not enough evidence to conclude that temperature affects thickness at 5% level of significance holding constant the effect of pressure. Hence, neither pressure nor temperature affects thickness individually.

Copyright ©2015 Pearson Education, Inc.

14.84
cont.

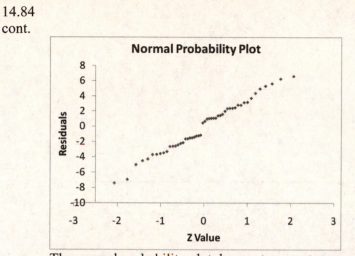

The normal probability plot does not suggest any potential violation of the normality assumption.

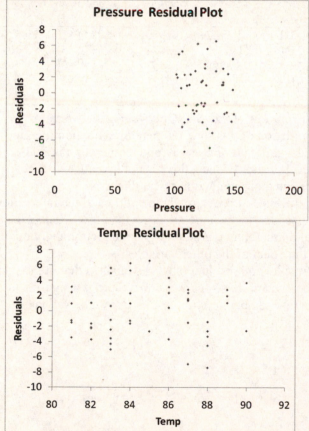

The residual plots do not indicate potential violation of the homoscedasticity assumption. The temperature residual plot, however, suggests that there might be nonlinear relationship between temperature and thickness.

Copyright ©2015 Pearson Education, Inc.

14.84   Excel output with the interaction term:
cont.

Regression Statistics	
Multiple R	0.2709
R Square	0.0734
Adjusted R Square	0.0129
Standard Error	3.4574
Observations	50

ANOVA

	df	SS	MS	F	Significance F
Regression	3	43.5348	14.5116	1.2140	0.3153
Residual	46	549.8556	11.9534		
Total	49	593.3904			

	Coefficients	Standard Error	t Stat	P-value	Lower 95%	Upper 95%
Intercept	197.8857	150.4571	1.3152	0.1950	-104.9687	500.7401
Pressure	-0.8178	1.2240	-0.6682	0.5074	-3.2815	1.6459
Temp	-1.4892	1.7731	-0.8398	0.4053	-5.0583	2.0800
Pressure x Temp	0.0096	0.0144	0.6623	0.5111	-0.0195	0.0386

The r^2 of the multiple regression is very low at 0.0734. Only 7.34 of the variation in thickness can be explained by the variation of pressure, temperature and their interaction. The F test statistic for the combined significant of pressure and temperature is 1.214 with a p-value of 0.3153. Hence, at a 5% level of significance, there is not enough evidence to conclude that pressure, temperature and their interaction affect thickness.

The p-value of the t test for the significance of pressure, temperature and the interaction term are 0.5074, 0.4053 and 0.5111, respectively, which are all larger than 5%. Hence, there is not sufficient evidence to conclude that pressure, temperature or the interaction individually affects thickness holding constant the effect of the other variables.

The pattern in the normal probability plot and residual plots is similar to that in the regression without the interaction term. Hence, the article's suggestion that there is a significant interaction between the pressure and the temperature in the tank cannot be validated.

Copyright ©2015 Pearson Education, Inc.

14.86   Excel output:

Regression Statistics	
Multiple R	0.5707
R Square	0.3257
Adjusted R Square	0.2615
Standard Error	11.3621
Observations	24

ANOVA

	df	SS	MS	F	Significance F
Regression	2	1309.5192	654.7596	5.0718	0.0160
Residual	21	2711.0379	129.0970		
Total	23	4020.5571			

	Coefficients	Standard Error	t Stat	P-value	Lower 95%	Upper 95%
Intercept	18.2892	71.4849	0.2558	0.8006	-130.3718	166.9502
Die Temperature	0.5976	0.4639	1.2883	0.2117	-0.3671	1.5622
Die Diameter	-13.5108	4.6386	-2.9127	0.0083	-23.1572	-3.8644

The r^2 of the multiple regression is 0.3257. So 32.57% of the variation in unit density can be explained by the variation of die temperature and die diameter.

The F test statistic for the combined significant of die temperature and die diameter is 5.0718 with a p-value of 0.0160. Hence, at a 5% level of significance, there is enough evidence to conclude that die temperature and die diameter affect unit density.

The p-value of the t test for the significance of die temperature is 0.2117, which is larger than 5%. Hence, there is not sufficient evidence to conclude that die temperature affects unit density holding constant the effect of die diameter.

The p-value of the t test for the significance of die diameter is 0.0083, which is smaller than 5%. There is enough evidence to conclude that die diameter affects unit density at 5% level of significance holding constant the effect of die temperature.

Excel output after dropping die temperature:

Regression Statistics	
Multiple R	0.5219
R Square	0.2724
Adjusted R Square	0.2393
Standard Error	11.5312
Observations	24

ANOVA

	df	SS	MS	F	Significance F
Regression	1	1095.2557	1095.2557	8.2370	0.0089
Residual	22	2925.3014	132.9682		
Total	23	4020.5571			

	Coefficients	Standard Error	t Stat	P-value	Lower 95%	Upper 95%
Intercept	107.9267	16.6438	6.4845	0.0000	73.4095	142.4439
Die Diameter	-13.5108	4.7076	-2.8700	0.0087	-23.2738	-3.7479

Copyright ©2015 Pearson Education, Inc.

14.86   Die diameter still remains statistically significant at the 5% level of significance. Hence, only
cont.   die diameter needs to be used in the model.

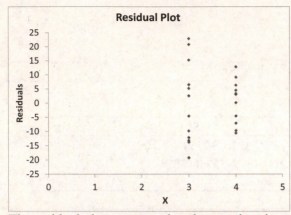

The residual plot suggests that the equal variance assumption is likely violated.

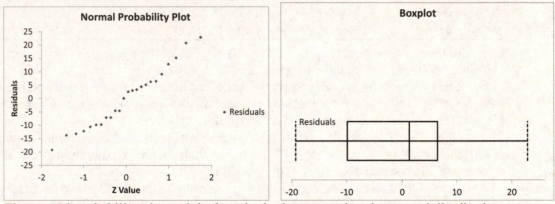

The normal probability plot and the boxplot both suggest that the normal distribution
assumption might be violated.

None of the observations have a Cook's $D_i > F_\alpha = 0.7155$ with d.f. = 2 and 22.

Hence, using the Studentized deleted residuals, hat matrix diagonal elements and Cook's
distance statistic together, there is insufficient evidence for removal of any observation from
the model.

Copyright ©2015 Pearson Education, Inc.

CHAPTER 15

OBJECTIVES

- To use quadratic terms in a regression model
- To use transformed variables in a regression model
- To measure the correlation among independent variables
- To build a regression model using either the stepwise or best-subsets approach
- To avoid the pitfalls involved in developing a multiple regression model

OVERVIEW AND KEY CONCEPTS

The Quadratic Regression Model

- In a quadratic regression model, the relationship between the dependent variable and one or more independent variable is a quadratic polynomial function.
- The quadratic regression model is useful when the residual plot reveals nonlinear relationship.
- The quadratic regression model:
  - $Y_i = \beta_0 + \beta_1 X_{1i} + \beta_2 X_{1i}^2 + \varepsilon_i$
  - The quadratic relationship can be between Y and more than one X variable as well.
- **Testing for the overall significance of the quadratic regression model:**
  - The test for the overall significance of the quadratic regression model is exactly the same as testing for the overall significance of any multiple regression model.
  - **Test statistic:** $F = \dfrac{MSR}{MSE}$.
- **Testing for quadratic effect:**
  - **The hypotheses:** $H_0 : \beta_2 = 0$ (no quadratic effect) vs. $H_1 : \beta_2 \neq 0$ (the quadratic term is needed)
  - **Test statistic:** $t = \dfrac{b_2 - \beta_2}{S_{b_2}}$.
  - This is a two-tail test with a left tail and a right-tail rejection region.

Using Transformation in Regression Models

- The following three transformation models are often used to overcome violations of the homoscedasticity assumption, as well as to transform a model that is not linear in form into one that is linear.
- **Square-root transformation:**
  - $Y_i = \beta_0 + \beta_1 \sqrt{X_{1i}} + \varepsilon_i$
  - The dependent variable is Y_i and the independent variable is $\sqrt{X_{1i}}$.

Copyright ©2015 Pearson Education, Inc. Copyright ©2015 Pearson Education, Inc.

- **Transformed multiplicative model:**
  - $\log Y_i = \log \beta_0 + \beta_1 \log X_{1i} + \cdots + \beta_k \log X_{ki} + \log \varepsilon_i$
  - The dependent variable is $\log Y_i$ and the independent variables are $\log X_{1i}$, $\log X_{2i}$, etc.
- **Transformed exponential model:**
  - $\ln Y_i = \beta_0 + \beta_1 X_{1i} + \cdots + \beta_k X_{ki} + \ln \varepsilon_i$
  - The dependent variable is $\ln Y_i$ and the independent variables are X_{1i}, X_{2i}, etc.

Collinearity

- Some of the explanatory variables are highly correlated with each other.
- The collinear variables do not provide new information and it becomes difficult to separate the effect of such variables on the dependent variable.

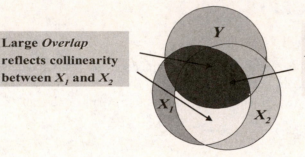

- The values of the regression coefficient for the correlated variables may fluctuate drastically depending on which independent variables are included in the model.
- Variance inflationary factor (VIF) is used to measure collinearity.

  - $VIF_j = \dfrac{1}{\left(1 - R_j^2\right)}$ where R_j^2 is the coefficient determination of regressing X_j on all the other explanatory variables.
  - If $VIF_j > 5$, X_j is considered highly correlated with the other explanatory variables.

Model Building

- The goal is to develop a good model with the fewest explanatory variables that is easier to interpret and has lower probability of collinearity.
- **Stepwise regression procedure:** Provides limited evaluation of alternative models.
- **Best-subsets approach:** Uses the Mallow's C_p and selects the models with small C_p near $k+1$.

Copyright ©2015 Pearson Education, Inc. Copyright ©2015 Pearson Education, Inc.

- **Model building flowchart:**

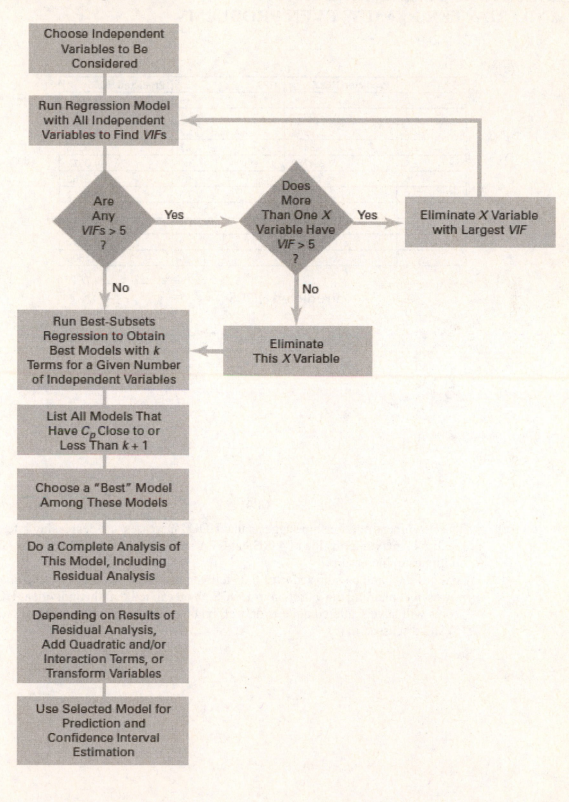

Copyright ©2015 Pearson Education, Inc. Copyright ©2015 Pearson Education, Inc.

SOLUTIONS TO END OF SECTION
AND CHAPTER REVIEW EVEN PROBLEMS

15.2 (a)

GPA	Predicted HOCS	GPA	Predicted HOCS
2	2.8600	3	3.9900
2.1	3.0342	3.1	4.0282
2.2	3.1948	3.2	4.0528
2.3	3.3418	3.3	4.0638
2.4	3.4752	3.4	4.0612
2.5	3.5950	3.5	4.0450
2.6	3.7012	3.6	4.0152
2.7	3.7938	3.7	3.9718
2.8	3.8728	3.8	3.9148
2.9	3.9382	3.9	3.8442
		4	3.7600

(b)

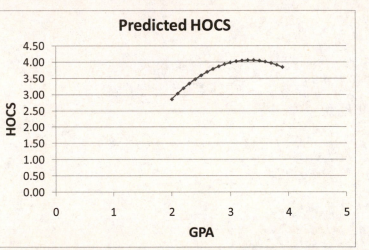

(c)   The curvilinear relationship suggests that HOCS increases at a decreasing rate. It reaches its maximum value of 4.0638 at GPA = 3.3 and declines after that as GPA continues to increase.

(d)   An r^2 of 0.07 and an adjusted r^2 of 0.06 tell you that GPA has very low explanatory power in explaining the variation in HOCS. You can tell that the individual HOCS scores will have scattered quite widely around the curvilinear relationship plotted in (b) and discussed in (c).

Copyright ©2015 Pearson Education, Inc. Copyright ©2015 Pearson Education, Inc.

15.4   (a)

Excel output:

Regression Statistics	
Multiple R	0.9866
R Square	0.9733
Adjusted R Square	0.9730
Standard Error	7.3289
Observations	152

ANOVA

	df	SS	MS	F	Significance F
Regression	2	292105.2471	146052.6236	2719.1357	0.0000
Residual	149	8003.2200	53.7129		
Total	151	300108.4671			

	Coefficients	Standard Error	t Stat	P-value	Lower 95%	Upper 95%
Intercept	-4.6280	2.2913	-2.0199	0.0452	-9.1556	-0.1005
Alcohol %	21.2075	0.4896	43.3180	0.0000	20.2401	22.1749
Carbohydrates	4.0040	0.1422	28.1481	0.0000	3.7229	4.2851

$\hat{Y} = -4.6280 + 21.2075 X_1 + 4.0040 X_2$, where X_1 = Alcohol % and X_2 = Carbohydrates.

(b)   Excel output:

Regression Statistics	
Multiple R	0.9875
R Square	0.9752
Adjusted R Square	0.9745
Standard Error	7.1159
Observations	152

ANOVA

	df	SS	MS	F	Significance F
Regression	4	292664.8874	73166.2218	1444.9277	0.0000
Residual	147	7443.5798	50.6366		
Total	151	300108.4671			

	Coefficients	Standard Error	t Stat	P-value	Lower 95%	Upper 95%
Intercept	9.8109	5.5487	1.7681	0.0791	-1.1546	20.7763
Alcohol %	15.2538	1.8655	8.1766	0.0000	11.5670	18.9405
Carbohydrates	4.4660	0.4018	11.1157	0.0000	3.6720	5.2601
Alcohol % Sq	0.4770	0.1442	3.3086	0.0012	0.1921	0.7619
Carbohydrates Sq	-0.0170	0.0145	-1.1674	0.2449	-0.0457	0.0118

(b) $\hat{Y} = 9.8109 + 15.2538 X_1 + 4.4660 X_2 + 0.4770 X_1^2 - 0.0170 X_2^2$, where X_1 = Alcohol % and X_2 = Carbohydrates.

Copyright ©2015 Pearson Education, Inc. Copyright ©2015 Pearson Education, Inc.

15.4   (c) $H_0: \beta_3 = \beta_4 = 0$ H_1: Not all $\beta_j = 0$ for $j = 3, 4$

cont.

$$F_{STAT} = \frac{[SSR\,(X_1, X_2, X_3, X_4) - SSR\,(X_1, X_2)]/2}{MSE\,(X_1, X_2, X_3, X_4)} = 5.5260 \text{ with 2 numerator and}$$

147 denominator degrees of freedom. $F_{crit} = 3.0576$. The p-value is 0.0049. Since the p-value = 0.0049 < 0.05, reject H_0. At 5% level of significance, the quadratic terms are significant together. Hence, the model in (b) is better.

$H_0: \beta_3 = 0$ vs. $H_1: \beta_3 \neq 0$

t statistic = 3.3086, p-value = 0.0012 < 0.05. Reject H_0. There is enough evidence that the quadratic term for alcohol % is significant at the 5% level of significance.

$H_0: \beta_4 = 0$ vs. $H_1: \beta_4 \neq 0$

t statistic = -1.1674, p-value = 0.2449 > 0.05. Do not reject H_0. There is not enough evidence that the quadratic term for carbohydrates is significant at the 5% level of significance.

Excel output after dropping the quadratic term for carbohydrates:

Regression Statistics	
Multiple R	0.9874
R Square	0.9750
Adjusted R Square	0.9745
Standard Error	7.1247
Observations	152

ANOVA

	df	SS	MS	F	Significance F
Regression	3	292595.8795	97531.9598	1921.4059	0.0000
Residual	148	7512.5876	50.7607		
Total	151	300108.4671			

	Coefficients	Standard Error	t Stat	P-value	Lower 95%	Upper 95%
Intercept	10.9172	5.4738	1.9944	0.0479	0.1002	21.7342
Alcohol %	15.7507	1.8186	8.6611	0.0000	12.1570	19.3444
Carbohydrates	4.0257	0.1385	29.0748	0.0000	3.7521	4.2993
Alcohol % Sq	0.4335	0.1394	3.1090	0.0023	0.1580	0.7091

$\hat{Y} = 10.9172 + 15.7507\,X_1 + 4.0257\,X_2 + 0.4335\,X_1^2$, where X_1 = Alcohol % and X_2 = Carbohydrates.

Copyright ©2015 Pearson Education, Inc. Copyright ©2015 Pearson Education, Inc.

15.4   (d)   PHStat output:
cont.

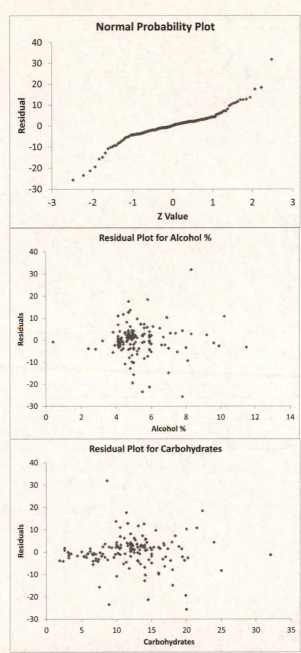

The normal probability plot suggests that the errors are left-skewed. However, because of the large sample size, the validity of the results is not seriously impacted. The residual plots of the alcohol percentage and carbohydrates in the quadratic model do not reveal any remaining non-linearity.

The number of calories in a beer depends quadratically on the alcohol percentage but linearly on the number of carbohydrates. The alcohol percentage along with its quadratic term and number of carbohydrates explain about 97.50% of the variation in the number of calories in a beer and about 97.45% of the variation in the number of calories in a beer after adjusting for the sample size and the number of independent variables.

Copyright ©2015 Pearson Education, Inc. Copyright ©2015 Pearson Education, Inc.

15.6   (a)

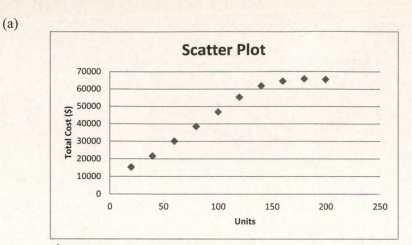

(b) $\hat{Y} = 710.0000 + 607.9773X - 1.3693X^2$

Regression Statistics	
Multiple R	0.9946
R Square	0.9892
Adjusted R Square	0.9861
Standard Error	2255.9071
Observations	10

ANOVA

	df	SS	MS	F	Significance F
Regression	2	3263096181.8182	1631548090.9091	320.5955	0.0000
Residual	7	35623818.1818	5089116.8831		
Total	9	3298720000.0000			

	Coefficients	Standard Error	t Stat	P-value	Lower 95%	Upper 95%
Intercept	710.0000	2653.2895	0.2676	0.7967	-5564.0326	6984.0326
Units	607.9773	55.4063	10.9731	0.0000	476.9622	738.9923
Units Sq	-1.3693	0.2454	-5.5790	0.0008	-1.9497	-0.7889

(c) $\hat{Y} = 710.0000 + 607.9773(145) - 1.3693(145)^2 = \$60,076.79$

(d)

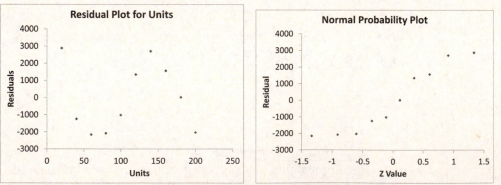

There appears to be a curvilinear pattern in the residual plot of the units and the units squared. The normal probability plot suggests possible departure from the normality assumption.

(e) $H_0: \beta_1 = \beta_2 = 0$ vs. H_1: At least one $\beta_j \neq 0$

$F_{STAT} = 320.5955 > 4.74$; reject H_0. There is a significant relationship between monthly unit production and total cost.

(f)   The p-value $= 0.0000$ indicates that the probability of having an F-test statistic of at least 320.5955 when $\beta_1 = \beta_2 = 0$ is essentially 0.

Copyright ©2015 Pearson Education, Inc. Copyright ©2015 Pearson Education, Inc.

15.6   (g) t_{STAT} = -5.5790 with p-value = 0.0008 < 0.05. Reject H_0. The quadratic effect is
cont.   significant.

        (h)   The p-value = 0.0008 indicates that the probability of having a t-test statistic with an
               absolute value of at least 5.5790 is equal to 0.0008 when $\beta_2 = 0$.

        (i) $r^2_{Y.12}$ = 0.9892. So, 98.92% of the variation in total cost can be explained by the
               quadratic relationship between total cost and unit production.

        (j) r^2_{adj} = 0.9861

        (k)   Total cost depends quadratically on unit production and 98.92% of the variation in
               total cost can be explained by the quadratic relationship between total cost and unit
               production.

15.8   (a) $\log \hat{Y} = \log(3.07) + 0.9 \log(8.5) + 1.41 \log(5.2) = 2.33318$

               $\hat{Y} = 10^{2.33318} = 215.37$

        (b)   Holding constant the effects of X_2, for each additional unit of the logarithm of X_1, the
               logarithm of Y is estimated to increase by a mean of 0.9. Holding constant the effects
               of X_1, for each additional unit of the logarithm of X_2, the logarithm of Y is estimated
               to increase by a mean of 1.41.

15.10   (a)   Excel output:

Regression Statistics	
Multiple R	0.9693
R Square	0.9396
Adjusted R Square	0.9388
Standard Error	11.0329
Observations	152

ANOVA

	df	SS	MS	F	Significance F
Regression	2	281971.5361	140985.7680	1158.2378	0.0000
Residual	149	18136.9310	121.7244		
Total	151	300108.4671			

	Coefficients	Standard Error	t Stat	P-value	Lower 95%	Upper 95%
Intercept	-154.0890	6.7312	-22.8917	0.0000	-167.3900	-140.7881
Sqrt Alcohol%	95.2628	3.3504	28.4329	0.0000	88.6423	101.8833
Sqrt Carbohydrates	27.3500	1.3864	19.7279	0.0000	24.6105	30.0894

$\hat{Y} = -154.0890 + 95.2628\sqrt{X_1} + 27.3500\sqrt{X_2}$, where X_1 = Alcohol % and X_2 =
Carbohydrates.

Copyright ©2015 Pearson Education, Inc. Copyright ©2015 Pearson Education, Inc.

15.10   (b)   PHStat output:
cont.

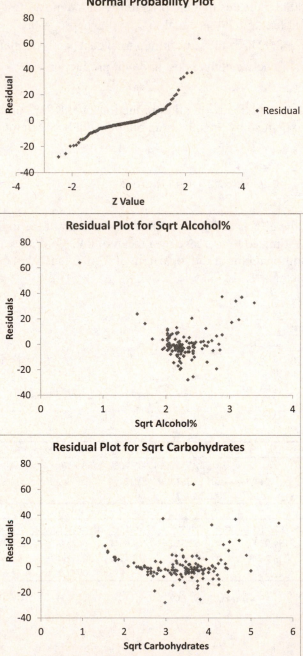

The normal probability plot suggests departure from the normality assumption. However, because of the large sample size, the validity of the results is not seriously impacted. The residual plots of the square-root transformation of alcohol percentage and carbohydrates reveal some remaining nonlinearity.

Copyright ©2015 Pearson Education, Inc. Copyright ©2015 Pearson Education, Inc.

15.10   (c) $H_0 : \beta_1 = \beta_2 = 0$ H_1 : Not all $\beta_j = 0$ for $j = 1, 2$

cont. $F_{STAT} = \dfrac{MSR}{MSE} = 1158.2378.$

Since the p-value is virtually zero, reject H_0 at 5% level of significance. There is evidence of a significant linear relationship between calories and the square root of the percentage of alcohol and the square root of the number of carbohydrates.

(d) $r^2 = 0.9396.$ So 93.96% of the variation in calories can be explained by the variations in the square root of the percentage of alcohol and the square root of the number of carbohydrates.

(e)   Adjusted $r^2 = 0.9388.$

(f)   The model in 15.4 is better for it has a higher r^2. Also, the residual analysis of the model in 15.4 does not reveal any remaining nonlinearity while residual analysis in (b) does reveal remaining nonlinearity.

15.12   (a) $\ln \hat{Y} = 9.7664 + 0.0080 X_1$

Regression Statistics	
Multiple R	0.9335
R Square	0.8714
Adjusted R Square	0.8553
Standard Error	0.1969
Observations	10

ANOVA

	df	SS	MS	F	Significance F
Regression	1	2.1019	2.1019	54.1987	0.0001
Residual	8	0.3102	0.0388		
Total	9	2.4121			

	Coefficients	Standard Error	t Stat	P-value	Lower 95%	Upper 95%
Intercept	9.7664	0.1345	72.5973	0.0000	9.4562	10.0766
Units	0.0080	0.0011	7.3620	0.0001	0.0055	0.0105

(b) $\ln \hat{Y} = 9.7664 + 0.0080\,(145)$ $\hat{Y} = e^{10.92363} = \$55471.75$

(c)

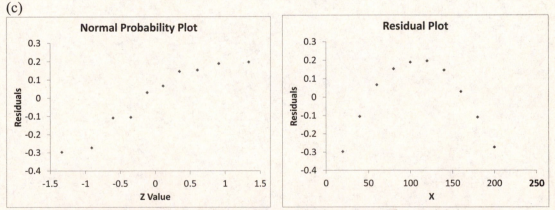

The residual analysis indicates a clear quadratic pattern. The model does not adequately fit the data.

Copyright ©2015 Pearson Education, Inc. Copyright ©2015 Pearson Education, Inc.

15.12 (d) $t_{STAT} = 7.3620$ with a p-value $= 0.0001 < 0.05$. Reject H_0. The model provides a
cont.   significant relationship.

     (e) $r^2 = 0.8714$. So, 87.14% of the variation in the natural logarithm of total cost can be
explained by variation in the unit production.

     (f) $r^2_{adj} = 0.8553$

     (g)   It is inappropriate to compare the r^2 of the model here with that of 15.6 because the
dependent variable here is logarithmically transformed.

15.14 $VIF = \dfrac{1}{1 - 0.2} = 1.25$

15.16 $R_1^2 = 0.64$, $VIF_1 = \dfrac{1}{1 - 0.64} = 2.778$

       $R_2^2 = 0.64$, $VIF_2 = \dfrac{1}{1 - 0.64} = 2.778$

There is no reason to suspect the existence of collinearity.

15.18 $R_1^2 = 0.008464$, $VIF_1 = \dfrac{1}{1 - 0.008464} = 1.009$

       $R_2^2 = 0.008464$, $VIF_2 = \dfrac{1}{1 - 0.008464} = 1.009$

There is no reason to suspect the existence of collinearity.

15.20 $VIF = \dfrac{1}{1 - 0.0104} = 1.0105$. There is no reason to suspect the existence of collinearity.

15.22 (a) $C_p = \dfrac{(1 - R_k^2)(n - T)}{1 - R_T^2} - [n - 2(k + 1)] = \dfrac{(1 - 0.274)(40 - 7)}{1 - 0.653} - [40 - 2(2 + 1)]$
         $= 35.04$

     (b) C_p overwhelmingly exceeds $k + 1 = 3$, the number of parameters (including the Y-
intercept), so this model does not meet the criterion for further consideration as the
best model.

Copyright ©2015 Pearson Education, Inc. Copyright ©2015 Pearson Education, Inc.

15.24   Let Y = assessed value, X_1 = size, X_2 = 1 if it has a fireplace, 0 otherwise, X_3 = number of bedrooms, X_4 = number of bathrooms.
Based on a full regression model involving all of the variables:
$VIF_1 = 2.3355$, $VIF_2 = 1.1873$, $VIF_3 = 1.9885$, $VIF_4 = 1.4428$ •
All the VIF values are less than 5.
The best-subsets output reveals the following models to be considered:
PHStat output:

Model	Cp	k+1	R Square	Adj. R Square	Std. Error	Consider This Model?
X1	-0.6401	2	0.3273	0.3033	60.9911	Yes
X1X2	1.1712	3	0.3323	0.2829	61.8788	Yes
X1X3	1.2893	3	0.3292	0.2795	62.0238	Yes
X1X4	1.3580	3	0.3274	0.2776	62.1080	Yes
X1X2X3	3.0022	4	0.3368	0.2603	62.8455	Yes
X1X2X4	3.1657	4	0.3325	0.2555	63.0506	Yes
X1X3X4	3.2826	4	0.3294	0.2520	63.1970	Yes
X1X2X3X4	5.0000	5	0.3369	0.2308	64.0873	Yes

The stepwise regression ends up with the model that includes only X_1.
PHStat output:

Stepwise Regression Analysis

Table of Results for General Stepwise

Size(000 sq. ft. entered.

	df	SS	MS	F	Significance F
Regression	1	50687.4669	50687.4669	13.6260	0.0010
Residual	28	104157.6411	3719.9158		
Total	29	154845.1080			

	Coefficients	Standard Error	t Stat	P-value	Lower 95%	Upper 95%
Intercept	276.8480	28.8074	9.6103	0.0000	217.8388	335.8572
Size(000 sq. ft.	50.8031	13.7628	3.6913	0.0009	22.6113	78.9949

No other variables could be entered into the model. Stepwise ends.

Copyright ©2015 Pearson Education, Inc. Copyright ©2015 Pearson Education, Inc.

15.24
cont.

The regression output of the full model:

Regression Statistics	
Multiple R	0.5804
R Square	0.3369
Adjusted R Square	0.2308
Standard Error	64.0873
Observations	30

ANOVA

	df	SS	MS	F	Significance F
Regression	4	52165.6097	13041.4024	3.1753	0.0307
Residual	25	102679.4983	4107.1799		
Total	29	154845.1080			

	Coefficients	Standard Error	t Stat	P-value	Lower 95%	Upper 95%
Intercept	244.4325	78.4366	3.1163	0.0046	82.8894	405.9757
Size(000 sq. ft.	43.5532	22.1005	1.9707	0.0599	-1.9636	89.0700
Fireplace Coded	16.0257	30.1438	0.5316	0.5997	-46.0566	78.1080
Bedrooms	8.1910	20.1244	0.4070	0.6875	-33.2559	49.6380
Bathrooms	0.9677	20.7664	0.0466	0.9632	-41.8016	43.7370

The t-test on the significant of individual independent variable suggests that only the size (X_1) should be retained.

PHStat output of the simple linear regression model with only the size as the independent variable:

Regression Statistics	
Multiple R	0.5721
R Square	0.3273
Adjusted R Square	0.3033
Standard Error	60.9911
Observations	30

ANOVA

	df	SS	MS	F	Significance F
Regression	1	50687.4669	50687.4669	13.6260	0.0010
Residual	28	104157.6411	3719.9158		
Total	29	154845.1080			

	Coefficients	Standard Error	t Stat	P-value	Lower 95%	Upper 95%
Intercept	276.8480	28.8074	9.6103	0.0000	217.8388	335.8572
Size(000 sq. ft.	50.8031	13.7628	3.6913	0.0009	22.6113	78.9949

15.24
cont.

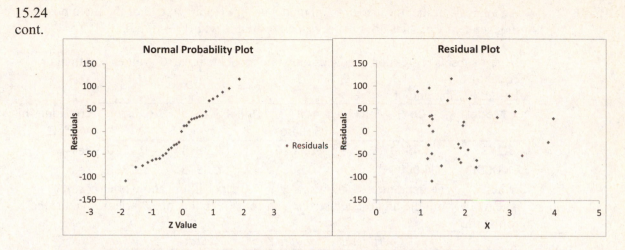

The residual analysis does not reveal any specific pattern so the model appears to be adequate.

None of the observations have a Cook's $D_i > F_{\alpha} = 0.7106$ with d.f. = 2 and 28.

Hence, using the Studentized deleted residuals, hat matrix diagonal elements and Cook's distance statistic together, there is insufficient evidence for removal of any observation from the model.

The final model you should use is:

$$\hat{Y} = 276.8480 + 50.8031X_1$$

15.26   In order to evaluate whether independent variables are intercorrelated, you can compute the Variance Inflationary Factor (*VIF*).

15.28   One way to choose among models that meet these criteria is to determine whether the models contain a subset of variables that are common, and then test whether the contribution of the additional variables is significant.

Copyright ©2015 Pearson Education, Inc. Copyright ©2015 Pearson Education, Inc.

15.30   An analysis of the linear regression model using PHStat with all of the three possible independent variables does not reveal any variable with $VIF > 5.0$.

A best subsets regression produces only one model that has C_p values less than or equal to $k+1$.

Partial PHStat output

Model	Cp	k+1	R Square	Adj. R Square	Std. Error	Consider This Model?
X2X3	2.4959	3	0.4816	0.3873	9.1710	Yes
X1X2X3	4.0000	4	0.5061	0.3579	9.3886	Yes

where X_1 = Temperature, X_2 = Pressure, X_3 = Cost (1 if low and 0 otherwise)
The model with the highest adjusted r^2 and contain all the three variables yields the following:

	Coefficients	Standard Error	t Stat	P-value
Intercept	-44.5795	40.3144	-1.1058	0.2947
Temperature	0.0849	0.1205	0.7042	0.4974
Pressure	0.8004	0.6027	1.3280	0.2137
Cost	-12.4788	5.1683	-2.4145	0.0364

The p-values for temperature and pressure are both > 0.05. Dropping temperature which has the largest p-value yields the following:

	Coefficients	Standard Error	t Stat	P-value
Intercept	-18.4899	15.5245	-1.1910	0.2587
Pressure	0.7879	0.5885	1.3389	0.2076
Cost	-13.1029	4.9737	-2.6345	0.0232

The p-value for pressure is still > 0.05. Dropping pressure yields the following:

Regression Statistics		Note:			
Multiple R	0.6301	**This worksheet does not recalculate.**			
R Square	0.3971	**If regression data changes, rerun procedure**			
Adjusted R Square	0.3468	**to create an updated version of this worksheet.**			
Standard Error	9.4690				
Observations	14				
ANOVA					
	df	SS	MS	F	Significance F
Regression	1	708.5829	708.5829	7.9028	0.0157
Residual	12	1075.9514	89.6626		
Total	13	1784.5343			
	Coefficients	Standard Error	t Stat	P-value	Lower 95%	Upper 95%
Intercept	1.7714	3.5790	0.4950	0.6296	-6.0265	9.5693
Cost	-14.2286	5.0614	-2.8112	0.0157	-25.2564	-3.2007

The best linear model is determined to be:

$\hat{Y} = 1.7714 - 14.2286 X_3$.

The overall model has $F = 7.9028$ (1 and 12 degrees of freedom) with a p-value = $0.0157 < 0.05$. $r^2 = 0.3971$, $r_{adj}^2 = 0.3468$.

A residual analysis does not reveal any strong patterns. The errors appear to be normally distributed.

Copyright ©2015 Pearson Education, Inc. Copyright ©2015 Pearson Education, Inc.

15.30
cont.

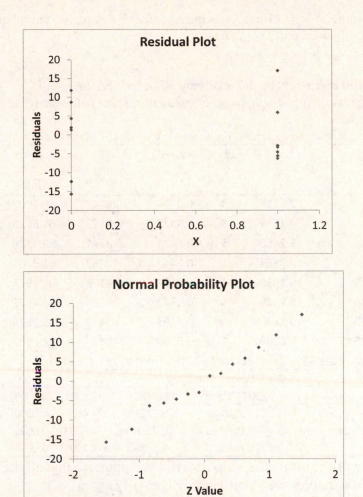

Copyright ©2015 Pearson Education, Inc. Copyright ©2015 Pearson Education, Inc.

15.32-15.34

Let Y = fair market value, X_1 = land area, X_2 = interior size, X_3 = age, X_4 = number of rooms, X_5 = number of bathrooms, X_6 = garage size.

(a)

Glencove:

Based on a full regression model involving all of the variables:

All *VIF*s are less than 5. So there is no reason to suspect collinearity between any pair of variables.

The best-subset approach yielded the following models to be considered:

Model	Cp	k+1	R Square	Adj. R Square	Std. Error	Consider This Model?
X1X2X3	2.1558	4	0.8424	0.8242	60.5007	Yes
X1X2X3X4	4.1117	5	0.8427	0.8175	61.6425	Yes
X1X2X3X5	3.2400	5	0.8484	0.8241	60.5180	Yes
X1X2X3X6	3.8887	5	0.8442	0.8192	61.3567	Yes
X1X2X3X4X5	5.1832	6	0.8488	0.8173	61.6903	Yes
X1X2X3X4X6	5.7825	6	0.8449	0.8125	62.4827	Yes
X1X2X3X5X6	5.1038	6	0.8493	0.8179	61.5846	Yes
X1X2X3X4X5X6	7.0000	7	0.8500	0.8108	62.7677	Yes

The stepwise regression approach reveals the following best model:

	Coefficients	Standard Error	t Stat	P-value
Intercept	260.6791	66.3288	3.9301	0.0006
Property Size (acres)	362.8318	48.6233	7.4621	0.0000
House Size (square feet)	0.1109	0.0228	4.8682	0.0000
Age	-1.7543	0.5483	-3.1996	0.0036

The *p*-value of the individual slope coefficients indicate that all the remaining independent variables are significant individually.

Combining the results of both approaches, the most appropriate multiple regression model for predicting fair market value in Glencove is

$$\hat{Y} = 260.6791 + 362.8318X_1 + 0.1109X_2 - 1.7543X_3$$

Copyright ©2015 Pearson Education, Inc. Copyright ©2015 Pearson Education, Inc.

15.32-15.34
cont.   **Roslyn:**

Based on a full regression model involving all of the variables:
All *VIF*s are less than 5. So there is no reason to suspect collinearity between any pair of variables.
The best-subset approach yielded the following models to be considered:

Model	Cp	k+1	R Square	Adj. R Square	Std. Error	Consider This Model?
X1X2	0.5528	3	0.9113	0.9047	97.3426	Yes
X1X2X3	1.5185	4	0.9151	0.9053	97.0851	Yes
X1X2X4	2.4581	4	0.9117	0.9015	99.0055	Yes
X1X2X5	2.4425	4	0.9117	0.9015	98.9740	Yes
X1X2X6	1.3027	4	0.9158	0.9061	96.6386	Yes
X1X2X3X4	3.4720	5	0.9152	0.9017	98.9099	Yes
X1X2X3X5	3.5164	5	0.9151	0.9015	99.0034	Yes
X1X2X3X6	3.0817	5	0.9166	0.9033	98.0841	Yes
X1X2X4X5	4.3936	5	0.9119	0.8978	100.8330	Yes
X1X2X4X6	3.2095	5	0.9162	0.9028	98.3553	Yes
X1X2X5X6	3.3019	5	0.9158	0.9024	98.5508	Yes
X1X2X3X4X5	5.4718	6	0.9152	0.8976	100.9491	Yes
X1X2X3X4X6	5.0164	6	0.9169	0.8995	99.9650	Yes
X1X2X3X5X6	5.0793	6	0.9166	0.8993	100.1014	Yes
X1X2X4X5X6	5.2051	6	0.9162	0.8987	100.3739	Yes
X1X2X3X4X5X6	7.0000	7	0.9169	0.8953	102.0786	Yes

The stepwise regression approach reveals the following best model:

	Coefficients	Standard Error	t Stat	P-value
Intercept	-168.9968	56.0905	-3.0129	0.0056
House Size (square feet)	0.2559	0.0226	11.3482	0.0000
Property Size (acres)	1094.5706	193.7733	5.6487	0.0000

The *p*-value of X_3, X_4, X_5, X_6 are all greater than 0.05 in the regression model with X_1, X_2, X_3, X_4, X_5, and X_6. Combing the results of both approaches, the most appropriate multiple regression model for predicting fair market value in Roslyn is

$$\hat{Y} = -168.9968 + 1094.5706 X_1 + 0.2559 X_2$$

Copyright ©2015 Pearson Education, Inc. Copyright ©2015 Pearson Education, Inc.

15.32-15.34
cont.   **Freeport:**

Based on a full regression model involving all of the variables:
All *VIF*s are less than 5. So there is no reason to suspect collinearity between any pair of variables.
The best-subset approach yielded the following models to be considered:

Model	Cp	k+1	R Square	Adj. R Square	Std. Error	Consider This Model?
X1X2	2.5499	3	0.8638	0.8538	27.2314	Yes
X1X2X3	3.8212	4	0.8676	0.8523	27.3666	Yes
X1X2X5	2.5555	4	0.8741	0.8595	26.6875	Yes
X1X2X6	2.0625	4	0.8766	0.8624	26.4182	Yes
X1X2X3X5	4.4527	5	0.8746	0.8545	27.1590	Yes
X1X2X3X6	3.9052	5	0.8774	0.8578	26.8532	Yes
X1X2X4X5	4.2508	5	0.8756	0.8557	27.0466	Yes
X1X2X4X6	3.9937	5	0.8770	0.8573	26.9029	Yes
X1X2X5X6	3.5681	5	0.8791	0.8598	26.6632	Yes
X1X2X3X4X6	5.6740	6	0.8786	0.8533	27.2741	Yes
X1X2X3X5X6	5.3826	6	0.8801	0.8551	27.1057	Yes
X1X2X4X5X6	5.4360	6	0.8798	0.8548	27.1366	Yes
X1X2X3X4X5X6	7.0000	7	0.8820	0.8513	27.4612	Yes

The *p*-value of the *t*-test for individual coefficient shows that X_1 is not significant at the 5% level of significance.

	Coefficients	Standard Error	t Stat	P-value
Intercept	145.1217	15.1661	9.5688	0.0000
Property size (acres	149.9337	86.1028	1.7413	0.0930
House Size (square	0.0913	0.0120	7.5956	0.0000

The stepwise regression approach reveals that the following best model:

	Coefficients	Standard Error	t Stat	P-value
Intercept	142.7398	15.6428	9.1249	0.0000
House Size (square feet)	0.1066	0.0085	12.5252	0.0000

Combining the results of both approaches, the most appropriate multiple regression model for predicting fair market value in Freeport is

$$\hat{Y} = 142.7398 + 0.1066 X_2$$

(b)   The adjusted r^2 for the best model in 15.32(a), 15.33(a), and 15.34(a) are, respectively, 0.8242, 0.9047 and 0.8431. The model in 15.33(a) has the highest explanatory power after adjusting for the number of independent variables and sample size.

Copyright ©2015 Pearson Education, Inc. Copyright ©2015 Pearson Education, Inc.

15.36 Let Y = fair market value, X_1 = land area, X_2 = interior size, X_3 = age, X_4 = number of rooms, X_5 = number of bathrooms, X_6 = garage size, X_7 = 1 if GlenCove and 0 otherwise, X_8 = 1 if Roslyn and 0 otherwise.

(a) Based on a full regression model involving all of the variables:
The *VIF* of X_2, X_3 and X_7 are greater than 5.
Dropping X_2 with the largest *VIF*, X_3 still has a *VIF* greater than 5.
After dropping X_2 and X_3, all remaining *VIF*s are less than 5. So there is no reason to suspect collinearity between any pair of variables.

Now let Y = fair market value, X_1 = land area, X_2 = number of rooms, X_3 = number of bathrooms, X_4 = garage size, X_5 = 1 if GlenCove and 0 otherwise, X_6 = 1 if Roslyn and 0 otherwise.

The best-subset approach yielded the following models to be considered:

Model	Cp	k+1	R Square	Adj. R Square	Std. Error	Consider This Model?
X1X3X4X6	4.3211	5	0.6958	0.6815	145.4771	Yes
X1X2X3X4X6	5.3213	6	0.6994	0.6815	145.4702	Yes
X1X2X3X4X5X6	7.0000	7	0.7005	0.6789	146.0615	Yes

The *p*-value of X_2, X_4 and X_5 are all greater than 0.05 in the regression model with X_1, X_2, X_3, X_4, X_5, and X_6.

	Coefficients	Standard Error	t Stat	P-value
Intercept	-19.7877	76.9121	-0.2573	0.7976
Property Size (acres)	551.1974	103.5799	5.3215	0.0000
Rooms	11.3359	10.7931	1.0503	0.2966
Baths	101.7208	26.0074	3.9112	0.0002
Garage	48.1114	29.1443	1.6508	0.1026
Glen Cove	23.1968	40.9252	0.5668	0.5724
Roslyn	226.0072	42.2948	5.3436	0.0000

The stepwise regression approach reveals the following best model:

	Coefficients	Standard Error	t Stat	P-value
Intercept	30.1063	44.6655	0.6740	0.5021
Baths	130.7788	21.7928	6.0010	0.0000
Property Size (acres)	611.6910	98.5954	6.2040	0.0000
Roslyn	214.2567	35.5299	6.0303	0.0000

Combining the results of both approaches, the most appropriate multiple regression model for predicting fair market value is

$$\hat{Y} = 30.1063 + 611.6910 X_1 + 130.7788 X_3 + 214.2567 X_6$$

(b) The estimated mean fair market value in Roslyn is $214.2567 thousands above Freeport for two otherwise identical properties. There is no significant difference in mean fair market value between two otherwise identical properties in Glen Cove and Freeport.

Copyright ©2015 Pearson Education, Inc. Copyright ©2015 Pearson Education, Inc.

15.38   In the multiple regression model with catalyst, pH, pressure, temperature and voltage as independent variables, none of the variables have a *VIF* value of 5 or larger.

The best-subset approach yielded only the following model to be considered:

Model	Cp	k+1	R Square	Adj. R Square	Std. Error
X1X2X3X4X5	6	6	0.875922	0.861822068	1.293575

where X_1 = catalyst, X_2 = pH, X_3 = pressure, X_4 = temp, and X_5 = voltage.

Looking at the *p*-values of the *t* statistics for each slope coefficient of the model that includes X_1 through X_5 reveals that pH level is not significant at 5% level of significance.

	Coefficients	Standard Error	t Stat	P-value
Intercept	4.454255233	8.222983547	0.541683588	0.590769119
Catalyst	0.162669323	0.036277562	4.484020293	5.18724E-05
pH	0.086375011	0.080013101	1.079510851	0.286242198
Pressure	-0.043059299	0.013464369	-3.198018263	0.002564899
Temp	-0.402556214	0.069704281	-5.775200729	7.21416E-07
Voltage	0.422370024	0.028413318	14.86521277	9.13658E-19

The multiple regression model with pH level deleted shows that all coefficients are significant individually at 5% level of significance.

	Coefficients	Standard Error	t Stat	P-value
Intercept	3.683340948	8.206951065	0.44880747	0.655724457
Catalyst	0.154754083	0.035594069	4.347749199	7.77444E-05
Pressure	-0.041971526	0.013451255	-3.120268445	0.003150939
Temp	-0.4035674	0.069825915	-5.779622062	6.62469E-07
Voltage	0.428756573	0.027841579	15.3998654	1.47975E-19

The best linear model is determined to be:

$\hat{Y} = 3.6833 + 0.1548X_1 - 0.04197X_3 - 0.4036X_4 + 0.4288X_5$.

The overall model has $F = 77.0793$ (4 and 45 degrees of freedom) with a *p*-value that is virtually 0. $r^2 = 0.8726$, $r^2_{adj} = 0.8613$.

None of the observations have a Cook's $D_i > F_\alpha = 0.8809$ with d.f. = 5 and 56.

Hence, using the Studentized deleted residuals, hat matrix diagonal elements and Cook's distance statistic together, there is insufficient evidence for removal of any observation from the model.

The normal probability plot does not suggest possible violation of the normality assumption. A residual analysis reveals a potential non-linear relationship in temperature.

Copyright ©2015 Pearson Education, Inc. Copyright ©2015 Pearson Education, Inc.

15.38
cont.

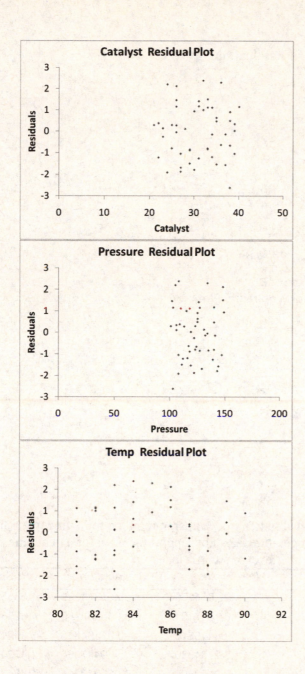

Copyright ©2015 Pearson Education, Inc. Copyright ©2015 Pearson Education, Inc.

15.38
cont.

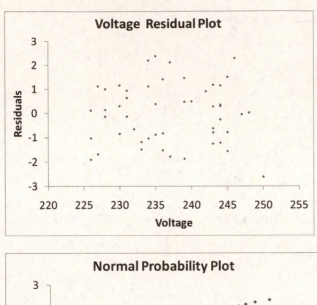

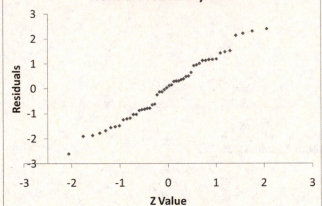

The *p*-value of the squared term for temperature in the following quadratic transformation of temperature does not support the need for a quadratic transformation at the 5% level of significance.

	Coefficients	Standard Error	t Stat	P-value
Intercept	-322.0541757	209.7341228	-1.535535426	0.131812685
Catalyst	0.16474942	0.035632189	4.623612047	3.30582E-05
Pressure	-0.044452151	0.01334035	-3.332157868	0.001753581
Temp	7.27648367	4.9417966	1.472436901	0.148020497
Temp Squared	-0.04508917	0.029010216	-1.554251433	0.127288634
Voltage	0.424662847	0.027539942	15.41988889	2.34994E-19

Copyright ©2015 Pearson Education, Inc. Copyright ©2015 Pearson Education, Inc.

15.38
cont.

The *p*-value of the interaction term between pressure and temperature below indicates that there is not enough evidence of an interaction at the 5% level of significance.

	Coefficients	Standard Error	t Stat	P-value
Intercept	103.5523674	55.92763384	1.851542078	0.070809822
Catalyst	0.144935857	0.035157935	4.122422311	0.000163315
Pressure	-0.859424944	0.453254189	-1.896121349	0.064522645
Temp	-1.586885548	0.659370559	-2.406667277	0.020363651
Pressure x Temp	0.009640768	0.005343284	1.804277709	0.078035623
Voltage	0.431941042	0.027226309	15.86484039	8.10114E-20

The best model is still the one that includes catalyst, pressure, temperature and voltage which manages to explain 87.26% of the variation in thickness.

Copyright ©2015 Pearson Education, Inc. Copyright ©2015 Pearson Education, Inc.

CHAPTER 16

OBJECTIVES
- To learn to construct different time-series forecasting models—moving averages, exponential smoothing, the linear trend, the quadratic trend, the exponential trend—and the autoregressive models and least-squares models for seasonal data
- To Learn to choose the most appropriate time-series forecasting model

OVERVIEW AND KEY CONCEPTS
Time series: A set of numerical data obtained at a regular interval.

Component factors of the classical multiplicative time series model
- **Trend:** Overall or persistent, long-term upward or downward pattern of movement. It is usually caused by changes in technology, growth in population, wealth and value, the duration of which is several years.
- **Seasonal:** Fairly regular periodic fluctuations that occurs within each 12-month period year after year. It is caused by weather conditions, social customs, or religion customs and the duration of which is within 12 months.
- **Cyclical:** Repeating up-and-down swings or movements through four phases: from peak (prosperity) to contraction (recession) to trough (depression) to expansion (recovery or growth). It is usually caused by the interactions of numerous combinations of factors that influence the economy. Its duration is usually two to ten years.
- **Irregular:** The erratic, or "residual" fluctuations in a series that exist after taking into account all the other three components. It is usually caused by random variations in data or due to unforeseen events, such as strikes or natural disasters.
- $Y_i = T_i \times C_i \times S_i \times I_i$ where T_i, C_i, I_i are value of trend, cyclical and irregular components in time period i, and S_i is the value of the seasonal component in time period i. There is no seasonal component for annual data.

Smoothing the Annual Time Series
- **Moving averages for a chosen period of length L:**
  - A series of arithmetic means computed over time such that each mean is calculated for a sequence of observed values having that particular length L.
  - It is denoted as $MA(L)$.
  - It is easy to compute.
- **Exponential smoothing:**
  - $E_1 = Y_1$

    $E_i = WY_i + (1-W)E_{i-1}$ where

    E_i = value of the exponentially smoothed series in time period i

    E_{i-1} = value of the exponentially smoothed series already computed in time period i-1

Copyright ©2015 Pearson Education, Inc.

Y_i = observed value of the time series in period i

W = subjectively assigned weight or smoothing coefficient $(0 < W < 1)$

- **Forecasting with exponentially smoothed series:** $\hat{Y}_{i+1} = E_i$
- Exponential smoothing can only be used to perform one period ahead forecast.
- Use a W close to 0 for smoothing out unwanted cyclical and irregular component; use a W close to 1 for forecasting.

Least-Squares Trend Fitting and Forecasting

- The least-squares trend fitting is used for intermediate and long-range forecast using the trend component of a time series.
- **Linear trend model:**
   - $Y_i = \beta_0 + \beta_1 X_i + \varepsilon_i$ where X_i is the coded year with a value of 0 for the first observation, a value of 1 for the second observation, etc.
   - **Linear trend forecasting equation:** $\hat{Y}_i = b_0 + b_1 X_i$
   - b_0 is interpreted as the predicted mean value of the time series for the 1st year.
   - b_1 measures the predicted change per year in the mean value of the time series.
- **Quadratic trend model:**
   - $Y_i = \beta_0 + \beta_1 X_i + \beta_2 X_i^2 + \varepsilon_i$
   - **Quadratic trend forecasting equation:** $\hat{Y}_i = b_0 + b_1 X_i + b_2 X_i^2$
- **Exponential trend model:**
   - $Y_i = \beta_0 \beta_1^{X_i} \varepsilon_i$ or $\log Y_i = \log \beta_0 + (\log \beta_1) X_i + \log \varepsilon_i$ where $(\beta_1 - 1) \times 100\%$ is the annual compound growth rate (in %).
   - **Exponential trend forecasting equation:** $\log \hat{Y}_i = b_0 + b_1 X_i$ or
   $\hat{Y}_i = 10^{(b_0 + b_1 X_i)} = (10^{b_0})(10^{b_1})^{X_i} = \hat{\beta}_0 \hat{\beta}_1^{X_i}$ where $10^{b_0} = \hat{\beta}_0$, $10^{b_1} = \hat{\beta}_1$ and
   $(\hat{\beta}_1 - 1) \times 100\%$ is the estimated annual compound growth rate in %.
- **Selecting the appropriate least-squares trend model:**
   - Use the linear trend model if the first differences are more or less constant
   $Y_2 - Y_1 = Y_3 - Y_2 = \cdots = Y_n - Y_{n-1}$
   - Use the quadratic trend model if the second differences are more or less constant
   $\left[(Y_3 - Y_2) - (Y_2 - Y_1) \right] = \cdots = \left[(Y_n - Y_{n-1}) - (Y_{n-1} - Y_{n-2}) \right]$
   - Use the exponential trend model if the percentage differences are more or less constant
   $$\left(\frac{Y_2 - Y_1}{Y_1} \right) 100\% = \left(\frac{Y_3 - Y_2}{Y_2} \right) 100\% = \cdots = \left(\frac{Y_n - Y_{n-1}}{Y_{n-1}} \right) 100\%$$

The Autoregressive Model

- The autoregressive model is appropriate for forecasting.

Copyright ©2015 Pearson Education, Inc.

- It takes advantage of autocorrelation in the time series, i.e. the fact that the values of a series of data at particular points in time are highly correlated with the values that precede and succeed them.
- p^{th} **order autoregressive model:**
  - $Y_i = A_0 + A_1 Y_{i-1} + A_2 Y_{i-2} + \cdots + A_p Y_{i-p} + \delta_i$
- p^{th} **order autoregressive equation:**
  - $\hat{Y}_i = a_0 + a_1 Y_{i-1} + a_2 Y_{i-2} + \cdots + a_p Y_{i-p}$
- p^{th} **order autoregressive forecasting equation:**
  - $\hat{Y}_{n+j} = a_0 + a_1 \hat{Y}_{n+j-1} + a_2 \hat{Y}_{n+j-2} + \cdots + a_p \hat{Y}_{n+j-p}$

    where

    $j = $ the number of years into the future

    $\hat{Y}_{n+j-p} = $ forecast of Y_{n+j-p} from the current time period for $j - p > 0$

    $\hat{Y}_{n+j-p} = $ the observed value for Y_{n+j-p} from the current time period for $j - p \leq 0$

- t **test for significance of the highest-order autoregressive parameter A_p:**
  - **The hypotheses:** $H_0 : A_p = 0$ vs. $H_1 : A_p \neq 0$.
  - **Test statistic:** $t = \dfrac{a_p - A_p}{S_{a_p}}$
  - This is a two-tail test with right-tail and left-tail rejection regions.
- **Autoregressive modeling steps:**
  1. Choose p: Note that the degree of freedom is $(n - 2p - 1)$.
  2. Form a series of "lag predictors" variables $Y_{i-1}, Y_{i-2}, \cdots, Y_{i-p}$.
  3. Estimate the autoregressive equation.
  4. Test the significance of the highest-order autoregressive parameter A_p : If the null hypothesis is rejected, this model is selected. Otherwise, decrease p by 1 and repeat steps 3-4.

Selecting a Forecasting Model

- **Perform a residual analysis:**
  - Obtain the residual plots and look for pattern.

Copyright ©2015 Pearson Education, Inc.

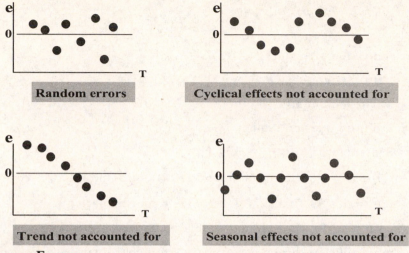

- **Measure Errors:**
    - Choose the model that gives the smallest measuring errors.
    - S_{YX} or $SSE = \sum_{i=1}^{n} \left(Y_i - \hat{Y}_i \right)^2$ is sensitive to outliers
    - Mean absolute deviation $MAD = \dfrac{\sum_{i=1}^{n} \left| Y_i - \hat{Y}_i \right|}{n}$ is not sensitive to extreme observations.

- **Principle of parsimony:**
    - When two or more models provide good fit to the data, select the simplest model.
    - Simplest model types: least-squares linear trend model, least-squares quadratic trend model, 1st order autoregressive model.
    - More complex types: 2nd or 3rd order autoregressive model, least-squares exponential trend model.

Forecasting with Seasonal Data

- Use categorical predictor variables with least-squares trend fitting.
- **Exponential model with quarterly data:**

Copyright ©2015 Pearson Education, Inc.

- $Y_i = \beta_0 \beta_1^{X_i} \beta_2^{Q_1} \beta_3^{Q_2} \beta_4^{Q_3} \varepsilon_i$

    where

    X = coded quarter values

    Q_1 = 1 if first quarter, 0 otherwise

    Q_2 = 1 if second quarter, 0 otherwise

    Q_3 = 1 if third quarter, 0 otherwise

    $\beta_0 = Y$ intercept

    $(\beta_1 - 1)100\%$ = quarterly compound growth rate (in %)

    β_2 = multiplier for first quarter relative to fourth quarter

    β_3 = multiplier for second quarter relative to fourth quarter

    β_4 = multiplier for third quarter relative to fourth quarter

    ε_i = value of the irregular component for time period i

- **The exponential growth with quarterly data forecasting equation:**

    - $\log(\hat{Y}) = b_0 + b_1 X_i + b_2 Q_1 + b_3 Q_2 + b_4 Q_3 + b_5 Q_4$

    - $\hat{Y}_i = \hat{\beta}_0 \hat{\beta}_1^{X_i} \hat{\beta}_2^{Q_1} \hat{\beta}_3^{Q_2} \hat{\beta}_4^{Q_3}$ where $\hat{\beta}_0 = 10^{b_0}$, $\hat{\beta}_1 = 10^{b_1}$, $\hat{\beta}_2 = 10^{b_2}$, $\hat{\beta}_3 = 10^{b_3}$, and $\hat{\beta}_4 = 10^{b_4}$

- Similarly for monthly data.

Online Topic: Index Numbers

- **Index numbers** measure the value of an item (or group of items) at a particular point in time as a percentage of the item's (or group of items') value at another point in time.

- A **price index** reflects the percentage change in the price of a commodity (or group of commodities) in a given period of time over the price paid for that commodity (or group of commodities) at a particular point of time in the past.

- **Simple price index:** $I_i = \left(\dfrac{P_i}{P_{\text{base}}} \right) 100$

    where I_i = price index for year i
    P_i = price for year i
    P_{base} = price for the base year

- Shifting the base for a simple price index: $I_{\text{new}} = \left(\dfrac{I_{\text{old}}}{I_{\text{new base}}} \right) 100$

    where I_{new} = new price index
    I_{old} = old price index
    $I_{\text{new base}}$ = value of the old price index for the new base year

- An **aggregate price index** reflects the percentage change in the price of a group of commodities (often referred to as a market basket) in a given period of time over the price paid for that group of commodities at a particular point of time in the past.

- An **unweighted aggregate price index** places equal weight on all the items in the market basket.

Copyright ©2015 Pearson Education, Inc.

- $$I_U^{(t)} = \left(\frac{\sum_{i=1}^{n} P_i^{(t)}}{\sum_{i=1}^{n} P_i^{(0)}} \right) 100$$

where t = time period (0, 1, 2, ...)

   i = item (1, 2, ..., n)

   n = total number of items under consideration

   $\sum_{i=1}^{n} P_i^{(t)}$ = sum of the prices paid for each of the n commodities at time period t

   $\sum_{i=1}^{n} P_i^{(0)}$ = sum of the prices paid for each of the n commodities at time period 0

   $I_U^{(t)}$ = value of the unweighted price index at time t

- A **weighted aggregate price index** allows for the differences in the consumption levels associated with the different items comprising the market basket by attaching a weight to each item to reflect the consumption quantity of that item.

- The **Laspeyres price index** is a weighted aggregate price index that uses the consumption quantities associated with the base year in the calculation of all price indexes in the series.

  - $$I_L^{(t)} = \left(\frac{\sum_{i=1}^{n} P_i^{(t)} Q_i^{(0)}}{\sum_{i=1}^{n} P_i^{(0)} Q_i^{(0)}} \right) 100$$

  where t = time period (0, 1, 2, ...)

     i = item (1, 2, ..., n)

     n = total number of items under consideration

     $Q_i^{(0)}$ = quantity of item i at time period 0

     $I_L^{(t)}$ = value of the Laspeyres price index at time t

- The **Paasche Price Index** uses the consumption quantities experienced in the year of interest instead of using the initial quantities.

  - $$I_P^{(t)} = \left(\frac{\sum_{i=1}^{n} P_i^{(t)} Q_i^{(t)}}{\sum_{i=1}^{n} P_i^{(0)} Q_i^{(t)}} \right) 100$$

  where t = time period (0, 1, 2, ...)

     i = item (1, 2, ..., n)

     n = total number of items under consideration

     $Q_i^{(t)}$ = quantity of item i at time period t

     $I_P^{(t)}$ = value of the Paasche price index at time t

  - Is a more accurate reflection of total consumption costs at time t.
  - Accurate consumption values for current purchases are often hard to obtain.
  - If a particular product increases greatly in price compared to the other items in the market basket, consumers will avoid the high-priced item out of necessity, not because of changes in what they might prefer to purchase.

Copyright ©2015 Pearson Education, Inc.

SOLUTIONS TO END OF SECTION
AND CHAPTER REVIEW EVEN PROBLEMS

16.2   (a)   Since you need data from four prior years to obtain the centered 9-year moving average for any given year and since the first recorded value is for 1984, the first centered moving average value you can calculate is for 1988.

       (b)   You would lose four years for the period 1984-1987 since you do not have enough past values to compute a centered moving average. You will also lose the final four years of recorded time series since you do not have enough later values to compute a centered moving average. Therefore, you will lose a total of eight years in computing a series of 9-year moving averages.

16.4   (a),(b),(c),(e)

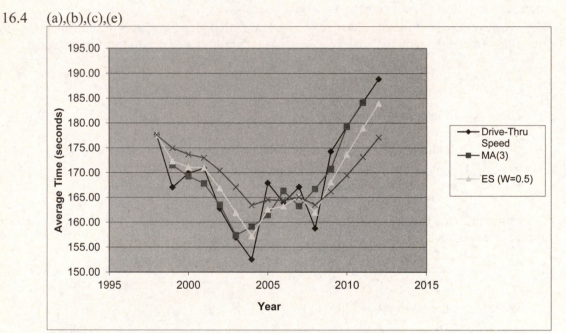

(b),(c),(e)

Year	Drive-Thru Speed	MA(3)	ES (W=0.5)	ES (W=0.25)
1998	177.59		177.5900	177.5900
1999	167.02	171.4967	172.3050	174.9475
2000	169.88	169.2500	171.0925	173.6806
2001	170.85	167.8167	170.9713	172.9730
2002	162.72	163.4967	166.8456	170.4097
2003	156.92	157.3867	161.8828	167.0373
2004	152.52	159.1133	157.2014	163.4080
2005	167.90	161.4400	162.5507	164.5310
2006	163.90	166.3000	163.2254	164.3732
2007	167.10	163.2567	165.1627	165.0549
2008	158.77	166.6967	161.9663	163.4837
2009	174.22	170.7533	168.0932	166.1678
2010	179.27	179.2300	173.6816	169.4433
2011	184.20	184.1000	178.9408	173.1325
2012	188.83		183.8854	177.0569

Copyright ©2015 Pearson Education, Inc.

16.4   (d) $W = 0.5$: $\hat{Y}_{2013} = E_{2012} = 183.8854$

cont. $W = 0.25$: $\hat{Y}_{2013} = E_{2012} = 177.0569$

(f)   The exponentially smoothed forecast for 2013 with $W = 0.5$ is higher than that with $W = 0.25$. A smoothing coefficient of $W = 0.25$ smoothes out the average time more than $W = 0.50$. The exponential smoothing with $W = 0.5$ assigns more weight to the more recent values and is better for forecasting, while the exponential smoothing with $W = 0.25$ which assigns more weight to more distance values is better suited for eliminating unwanted cyclical and irregular variations.

16.6   (a),(b),(c)

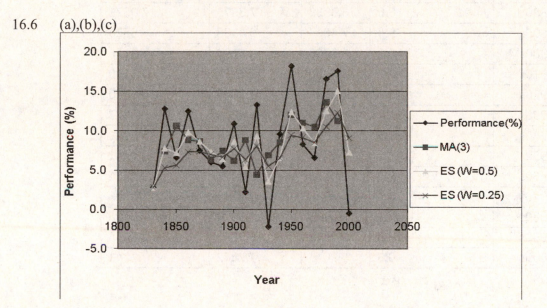

Copyright ©2015 Pearson Education, Inc.

16.6 (b),(c),(e)
cont.

Decade	Performance(%)	MA(3)	ES (W=0.5)	ES (W=0.25)
1830s	2.8		2.8000	2.8000
1840s	12.8	7.4000	7.8000	5.3000
1850s	6.6	10.6333	7.2000	5.6250
1860s	12.5	8.8667	9.8500	7.3438
1870s	7.5	8.6667	8.6750	7.3828
1880s	6.0	6.3333	7.3375	7.0371
1890s	5.5	7.4667	6.4188	6.6528
1900s	10.9	6.2000	8.6594	7.7146
1910s	2.2	8.8000	5.4297	6.3360
1920s	13.3	4.4333	9.3648	8.0770
1930s	-2.2	6.9000	3.5824	5.5077
1940s	9.6	8.5333	6.5912	6.5308
1950s	18.2	12.0333	12.3956	9.4481
1960s	8.3	11.0333	10.3478	9.1611
1970s	6.6	10.5000	8.4739	8.5208
1980s	16.6	13.6000	12.5370	10.5406
1990s	17.6	11.2333	15.0685	12.3055
2000s	-0.5		7.2842	9.1041

(d) $\hat{Y}_{2010s} = E_{2000s} = 7.2842$

(e) (d) $\hat{Y}_{2010s} = E_{2000s} = 9.1041$

(f)   The exponentially smoothed forecast for 2010 with $W = 0.5$ is lower than that with $W = 0.25$. The exponential smoothing with $W = 0.5$ assigns more weight to the more recent values and is better for forecasting, while the exponential smoothing with $W = 0.25$ which assigns more weight to more distance values is better suited for eliminating unwanted cyclical and irregular variations.

(g)   According to the exponential smoothing with $W = 0.25$, there appears to be a general upward trend in the performance of the stocks in the past.

Copyright ©2015 Pearson Education, Inc.

16.8   (a),(b),(c),(e)

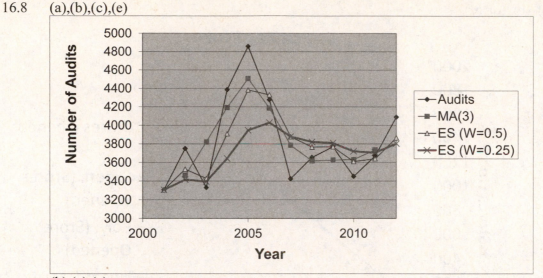

(b),(c),(e)

Year	Audits	MA(3)	ES (W=0.5)	ES (W=0.25)
2001	3305		3305.00	3305.00
2002	3749	3461.33	3527.00	3416.00
2003	3330	3821.67	3428.50	3394.50
2004	4386	4191.67	3907.25	3642.38
2005	4859	4507.00	4383.13	3946.53
2006	4276	4186.33	4329.56	4028.90
2007	3424	3784.67	3876.78	3877.67
2008	3654	3616.33	3765.39	3821.76
2009	3771	3625.00	3768.20	3809.07
2010	3450	3630.00	3609.10	3719.30
2011	3669	3736.00	3639.05	3706.72
2012	4089		3864.02	3802.29

(d) $W = 0.5$: $\hat{Y}_{2013} = E_{2012} = 3864.02$

       $W = 0.25$: $\hat{Y}_{2013} = E_{2012} = 3802.29$

(f)   The exponentially smoothed forecast for 2013 with $W = 0.5$ is higher than that with $W = 0.25$.

(g)   The exponential smoothing with $W = 0.5$ assigns more weight to the more recent values and is better for forecasting, while the exponential smoothing with $W = 0.25$ which assigns more weight to more distance values is better suited for eliminating unwanted cyclical and irregular variations.

16.10 (a)   The Y-intercept $b_0 = 4.0$ is the fitted trend value reflecting the real total revenues (in millions of dollars) during the origin or base year 1992.

(b)   The slope $b_1 = 1.5$ indicates that the real total revenues are increasing at an estimated rate of 1.5 million dollars per year.

(c)   Year is 1996, $X = 1996 - 1992 = 4$

       $\hat{Y}_5 = 4.0 + 1.5(4) = 10.0$ million dollars

(d)   Year is 2013, $X = 2013 - 1992 = 21$,

       $\hat{Y}_{20} = 4.0 + 1.5(21) = 35.5$ million dollars

(e)   Year is 2016, $X = 2016 - 1992 = 24$

       $\hat{Y}_{23} = 4.0 + 1.5(24) = 40$ million dollars

Copyright ©2015 Pearson Education, Inc.

16.12 (a), (b), (c), (d)

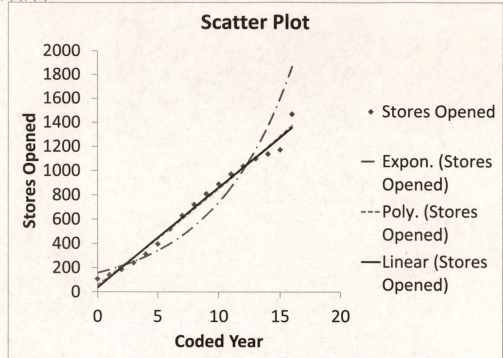

(b) Linear trend: $\hat{Y} = 35.9216 + 82.5686X$ where X is relative to 1997.

(c) Quadratic trend: $\hat{Y} = 53.6925 + 75.4603X + 0.4443X^2$ where X is relative to 1997.

(d) Exponential trend: $\log_{10}\hat{Y} = 2.1981 + 0.0671X$ where X is relative to 1997.

(e) Linear trend: $\hat{Y}_{2014} = 35.9216 + 82.5686(17) = 1439.5882 = 1440$

$\hat{Y}_{2015} = 35.9216 + 82.5686(18) = 1522.1569 = 1522$

Quadratic trend: $\hat{Y}_{2014} = 53.6925 + 75.4603(17) + 0.4443(17)^2 = 1464.9118 = 1465$

$\hat{Y}_{2015} = 53.6925 + 75.4603(18) + 0.4443(18)^2 = 1555.9216 = 1556$

Exponential trend: $\hat{Y}_{2014} = 10^{2.1981+0.0671(17)} = 2180.1029 = 2180^*$

$\hat{Y}_{2015} = 10^{2.1981+0.0671(18)} = 2544.2451 = 2544$

Note *: The result is obtained using Excel. Your answer might be slightly different if you use the rounded values in the last stage of the computation.

(f) The linear and quadratic trend model fit the data better than the exponential trend model and, hence, either forecast should be used.

Copyright ©2015 Pearson Education, Inc.

16.14   (a)

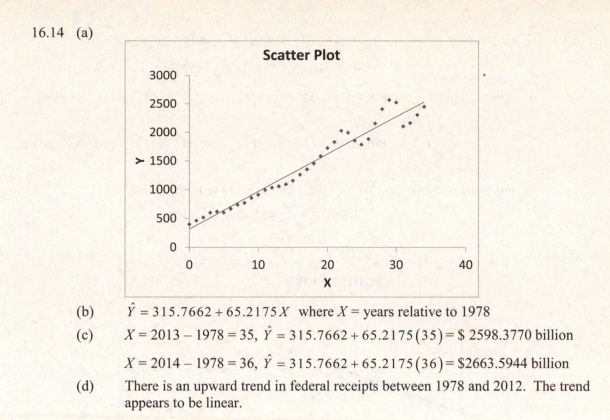

(b) $\hat{Y} = 315.7662 + 65.2175X$ where X = years relative to 1978

(c) $X = 2013 - 1978 = 35$, $\hat{Y} = 315.7662 + 65.2175(35) = \$ 2598.3770$ billion

$X = 2014 - 1978 = 36$, $\hat{Y} = 315.7662 + 65.2175(36) = \$2663.5944$ billion

(d)   There is an upward trend in federal receipts between 1978 and 2012. The trend appears to be linear.

16.16   (a), (b), (c), (d)

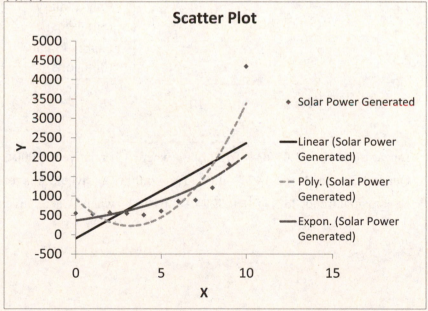

(b)   Linear trend: $\hat{Y} = -95.0000 + 245.4909X$ where X is relative to 2002.

(c)   Quadratic trend: $\hat{Y} = 930.2098 - 437.9823X + 68.3473X^2$ where X is relative to 2002.

(d)   Exponential trend: $\log_{10}\hat{Y} = 2.5659 + 0.0747X$ where X is relative to 2002.

Copyright ©2015 Pearson Education, Inc.

16.16   (e)   Linear trend: $\hat{Y}_{2013} = -95.0000 + 245.4909(11) = 2605.4$ million KWh

cont. $\hat{Y}_{2014} = -95.0000 + 245.4909(12) = 2850.89$ million KWh

Quadratic trend: $\hat{Y}_{2013} = 930.2098 - 437.9823(11) + 68.3473(11)^2 = 4382.43$ million KWh

$\hat{Y}_{2014} = 930.2098 - 437.9823(12) + 68.3473(12)^2 = 5516.44$ million KWh

Exponential trend: $\hat{Y}_{2013} = 10^{2.5659+0.0747(11)} = 2438.44$ million KWh

$\hat{Y}_{2014} = 10^{2.5659+0.0747(12)} = 2895.82$ million KWh

16.18   (a), (b), (c), (d)

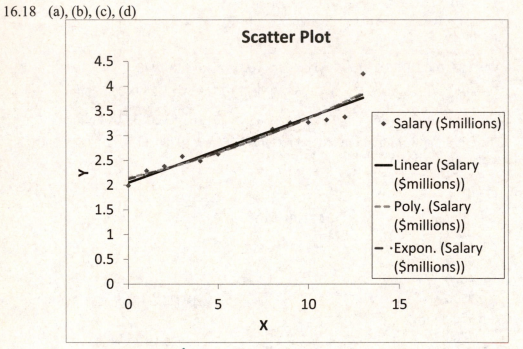

(b)   Linear trend: $\hat{Y} = 2.0500 + 0.1321X$ where X is relative to 2000

(c)   Quadratic trend: $\hat{Y} = 2.1471 + 0.0835X + 0.0037X^2$ where X is relative to 2000.

(d)   Exponential trend: $\log_{10}\hat{Y} = 0.3274 + 0.0198X$ where X is relative to 2000.

Copyright ©2015 Pearson Education, Inc.

16.18 (e)
cont.

1st Difference	2nd Difference	% Difference
0.30		15.08
0.09	-0.21	3.93
0.20	0.11	8.40
-0.09	-0.29	-3.49
0.14	0.23	5.62
0.20	0.06	7.60
0.09	-0.11	3.18
0.21	0.12	7.19
0.13	-0.08	4.15
0.01	-0.12	0.31
0.05	0.04	1.53
0.06	0.01	1.81
0.87	0.81	25.74

(e)

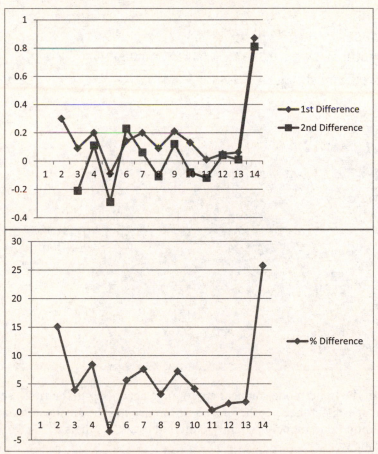

Investigating the first, second, and percentage differences suggests that the linear and exponential trend models have the best fit.

(f) The forecasts using the 2 models are:

Linear trend: $\hat{Y} = 2.0500 + 0.1321(14) = \$3.8992$ millions

Exponential trend: $\hat{Y} = 10^{0.3274 + 0.0198(14)} = \$4.0184$ millions

Copyright ©2015 Pearson Education, Inc.

16.20 (a),(c),(d),(e)

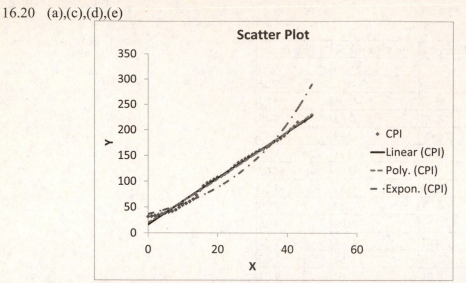

(b) There has been an upward trend in the CPI in the United States over the 48-year period. The rate of increase became faster in the late 70s but tapered off in the early 80s.

(c) Linear trend: $\hat{Y} = 16.2540 + 4.4919X$

(d) Quadratic trend: $\hat{Y} = 19.7334 + 4.0381X + 0.0097X^2$

(e) Exponential trend: $\log_{10}\hat{Y} = 1.5612 + 0.0192X$

(f)

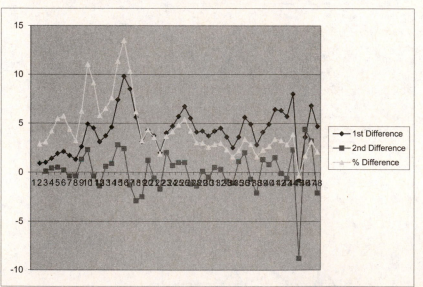

None of the trend models appear appropriate according to the first-, second- and percentage-difference but the second-difference has the smallest variation in general. So a quadratic trend model is slightly preferred over the others.

(g) Quadratic trend:

For 2013: $\hat{Y} = 19.7334 + 4.0381(48) + 0.0097(48)^2 = 235.8101$

For 2014: $\hat{Y} = 19.7334 + 4.0381(49) + 0.0097(49)^2 = 240.7848$

Copyright ©2015 Pearson Education, Inc.

16.22   (a)

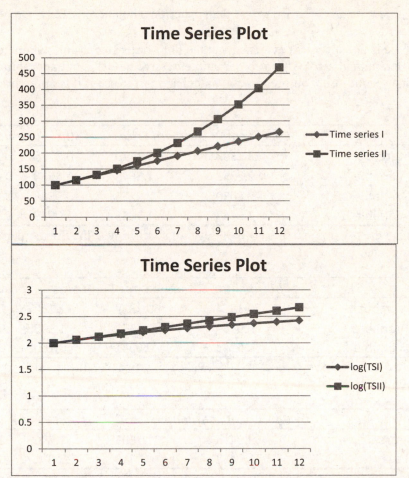

For Time Series I, the graph of Y vs. X appears to be more linear than the graph of log Y vs. X, so a linear model appears to be more appropriate. For Time Series II, the graph of log Y vs. X appears to be more linear than the graph of Y vs. X, so an exponential model appears to be more appropriate.

(b)   Time Series I: $\hat{Y} = 100.0731 + 14.9776X$, where X = years relative to 2001

Time Series II: $\hat{Y} = 10^{1.9982 + 0.0609X}$, where X = years relative to 2001

(c) $X = 12$ for year 2013 in all models. Forecasts for the year 2013:

Time Series I: $\hat{Y} = 100.0731 + 14.9776(12) = 279.8045$

Time Series II: $\hat{Y} = 10^{1.9982 + 0.0609(12)} = 535.6886$

16.24 $t_{STAT} = \dfrac{a_3}{S_{a_3}} = \dfrac{0.24}{0.10} = 2.4$ is greater than the critical bound of 2.2281. Reject H_0. There is

sufficient evidence that the third-order regression parameter is significantly different from zero. A third-order autoregressive model is appropriate.

Copyright ©2015 Pearson Education, Inc.

16.26   (a) $t_{STAT} = \dfrac{a_3}{S_{a_3}} = \dfrac{0.24}{0.15} = 1.6$ is less than the critical bound of 2.2281. Do not reject H_0. .

There is not sufficient evidence that the third-order regression parameter is significantly different than zero. A third-order autoregressive model is not appropriate.

(b)   Fit a second-order autoregressive model and test to see if it is appropriate.

16.28   (a)

	Coefficients	Standard Error	t Stat	P-value
Intercept	73.0383	79.1710	0.9225	0.3780
X Variable 1	2.2358	1.5648	1.4288	0.1835
X Variable 2	-2.8050	2.9255	-0.9588	0.3603
X Variable 3	1.6443	1.5045	1.0929	0.3001

Since the p-value $= 0.3001 > 0.05$ level of significance, the third order term can be dropped.

(b)

	Coefficients	Standard Error	t Stat	P-value
Intercept	70.1584	60.1327	1.1667	0.2660
X Variable 1	0.9157	0.6571	1.3935	0.1888
X Variable 2	0.1243	0.6541	0.1900	0.8525

Since the p-value $= 0.8525 > 0.05$ level of significance, the second order term can be dropped..

(c)

	Coefficients	Standard Error	t Stat	P-value
Intercept	53.9415	31.1693	1.7306	0.1055
YLag1	1.0482	0.0418	25.0917	0.0000

Since the p-value is virtually zero, the first order term cannot be dropped.

(d)   The most appropriate model for forecasting is the first-order autoregressive model:

$\hat{Y}_{2014} = 53.9415 + 1.0482 Y_{2013} = 1595.8650 = 1596$ stores.

$\hat{Y}_{2015} = 53.9415 + 1.0482 \hat{Y}_{2014} = 1726.7503 = 1727$ stores.

Copyright ©2015 Pearson Education, Inc.

16.30   (a)

	Coefficients	Standard Error	t Stat	P-value
Intercept	-0.1927	0.7859	-0.2452	0.8133
YLag1	0.4966	1.0298	0.4822	0.6444
YLag2	0.3137	1.1551	0.2716	0.7938
YLag3	0.3507	0.8621	0.4068	0.6963

Since the p-value = 0.6963 > 0.05 level of significance, the third order term can be dropped.

(b)

	Coefficients	Standard Error	t Stat	P-value
Intercept	-0.2268	0.6014	-0.3771	0.7149
YLag1	0.7751	0.8212	0.9438	0.3699
YLag2	0.3759	0.7459	0.5039	0.6264

Since the p-value = 0.6264 > 0.05 level of significance, the second order term can be dropped.

(c)

	Coefficients	Standard Error	t Stat	P-value
Intercept	-0.0479	0.4358	-0.1100	0.9144
YLag1	1.0791	0.1535	7.0278	0.0000

Since the p-value is virtually zero, the first order term cannot be dropped.

(d)   The most appropriate model for forecasting is the first-order autoregressive model:

$$\hat{Y}_{2014} = -0.0479 + 1.0791 Y_{2013} = \$4.5380 \text{ million}$$

16.32   (a)

$$S_{YX} = \sqrt{\frac{\sum_{i=1}^{n}(Y_i - \hat{Y}_i)^2}{n - p - 1}} = \sqrt{\frac{45}{12 - 1 - 1}} = 2.121 \text{ . The standard error of the estimate is}$$

2.121.

(b) $$MAD = \frac{\sum_{i=1}^{n}\left|Y_i - \hat{Y}_i\right|}{n} = \frac{18}{12} = 1.5 \text{ . The mean absolute deviation is } 1.5.$$

Copyright ©2015 Pearson Education, Inc.

16.34   (a)

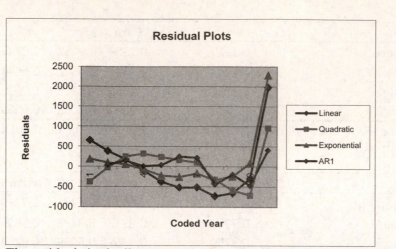

The residuals in the linear, quadratic and exponential trend model show strings of consecutive positive and negative values.

(b), (c)

	Linear	Quadratic	Exponential	AR1
SSE	6275572.218	2267548.717	5613646.138	760222.4864
Syx	835.0364076	532.3942051	789.771144	308.2658119
MAD	580.8396694	367.8580208	364.4034464	222.0913936

(d)   The residuals in the three trend models show strings of consecutive positive and negative values. The autoregressive model performs well for the historical data and have a fairly random pattern of residuals. It also has the smallest values in MAD and S_{YX}. Based on the principle of parsimony, the autoregressive model would be the best model for forecasting.

16.36   (a)

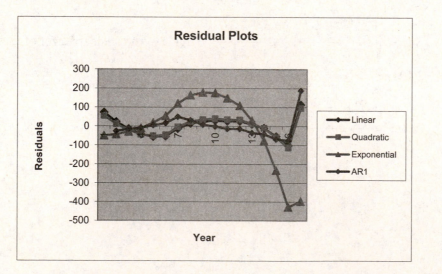

(b),(c)

	Linear	Quadratic	Exponential	AR1
SSE	43144.31373	41614.23942	547380.1537	53441.70015
Syx	53.63103189	54.52014007	191.0288205	61.78401328
MAD	40.19146482	40.60960359	133.0123643	37.09222979

Copyright ©2015 Pearson Education, Inc.

16.36   (d)   The residuals in the three trend models show strings of consecutive positive and
cont.   negative values. The autoregressive model performs well for the historical data and
               has a fairly random pattern of residuals. The autoregressive model also has the
               smallest values in MAD. Based on the principle of parsimony, the autoregressive
               model would be the best model for forecasting.

16.38   (a)

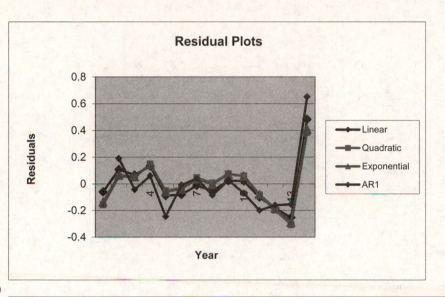

        (b),(c)

	Linear	Quadratic	Exponential	AR1
SSE	0.39772967	0.357079121	0.353788238	0.629926981
Syx	0.182055319	0.180171414	0.171704261	0.239303341
MAD	0.119262166	0.118210361	0.116457278	0.148959242

        (d)   The residuals in the linear, quadratic and exponential trend models show strings of
               consecutive positive and negative values. The autoregressive model has a fairly
               random pattern of residuals. The exponential trend model, however, has the smallest
               values in *MAD* and S_{YX}. Based on the principle of parsimony, the exponential trend
               model would be the best model for forecasting.

16.40   (a) $\log \hat{\beta}_0 = 2$. $\hat{\beta}_0 = 10^2 = 100$. This is the fitted value for January 2009 prior to
               adjustment by the January multiplier.

        (b) $\log \hat{\beta}_1 = 0.01$. $\hat{\beta}_1 = 10^{0.01} = 1.0233$. The estimated average monthly compound growth
               rate is $(\hat{\beta}_1 - 1)100\% = 2.33\%$.

        (c) $\log \hat{\beta}_2 = 0.1$. $\hat{\beta}_2 = 10^{0.1} = 1.2589$. The January values in the time series are estimated
               to have a mean 25.89% higher than the December values.

16.42   (a) $\log \hat{\beta}_0 = 3.0$. $\hat{\beta}_0 = 10^{3.0} = 1{,}000$. This is the fitted value for the first quarter of 2009
               prior to adjustment by the quarterly multiplier.

        (b) $\log \hat{\beta}_1 = 0.1$. $\hat{\beta}_1 = 10^{0.1} = 1.2589$. The estimated average quarterly compound growth
               rate is $(\hat{\beta}_1 - 1)100\% = 25.89\%$.

        (c) $\log \hat{\beta}_3 = 0.2$. $\hat{\beta}_3 = 10^{0.2} = 1.5849$. The second quarter values in the time series are
               estimated to have a mean 58.49% higher than the fourth quarter values.

Copyright ©2015 Pearson Education, Inc.

16.44   (a)   The retail industry is heavily subject to seasonal variation due to the holiday seasons and so are the revenues for Toys R Us.

(b)

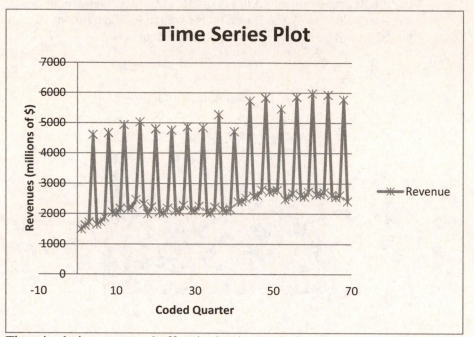

There is obvious seasonal effect in the time series.

(c) $\log_{10} \hat{Y} = 3.6291 + 0.0025X - 0.3670Q_1 - 0.3676Q_2 - 0.3438Q_3$

(d) $\log_{10} \hat{\beta}_1 = 0.0025.$ $\hat{\beta}_1 = 10^{0.0025} = 1.0058.$ The estimated quarterly compound growth rate is $(\hat{\beta}_1 - 1)\,100\% = 0.58\%$

(e) $\log_{10} \hat{\beta}_2 = -0.3670.$ $\hat{\beta}_2 = 10^{-0.3670} = 0.4296.$ $(\hat{\beta}_2 - 1)\,100\% = -57.04\%.$ The 1st quarter values in the time series are estimated to have a mean 57.04% below the 4th quarter values.

$\log_{10} \hat{\beta}_3 = -0.3676.$ $\hat{\beta}_3 = 10^{-0.3676} = 0.4289.$ $(\hat{\beta}_3 - 1)\,100\% = -57.11\%.$ The 2nd quarter values in the time series are estimated to have a mean 57.11% below the 4th quarter values.

$\log_{10} \hat{\beta}_4 = -0.3438.$ $\hat{\beta} = 10^{-0.3438} = 0.4531.$ $(\hat{\beta}_4 - 1)\,100\% = -54.69\%.$ The 3rd quarter values in the time series are estimated to have a mean 54.69% below the 4th quarter values.

(f)   Forecasts:

2013-2	69	0	1	0	2723.336
2013-3	70	0	0	1	2893.926
2013-4	71	0	0	0	6423.647
2014-1	72	1	0	0	2775.405
2014-2	73	0	1	0	2787.204
2014-3	74	0	0	1	2961.794
2014-4	75	0	0	0	6574.295

Copyright ©2015 Pearson Education, Inc.

16.46   (a)

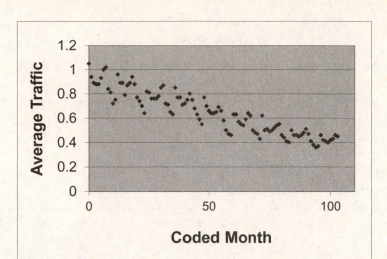

(b)

	Coefficients	Standard Error	t Stat	P-value
Intercept	-0.0916	0.0070	-13.1771	0.0000
Coded Month	-0.0037	0.0001	-64.4666	0.0000
M1	0.1245	0.0086	14.5072	0.0000
M2	0.0905	0.0086	10.5454	0.0000
M3	0.0806	0.0086	9.3975	0.0000
M4	0.0668	0.0086	7.7810	0.0000
M5	0.0793	0.0086	9.2457	0.0000
M6	0.1001	0.0086	11.6725	0.0000
M7	0.1321	0.0086	15.3949	0.0000
M8	0.1238	0.0086	14.4279	0.0000
M9	0.0577	0.0088	6.5372	0.0000
M10	0.0356	0.0088	4.0317	0.0001
M11	0.0103	0.0088	1.1646	0.2472

(c) $\hat{Y}_{103} = 0.4451$

(d)   Forecasts for the last four months of 2012:

Month	$\hat{Y}$
September	0.3790
October	0.3571
November	0.3340
December	0.3234

(e) $\log_{10} \hat{\beta}_1 = -0.0037$; $\hat{\beta}_1 = 10^{-0.0037} = 0.9915$. The estimated monthly compound growth rate is $(\hat{\beta}_1 - 1) 100\% = -0.8542\%$.

(f) $\log_{10} \hat{\beta}_8 = 0.1321$; $\hat{\beta}_8 = 10^{0.1321} = 1.3554$. $(\hat{\beta}_8 - 1) 100\% = 35.5382\%$.

The July values in the time series are estimated to have a mean 35.5382% above the December values.

Copyright ©2015 Pearson Education, Inc.

16.48 (a)

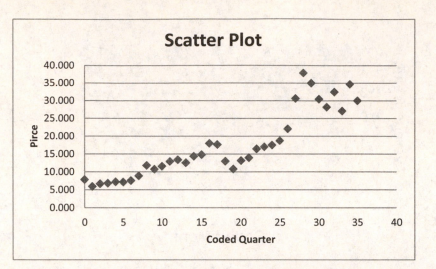

(b)

	Coefficients	Standard Error	t Stat	P-value
Intercept	0.7884	0.0362	21.8058	0.0000
Coded Quarter	0.0213	0.0013	16.5210	0.0000
Q1	0.0545	0.0378	1.4406	0.1597
Q2	0.0044	0.0377	0.1165	0.9080
Q3	0.0080	0.0377	0.2117	0.8338

(c) $\log_{10} \hat{\beta}_1 = 0.0213$; $\hat{\beta}_1 = 10^{0.0213} = 1.050226$; $(\hat{\beta}_1 - 1)\,100\% = 5.0226\%$

The estimated *quarterly* compound mean growth rate in the price of silver is 5.0226%, after adjusting for the seasonal component.

(d) $\log_{10} \hat{\beta}_2 = 0.0545$; $\hat{\beta}_2 = 10^{0.0545} = 1.1337$; $(\hat{\beta}_2 - 1)\,100\% = 13.3700\%$. The 1st quarter values in the time series are estimated to have a mean 13.37% above the 4th quarter values.

(e) Last quarter, 2012: $\hat{Y}_{35} = \$\,34.1414$

(f) 2013:

Quarter	$\hat{Y}$
1st	40.6502
2nd	38.0402
3rd	40.2810
4th	41.5349

(g) The forecasts in (f) were not accurate because there is not a strong seasonable component in the price of silver.

16.50 A time series is a set of numerical data obtained at regular periods over time.

16.52 Moving averages take into account the results of a limited number of periods of time. Exponential smoothing takes into account all the time periods but gives increased weight to more recent time periods.

16.54 The linear trend model in this chapter has the time period as the *X* variable.

Copyright ©2015 Pearson Education, Inc.

16.56   The different methods for choosing an appropriate forecasting model are residual analysis, the sum of squared deviations, the mean absolute deviation and parsimony.

16.58   Forecasting for monthly or quarterly data uses an exponential trend model with dummy variables to represent either months or quarters.

16.60   (a)

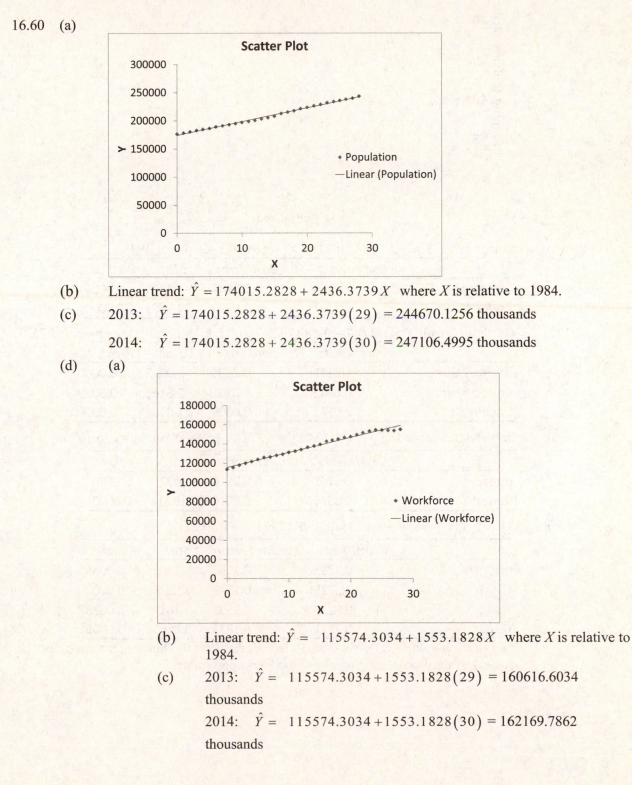

(b)   Linear trend: $\hat{Y} = 174015.2828 + 2436.3739X$ where X is relative to 1984.

(c)   2013: $\hat{Y} = 174015.2828 + 2436.3739(29) = 244670.1256$ thousands

         2014: $\hat{Y} = 174015.2828 + 2436.3739(30) = 247106.4995$ thousands

(d)   (a)

(b)   Linear trend: $\hat{Y} = 115574.3034 + 1553.1828X$ where X is relative to 1984.

(c)   2013: $\hat{Y} = 115574.3034 + 1553.1828(29) = 160616.6034$ thousands

         2014: $\hat{Y} = 115574.3034 + 1553.1828(30) = 162169.7862$ thousands

Copyright ©2015 Pearson Education, Inc.

16.62 (a)

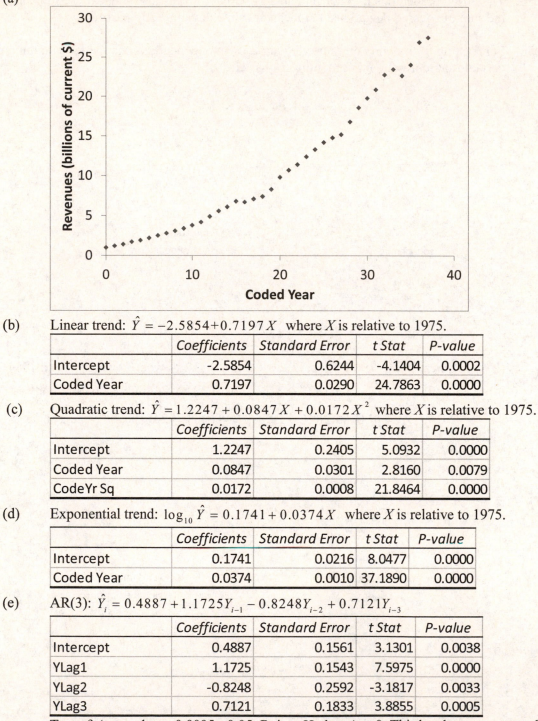

(b) Linear trend: $\hat{Y} = -2.5854 + 0.7197X$ where X is relative to 1975.

	Coefficients	Standard Error	t Stat	P-value
Intercept	-2.5854	0.6244	-4.1404	0.0002
Coded Year	0.7197	0.0290	24.7863	0.0000

(c) Quadratic trend: $\hat{Y} = 1.2247 + 0.0847X + 0.0172X^2$ where X is relative to 1975.

	Coefficients	Standard Error	t Stat	P-value
Intercept	1.2247	0.2405	5.0932	0.0000
Coded Year	0.0847	0.0301	2.8160	0.0079
CodeYr Sq	0.0172	0.0008	21.8464	0.0000

(d) Exponential trend: $\log_{10}\hat{Y} = 0.1741 + 0.0374X$ where X is relative to 1975.

	Coefficients	Standard Error	t Stat	P-value
Intercept	0.1741	0.0216	8.0477	0.0000
Coded Year	0.0374	0.0010	37.1890	0.0000

(e) AR(3): $\hat{Y}_i = 0.4887 + 1.1725Y_{i-1} - 0.8248Y_{i-2} + 0.7121Y_{i-3}$

	Coefficients	Standard Error	t Stat	P-value
Intercept	0.4887	0.1561	3.1301	0.0038
YLag1	1.1725	0.1543	7.5975	0.0000
YLag2	-0.8248	0.2592	-3.1817	0.0033
YLag3	0.7121	0.1833	3.8855	0.0005

Test of A_3: p-value = 0.0005 < 0.05. Reject H_0 that $A_3 = 0$. Third-order term cannot be deleted. A third-order autoregressive model is appropriate.

Copyright ©2015 Pearson Education, Inc.

16.62   (f)
cont.

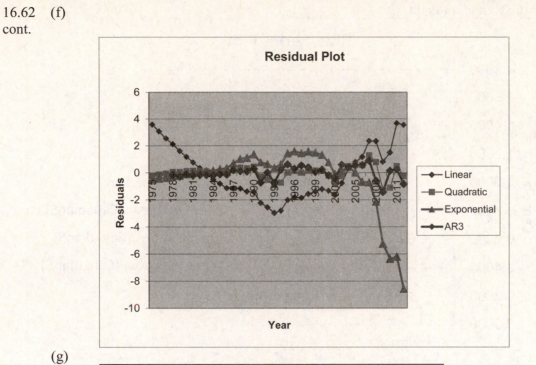

(g)

	Linear	Quadratic	Exponential	AR3
SSE	138.6905	9.4759	206.5249	7.7632
Syx	1.9628	0.5203	2.3952	0.5004
MAD	1.6711	0.3576	1.3060	0.3682

(h)   The residuals in the first three models show strings of consecutive positive and negative values. The autoregressive model performs well for the historical data and has a fairly random pattern of residuals. It also has the smallest values in the standard error of the estimate, *MAD* and *SSE*. Based on the principle of parsimony, the autoregressive model would probably be the best model for forecasting.

(i) $\hat{Y}_{2013} = 0.4887 + 1.1725Y_{2012} - 0.8248Y_{2011} + 0.7121Y_{2010} = \$27.7445$ billions

Copyright ©2015 Pearson Education, Inc.

16.64   **For the Canadian dollar:**

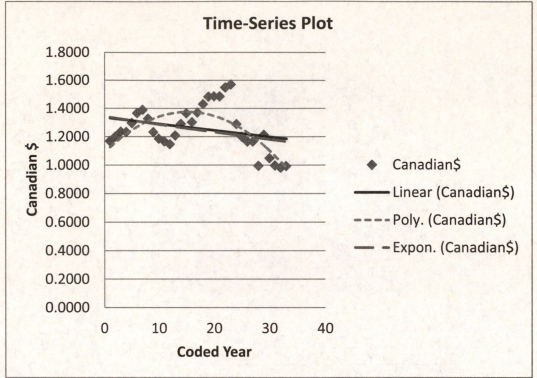

Linear Trend: $\hat{Y} = 1.3312 - 0.0046X$, where X = years relative to 1980

Quadratic Trend: $\hat{Y} = 1.1253 + 0.0353X - 0.0012X^2$, where X = years relative to 1980

Exponential Trend: $\log_{10}\hat{Y} = 0.1260 - 0.0019X$ where X is relative to 1980

AR(3):

	Coefficients	Standard Error	t Stat	P-value
Intercept	0.2058	0.1702	1.2089	0.2376
YLag1	0.8778	0.1935	4.5373	0.0001
YLag2	0.1202	0.2582	0.4655	0.6454
YLag3	-0.1652	0.2055	-0.8037	0.4289

Test of A_3: p-value 0.4289> 0.05. Do not reject H_0 that $A_3 = 0$. Third-order term can be deleted.

AR(2):

	Coefficients	Standard Error	t Stat	P-value
Intercept	0.1588	0.1511	1.0507	0.3024
YLag1	0.8837	0.1890	4.6766	0.0001
YLag2	-0.0139	0.1992	-0.0699	0.9448

Test of A_2: p-value = 0.9448> 0.05. Do not reject H_0 that $A_2 = 0$. The second-order term can be dropped.

Copyright ©2015 Pearson Education, Inc.

16.64
cont.

AR(1):

	Coefficients	Standard Error	t Stat	P-value
Intercept	0.1594	0.1337	1.1918	0.2427
YLag1	0.8698	0.1048	8.2995	0.0000

Test of A_1: p-value is virtually zero. Reject H_0 that $A_1 = 0$. The first-order autoregressive model is appropriate.

Residual plots:

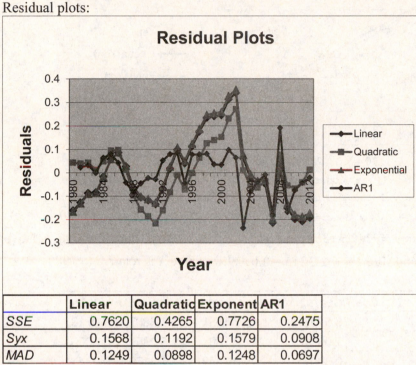

	Linear	Quadratic	Exponent	AR1
SSE	0.7620	0.4265	0.7726	0.2475
Syx	0.1568	0.1192	0.1579	0.0908
MAD	0.1249	0.0898	0.1248	0.0697

The residuals in the linear, quadratic and exponential trend models show strings of consecutive positive and negative values. There is no apparent pattern in the residuals of the AR(1) model . The autoregressive model has the smallest values in the standard error of the estimate, SSE and MAD. Based on the principle of parsimony, the autoregressive model would probably be the best model for forecasting.

$$\hat{Y}_{2013} = 0.1594 + 0.8698Y_{2012} = 1.0227$$

$$\hat{Y}_{2014} = 0.1594 + 0.8698\hat{Y}_{2013} = 1.0489$$

Copyright ©2015 Pearson Education, Inc.

16.64 **For the Japanese Yen:**
cont.

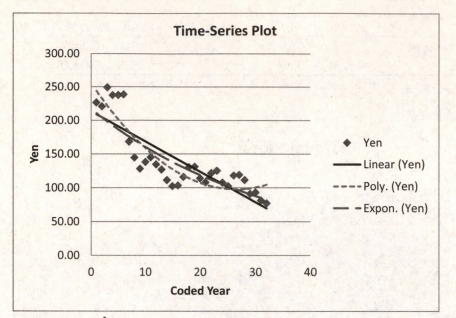

Linear Trend: $\hat{Y} = 207.7707 - 4.3784X$, where X = years relative to 1980

Quadratic Trend: $\hat{Y} = 242.3133 - 11.0640X + 0.2089X^2$, where X = years relative to 1980

Exponential Trend: $\log_{10}\hat{Y} = 2.3215 - 0.0129X$ where X is relative to 1980

AR(3):

	Coefficients	Standard Error	t Stat	P-value
Intercept	16.5738	8.8151	1.8802	0.0713
YLag1	1.0551	0.1692	6.2352	0.0000
YLag2	-0.3007	0.2469	-1.2179	0.2342
YLag3	0.0857	0.1644	0.5211	0.6067

Test of A_3: p-value 0.6067 > 0.05. Do not reject H_0 that $A_3 = 0$. Third-order term can be deleted.

AR(2):

	Coefficients	Standard Error	t Stat	P-value
Intercept	11.0570	9.3411	1.1837	0.2465
YLag1	1.0744	0.1861	5.7747	0.0000
YLag2	-0.1807	0.1812	-0.9972	0.3272

Test of A_2: p-value = 0.3272 > 0.05. Do not reject H_0 that $A_2 = 0$. Second-order term can be deleted.

AR(1):

	Coefficients	Standard Error	t Stat	P-value
Intercept	8.4239	8.7778	0.9597	0.3449
YLag1	0.9082	0.0594	15.2990	0.0000

Test of A_1: p-value is virtually 0. Reject H_0 that $A_1 = 0$. A first-order autoregressive model is appropriate.

Copyright ©2015 Pearson Education, Inc.

16.64   Residual plots:
cont.

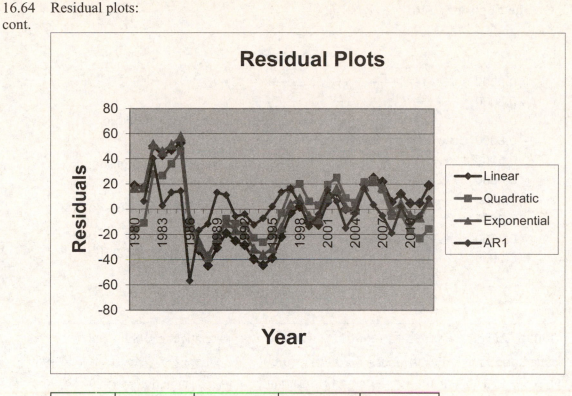

	Linear	Quadratic	Exponential	AR1
SSE	24027.0833	14580.1927	19885.9257	8319.9051
Syx	27.8400	22.0456	25.3275	16.6532
MAD	22.0604	18.2687	18.9365	11.9083

The residuals in the linear, quadratic and exponential trend models show strings of consecutive positive and negative values. There is no apparent pattern in the residuals of the AR(1) model . The autoregressive model has the smallest values in the standard error of the estimate, SSE and MAD. Based on the principle of parsimony, the autoregressive model would probably be the best model for forecasting.

$$\hat{Y}_{2013} = 8.4239 + 0.9082 Y_{2012} = 87.2062$$

$$\hat{Y}_{2014} = 8.4239 + 0.9082 \hat{Y}_{2013} = 87.6204$$

Copyright ©2015 Pearson Education, Inc.

16.64
cont.   **For the English Pound:**

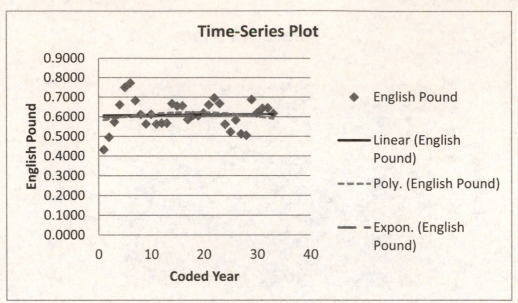

Linear Trend: $\hat{Y} = 0.6059 + 0.0002X$, where X = years relative to 1980

Quadratic Trend: $\hat{Y} = 0.5829 + 0.0047X - 0.0001X^2$, where X = years relative to 1980

Exponential Trend: $\log_{10}\hat{Y} = -0.2238 + 0.0004X$ where X is relative to 1980

AR(3):

	Coefficients	Standard Error	t Stat	P-value
Intercept	0.4667	0.1174	3.9771	0.0005
YLag1	0.5855	0.1879	3.1158	0.0044
YLag2	-0.0878	0.2191	-0.4006	0.6920
YLag3	-0.2547	0.1684	-1.5125	0.1425

Test of A_3: p-value = 0.1425 > 0.05. Do not reject H_0 that $A_3 = 0$. Third-order term can be deleted.

AR(2):

	Coefficients	Standard Error	t Stat	P-value
Intercept	0.3722	0.0949	3.9221	0.0005
YLag1	0.6800	0.1789	3.8016	0.0007
YLag2	-0.2818	0.1610	-1.7505	0.0910

Test of A_2: p-value = 0.0910 > 0.05. Do not reject H_0 that $A_2 = 0$. Second-order term can be deleted.

AR(1):

	Coefficients	Standard Error	t Stat	P-value
Intercept	0.2923	0.0811	3.6059	0.0011
YLag1	0.5299	0.1321	4.0131	0.0004

Test of A_1: p-value = 0.0004 < 0.05. Reject H_0 that $A_1 = 0$. A first-order autoregressive model is appropriate.

Copyright ©2015 Pearson Education, Inc.

16.64   Residual plots:
cont.

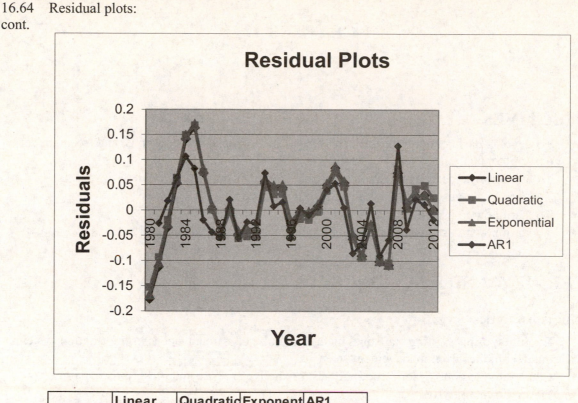

	Linear	Quadratic	Exponent	AR1
SSE	0.1691	0.1649	0.1700	0.0886
Syx	0.0739	0.0741	0.0740	0.0543
MAD	0.0557	0.0572	0.0558	0.0419

The residuals in the linear, quadratic and exponential trend models show strings of consecutive positive and negative values. There is no apparent pattern in the residuals of the AR(1) model . The autoregressive model has the smallest values in the standard error of the estimate, SSE and MAD. Based on the principle of parsimony, the autoregressive model would probably be the best model for forecasting.

$$\hat{Y}_{2013} = 0.2923 + 0.5299Y_{2012} = 0.6184$$

$$\hat{Y}_{2014} = 0.2923 + 0.5299\hat{Y}_{2013} = 0.6200$$

Copyright ©2015 Pearson Education, Inc.

CHAPTER 17

OBJECTIVES

- To develop dashboard elements such as sparklines, gauges, bullet graphs, and treemaps for descriptive analytics.
- To learn how to use classification and regression trees for predictive analytics
- To learn how to use neural nets for predictive analytics
- To learn how to use cluster analysis for predictive analytics
- To learn how to use multidimensional scaling for predictive analytics

OVERVIEW AND KEY CONCEPTS

Business Analytics

- Evolution of preexisting statistical methods combined with advances in information systems and techniques from management science.
- Can be divided into descriptive analytics, predictive analytic and prescriptive analytic.
- **Descriptive analytics**
  - Explores business activities that have occurred or are occurring in the present moment.
- **Predictive analytics**
  - Identifies what is likely to occur in the (near) future and finds relationships in data that may not be readily apparent using descriptive analytics.
- **Prescriptive analytics**
  - Investigates what should occur and prescribes the best course of action for the future.

Descriptive Analytics

- An analytic dashboard provides information in a visual form that is intended to be easy to comprehend and review. They include
  - **Sparklines** summarize time-series data as small, compact graphs designed to appear as part of a table (or a written passage).
  - **Gauges** can consume a lot of visual space in a dashboard.
  - **Bullet graphs** foster the direct comparison of each measurement.
  - **Treemaps** are useful when categories can be grouped to form a multilevel hierarchy or tree.

Data Discovery

- Data discovery methods allow decision makers to interactively organize or visualize data and perform preliminary analyses.
- Data discovery involves
  - Drill-down - the revealing of the data that underlies a higher-level summary
  - Slicers allow one to work with more than three or four variables at the same time in a way that avoids creating overly complex multidimensional contingency tables that would be hard to read.

Copyright ©2015 Pearson Education, Inc.

Predictive Analytics

- Predictive analytics methods fall into one of four categories:
    - Prediction: Assigning a value to a target based on a model
    - Classification: Assigning items in a collection to target categories or classes
    - Clustering: Finding natural groupings in data
    - Association: Finding items that tend to co-occur and specifying the rules that govern their co-occurrence
- Classification of predictive analytics methods:

METHOD	METHOD FOR			
	Prediction	Classification	Clustering	Association
Classification and Regression Trees	•	•		
Neural Networks	•	•	•	
Cluster Analysis			•	
Multidimensional Scaling (MDS)		•		•

Classification and Regression Trees

- Classification and regression trees are decision trees that split data into groups based on the values of independent or explanatory variables.
- The dependent variable in a classification tree is categorical while the dependent variable of a regression tree is continuous.
- Successfully completing a classification or regression tree requires:
    - Rules for splitting the data at each node based on one independent variable.
    - Rules for deciding when a branch cannot be split any more.
    - A prediction for the target variable at each node.
- Classification and regression trees are not affected by the distribution of the variables that make up the data and, hence, are robust to departure from the normality assumption of many parametric models.

Neutral Networks

- A powerful, flexible data mining techniques that construct models from patterns and relationships uncovered in data.
- Learn from the data to construct a model.
- Flexible and can be applied to prediction, classification, and clustering problems.
- A nonparametric method that does not make a priori assumptions about the distribution of the data.
- Neural networks used for prediction and classification are typically multilayer perceptrons that contain an input layer, a hidden layer, and an output layer.
- To construct models, multilayer perceptrons use error back propagation.
    1. The input layer nodes send the various inputs to the nodes of the hidden layer.
    2. The results of the processing element computations in the hidden layer are sent to the output layer.
    3. The output layer combines the results it receives from the hidden layer and compares it to the target Y value.
    4. The output layer then sends back to the hidden layer nodes (the start of the back propagation) its estimate of the difference between the predicted results and the target value (the error rate).

Copyright ©2015 Pearson Education, Inc.

5. Computations in the hidden layer then backwardly influence the weighting done near the input layer.
6. This forward-and-backward computation among the three layers continues until the output layer detects that the error rate has been minimized or is at an acceptable level.
7. The model is established.

- Neural networks use the training data to uncover a model that by some criteria best describes the patterns and relationships in the data.
- The model is then applied to the validation data to see if the model can make the correct prediction or classification.
- Neural networks can suffer from poor quality of data, insufficient data, or overfitted models, models that only work well with the data used to construct that model.

Cluster Analysis

- Seeks to classify data into a sequence of groupings such that objects in each group are more alike other objects in their group than they are to objects found in other groups.
- **Hierarchical clustering**:
    1. Starts with each object in its own cluster.
    2. Then, the two objects that are determined to be the closest to each other are merged into a single cluster.
    3. The merging of the two closest objects repeats until there remains only one cluster that includes all objects.
- *k*-means clustering:
    1. The number of clusters (*k*) is set at the start of the process.
    2. Objects are then assigned to clusters in an iterative process that seeks to make the means of the *k* clusters as different as possible.
    3. During the iterative process, objects may be reassigned to a different cluster later in the process.
- To perform a cluster analysis, one must determine (1) how to measure the distance between objects and (2) how to measure the distance between clusters.
- The most common measure of distance between objects used in cluster analysis is Euclidean distance:

    $$d_{ij} = \sqrt{\sum_{k=1}^{r} \left(X_{ik} - X_{jk} \right)^2}$$

    where

    d_{ij} = distance between object *i* and object *j*

    X_{ik} = value of object *i* in dimension *k*

    X_{jk} = value of object *j* in dimension *k*

    r = number of dimensions

- There are four common measures of distance between clusters:
    - **Complete linkage** bases the distance between clusters on the maximum distance between objects in one cluster and another cluster.
    - **Single linkage** bases the distance between clusters on the minimum distance between objects in one cluster and another cluster.
    - **Average linkage** bases the distance between clusters on the mean distance between objects in one cluster and another cluster.
    - **Ward's minimum variance method** bases the distance between clusters on the sum of squares over all variables between objects in one cluster and another cluster.

Copyright ©2015 Pearson Education, Inc.

Multidimensional Scaling

- Visualizes objects in a two or more dimensional space, or map, with the goal of discovering patterns of similarities or dissimilarities among the objects.
- Two main types of multidimensional scaling:
  - **Metric multidimensional scaling** that assumes that the distance between objects is ratio scaled
  - **Nonmetric multidimensional scaling** that assumes that the distance between objects is ordinal scaled.
- To perform an MDS analysis, one must (1) determine how to measure the distance between objects (the basis for placing objects in the map) and (2) the number of map dimensions to be interpreted.
- The most common measure of distance between objects used is the Euclidean distance:
  - $$d_{ij} = \sqrt{\sum_{k=1}^{r} \left(X_{ik} - X_{jk} \right)^2}$$

    where

    d_{ij} = distance between object i and object j

    X_{ik} = value of object i in dimension k

    X_{jk} = value of object j in dimension k

    r = number of dimensions
- The goal of MDS analysis is to minimize the number of dimensions used to interpret the results while maximizing the goodness of fit of the results to the original data.
- The goodness of fit is measured by the stress statistic:
  - $$Stress = \sqrt{\frac{\sum_{i,j=1}^{m} \left(d_{ij} - \hat{d}_{ij} \right)^2}{\sum_{i,j=1}^{m} \left(d_{ij} - \overline{d} \right)^2}}$$

    where

    d_{ij} = distance between object i and object j

    $\hat{d}_{ij}$ = the fitted regression value estimated by the multidimensional scaling algorithm from the original data for objects i and j

    $\overline{d}$ = mean distance between objects

    $m = n\left(n - 1 \right) / 2$

    n = number of objects
- A good rule in deciding the number of dimensions is to increase dimensions as long as the stress statistic decreases substantially.

Copyright ©2015 Pearson Education, Inc.

SOLUTIONS TO END OF SECTION
AND CHAPTER REVIEW EVEN PROBLEMS

17.2   (a)   Bullet graph for one-year return:

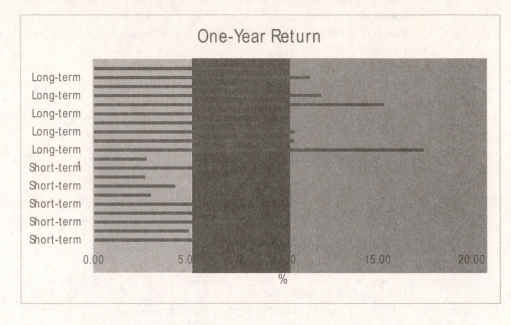

Bullet graph for three-year return:

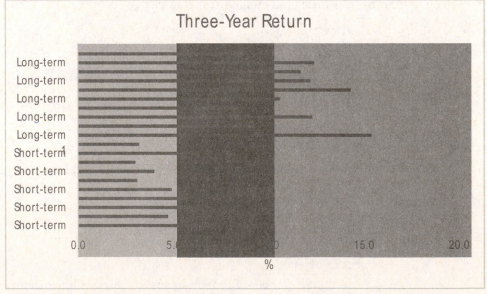

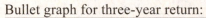

(b)   Gauges take up too much visual space that would be needed for the 20 funds.
(c)   The one-year return and the three-year return is much higher for the long-term funds than for the short-term funds.

Copyright ©2015 Pearson Education, Inc.

17.4   (a)

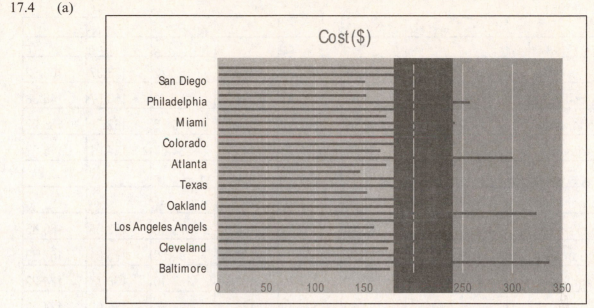

(b)   The bullet graph shows that four teams have costs considered as expensive while the stem-and-leaf display shows that the costs are concentrated between $172 and $225.

(c)   The bullet graph enables you to see the names of the individual teams and which teams are inexpensive, typical, and expensive whereas the stem-and-leaf display only shows the distribution of the costs.

(d)   The bullet graphs shows the costs for each team and which teams fall into the inexpensive, typical, and expensive categories.

17.6   (a)

Stock Indexes		2006	2007	2008	2009	2010	2011	2012
DJIA		16.3	6.4	-33.8	18.8	11.0	5.5	7.3
S&P 500		13.6	3.5	-38.5	23.5	12.8	0.0	13.4
NASDAQ		9.5	9.8	-40.5	43.9	16.9	-1.8	15.9

(b)   The rates of return of the three indices vary a great deal from year to year, but the pattern for the three indices are similar except for the NASDAQ in 2009 which had a much higher return in that year than the DJIA or the S&P500.

(c)   Unlike the three stock indices which had similar patterns between 2006–2012, the returns of the three metals differed greatly from year to year.

Copyright ©2015 Pearson Education, Inc.

17.8   (a)

Fast Food Chain				**Year**		
		1	**2**	**3**	**4**	**5**	**6**
Burger King |〰️	178.45	171.33	178.20	162.22	173.37	160.52
Chick-Fil-A	〰️	219.39	198.81	194.80	167.21	150.57	146.38
McDonald's	〰️	177.59	167.02	169.88	170.85	162.72	156.92
Wendy's	〰️	171.30	150.29	141.73	134.67	127.21	116.22

Fast Food Chain				**Year**		
Burger King		**7**	**8**	**9**	**10**	**11**	**12**
Chick-Fil-A		173.19	166.10	166.00	179.90	153.06	166.85
McDonald's		163.74	168.60	191.90	194.30	175.01	167.59
Wendy's		152.52	167.90	163.90	167.10	158.77	174.22
		124.69	135.70	135.10	138.50	131.08	134.09

(b)   Wendy's consistently has the fastest service time. The service time at McDonald's and Burger King are similar over the years. The service time at Chick-Fil-A was slower in the earlier and later years than the other fast food chains.

17.10   (a)

Copyright ©2015 Pearson Education, Inc.

17.10   (b)   The values of the teams varied from $312 million for the Milwaukee Bucks to $1,100
cont.   million for the New York Knicks. The change in values was not consistent across the
                teams. The two most valuable teams, the Los Angeles Lakers, and the New York
                Knicks had very different increases in value (11% and 41% respectively.)

17.12   (a)

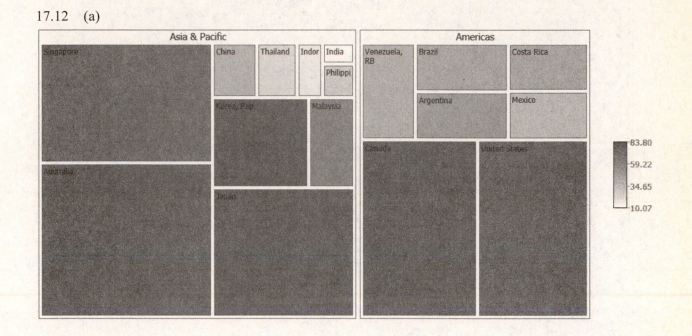

Copyright ©2015 Pearson Education, Inc.

17.12   (b)
cont.

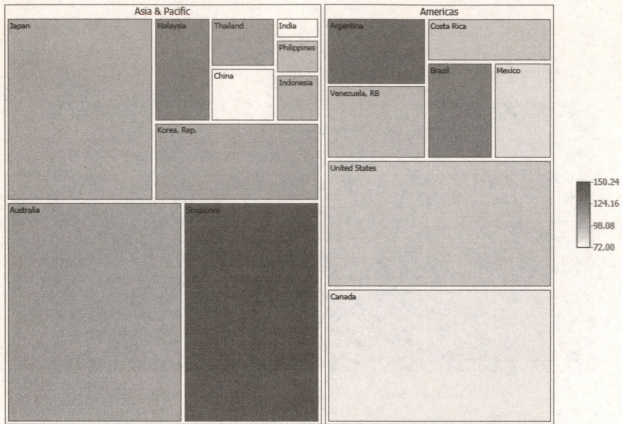

(c)   Almost all the countries that had lower GDP had lower Internet use except for the
         Republic of Korea. The pattern of mobile cellular subscriptions does not seem to
         depend on the GDP of the country.

17.14   (a)

Count of Market Cap	Column Labels					
Row Labels	Five	Four	One	Three	Two	Grand Total
Growth		**18**	**76**	**16**	**74**	**43**	**227**
Large		9	31	5	37	21	103
Mid-Cap		7	28	4	20	13	72
Small		2	17	7	17	9	52
Value		**5**	**22**	**7**	**36**	**19**	**89**
Large		2	13	5	21	9	50
Mid-Cap		1	4		9	5	19
Small		2	5	2	6	5	20
Grand Total		**23**	**98**	**23**	**110**	**62**	**316**

Copyright ©2015 Pearson Education, Inc.

17.14   (b)   There are 37 of such funds.
cont.   PHStat output of the summary statistics of the variables:

	Assets	Turnover Ratio	Beta	SD	1YrReturn%	3YrReturn%	5YrReturn%	10YrReturn%	Expense Ratio
Mean	649.0489189	57.6627027	1.071081081	16.97513514	14.87432432	9.263243243	0.802972973	6.178648649	1.418378378
Median	123.8	38	1.1	17.32	14.65	9.25	0.84	6.4	1.21
Mode	#N/A	13	1.1	17.93	11.8	9.46	1.22	6.81	1.07
Minimum	0.1	0	0.85	13.29	9.16	6.62	-3.27	0.9	0.58
Maximum	6190	413	1.25	19.9	20.85	12.59	3.36	9.69	6.97
Range	6189.9	413	0.4	6.61	11.69	5.97	6.63	8.79	6.39
Variance	1650071.1335	5340.2103	0.0069	2.1347	7.3247	1.5361	1.7426	2.8816	1.0450
Standard Deviation	1284.5509	73.0767	0.0833	1.4610	2.7064	1.2394	1.3201	1.6975	1.0223
Coeff. of Variation	197.91%	126.73%	7.77%	8.61%	18.20%	13.38%	164.40%	27.47%	72.07%
Skewness	3.0908	3.4983	-1.0282	-0.7817	0.1305	0.2500	-0.8352	-1.1914	4.6897
Kurtosis	10.4021	15.5456	1.1615	0.5130	-0.3423	0.2923	1.8633	2.6974	25.3885
Count	37	37	37	37	37	37	37	37	37
Standard Error	211.1789	12.0137	0.0137	0.2402	0.4449	0.2038	0.2170	0.2791	0.1681

17.16   (a)

Count of Market Cap	Column Labels					
Row Labels	**Five**	**Four**	**One**	**Three**	**Two**	**Grand Total**
Growth	**18**	**76**	**16**	**74**	**43**	**227**
Average	3	15	6	28	22	74
High		1	5	1	3	10
Low	15	60	5	45	18	143
Value	**5**	**22**	**7**	**36**	**19**	**89**
Average	1		3	7	6	17
High			2		1	3
Low	4	22	2	29	12	69
Grand Total	**23**	**98**	**23**	**110**	**62**	**316**

(b)   There is only one such fund.

17.18   The five-year returns for the four funds that are small market cap funds that have a
                 rating of five stars are 5.29, 6.97, 10.75, and 11.35.

Type		Market Cap		Star Rating		Risk		5YrReturn%	
Growth		Large		Five		Average		5.29	
Value		Mid-Cap		Four		High		6.97	
		Small		One		Low		10.75	
				Three				11.35	
				Two				-9.03	
								-5.78	
								-5.17	
								-4.89	

17.20   The highest five-year return of 12.33 is for a large cap growth fund.

17.22   (a)   JMP output:

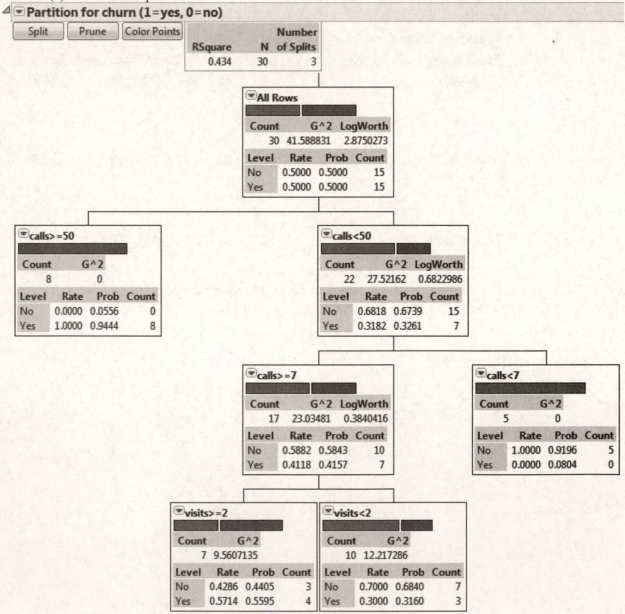

Copyright ©2015 Pearson Education, Inc.

17.22   (b)   The r^2 for the classification tree model is 0.434. The first split is for the 8 customers
cont.   who called 50 or more times. Among customers who called fewer than 50 times, those
                 who called at least seven times and visited two or more times are more likely to be
                 churned.

17.24   Because half the data will be used for a validation sample, the results will differ
                 depending on which values are in the training sample and which are in the validation
                 sample.

17.26   (a)

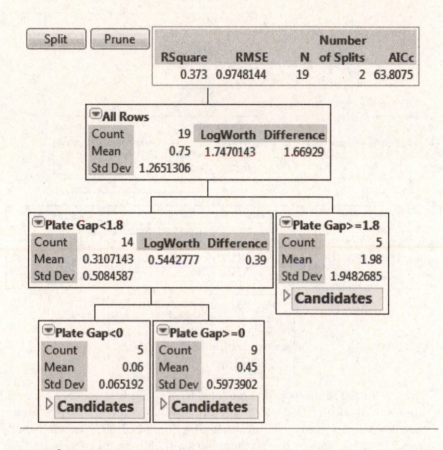

        (b)   The r^2 for the regression tree model is 0.373. The first split is based on a plate gap of
               1.8. For those bags with a plate gap less than 1.8, the mean tear is 0.3107. For those bags
               with a plate gap at least 1.8, the mean tear is 1.98. For those bags with a plate gap less
               than 0.0, the mean tear is 0.06. For those bags with a plate gap less than 1.8 but greater
               than 0, the mean tear is 0.45. Thus, you would recommend that a plate gap of less than 0
               be used to minimize tears in the bag.

Copyright ©2015 Pearson Education, Inc.

17.28 (a)   JMP output:

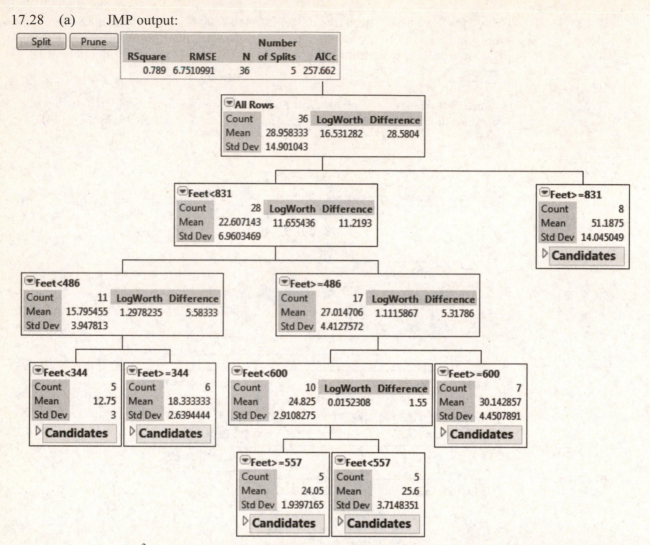

(b)   The r^2 for the regression tree model is 0.789. The first split is based on 831 square feet.
Moves of at least 831 sq. ft. have a mean moving time of 51.1875 hours. Moves of less
than 831 square feet have a mean moving time of 22.6071 hours. Among moves of less
than 831 sq. ft., moves of less than 486 sq. ft., have a mean moving time of 15.7955
hours. Moves of less than 344 sq. ft. have a mean moving time of 12.75 hours. Moves of
between 344 and 486 sq. ft. have a mean moving time of 18.3333 hours. Moves of
between 486 and 830 sq. ft. have a mean moving time of 27.0147 hours. Moves between
486 and 599 sq. ft. have a mean moving time of 24.825 hours. Moves between 600 and
830 have a mean moving time of 30.1429 hours. Moves between 557 and 599 sq. ft.
have a mean moving time of 24.05 hours. Moves between 486 and 557 sq. ft have a
mean moving time of 25.6 hours.

Copyright ©2015 Pearson Education, Inc.

17.30 – 17.36   Because some of the data will be used for a validation sample, the results will differ depending on which values are in the training sample and which are in the validation sample.

17.38   (a)   JMP output:

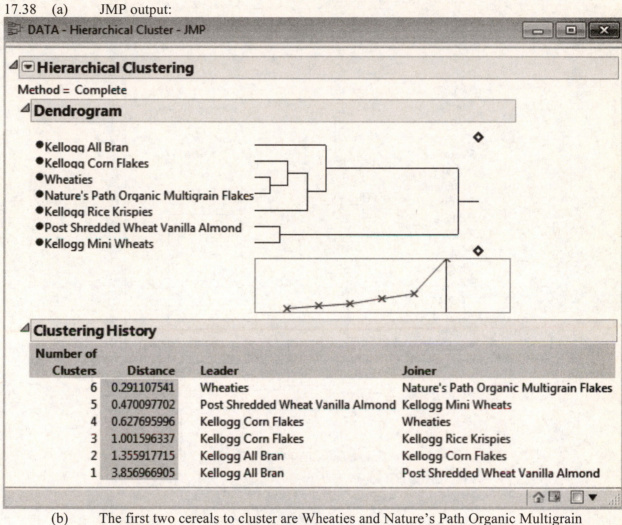

(b)   The first two cereals to cluster are Wheaties and Nature's Path Organic Multigrain Flakes followed by Post Shredded Wheat Vanilla Almond and Kellogg's Mini Wheats. At the two cluster level, one cluster contains Post Shredded Wheat Vanilla Almond and Kellogg's Mini Wheats and the other cluster contains the other five cereals. The first cluster appears to contain brands with similar amount of calories, carbohydrates, and sugar.

Copyright ©2015 Pearson Education, Inc.

17.40   (a)   Partial JMP output:

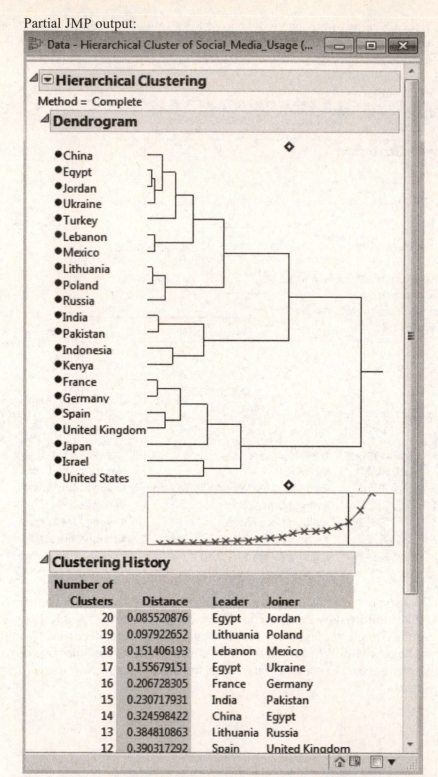

Number of Clusters	Distance	Leader	Joiner
20	0.085520876	Egypt	Jordan
19	0.097922652	Lithuania	Poland
18	0.151406193	Lebanon	Mexico
17	0.155679151	Egypt	Ukraine
16	0.206728305	France	Germany
15	0.230717931	India	Pakistan
14	0.324598422	China	Egypt
13	0.384810863	Lithuania	Russia
12	0.390317292	Spain	United Kingdom

(b)   The first two countries to cluster are Egypt and Jordan followed by Lithuania and Poland. At the two cluster level one cluster is France, Germany, Spain, United Kingdom, Japan, Israel, and the United States and the other cluster contains the remaining countries. The first cluster appears to contain the western European countries and the United States and Israel.

Copyright ©2015 Pearson Education, Inc.

17.42   (a)   JMP output:

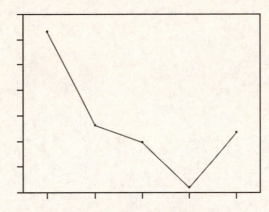

Number of Dimensions	Stress Values
1	0.314699327
2	0.130783113
3	0.097315357
4	0.009119312
5	0.116426662

Since the stress value shows steep decline for one-dimension and two-dimension,

two-dimensional MDS is investigated.

Copyright ©2015 Pearson Education, Inc.

17.42 (a)
cont.

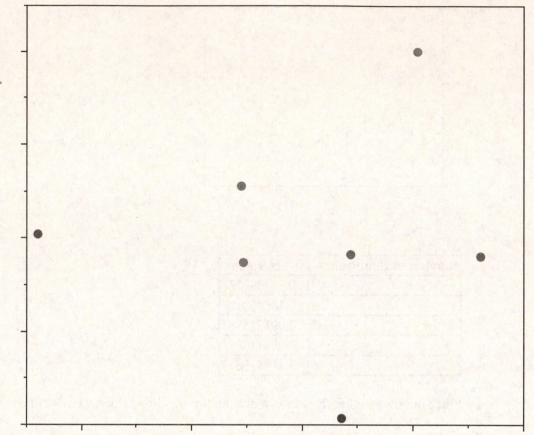

(b) Since the stress statistic is 0.0973 in three dimensions, 0.1308 in two dimensions, and 0.3147 in one dimension, it is reasonable to try to interpret a two-dimensional mapping of the cereals. Looking at a 45° rotation, one dimension separates Post Shredded Wheat Vanilla Almond and Kellogg's Mini Wheats based on their higher calorie and sugar content. A second dimension does not seem to be interpretable. In addition, All Bran, which has lower calories and higher sugar is separated from the other cereals.

Copyright ©2015 Pearson Education, Inc.

17.44   (a)   JMP output:

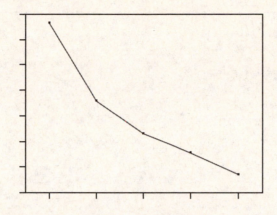

Number of Dimensions	Stress Values
1	0.53228397
2	0.37868642
3	0.31505665
4	0.27729418
5	0.23542606

Copyright ©2015 Pearson Education, Inc.

17.44   (a)
cont.

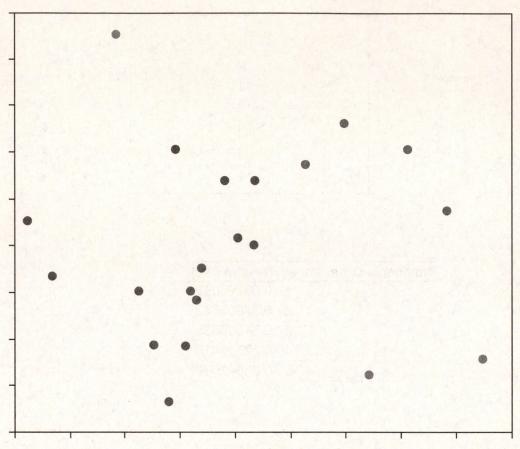

(b)   Since the stress statistic is 0.2773 in four dimensions, 0.3151 in three dimensions, 0.3787 in two dimensions, and 0.5323 in one dimension, it is reasonable to try to first try interpret a two-dimensional mapping of the countries. There does not seem to be a clear interpretation of the dimensions along the lines of GDP and social media usage. Pakistan seems very separated from the other countries with Indonesia on the other side of the graph. Russia and Lithuania are close as are Mexico and Spain, and Israel and Egypt.

17.46   Sparklines summarize time-series as small, compact graphs designed to appear as part of a table (or a written passage) while time-series plots are stand along grahic displays.

17.48   Classification trees and regression trees are decision trees that split data into groups based on the values of independent or explanatory variables. Classificaiton trees use categorical dependent variable while regression trees use numerical dependent variables.

17.50   Cluster analysis seeks to classify data into a sequence of groupings such that objects in each group are more alike other objects in their group than they are to objects found in other groups. Multidimensional scaling visualizes objects in a two or more dimensional space, or map, with the goal of discovering patterns of similarities or dissimilarities among the objects.

Copyright ©2015 Pearson Education, Inc.

17.52   (a)

Currency (Value of $1 U.S.)		2002	2003	2004	2005	2006	2007	2008	2009	2010
					Year					
Canada		1.57	1.29	1.20	1.17	1.17	0.99	1.21	1.05	1.00
English Pound		0.67	0.56	0.52	0.58	0.51	0.50	0.69	0.62	0.64
Euro		0.96	0.79	0.74	0.85	0.76	0.69	0.72	0.70	0.75

Currency (Value of $1 U.S.)		2008	2009	2010	2011	2012				
				Year						
Canada		1.21	1.05	1.00	0.98	0.99				
English Pound		0.69	0.62	0.64	0.64	0.62				
Euro		0.72	0.70	0.75	0.77	0.76				

(b)   The sparklines show differences in the values of the U. S. dollar in terms of the Canadian dollar, the English pound, and the Euro over the time period 2002 – 2012. The value of the U. S. dollar in terms of the Canadian dollar declined drastically from 2002 to 2007, but has remained steady since 2009. The value of the U. S. dollar in terms of the English pound has remained relatively steady between 2002 and 2012. The value of the U. S. dollar in terms of the Euro declined between 2002 and 2007 (with an increase in 2005) but has remained steady since 2008.

17.54   Because half the data will be used for a validation sample, the results will differ depending on which values are in the training sample and which are in the validation sample.

17.56   Because half the data will be used for a validation sample, the results will differ depending on which values are in the training sample and which are in the validation sample.

Copyright ©2015 Pearson Education, Inc.

17.58   (a)   JMP output:

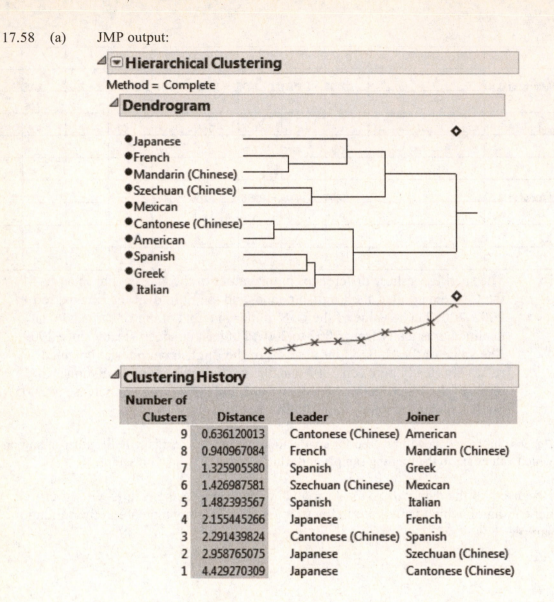

Number of Clusters	Distance	Leader	Joiner
9	0.636120013	Cantonese (Chinese)	American
8	0.940967084	French	Mandarin (Chinese)
7	1.325905580	Spanish	Greek
6	1.426987581	Szechuan (Chinese)	Mexican
5	1.482393567	Spanish	Italian
4	2.155445266	Japanese	French
3	2.291439824	Cantonese (Chinese)	Spanish
2	2.958765075	Japanese	Szechuan (Chinese)
1	4.429270309	Japanese	Cantonese (Chinese)

Copyright ©2015 Pearson Education, Inc.

17.58   (b)   JMP output:
cont.

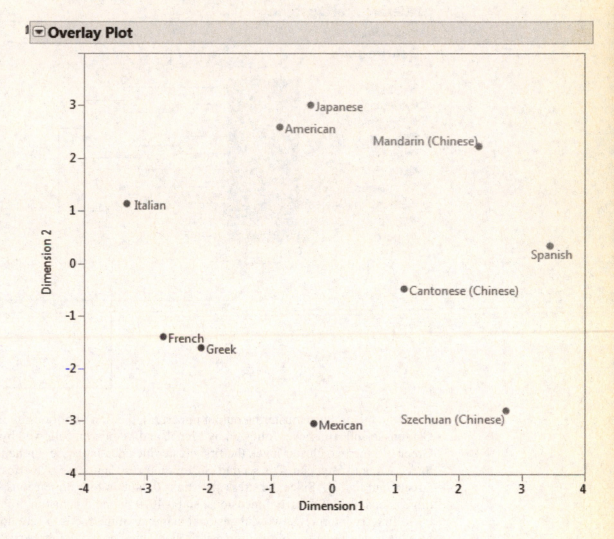

Copyright ©2015 Pearson Education, Inc.

17.58   (b)
cont.

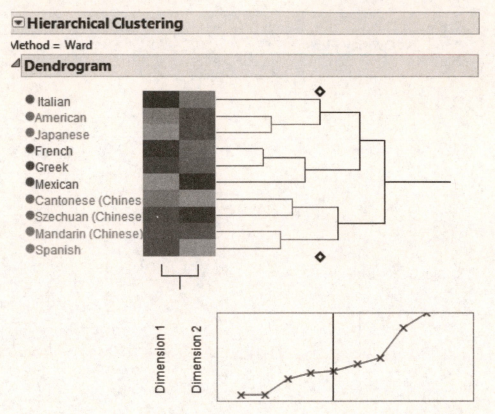

(c)   From the hierarchical clustering output in part (a), the first two foods to cluster are Cantonese and American, followed by French and Mandarin, followed by Spanish and Greek. At the two cluster level, the first cluster includes Japanese, French, Mandarin, Szechuan, and Mexican. The second cluster includes Cantonese, American, Spanish, Greek, and Italian. Since the stress statistic is 0.0468 in four dimensions, 0.1164 in three dimensions, 0.2339 in two dimensions, and 0.4079 in one dimension, it is reasonable to try to first try interpret a two-dimensional mapping of the foods. There does not seem to be a clear interpretation of the dimensions along the lines of the three scales. The two spicy foods, Mexican and Szechuan are close to each other as are French and Greek, and Japanese and American. Italian is separated by itself as is Spanish.

Copyright ©2015 Pearson Education, Inc.

CHAPTER 18

OBJECTIVES
- Identify the questions to ask when choosing which statistical methods to use to conduct data analysis
- Generate rules for applying statistics in future studies and analyses

OVERVIEW AND KEY CONCEPTS
Data Analysis Tasks Discussed in the Book

DESCRIBING A GROUP OR SEVERAL GROUPS

For Numerical Variables:
Ordered array, stem-and-leaf display, frequency distribution, relative frequency distribution, percentage distribution, cumulative percentage distribution, histogram, polygon, cumulative percentage polygon (**Sections 2.2 and 2.4**)
Boxplot (**Section 3.3**)
Normal probability plot (**Section 6.3**)
Bullet graph, gauge, treemap (**Section 17.1**)
Mean, median, mode, quartiles, geometric mean, range, interquartile range, standard deviation, variance, coefficient of variation, skewness, kurtosis (**Sections 3.1, 3.2, and 3.3**)
Index numbers (**online Section 16.8**)

For Categorical Variables:
Summary table, bar chart, pie chart, Pareto chart (**Sections 2.1 and 2.3**)
Contingency tables and multidimensional tables (**Sections 2.1 and 2.6**)

MAKING INFERENCES ABOUT ONE GROUP

For Numerical Variables:
Confidence interval estimate of the mean (**Sections 8.1 and 8.2**)
t test for the mean (**Section 9.2**)
Chi-square test for a variance or standard deviation (**online Section 12.7**)

For Categorical Variables:
Confidence interval estimate of the proportion (**Section 8.3**)
Z test for the proportion (**Section 9.4**)

Copyright ©2015 Pearson Education, Inc.

COMPARING TWO GROUPS

For Numerical Variables:
   Tests for the difference in the means of two independent populations **(Section 10.1)**
   Wilcoxon rank sum test **(Section 12.4)**
   Paired t test **(Section 10.2)**
   F test for the difference between two variances **(Section 10.4)**
   Wilcoxon signed rank test **(online Section 12.8)**

For Categorical Variables:
   Z test for the difference between two proportions **(Section 10.3)**
   Chi-square test for the difference between two proportions **(Section 12.1)**
   McNemar test for two related samples **(online Section 12.6)**

COMPARING MORE THAN TWO GROUPS

For Numerical Variables:
   One-way analysis of variance **(Section 11.1)**
   Kruskal-Wallis rank test **(Section 12.5)**
   Randomized block design **(Section 11.2)**
   Two-way analysis of variance **(Section 11.3)**
   Friedman rank test **(online Section 12.9)**

For Categorical Variables:
   Chi-square test for differences among more than two proportions **(Section 12.2)**

ANALYZING THE RELATIONSHIP BETWEEN TWO VARIABLES

For Numerical Variables:
   Scatter plot, time-series plot **(Section 2.5)**
   Covariance, coefficient of correlation, t test of correlation **(Sections 3.5 and 13.7)**
   Simple linear regression **(Chapter 13)**
   Time-series forecasting **(Chapter 16)**

For Categorical Variables:
   Contingency table, side-by-side bar chart **(Sections 2.1 and 2.3)**
   Chi-square test of independence **(Section 12.3)**

Copyright ©2015 Pearson Education, Inc.

ANALYZING THE RELATIONSHIP BETWEEN TWO OR MORE VARIABLES

For Numerical Dependent Variables:
Multiple regression **(Chapters 14 and 15)**
Regression tree **(Section 17.3)**
Neural network **(Section 17.4)**

For Categorical Dependent Variables:
Logistic regression **(Section 14.7)**
Classification tree **(Section 17.3)**
Neural network **(Section 17.4)**

CLASSIFYING OBJECTS INTO GROUPS

For a Set of Variables:
Cluster analysis **(Section 17.5)**
Multidimensional scaling **(Section 17.6)**

ANALYZING PROCESS DATA

For Numerical Variables:
$\overline{X}$ and R control charts **(online Section 19.5)**

For Categorical Variables:
p chart **(online Section 19.2)**

For Counts of Nonconformities:
c chart **(online Section 19.4)**

To Describe the Characteristics of Numerical Variables
- Create stem-and-leaf display, percentage distribution, histogram, polygon, boxplot, normal probability plot, bullet graph, gauge, and treemap (Sections 2.2, 2.4, 3.3, 6.3, and 17.1).
- Compute statistics such as the mean, median, mode, quartiles, range, interquartile range, standard deviation, variance, coefficient of variation, skewness and kurtosis (Section 3.1, 3.2 and 3.3).

To Draw Conclusions about the Population Mean or Standard Deviation for Numerical Variables
- Construct confidence interval for the mean or perform the t test (Sections 8.2 and 9.2).
- Conduct a χ^2 test of hypothesis for the standard deviation or variance (Section 12.7).

To Determine Whether the Mean or Standard Deviation Differs Depending On the Group for Numerical Variables
- Two Independent Groups
  - Variables are normally distributed and variances are equal
    - Conduct a pooled t test for the difference between the means (Section 10.1).
    - Develop boxplots and normal probability plots for each group to evaluate the assumption of normality (Section 3.3, and 6.3).
    - Conduct an F test for the differences between the variances to determine whether the variances are equal (Section 10.4).
  - Variables are normally distributed but variances are not equal
    - Conduct a separate-variance t test for the difference between the means (Section 10.1).
  - Variables are not normally distributed

Copyright ©2015 Pearson Education, Inc.

- Perform a Wilcoxon rank sum test (Section 12.4) and compare these results to those of the pooled t test or separate-variance t test (Section 10.1).
- Two Dependent Groups
  - The paired differences are normally distributed
    - Conduct a paired t test (Section 10.2)
  - The paired differences are not normally distributed
    - Conduct a Wilcoxon signed rank test (online Section 12.8)
- More than Two Independent Groups
  - Variables are normally distributed and variances are equal
    - Conduct a One Way Analysis of Variance (Section 11.1)
  - Variables are not normally distributed and variances are not equal
    - Conduct a Kruskal-Wallis rank test (Section 12.5)
- More than Two Dependent Groups Where the Rows Represent the Blocks and the Columns Represent the Factors
  - Variables are normally distributed
    - Conduct a randomized block design (Section 11.3).
  - Variables are not normally distributed
    - Conduct a Friedman rank test (online Section 12.9).

To Determine Which Factors (Categorical Variables) Affect the Value of a Numerical Variable

- Perform a two-way ANOVA (Section 11.3)

To Predict the Value of a Numerical Variable Based On the Value of Other Variables

- Conduct simple linear least-squares regression analysis if there is only one independent variable (Chapter 13).
- Conduct multiple linear least-squares regression analysis if there is more than one independent variable (Chapter 14 and 15) or a regression tree (Section 17.3) or a neural network (Section 17.4)..
- Use moving averages, exponential smoothing, least-squares forecasting, and autoregressive modeling to forecast values for future time periods or if you have values over a period of time (Chapter 16).

To Determine Whether the Values of a Numerical Variable Are Stable Over Time

- Develop R and $\bar{X}$ charts to study a process over a time period for numerical variables (Section 19.5).
- Construct c chart to study a process over a time period for counts of the number of nonconformities (Section 19.4).

To Describe the Proportion of Items of Interest in Each Category of Categorical Variables

- Create summary tables and use the bar chart, pie chart, Pareto chart, or side-by-side bar chart (Sections 2.1 and 2.3)

To Draw Conclusions about the Proportion of Items of Interest of Categorical Variables

- Develop a confidence interval estimate of the proportion (Section 8.3).
- Conduct a Z test of hypothesis for the proportion to determine whether the population proportion is equal to a specific value by (Section 9.4)

Copyright ©2015 Pearson Education, Inc.

To Determine Whether the Proportion of Items of Interest Differs Depending on the Group of Categorical Variables

- Two categories and two independent groups
  - Conduct either the Z test for the difference between two proportions (Section 10.3) or the χ^2 test for the difference between two proportions (Section 12.1).
- Two categories and two groups of matched or repeated measurements
  - Conduct the McNemar test (Section 12.6).
- Two categories and more than two independent groups
  - Conduct a χ^2 test for the difference among several proportions (Section 12.2).
- More than two categories and more than two groups
  - Conduct a χ^2 test of independence (Section 12.3).

To Predict the Proportion of Items of Interest of a Categorical Variable Based on the Value of Other Categorical and/or Numerical Variables

- Develop a logistic regression model (Section 14.7) or use classification trees (Section 17.3) or neural networks (see Section 17.4).

To Determine Whether the Proportion or Number of Items of Interest Is Stable Over Time

- Develop a p chart (Section 19.2).

Copyright ©2015 Pearson Education, Inc.

SOLUTIONS TO END OF SECTION
AND CHAPTER REVIEW EVEN PROBLEMS

18.2   Let X_1 = Temp X_2 = Win% X_3 = OpWin% X_4 = Weekend X_5 = Promotion

With all the 5 independent variables in the model: None of the *VIF* is > 5.

The best-subset regression produces the following potential models:

Model	Cp	k	R Square	Adj. R Square	Std. Error	Consider This Model?
X1X2X3X4X5	6	6	0.301052	0.253826288	6442.446	Yes
X1X2X3X5	4.0174	5	0.300888	0.263602154	6400.104	Yes
X1X3X5	3.703162	4	0.284966	0.256740664	6429.852	Yes
X2X3X4X5	4.674724	5	0.29468	0.257062456	6428.46	Yes
X2X3X5	2.680286	4	0.294627	0.26678334	6386.265	Yes

Based on the smallest C_p value and the highest adjusted *r*-square, the best model is the following:

	Coefficients	Standard Error	t Stat	P-value	Lower 95%	Upper 95%
Intercept	-1669.988177	5531.248104	-0.30191887	0.763538564	-12686.43764	9346.46129
Win%	27.4932005	14.0652218	1.954693705	0.054297102	-0.520152407	55.50655341
OpWin%	10.53699651	6.324477812	1.666065851	0.099817096	-2.059308864	23.13330188
Promotion	7089.212249	1455.76966	4.869734852	5.9398E-06	4189.791975	9988.632523

Since only X_5 makes significant contribution to the regression model at 5% level of significance, the more parsimonious model includes only X_5.

$$\hat{Y} = 13,935.703 + 6,813.228 X_5$$

	Coefficients	Standard Error	t Stat	P-value
Intercept	13935.7027	1096.695459	12.70699408	1.09284E-20
Promotion	6813.22753	1495.880191	4.554661244	1.90736E-05

The estimated mean paid attendance on a non-promotion day is 13,935.70. The estimated mean paid attendance on a promotion day will be 6,813.23 higher than when there is no promotion.

$$H_0 : \beta_5 = 0 \text{ vs } H_1 : \beta_5 \neq 0$$

Since the *p*-value is virtually zero, reject H_0. At the 0.05 level of significance, promotion makes a significant contribution to the regression model.

$r^2 = 0.2101$. Hence, 21.02% of the variation in attendance can be explained by promotion.

Copyright ©2015 Pearson Education, Inc.

18.2
cont.

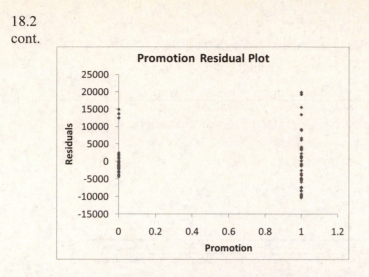

Normal Probability Plot

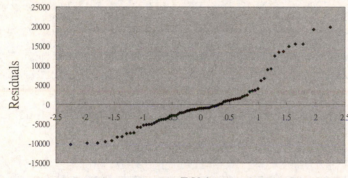

Z Value

The normal probability plot reveals non-normality in the residuals. The residual plot suggests possible violation of the homoscedasticity assumption.

Copyright ©2015 Pearson Education, Inc.

18.4 Let $X_1 = \text{Temp}$ $X_2 = \text{Win\%}$ $X_3 = \text{OpWin\%}$ $X_4 = \text{Weekend}$ $X_5 = \text{Promotion}$

With all the 5 independent variables in the model: None of the *VIF* is > 5.

The best-subset regression produces only one potential model:

Model	Cp	k	R Square	Adj. R Square	Std. Error	Consider This Model?
X1X2X3X4X5	6	6	0.390987	0.350386138	4320.381	Yes

The best model is the full model that includes all the independent variables.

Regression Statistics	
Multiple R	0.625289536
R Square	0.390987004
Adjusted R Square	0.350386138
Standard Error	4320.381297
Observations	81

ANOVA

	df	SS	MS	F	Significance F
Regression	5	898754711.7	179750942.3	9.630016278	3.94963E-07
Residual	75	1399927091	18665694.55		
Total	80	2298681803			

	Coefficients	Standard Error	t Stat	P-value	Lower 95%	Upper 95%
Intercept	10682.45521	6013.474857	1.776419701	0.079719211	-1297.003842	22661.91425
Temp	82.20546833	38.59788228	2.129792192	0.036469445	5.314525708	159.096411
Win%	26.26250802	12.37716144	2.121852263	0.037152917	1.60593222	50.91908383
OpWin%	7.367011607	5.929542741	1.24242491	0.217950544	-4.445246053	19.17926927
Weekend	3369.907577	1026.248391	3.283715332	0.001558126	1325.515463	5414.299691
Promotion	3129.013192	1030.12174	3.037517868	0.003280737	1076.904969	5181.121414

Since X_3 does not make significant contribution to the regression model at 5% level of significance, it can be dropped from the model. The more parsimonious model includes X_1, X_2, X_4 and X_5.

$$\hat{Y} = 14{,}965.626 + 88.888X_1 + 23.269X_2 + 3{,}562.425X_4 + 3{,}029.087X_5$$

	Coefficients	Standard Error	t Stat	P-value
Intercept	14965.62623	4944.771809	3.026555483	0.003375413
Temp	88.88797075	38.35774548	2.317340856	0.023179453
Win%	23.26917677	12.1837526	1.909853026	0.059925592
Weekend	3562.425371	1018.104525	3.499076257	0.000784145
Promotion	3029.087074	1030.643544	2.939024935	0.004358397

Since X_2 does not make significant contribution to the regression model at 5% level of significance, it can be dropped from the model. The more parsimonious model includes only X_1, X_4 and X_5.

$$\hat{Y} = 22601.7676 + 108.6331X_1 + 3907.6538X_4 + 3433.9977X_5$$

	Coefficients	Standard Error	t Stat	P-value
Intercept	22601.76761	2958.970207	7.638389719	5.03953E-11
Temp	108.633101	37.56787033	2.891649169	0.004978867
Weekend	3907.653774	1019.008546	3.834760553	0.000255422
Promotion	3433.997688	1025.794791	3.347645862	0.001263126

Since the non-dummy independent variable, day high temperature, is unlikely to have zero values, the intercept should be interpreted as the portion of paid attendance that varies with factors other than those already included in the model.

Copyright ©2015 Pearson Education, Inc.

18.4
cont.

As the high temperature increases by one degree, the estimated mean paid attendance will increase by 108.6331 taking into consideration all the other independent variables included in the model.

The estimated mean paid attendance of a game played on a weekend will be 3907.6538 higher than when the game is played on a weekday taking into consideration all the other independent variables included in the model.

The estimated mean paid attendance on a promotion day will be 3433.9977 higher than when there is no promotion taking into consideration all the other independent variables included in the model.

$$H_0 : \beta_j = 0 \qquad H_1 : \beta_j \neq 0 \qquad \text{for } j = 1, 2, 4, 5$$

At the 0.05 level of significance, temperature, and the weekend and promotion dummy variables make a significant contribution to the regression model individually.

Adjusted $r^2 = .3232$. Hence, 32.32% of the variation in attendance can be explained by the 3 independent variables after adjusting for the number of independent variables and the sample size.

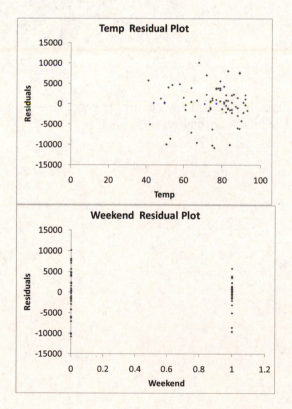

Copyright ©2015 Pearson Education, Inc.

18.4
cont.

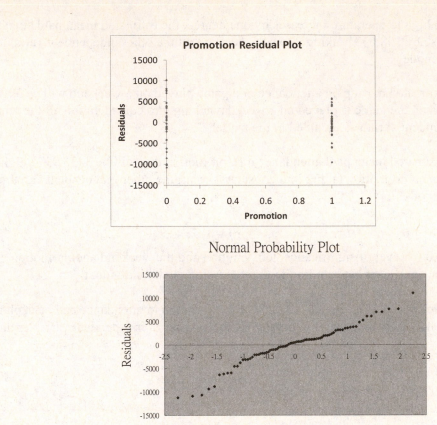

The residual plots do not reveal any obvious pattern. The normal probability plot does not reveal departure from the normality assumption.

Copyright ©2015 Pearson Education, Inc.

18.6 Let X_1 = Business Travel & Tourism Spending 2012 (US $Millions), X_2 = International Visitors 2012 (Number), X_3 = Tourism Establishments (Number).

Based on a full regression model involving all of the variables: None of the VIF > 5.

Based on the C_p values and the adjusted r-square obtained using PHStat, the best-subset regression produces the following potential models.

Portion of the PHStat Output for Best-subset Regression:

Model	Cp	k+1	R Square	Adj. R Square	Std. Error	Consider This Model?
X1X2	2.4622	3	0.8925	0.8836	106434.4506	Yes
X1X2X3	4.0000	4	0.8946	0.8809	107647.3042	Yes

PHStat output for the full model that include all the 3 independent variables:

	Coefficients	Standard Error	t Stat	P-value
Intercept	53568.1665	26921.5424	1.9898	0.0586
Business Travel & Tourism Spending 2012 (US $Millions)	12.6866	2.7076	4.6855	0.0001
International Visitors 2012 (Number)	7.4693	1.6407	4.5524	0.0001
Tourism Establishments (Number)	-0.7211	1.0606	-0.6799	0.5034

The t-test for the significance of the individual slope coefficient has a p-value > 0.05 for X_3. Therefore, X_3 should be dropped from the model. The best model to predict the number of jobs generated in the travel and tourism industry should include only Business Travel & Tourism Spending 2012 (US $Millions) and International Visitors 2012 (Number).

Spain has a Cook's $D_i = 0.9613 > F_\alpha = 0.8115$ with d.f. = 3 and 24. It also has a Studentized deleted residual $|t_i| = |-2.6988| > t_{\alpha/2}$ 1.7139 with d.f. = 23 and a hat matrix element $h_i = 0.3332 > 2(k+1)/n = 0.2222$.

Hence, using the Studentized deleted residuals, hat matrix diagonal elements and Cook's distance statistic together, there is sufficient evidence for removal of Spain from the model.

Copyright ©2015 Pearson Education, Inc.

18.6   PHStat output with Spain removed from the data set:
cont.

| Regression Analysis | | | | | | |

Regression Statistics						
Multiple R	0.9576
R Square	0.9169
Adjusted R Square	0.9097
Standard Error	94751.0387
Observations	26

ANOVA

	df	SS	MS	F	Significance F
Regression	2	2278843815344.3100	1139421907672.1600	126.9161	0.0000
Residual	23	206488464655.6870	8977759332.8560		
Total	25	2485332280000.0000			

	Coefficients	Standard Error	t Stat	P-value	Lower 95%	Upper 95%
Intercept	46574.3143	23761.8543	1.9600	0.0622	-2580.8265	95729.4550
Business Travel & Tourism Spending 2012 (	9.4572	2.3438	4.0349	0.0005	4.6086	14.3057
International Visitors 2012 (Number)	9.2881	1.5565	5.9671	0.0000	6.0681	12.5081

The F-test for the full model has a p-value $= 0.0000 < 0.05$ and the t-test for the significance of the individual slope coefficient has a p-value < 0.05 for both X_1 and X_2. The model with both X_1 and X_2 should be used.

None of the observations have a Cook's $D_i > F_\alpha = 0.8125$ with d.f. $= 3$ and 23.

Hence, using the Studentized deleted residuals, hat matrix diagonal elements and Cook's distance statistic together, there is insufficient evidence for removal of any additional observation from the model.

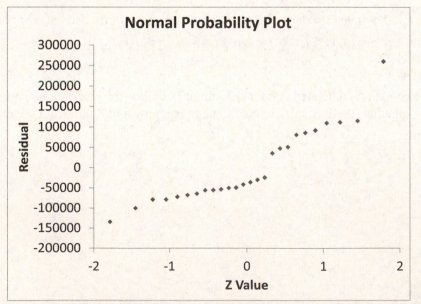

The normal probability plot reveals potential departure from the normality assumption. With a sample size of 27, this departure from the normality assumption may not have severe consequences on the estimates and prediction.

Copyright ©2015 Pearson Education, Inc.

18.6
cont.

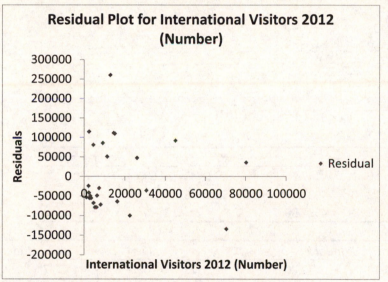

The residual plots do not reveal any obvious pattern.

The best model to predict the number of jobs generated in the travel and tourism industry should include only Business Travel & Tourism Spending 2012 (US $Millions) and International Visitors 2012 (Number) with Spain eliminated.

$$\hat{Y} = 46574.3143 + 9.4572X_1 + 9.2881X_2$$

Copyright ©2015 Pearson Education, Inc.

18.8   Let Y = Wins, X_1 = Points Scored, X_2 = Points allowed, X_3 = Field Goals %, X_4 = Field Goals % Allowed, X_5 = Own Turnovers, X_6 = Opponent Turnovers, X_7 = Rebound %.
Based on a full regression model involving all of the variables:
The *VIF*s for X_1 and X_2 are > 5. X_2 with the highest *VIF* is dropped.
All *VIFs* < 5 after dropping X_2. So there is no reason to suspect collinearity between any pair of the remaining variables.

Now let Y = Wins, X_1 = Points scored, X_2 = Field Goals %, X_3 = Field Goals % Allowed, X_4 = Own Turnovers, X_5 = Opponent Turnovers, X_6 = Rebound %.

The best-subset approach yields the following models to be considered:
Partial PHStat output from the best-subsets selection:

Model	Cp	k+1	R Square	Adj. R Square	Std. Error	Consider This Model?
X1X2X3X4X5X6	7.0000	7	0.8853	0.8554	4.8334	Yes

PHStat output of the full regression model with X_1 through X_6:

Regression Statistics	
Multiple R	0.9409
R Square	0.8853
Adjusted R Square	0.8554
Standard Error	4.8334
Observations	30

ANOVA

	df	SS	MS	F	Significance F
Regression	6	4147.6457	691.2743	29.5900	0.0000
Residual	23	537.3209	23.3618		
Total	29	4684.9667			

	Coefficients	Standard Error	t Stat	P-value	Lower 95%	Upper 95%
Intercept	-94.8014	72.2093	-1.3129	0.2022	-244.1777	54.5750
Points Scored	0.8565	0.3696	2.3171	0.0298	0.0918	1.6211
Field Goal%	2.5218	0.9033	2.7919	0.0104	0.6533	4.3903
Field Goal % Allowe	-3.4399	0.7568	-4.5453	0.0001	-5.0055	-1.8743
Own Turnovers	-5.2657	1.2674	-4.1548	0.0004	-7.8875	-2.6440
Opponent Turnover	1.6922	1.0897	1.5529	0.1341	-0.5620	3.9463
Rebound %	2.8621	0.7020	4.0773	0.0005	1.4100	4.3143

18.8   None of the observations have a Cook's $D_i > F_\alpha = 0.9336$ with d.f. = 7 and 23.

cont.   Hence, using the Studentized deleted residuals, hat matrix diagonal elements and Cook's distance statistic together, there is insufficient evidence for removal of any observation from the model.

The p-value for the t test for the significance of the individual slope coefficients are all < 0.05 with the exception of X_5.

X_5 is dropped from the regression.

PHStat output:

Regression Statistics	
Multiple R	0.9345
R Square	0.8733
Adjusted R Square	0.8469
Standard Error	4.9735
Observations	30

ANOVA

	df	SS	MS	F	Significance F
Regression	5	4091.3072	818.2614	33.0800	0.0000
Residual	24	593.6595	24.7358		
Total	29	4684.9667			

	Coefficients	Standard Error	t Stat	P-value	Lower 95%	Upper 95%	Lower 95%	Upper 95%
Intercept	-59.0934	70.4346	-0.8390	0.4098	-204.4634	86.2766	-204.4634	86.2766
Points Scored	1.0010	0.3681	2.7192	0.0120	0.2412	1.7607	0.2412	1.7607
Field Goal%	2.4898	0.9292	2.6795	0.0131	0.5720	4.4076	0.5720	4.4076
Field Goal % Allowe	-3.5959	0.7719	-4.6587	0.0001	-5.1889	-2.0028	-5.1889	-2.0028
Own Turnovers	-5.5978	1.2854	-4.3549	0.0002	-8.2508	-2.9449	-8.2508	-2.9449
Rebound %	2.5994	0.7010	3.7080	0.0011	1.1526	4.0463	1.1526	4.0463

The p-values of the t test for the significance of the individual slope coefficients are all < 0.05. The F test for the significance of all the independent variables as a group has a p-value < 0.05.

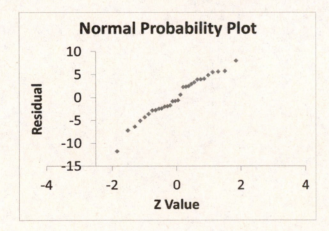

Copyright ©2015 Pearson Education, Inc.

18.8
cont.

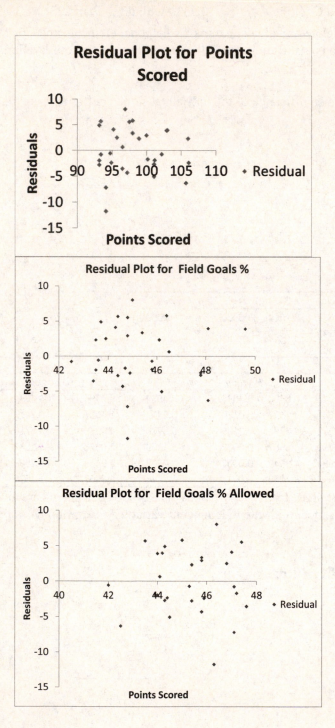

Copyright ©2015 Pearson Education, Inc.

18.8
cont.

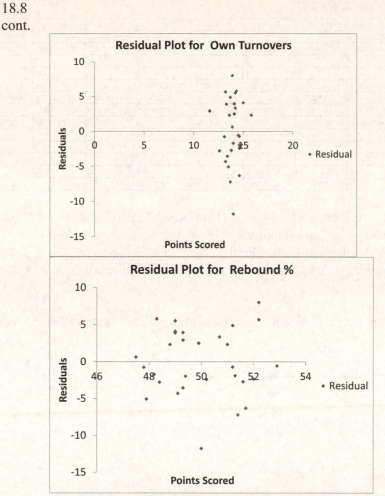

The normal probability plot does not reveal severe departure from the normality assumption. The residual plots for Points Scores and Field Goal % reveal potential violation of the equal variance assumption as the variance appears to decrease as the Points Scores and Field Goal % increase.

The best model to use to predict the number of wins should include Point Scores, Field Goals %, Field Goals % Allowed, Own Turnovers and Rebound %.

Copyright ©2015 Pearson Education, Inc.

18.10   Summary Statistics:

	Salary	Competence Rating	M to M	F to M	M to F	Public	Biology	Chemistry	Age-Rater
Mean	29.4025	3.733333333	0.25	0.25	0.25	0.5	0.333333333	0.333333333	54.05833333
Standard Error	0.475963511	0.140394269	0.039694209	0.039694209	0.039694209	0.045834925	0.043213582	0.043213582	0.52504446
Median	28.95	4	0	0	0	0.5	0	0	55
Mode	28.3	4	0	0	0	1	0	0	56
Standard Deviation	5.213919033	1.537942166	0.434828277	0.434828277	0.434828277	0.502096445	0.473381068	0.473381068	5.751573893
Sample Variance	27.18495168	2.365266106	0.18907563	0.18907563	0.18907563	0.25210084	0.224089636	0.224089636	33.08060224
Kurtosis	3.019432897	-0.510058795	-0.643584915	-0.643584915	-0.643584915	-2.034188034	-1.512711864	-1.512711864	0.264824682
Skewness	1.085010708	0.219536333	1.169368699	1.169368699	1.169368699	0	0.716089158	0.716089158	-0.185855334
Range	31.5	6	1	1	1	1	1	1	34
Minimum	18.5	1	0	0	0	0	0	0	37
Maximum	50	7	1	1	1	1	1	1	71
Sum	3528.3	448	30	30	30	60	40	40	6487
Count	120	120	120	120	120	120	120	120	120

Let Y = Salary, X_1 = Competence Rating, X_2 = M to M (1 if Rater = M and Candidate = M, 0 otherwise), X_3 = F to M (1 if Rater = F and Candidate = M, 0 otherwise), X_4 = M to F (1 if Rater = M and Candidate = F, 0 otherwise), X_5 = Public (1 if public, 0 otherwise), X_6 = Biology (1 if Biology, 0 otherwise), X_7 = Chemistry (1 if Chemistry, 0 otherwise), X_8 = Age-Rater.

The regression with all eight potential independent variable indicates that none of the VIF is > 5.

Regression output that include all eight independent variables:

Regression Statistics	
Multiple R	0.9358
R Square	0.8757
Adjusted R Square	0.8667
Standard Error	1.9035
Observations	120

ANOVA

	df	SS	MS	F	Significance F
Regression	8	2832.8317	354.1040	97.7318	0.0000
Residual	111	402.1776	3.6232		
Total	119	3235.0093			

	Coefficients	Standard Error	t Stat	P-value	Lower 95%	Upper 95%	Lower 95%
Intercept	15.7064	1.9022	8.2570	0.0000	11.9371	19.4758	11.9371
Competence Rating	2.9869	0.1159	25.7765	0.0000	2.7573	3.2166	2.7573
M to M	1.2944	0.4989	2.5946	0.0107	0.3058	2.2830	0.3058
F to M	1.7188	0.4984	3.4486	0.0008	0.7312	2.7065	0.7312
M to F	-0.8224	0.4964	-1.6567	0.1004	-1.8062	0.1613	-1.8062
Public	0.3157	0.3541	0.8917	0.3745	-0.3859	1.0174	-0.3859
Biology	-0.3072	0.4268	-0.7196	0.4733	-1.1530	0.5387	-1.1530
Chemistry	0.2041	0.4291	0.4755	0.6353	-0.6462	1.0543	-0.6462
Age-Rater	0.0347	0.0315	1.1001	0.2737	-0.0278	0.0971	-0.0278

The full-model F_{stat} = 97.7318 with a p-value = 0.0000. Hence, the eight independent variables as a group are significant in explaining the variation in Salary at the 5% level of significance.

Copyright ©2015 Pearson Education, Inc.

18.10
cont.
The individual *t* test indicates that "M to F", "Public", "Biology", "Chemistry", and "Age-Rater" all have *p*-value > 0.05 and, hence, are not significant individually at the 5% level of significance.

Regression output after dropping "M to F", "Public", "Biology", "Chemistry", and "Age-Rater":

Regression Statistics						
Multiple R	0.9321					
R Square	0.8687					
Adjusted R Square	0.8653					
Standard Error	1.9134					
Observations	120					

ANOVA						
	df	SS	MS	F	Significance F	
Regression	3	2810.3354	936.7785	255.8818	0.0000	
Residual	116	424.6739	3.6610			
Total	119	3235.0093				

	Coefficients	Standard Error	t Stat	P-value	Lower 95%	Upper 95%
Intercept	17.3144	0.4705	36.8036	0.0000	16.3826	18.2462
Competence Rating	2.9823	0.1161	25.6975	0.0000	2.7524	3.2122
M to M	1.6897	0.4326	3.9062	0.0002	0.8330	2.5465
F to M	2.1270	0.4332	4.9103	0.0000	1.2691	2.9849

Partial *F*-test for portion of the multiple regression model:

$$H_0 : \beta_4 = \beta_5 = \beta_6 = \beta_7 = \beta_8 = 0 \quad \text{vs.} \quad H_1 : \text{Not all } \beta_j = 0 \text{ for } j = 4,5,6,7,8$$

$$F_{\text{STAT}} =$$

$$\frac{\left(SSR\left(X_4, X_5, X_6, X_7, X_8 \mid X_1, X_2, X_3\right)\right)/5}{MSE\left(\text{All } Xs\right)} = \frac{\left(SSR\left(\text{All } Xs\right) - SSR\left(X_1, X_2, X_3\right)\right)/5}{MSE\left(\text{All } Xs\right)}$$

= 1.2418 with 5 and 111 degrees of freedom.

Since *p*-value = 0.2945 > 0.05, do not reject H_0. There is not enough evidence that at least one of "M to F", "Public", "Biology", "Chemistry", and "Age-Rater" is significant.

The best model is

$$\text{Salary} = 17.3144 + 2.9823\left(\text{Competence Rating}\right) + 1.6897\left(\text{M to M}\right) + 2.1270\left(\text{F to M}\right)$$

Copyright ©2015 Pearson Education, Inc.

18.10 The normal probability plot of the residuals:
cont.

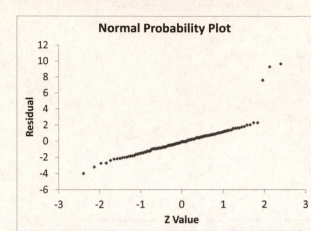

The normal probability plot suggests that the residuals are quite normally distributed except the 3 outliers in the right-tail, which could severly bias the result.

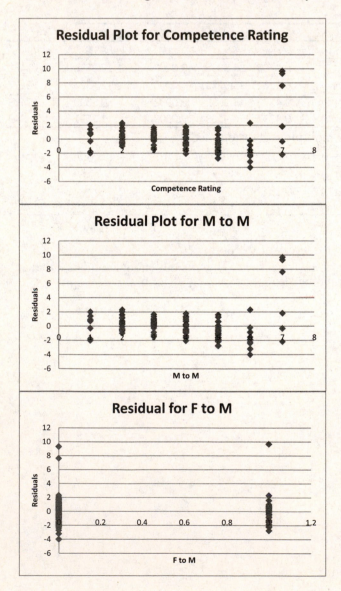

Copyright ©2015 Pearson Education, Inc.

18.10   The residual plots suggest violation of the equal variance assumption. Hence, the conclusion
cont.   from the regression result might not be reliable.

The best regression model suggests that after taking into consideration the other factors like
competence rating that could have affected salary, the mean salary of a femal candidate is
estimated to be the same regardless of the gender of the rater. The mean salary of a male
candidate is estimated to be $1.6897 thousands higher than his female counterpart when
rated by a male and estimated to be $2.1270 thousands higher than his female counterpart
when rated by a female.

18.12   Pivital table in terms of counts (Job by Term Deposit):

Count of Job	Column Labels ▼		
Row Labels ▼	no	yes	Grand Total
admin.	134	4	138
blue-collar	270	17	287
entrepreneur	29		29
housemaid	8		8
management	133	7	140
retired	36	2	38
self-employed	24	3	27
services	121	3	124
student	10		10
technician	152	5	157
unemployed	19		19
unknown	2		2
Grand Total	**938**	**41**	**979**

Pivital table in terms of row totals (Job by Term Deposit):

Count of Term Deposit	Column Labels ▼		
Row Labels ▼	no	yes	Grand Total
admin.	97.10%	2.90%	100.00%
blue-collar	94.08%	5.92%	100.00%
entrepreneur	100.00%	0.00%	100.00%
housemaid	100.00%	0.00%	100.00%
management	95.00%	5.00%	100.00%
retired	94.74%	5.26%	100.00%
self-employed	88.89%	11.11%	100.00%
services	97.58%	2.42%	100.00%
student	100.00%	0.00%	100.00%
technician	96.82%	3.18%	100.00%
unemployed	100.00%	0.00%	100.00%
unknown	100.00%	0.00%	100.00%
Grand Total	**95.81%**	**4.19%**	**100.00%**

Copyright ©2015 Pearson Education, Inc.

18.12   PHStat output for the Chi-square test for the difference in proportions: cont.

Chi-Square Test													

Observed Frequencies

					Column variable								
Row variable	admin.	blue-colla	entrepren	housemai	managem	retired	self-empl	services	student	techniciar	unemploy	unknown	Total
No	134	270	29	8	133	36	24	121	10	152	19	2	938
Yes	4	17			7	2	3	3		5			41
Total	138	287	29	8	140	38	27	124	10	157	19	2	979

Expected Frequencies

					Column variable								
Row variable	admin.	blue-collar	ntreprene	housemaid	anagemer	retired	lf-employ	services	student	technician	nemploye	unknown	Total
No	132.2206	274.9806	27.7855	7.664964	134.1369	36.40858	25.86925	118.8069	9.581205	150.4249	18.20429	1.916241	938
Yes	5.779367	12.01941	1.214505	0.335036	5.863126	1.59142	1.130746	5.193054	0.418795	6.575077	0.79571	0.083759	41
Total	138	287	29	8	140	38	27	124	10	157	19	2	979

Data	
Level of Significance	0.05
Number of Rows	2
Number of Columns	12
Degrees of Freedom	11

Results	
Critical Value	19.67514
Chi-Square Test Statistic	10.62328
p-Value	0.475342
Do not reject the null hypothesis	

Expected frequency assumption
  is violated.

The p-value = 0.4753 > 0.05, do not reject H_0. There is not enough evidence that the proportions are different across the different type of jobs at the 5% level of significance. However, the expected frequency assumption for the chi-square test is violated.

Pivital table in terms of counts (Marital by Term Deposit):

Count of Term Deposit	Column Labels		
Row Labels	no	yes	Grand Total
divorced	120	9	129
married	572	18	590
single	246	14	260
Grand Total	938	41	979

Pivital table in terms of row totals (Marital by Term Deposit):

Count of Term Deposit	Column Labels		
Row Labels	no	yes	Grand Total
divorced	93.02%	6.98%	100.00%
married	96.95%	3.05%	100.00%
single	94.62%	5.38%	100.00%
Grand Total	95.81%	4.19%	100.00%

Copyright ©2015 Pearson Education, Inc.

18.12   PHStat output for the Chi-square test for the difference in proportions:
cont.

Chi-Square Test

Observed Frequencies			
	Column variable		
Row variable	divorced	married	single	Total
No	120	572	246	938
Yes	9	18	14	41
Total	129	590	260	979

Expected Frequencies			
	Column variable		
Row variable	divorced	married	single	Total
No	123.5975	565.2911	249.1113	938
Yes	5.402451	24.70889	10.88866	41
Total	129	590	260	979

Data	
Level of Significance	0.05
Number of Rows	2
Number of Columns	3
Degrees of Freedom	2

Results	
Critical Value	5.991465
Chi-Square Test Statistic	5.329455
p-Value	0.069618
Do not reject the null hypothesis	

Expected frequency assumption is met.

The p-value = 0.0696 > 0.05, do not reject H_0. There is not enough evidence that the proportions are different across the different marital status at the 5% level of significance.

Pivital table in terms of counts (Education by Term Deposit):

Count of Term Deposit	Column Labels		
Row Labels	no	yes	Grand Total
primary	139	10	149
secondary	576	21	597
tertiary	183	9	192
unknown	40	1	41
Grand Total	938	41	979

Copyright ©2015 Pearson Education, Inc.

18.12   Pivital table in terms of row totals (Education by Term Deposit):
cont.

Count of Term Deposit	Column Labels ▼		
Row Labels ▼	no	yes	Grand Total
primary	93.29%	6.71%	100.00%
secondary	96.48%	3.52%	100.00%
tertiary	95.31%	4.69%	100.00%
unknown	97.56%	2.44%	100.00%
Grand Total	**95.81%**	**4.19%**	**100.00%**

PHStat output for the Chi-square test for the difference in proportions:

Chi-Square Test

	Observed Frequencies				
	Column variable				
Row variable	primary	secondary	tertiary	unknown	Total
No	139	576	183	40	938
Yes	10	21	9	1	41
Total	149	597	192	41	979

	Expected Frequencies				
	Column variable				
Row variable	primary	secondary	tertiary	unknown	Total
No	142.76	571.998	183.9591	39.28294	938
Yes	6.240041	25.00204	8.040858	1.717058	41
Total	149	597	192	41	979

Data	
Level of Significance	0.05
Number of Rows	2
Number of Columns	4
Degrees of Freedom	3

Results	
Critical Value	7.814728
Chi-Square Test Statistic	3.465157
p-Value	0.325309
Do not reject the null hypothesis	

Expected frequency assumption
  is met.

The p-value $= 0.3253 > 0.05$, do not reject H_0. There is not enough evidence that the proportions are different across the different education levels at the 5% level of significance.

Copyright ©2015 Pearson Education, Inc.

18.12 Pivital table in terms of counts (Default by Term Deposit):
cont.

Count of Term Deposit Row Labels	Column Labels ▼ no	yes	Grand Total
no	914	40	954
yes	24	1	25
Grand Total	**938**	**41**	**979**

Pivital table in terms of row totals (Default by Term Deposit):

Count of Term Deposit Row Labels	Column Labels ▼ no	yes	Grand Total
no	95.81%	4.19%	100.00%
yes	96.00%	4.00%	100.00%
Grand Total	**95.81%**	**4.19%**	**100.00%**

PHStat output for the Chi-square test for the difference in proportions:

Chi-Square Test

Observed Frequencies			
	Column variable		
Row variable	No	Yes	Total
No	914	24	938
Yes	40	1	41
Total	954	25	979

Expected Frequencies			
	Column variable		
Row variable	No	Yes	Total
No	914.047	23.95301	938
Yes	39.95301	1.046987	41
Total	954	25	979

Data	
Level of Significance	0.05
Number of Rows	2
Number of Columns	2
Degrees of Freedom	1

Results	
Critical Value	3.841459
Chi-Square Test Statistic	0.002259
p-Value	0.962096
Do not reject the null hypothesis	

Expected frequency assumption
  is violated.

The p-value $= 0.9621 > 0.05$, do not reject H_0. There is not enough evidence that the proportions are different across whether credit is in default at the 5% level of significance. However, the expected frequency assumption needed for the chi-square test is violated.

Copyright ©2015 Pearson Education, Inc.

18.12 Pivital table in terms of counts (Housing Loan by Term Deposit):
cont.

Count of Term Deposit	Column Labels ▼		
Row Labels ▼	no	yes	Grand Total
no	101	4	105
yes	837	37	874
Grand Total	938	41	979

Pivital table in terms of row totals (Housing Loan by Term Deposit):

Count of Term Deposit	Column Labels ▼		
Row Labels ▼	no	yes	Grand Total
no	96.19%	3.81%	100.00%
yes	95.77%	4.23%	100.00%
Grand Total	95.81%	4.19%	100.00%

PHStat output for the Chi-square test for the difference in proportions:

Chi-Square Test			

Observed Frequencies			
	Column variable		
Row variable	No	Yes	Total
No	101	837	938
Yes	4	37	41
Total	105	874	979

Expected Frequencies			
	Column variable		
Row variable	No	Yes	Total
No	100.6027	837.3973	938
Yes	4.397344	36.60266	41
Total	105	874	979

Data	
Level of Significance	0.05
Number of Rows	2
Number of Columns	2
Degrees of Freedom	1

Results	
Critical Value	3.841459
Chi-Square Test Statistic	0.041975
p-Value	0.837667
Do not reject the null hypothesis	

Expected frequency assumption	
is violated.	

The p-value $= 0.8377 > 0.05$, do not reject H_0. There is not enough evidence that the proportions are different across whether there is a housing loan at the 5% level of significance. However, the expected frequency assumption needed for the chi-square test is violated.

Copyright ©2015 Pearson Education, Inc.

18.12 Pivital table in terms of counts (Personal Loan by Term Deposit):
cont.

Count of Term Deposit	Column Labels ▼		
Row Labels ▼	no	yes	Grand Total
no	101	4	105
yes	837	37	874
Grand Total	938	41	979

Pivital table in terms of row totals (Personal Loan by Term Deposit):

Count of Term Deposit	Column Labels ▼		
Row Labels ▼	no	yes	Grand Total
no	95.40%	4.60%	100.00%
yes	98.04%	1.96%	100.00%
Grand Total	95.81%	4.19%	100.00%

PHStat output for the Chi-square test for the difference in proportions:

Chi-Square Test

Observed Frequencies			
	Column variable		
Row variable	No	Yes	Total
No	788	150	938
Yes	38	3	41
Total	826	153	979

Expected Frequencies			
	Column variable		
Row variable	No	Yes	Total
No	791.4076	146.5924	938
Yes	34.59244	6.407559	41
Total	826	153	979

Data	
Level of Significance	0.05
Number of Rows	2
Number of Columns	2
Degrees of Freedom	1

Results	
Critical Value	3.841459
Chi-Square Test Statistic	2.241695
p-Value	0.134334
Do not reject the null hypothesis	
Expected frequency assumption	
is met.	

The p-value $= 0.1343 > 0.05$, do not reject H_0. There is not enough evidence that the proportions are different across whether there is a personal loan at the 5% level of significance.

Copyright ©2015 Pearson Education, Inc.

18.14   Below are some of the summary characteristics of the variables in the data set that the students can use to write a report describing their conclusions depending on the various aspects of the variables they have chosen to analyze.

	Age	Age of Dwelling	Years at Dwelling	Bedrooms	Vehicles	Fuel Cost
Mean	45.02975255	33.79965442	9.2139474	2.120300752	1.082706767	89.85827145
Standard Error	0.705769554	1.152810723	0.342782478	0.069056259	0.039892829	0.559921397
Median	43.75442855	32.48917338	8.948247655	2	1	90.46724522
Mode	49	#N/A	1	3	1	95
Standard Deviation	11.51075308	18.80177391	5.590613026	1.126273495	0.650632352	9.132041622
Sample Variance	132.4974365	353.506702	31.254954	1.268491985	0.423322457	83.39418418
Kurtosis	0.031307707	-1.255923243	-1.219017271	-0.675904939	-0.635503488	0.555925635
Skewness	0.339425495	0.019065124	0.195702678	0.064456196	-0.082617089	-0.143141799
Range	56	63.76007056	18.83411217	5	2	63.13892164
Minimum	21	1.164978062	1	0	0	52.86107836
Maximum	77	64.92504862	19.83411217	5	2	116
Sum	11977.91418	8990.708076	2450.910008	564	288	23902.30021
Count	266	266	266	266	266	266
First Quartile	37.41105795	17.7164396	4.067588443	1	1	83.56048067
Third Quartile	52	50.94207517	13.84755467	3	2	96.34071552
Interquartile Range	14.58894205	33.22563556	9.779966227	2	1	12.78023485
CV	25.56%	55.63%	60.68%	53.12%	60.09%	10.16%

	Commuting Time (minutes)	Hours Worked	Annual Earned Income	Total Annual Income
Mean	36.13163852	37.40878791	46.15825738	49.4676592
Standard Error	1.187797971	0.723252762	1.027240886	1.085540136
Median	40.75386115	39.80193024	49.27415319	52.98579124
Mode	0	0	0	0
Standard Deviation	19.37239865	11.79589557	16.75379184	17.70462382
Sample Variance	375.2898295	139.1431523	280.6895409	313.4537046
Kurtosis	-0.454039967	4.019858826	1.406214288	1.478263003
Skewness	-0.681350273	-1.845682346	-1.132319043	-1.165455659
Range	75.4025378	63.85282643	77.25577829	82.97470766
Minimum	0	0	0	-1.1
Maximum	75.4025378	63.85282643	77.25577829	81.87470766
Sum	9611.015845	9950.737585	12278.09646	13158.39735
Count	266	266	266	266
First Quartile	28.34918331	33.74792776	37.26373866	40.75810124
Third Quartile	49.37348862	44.27061018	58.17911369	62.16256804
Interquartile Range	21.02430531	10.52268242	20.91537503	21.4044668
CV	53.62%	31.53%	36.30%	35.79%

Copyright ©2015 Pearson Education, Inc.

18.14
cont.

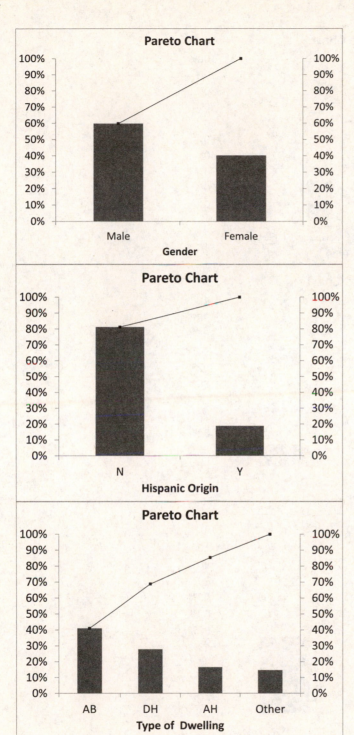

Copyright ©2015 Pearson Education, Inc.

18.14
cont.

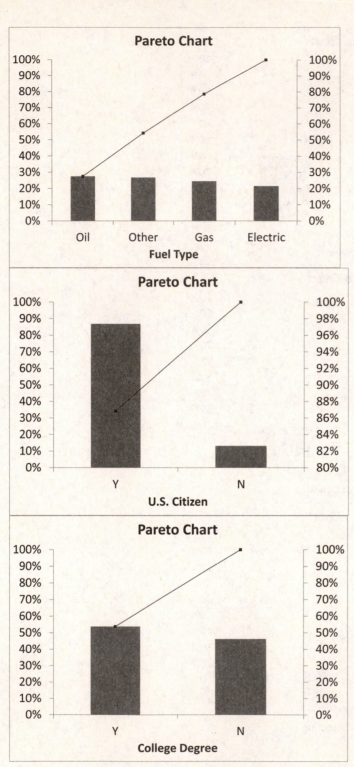

Copyright ©2015 Pearson Education, Inc.

18.14
cont.

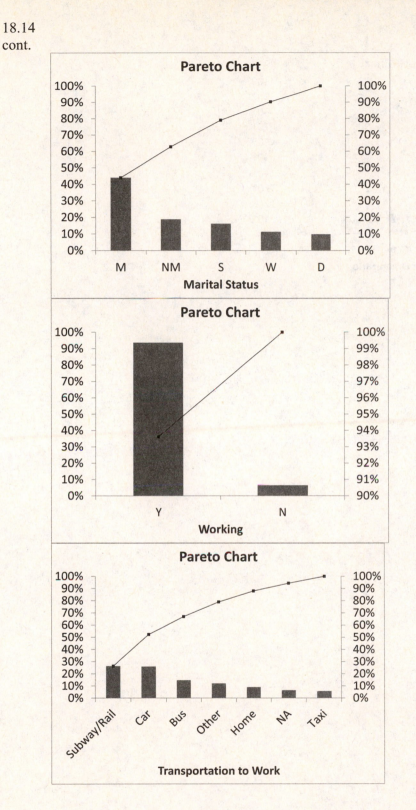

Copyright ©2015 Pearson Education, Inc.

18.14
cont.

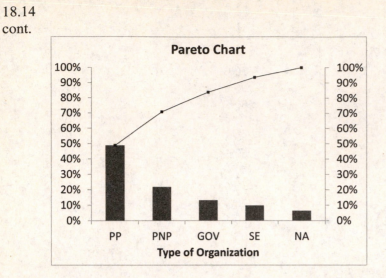

Copyright ©2015 Pearson Education, Inc.

CHAPTER 19 (ONLINE)

OBJECTIVES
- To learn to construct a variety of control charts
- To know which control chart to use for a particular type of data
- To be familiar with the basic themes of total quality management and Deming's 14 points
- To know the basic aspects of Six Sigma

OVERVIEW AND KEY CONCEPTS
Themes of Quality Management
1. The primary focus is on process improvement.
2. Most of the variation in a process is due to the system and not the individual.
3. Teamwork is an integral part of a quality management organization.
4. Customer satisfaction is a primary organizational goal.
5. Organizational transformation must occur in order to implement quality management.
6. Fear must be removed from organizations.
7. Higher quality costs less not more but it requires an investment in training.

Deming's 14 Points for Management
1. Create constancy of purpose for improvement of product and service.

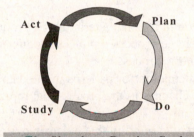

The Shewhart-Deming Cycle Focuses on Constant Improvement

2. Adopt the new philosophy.
3. Cease dependence on inspection to achieve quality.
4. End the practice of awarding business on the basis of price tag alone. Instead, minimize total cost by working with a single supplier.
5. Improve constantly and forever every process for planning, production and service.
6. Institute training on the job.
7. Adopt and institute leadership.
8. Drive out fear.
9. Break down barriers between staff areas.
10. Eliminate slogans, exhortations, and targets for the workforce.
11. Eliminate numerical quotas for the workforce and numerical goals for management.
12. Remove barriers that rob people of pride of workmanship. Eliminate the annual rating or merit system.
13. Institute a vigorous program of education and self-improvement for everyone.
14. Put everyone in the company to work to accomplish the transformation.

Copyright ©2015 Pearson Education, Inc.

Six Sigma Management

- A method for breaking processes into a series of steps in order to eliminate defects and produce near perfect results.
- Has a clear focus on obtaining bottom-line results in a relatively short three to six-month period of time.
- **The Six Sigma DMAIC model:**
    - **Define:** The problem to be solved needs to be defined along with the costs, benefits of the project, and the impact on the customer.
    - **Measure:** Operational definitions for each Critical-To-Quality (CTQ) characteristic must be developed. In addition, the measurement procedure must be verified so that it is consistent over repeated measurements.
    - **Analyze:** The root causes of why defects can occur need to be determined along with the variables in the process that cause these defects to occur. Data are collected to determine the underlying value for each process variable often using control charts.
    - **Improve:** The importance of each process variable on the CTQ characteristic is studied using designed experiments. The objective is to determine the best level for each variable that can be maintained in the long term.
    - **Control:** The objective is to maintain the gains that have been made with a revised process in the long term by avoiding potential problems that can occur when a process is changed.
- Its implementation requires a data-oriented approach using statistical tools such as control charts and designed experiments.
- Involves training everyone in the company in the DMAIC model.

Control Charts

- The **control chart** is a means of monitoring variation in the characteristic of a product or services by focusing on the time dimension in which the process produces products or services and studying the nature of the variability in the process.
- **Special (assignable) causes of variation:** Large fluctuations or patterns in the data that are not inherent to a process. They are often caused by changes in the process that represents either problems to be fixed or opportunities to exploit.
- **Chance (common) causes of variation:** The inherent variability that exists in a process. These consist of the numerous small causes of variability that operate randomly or by chance.
- An **out-of-control process** contains both common causes of variation and assignable causes of variation. Because assignable causes of variation are not part of the process design, an out-of-control process is unpredictable.
- An **in-control process** contains only common causes of variation. Because theses causes of variation are inherent to the process, an in-control process is predictable. An in-control-process is sometimes said to be in a **state of statistical control**.
- **Control limits:**
    - Statistical measure of interest $\pm$ 3 standard deviations

Copyright ©2015 Pearson Education, Inc.

- **Identifying pattern in control charts:**

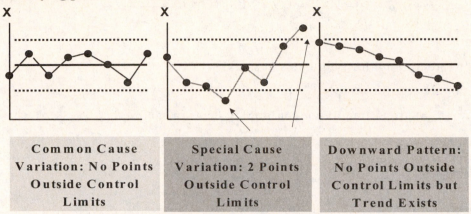

Common Cause Variation: No Points Outside Control Limits	Special Cause Variation: 2 Points Outside Control Limits	Downward Pattern: No Points Outside Control Limits but Trend Exists

  - A trend exists if there are 8 consecutive points above (or below) the centerline or 8 consecutive points that are increasing (or decreasing).

- **The first type of control error:** The belief that observed value represents special cause when in fact it is due to common cause.

- **The second type of control error:** Treating special cause variation as if it is common cause variation.

- When a process is out-of-control, the assignable causes of variation must be identified. If the assignable causes of variation are detrimental to the quality of the product or service, a plan to eliminate this source of variation must be implemented. If an assignable cause of variation increases quality, the process should be change so that it is incorporated into the process design and becomes a common cause source of variation and the process is improved.

- When a process is in control, it must be determined whether the amount of common cause variation in the process is small enough to satisfy the customers of the products or services. If it is small enough to consistently satisfy the customers, the control charts can be used to monitor the process on a continuous basis to make sure that it does not go out-of-control. If it is too large, the process should be altered.

Control Chart for the Proportion of Nonconforming Item (the *p* Chart)

- It is an attribute chart, which is used when sampled items are classified according to whether they conform or do not conform to operationally defined requirement.

- When used with unequal sample sizes over time, the unequal sample sizes should not differ by more than 25% from average sample size.

Copyright ©2015 Pearson Education, Inc.

- $LCL_p = \max\left(0, \bar{p} - 3\sqrt{\dfrac{\bar{p}(1-\bar{p})}{\bar{n}}}\right)$, $UCL_p = \bar{p} + 3\sqrt{\dfrac{\bar{p}(1-\bar{p})}{\bar{n}}}$

  where

  X_i = number of nonforming items in sample i

  n_i = sample size for sample i

  $p_i = X_i / n_i$ = proportion of nonconforming items in sample i

  $$\bar{n} = \frac{\displaystyle\sum_{i=1}^{k} n_i}{k}$$

  $$\bar{p} = \frac{\displaystyle\sum_{i=1}^{k} X_i}{\displaystyle\sum_{i=1}^{k} n_i}$$

  k = number of samples

Morals of the Red Bead Example
- Variation is an inherent part of any process.
- The system is primarily responsible for worker performance.
- Only management can change the system.
- Some workers will always be above average and some will be below.

The c Chart
- It is an attribute chart and a control chart for the number of nonconformities (or occurrences) in a unit (called an area of opportunity).
- $LCL_c = \bar{c} - 3\sqrt{\bar{c}}$, $UCL_c = \bar{c} + 3\sqrt{\bar{c}}$

  where

  $$\bar{c} = \frac{\displaystyle\sum_{i=1}^{k} c_i}{k}$$

  $\bar{c}$ = average number of occurrences

  k = number of units sampled

  c_i = number of occurrences in unit i

Control Chart for the Range (R) and Mean $(\bar{X})$
- They are variable control charts.
- They are more sensitive in detecting special-cause variation than the p chart.
- They are typically used in pairs
- The R chart monitors the variation in the process while the $\bar{X}$ chart monitors the process average.
- The R chart should be examined first because if it indicates the process is out-of-control, the interpretation of the $\bar{X}$ chart will be misleading.

Copyright ©2015 Pearson Education, Inc.

- **Control chart for the range (*R* chart):**
  - $LCL_R = D_3 \bar{R}$, $UCL_R = D_4 \bar{R}$
    where

    $$\bar{R} = \frac{\sum\limits_{i=1}^{k} R_i}{k}$$

    D_3 and D_4 are to obtained from a table.
- **Control chart for the mean ($\bar{X}$ chart):**
  - $LCL_{\bar{X}} = \bar{\bar{X}} - A_2\bar{R}$, $UCL_{\bar{X}} = \bar{\bar{X}} + A_2\bar{R}$
    where

    $$\bar{\bar{X}} = \frac{\sum\limits_{i=1}^{k} \bar{X}_i}{k}$$

    $$\bar{R} = \frac{\sum\limits_{i=1}^{k} R_i}{k}$$

    $\bar{X} =$ the sample mean of n observations at time i

    $R_i =$ the range of n observations at time i

    $k =$ number of subgroups

    and A_2 is obtained from a table.

Process Capability
- **Process capability** is the ability of a process to consistently meet specified customer-driven requirement.
- **Specification limits** are technical requirements set by management in response to customer's expectations.
- The **upper specification limit** (*USL*) is the largest value a characteristic of interest can have and still conform to customer's expectation.
- The **lower specification limit** (*LSL*) is the smallest value that is still conforming.

Estimating Process Capability:
- Must have an in-control process first before being able to estimate process capability.
- Estimate process capability by estimating the percentage of product or service within specification.
- **For a characteristic with an *LSL* and a *USL*:**

  P(an outcome will be within specification)

  $= P(LSL < X < USL)$

  $$= P\left(\frac{LSL - \bar{\bar{X}}}{\bar{R}/d_2} < Z < \frac{USL - \bar{\bar{X}}}{\bar{R}/d_2} \right)$$

  where Z is the standardized normal random variable.

Copyright ©2015 Pearson Education, Inc.

- **For a characteristic with only an *LSL*:**

  P(an outcome will be within specification)

  $$= P(LSL < X)$$

  $$= P\left(\frac{LSL - \overline{\overline{X}}}{\overline{R}/d_2} < Z \right)$$

- **For a characteristic with only a *USL*:**

  P(an outcome will be within specification)

  $$= P(X < USL)$$

  $$= P\left(Z < \frac{USL - \overline{\overline{X}}}{\overline{R}/d_2} \right)$$

- A **Capability Index** is an aggregate measure of a process' ability to meet specification limits. The larger the value of a capability index, the more capable a process is of meeting customer requirement.

- **To measure a process' potential:**

  - **The C_p index:** $C_p = \dfrac{USL - LSL}{6\left(\overline{R}/d_2\right)} = \dfrac{\text{specification spread}}{\text{process spread}}$

  - C_p is a measure of process potential, not of actual performance, because it does not consider the current process average.

  - $C_p > 1$ indicates that if the process average can be centered, then more than 99.73% of the observations will be inside the specification limits.

  - $C_p < 1$ indicates that the process is not very capable of meeting requirement for even if the process average can be centered, less than 99.73% of the observations will be inside the specification limits.

- **To measure a process' actual performance:**

  - For one-sided specification limits:

    $$CPL = \frac{\overline{\overline{X}} - LSL}{3\left(\overline{R}/d_2\right)}$$

    $$CPU = \frac{USL - \overline{\overline{X}}}{3\left(\overline{R}/d_2\right)}$$

    CPL (*CPU*) >1 implies that the process mean is more than 3 standard deviation away from the lower (upper) specification limit.

  - For two-sided specification limits:

    $$C_{pk} = \min\left(CPL, CPU\right)$$

    $C_{pk} = 1$ indicates that the process average is 3 standard deviations away from the closest specification limit.

    Larger C_{pk} indicates larger capability of meeting the requirements.

Copyright ©2015 Pearson Education, Inc.

SOLUTIONS TO END OF SECTION
AND CHAPTER REVIEW EVEN PROBLEMS

19.2   (a)   Proportion of nonconformances largest on Day 4, smallest on Day 3.

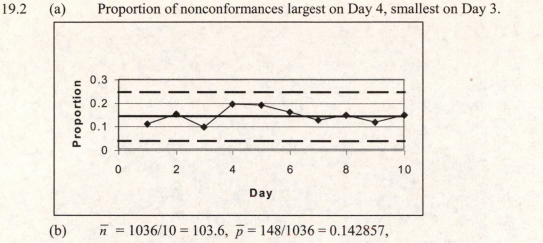

(b) $\bar{n} = 1036/10 = 103.6$, $\bar{p} = 148/1036 = 0.142857$,

$$LCL = \bar{p} - 3\sqrt{\frac{\bar{p}(1-\bar{p})}{\bar{n}}} = 0.142857 - 3\sqrt{\frac{0.142857(1-0.142857)}{103.6}} = 0.039719$$

$$UCL = \bar{p} + 3\sqrt{\frac{\bar{p}(1-\bar{p})}{\bar{n}}} = 0.142857 + 3\sqrt{\frac{0.142857(1-0.142857)}{103.6}} = 0.245995$$

(c)   Proportions are within control limits, so there do not appear to be any special causes of variation.

19.4   (a) $n = 500$, $\bar{p} = 761/16000 = 0.0476$

$$LCL = \bar{p} - 3\sqrt{\frac{\bar{p}(1-\bar{p})}{n}} = 0.0476 - 3\sqrt{\frac{0.0476(1-0.0476)}{500}} = 0.0190 > 0$$

$$UCL = \bar{p} + 3\sqrt{\frac{\bar{p}(1-\bar{p})}{n}} = 0.0476 + 3\sqrt{\frac{0.0476(1-0.0476)}{500}} = 0.0761$$

Copyright ©2015 Pearson Education, Inc.

19.4
cont.

(a)

p Chart

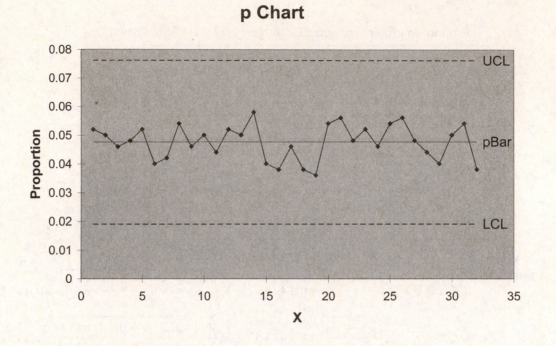

(b)   Since the individual points are distributed around $\overline{p}$ without any pattern and all the points are within the control limits, the process is in a state of statistical control.

19.6   (a) $\overline{n}$ = 113345/22 = 5152.0455, $\overline{p}$ = 1460/113345 = 0.01288,

$$LCL = \overline{p} - 3\sqrt{\frac{\overline{p}(1-\overline{p})}{\overline{n}}} = 0.01288 - 3\sqrt{\frac{0.01288\ (1-0.01288\ )}{5152\ .0455}} = 0.00817$$

$$UCL = \overline{p} + 3\sqrt{\frac{\overline{p}(1-\overline{p})}{\overline{n}}} = 0.01288 + 3\sqrt{\frac{0.01288(1-0.01288)}{5152.0455}} = 0.01759$$

Copyright ©2015 Pearson Education, Inc.

19.6
cont.   **PHStat output:**

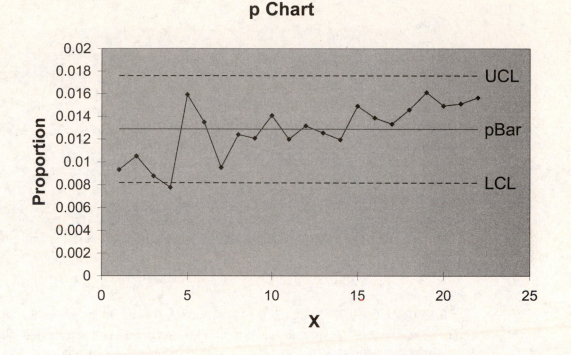

The proportion of unacceptable cans is below the LCL on Day 4. There is evidence
of a pattern over time, since the last eight points are all above the mean and most of
the earlier points are below the mean. Thus, the special causes that might be
contributing to this pattern should be investigated before any change in the system of
operation is contemplated.

(b)   Once special causes have been eliminated and the process is stable, Deming's
fourteen points should be implemented to improve the system. They might also look
at day 4 to see if they could identify and exploit the special cause that led to such a
low proportion of defects on that day.

Copyright ©2015 Pearson Education, Inc.

19.8   (a)

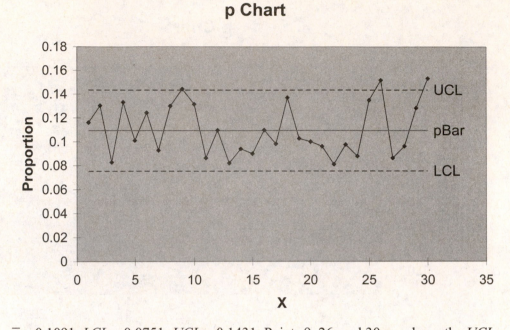

p Chart

$\bar{p} = 0.1091$, $LCL = 0.0751$, $UCL = 0.1431$. Points 9, 26, and 30 are above the UCL.

(b)   First, the reasons for the special cause variation would need to be determined and local corrective action taken. Once special causes have been eliminated and the process is stable, Deming's fourteen points should be implemented to improve the system.

19.12   (a) $\bar{c} = 115/10 = 11.5$, $LCL = \bar{c} - 3\sqrt{\bar{c}} = 11.5 - 3\sqrt{11.5} = 1.32651$

$UCL = \bar{c} + 3\sqrt{\bar{c}} = 11.5 + 3\sqrt{11.5} = 21.67349$

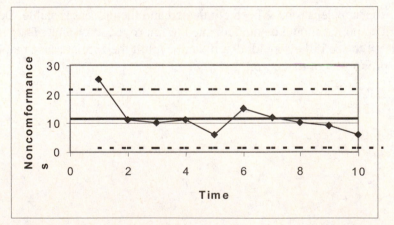

(b)   Yes, the number of nonconformances per unit for Time Period 1 is above the upper control limit.

Copyright ©2015 Pearson Education, Inc.

19.14   (a)   The twelve errors committed by Gina appear to be much higher than all others, and Gina would need to explain her performance.

        (b)

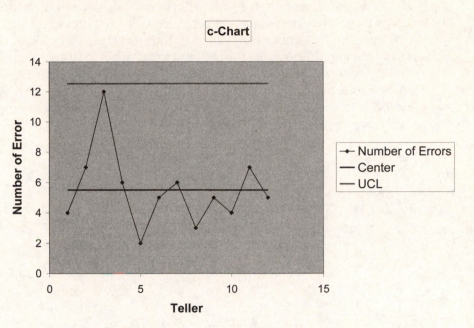

$\bar{c} = 5.5$, $UCL = 12.56$, LCL does not exist. The number of errors is in a state of statistical control since none of the tellers are outside the UCL.

        (c)   Since Gina is within the control limits, she is operating within the system, and should not be singled out for further scrutiny.

        (d)   The process needs to be studied and potentially changed using principles of Six Sigma® management and/or Deming's 14 points for management.

19.16   (a) $\bar{c} = 3.057$

        (b)

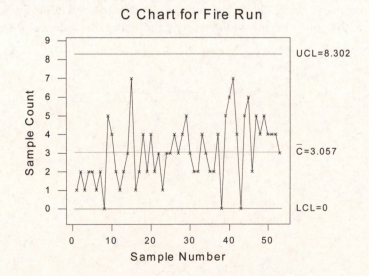

Copyright ©2015 Pearson Education, Inc.

19.16   (c)   There is evidence of a pattern over time, since the first eight points are all below the
cont.   mean. Thus, the special causes that might be contributing to this pattern should be
                         investigated before any change in the system of operation is contemplated.

        (d)   Even though weeks 15 and 41 experienced seven fire runs each, they are both below
                 the upper control limit. They can, therefore, be explained by chance causes.

        (e)   After having identified the special causes that might have contributed to the first
                 eight points that are below the average, the fire department can use the c-chart to
                 monitor the process in future weeks in real-time and identify any potential special
                 causes of variation that might have arisen and could be attributed to increased arson,
                 severe drought, or holiday-related activities.

19.18   (a) $d_2 = 2.059$ (d) $D_4 = 2.282$
        (b) $d_3 = 0.88$ (e) $A_2 = 0.729$
        (c) $D_3 = 0$

19.20   (a) $\bar{R} = 0.247$, R chart: $UCL = 0.636$; LCL does not exist

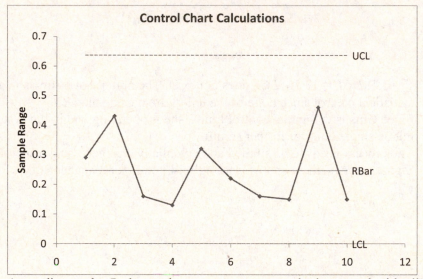

        (b)   According to the R-charts, the process appears to be in control with all points lying
                 inside the control limits without any pattern and no evidence of special cause
                 variation.

Copyright ©2015 Pearson Education, Inc.

19.20 (c) $\bar{\bar{X}} = 47.998$, $\bar{X}$ chart: $UCL = 48.2507$; $LCL = 47.7453$
cont.

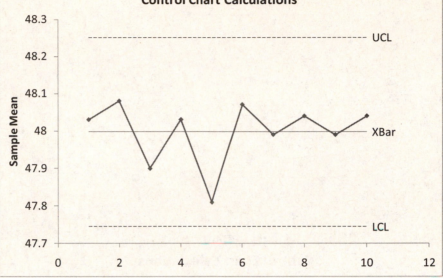

(d)   According to the $\bar{X}$-chart, the process appears to be in control with all points lying inside the control limits without any pattern and no evidence of special cause variation.

19.22 (a)

$$\bar{R} = \frac{\sum\limits_{i=1}^{k} R_i}{k} = 3.275, \quad \bar{\bar{X}} = \frac{\sum\limits_{i=1}^{k} \bar{X}_i}{k} = 5.9413.$$

R chart:

$$UCL = D_4 \bar{R} = 2.282(3.275) = 7.4736$$

LCL does not exist.

$\bar{X}$ chart:

$$UCL = \bar{\bar{X}} + A_2 \bar{R} = 5.9413 + 0.729(3.275) = 8.3287$$

$$LCL = \bar{\bar{X}} - A_2 \bar{R} = 5.9413 - 0.729(3.275) = 3.5538$$

Copyright ©2015 Pearson Education, Inc.

19.22
cont.

PHStat R Chart output:

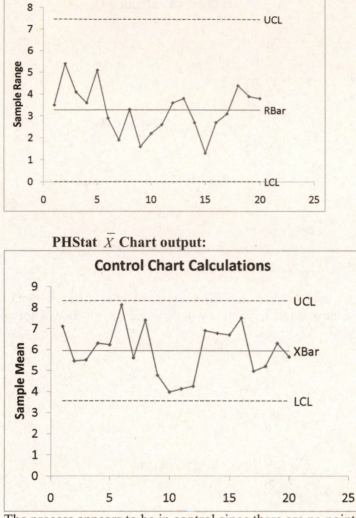

PHStat $\overline{X}$ Chart output:

(b)   The process appears to be in control since there are no points outside the control
limits and there is no evidence of a pattern in the range chart, and there are no points
outside the control limits and there is no evidence of a pattern in the $\overline{X}$ chart.

Copyright ©2015 Pearson Education, Inc.

19.24   (a) $\overline{R} = 0.8794$, R chart: $UCL = 2.0068$; LCL does not exist

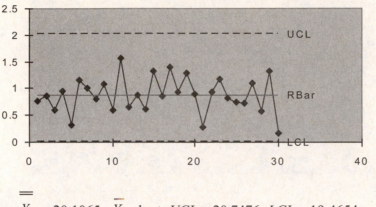

R Chart

$\overline{\overline{X}} = 20.1065$, $\overline{X}$ chart: $UCL = 20.7476$; $LCL = 19.4654$

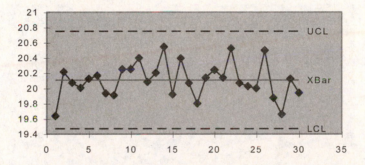

XBar Chart

(c)   The process appears to be in control since there are no points outside the lower and upper control limits of either the *R*-chart and *X*bar-chart, and there is no pattern in the results over time.

Copyright ©2015 Pearson Education, Inc.

19.26   (a)

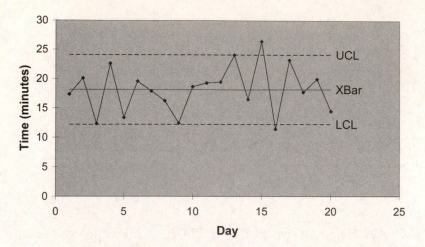

X Bar Chart

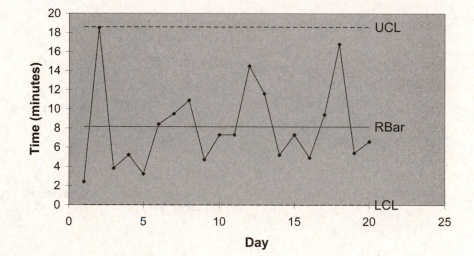

R Chart

$\overline{R} = 8.145$, $\overline{\overline{X}} = 18.12$.

R chart: $LCL = D_3 \, \overline{R} = 0 \,(8.145) = 0$. LCL does not exist.

$UCL = D_4 \, \overline{R} = (2.282)\,(8.145) = 18.58689$.

For $\overline{X}$ chart: $LCL = \overline{\overline{X}} - A_2 \, \overline{R} = 18.12 - (0.729)\,(8.145) = 12.1823$

$UCL = \overline{\overline{X}} + A_2 \, \overline{R} = 18.12 + (0.729)\,(8.145) = 24.0577$

(b)   There are no sample ranges outside the control limits and there does not appear to be a pattern in the range chart. The sample mean on Day 15 is above the *UCL* and the sample mean on Day 16 is below the *LCL*, which is an indication there is evidence of special cause variation in the sample means.

Copyright ©2015 Pearson Education, Inc.

19.28   (a) $\overline{\overline{R}}$ = 0.3022, *R* chart: *UCL* = 0.6389; *LCL* does not exist

$\overline{\overline{X}}$ = 90.1317, $\overline{X}$ chart: *UCL* = 90.3060; *LCL* = 89.9573

R Chart

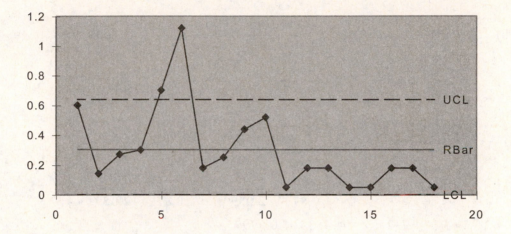

XBar Chart

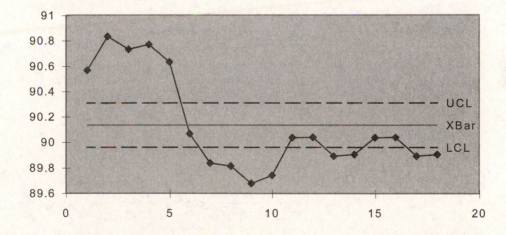

(b)   The *R*-chart is out-of-control because the 5th and 6th data points fall above the upper control limit. There is also a downward trend in the right tail of the *R*-chart, which signifies that special causes of variation must be identified and corrected. Even though the *X*-bar chart also appears to be out-of-control because a majority of the data point fall above or below the control limit, any interpretation will be misleading because the *R*-chart has indicated the presence of out-of-control conditions. There is also a downward trend in both control charts. Special causes of variation should be investigated and eliminated.

Copyright ©2015 Pearson Education, Inc.

19.30   (a)   Estimate of the population mean $= \overline{\overline{X}} = 100$

Estimate of population standard deviation $= \overline{R} / d_2 = \dfrac{3.386}{1.693} = 2$

$$P\left(98 < X < 102\right) = P\left(\dfrac{98-100}{2} < Z < \dfrac{102-100}{2}\right) = 0.6827$$

  (b) $P\left(93 < X < 107.5\right) = P\left(\dfrac{93-100}{2} < Z < \dfrac{107.5-100}{2}\right) = .9997$

  (c) $P\left(X > 93.8\right) = P\left(Z > \dfrac{93.8-100}{2}\right) = .9990$

  (d) $P\left(X < 110\right) = P\left(Z < \dfrac{110-100}{2}\right) \cong 1$

19.32   (a) $P\left(18 < X < 22\right) = P\left(\dfrac{18-20.1065}{0.8794/2.059} < Z < \dfrac{22-20.1065}{0.8794/2.059}\right)$

$$= P\left(-4.932 < Z < 4.4335\right) = 0.9999$$

  (b) $C_p = \dfrac{(USL - LSL)}{6\left(\overline{R}/d_2\right)} = \dfrac{(22-18)}{6\left(0.8794/2.059\right)} = 1.56$

$$CPL = \dfrac{\left(\overline{\overline{X}} - LSL\right)}{3\left(\overline{R}/d_2\right)} = \dfrac{(20.1065-18)}{3\left(0.8794/2.059\right)} = 1.644$$

$$CPU = \dfrac{\left(USL - \overline{\overline{X}}\right)}{3\left(\overline{R}/d_2\right)} = \dfrac{(22-20.1065)}{3\left(0.8794/2.059\right)} = 1.4778$$

$$C_{pk} = \min(CPL, CPU) = 1.4778$$

19.34   (a)

$$P\left(5.2 < X < 5.8\right) = P\left(\dfrac{5.2-5.509}{0.2248/2.059} < Z < \dfrac{5.8-5.509}{0.2248/2.059}\right)$$

$$= P\left(-2.830 < Z < 2.665\right) = 0.9938$$

  (b)   According to the estimate in (a), only 99.38% of the tea bags will have weight fall between 5.2 grams and 5.8 grams. The process is, therefore, incapable of meeting the 99.7% goal.

19.36   Chance or common causes of variation represent the inherent variability that exists in a system. These consist of the numerous small causes of variability that operate randomly or by chance. Special or assignable causes of variation represent large fluctuations or patterns in the data that are not inherent to a process. These fluctuations are often caused by changes in a system that represent either problems to be fixed or opportunities to exploit.

19.38   When only common causes of variation are present, it is up to management to change the system.

Copyright ©2015 Pearson Education, Inc.

19.40   Attribute control charts are used for categorical or discrete data such as the number of nonconformances. Variables control charts are used for numerical variables and are based on statistics such as the mean and standard deviation.

19.42   From the red bead experiment you learned that variation is an inherent part of any process, that workers work within a system over which they have little control, that it is the system that primarily determines their performance, and that only management can change the system.

19.44   If a process has a $C_p = 1.5$ and a $C_{pk} = 0.8$, it indicates that the process has the potential of meeting production specification limits but fails to meet the specification limits in actual performance. The process should be investigated and adjusted to increase either the *CPU* or *CPL* or both.

19.46   (a)   One the main reason that service quality is lower than product quality is because the former involves human interaction which is prone to variation. Also, the most critical aspects of a service are often timeliness and professionalism, and customers can always perceive that the service could be done quicker and with greater professionalism. For products, customers often cannot perceive a better or more ideal product than the one they are getting. For example, a new laptop is better and contains more interesting features than any laptop that he or she has ever imagined.

   (b)   Both services and products are the results of processes. However, measuring services is often harder because of the dynamic variation due to the human interaction between the service provider and the customer. Product quality is often a straightforward measurement of a static physical characteristic like the amount of sugar in a can of soda. Categorical data are also more common in service quality.

   (c)   Yes.

   (d)   Yes.

19.48   (a)

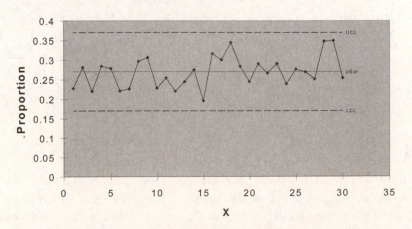

   (b)   Yes, RudyBird's market share is in control before the start of the in-store promotion since all sample proportions fall within the control limits.

Copyright ©2015 Pearson Education, Inc.

19.48   (c)
cont.

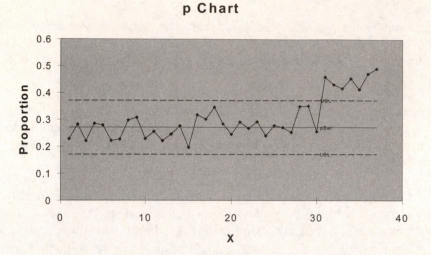

p Chart

After including the data for days 31-37, there is an apparent upward trend in the *p* chart during the promotion period and all the market share proportions in that period are above the upper control limit. The process became out-of-control. This assignable-cause variation can be attributed to the in-store promotion. The promotion was successful in increasing the market share of RudyBird.

19.50   (a)

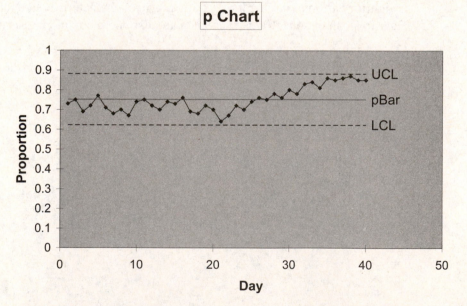

p Chart

$\bar{p} = 0.75175$, $LCL = 0.62215$, $UCL = 0.88135$. Although none of the points are outside either the *LCL* or *UCL*, there is a clear pattern over time with lower values occurring in the first half of the sequence and higher values occurring toward the end of the sequence.

(b)   This would explain the pattern in the results over time.

(c)   The control chart would have been developed using the first 20 days and then, using those limits, the additional proportions could have been plotted.

Copyright ©2015 Pearson Education, Inc.

19.52   (a) $\overline{p} = 0.1198$, $LCL = 0.0205$, $UCL = 0.2191$.

(b)   The process is out of statistical control. The proportion of trades that are undesirable is below the *LCL* on Day 24 and are above the *UCL* on Day 4.

(c)   Special causes of variation should be investigated and eliminated. Next, process knowledge should be improved to decrease the proportion of trades that are undesirable.

19.54   **Kidney- Shift 1**

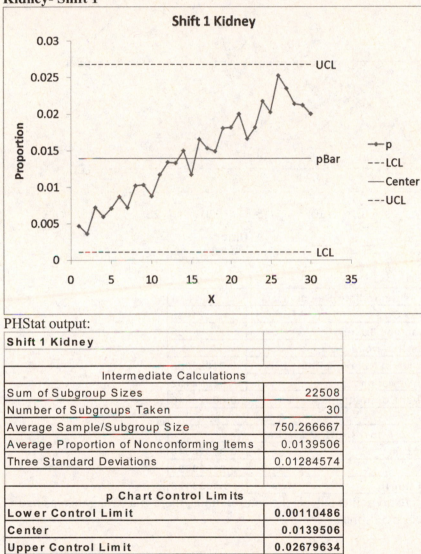

PHStat output:

Shift 1 Kidney	
Intermediate Calculations	
Sum of Subgroup Sizes	22508
Number of Subgroups Taken	30
Average Sample/Subgroup Size	750.266667
Average Proportion of Nonconforming Items	0.0139506
Three Standard Deviations	0.01284574
p Chart Control Limits	
Lower Control Limit	0.00110486
Center	0.0139506
Upper Control Limit	0.02679634

Although there are no points outside the control limits, there is a strong increasing trend in nonconformances over time.

Copyright ©2015 Pearson Education, Inc.

19.54   **Kidney- Shift 2**
cont.

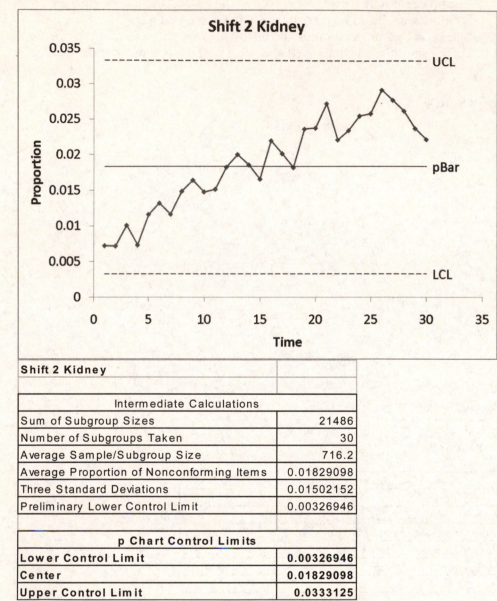

Shift 2 Kidney	

Intermediate Calculations	
Sum of Subgroup Sizes	21486
Number of Subgroups Taken	30
Average Sample/Subgroup Size	716.2
Average Proportion of Nonconforming Items	0.01829098
Three Standard Deviations	0.01502152
Preliminary Lower Control Limit	0.00326946

p Chart Control Limits	
Lower Control Limit	0.00326946
Center	0.01829098
Upper Control Limit	0.0333125

Although there are no points outside the control limits, there is a strong increasing trend in nonconformances over time.

Copyright ©2015 Pearson Education, Inc.

19.54   **Shift 1 Shrimp**
cont.

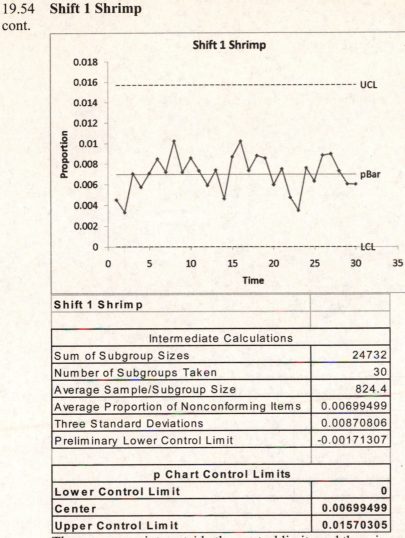

Shift 1 Shrimp	
Intermediate Calculations	
Sum of Subgroup Sizes	24732
Number of Subgroups Taken	30
Average Sample/Subgroup Size	824.4
Average Proportion of Nonconforming Items	0.00699499
Three Standard Deviations	0.00870806
Preliminary Lower Control Limit	-0.00171307
p Chart Control Limits	
Lower Control Limit	0
Center	0.00699499
Upper Control Limit	0.01570305

There are no points outside the control limits and there is no pattern over time.

Copyright ©2015 Pearson Education, Inc.

19.54
cont.   **Shift 2 Shrimp**

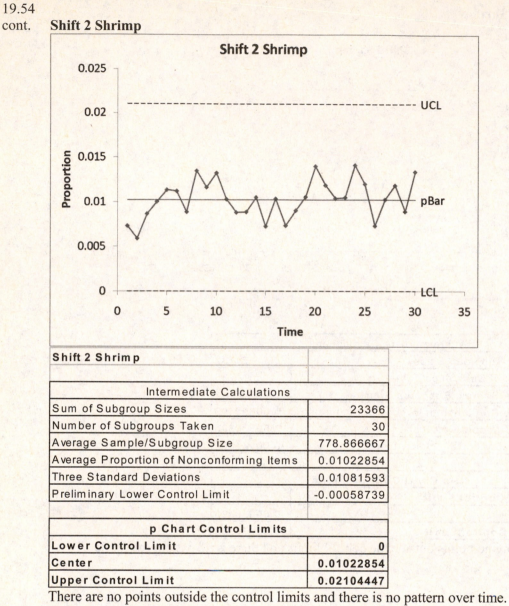

Shift 2 Shrimp	
Intermediate Calculations	
Sum of Subgroup Sizes	23366
Number of Subgroups Taken	30
Average Sample/Subgroup Size	778.866667
Average Proportion of Nonconforming Items	0.01022854
Three Standard Deviations	0.01081593
Preliminary Lower Control Limit	-0.00058739

p Chart Control Limits	
Lower Control Limit	0
Center	0.01022854
Upper Control Limit	0.02104447

There are no points outside the control limits and there is no pattern over time.

The team needs to determine the reasons for the increase in nonconformances for the kidney product. The production volume for kidney is clearly decreasing for both shifts. This can be observed from a plot of the production volume over time. The team needs to investigate the reasons for this.

Copyright ©2015 Pearson Education, Inc.

CHAPTER 20 (ONLINE)

OBJECTIVES
- To learn to use payoff tables and decision trees to evaluate alternative courses of action
- To learn to use several criteria to select an alternative course of action
- To learn to use Bayes' theorem to revise probabilities in light of sample information
- To learn about the concept of utility

OVERVIEW AND KEY CONCEPTS
Some Basic Features of Decision Making
- **Alternative courses of action:** The decision maker must have two or more possible choices to evaluate prior to selecting one course of action.
- **Events or states of the world:** The decision maker must list the events that can occur and consider each event's possibility of action.
- **Payoffs:** The decision maker must associate a monetary value or payoff with the result of each event.
- **Decision criteria:** The decision maker must determine how the best course of action is to be selected.

Payoff Table
- A payoff table contains each possible event that can occur for each alternative course of action.

Consider a food vendor determining whether to sell soft drinks or hot dogs.

Event (E_i)	Course of Action (A_j)	
	Sell Soft Drinks (A_1)	Sell Hot Dogs (A_2)
Cool Weather (E_1)	$x_{11} = \$50$	$x_{12} = \$100$
Warm Weather (E_2)	$x_{21} = \$200$	$x_{22} = \$125$

x_{ij} = payoff (profit) for event i and action j

Copyright ©2015 Pearson Education, Inc.

Decision Tree

- A decision tree pictorially represents the events and courses of action through a set of branches and nodes.

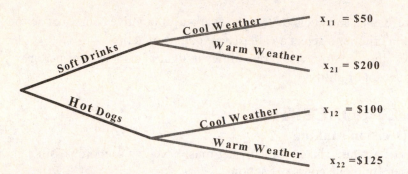

Food Vendor Profit Tree Diagram

Cool Weather $x_{11} = \$50$

Warm Weather $x_{21} = \$200$

Soft Drinks

Hot Dogs

Cool Weather $x_{12} = \$100$

Warm Weather $x_{22} = \$125$

Opportunity Loss

- The opportunity loss is the difference between the highest possible profit (payoff or monetary value) for an event and the actual profit obtained for an action taken.
- **The opportunity loss table:**

Event	Optimal Action	Profit of Optimal Action	Alternative Course of Action	
			Sell Soft Drinks	Sell Hot Dogs
Cool Weather	Hot Dogs	100	100 - 50 = 50	100 - 100 = 0
Warm Weather	Soft Drinks	200	200 - 200 = 0	200 - 125 = 75

Copyright ©2015 Pearson Education, Inc.

Some Decision Criteria
- **Maximax**
  - Is an optimistic payoff criterion.
  - Find the maximum payoff for each action.
  - Choose the action that has the highest of these maximum payoffs.
- **Maximin**
  - Is a pessimistic payoff criterion.
  - Find the minimum payoff for each action.
  - Choose the action that has the highest of these minimum payoffs.
- **Expected monetary value (*EMV*):**
  - The expected profit (payoff or monetary value) for taking an action.
  - $$EMV(j) = \sum_{i=1}^{N} x_{ij} P_i$$

    where

    $EMV(j) =$ expected monetary value of action j

    $x_{ij} =$ payoff that occurs when action j is taken and event i occurs

    $P_i =$ probability of occurence of event i
- **Expected opportunity loss (*EOL*):**
  - $$EOL(j) = \sum_{i=1}^{N} L_{ij} P_i$$

    where

    $EOL(j) =$ expected opportunity loss of action j

    $L_{ij} =$ opportunity loss that occurs when action j is taken and event i occurs

    $P_i =$ probability of occurence of event i
- **Expected profit under certainty (*EPUC*):** The expected profit one could make if one has perfect information about which event will occur.
- **Expected value of perfect information:**
  - The expected value of perfect information is the expected opportunity loss from the best decision, i.e. the minimum *EOL* among all the courses of action.
  - It also represents the maximum amount one would pay to obtain perfect information.
  - The difference between expected profit under certainty and the expected monetary value from he best action.
  - $EVPI = EPUC - \max_j EMV(j) = \min_j EOL(j)$
- **Return to risk ratio:**
  - Expressed the relationship between the return (expected payoff) and the risk (standard deviation).
  - $$RTRR(j) = \frac{EMV(j)}{\sigma_j}$$
- **Coefficient of variation:**
  - Coefficient of variation is the inverse of return to risk ratio.

Copyright ©2015 Pearson Education, Inc.

$$\blacksquare \quad CV(j) = \frac{\sigma_j}{EMV(j)} = \frac{1}{RTRR(j)}$$

Decision Making with Sample Information

- Decision maker chooses the best course of action A_j using some prior probabilities of events $P(E_i)$. When new information becomes available in the form of conditional probabilities of an action given a specific event, $P(A_j | E_i)$, one can update the probabilities of the events using the Bayes's theorem to obtain the posterior probabilities of events, $P(E_i | A_j)$, and re-evaluate all the decision criteria.

Utility

- Each incremental amount of profit or loss does not have the same value to every individual.
  - A **risk adverse** person, once reaching a goal, assigns less value to each incremental amount of profit.
  - A **risk seeker** assigns more value to each incremental amount of profit.
  - A **risk neutral** person assigns the same value to each incremental amount of profit.

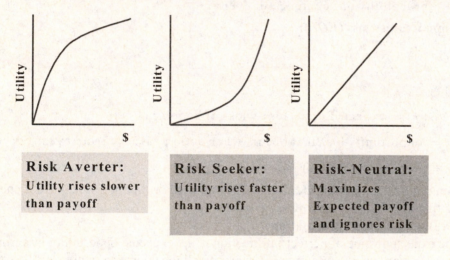

Risk Averter:
Utility rises slower
than payoff

Risk Seeker:
Utility rises faster
than payoff

Risk-Neutral:
Maximizes
Expected payoff
and ignores risk

Copyright ©2015 Pearson Education, Inc.

SOLUTIONS TO END OF SECTION
AND CHAPTER REVIEW EVEN PROBLEMS

20.2   (a)

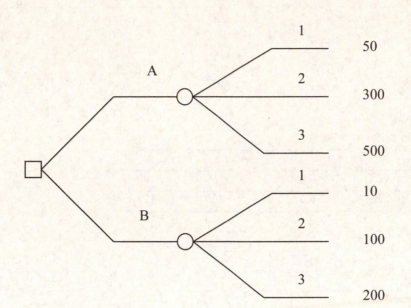

(b)   Opportunity loss table:

Event	Optimum Action	Profit of Optimum Action	Alternative Courses of Action	
			A	B
1	A	50	$50 - 50 = 0$	$50 - 10 = 40$
2	A	300	$300 - 300 = 0$	$300 - 100 = 200$
3	A	500	$500 - 500 = 0$	$500 - 200 = 300$

20.4   (a)-(b) Payoff table:

Event	Company A		Company B	
1	$\$10,000 + \$2 \cdot 1,000 =$	$\$12,000$	$\$2,000 + \$4 \cdot 1,000 =$	$\$6,000$
2	$\$10,000 + \$2 \cdot 2,000 =$	$\$14,000$	$\$2,000 + \$4 \cdot 2,000 =$	$\$10,000$
3	$\$10,000 + \$2 \cdot 5,000 =$	$\$20,000$	$\$2,000 + \$4 \cdot 5,000 =$	$\$22,000$
4	$\$10,000 + \$2 \cdot 10,000 =$	$\$30,000$	$\$2,000 + \$4 \cdot 10,000 =$	$\$42,000$
5	$\$10,000 + \$2 \cdot 50,000 =$	$\$110,000$	$\$2,000 + \$4 \cdot 50,000 =$	$\$202,000$

(c)

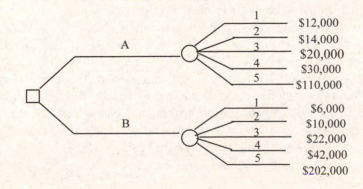

Copyright ©2015 Pearson Education, Inc.

20.4   (d)   Opportunity loss table:
cont.

Event	Optimum Action	Profit of Optimum Action	Alternative Courses of Action	
			A	*B*
1	*A*	12,000	0	6,000
2	*A*	14,000	0	4,000
3	*B*	22,000	2,000	0
4	*B*	42,000	12,000	0
5	*B*	202,000	92,000	0

20.6   Excel output:

Probabilities & Payoffs Table:				
	P	**A**	**B**	
E1	0.5	50	100	
E2	0.5	200	125	
Max		200	125	
Min		50	100	
Maximax		(a) 200		
maximin			(b) 100	
Statistics for:		**A**	**B**	
Expected Monetary Value		(c) 125	(c) 112.5	
Variance		5625	156.25	
Standard Deviation		75	12.5	
Coefficient of Variation		0.6	0.111111	
Return to Risk Ratio		1.666667	9	

Opportunity Loss Table:				
	Optimum Action	Optimum Profit	Alternatives	
			A	B
E1	B	100	50	0
E2	A	200	0	75
			A	**B**
Expected Opportunity Loss			(d) 25	(d) 37.5
			EVPI	

(a)   The optimal action based on the maximax criterion is *Action A*.

(b)   The optimal action based on the maximin criterion is *Action B*.

(c) $EMV_A = 50(0.5) + 200(0.5) = 125$ $EMV_B = 100(0.5) + 125(0.5) = 112.50$

(d) $EOL_A = 50(0.5) + 0(0.5) = 25$ $EOL_B = 0(0.5) + 75(0.5) = 37.50$

(e)   Perfect information would correctly forecast which event, 1 or 2, will occur. The value of perfect information is the increase in the expected value if you knew which of the events 1 or 2 would occur prior to making a decision between actions. It allows us to select the optimum action given a correct forecast.

EMV with perfect information $= 100 (0.5) + 200 (0.5) = 150$

$EVPI = EMV$ with perfect information $- EMV_A = 150 - 125 = 25$

Copyright ©2015 Pearson Education, Inc.

20.6   (f)   Based on (c) and (d) above, select action A because it has a higher expected
cont.   monetary value (a) and a lower opportunity loss (b) than action B.

    (g) $\sigma_A^2 = (50 - 125)^2 (0.5) + (200 - 125)^2 (0.5) = 5625$ $\sigma_A = 75$

$$CV_A = \frac{75}{125} \cdot 100\% = 60\%$$

$\sigma_B^2 = (100 - 112.5)^2 (0.5) + (125 - 112.5)^2 (0.5) = 156.25$ $\sigma_B = 12.5$

$$CV_B = \frac{12.5}{112.5} \cdot 100\% = 11.11\%$$

    (h)   Return-to-risk ratio for $A = \dfrac{125}{75} = 1.667$

Return-to-risk ratio for $B = \dfrac{112.5}{12.5} = 9.0$

    (i)   Based on (g) and (h), select action B because it has a lower coefficient of variation
and a higher return-to-risk ratio.

    (j)   The best decision depends on the decision criteria. In this case, expected monetary
value leads to a different decision than the return-to-risk ratio.

20.8   (a)   Rate of return $= \dfrac{\$100}{\$1,000} \cdot 100\% = 10\%$

    (b) $CV = \dfrac{\$25}{\$100} \cdot 100\% = 25\%$

    (c)   Return-to-risk ratio $= \dfrac{\$100}{\$25} = 4.0$

20.10   Select stock A because it has a higher expected monetary value while it has the same
standard deviation as stock B.

20.12   PHStat output:

Expected Monetary Value				
Probabilities & Payoffs Table:				
	P	**Sell Soft Drinks**	**Sell Ice Cream**	
Cool weather	0.4	50	30	
Warm weather	0.6	60	90	
max		60	90	
min		50	30	
Maximax			90	
Maximin		50		
Statistics for:		**Sell Soft Drinks**	**Sell Ice Cream**	
Expected Monetary Value		56	66	
Variance		24	864	
Standard Deviation		4.898979	29.39388	
Coefficient of Variation		0.087482	0.445362	
Return to Risk Ratio		11.43095	2.245366	
Opportunity Loss Table:				
	Optimum Action	Optimum Profit	Alternatives	
			Sell Soft Drinks	Sell Ice Cream
Cool weather	Sell Soft Drinks	50	0	20
Warm weather	Sell Ice Cream	90	30	0
			Sell Soft Drinks	**Sell Ice Cream**
Expected Opportunity Loss			18	8
				EVPI

Copyright ©2015 Pearson Education, Inc.

20.12 (a)   The optimal action based on the maximax criterion is to sell ice cream.

cont. (b)   The optimal action based on the maximin criterion is to sell soft drinks.

(c) EMV(Soft drinks) = 50(0.4) + 60(0.6) = 56

       EMV(Ice cream) = 30(0.4) + 90(0.6) = 66

(d) EOL(Soft drinks) = 0(0.4) + 30(0.6) = 18

       EOL(Ice cream) = 20(0.4) + 0(0.6) = 8

(e) $EVPI$ is the maximum amount of money the vendor is willing to pay for the information about which event will occur.

(f)   Based on (c) and (d), choose to sell ice cream because you will earn a higher expected monetary value and incur a lower opportunity loss than choosing to sell soft drinks.

(g) CV(Soft drinks) = $\dfrac{4.899}{56} \cdot 100\% = 8.748\%$

       CV(Ice cream) = $\dfrac{29.394}{66} \cdot 100\% = 44.536\%$

(h)   Return-to-risk ratio for soft drinks = $\dfrac{56}{4.899} = 11.431$

       Return-to-risk ratio for ice cream = $\dfrac{66}{29.394} = 2.245$

(i)   To maximize return and minimize risk, you will choose to sell soft drinks because it has the smaller coefficient of variation and the larger return-to-risk ratio.

(j)   Ignoring the variability of the payoff in (f), you will choose to sell ice cream. However, when risk, which is measured by standard deviation, is taken into consideration as in coefficient of variation or return-to-risk ratio, you will choose to sell soft drinks because it has the lower variability per unit of expected return or the higher expected return per unit of variability.

Copyright ©2015 Pearson Education, Inc.

20.14   PHStat output:

Probabilities & Payoffs Table:					
	P	**A**	**B**	**C**	
Economy declines	0.3	500	-2000	-7000	
No change	0.5	1000	2000	-1000	
Economy expands	0.2	2000	5000	20000	
Max		2000	5000	20000	
Min		500	-2000	-7000	
Maximax				20000	
Maximin		500			
Statistics for:		**A**	**B**	**C**	
Expected Monetary Value		1050	1400	1400	
Variance		272500	6240000	93240000	
Standard Deviation		522.0153	2497.999	9656.086	
Coefficient of Variation		0.497157	1.784285	6.897204	
Return to Risk Ratio		2.011435	0.560449	0.144986	

Opportunity Loss Table:					
	Optimum Action	Optimum Profit	Alternatives		
			A	B	C
Economy declines	A	500	0	2500	7500
No change	B	2000	1000	0	3000
Economy expands	C	20000	18000	15000	0
			A	B	C
Expected Opportunity Loss			4100	3750	3750
				EVPI	EVPI

(a)   The optimal action based on the maximax criterion is to choose investment C.

(b)   The optimal action based on the maximin criterion is to choose investment A.

(c) $EMV_A = 500(0.3) + 1,000(0.5) + 2,000(0.2) = 1,050$

  $EMV_B = -2,000(0.3) + 2,000(0.5) + 5,000(0.2) = 1,400$

  $EMV_C = -7,000(0.3) - 1,000(0.5) + 20,000(0.2) = 1,400$

(d)   See the table above.

  $EOL_A = 0(0.3) + 1,000(0.5) + 18,000(0.2) = 4,100$

  $EOL_B = 2,500(0.3) + 0(0.5) + 15,000(0.2) = 3,750$

  $EOL_C = 7,500(0.3) + 3,000(0.5) + 0(0.2) = 3,750$

(e) EMV with perfect information $= 500(0.3) + 2,000(0.5) + 20,000(0.2) = 5,150$

  $EVPI = EMV$ with perfect information $- EMV_{B \text{ or } C} = 5,150 - 1,400 = 3,750$

  The investor should not be willing to pay more than \$3,750 for a perfect forecast.

(f)   Action B and C maximize the expected monetary value and have the lower opportunity loss

Copyright ©2015 Pearson Education, Inc.

20.14   (g)
cont.

$$\sigma_A^2 = (500 - 1{,}050)^2 (0.3) + (1{,}000 - 1{,}050)^2 (0.5) + (2{,}000 - 1{,}050)^2 (0.2)$$
$$= 272{,}500$$
$$\sigma_A = 522.02$$
$$\sigma_B^2 = (-2{,}000 - 1{,}400)^2 (0.3) + (2{,}000 - 1{,}400)^2 (0.5) + (5{,}000 - 1{,}400)^2 (0.2)$$
$$= 6{,}240{,}000$$
$$\sigma_B = 2{,}498.00$$
$$\sigma_C^2 = (-7{,}000 - 1{,}400)^2(0.3) + (-1{,}000 - 1{,}400)^2(0.5) + (20{,}000 - 1{,}400)^2(0.2)$$
$$= 93{,}240{,}000$$
$$\sigma_C = 9656.09$$
$$CV_A = \frac{522.02}{1050} \cdot 100\% = 49.72\%$$
$$CV_B = \frac{2498.00}{1400} \cdot 100\% = 178.43\%$$
$$CV_C = \frac{9656.09}{1400} \cdot 100\% = 689.72\%$$

(h)   Return-to-risk ratio for $A = \dfrac{1050}{522.02} = 2.01$

Return-to-risk ratio for $B = \dfrac{1400}{2498} = 0.56$

Return-to-risk ratio for $C = \dfrac{1400}{9656.09} = 0.14$

(i)-(j)   Action A minimizes the coefficient of variation and maximizes the investor's return-to-risk.

(k)

	(1) 0.1, 0.6, 0.3	(2) 0.1, 0.3, 0.6	(3) 0.4, 0.4, 0.2	(4) 0.6, 0.3, 0.1
(c) Max *EMV*	C: 4,700	C: 11,000	A or B: 800	A: 800
σ Max *EMV*	σ_C: 10,169	σ_C: 11,145	σ_A: 548 σ_B: 2,683	σ_A: 458
(d) Min *EOL* & (e) *EVPI*	C: 2,550	C: 1,650	A: 4,000 or B: 4,000	A: 2,100
(g) Min *CV*	A: 40.99%	A: 36.64%	A: 54.77%	A: 57.28%
(h) Max Return- to-risk	A: 2.4398	A: 2.7294	A: 1.8257	A: 1.7457
(i) Choice on (g), (h)	Choose A	Choose A	Choose A	Choose A
(j) Compare (c) and (i)	Different: (c) C (j) A	Different: (c) C (j) A	Different: (c) A or B (j) A	Same: A

Copyright ©2015 Pearson Education, Inc.

20.16 PHStat output:

Probabilities & Payoffs Table:

	P	A	B	
Demand 1000	0.45	12000	6000	
Demand 2000	0.2	14000	10000	
Demand 5000	0.15	20000	22000	
Demand 10000	0.1	30000	42000	
Demand 50000	0.1	110000	202000	
Max		110000	202000	
Min		14000	10000	
Maximax			202000	
Maximin		14000		

Statistics for:	A	B	
Expected Monetary Value	25200	32400	
Variance	8.29E+08	3.32E+09	
Standard Deviation	28791.67	57583.33	
Coefficient of Variation	1.142526	1.777263	
Return to Risk Ratio	0.875253	0.562663	

Opportunity Loss Table:

	Optimum Action	Optimum Profit	Alternatives A	B
Demand 1000	A	12000	0	6000
Demand 2000	A	14000	0	4000
Demand 5000	B	22000	2000	0
Demand 10000	B	42000	12000	0
Demand 50000	B	202000	92000	0

			A	B
Expected Opportunity Loss			10700	3500
				EVPI

(a)   The optimal action based on the maximax criterion is to sign with company B.

(b)   The optimal action based on the maximin criterion is to sign with company A.

(c) $EMV_A = 12,000(0.45) + 14,000(0.2) + 20,000(0.15) + 30,000(0.1)$
$+ 110,000(0.1) = 25,200$

$EMV_B = 6,000(0.45) + 10,000(0.2) + 22,000(0.15) + 42,000(0.1)$
$+ 202,000(0.1) = 32,400$

(d) $EOL_A = 0(0.45) + 0(0.2) + 2,000(0.15) + 12,000(0.1) + 92,000(0.1)$
$= 10,700$

$EOL_B = 6,000(0.45) + 4,000(0.2) + 0(0.15) + 0(0.1) + 0(0.1)$
$= 3,500$

(e) EMV with perfect information $= 12,000(0.45) + 14,000(0.2) + 22,000(0.15)$
$+ 42,000(0.1) + 202,000(0.1) = 35,900$

$EVPI = EMV,$ perfect information $- EMV_B = 35,900 - 32,400 = 3,500$
The author should not be willing to pay more than $3,500 for a perfect forecast.

(f)   Sign with company B to maximize the expected monetary value ($32,400) and minimize the expected opportunity loss ($3,500).

(g) $CV_A = \dfrac{28,792}{25,200} \cdot 100\% = 114.25\%$ $CV_B = \dfrac{57,583}{32,400} \cdot 100\% = 177.73\%$

(h)   Return-to-risk ratio for $A = \dfrac{25,200}{28,792} = 0.8752$

Return-to-risk ratio for $B = \dfrac{32,400}{57,583} = 0.5627$

Copyright ©2015 Pearson Education, Inc.

20.16 (i) Signing with company *A* will minimize the author's risk and yield the higher return-
cont. to-risk. Company *B* has a higher *EMV* than *A*, but choosing company *B* also entails
more risk and has a lower return-to-risk ratio than *A*.

(k) (c)-(j) See the table below.

Probabilities & Payoffs Table:				
	P	**A**	**B**	
Demand 1000	0.3	12000	6000	
Demand 2000	0.2	14000	10000	
Demand 5000	0.2	20000	22000	
Demand 10000	0.1	30000	42000	
Demand 50000	0.2	110000	202000	
Max		110000	202000	
Min		14000	10000	
Maximax			202000	
Maximin		14000		
Statistics for:		**A**	**B**	
Expected Monetary Value		35400	52800	
Variance		1.42E+09	5.68E+09	
Standard Deviation		37672.8	75345.6	
Coefficient of Variation		1.064203	1.427	
Return to Risk Ratio		0.93967	0.700771	

Opportunity Loss Table:				
	Optimum	Optimum	Alternatives	
	Action	Profit	A	B
Demand 1000	A	12000	0	6000
Demand 2000	A	14000	0	4000
Demand 5000	B	22000	2000	0
Demand 10000	B	42000	12000	0
Demand 50000	B	202000	92000	0
			A	B
Expected Opportunity Loss			20000	2600
				EVPI

The author's decision is not affected by the changed probabilities.

20.18 (a) $P(E_1 \mid F) = \dfrac{P(F \mid E_1) \cdot P(E_1)}{P(F \mid E_1) \cdot P(E_1) + P(F \mid E_2) \cdot P(E_2)} = \dfrac{0.6(0.5)}{0.6(0.5) + 0.4(0.5)} = 0.6$

$P(E_2 \mid F) = 1 - P(E_1 \mid F) = 1 - 0.6 = 0.4$

(b) $EMV_A = (0.6)(50) + (0.4)(200) = 110$
$EMV_B = (0.6)(100) + (0.4)(125) = 110$

(c) $EOL_A = (0.6)(50) + (0.4)(0) = 30$
$EOL_B = (0.6)(0) + (0.4)(75) = 30$

(d) $EVPI = (0.6)(100) + (0.4)(200) = 30$
You should not be willing to pay more than $30 for a perfect forecast.

(e) Both have the same *EMV* and the same *EOL*.

(f) $\sigma_A^2 = (0.6)(-60)^2 + (0.4)(90)^2 = 5400$ $\sigma_A = 73.4847$
$\sigma_B^2 = (0.6)(-10)^2 + (0.4)(15)^2 = 150$ $\sigma_B = 12.2474$
$CV_A = \dfrac{73.4847}{110} \cdot 100\% = 66.8\%$ $CV_B = \dfrac{12.2474}{110} \cdot 100\% = 11.1\%$

(g) Return-to-risk ratio for $A = \dfrac{110}{73.4847} = 1.497$
Return-to-risk ratio for $B = \dfrac{110}{12.2474} = 8.981$

Copyright ©2015 Pearson Education, Inc.

20.18 (h)   Action *B* has a better return-to-risk ratio.
cont. (i)   Both have the same *EMV*, but action *B* has a better return-to-risk ratio.

20.20 (a) P(forecast cool | cool weather) = 0.80
              P(forecast warm | warm weather) = 0.70

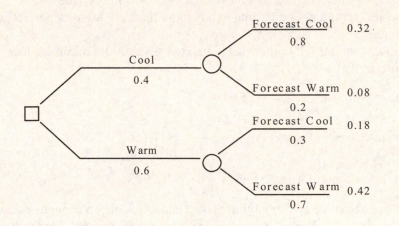

	Forecast Cool	Forecast Warm	Totals
Cool	0.32	0.08	0.4
Warm	0.18	0.42	0.6
Totals	0.5	0.5	

Revised probabilities: P(cool | forecast cool) $= \dfrac{0.32}{0.5} = 0.64$

P(warm | forecast cool) $= \dfrac{0.18}{0.5} = 0.36$

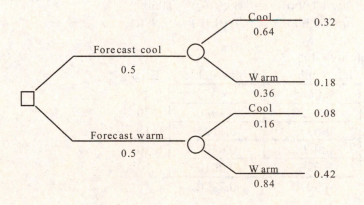

Copyright ©2015 Pearson Education, Inc.

20.20   (b)
cont.

EMV(Soft drinks) = 50(0.64) + 60(0.36) = 53.6

EMV(Ice cream) = 30(0.64) + 90(0.36) = 51.6

EOL(Soft drinks) = 0(0.64) + 30(0.36) = 10.8

EOL(Ice cream) = 20(0.64) + 0(0.36) = 12.8

EMV with perfect information = 50(0.64) + 90(0.36) = 64.4

$EVPI = EMV,$ perfect information $- EMV_A = 64.4 - 53.6 = 10.8$

The vendor should not be willing to pay more than \$10.80 for a perfect forecast of the weather.

The vendor should sell soft drinks to maximize value and minimize loss.

CV(Soft drinks) = $\frac{4.8}{53.6} \cdot 100\% = 8.96\%$

CV(Ice cream) = $\frac{28.8}{51.6} \cdot 100\% = 55.81\%$

Return-to-risk ratio for soft drinks = $\dfrac{53.6}{4.8} = 11.1667$

Return-to-risk ratio for ice cream = $\dfrac{51.6}{28.8} = 1.7917$

Based on these revised probabilities, the vendor's decision changes because of the increased likelihood of cool weather given a forecast for cool. Under these conditions, she should sell soft drinks to maximize the expected monetary value and also to minimize her expected opportunity loss, as well as minimizing risk and maximizing return.

20.22   (a)

P(favorable | 1,000) = 0.01 P(favorable | 2,000) = 0.01

P(favorable | 5,000) = 0.25 P(favorable | 10,000) = 0.60

P(favorable | 50,000) = 0.99

P(favorable *and* 1,000)   = 0.01(0.45) = 0.0045

P(favorable *and* 2,000)   = 0.01(0.20) = 0.0020

P(favorable *and* 5,000)   = 0.25(0.15) = 0.0375

P(favorable *and* 10,000)   = 0.60(0.10) = 0.0600

P(favorable *and* 50,000)   = 0.99(0.10) = 0.0990

Joint probability table:

	Favorable	Unfavorable	Totals
1,000	0.0045	0.4455	0.45
2,000	0.0020	0.1980	0.20
5,000	0.0375	0.1125	0.15
10,000	0.0600	0.0400	0.10
50,000	0.0990	0.0010	0.10
Totals	0.2030	0.7970	

Given an unfavorable review, the revised conditional probabilities are:

P(1,000 | unfavorable)   = 0.4455/0.7970 = 0.5590

P(2,000 | unfavorable)   = 0.1980/0.7970 = 0.2484

P(5,000 | unfavorable)   = 0.1125/0.7970 = 0.1412

P(10,000 | unfavorable)   = 0.0400/0.7970 = 0.0502

P(50,000 | unfavorable)   = 0.0010/0.7970 = 0.0013

Copyright ©2015 Pearson Education, Inc.

20.22   (b)   Payoff table, given unfavorable review:
cont.

	Pr	A	B
1,000	0.5590	12,000	6,000
2,000	0.2484	14,000	10,000
5,000	0.1412	20,000	22,000
10,000	0.0502	30,000	42,000
50,000	0.0013	110,000	202,000
EMV		14,658.60	11,315.4
σ^2		31,719,333.50	126877326.67
σ		5,631.99	11263.98
CV		38.42%	99.55%
Return-to-risk		2.6027	1.0046

Opportunity loss table:

	Pr	A	B
Event 1	0.5590	0	6,000
Event 2	0.2484	0	4,000
Event 3	0.1412	2,000	0
Event 4	0.0502	12,000	0
Event 5	0.0013	92,000	0
EOL		1,004.40	4,347.60

(c)   The author's decision is affected by the changed probabilities. Under the new
           circumstances, signing with company A maximizes the expected monetary value
           ($14,658.60), minimizes the expected opportunity loss ($1,004.40), minimizes risk
           with a smaller coefficient of variation and yields a higher return-to-risk than
           choosing company B.

20.26   A payoff table presents the alternatives in a tabular format, while the decision tree organizes
        the alternatives and events visually.

20.28   Since it is the difference between the *highest* possible profit for an event and the actual profit
        obtained for an action taken. It can never be negative.

20.30   The expected value of perfect information represents the maximum amount you would pay to
        obtain perfect information. It represents the alternative course of action with the smallest
        expected opportunity loss. It is also equal to the expected profit under certainty minus the
        expected monetary value of the best alternative course of action.

20.32   Expected monetary value measures the mean return or profit of an alternative course of
        action over the long run without regard for the variability in the payoffs under different
        events. The return-to-risk ratio considers the variability in the payoffs in evaluating which
        alternative course of action should be chosen.

20.34   A risk averter attempts to reduce risk, while a risk seeker looks for increased return usually
        associated with greater risk.

Copyright ©2015 Pearson Education, Inc.

20.36   (a), (c), (g), (h)   Payoff table:

Event		Pr	A: Buy 6,000	B: Buy 8,000	C: Buy 10,000	D: Buy 12,000
1	Sell 6,000	0.1	2,100	1,400	700	0
2	Sell 8,000	0.5	2,100	2,800	2,100	1,400
3	Sell 10,000	0.3	2,100	2,800	3,500	2,800
4	Sell 12,000	0.1	2,100	2,800	3,500	4,200
		EMV	2,100	2,660	2,520	1,960
		σ	0	420	896	1,120
		CV	0	15.79%	35.57%	57.14%
		Return-to-risk	undefined	6.3333	2.8111	1.7500

(d)   Opportunity loss table:

Event		Pr	A: Buy 6,000	B: Buy 8,000	C: Buy 10,000	D: Buy 12,000
1	Sell 6,000	0.1	0	700	1,400	2,100
2	Sell 8,000	0.5	700	0	700	1,400
3	Sell 10,000	0.3	1,400	700	0	700
4	Sell 12,000	0.1	2,100	1,400	700	0
		EOL	980	420	560	1,120

(b)

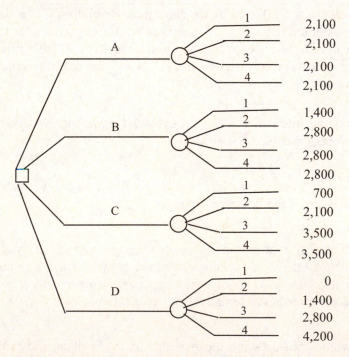

(e)   *EVPI* = $420. The management of Shop-Quick Supermarkets should not be willing to pay more than $420 for a perfect forecast.

(f)   To maximize the expected monetary value and minimize expected opportunity loss, the management should buy 8,000 loaves.

(i)   Action *B* (buying 8,000 loaves) maximizes the return-to-risk and, while buying 6,000 loaves reduces the coefficient of variation to zero, action *B* has a smaller coefficient of variation than *C* or *D*.

Copyright ©2015 Pearson Education, Inc.

2.36 (j) There are no differences.
cont. (k) (a), (c), (g), (h)
Payoff table:

	Pr	A: Buy 6,000	B: Buy 8,000	C: Buy 10,000	D: Buy 12,000
Sell 6,000	0.3	2,100	1,400	700	0
Sell 8,000	0.4	2,100	2,800	2,100	1,400
Sell 10,000	0.2	2,100	2,800	3,500	2,800
Sell 12,000	0.1	2,100	2,800	3,500	4,200
	EMV	2,100	2,380	2,100	1,540
	σ	0	642	1,084	1,321
	CV	0	26.96%	51.64%	85.76%
	Return-to-risk	undefined	3.7097	1.9365	1.1660

(k) (d)
Opportunity loss table:

	Pr	A: Buy 6,000	B: Buy 8,000	C: Buy 10,000	D: Buy 12,000
Sell 6,000	0.3	0	700	1,400	2,100
Sell 8,000	0.4	700	0	700	1,400
Sell 10,000	0.2	1,400	700	0	700
Sell 12,000	0.1	2,100	1,400	700	0
	EOL	700	490	770	1,330

(e) *EVPI* = $490. The management of Shop-Quick Supermarkets should not be willing to pay more than $490 for a perfect forecast.

(f) To maximize the expected monetary value and minimize expected opportunity loss, the management should buy 8,000 loaves.

(i) Action *B* (buying 8,000 loaves) maximizes the return-to-risk and, while buying 6,000 loaves reduces the coefficient of variation to zero, action *B* has a smaller coefficient of variation than *C* or *D*.

(j) There are no differences.
The management's decision is not affected by the changed probabilities.

20.38 (a)

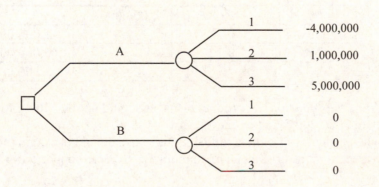

Copyright ©2015 Pearson Education, Inc.

20.38   (c), (f) Payoff table:
cont.

Event		Pr	New	Old
1	Weak	0.3	− 4,000,000	0
2	Moderate	0.6	1,000,000	0
3	Strong	0.1	5,000,000	0
	EMV		− 100,000	0
	σ		2,808,914	0
	CV		− 2,808.94%	undefined
	Return-to-risk		− 0.0356	undefined

(b), (d), (e)   Opportunity loss table:

	Pr	New	Old
Weak	0.3	4,000,000	0
Moderate	0.6	0	1,000,000
Strong	0.1	0	5,000,000
EOL		1,200,000	1,100,000

$EVPI = \$1,100,000$. The product manager should not be willing to pay more than $1,100,000 for a perfect forecast.

(g)   The product manager should continue to use the old packaging to maximize expected monetary value and to minimize expected opportunity loss and risk.

(h)   (c), (f)   Payoff table:

	Pr	New	Old
Weak	0.6	− 4,000,000	0
Moderate	0.3	1,000,000	0
Strong	0.1	5,000,000	0
EMV		− 1,600,000	0
σ		3,136,877	0
CV		− 196.05%	undefined
Return-to-risk		− 0.5101	undefined

(b), (d), (e) Opportunity loss table:

	Pr	New	Old
Weak	0.6	4,000,000	0
Moderate	0.3	0	1,000,000
Strong	0.1	0	5,000,000
EOL		2,400,000	800,000

$EVPI = \$800,000$. The product manager should not be willing to pay more than $800,000 for a perfect forecast.

(g)   The product manager should continue to use the old packaging to maximize expected monetary value and to minimize expected opportunity loss and risk.

Copyright ©2015 Pearson Education, Inc.

20.38   (i)
cont.

(c), (f) Payoff table:

	Pr	New	Old
Weak	0.1	− 4,000,000	0
Moderate	0.3	1,000,000	0
Strong	0.6	5,000,000	0
EMV		2,900,000	0
σ		2,913,760.457	0
CV		100.47%	undefined
Return-to-risk		0.9953	undefined

(b), (d), (e) Opportunity loss table:

	Pr	New	Old
Weak	0.1	4,000,000	0
Moderate	0.3	0	1,000,000
Strong	0.6	0	5,000,000
EOL		400,000	3,300,000

EVPI = $400,000. The product manager should not be willing to pay more than $400,000 for a perfect forecast.

(g)   The product manager should use the new packaging to maximize expected monetary value and to minimize expected opportunity loss.

(j) P(Sales decreased | weak response) = 0.6
P(Sales stayed same | weak response) = 0.3
P(Sales increased | weak response) = 0.1
P(Sales decreased | moderate response) = 0.2
P(Sales stayed same | moderate response) = 0.4
P(Sales increased | moderate response) = 0.4
P(Sales decreased | strong response) = 0.05
P(Sales stayed same | strong response) = 0.35
P(Sales increased | strong response) = 0.6
P(Sales decreased *and* weak response) = 0.6(0.3) = 0.18
P(Sales stayed same *and* weak response) = 0.3(0.3) = 0.09
P(Sales increased *and* weak response) = 0.1(0.3) = 0.03
P(Sales decreased *and* moderate response) = 0.2(0.6) = 0.12
P(Sales stayed same *and* moderate response) = 0.4(0.6) = 0.24
P(Sales increased *and* moderate response) = 0.4(0.6) = 0.24
P(Sales decreased *and* strong response) = 0.05(0.1) = 0.005
P(Sales stayed same *and* strong response) = 0.35(0.1) = 0.035
P(Sales increased *and* strong response) = 0.6(0.1) = 0.06

Joint probability table:

	Pr	Sales Decrease	Sales Stay Same	Sales Increase
Weak	0.3	0.180	0.090	0.030
Moderate	0.6	0.120	0.240	0.240
Strong	0.1	0.005	0.035	0.060
Total		0.305	0.365	0.330

Copyright ©2015 Pearson Education, Inc.

20.38   (j)   Given the sales stayed the same, the revised conditional probabilities are:
cont.
P(weak response | sales stayed same) = $\frac{.09}{.365}$ = 0.2466

P(moderate response | sales stayed same) = $\frac{.24}{.365}$ = 0.6575

P(strong response | sales stayed same) = $\frac{.035}{.365}$ = 0.0959

(k)   (c), (f)   Payoff table:

	Pr	New	Old
Weak	0.2466	− 4,000,000	0
Moderate	0.6575	1,000,000	0
Strong	0.0959	5,000,000	0
EMV		150,600	0
σ		2,641,575.219	0
CV		1,754.03%	undefined
Return-to-risk		0.0570	undefined

(b), (d), (e)   Opportunity loss table:

	Pr	New	Old
Weak	0.2466	4,000,000	0
Moderate	0.6575	0	1,000,000
Strong	0.0959	0	5,000,000
EOL		986,400	1,137,000

$EVPI$ = $986,400. The product manager should not be willing to pay more than $986,400 for a perfect forecast.

(g)   The product manager should use the new packaging to maximize expected monetary value and to minimize expected opportunity loss.

(l)   Given the sales decreased, the revised conditional probabilities are:
P(weak response | sales decreased) = $\frac{.18}{.305}$ = 0.5902

P(moderate response | sales decreased) = $\frac{.12}{.305}$ = 0.3934

P(strong response | sales decreased) = $\frac{.005}{.305}$ = 0.0164

(m)   (c), (f)   Payoff table:

	Pr	New	Old
Weak	0.5902	− 4,000,000	0
Moderate	0.3934	1,000,000	0
Strong	0.0164	5,000,000	0
EMV		− 1,885,400	0
σ		2,586,864.287	0
CV		− 137.21%	undefined
Return-to-risk		− 0.7288	undefined

20.38   (m)   (b), (d), (e)   Opportunity loss table:
cont.

	Pr	New	Old
Weak	0.5902	4,000,000	0
Moderate	0.3934	0	1,000,000
Strong	0.0164	0	5,000,000
	EOL	2,360,800	475,400

EVPI = $475,400. The product manager should not be willing to pay more than $475,400 for a perfect forecast.

(g)   The product manager should continue to use the old packaging to maximize expected monetary value and minimize expected opportunity loss.

20.40   (a)

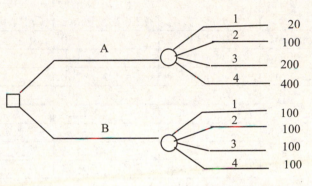

(c), (e), (f) Payoff table:*

Event		Pr	A: Do Not Call Mechanic	B: Call Mechanic
1	Very low	0.25	20	100
2	Low	0.25	100	100
3	Moderate	0.25	200	100
4	High	0.25	400	100
	EMV		180	100
	σ		142	0
	CV		78.96%	0
	Return-to-risk		1.2665	undefined

*Note: The payoff here is cost and not profit. The opportunity cost is therefore calculated as the difference between the payoff and the minimum in the same row.

(b), (d) Opportunity loss table:

	Pr	A: Do Not Call Mechanic	B: Call Mechanic
Very low	0.25	80	0
Low	0.25	0	0
Moderate	0.25	0	100
High	0.25	0	300
	EOL	20	100

(e)   EVPI = $20. The manufacturer should not be willing to pay more than $20 for the information about which event will occur.

Copyright ©2015 Pearson Education, Inc.

20.40 (g)   We want to minimize the expected monetary value because it is a cost. To minimize
cont.   the expected monetary value, call the mechanic.

(h)   Given 2 defectives out of 15, the binomial probabilities and their related revised
conditional probabilities are:

	Pr	Binomial Probabilities	Revised Conditional Probabilities
Very low	0.01	0.0092	0.0092/0.6418 = 0.0143
Low	0.05	0.1348	0.1348/0.6418 = 0.2100
Moderate	0.10	0.2669	0.2669/0.6418 = 0.4159
High	0.20	0.2309	0.2309/0.6418 = 0.3598
		0.6418	

(i)   (c), (e), (f) Payoff table:

	Pr	*A:* Do Not Call Mechanic	*B:* Call Mechanic
Very low	0.0143	20	100
Low	0.2100	100	100
Moderate	0.4159	200	100
High	0.3598	400	100
EMV		248.3860	100
σ		121	0
CV		48.68%	0
Return-to-risk		2.0544	undefined

(i)   (b), (d) Opportunity loss table:

	Pr	*A:* Do Not Call Mechanic	*B:* Call Mechanic
Very low	0.0143	80	0
Low	0.2100	0	0
Moderate	0.4159	0	100
High	0.3598	0	300
EOL		1.1440	149.53

(e)   *EVPI* = \$1.14. The manufacturer should not be willing to pay more than
\$1.14 for the information about which event will occur.

(g)   We want to minimize the expected monetary value because it is a cost. To
minimize the expected monetary value, call the mechanic.

Copyright ©2015 Pearson Education, Inc.

SOLUTIONS TO END OF SECTION
AND CHAPTER REVIEW EVEN PROBLEMS

Chapter 5

5.66   You can use the Poisson distribution to approximate the binomial distribution when n is large and π is very small. The approximation gets better as n gets larger and p gets smaller.

5.68

Poisson Probabilities					
Data					
Mean/Expected number of events of interest:			1		
Poisson Probabilities Table					
	X	P(X)	P(<=X)	P(<X)	P(>X)	P(>=X)
	0	0.3679	0.3679	0.0000	0.6321	1.0000
	1	0.3679	0.7358	0.3679	0.2642	0.6321
	2	0.1839	0.9197	0.7358	0.0803	0.2642

(a) $P(X = 0) = 0.3679$
(b) $P(X = 1) = 0.3679$
(c) $P(X = 2) = 0.1839$
(d) $P(X \leq 2) = 0.9197$
(e) $P(X > 2) = 0.0803$

5.70

Binomial Probabilities					
Data					
Sample size	20				
Probability of an event of interest	0.01				
Statistics					
Mean	0.2				
Variance	0.198				
Standard deviation	0.4450				
Binomial Probabilities Table					
	X	P(X)	P(<=X)	P(<X)	P(>X)	P(>=X)
	0.0000	0.8179	0.8179	0.0000	0.1821	1.0000
	1.0000	0.1652	0.9831	0.8179	0.0169	0.1821
	2.0000	0.0159	0.9990	0.9831	0.0010	0.0169

Copyright ©2015 Pearson Education, Inc.

5.70
cont.
$P(X \geq 1) = 0.1821$

Poisson Probabilities						
Data						
Mean/Expected number of events of interest:			0.2			
Poisson Probabilities Table						
	X	P(X)	P(<=X)	P(<X)	P(>X)	P(>=X)
	0	0.8187	0.8187	0.0000	0.1813	1.0000
	1	0.1637	0.9825	0.8187	0.0175	0.1813
	2	0.0164	0.9989	0.9825	0.0011	0.0175

$P(X \geq 1) = 0.1813$
The probability of 0.1813 obtained using a Poisson approximation is quite close to the exact binomial probability of 0.1821.

5.72   Since $n = 10,000$ is large and $\pi = 0.002$ is quite small, you can use the Poisson distribution to approximate the binomial distribution.

Poisson Probabilities						
Data						
Mean/Expected number of events of interest:			20			
Poisson Probabilities Table						
	X	P(X)	P(<=X)	P(<X)	P(>X)	P(>=X)
	0	0.0000	0.0000	0.0000	1.0000	1.0000
	5	0.0001	0.0001	0.0000	0.9999	1.0000
	10	0.0058	0.0108	0.0050	0.9892	0.9950
	20	0.0888	0.5591	0.4703	0.4409	0.5297

(a) $P(X = 0)$ is virtually 0
(b) $P(X \leq 5) = 0.0001$
(c) $P(X \leq 10) = 0.0108$
(d) $P(X \leq 20) = 0.5591$

Copyright ©2015 Pearson Education, Inc.

Chapter 6

6.56 $n = 100, p = 0.40.$ $n\pi = 40 \geq 5$ and $n(1 - \pi) = 60 \geq 5$

$\mu = n\pi = 40$ $\sigma = \sqrt{n\pi(1 - \pi)} = 4.8990$

(a)

Probability for a Range	
From X Value	39.5
To X Value	40.5
Z Value for 39.5	-0.102062
Z Value for 40.5	0.102062
P(X<=39.5)	0.4594
P(X<=40.5)	0.5406
P(39.5<=X<=40.5)	0.0813

$P(X = 40) \cong P(39.5 \leq X \leq 40.5) = P(-0.1021 \leq Z \leq 0.1021) = 0.0813$

(b)

Probability for X >	
X Value	40.5
Z Value	0.1020616
P(X>40.5)	0.4594

$P(X > 40) = P(X \geq 41) \cong P(X \geq 40.5) = P(Z \geq 0.1021) = 0.4594$

(c)

Probability for X <=	
X Value	40.5
Z Value	0.1020616
P(X<=40.5)	0.5406461

$P(X \leq 40) \cong P(X \leq 40.5) = P(Z \leq 0.1021) = 0.5406$

(d)

Probability for X <=	
X Value	39.5
Z Value	-0.102062
P(X<=39.5)	0.4593539

$P(X < 40) = P(X \leq 39) \cong P(X \leq 39.5) = P(Z \leq -0.1021) = 0.4594$

6.58 $\pi = \dfrac{1}{3} = 0.3333$, $n = 150$, $n\pi = 50 > 5$, $n(1 - \pi) = 100 > 5$

(a) $P(X \geq 60) = P\left(\dfrac{X - n\pi}{\sqrt{n\pi(1 - \pi)}} = \dfrac{59.5 - 150(0.3333)}{\sqrt{150(0.3333)(1 - 0.3333)}} \right)$

$= P(Z > 1.6454) = 0.0499$

(b) $P(X = 60) = P(59.5 \leq X_a \leq 60.5) = P(1.6454 \leq Z \leq 1.8187) = 0.0155$

(c) $P(X < 60) = P(X_a \leq 59.5) = P(Z \leq 1.6454) = 0.9501$

(d) $P(X = 71) = P(70.5 \leq X_a \leq 71.5) = P(3.5507 \leq Z \leq 3.7239) = 0.0001$

Copyright ©2015 Pearson Education, Inc.

Chapter 7

7.36 $\qquad \sqrt{\dfrac{N-n}{N-1}} = \sqrt{\dfrac{400-100}{400-1}} = 0.8671 \qquad\qquad \sqrt{\dfrac{N-n}{N-1}} = \sqrt{\dfrac{900-200}{900-1}} = 0.8824$

A sample of size 100 selected without replacement from a population a population of size 400 has a greater effect in reducing the standard error.

7.38 $\qquad \mu = 1.30, \ \sigma = 0.04$

Since $n/N = 16/200 > 0.05$ and the sample is selected without replacement, we need to perform the finite population correction.

$$\mu_{\bar{X}} = \mu = 1.3 \qquad\qquad \sigma_{\bar{X}} = \frac{\sigma}{\sqrt{n}}\sqrt{\frac{N-n}{N-1}} = 0.0096$$

PHstat output:

Common Data	
Mean	1.3
Standard Deviation	0.0096
Probability for a Range	
From X Value	1.31
To X Value	1.33
Z Value for 1.31	1.041667
Z Value for 1.33	3.125
P(X<=1.31)	0.8512
P(X<=1.33)	0.9991
P(1.31<=X<=1.33)	0.1479

$P(1.31 < \bar{X} < 1.33) = P(1.0417 < Z < 3.125) = 0.1479$

7.40 $\qquad \pi = .10$

Since $n/N = 400/5000 > 0.05$ and the sample is selected without replacement, we need to perform the finite population correction.

$$\mu_p = .1 \qquad\qquad \sigma_p = \sqrt{\frac{\pi(1-\pi)}{n}}\sqrt{\frac{N-n}{N-1}} = 0.0144$$

PHstat output:

Common Data			Probability for a Range	
Mean	0.1		**From X Value**	0.09
Standard Deviation	0.0144		**To X Value**	0.1
			Z Value for 0.09	-0.694444
Probability for X <=			**Z Value for 0.1**	0
X Value	0.08		**P(X<=0.09)**	0.2437
Z Value	-1.388889		**P(X<=0.1)**	0.5000
P(X<=0.08)	0.0824333		**P(0.09<=X<=0.1)**	0.2563

(a) $\qquad P(0.09 < p < 0.10) = P(-0.6944 < Z < 0) = 0.2563$

(b) $\qquad P(p < .08) = P(Z < -1.3889) = 0.0824$

Copyright ©2015 Pearson Education, Inc.

Chapter 8

8.70 $N \cdot \bar{X} \pm N \cdot t \cdot \dfrac{S}{\sqrt{n}} \sqrt{\dfrac{N-n}{N-1}} = 500 \cdot 25.7 \pm 500 \cdot 2.7969 \cdot \dfrac{7.8}{\sqrt{25}} \cdot \sqrt{\dfrac{500-25}{500-1}}$

$\$10{,}721.53 \le \text{Population Total} \le \$14{,}978.47$

8.72 (a) $p + Z \cdot \sqrt{\dfrac{p(1-p)}{n}} \sqrt{\dfrac{(N-n)}{(N-1)}} = 0.04 + 1.2816 \cdot \sqrt{\dfrac{0.04(1-0.04)}{300}} \sqrt{\dfrac{(5000-300)}{(5000-1)}}$

$\pi < 0.05406$

(b) $p + Z \cdot \sqrt{\dfrac{p(1-p)}{n}} \sqrt{\dfrac{(N-n)}{(N-1)}} = 0.04 + 1.645 \cdot \sqrt{\dfrac{0.04(1-0.04)}{300}} \sqrt{\dfrac{(5000-300)}{(5000-1)}}$

$\pi < 0.05804$

(c) $p + Z \cdot \sqrt{\dfrac{p(1-p)}{n}} \sqrt{\dfrac{(N-n)}{(N-1)}} = 0.04 + 2.3263 \cdot \sqrt{\dfrac{0.04(1-0.04)}{300}} \sqrt{\dfrac{(5000-300)}{(5000-1)}}$

$\pi < 0.06552$

8.74 $N \cdot \bar{X} \pm N \cdot t \cdot \dfrac{S}{\sqrt{n}} \sqrt{\dfrac{N-n}{N-1}} = 3000 \cdot \$261.40 \pm 3000 \cdot 1.8331 \cdot \dfrac{\$138.8046}{\sqrt{10}} \cdot \sqrt{\dfrac{3000-10}{3000-1}}$

$\$543{,}176.96 \le \text{Population Total} \le \$1{,}025{,}223.04$

8.76 $N \cdot \bar{D} \pm N \cdot t \cdot \dfrac{S_D}{\sqrt{n}} \sqrt{\dfrac{N-n}{N-1}} = 4000 \cdot \$7.45907 \pm 4000 \cdot 2.6092 \cdot \dfrac{\$29.5523}{\sqrt{150}} \cdot \sqrt{\dfrac{4000-150}{4000-1}}$

$\$5{,}126.26 \le \text{Total Difference in the Population} \le \$54{,}546.28$

Note: The *t*-value of 2.6092 for 99% confidence and d.f. = 149 was derived on Excel.

8.78 (a) $p + Z \cdot \sqrt{\dfrac{p(1-p)}{n}} \sqrt{\dfrac{N-n}{N-1}} = 0.0367 + 1.645 \cdot \sqrt{\dfrac{0.0367(1-0.0367)}{300}} \sqrt{\dfrac{10000-300}{10000-1}}$

$\pi < 0.0542$

(b) Since the upper bound is higher than the tolerable exception rate of 0.04, the auditor should request a larger sample.

8.80 $\bar{X} \pm t_{n-1} \dfrac{S}{\sqrt{n}} \sqrt{\dfrac{N-n}{N-1}} = 75 \pm 2.0301 \dfrac{24}{\sqrt{36}} \sqrt{\dfrac{200-36}{200-1}}$ $67.63 \le \mu \le 82.37$

Copyright ©2015 Pearson Education, Inc.

8.82 (a) $\bar{X} \pm Z \dfrac{\sigma}{\sqrt{n}} \sqrt{\dfrac{N-n}{N-1}} = 350 \pm 1.96 \dfrac{100}{\sqrt{50}} \sqrt{\dfrac{2000-50}{2000-1}}$ $322.6238 \le \mu \le 377.3762$

(b) $n_0 = \dfrac{Z^2 \sigma^2}{e^2} = \dfrac{1.96^2 (100)^2}{20^2} = 96.0364$

$n = \dfrac{n_0 N}{n_0 + (N-1)} = \dfrac{96.0364 (2000)}{96.0364 + (2000-1)} = 91.6799$ Use $n = 92$

(c) (a) $\bar{X} \pm Z \dfrac{\sigma}{\sqrt{n}} \sqrt{\dfrac{N-n}{N-1}} = 350 \pm 1.96 \dfrac{100}{\sqrt{50}} \sqrt{\dfrac{1000-50}{1000-1}}$

$322.9703 \le \mu \le 377.0297$

(b) $n_0 = \dfrac{Z^2 \sigma^2}{e^2} = \dfrac{1.96^2 (100)^2}{20^2} = 96.0364$

$n = \dfrac{n_0 N}{n_0 + (N-1)} = \dfrac{96.0364 (1000)}{96.0364 + (1000-1)} = 87.7015$ Use $n = 88$

8.84 (a) $p \pm Z \sqrt{\dfrac{p(1-p)}{n}} \sqrt{\dfrac{N-n}{N-1}} = 0.3 \pm 1.6449 \sqrt{\dfrac{0.3(1-0.3)}{100}} \sqrt{\dfrac{1000-100}{1000-1}}$

$0.2285 \le \pi \le 0.3715$

(b) $n_0 = \dfrac{Z^2 p(1-p)}{e^2} = \dfrac{1.6449^2 (0.3)(1-0.3)}{0.05^2} = 227.2656$

$n = \dfrac{n_0 N}{n_0 + (N-1)} = \dfrac{227.2656 (1000)}{227.2656 + (1000-1)} = 185.3315$ Use $n = 186$

(c) (a)

$p \pm Z \sqrt{\dfrac{p(1-p)}{n}} \sqrt{\dfrac{N-n}{N-1}} = 0.3 \pm 1.6449 \sqrt{\dfrac{0.3(1-0.3)}{100}} \sqrt{\dfrac{2000-100}{2000-1}}$

$0.2265 \le \pi \le 0.3735$

(b)

$n_0 = \dfrac{Z^2 p(1-p)}{e^2} = \dfrac{1.6449^2 (0.3)(1-0.3)}{0.05^2} = 227.2656$

$n = \dfrac{n_0 N}{n_0 + (N-1)} = \dfrac{227.2656 (2000)}{227.2656 + (2000-1)} = 204.1676$ Use $n = 205$

Copyright ©2015 Pearson Education, Inc.

8.86   (a) $\overline{X} \pm Z \dfrac{\sigma}{\sqrt{n}} \sqrt{\dfrac{N-n}{N-1}} = 1.99 \pm 1.96 \dfrac{0.05}{\sqrt{100}} \sqrt{\dfrac{2000-100}{2000-1}}$ $1.9804 \le \mu \le 2.0000$

(b) $n_0 = \dfrac{Z^2 \sigma^2}{e^2} = \dfrac{1.96^2 (0.05)^2}{0.01^2} = 96.0364$

$n = \dfrac{n_0 N}{n_0 + (N-1)} = \dfrac{96.0364(2000)}{96.0364 + (2000-1)} = 91.6799$ Use $n = 92$

(c)   (a) $\overline{X} \pm Z \dfrac{\sigma}{\sqrt{n}} \sqrt{\dfrac{N-n}{N-1}} = 1.99 \pm 1.96 \dfrac{0.05}{\sqrt{100}} \sqrt{\dfrac{1000-100}{1000-1}}$

$1.9807 \le \mu \le 1.9993$

(b) $n_0 = \dfrac{Z^2 \sigma^2}{e^2} = \dfrac{1.96^2 (0.05)^2}{0.01^2} = 96.0364$

$n = \dfrac{n_0 N}{n_0 + (N-1)} = \dfrac{96.0364(1000)}{96.0364 + (1000-1)} = 87.7015$ Use $n = 88$

Copyright ©2015 Pearson Education, Inc.

Chapter 9

9.80 $H_0 : \mu \geq 7$, $H_1 : \mu < 7$, $\alpha = 0.05$, $n = 16$, $\sigma = 0.2$

Lower critical value: $Z_L = -1.6449$, $\overline{X}_L = \mu + Z_L \left(\dfrac{\sigma}{\sqrt{n}} \right) = 7 - 1.6449 \left(\dfrac{.2}{\sqrt{16}} \right) = 6.9178$

(a) $Z_{STAT} = \dfrac{\overline{X}_L - \mu_1}{\dfrac{\sigma}{\sqrt{n}}} = \dfrac{6.9178 - 6.9}{\dfrac{.2}{\sqrt{16}}} = 0.3551$

power $= 1 - \beta = P\left(\overline{X} < \overline{X}_L \right) = P\left(Z < 0.3551 \right) = 0.6388$

$\beta = 1 - 0.6388 = 0.3612$

(b) $Z_{STAT} = \dfrac{\overline{X}_L - \mu_1}{\dfrac{\sigma}{\sqrt{n}}} = \dfrac{6.9178 - 6.8}{\dfrac{.2}{\sqrt{16}}} = 2.3551$

power $= 1 - \beta = P\left(\overline{X} < \overline{X}_L \right) = P\left(Z < 2.3551 \right) = 0.9907$

$\beta = 1 - 0.9907 = 0.0093$

9.82 $H_0 : \mu \geq 7$, $H_1 : \mu < 7$, $\alpha = 0.05$, $n = 25$, $\sigma = 0.2$

Lower critical value: $Z_L = -1.6449$, $\overline{X}_L = \mu + Z_L \left(\dfrac{\sigma}{\sqrt{n}} \right) = 7 - 1.6449 \left(\dfrac{.2}{\sqrt{25}} \right) = 6.9342$

(a) $Z_{STAT} = \dfrac{\overline{X}_L - \mu_1}{\dfrac{\sigma}{\sqrt{n}}} = \dfrac{6.9342 - 6.9}{\dfrac{.2}{\sqrt{25}}} = 0.8551$

power $= 1 - \beta = P\left(\overline{X} < \overline{X}_L \right) = P\left(Z < 0.8551 \right) = 0.8038$

$\beta = 1 - 0.8038 = 0.1962$

(b) $Z_{STAT} = \dfrac{\overline{X}_L - \mu_1}{\dfrac{\sigma}{\sqrt{n}}} = \dfrac{6.9342 - 6.8}{\dfrac{.2}{\sqrt{25}}} = 3.3551$

power $= 1 - \beta = P\left(\overline{X} < \overline{X}_L \right) = P\left(Z < 3.3551 \right) = 0.9996$

$\beta = 1 - 0.9996 = 0.0004$

(c) Holding everything else constant, the larger the sample size, the higher the power of the test will be and the lower the probability of committing a Type II error will be.

Copyright ©2015 Pearson Education, Inc.

9.84 $H_0 : \mu \geq 25,000$ vs. $H_1 : \mu < 25,000$, $\alpha = 0.01$, $n = 100$, $\sigma = 3500$

Lower critical value: $Z_L = -2.3263$,

$$\bar{X}_L = \mu + Z_L \left(\frac{\sigma}{\sqrt{n}} \right) = 25,000 - 2.3263 \left(\frac{3,500}{\sqrt{100}} \right) = 24,185.7786$$

(a) $Z_{STAT} = \dfrac{\bar{X}_L - \mu_1}{\dfrac{\sigma}{\sqrt{n}}} = \dfrac{24,185.7786 - 24,000}{\dfrac{3500}{\sqrt{100}}} = 0.5308$

power $= 1 - \beta = P(\bar{X} < \bar{X}_L) = P(Z < 0.5308) = 0.7022$

$\beta = 1 - 0.7022 = 0.2978$

(b) $Z_{STAT} = \dfrac{\bar{X}_L - \mu_1}{\dfrac{\sigma}{\sqrt{n}}} = \dfrac{24,185.7786 - 24,900}{\dfrac{3500}{\sqrt{100}}} = -2.0406$

power $= 1 - \beta = P(\bar{X} < \bar{X}_L) = P(Z < -2.0406) = 0.0206$

$\beta = 1 - 0.0206 = 0.9794$

(c)   Holding everything else constant, the greater the distance between the true mean and the hypothesized mean, the higher the power of the test will be and the lower the probability of committing a Type II error will be. Holding everything else constant, the smaller the level of significance, the lower the power of the test will be and the higher the probability of committing a Type II error will be.

9.86 $H_0 : \mu = 25,000$, $H_1 : \mu \neq 25,000$, $\alpha = 0.05$, $n = 100$, $\sigma = 3500$

Critical values: $Z_L = -1.960$, $Z_U = 1.960$

$$\bar{X}_L = \mu + Z_L \left(\frac{\sigma}{\sqrt{n}} \right) = 25,000 - 1.960 \left(\frac{3,500}{\sqrt{100}} \right) = 24,314.0130$$

$$\bar{X}_U = \mu + Z_U \left(\frac{\sigma}{\sqrt{n}} \right) = 25,000 + 1.960 \left(\frac{3,500}{\sqrt{100}} \right) = 25,685.9870$$

(a) $\beta = P(\bar{X}_L < \bar{X} < \bar{X}_U) = P(0.8972 < Z < 4.8171) = 0.1848$

power $= 1 - \beta = 1 - 0.1848 = 0.8152$

(b) $\beta = P(\bar{X}_L < \bar{X} < \bar{X}_U) = P(-1.6742 < Z < 2.2457) = 0.9406$

power $= 1 - \beta = 1 - 0.9406 = 0.0594$

(c)   A one-tail test is more powerful than a two-tail test, holding everything else constant.

Copyright ©2015 Pearson Education, Inc.

Chapter 12

12.60 (a) $H_0 : \pi_1 = \pi_2$ $H_1 : \pi_1 \neq \pi_2$ where 1 = group1, 2 = group2

Decision rule: If $Z_{STAT} < -1.96$ or $Z_{STAT} > 1.96$, reject H_0.

Test statistic: $Z_{STAT} = \dfrac{B - C}{\sqrt{B + C}} = \dfrac{25 - 16}{\sqrt{25 + 16}} = 1.4056$

Decision: Since $Z_{STAT} = 1.4056$ is between the critical bounds of -1.96 and the upper critical bound of 1.96, do not reject H_0. There is not enough evidence of a difference between group 1 and group 2.

12.62 (a) $H_0 : \pi_1 = \pi_2$ $H_1 : \pi_1 \neq \pi_2$ where 1 = prior, 2 = after

Decision rule: If $Z < -2.5758$ or $Z > 2.5758$, reject H_0.

Test statistic: $Z_{STAT} = \dfrac{B - C}{\sqrt{B + C}} = \dfrac{21 - 36}{\sqrt{21 + 36}} = -1.9868$

Decision: Since $Z_{STAT} = -1.9868$ is in between the two critical bounds, do not reject H_0. There is not enough evidence to conclude there is a difference in the proportion of voters who favored Candidate A prior to and after the debate.

(b) p-value = 0.0469. The probability of obtaining a sample which gives rise to a test statistic that differs from 0 by -1.9868 or more in either direction is 0.0469 if there is not a difference in the proportion of voters who favor Candidate A prior to and after the debate.

12.64 (a) $H_0 : \pi_1 \geq \pi_2$ $H_1 : \pi_1 < \pi_2$ where 1 = last year, 2 = now

Decision rule: If $Z_{STAT} < -1.645$, reject H_0.

Test statistic: $Z_{STAT} = \dfrac{B - C}{\sqrt{B + C}} = \dfrac{5 - 20}{\sqrt{5 + 20}} = -3$

Decision: Since $Z_{STAT} = -3 < -1.645$, reject H_0. There is enough evidence to conclude that satisfaction was lower last year prior to introduction of Six Sigma management.

(b) p-value = 0.0014. The probability of obtaining a data set which gives rise to a test statistic smaller than -3 is 0.0014 if the satisfaction was not lower last year prior to introduction of Six Sigma management.

12.66 (a)   For $df = 25$ and $\alpha = 0.01$, $\chi^2_{\alpha/2} = 10.520$ and $\chi^2_{1-\alpha/2} = 46.928$.

(b)   For $df = 16$ and $\alpha = 0.05$, $\chi^2_{\alpha/2} = 6.908$ and $\chi^2_{1-\alpha/2} = 28.845$.

(c)   For $df = 13$ and $\alpha = 0.10$, $\chi^2_{\alpha/2} = 5.892$ and $\chi^2_{1-\alpha/2} = 22.362$.

12.68 $\chi^2_{STAT} = \dfrac{(n-1) \cdot S^2}{\sigma^2} = \dfrac{24 \cdot 150^2}{100^2} = 54$

12.70 $df = n - 1 = 16 - 1 = 15$

Copyright ©2015 Pearson Education, Inc.

12.72   (a)   If $H_1 : \sigma \neq 12$, do not reject H_0 since the test statistic $\chi^2 = 10.417$ falls between the two critical bounds, $\chi^2_{\alpha/2} = 6.262$ and $\chi^2_{1-\alpha/2} = 27.488$.

(b)   If $H_1 : \sigma < 12$, do not reject H_0 since the test statistic $\chi^2 = 10.417$ is greater than the critical bound 7.261.

12.74   (a) H_0: $\sigma \leq 1.2^0$ F. The standard deviation of the oven temperature has not increased above 1.2^0F.

H_1: $\sigma > 1.2^0$ F. The standard deviation of the oven temperature has increased above 1.2^0F.

Decision rule: $df = 29$. If $\chi^2_{STAT} > 42.557$, reject H_0.

Test statistic: $\chi^2_{STAT} = \dfrac{(n-1) \cdot S^2}{\sigma^2} = \dfrac{29 \cdot 2.1^2}{1.2^2} = 88.813$

Decision: Since the test statistic of $\chi^2_{STAT} = 88.813$ is greater than the critical boundary of 42.557, reject H_0. There is sufficient evidence to conclude that the standard deviation of the oven temperature has increased above 1.2^0F.

(b)   You must assume that the data in the population are normally distributed to be able to use the chi-square test of a population variance or standard deviation.

(c) p-value $= 5.53 \times 10^{-8}$ or 0.00000005. The probability that a sample is obtained whose standard deviation is equal to or larger than 2.1^0F when the null hypothesis is true is 5.53×10^{-8}, a very small probability.

Note: The p-value was found using Excel.

12.76   (a) H_0: $\sigma = \$12$. The standard deviation of the monthly cost of calls within the local calling region is \$12.

H_1: $\sigma \neq \$12$. The standard deviation of the monthly cost of calls within the local calling region differs from \$12.

Decision rule: $df = 14$. If $\chi^2_{STAT} < 6.571$ or $\chi^2_{STAT} > 23.685$, reject H_0.

Test statistic: $\chi^2_{STAT} = \dfrac{(n-1) \cdot S^2}{\sigma^2} = \dfrac{14 \cdot 9.25^2}{12^2} = 8.319$

Decision: Since the test statistic of $\chi^2_{STAT} = 8.319$ is between the critical boundaries of 6.571 and 23.685, do not reject H_0. There is insufficient evidence to conclude that the standard deviation of the monthly cost of calls within the local calling region differs from \$12.

(b)   You must assume that the data in the population are normally distributed to be able to use the chi-square test of a population variance or standard deviation.

(c) p-value $= 2(1 - 0.8721) = 0.2558$. The probability of obtaining a test statistic equal to or more extreme than the result obtained from this sample data is 0.2558 if the standard deviation of the monthly cost of calls within the local calling region is \$12.

Note: Excel returns an upper-tail area of 0.8721 for $\chi^2_{STAT} = 8.319$. But since the sample standard deviation is smaller than the hypothesized value, the amount of area in the lower tail is $(1 - 0.8721)$. That value is doubled to accommodate the two-tail hypotheses.

Copyright ©2015 Pearson Education, Inc.

12.78   (a) $W_L = 13, W_U = 53$ (b) $W_L = 10, W_U = 56$ (c) $W_L = 7, W_U = 59$
            (d) $W_L = 5, W_U = 61$

12.80   (a) $W_L = 13$ (b) $W_L = 10$ (c) $W_L = 7$
            (d) $W_L = 5$

12.82 $n' = 10, \alpha = 0.05, W_L = 8, W_U = 47$

12.84 $W = \Sigma_{i=1}^{n'} R_i^{(+)} = 67.5$

12.86   Since $W = 67.5 > W_U = 61$, reject H_0.

12.88   (a) $H_0: M_D = 0$ where Populations: 1 = TV   2 = Phone
                      $H_1: M_D \neq 0$
                      Minitab output:

Wilcoxon Signed Rank Test: Difference

```
Test of median = 0.000000 versus median not = 0.000000

                  N for    Wilcoxon               Estimated
             N    Test    Statistic       P        Median
Difference   13    13        0.0       0.002       -9.000
```

Since the p-value = 0.002 is smaller than the 0.05 level of significance, reject H_0.

There is sufficient evidence of a difference in the median service rating between TV and phone services.

(b)   Using the paired-sample t-test in Problem 10.21, you reject the null hypothesis; you conclude that there is evidence of a difference in the mean service rating between TV and phone. Using the Wilcoxon signed rank test, you reject the null hypothesis; you conclude that there is enough evidence of a difference in the median service rating between TV and phone services.

12.90   (a) $H_0: M_D = 0$ where Populations: 1 = Global 2 = U.S.
                      $H_1: M_D \neq 0$
                      Minitab output:

Wilcoxon Signed Rank Test: Difference

```
Test of median = 0.000000 versus median not = 0.000000

                  N for    Wilcoxon               Estimated
             N    Test    Statistic       P        Median
Difference   13    12       36.0       0.845       -1.000
```

Since the p-value = 0.845 is greater than the 0.05 level of significance, do not reject H_0. There is insufficient evidence of a difference in the median rating between global and U.S. employees.

Copyright ©2015 Pearson Education, Inc.

12.90   (b)   Using the paired-sample t-test in Problem 10.23, you do not reject the null
cont.   hypothesis; you conclude that there is insufficient evidence of a difference in the
             mean rating between global and U.S. employees. Using the Wilcoxon signed rank
             test, you do not reject the null hypothesis; you conclude that there is insufficient
             evidence of a difference in the median rating between global and U.S. employees.

12.92 $d.f. = 5$, $\alpha = 0.1$, $\chi_U^2 = 9.2363$

12.93   (a) $H_0: M_1 = M_2 = M_3 = M_4 = M_5 = M_6$ H_1: At least one of the medians differs.
             Reject H_0 if $F_R > 9.2363$.
        (b)   Since $F_R = 11.56 > 9.2363$, reject H_0. There is enough evidence that the medians are
             different.

12.94   Minitab output:
        Friedman Test: Rating versus Brand, Expert

```
Friedman test for Rating by Brand blocked by Expert

S = 20.03  DF = 3  P = 0.000
S = 20.72  DF = 3  P = 0.000 (adjusted for ties)

                  Est    Sum of
Brand       N   Median   Ranks
A           9   25.000    25.0
B           9   26.750    34.5
C           9   24.000    20.0
D           9   22.250    10.5

Grand median  =   24.500
```

        (a) $H_0: M_A = M_B = M_C = M_D$ H_1: Not all medians are the equal.
             Since the p-value is virtually zero, reject H_0 at 0.05 level of significance. There is
             evidence of a difference in the median summated ratings of the four brands of
             Colombian coffee.
        (b)   In (a), you conclude that there is evidence of a difference in the median summated
             ratings of the four brands of Colombian coffee while in problem 11.23, you conclude
             that there is evidence of a difference in the mean summated ratings of the four
             brands of Colombian coffee.

12.96   Minitab output:

        Friedman Test: Value versus Group blocked by Shopping Item

```
S = 23.79  DF = 3  P = 0.000
S = 24.69  DF = 3  P = 0.000 (adjusted for ties)

                           Sum of
Group        N  Est Median  Ranks
Publix      33    2.7887     92.0
Target      33    2.6262     76.5
Walmart     33    2.5088     56.5
Winn-Dixie  33    2.9712    105.0

Grand median = 2.7237
```

Copyright ©2015 Pearson Education, Inc.

12.96 (a) $H_0 : M_A = M_B = M_C = M_D$ H_1 : Not all medians are the equal.
cont. Since the *p*-value is virtually zero, reject H_0 at 0.05 level of significance. There is evidence of a difference in the median prices for these items at the four supermarkets.

(b) In (a), you conclude that there is evidence of a difference in the median prices for these items at the four supermarkets while in problem 11.25, you conclude that there is evidence of a difference between the mean price of these items at the four supermarkets.

12.98 Minitab output:
Friedman Test: Strength versus Days, Samples

```
Friedman test for Strength by Days blocked by Samples

S = 80.00   DF = 2   P = 0.000

                      Est      Sum of
Days          N    Median      Ranks
  2          40    3.0863       40.0
  7          40    3.5888       80.0
 28          40    4.5838      120.0

Grand median  =    3.7529
```

(a) $H_0 : M_2 = M_7 = M_{28}$ H_1 : Not all medians are equal.
Since the *p*-value is virtually zero, reject H_0 at 0.05 level of significance. There is evidence of a difference in the median compressive strength after 2, 7 and 28 days.

(b) In (a), you conclude that there is evidence of a difference in the median compressive strength after 2, 7 and 28 days, and in problem 11.28, you conclude that there is evidence of a difference in the mean compressive strength after 2, 7 and 28 days.

Copyright ©2015 Pearson Education, Inc.

Chapter 16

16.66 (a)   2011 as the base year:

$$I_{2011} = \frac{P_{2011}}{P_{2011}}(100) = \frac{\$5}{\$5}(100) = 100$$

$$I_{2012} = \frac{P_{2012}}{P_{2011}}(100) = \frac{\$8}{\$5}(100) = 160$$

$$I_{2013} = \frac{P_{2013}}{P_{2011}}(100) = \frac{\$7}{\$5}(100) = 140$$

(b)   2012 as the base year:

$$I_{2011} = \frac{P_{2011}}{P_{2012}}(100) = \frac{\$5}{\$8}(100) = 62.5$$

$$I_{2012} = \frac{P_{2012}}{P_{2012}}(100) = \frac{\$8}{\$8}(100) = 100$$

$$I_{2013} = \frac{P_{2013}}{P_{2012}}(100) = \frac{\$7}{\$8}(100) = 87.5$$

Copyright ©2015 Pearson Education, Inc.

16.68   (a),(b)

Year	DJIA	Price Index (base = 1979)	Price Index (base = 2000)
1979	838.7	100	7.77437894
1980	964.0	114.9397878	8.935854653
1981	875.0	104.3281269	8.110863923
1982	1046.5	124.7764397	9.700593252
1983	1258.6	150.0655777	11.66666667
1984	1211.6	144.4616669	11.2309974
1985	1546.7	184.4163587	14.33722655
1986	1896.0	226.0641469	17.57508343
1987	1938.8	231.1672827	17.97182054
1988	2168.6	258.5668296	20.10196515
1989	2753.2	328.2699416	25.5209492
1990	2633.7	314.0217003	24.41323693
1991	3168.8	377.822821	29.37337783
1992	3301.1	393.5972338	30.59974045
1993	3754.1	447.6093955	34.79885057
1994	3834.4	457.1837367	35.54319614
1995	5117.1	610.1228091	47.43325918
1996	6448.3	768.8446405	59.77289581
1997	7908.3	942.9235722	73.30645161
1998	9181.4	1094.718016	85.10752688
1999	11497.1	1370.823894	106.5730441
2000	10788.0	1286.27638	100
2001	10021.5	1194.884941	92.8948832
2002	8341.6	994.5868606	77.32295143
2003	10453.9	1246.44092	96.90304042
2004	10788.0	1286.27638	100
2005	10717.5	1277.870514	99.34649611
2006	12463.2	1486.014069	115.5283648
2007	13264.8	1581.590557	122.9588432
2008	8772.3	1045.934184	81.31488691
2009	10430.7	1243.673542	96.68789396
2010	11577.4	1380.398235	107.3173897
2011	12221.2	1457.15989	113.2851316
2012	13104.1	1562.429951	121.4692251

(c)   The price index using 2000 as the base year is more useful because it is closer to the present and the DJIA has grown more than 1500% over the period.

Copyright ©2015 Pearson Education, Inc.

16.70 (a), (c)

Year	Price	Price Index (base = 1980)	Price Index (base = 1990)
1980	0.703	100	40.51873199
1981	0.792	112.6600284	45.64841499
1982	0.763	108.5348506	43.97694524
1983	0.726	103.2716927	41.8443804
1984	0.854	121.4793741	49.22190202
1985	0.697	99.14651494	40.17291066
1986	1.104	157.0412518	63.63112392
1987	0.943	134.1394026	54.35158501
1988	0.871	123.8975818	50.20172911
1989	0.797	113.371266	45.93659942
1990	1.735	246.799431	100
1991	0.912	129.7297297	52.5648415
1992	0.936	133.14367	53.9481268
1993	1.141	162.3044097	65.76368876
1994	1.604	228.1650071	92.44956772
1995	1.323	188.1934566	76.25360231
1996	1.103	156.8990043	63.57348703
1997	1.213	172.5462304	69.91354467
1998	1.452	206.5433855	83.68876081
1999	1.904	270.8392603	109.740634
2000	1.443	205.2631579	83.17002882
2001	1.414	201.1379801	81.49855908
2002	1.451	206.401138	83.63112392
2003	1.711	243.3854908	98.6167147
2004	1.472	209.3883357	84.84149856
2005	1.66	236.1308677	95.67723343
2006	2.162	307.5391181	124.610951
2007	1.647	234.2816501	94.92795389
2008	1.734	246.6571835	99.94236311
2009	1.961	278.9473684	113.0259366
2010	1.591	226.3157895	91.70028818
2011	1.531	217.7809388	88.24207493
2012	1.604	228.1650071	92.44956772

(b) The average price per pound of fresh tomatoes in 2012 in the U.S. is 128.17% higher than it was in 1980.

(d) The average price per pound of fresh tomatoes in 2012 in the U.S. is 92.44% of that in 1990 or 7.56% lower than it was in 1990.

Copyright ©2015 Pearson Education, Inc.

16.70 (e)
cont.

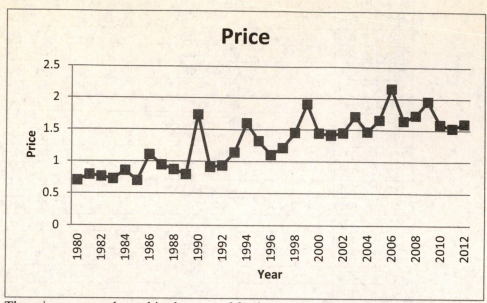

There is an upward trend in the cost of fresh tomatoes from 1980 to 2012 with a prominent cyclical component.

Copyright ©2015 Pearson Education, Inc.